Advance Reviews for AutoCAD Power Tools

"I use AutoCAD every day. Still—*AutoCAD Power Tools* taught me eight new tricks."

—*Theo Armour, Autodesk, Inc.*

"*AutoCAD Power Tools* could fairly be called a wizard's training manual. It pulls together a broad range of invaluable technical information and presents it in very cogent fashion. Further, it provides the kind of secret tips that would be hard to find elsewhere. This book is the ideal starting point for AutoCAD users who aspire to wizardry."

—*Evan Yares, CAD Consultant,*
Design Automation Systems, Inc.

"I especially like the tips in *AutoCAD Power Tools* and the reasons the authors give for preferring one method over another. This approach provides the reader with insight into why some methods might be useful, without implying that they're the *only* acceptable ways to work."

—*Peter Sheerin, Technical Editor,*
CADENCE Magazine

"*AutoCAD Power Tools* breaks new ground ... providing both the knowledge and the software tools to make you truly an AutoCAD power user."

—*Bob McNeel, Robert McNeel & Associates*

AutoCAD
Power Tools®

AutoCAD Power Tools®

Bud Smith
Jake Richter
Mark Middlebrook

RANDOM HOUSE
ELECTRONIC PUBLISHING

New York   Toronto   London   Sydney   Auckland

Contents

P A R T   I

Introducing Release 12 for DOS and Windows 1

3 *Performance*   51

P A R T   I I

Power User's Guide to Release 12   67

4 *Basic Setup and Prototypes*   69

5 *Drawing-Specific Setup*   87

Preface

The book and disk package that you hold in your hands is the culmination of a great deal of work by many people. This preface will explain what it contains and how it came about so you can better understand, before you start, what you're getting into and what we hope you'll get out of it. It also includes a request for your help in making future versions of this package even better than the current one.

About the Book

The best way to learn about the structure of this book is to read the Table of Contents and the first chapter in each of the four parts. Here, we want to talk in a more general way about what we have tried to do in this book.

Possibly the biggest single concern we faced in putting together the book and the disk was performance versus productivity. In research we conducted, users of Panacea's AutoCAD drivers consistently identified performance as their most important concern. Yet we, like many self-appointed experts, wanted to talk about productivity—the amount of work you can get done in a day—just as much as performance. So we tackled both. You'll find detailed coverage of performance issues and a display list driver to speed up your computer's performance. But taking up even more of the book is a focus on using techniques and approaches that maximize productivity.

There were a lot of other concerns that we tried to address in making this book as useful as possible; the most important of these are described below.

Organizing Principles

The overall concept for *AutoCAD Power Tools* is unique. There are an awful lot of books about AutoCAD, some of which are very good. Many of them try to cover the entire program and reach all potential readers; these books only scratch the surface. Others only cover one aspect, such as AutoLISP programming, in great depth. This approach is valuable, but if you want to learn more than one or two topics, you end up having to read thousands of pages of AutoCAD documentation and third-party books.

We have taken a different approach, with three main tenets: leave out beginners, focus on new features, and do the things the documentation doesn't.

Leaving out beginners means cutting out a lot of stuff—baby talk aimed at new users and nonusers, lengthy descriptions of obvious intermediate steps, and the most basic conceptual information. Leaving out all of this enabled us to state organizing principles clearly, then get straight to the important points we wanted to make. By leaving out the basics, we were able to make descriptions of features and how to use them, tutorials, and especially the customization chapters much easier to read. We were also able to find room for a lot of little-known intermediate and advanced material because of this approach.

Focusing on new features was also key to this book. Based on experience with AutoCAD and other programs, we believe that most AutoCAD users have absorbed most of the program's features up through Release 9 or 10. These early releases seem to have been primarily concerned with making the program a better direct replacement for the drafting table; and, they've been around long enough for most people to "get" what's in them. But many of the features introduced in Releases 11 and 12 are both newer and less obvious than earlier ones. They are more concerned with power and ease of use than with pure replacement of manual drafting. Concentrating on these newer features has again enabled us to move quickly to the most interesting stuff.

Our third tenet, covering things the documentation doesn't, seems obvious, but it isn't. Many computer users would rather get all their information from third-party books and never read documentation. Other users are just as glad to get a combination of new information and approaches with excerpts from the documentation. So many existing computer books are largely or entirely a rehash of the documentation.

In the case of AutoCAD, however, rehashes just don't work. The program is so massive that serious users need the information in the documentation, plus all the new information and different approaches they can get. So we cover new material and approaches almost exclusively, then refer you to specific parts of the documentation wherever it has valuable reference material. By building on and referring to Autodesk's documentation in this way, we avoid rehashing it—without making the rash assumption that you've read every word of it.

All of these approaches, though, are statements of direction rather than absolute rules. Only you can tell us if we have done the right things. Are these principles the right ones for creating a book that is useful to you? Did we follow them to the appropriate degree, and in the right places? Where is this book/disk package most useful, and where is it not very useful? Our e-mail addresses are given below; write and let us know how we can improve future versions of this book.

Release 12, Windows, and Customization

There are some key issues that any author, or writing team, tries to address in writing a book. We believe that the three most important issues facing AutoCAD users today are the following: taking full advantage of Release 12; preparing for the transition to Windows; and managing AutoCAD, especially in workgroups. We have tried to address these issues in *AutoCAD Power Tools*.

Taking full advantage of Release 12 is difficult. Billed as "the interface release," it doesn't break a lot of new conceptual ground. Instead, it tries to make the existing functionality easier to access. Unfortunately, experienced users face a J-shaped curve in getting up to speed; one's productivity actually drops (going down the first part of the J) in the early stages of moving to new techniques, only rising later (moving up the rest of the J) when the new techniques are mastered. With the material in this book, we've tried to help you get through the Release 12 learning curve as quickly as possible, while enabling you to obtain the most from the improvements in Releases 10 and 11 as well.

Like it or not, Windows is the number one strategic platform for the future of AutoCAD. But we think that in the Release 12 time frame, many users will be experimenting with Windows, or moving back and forth between DOS (speed, tools, third-party applications) and Windows (ease of use, new capabilities). So we covered both in this book, with emphasis on the DOS 386 version. The tools on the disk either have both DOS and Windows versions, or are usable on both, except for the display list driver. We hope that our gentle introduction to the Windows environment will fit the needs of most of our readers. If you want a Windows-only book, tell us, and let us know what you think should be in it.

Workgroup management of AutoCAD must have some kind of social stigma, because no one talks about it much. But all of the authors agree that this is a big problem in using any kind of CAD and that the problem is only growing larger with time. So we have discussed workgroup topics in nearly every chapter, mostly in separate discussions near the end. If we can at least get people thinking and talking about these issues, we'll have made a contribution.

Customization and Power Tools

As with performance versus productivity, the Power Tools on the enclosed disk will probably get a lot of use and attention. And they deserve to; this is probably the most powerful set of software ever made available as part of a book of this type. You would have to spend over $200 to purchase the enclosed programs. But they're all free; even the shareware fees are paid automatically in the purchase price. The customization emphasis in this book, while less sexy, may prove to be just as valuable to you. Most serious AutoCAD users recognize that AutoCAD is an environment that is only fully useful if it's customized to your needs. Third-party programs for specific disciplines only cover part of the gap. Even programs such as those included with this book don't make AutoCAD completely specific to your needs.

To really get the most out of AutoCAD you need customization down to the subdiscipline, company, and workgroup level. Then you need a little more flexibility to make AutoCAD do everything it can for you as an individual. In this book, we tell you how to use most of the customization tools AutoCAD makes available to you, from scripts and ACAD.PGP all the way up through AutoLISP and dialogue box programming.

We hope that this emphasis will inspire you to begin customizing AutoCAD if you've never done so before, or reinvigorate your interest and expand your customization abilities if you are familiar with menus or AutoLISP. Let us know whether we've achieved this goal.

How the Book Was Created

The original idea for the book came from the author of this preface, Bud Smith. He wrote Part I and Part II of the book, which describe AutoCAD and explain how to use most of its features. Besides doing a lot of writing and developing the concept and book outline, he brought some publishing expertise to the project.

Bud is an ex-programmer (Four-Phase database programming, 6502 assembler, Pascal, spreadsheet design) who came to Silicon Valley five years ago to make his mark as a technical writer. He has written books, magazine articles, and user manuals covering many topics, with an emphasis on technical areas, such as microprocessors, and currently works for a company developing object-oriented software.

The software for this book was mostly developed by Jake Richter, president of Panacea, Inc. Jake has been a friend and writing partner of Bud's for years, and they worked on a previous book about the 8514/A graphics standard. (Shows how smart they are! Four years after publication, they just got their first royalty check—for $65.)

Panacea has developed the DLD® line of software accelerators for AutoCAD and has a new product, PanaIcon_, which is receiving quite a bit of favorable attention. Jake is a fixture at computer industry and CAD trade shows, and he has written a number of articles as well as a couple of other books.

A few months into this project, Bud and Jake joined forces with Mark Middlebrook, a longtime AutoCAD user, consultant, trainer, and contributing editor for *CADalyst* magazine. He is cochair of the San Francisco AutoCAD User's Group, one of the most active of such groups, and an assistant sysop on CompuServe's ACAD forum. Before launching his computer consulting firm, Daedalus Consulting, Mark studied and worked in the structural engineering profession.

Mark wrote Part III of the book dealing with customization, and he also did a tremendous amount of work on Parts I and II. He also contributed other writing and helped with the software too. This book/disk package is now just as much Mark's as Bud or Jake's.

Mike Roney, our editor, pushed us to include great software along with the best book we could write. He built the original agreement between the authors and Bantam Books, and kept it alive during the acquisition of his Bantam division by Random House Electronic Publishing. His enormous patience and gentle persistence throughout the project have been crucial.

We also enlisted two expert technical editors. Randy Bush works in the training department of a large CAD software company in Sausalito, California. He is an active member of the San Francisco AutoCAD User's Group and CompuServe ACAD forum, and has taught AutoCAD to hundreds of users and dealers. His insider's perspective has been invaluable. Convincing Peter Sheerin to serve as a technical editor for the book was a real stroke of luck. He is the technical editor for *CADENCE* magazine and coauthor of another AutoCAD book. Thanks to Randy and Peter, we feel very confident about the quality of both the text and the software.

The writing and editorial team obviously has broad experience in publishing, computing, graphics, CAD in general, and AutoCAD in particular. This book and disk package represents the best each of us could bring to this rare opportunity to do something really different and exciting. We're confident that you will find it to be both interesting and useful.

Ongoing Effort

This book is not intended to be just a shot in the dark; we intend to keep revising it as we get feedback from our readers and as new versions of AutoCAD proliferate. Please tell us what you think of the current book, and let us know what you would like to see in future versions.

We would like to hear your comments and use them as input for the next edition; however, we can't answer regular letters, due to the amount of time and expense required to do so. We prefer to receive questions and comments on CompuServe when possible. You can leave a CompuServe mail message or, if you want to start a general discussion, post a message in the ACAD forum. (See Appendix B for more information on the value of CompuServe, and details on how to sign up. Appendix B also tells you how to send e-mail to CompuServe via the Internet.) Our user IDs for CompuServe and the Internet are as follows:

Mark Middlebrook, CIS	73030,1604
Internet	73030.1604@compuserve.com
Bud Smith, CIS	71023,1775
Internet	71023.1775@compuserve.com
Jake Richter	75130,2705
Internet	jake@panacea.com

Send your comments to any of us. We will respond and use your comments as input for the next book.

Special Offer. If we use your comments in our next book, we will put your name in a drawing for a free copy. The five people with the most useful comments will receive a copy; five others, selected at random from among those who commented, will also get one. This is just a small "thank you" for what we expect will be a number of very useful suggestions.

Thanks for Your Trust

We understand that deciding to spend $50 or so on a book, even one with software enclosed, is somewhat of an act of faith. And investing many hours in setting up and using the software, as well as reading some or all of the book, is an even bigger deal. Thanks for the vote of confidence you have given our efforts by purchasing *AutoCAD Power Tools*; we hope that you feel you've been amply repaid by what you find herein.

Acknowledgments

Mike Roney, our editor at Random House, showed an extraordinary amount of faith in our efforts. He carried the torch for us within two of the world's leading publishing houses: Bantam, which originally bought the book, and Random House, which bought the Electronic Publishing division of Bantam. Thanks, Mike.

AutoCAD has a large and active user's-group community. The San Francisco AutoCAD User's Group is cochaired by Mark and has warmly welcomed me as a new member. SFAUG, and its Customization SIG (Special Interest Group), have given us many opportunities to test our theories and methods of presentation.

It seems corny to thank the company whose product you're writing about, but Autodesk really has created a great product in AutoCAD, and has shown vision in their products, investments, and plans for the future. The company gave us free software and other support, and encouraged Randy Bush, an employee, to work with us as a technical editor.

Mark wishes to thank the members of the ACAD forum on CompuServe, who have taught him much about AutoCAD customization, despite his insufferable tendency to deliver lectures on grammar. He particularly thanks Pierre Gasztowtt, an AutoCAD applications programmer with Computers & Structures, Inc. and a valued friend. Pierre's insight and instruction were crucial at several junctures, and especially during the writing of the programmable dialogue box chapter. Special thanks also go to Robert Schutz of Off Broadway, an AutoCAD dealership in Oakland, CA. Ever since Mark's naïve debut as AutoCAD consultant in 1988, Robert has been a continual source of ideas, encouragement, and friendship.

Jake wants to thank Linda Richter, his wife and best friend.

My own special thanks go to my family—my wife, Jacyn, and kids, James and Veronica. One who hasn't been through it can't really know what it's like to be married to someone working on a book. My wife and kids heard endless tall tales about how close this book was to being finished, and when the next check was coming in. They saw little of me but the back of my head for the year it took to complete this project. They helped me keep a foothold in real life while I got this done and, as a reward, are now suffering further as I visit user's groups and trade shows in our marketing efforts.

—*Bud Smith*

Introducing Release 12 for DOS and Windows

1

Introducing Release 12

Note to the new user: This chapter introduces Release 12 to AutoCAD users who are familiar with a previous version. If you are a new user with Release 12, make sure you are skilled in the basic features of the program before using this chapter. The Tutorial manual in the AutoCAD Release 12 documentation is a good place to start. Once you're familiar with the basics, re-read this chapter to get a better feel for the new release and how it differs from previous versions.

Release 12 is the most important upgrade to AutoCAD in years, perhaps in the program's history. While maintaining file compatibility with Release 11, Autodesk has moved the program in a new direction that brings it up to date with other CAD and productivity programs and takes a big step into the era of graphical user interfaces (see Figure 1.1).

The word "productivity" is important here. Most AutoCAD users are very concerned with the program's performance—the speed with which it updates the screen or generates a plot file, for instance. For DOS users, *AutoCAD Power Tools* meets the need for improved performance with the TurboDLD*Lite*™ display list driver found on the enclosed disk. (A similar driver is already built into the new Windows version.) But performance is really only one element in the more important area of productivity: how much work you can get done each day with a given amount of effort. Most of the improvements that you will find in AutoCAD Release 12, and many of the tips and techniques discussed in this book, have to do with helping you increase your productivity.

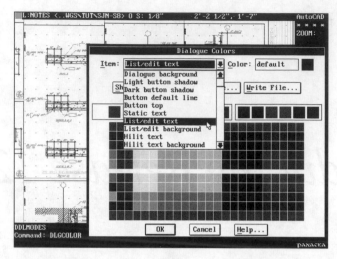

Figure 1.1   AutoCAD 386 Release 12's graphical user interface.

With Release 12, AutoCAD is brought up to date with features like cascading menus, increased use of dialogue boxes, autosave capability, and a point-and-click interface that supports (with some limitations) a new style of editing. These features make it possible to work more productively. But it's all too easy to upgrade to Release 12, then continue to work in the same way that you did in earlier releases. If you don't upgrade your working habits along with the software, you won't get the full benefit of Release 12 or future releases of AutoCAD. Use the text and tutorials in this book to learn how to get the most out of Release 12.

Release 12 for DOS and Release 12 for Windows

Release 12 for DOS 386 is a worthwhile story in itself, but Release 12 for Windows is of equal importance. The new version is a full-fledged Windows program, with multiple sessions running simultaneously, cut-and-paste between programs, intelligent drag-and-drop file manipulation, and a host of other new features (see Figure 1.2).

This book discusses, in the main flow of the text, features common to Release 12 for DOS and Windows. The Power Tools on disk are equally useful for either version, except for the TurboDLD*Lite* display list driver, which brings the most important performance feature built into the Windows version to the DOS version (moving the DOS version ahead again in performance). Whichever version you have, you can read 90 percent of the book and apply it equally to either one.

In addition, this book includes a Windows-specific chapter (the next chapter) and Windows-specific paragraphs and tips in other chapters. The word "Windows" is right up front in these sections, so you can skip them if you have the

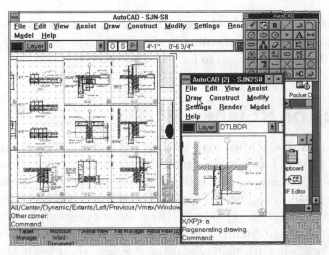

Figure 1.2 AutoCAD Release 12 for Windows.

DOS version and don't care about Windows or you can hone in on them if you have the Windows version and don't care about DOS.

But if you, like most users, are sitting on the fence between the two versions, trying to make a successful conversion to Windows or still mulling it over, you should find the interweaving of DOS and Windows information helpful and revealing. By studying the similarities and differences between both versions, you'll be able to decide which platform is best for you. And if you're a long-time DOS AutoCAD user, you'll be ready to plot a transition strategy.

About This Chapter

This chapter describes some of the most important new features in Release 12 and demonstrates them in a guided tour. It is just as applicable to Windows as to DOS. The remaining chapters in Part I discuss Release 12 for Windows and performance on both platforms. Part II covers Release 12 features in greater depth. The idea behind the chapters in this section is to give you a quick survey of both new versions of AutoCAD and of how you can get the best performance out of them.

Upgrading

This chapter, like the others in Parts I and II, assumes that you are an experienced AutoCAD user and have already upgraded to Release 12, but are not yet taking full advantage of it. If you are still deciding whether to upgrade, or if you need to serve as a resource to others on this decision, please see Appendix A, *Making the Upgrade Decision*. It sets out the pros and cons in clear, unbiased terms that will help you decide whether to upgrade, which platform (DOS or Windows) to look at, and when to do so.

Key Features of Release 12

Previous releases of AutoCAD (through Release 11) had not done enough to keep it up to date. Its interface had not improved as quickly as that of the best spreadsheets, word processors, and other mainstream software packages. The AutoCAD Main Menu had been a real source of frustration, the number of commands and options had exploded to the point that remembering even a basic working set was difficult, and features widely available in other programs—like the ability to display a print preview—had been lacking. With Release 12, however, AutoCAD takes a big step forward. With the changes found in Release 12 for DOS and Release 12 for Windows (see Chapter 2), Autodesk has fixed a lot of limitations and positioned AutoCAD solidly for further improvements.

For most users of AutoCAD, the key changes in Release 12 for DOS are in four areas: the program's user interface, editing and selection, speed, and plotting. We demonstrate some key features in this chapter, and discuss all the important new 2D drafting and plotting features in detail in Part II.

The introduction of modeling and rendering features into the standard AutoCAD package is another important change that will affect more people as the use of AutoCAD evolves. We briefly demonstrate rendering in this chapter, and describe 3D-related features more extensively in Chapter 12.

The final key set of improvements in Release 12—enhancements in customizability—are used directly by fewer people, but will have far-reaching effects. We discuss customizability at length in Part III, and we've used the improvements in this area to create the programs on the accompanying disk described in Part IV.

We use brief tutorial sections to describe and demonstrate some of the major changes in the interface, improvements in editing and selection, changes in program speed, plotting improvements, and 3D features. The tutorial sections are intended for use with Release 12; if you don't yet have it installed, reading through the tutorial and looking at the figures will serve almost the same purpose as actually performing the steps in it.

Here is a quick list of the top 10 features in Release 12:

1. Better file handling (no Main Menu)
2. Cursor pop-up menu
3. Hatching improvements

   4. Selection enhancements
   5. Layer locking
   6. Grips
   7. Plotting improvements
   8. File compatibility with Release 11
   9. Faster entity selection and object snaps
   10. Programmable dialogue boxes

Features Demonstrated in This Chapter

The features demonstrated in this chapter represent many of the improvements in AutoCAD Release 12. Among them are:

- "No regens"
- Interface improvements, including increased use of dialogue boxes
- Improved on-line help
- Automatic timed saves of drawings
- A new geometry calculator
- Noun/verb editing and grips
- Plot preview

"No Regens"

One of the most discussed features of Release 12 is the reduced number of times it needs to regenerate the screen display ("do a regen") when the user pans across the display or zooms in or out. AutoCAD now maintains a 32-bit display list, rather than a 16-bit one, so it can store in memory a more detailed version of the information in the drawing database. This allows the user to zoom in much farther without causing a regen. Release 12 also uses the larger display list to store information about a wider area around the edges of the initial display, so pans and zooms near the edge of the screen are less likely to cause a regen (see Figure 1.3). However, this feature won't speed up AutoCAD for all users. To minimize regens, experienced users of previous versions have already adjusted the way they use AutoCAD. For instance, panning and zooming near the edge of the screen is less likely to cause a regen if it's done carefully. And many users don't often need to zoom in close enough to cause a regen (or have learned to avoid needing to do so).

Additionally, the 32-bit display list can cause problems, because it takes up about twice as much memory as the old 16-bit one. Display lists that used to fit entirely in RAM now must be stored partly on disk. If you're already tight on disk space, the bigger temporary files can send you over the edge. If you use large drawings, you will probably need to add memory and, perhaps,

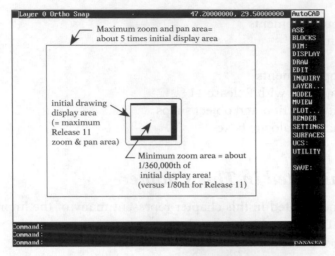

Figure 1.3   Regen-less panning and zooming zone in Release 12.

also free up some disk space on your system in order to maintain the same performance with Release 12 and its 32-bit display list that you got used to with Release 11.

For large and complex drawings, such as maps or detailed architectural plans, however, the larger display list is a great boon. Experienced users can zoom more tightly without fear of a regen, and new users won't have to struggle with learning cumbersome techniques for avoiding regens. As a result, AutoCAD's new 32-bit display list and accompanying reduction in the number of regens will be a benefit to most users over the long term, if not the short term. The use and value of this feature are described in more detail in Chapter 3, *Performance*.

Interface Improvements

Release 12 brings the AutoCAD interface up to date with other graphical programs, while still keeping compatibility with previous versions. The Main Menu is gone, replaced by a new File menu with an Open command that brings up a dialogue box to select the file you want to open (see Figure 1.4). The pull-down menu bar is arranged more like that of other graphical programs, and (as with previous versions) can be reconfigured to support the way you want to do your job. Support for cascading menus increases the number of features available through the menu bar. Inactive choices can be grayed out. There is also a "double-click" feature that is useful, once you get the hang of it: Double-click on a menu title, such as View, to repeat the last command you picked in that menu.

A pop-up cursor menu, also customizable, further increases the number of features that you can easily access. Hitting the third button on your mouse or

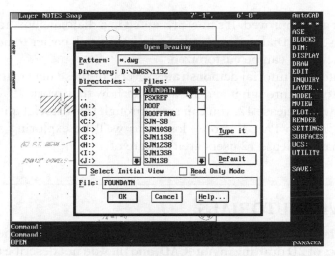

Figure 1.4 The Open Drawing dialogue box.

digitizer puck brings up the Osnap menu that occupied first place in the Release 11 menu bar. (If you have a 2-button mouse, hold down the <Shift> key and press the second button.)

The side-screen menu now follows the current command, however you entered it. For instance, whether you enter the ELLIPSE command from the side menu, the command line, a digitizer entry, or a pull-down menu choice, the options for the ELLIPSE command appear in the side menu. There aren't side menus for every command, but the commands that do have them now display them consistently.

The increased use of dialogue boxes throughout Release 12 improves ease of use, simplifies training, and makes some of the more arcane features of AutoCAD accessible. A dialogue language allows you to modify and create dialogue boxes from within AutoLISP or ADS programs, thereby greatly improving customizability. Looking at Release 12's dialogue boxes is a good way to introduce yourself to most of its new ease of use and other features. (If you browse through the figures in this book, you'll see most of the Release 12 for DOS dialogue boxes.)

We also describe other customization features in detail in Part III. Among the user interface features you can customize are the menu that appears when you hit the third button on your mouse or puck, the menus in general, and the status line at the top of the screen.

A new geometry calculator is also an important feature. The good news is that it includes a lot of useful functions for locating points and determining distances. The bad news is that the functionality is hidden within a command-line interface, rather than put in a dialogue box or equation-builder interface that would make the functions more readily available.

On-line help is also improved. It's now presented in a dialogue box, rather than on the text screen. Dialogue controls make help much easier to access and, as before, help text can be customized.

The coming interface tutorial demonstrates several of these new features. Take a moment to step through it and get a feel for how they work. If you're already familiar with Release 12, you can scan through this tutorial quickly. But look at the ones in Part II more closely, as we'll be exploring some subtleties that many Release 12 users aren't aware of.

HIGH-LEVEL TUTORIALS

The tutorials in this book are high-level; they assume that you understand the basics of 2D drafting in AutoCAD, and they do not describe all minor or intermediate steps. If you have trouble following the steps in this book, please work through the *AutoCAD Tutorial Manual* that comes with Release 12 before proceeding.

Interface Tutorial

The first part of this tutorial demonstrates some of the new interface features of Release 12, including the updated menu bar and the demise of the AutoCAD Main Menu.

 NOTE

In all future tutorials, you'll be saving tutorial files to their own subdirectory. For this chapter, the location of drawings isn't important but, if you like, you may follow the steps in the "Project subdirectories" sidebar in Chapter 4 before starting AutoCAD.

---

1. Start AutoCAD and begin a new, unnamed file.

On starting AutoCAD, you're taken immediately into the drawing editor's graphics screen—no text-mode menu. Follow these detailed steps:

Move the mouse pointer to the top edge of the screen.

The new menu bar appears.

Pick the File menu.

Tip

The <*> character (<Shift>+8) serves as a wildcard. For instance, you can enter N* to see a scrolling box with help for all help entries starting with N. (NEW is the only such entry, but other letters will get you more entries.) To get on-line help for an entry with a long name, try typing the first few characters, the * character, then <Enter>.

Pick the NEW... command.

The Create New Drawing dialogue box pops up (see Figure 1.5). This dialogue box is discussed in more detail in Chapter 6, *Creating New Geometry*.

Pick the OK button.

AutoCAD reinitializes the drawing editor. You're now editing an unnamed file.

2. Look at on-line help for the NEW command.

Pick the Assist menu.

Pick the Help! command.

The new Help dialogue box pops up.

Enter NEW as the command name you want help for.

On-line help for the NEW command appears.

Read the help entry (see Figure 1.6).

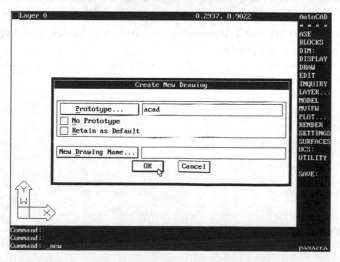

Figure 1.5   The Create New Drawing dialogue box.

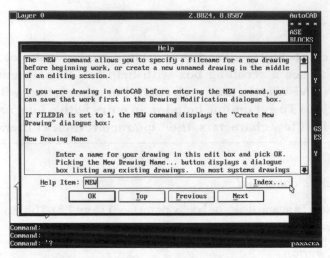

Figure 1.6   Help for the NEW command.

3. Look at on-line help for all commands.

Pick the Index... button (or press <Alt>+<I>).

The Help Index dialogue box pops up, with the command NEW highlighted.

 Tip

The underlined letter in the name of a button or option is the keyboard shortcut that will take you directly to that option. However, if you're in a text entry box, typing the letter will simply enter it into the text entry box. To avoid this, press <Alt> along with the shortcut letter to go to the corresponding option, instead of typing the letter into the text entry box.

Enter the name of an entry you wish to look up, or

Pick a name from the scrolling list.

Pick OK to exit the Help Index.

Pick OK to exit help.

4. Set the SAVETIME system variable to 10 minutes.

```
Command: SAVETIME
```

```
New Value for SAVETIME <120>: 10
```

120 minutes is the default value of the SAVETIME system variable. If you changed this value during system configuration, the number shown in the prompt on your system will be different.

 ## *Tip*

The SAVETIME system variable saves the currently open drawing in a file named AUTO.SV$ in the current subdirectory. If your computer locks up, or you accidentally tell AutoCAD to exit without saving changes, simply rename AUTO.SV$ to a filename ending in .DWG and you can pick up from the most recent automatic save. The timer for automatic saves is reset each time you enter a command that saves the file; enter the command TIME to see how long it will be until the next automatic save.

The setting for SAVETIME is stored in the configuration file, not the drawing file, so you don't need to reset it for each drawing.

Automatic saves don't happen unless there's command-line activity, so save your file explicitly if you're going to be away from the keyboard. Also, you'll need to delete any extra AUTO.SV$ files once you return to DOS; AutoCAD doesn't delete them for you.

---

5. Draw a line.

```
Command: LINE
LINE From point: Pick a point at the lower left of the screen.
To point: Pick a point at the upper right of the screen.
To point: <Enter>
```

6. Use the cursor menu to start the Geometry Calculator and construct a circle one-third of the way along the line.

```
Command: CIRCLE
3P/2P/TTR/<Center point>:
```

Instead of picking a center point with the first button of your mouse or digitizer puck, pick anywhere on the screen with the third button. (Hold down the <Shift> key and pick with the second button if you're using a 2-button mouse.)

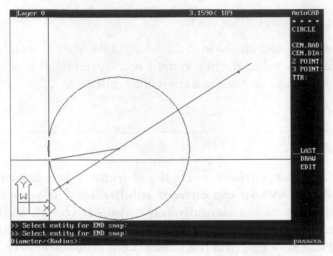

Figure 1.7   Geometry Calculator trisects a line.

The menu will stay on-screen even if you release the button and move the mouse around; it disappears only if you click outside of it.

Pick the last option, Calculator.

The calculator will start up; use the plt( ) function (Point along a Line with the distance defined by ratio *T*) to locate the third point of the line.

```
Command: 'cal >> Expression: PLT(END,END,1/3).
>> Select entity for END snap: Pick near one end of the line.
>> Select entity for END snap: Pick near the other end of the line.
```

The Geometry Calculator locates the third point nearest the end you picked first (see Figure 1.7).

Tip

The cursor menu is defined in ACAD.MNU under the label ***POP0, and can be modified. See Chapter 17 for details.

Note that if the cursor location is high in the drawing area, the cursor menu appears with the first option, Center, highlighted. If the cursor location is near the bottom of the drawing area, the cursor menu appears with its bottom edge at the bottom of the drawing screen, and the option at the same height as the current cursor location is highlighted. So, if you move the mouse almost to the bottom of the drawing area before pressing your third button, you'll "preselect" the Calculator option.

New Editing Modes

Anyone who has used an illustration software package has experienced the frustration of then going back to AutoCAD. There is a natural way of working in such packages—selecting an object or group of objects, grab them with the mouse, or move or rotating them—that AutoCAD does not support. Instead, planning and forethought are needed to figure out the correct command, to specify the needed object or group of objects, then complete the operation. This style of working is called "verb/noun" editing.

While most AutoCAD users have adjusted to this way of working, it can be a benefit to have the selection-first, or noun/verb, method available at least some of the time. Release 12 supports both styles of editing. You still can enter a command, then select the objects it applies to. But often you have the additional option of selecting an object or group of objects, then entering a command.

This new approach is not completely consistent, however. Not all selection options are available before a command is selected, and not all commands can use the current noun/verb selection set. This is unfortunate because Release 12 also includes new Fence, WPolygon, CPolygon, and ALL selection options that would be more useful if they were available at all times, not just after a command is entered. We describe the commands and variables that let you choose the editing style, and the limitations on noun/verb editing and selecting entities, in Chapter 7, *Selecting and Editing*.

Grips are another Release 12 feature that allows you to work with AutoCAD in a way similar to the way you use an illustration program. Grips are handles that appear on an entity when it is selected with the mouse. (If the system variable GRIPS is set to 0, then grips do not appear.) Once you have selected one or more entities, you can stretch, move, rotate, scale, or mirror the entities simply by dragging the mouse. All of these options have a Copy suboption to apply the change to a copy of the selected entities, rather than the entities themselves.

In this chapter, we'll give a brief demonstration of editing with grips. In Chapter 7, we'll describe all these features in more depth, and include them in a more substantive example.

Editing Tutorial

This tutorial demonstrates the new Grips editing feature of Release 12. If you haven't used this style of editing (called "direct manipulation") before, it may seem unnatural to you. Even if you have used it in other programs, the way it's implemented in AutoCAD will take some getting used to. Stick with it; once you overcome the initial unfamiliarity, grip editing will significantly increase your productivity.

1. Make sure grips and noun/verb editing are on.

```
Command: GRIPS 1
Command: PICKFIRST 1
```

2. Draw a circle with a radius of about 2".

```
Command: Circle
3P/2P/TTR/<Center point>: 
```
Pick a point in the lower middle of your screen.
```
Diameter/<Radius>: 
```
Pick any point about 2" from the center of the circle.

3. Select the circle.

Pick any point on the circle.

Grips will appear and the circle will highlight.

4. Make a concentric copy of the circle that's about half the size of the original.

Pick any of the four grips on the perimeter of the circle.

The selected grip will change color to indicate that it's the "hot grip."

Hold down the <Shift> key.

The <Shift> key invokes the Copy suboption of the STRETCH grip editing mode. "Stretching" a circle with grips is similar to using the OFFSET command.

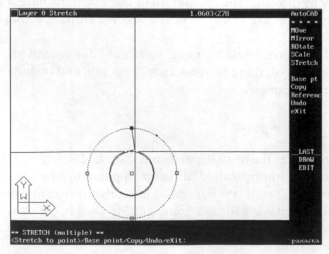

Figure 1.8   Concentric circles with grips.

While holding down the <Shift> key, pick a point within the circle about halfway between the center and the perimeter.

A new circle will appear within the first one. See Figure 1.8 for an example of how the screen should look.

Press <Enter> or <Spacebar>.

The grip editing operation will be concluded.

5. Get rid of the grips on the larger circle.

Press <Ctrl>+C twice.

The first <Ctrl>+C removes the highlighting, and the second <Ctrl>-C removes the grips. You must press <Ctrl>+C from the keyboard in order to cancel the highlighting and grips; unfortunately, the fourth digitizer button doesn't do the job here.

6. Move the smaller circle so that it sits atop the larger one.

Pick any point on the perimeter of the smaller circle.

The smaller circle will be selected.

Pick the center of the smaller circle.

Why pick the center? Because if you pick the center, AutoCAD will move the circle; if you pick a point on the perimeter, AutoCAD will stretch it.

Move the mouse so that the smaller circle appears, aligned, atop the larger one.

7. Repeat the process to create a third circle, smaller yet, and place it atop the second one.

Use steps 4 through 6 to guide you if you don't quite have the hang of this yet.

8. Create three small circles and arrange them within the topmost circle so that the result looks like Figure 1.9.

9. Save your drawing as SNOWMAN; you will use it in the coming plotting tutorial.

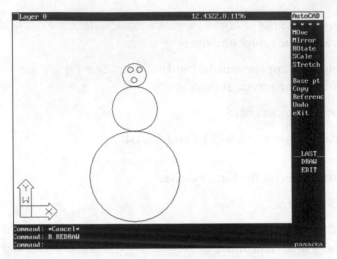

Figure 1.9   Snowman created with grips.

Plotting

AutoCAD plotting traditionally has been slow, mistake-prone, and expensive. Switching between plotters required loading AutoCAD from different batch files or reconfiguring. Verifying paper size, rotation, plot scale, and other parameters was a trial and error process. Release 12 moves AutoCAD plotting from a major liability to a powerful, easy-to-use feature. Major improvements include the use of dialogue boxes to specify options, a plot preview to view the effects of different options, and the ability to store multiple plotter configurations (up to 29) and choose among them without reconfiguring AutoCAD each time you want to use a different one.

It's taken Autodesk some time to get all these changes right, however. The first shipping version of Release 12 for DOS had problems with the plot dialogue box and slow performance from several of the bundled plotter drivers. Release 12c1 for DOS, a bug-fix release that came out in the fall of 1992, fixed some of the problems, but it took a second bug-fix release, 12c2, to fix many of them. If you encounter plot (or other) problems, you may need to get the 12c2 bug-fix from your dealer.

Tip

If you're not sure which version of Release 12 you have, watch AutoCAD's sign-on screen as it loads, or select "About AutoCAD..." from the File menu (the Help menu in Release 12 for Windows).

The plotting tutorial briefly demonstrates the plot dialogue box and one of its new options, plot preview. See Chapter 11, *Paper Space and Plotting,* for more detail on plotting.

Tip

Use the plot dialogue box to preview a plot of your drawing or drawing area when you are first setting it up and when you make major changes to the drawing. This will make it easier to end up with a drawing that will look good when plotted.

Plotting Tutorial

To complete this chapter's tutorial, we'll preview a plot using the new plot dialogue box, then exit.

1. Open the SNOWMAN drawing you created in the Editing tutorial above.

If you did not create the SNOWMAN drawing, take a moment and create or load any simple drawing; you will not need the results of this tutorial in any other tutorials.

2. Open the plot dialogue box.

Pick the PLOT... command from the File menu.

The Plot Configuration dialogue appears (see Figure 1.10). From this dialogue, you can configure and control plotting with a great deal of flexibility. For now, we'll keep things simple.

3. Rotate the plot 90 degrees.

Pick the Rotation and Origin button in the Scale, Rotation and Origin area located in the right center of the dialogue box.

The *Plot Rotation and Origin* subdialogue will appear.

Pick 90 and pick OK.

The subdialogue disappears.

4. Preview the result.

In the Plot Configuration dialogue box, pick Full.

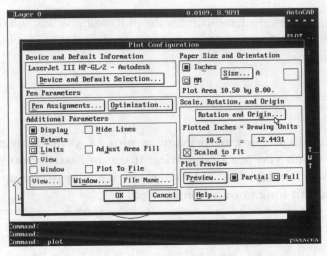

Figure 1.10   The Plot Configuration dialogue box.

NO PLOTTER

If you get the message shown in Figure 1.11, you have not yet configured a plotter. Press <Enter> or <Spacebar> to cancel the warning, then enter CONFIG. Configure a plotter (if you aren't connected to a real one, you can invent one and plot to a file on disk instead). If you're not familiar with how to configure a plotter, follow the steps under "Plotting with Scripts" in Chapter 16. Then return to the drawing editor and start again with step 1 under the Plotting Tutorial.

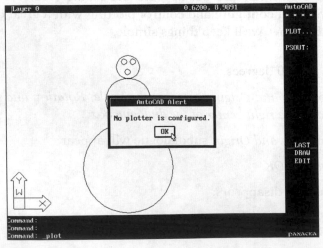

Figure 1.11   The "No plotter" alert box.

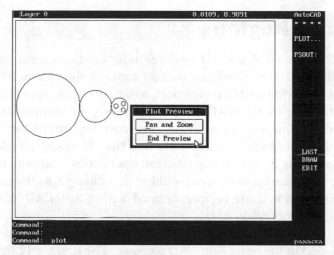

Figure 1.12   Plot Preview shows how plots will appear on paper.

Pick Preview... (not OK)

The drawing window displays the image that will be plotted and a subdialog, Plot Preview, with some options (see Figure 1.12). Note that the drawing is rotated 90 degrees.

5. Return to the drawing editor.

Pick End Preview.

In the Plot Configuration dialogue, pick Cancel.

The Plot Configuration dialogue box disappears.

6. Exit AutoCAD.

```
Command: QUIT
```
Or pick Exit AutoCAD from the File menu.

 Tip

When you quit a drawing that you've changed without saving, AutoCAD now displays a dialogue box instead of the old command-line prompt. The three choices are Save Changes..., Discard Changes, and Cancel Command. Notice that the default is Save Changes..., and that you have to type D for Discard (instead of Y for Yes) followed by <Enter> in order to quit without saving changes.

Rendering and Regions

As of Release 12, the basic AutoCAD package now contains most of the rendering capabilities of AutoShade, as well as some of the capabilities of AME. You can do rendering within a viewport, assign different appearances ("finishes") to entities or to AutoCAD colors, and save your renderings and replay them within a viewport. Less flashy, but more important for some users, is the new Region Modeler, a 2D version of the 3D modeler in AME. With it, you can combine entities using Boolean operations, compute properties of a region, and create associative hatching that changes as the region it fills changes. You can extrude regions created within AutoCAD into 3D solids that you can operate on in AME.

Chapter 12 of this book provides a brief look at some of the rendering features now included in the basic AutoCAD package. The Release 12 *Render Reference Manual* covers rendering in more detail, and Chapter 3 of the *AutoCAD Extras Manual* documents and includes a tutorial for the Region Modeler. If you want to see a quick, dramatic demonstration of 3D rendering, open the KITCHEN2 tutorial drawing that comes with AutoCAD, and pick the Render option from the Render menu. Once you have configured your display driver for rendering, AutoCAD will churn for a minute or two and then show a rendered version of the kitchen (see Figure 1.13). Repeat this little demonstration to impress friends and family who don't understand what you do for a living.

Figure 1.13   A rendered KITCHEN2.DWG.

Release 12 and Workgroups

If you're a consultant (paid or informal) who gives advice to others, a manager responsible for a workgroup, or just someone who wants to use some forethought and organizational skills to get the most out of AutoCAD, you frequently need to take a step back from the details and look at the big picture. This section and others like it in this book will discuss important considerations for workgroups who want to get the most out of AutoCAD.

The most important consideration for workgroups in using Release 12 is that everyone who can take advantage of at least some of the new release's features should be using it. See Appendix A, *Making the Upgrade Decision*, for a discussion of upgrade considerations for individuals and workgroups, including discussion of the choice between DOS and Windows versions.

Once everyone's on the right release, there are several things that Release 12 users within workgroups need to consider. The first is training. Training not only increases individual efficiency, it decreases the amount of time that users will spend explaining basic commands and techniques to one another. This chapter has introduced several new features of Release 12, and this book is one source of training. Part II includes tutorials that cover its most important 2D-drafting features and introduce you to 3D capabilities. Part III describes how to customize AutoCAD for users and CAD managers who won't be spending their lives programming, but who need real-world customization solutions. Other books, instructor-led classes, and self-paced, video- or disk-based courses are also sources of training. Make sure that each Release 12 user in your workgroup receives some form of training.

Getting the people in your workgroup trained also increases the chances that they will come across tips and tricks or ways to customize AutoCAD that will be useful to the whole group. Treat this kind of activity as "real work" and try to ensure that it's recognized as such within your group.

We cover each of the features described in this chapter in more detail later, and discuss considerations affecting a workgroup in the pertinent chapters. The only feature described in this chapter and not in later chapters is the SAVETIME variable. Make sure the users in your group set SAVETIME to 10 or 15 minutes, rather than accepting the default value of 120 minutes. This change alone can help avoid considerable lost work when there's a system crash, power failure, or network breakdown.

2

Introducing Release 12 for Windows

AutoCAD Release 12 for Windows has caused as much excitement as any previous AutoCAD release, and possibly more confusion. Before, platform decisions were easy: You got the most current version that ran on your hardware. But now, as an Intel-based PC user, you have a choice: two very good, up-to-date versions of AutoCAD that run on your hardware, each with its own advantages and disadvantages.

To alleviate some of the confusion, we'll cut to the chase and give you an overall assessment. First, AutoCAD Release 12 for Windows is a very good product with substantial advantages over the DOS 386 version. Autodesk has stated that Windows will be the standard operating platform for the majority of AutoCAD users by the mid-90s, and that AutoCAD for Windows will take the place of AutoCAD 386 as the "flagship" product. If there are no significant obstacles to your moving to it, you should.

However, we believe that most users will need to wait. AutoCAD Release 12 for Windows has stiff hardware requirements, lacks a full range of third-party applications and hardware drivers, imposes a new operating environment learning curve on DOS users who are not yet familiar with Windows, and is somewhat slower than Release 12/386 with a display list processor. Some combination of these factors will keep most AutoCAD users on DOS during the Release 12 time frame.

So, why learn about Release 12 for Windows? First, you may be one of the lucky few who can afford the time and money to move to it soon. Or, you may have the wherewithal to run both versions, possibly using DOS for heavy production work and Windows for software development, rendering, and linking between multiple applications.

But, even if you're completely stuck in DOS for now, it's worth knowing something about Release 12 for Windows, because you'll probably be moving to a Windows version of AutoCAD within the next few years. It may be the current Windows version (as soon as your third-party applications, drivers, and hardware catch up to it), the NT version (now running in Autodesk's labs) when that becomes available, or Release 13 for Windows (whenever that comes out). You may time the upgrade to coincide with the acquisition of a Pentium system, as those become affordable and the bugs get shaken out. In any case, you probably will be looking at the Windows desktop within the next two years. Come along with us for a tour of the new Windows version and highlights of its features, and get a jump on one of the biggest transitions you'll make as an AutoCAD user.

Key Features of Release 12 for Windows

AutoCAD Release 12 for Windows is the best AutoCAD in a long time in terms of taking advantage of the capabilities of its host platform. The "dumbing down" of AutoCAD that had been occurring in an effort to most easily meet the conflicting demands of multiple platforms was halted with Release 12 for DOS, and has begun to be reversed with Release 12 for Windows. The new Windows version takes advantage of Windows features to almost as great an extent as one could hope for, short of completely redesigning the program. For instance, many Windows 3.1 features, such as object linking and embedding (OLE) and drag-and-drop, are not yet available in other Windows programs, but are well-implemented in AutoCAD.

We believe the most important features of Release 12 for Windows are as follows (of course, your own list might be a little different). With apologies to David Letterman, we'll count down from our tenth most important reason to our first:

10. **Customization**   Autodesk says about 30 percent of AutoCAD users customize their systems. Release 12 for Windows brings a multitasking customization environment to PC users, so now you can keep the AutoCAD drawing editor, a text editor, and customization tools like compilers open and on-screen at the same time.

9. **Rendering**   If you're a heavy user of rendering, this feature will be #1. Release 12 for Windows supports multiple open rendering windows, renders in the background, tiles a rendered image across dozens of A-size sheets for you to assemble into a huge image, and more. As with all rendering, these features use immense amounts of memory.

8. **File access**   Not as capable as the DWGDB program included with *AutoCAD Power Tools*, but fine as base functionality. The last four open files are listed on the File menu, and a simple Find File dialogue is available.

7. **Aerial view**   At last, AutoCAD has its own bird's-eye view! The aerial view is simple and elegant, and will make DOS users who don't have this feature in their display drivers aware of how useful it is. Of course, for those who want more features and speed, third-party developers will improve on Autodesk's effort.

6. **Performance**   Release 12 for Windows uses a 32-bit Windows extender to accelerate overall performance and a built-in display list processor to speed up zooms and pans. As a result, R12Win (out of the box) roughly matches the performance of Release 12/386 without an extender—if you have enough memory. So, Release 12/386 with a display list processor is still the hot ticket for performance, but, for many users, the Windows version does fine. Hot tip: Buy more memory.

5. **Release 12/386 features**   AutoCAD Release 12 for Windows includes all the features in Release 12/386. (The first release of R12 for Windows was the c1 version, a few bug fixes behind the latest c2 version for DOS.)

4. **Multiple application**   This feature will move higher on the list as soon as most AutoCAD users learn that there *are* other applications (Hey, it was a *joke*!). You can multitask between AutoCAD and other Windows applications and paste AutoCAD drawings into other applications with hot or cold links. Eats memory for breakfast.

3. **Cut and paste**   Not such a big deal, you say? Wait until you paste between your AutoCAD sessions; whatever you paste is dropped in as a block and keeps its attributes, extended entity data, and so on. Cut and paste to other applications loses the nongraphical data but otherwise works fine.

2. **Toolbar and Toolbox**   These are the two features that "feel" most like Windows. You quickly will get so used to them that changing the current layer any other way, for instance, will seem stupid.

1. **Two words: Multiple sessions**   If you have enough memory in your system (about 16MB to start), you can run three AutoCAD sessions simultaneously. You can plot and render in the background while working (slowly?) in the foreground. Hot tip: Buy a faster system with more memory.

A Real AutoCAD for Windows

Most of the benefits of AutoCAD Release 12 for Windows flow logically from the fact that it's a well-implemented Windows version of AutoCAD. This comment is not meant to minimize Autodesk's accomplishment; it takes a lot of good design and programming work to make a solid Windows program. The development team must have a thorough understanding of its own product and of the Windows environment, then combine the two appropriately so that the result doesn't violate either the Windows interface paradigm or the functionality AutoCAD users have come to expect. If you think this sounds simple, think again. The number of unsuccessful ports of various DOS programs for Windows and the Macintosh (including the first version of AutoCAD on the Mac) shows that it is not easy.

The other important characteristic of Release 12 for Windows is that it's a real AutoCAD. It includes all the features of Release 12/386, and then some. Most importantly, it isn't hamstrung by the performance limitations that made the Release 11 Extension for Windows nearly useless as a production platform.

In the following sections, we divide the new features of Release 12 for Windows into groups and describe them briefly. We also discuss any limitations and problems. The intent is to "drive you through" this new version, whether you simply read this book or carry out the tutorials on a system with Release 12 for Windows installed. For more details about each feature, see the *Using AutoCAD for Windows* and *AutoCAD Installation and Performance Guide for Windows* manuals.

Getting into Windows

Some of the best features of AutoCAD Release 12 for Windows come from meeting certain Windows "basics." One of the primary benefits of the Windows environment is a fundamental consistency among applications, so a credible Windows AutoCAD has to "look" like other Windows programs and share a core set of functions and ways of accessing them (file dialogues, <F1> for help, etc.).

Consistency. In most of its operations, Release 12 for Windows is consistent with other Windows applications. The biggest visible exception is the lack of scrollbars on the drawing editor windows when you use the display-list driver. Smaller exceptions apply to the way selections and commands work; while noun/verb editing is a step in the right direction, some of the compromises are in the direction of AutoCAD history, not Windows consistency.

Multiple sessions. Windows users expect to be able to open multiple documents in a program, and AutoCAD includes this feature. However, 4MB

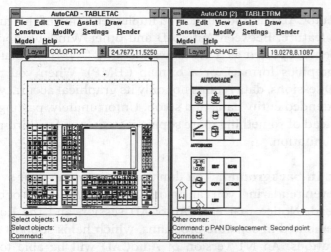

Figure 2.1   Two AutoCAD sessions.

or so per additional open document is a pretty heavy price to pay, and three is a low limit on the number of open documents. Release 12 for Windows actually launches another copy of itself for each additional document; a future version should have more "lightweight" additional windows. Figure 2.1 shows two sessions running at once.

Toolbar. Toolbars are becoming a standard feature of Windows programs, and AutoCAD has a good one, part of which you can customize. Selecting the current layer from a pull-down list is one example of a feature that will be hard to live without if you have to go back to Release 12/386 sometimes. Figure 2.2 shows the toolbar.

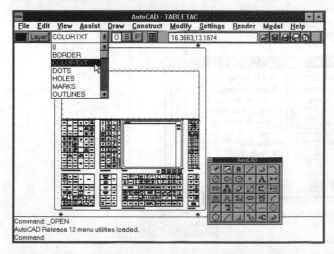

Figure 2.2   The AutoCAD Release 12 for Windows toolbar.

Cut and paste. AutoCAD has a sophisticated implementation of this fundamental Windows feature. Between AutoCAD and other Windows applications, data can be transported as a Windows Metafile (.WMF format—an efficient vector graphics format), or a bitmap (.BMP). When you paste between AutoCAD sessions, data retains not only its graphical accuracy, but also attributes, extended entity data, and so on. Unfortunately, pasting text starts DTEXT instead of something more sophisticated; look for third-party solutions to this limitation.

Plot, render, etc. in background. You don't have to give up your system while plotting or even rendering; you can do other work in AutoCAD or other applications instead. Notice that each AutoCAD session and the Render module are implemented in separate programs, which helps support such background operations. An NT version of AutoCAD will be able to use threads to achieve the same thing much more "cheaply."

Preferences dialogue. This dialogue gives you one place to set several Windows-specific and general AutoCAD functions. (We'll discuss the Environment button and dialogue shortly.) The PREFERENCES command allows you to change the look of your AutoCAD Release 12 for Windows setup and make other changes as well; see Figure 2.3.

Uses Windows drivers. Device-independence is no doubt one reason why Autodesk wants to move its DOS users to Windows. The wide availability of Windows drivers makes it easier for Autodesk to justify writing fewer AutoCAD-specific drivers, and, thus, leaves them with fewer worries about

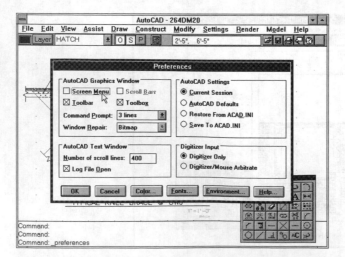

Figure 2.3 Preferences dialogue with settings at default values.

buggy drivers or late third-party ADI drivers after each AutoCAD release—at least, in theory. Unfortunately, there still are problems with many Windows drivers not being robust enough for AutoCAD users, but device manufacturers soon will need to provide excellent Windows drivers or lose large numbers of potential customers.

Windows Guided Tour–Part 1: Basics

In the following tour, we'll open a drawing, set our preferences, change layers from the toolbar, then start another AutoCAD session and use the Windows Clipboard to transfer geometry between the sessions. We'll assume that you understand the basics of DOS AutoCAD and of moving around in Windows.

1. Start Release 12 for Windows.

Double-click on the AutoCAD program icon.

The AutoCAD drawing window and toolbox appears (see Figure 2.2).

2. Establish your preferences.

From the File menu, pick Preferences... or
Enter PREFERENCES at the Command: prompt.

The Preferences dialogue appears (see Figure 2.3).

Change any of the settings in the AutoCAD Graphics Window section of the dialogue to suit your preferences. For instance, turn on Screen Menu if you want to use the side menu.

Note also the Color and Fonts buttons for changing the colors and fonts used by the AutoCAD graphics and text windows.

If you make any changes and want them to remain for future sessions, pick the Save to ACAD.INI radio button.

Pick OK.

3. Open TABLETAC.DWG in the SAMPLE subdirectory.

Pick the Open icon on the toolbar (the file folder just to the right of the coordinate read-out display area).

The Open Drawing dialogue appears.

In the Directories window, navigate to the \ACADWIN\SAMPLE subdirectory.

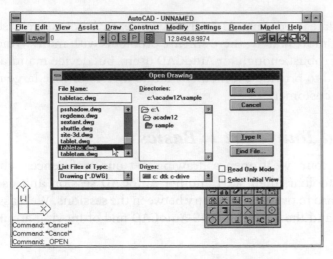

Figure 2.4   Loading the TABLETAC sample drawing.

In the File Name window, scroll down until you see tabletac.dwg.

Double-click on tabletac.dwg to load it (see Figure 2.4).

4. Use the toolbar to change to the COLORTXT layer.

Pick on the drop-down list arrow to the right of the Layer display area.

A scrolling list of layers defined in the current drawing appears; see Figure 2.2.

Click on COLORTXT.

AutoCAD runs the LAYER command and makes COLORTXT current.

5. Make the current window smaller.

Stretch the right border of the current AutoCAD window to the left by clicking on the border and dragging it.

Stretch the border so that the drawing window takes up about half of the screen.

6. Start another AutoCAD session and load TABLETRM.DWG.

Repeat steps 1 and 3, but this time load TABLETRM.DWG.

You may need to temporarily minimize the first AutoCAD session by clicking on the down arrow at the top right of the screen.

Stretch the new AutoCAD window so that it occupies the other half of the screen.

Zoom and pan as necessary in each window so that you can see the drawings.

If your screen gets too crowded, close the toolboxes by double-clicking on their Control-menu boxes. The screen should now look something like Figure 2.1.

7. Use the Windows Clipboard to insert the AutoShade menu into TABLETAC.

Make sure you're in the TABLETRM window.

Pick Copy Vectors from the Edit menu.

Select objects: *Use a selection window to select the AutoShade menu.*

AutoCAD copies the geometry to the Clipboard in both Windows Metafile Format and AutoCAD format.

Change to the TABLETAC window.

Pick Paste from the Edit menu.

AutoCAD constructs a name for the Block.

Insertion point: 0,0

Notice that AutoCAD used the 0,0 point of the TABLETRM drawing as the Block's basepoint.

Accept the defaults for the remaining values.

AutoCAD inserts the Block; see Figure 2.5.

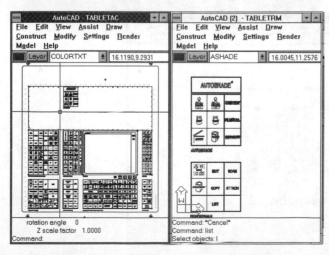

Figure 2.5 TABLETAC after pasting the Block.

8. Quit the second AutoCAD session and get rid of TABLETAC in the first one.

Close the TABLETRM session by double-clicking on its Control-menu box at the upper-left corner of the window. Tell AutoCAD to discard changes.

Pick New… from the File menu, discard changes, and then click on OK in the Create New Drawing dialogue in order to start a new unnamed drawing.

Advanced Windows Features

In addition to the benefits that come from meeting the basic requirements of Windows, AutoCAD gets a lot of mileage from implementing many advanced features as well. These are features that are not required for Windows applications but that AutoCAD has implemented to good advantage.

Toolbox. The toolbox is a collection of icons that allow you to choose a command by picking its icon, then using the cursor as a "tool" to carry out the operation. You can turn the toolbox off or place it on the screen in one of three ways: as a strip down the left of the screen, as a strip down the right (in the side-screen menu spot), or (our favorite) as a "floating" square block that you can move anywhere on the screen. In this last version, the name of the command that you're currently pointing at appears in the toolbox title bar (see Figure 2.6).

Scrollable command window. Anyone who's used a good communications program with its scrolling text window and retrieval of several hundred lines of text has long bemoaned the limited 24-line, use-it-or-lose-it AutoCAD text screen. Release 12 for Windows gives you a resizable and scrollable text

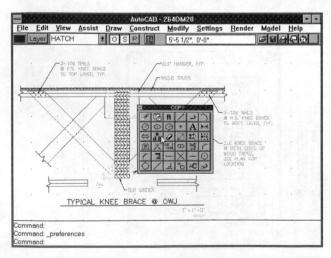

Figure 2.6   Toolbox with command name displayed in the title bar.

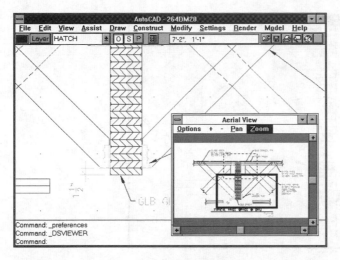

Figure 2.7   Aerial view.

window for command-line history, and it can save up to 1,500 lines of text. You can even log command-line activity to a text file for writing scripts or training documents (or books!).

Aerial view. This is an easy-to-use and very nice bird's-eye viewer for free (see Figure 2.7). It lets you zoom and pan at display-list speed by picking points in a zoomed-out view, no matter what the main drawing window shows. In addition, the Locate option acts as a magnifying glass: It dynamically displays in the aerial view window a zoomed-in view of wherever your cursor is located in the drawing window. This feature is great for inspecting drawings without having to zoom repeatedly.

Drag-and-drop. You can drag-and-drop all sorts of files into your drawing, and AutoCAD intelligently adds them in. Just open the Windows File Manager next to your drawing window, go to the subdirectory where the Block, font file, linetype, AutoLISP program, script, etc. is located, and "drag" the name of the file into the drawing window. AutoCAD will then "do the right thing" with it, based on the file extension; for instance, DWG files get inserted as blocks. There are two limitations, though: You can't load a drawing or attach an Xref this way.

Last four drawings. The last four drawings you've opened show up at the bottom of the File menu. Again, it's a minor feature that you'll get attached to very fast. See Figure 2.8 for an example.

Find file. When it's time to load drawings that you've accessed less recently, bring up the Find File dialogue. It's helpful but limited. The *AutoCAD Power*

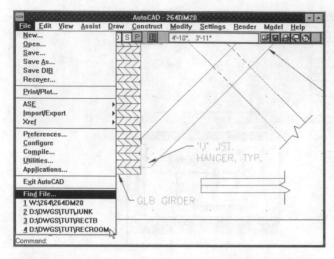

Figure 2.8   File access options: last four drawings and Find File.

Tools disk includes a DWGDB dialogue that works under both the DOS and Windows versions of AutoCAD and offers better searching capabilities. Figure 2.9 shows the version built into AutoCAD.

On-line help.   R12Win's help facility is far superior to the one in Release 12/ 386—it's practically the equivalent of having the AutoCAD manuals on-line. Release 12 for Windows uses the standard Windows help engine, so users of other Windows programs will immediately be familiar with how to use it. With Release 12 for Windows help, there's an amazing amount of information only a few cursor picks away, including "how to" screens that you won't find in the printed manuals. You can search, follow links, get glossary

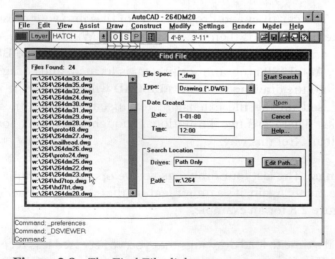

Figure 2.9   The Find File dialogue.

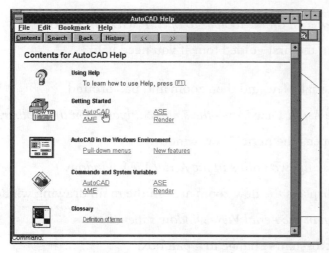

Figure 2.10   On-line help.

definitions in pop-up windows, add annotations, place bookmarks, and more. Figure 2.10 shows a Help window.

Object Linking and Embedding (OLE). With OLE, you can paste AutoCAD drawings directly into another OLE-supporting application, either by embedding (a cold, dead copy) or linking (a live copy that changes as the original drawing changes). Even more impressively, you can edit the pasted drawing in place by double-clicking on it to bring up AutoCAD! Though great for users, this feature also may become a gold mine for Autodesk and a bad dream for AutoCAD support people. Users who normally would not need AutoCAD will want a license so they can edit drawings pasted into documents they receive. But these same users will know nothing about CAD in general or AutoCAD in particular; we can hear the tech-support lines ringing now. There are a few negatives to AutoCAD's OLE support: You can link from model space, but not from paper space; you can only link from the first AutoCAD session; and AutoCAD is an OLE server but not a client—you can't link other documents, such as text from a word processor, into an AutoCAD drawing.

Windows Guided Tour–Part 2: Advanced Features

In our second tour, we'll try out the Aerial View, look up help for it, and use OLE to link a drawing to a Windows Write document.

1. Open PSGLOBE.DWG in the SAMPLE subdirectory.

Maximize the AutoCAD Window first (i.e., pick the up-arrow symbol at the upper-right corner of the window).

Use the Open icon on the toolbar to open PSGLOBE.DWG.

See step 3 in the first guided tour if you need help.

2. Open the Aerial View and then zoom and pan around.

Click on the Aerial View icon—the small compass—on the toolbar.

AutoCAD opens the Aerial View window.

Zoom by picking two points in the Aerial View window.

AutoCAD displays the new zoom area in the main drawing window.

Click on Pan in the Aerial View window's menu.

The zoom crosshairs change to a pan box.

Pick anywhere in the Aerial View window to pan.

3. Use Locate to review the drawing.

Pick Options and then Locate in the Aerial View window's menu.

Move your cursor outside the Aerial View window.

Now the Aerial View window displays a magnified view of the location at your cursor. As you move the cursor, the view updates.

Change the magnification by pressing your right mouse button.

The Magnification dialogue appears; see Figure 2.11.

When you're finished using Locate, pick in the Aerial View window to restore the bird's-eye view.

4. Look up Aerial View in the on-line help system.

Pick Contents from the Help menu or
Press the <F1> key.

The AutoCAD Help dialogue appears; see Figure 2.10.

Pick on the word AutoCAD under Getting Started, as shown in Figure 2.10.

The Getting Started with AutoCAD page appears.

Use the scrollbar to move down, and pick on New Features at the end of the page.

The New Features page appears.

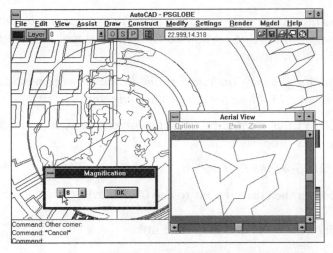

Figure 2.11   Changing the magnification for Locate.

> *Pick on the Aerial View.*
>
> The Aerial View page appears; see Figure 2.12.
>
> *Read the help screen, and click on any phrases in green for more information.*
>
> *When you're finished, double-click on the AutoCAD Help window Control-menu box to close help.*

5. Prepare to make an OLE link to a Windows Write document.

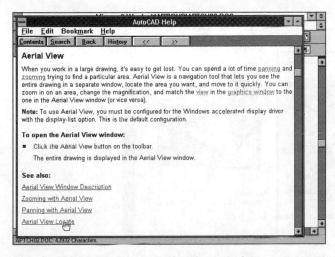

Figure 2.12   On-line Help for the Aerial View.

Restore the AutoCAD drawing window to its half-screen size by picking on the Restore button (the up-and-down-arrow symbol at the upper-right corner of the window).

Zoom so that the drawing fits comfortably in the drawing window, as shown in Figure 2.13. Close the Aerial View window.

The OLE COPYLINK command uses the current view, so you need to arrange the view properly first.

Pick Copy Link from the Edit menu.

AutoCAD copies the current view to the Clipboard.

6. Launch Windows Write and make the link.

Start Windows Write from the Program Manager.

Windows Write should be in your Accessories group.

Arrange the Write window so that you can see both your AutoCAD drawing and Write document, as shown in Figure 2.13.

Type some text at the top of the document.

From Write's Edit menu, pick Paste Link.

The AutoCAD drawing is linked into the Write document via OLE.

Add more text and any formatting you want; see Figure 2.13 for an example.

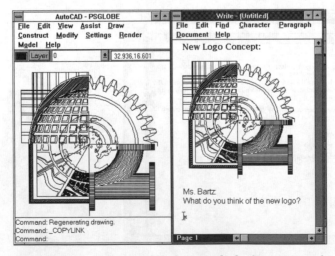

Figure 2.13 An AutoCAD drawing linked to a Write document.

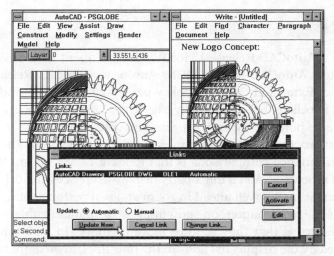

Figure 2.14 The updated OLE link.

7. Revise the drawing and update the link.

Return to the AutoCAD window and make a change to the drawing, such as adding some circles to the annular ring (see Figure 2.14).

The Write document still displays the old version.

Return to the Write Window and pick Links... from the Edit menu.

The Links dialogue box appears.

Pick the Update Now button.

The Write document updates; see Figure 2.14.

Quit both Write and AutoCAD. You can discard changes.

This is just one simple example of linking drawings with OLE. OLE makes it much easier to create and update reports containing drawings, and as more and more programs support OLE, the possibilities will multiply. Although Windows Write works fine for simple documents, many full-fledged Windows word processors, such as Microsoft Word for Windows and WordPerfect for Windows (version 5.2), support OLE as well.

 Tip

OLE can be a valuable tool for developing CAD standards manuals. Instead of relying on text alone or paste-up with scissors and glue, use OLE to link drawings with text. This approach will make it easier to update your CAD standards manual.

Performance

The performance of AutoCAD Release 12 for Windows is about as good as the performance of stock AutoCAD Release 12/386. Anyone who used the Release 11 AutoCAD Windows Extension (with its pokey performance) might find this statement difficult to believe, but it's generally true. The 32-bit Windows extender used by R12Win is responsible for faster regens and other operations, and the built-in display-list processor further improves zoom and pan speed. The only problem with performance comparisons is that Release 12/386 doesn't come with a display-list processor. Add a third-party display-list processing driver to the 386 version, and it moves well ahead in zoom and pan performance.

As we discuss in the next chapter, one potential performance problem with display-list processors is that they require more memory. In R12Win, the extra memory used by the display list adds to the multimegabyte demands of Windows, AutoCAD, and any additional AutoCAD sessions. In DOS, using display-list processing with big drawings might cause you to need "a lot" of system memory, perhaps 12MB or so. Under Windows, using display-list processing with multiple sessions will force your memory requirements into the 20MB-plus range. And in the Windows version, losing display-list processing due to lack of memory is likely to force performance well below what the DOS version, even without display-list processing, can support.

To further increase performance, Release 12 for Windows bypasses part of the Windows Graphics Display Interface (GDI). This speeds up AutoCAD, but might cause incompatibilities with some Windows display drivers. Also, you might see AutoCAD windows "popping up" over another application if you've left an AutoCAD window processing in the background. If you run into these sorts of problems, you can turn off the GDI bypass from the CONFIG menu.

A Few More Features

There are several features that AutoCAD has in its Windows version that it lacks under DOS. These features aren't required or specifically enabled by Windows; they're just useful add-ons that Autodesk has included at this point.

Environment dialogue. This dialogue is brought up by picking the Environment... button in the Preferences dialogue described earlier. The Environment dialogue (see Figure 2.15) is one way of instructing AutoCAD where to look for support files and how to handle its pager (swap) file. You also can use environment variables, as you do with AutoCAD 386.

Rendering improvements. Rendering under Release 12 for Windows is much better than in the DOS version. You can render to a window and

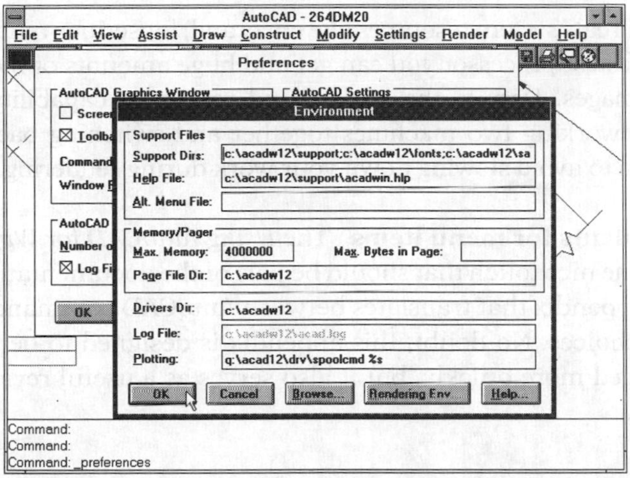

Figure 2.15   The Environment dialogue.

render in the background; no longer does rendering need to take over your computer. The rendering program, which is separate from the main AutoCAD program, uses the Windows Multiple Document Interface (MDI), so you don't need a separate copy of AVE Render running in each rendering window. This reduces program overhead. And finally, it's much easier to do something useful with your renderings in R12Win: You can copy rendered images to the Clipboard or save them to bitmaps (.BMP) or metafiles (.WMF) for importing into other Windows programs. As an added bonus, you can print across multiple A-size pages (see Figure 2.16 to see how this is specified). With some taping or gluing, you can produce big, beautiful poster-size or larger images.

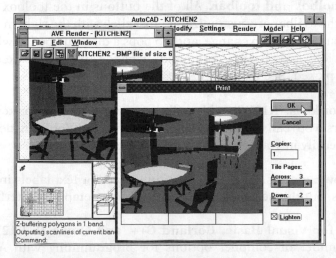

Figure 2.16   Printing a rendered image across multiple pages.

But rendering still eats system resources like crazy and, for serious rendering, you will need the fastest processor you can get and huge amounts of memory for complicated images. Despite the background rendering capability, you might consider networking two machines together and switching back and forth between them to avoid slowing down your work during rendering.

Command equivalents for menu items. The *Using AutoCAD for Windows* manual includes one nice touch that should be part of the documentation for all platforms: an appendix that translates between AutoCAD commands and pull-down menu choices. No doubt, this appendix is designed to help new users get up to speed more quickly, but it also serves as a useful review for experienced users.

Customization

Like serious rendering users, serious AutoCAD customizers will be tempted by Release 12 for Windows because of the multitasking environment and links to other applications. On the other hand, ADS-based text editors and other development tools for AutoCAD 386 make it a workable and efficient customization environment for many people, and it will take some time for these tools to migrate to Windows.

R12Win has clear advantages for ordinary users who want to make modest changes to AutoCAD. Several of the interface improvements in the Windows version are trivially easy to modify, even for people who tremble at the mention of the word "AutoLISP."

Customizable toolbox and toolbar. All of the buttons in the toolbox and most of those in the toolbar are customizable. Just click with the right mouse button on the icon you want to change, and up pops a dialogue box in which you can select an icon and type in a command string for AutoCAD to execute when the icon is picked. See Figure 2.17 for an example.

Menu accelerator keys. R12Win adds pull-down menu accelerator keys— underlined letters you can use to select menu choices. You can define accelerator keys easily in your own custom menus. See Chapter 17.

Icons in pull-down menus. You can substitute icons for text labels in the pull-down menus, but this seems like a bizarre "mixed metaphor" interface.

ADS interfaces for Visual Basic, Borland C++, and Quick C. R12Win increases the number of compiler options for programming with ADS. Visual Basic programmers now can write ADS programs without having to

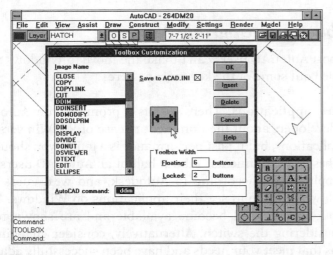

Figure 2.17   Customizing the toolbox.

learn C, and C programmers can use one of the popular Windows compilers from Borland or Microsoft. Note that existing Release 12/386 ADS applications must be recompiled in order to run under Release 12 for Windows, so many current third-party applications won't work with R12Win.

DDE. Dynamic Data Exchange is the "communications pipeline" between Windows applications; it lets one program exchange data with or even drive another program.

ODBC ASE driver. Release 12 for Windows adds support for Microsoft's Open Database Connectivity (ODBC) interface to the AutoCAD SQL Extension (ASE). The ODBC driver lets AutoCAD link to external databases created by ODBC-compliant database management systems. We discuss ASE briefly in Chapter 10 (*Xrefs, Blocks, and Attributes*), and Chapter 13 (*Customization Overview*).

Moving Up to Windows

Moving to Windows is technically a platform switch rather than an upgrade. But the Windows version really is an improvement over the DOS version in terms of raw AutoCAD functionality. Just the ability to run multiple sessions makes the effort of switching worthwhile. But most users can't make the move right away. You already know the benefits of R12Win from the previous parts of this chapter; now we'll describe the issues you need to consider before switching to it. Spend some time learning about Release 12 for Windows and plan a realistic migration strategy for your situation.

Why You Probably Can't Upgrade Now

Unfortunately, most AutoCAD users can't make the move to Windows right away. We've spelled out some of the key reasons here.

Lack of third-party applications. There are lots of promises from Autodesk and third-party developers about the imminent release of R12Win versions of third-party applications, but if past performance is a guide, you shouldn't bet your job on these "commitments." About half of all AutoCAD users rely on third-party applications, according to Autodesk, and we'd guess that most of them will wait awhile to see their applications on Windows. Wait until the applications you need become available and are shown to be robust before considering the switch. Alternatively, consider changing to other applications that meet your needs and have been successfully adapted to Windows.

The "first on your block" syndrome. The earlier you move to Windows, the more likely it will be that you'll go it alone. The obstacles to switching are significant enough that many people you know will hold off, and that means a smaller pool of formal and informal support, training, and customization resources will be available. If you can, coordinate your migration strategy with others with whom you work or on whom you rely for help.

Lack of drivers and inadequate drivers. There's a lot of hardware that needs new or improved Windows drivers to be useful with Release 12 for Windows. Tablet makers, in particular, face challenges getting their products to work in a multitasking, mouse-based environment. Again, wait until the drivers you need are shipping and reliable, or switch to hardware that's made the transition.

System requirements. Windows needs more of everything than DOS to gain equivalent performance, and AutoCAD Release 12 for Windows needs even more: a bigger monitor to manage all those windows, faster video, much more memory, a bigger, faster hard disk, and a faster processor to drive it all. The cost and hassle of upgrading or replacing your hardware is a big impediment to change.

Loss of graphics performance. The better your AutoCAD 386 graphics card and driver, the more reluctant you'll be to move to Windows. Graphics hardware and driver makers have spent a lot of time tuning their products for AutoCAD 386, and it shows. It's likely to be some time before R12Win drivers come close.

Licensing problems. If you switch from AutoCAD 386 to Release 12 for Windows, the license agreement gives you 90 days to erase the 386 version from your hard disk. Now, Autodesk seems to be winking at violations of this clause, but who wants to be the first one brought up on charges by the Software Publishers Association over it? To legally run both versions for more than 90 days, you'll need to buy an additional AutoCAD license, which isn't a very appealing prospect for many people.

General configuration issues. People who have spent years optimizing their hardware and software for AutoCAD 386 are not going to be in a hurry to make any big changes. Also, Windows is a complicated environment in which trouble-shooting problems or tuning performance requires taking into account the inter-actions among DOS, Windows, AutoCAD, other programs, and various drivers.

Benefits of waiting. One of the biggest impediments to upgrading to Windows now is that all of the problems associated with the move are going to get smaller with time. Hardware will get faster and cheaper; device support for Windows will increase; more third-party applications for Windows will become available; and the need to have two versions at once (an expensive choice under current licensing policies) will decrease.

When to Upgrade

Despite the issues raised above, you must be careful not to wait too long to switch. In the computer world, it's always tempting to hold off just a little longer while prices drop, features increase, and incompatibilities work themselves out. Just realize that, at some point, you'll have to bite the bullet and move; don't put it off so long that you miss out on needed benefits or end up playing a long catch-up game with people who started the transition earlier.

In general, we recommend that you make the move as soon as you reasonably can. If you can't move right away, consider that an NT version and AutoCAD Release 13 are in progress. Also, you probably will need to upgrade your hardware within six to twelve months after Pentium-based machines come out. Moving to Windows on your new hardware is probably a good idea. Gather the information you need, make a decision you can live with, and revisit it as new information becomes available.

What to Look For Next Time

If Autodesk does nothing but fill holes in its next major release of AutoCAD for Windows, there are some logical fixes to be made. Better support for noun/verb editing is one. Try a Windows-based illustration program to get a feel for how this might work. Text editing needs to become much better; at minimum, AutoCAD needs to be an OLE client as well as a server. Then you'll be able to maintain text in a word processor—even one as simple as Windows Write would be a big improvement—and paste it into AutoCAD via a live link. The regen required every time you resize a drawing window desperately needs to be eliminated.

The AutoCAD drawing editor also needs Multiple Document Interface support. This would allow more documents to be open simultaneously and cut memory usage, since each open document would not need to start a separate instance of AutoCAD. MDI also should remove restrictions, such as only being able to link the first drawing via OLE, and could speed up background tasks. But it will probably take an NT version with multithreading support to really improve background processing performance.

Despite these needs, the Release 12 for Windows is about as good an implementation of AutoCAD Release 12 as one could hope for under Windows. But it's not the best CAD program one could imagine under Windows. Balancing backward compatibility with new features to create a much better program is a hard task, and one that big companies often fail at. If Autodesk decides to redesign AutoCAD for a "best possible" Windows version, the look, feel, and features of the resulting product are unpredictable.

Release 12 for Windows and Workgroups

While an individual's decision to move to Windows is complicated, the same decision, when multiplied by all the considerations facing a workgroup, is huge. If you compare it to switching over to AutoCAD on Sun workstations, you'll be in the right ballpark for the magnitude of the change.

But the move to a Windows version of AutoCAD also provides additional opportunities for the workgroup beyond those available to an individual. For instance, if your workgroup has been getting by with a hodgepodge of hardware, drivers, operating systems, third-party applications, and AutoCAD versions, now is the time to reduce the confusion. Make some choices in hardware and software and stick with them. As users move to AutoCAD for Windows, get them on the new hardware and software, as well.

The main need for a workgroup is not necessarily to move to AutoCAD for Windows quickly, but to move together. You will waste a great deal of decision-making time, training, customization, and other efforts if you let your shop stay split for too long. Try to keep all but a few well-qualified early adopters from making the switch ahead of the pack (and make sure they keep current DOS licenses, as well), then move everyone else over in a relatively short time frame. Minimize early support—make clear that it's what the British call a "DIY," (Do It Yourself)—for Windows. Then, once the transition is made, cut down fast on support for DOS.

Described below are a few more points you should consider about this transition.

Politics. We've written this section as if you were an omnipotent CAD decision-maker for your workgroup or company, but reality is much more complicated. In some workgroups and companies, one or two people can make decisions and enforce them; in others, consensus will need to be carefully built over months or years. In many environments, near-anarchy prevails, and the best you can hope to do is make the right decisions for yourself and try to exert some influence on others. One worthwhile effort is to ask about successful and unsuccessful hardware and software transitions in your company and learn from them.

Use consultants and dealers. More politics: Beyond the technical expertise they can bring to a situation, consultants and dealers can be wonderful for forcing everyone away from turf wars and into supporting and implementing a decision. Look for someone who has handled this kind of transition before, and get his or her help in the changes that need to be made in your workgroup or company.

New users. One of the key arguments for AutoCAD for Windows is that it will make things easier for new users. At least for this version, we're not so sure. Autodesk emphasizes that people use 20 percent of the operations 80 percent of the time, and they've worked hard to simplify those most-used operations. The trouble is that the user then gets completely lost when faced with the remaining, unsimplified parts of the program; old, dusty applications and AutoLISP routines with primitive interfaces; configuration problems; and so on.

If people in your company start using OLE to put AutoCAD drawings in all sorts of documents, you're going to get a lot of calls from actual and would-be new AutoCAD users. Then, your management will want to know who needs a $3,000-plus AutoCAD license, plus a hardware upgrade, and why. Try to put some planning effort into this before you're deluged with in-house support calls and complaints. Keeping AutoCAD for Windows' use low until your whole group makes the transition will help.

Marking time. What should you do if you decide to wait before moving to Windows? The tools in this book help accentuate the positive in the DOS environment. The TurboDLD*Lite* display-list driver will speed DOS users ahead of Windows users, while requiring a smaller hardware investment. The DWGDB dialogue gives capabilities to either DOS or Windows that go beyond the base functionality of the Windows version. The File Viewer, in particular, reduces the need for multitasking.

This chapter and various notes throughout the book will help you get a feel for Release 12 for Windows and decide how to best make the transition. The descriptions in this book of how to get the most out of using, managing, and customizing Release 12 contain a lot of information that you can use to maximize productivity in your current environment. Use them to keep things moving forward up to and beyond the time you move to Windows.

Early adopters. Get one or more users to serve as "guinea pigs" for the move to AutoCAD for Windows. The most proficient users should have less trouble with the change and might enjoy helping prepare for a move by everyone else. Make sure early adopters have the hardware they need to run Windows well. Ask them about their experiences and note the high and low points for your planning. Early adopters will serve as your first line of support when the phone starts ringing after a full-scale move to AutoCAD for Windows.

Standard customization. The move to Windows is a great chance to do some up-front customizing. Get your early users to help you configure the toolbar and toolbox for your group's needs. Augment your AutoLISP routines with dialogue boxes if you have the in-house talent, or outside help to do it efficiently. Get away from the side-screen menu. Make sure that everyone gets started with an appropriate set of prototype drawings, fonts, linetypes, Blocks, Xrefs, and so on. (The rest of this book contains details on all of these things.)

Migration strategies. Our previous advice about migration strategies is even more pertinent for workgroups. You may decide to move as soon as possible or to wait for other major transitions, such as moving to Pentium machines, moving to AutoCAD for Microsoft Windows NT when that becomes an option, and/or moving to the next major release of AutoCAD. Make those who complain loudest early adopters and do what you can to hold off the rest.

One last reminder. Remember that the move to AutoCAD for Windows resembles a platform switch to a different operating system more than it resembles a normal release-number upgrade. This is especially true if you're fairly new to Windows. You will need to make wide-ranging decisions about hardware and software that will affect your group's work well into the future. Don't be afraid to say "no," and be sure to pick a definite time frame in which to say "yes."

3
Performance

Speed is a top concern of all AutoCAD users. CAD users in general, and AutoCAD users in particular, probably have done more to drive the sales of high-performance PCs and fast graphics subsystems than any other user groups. The growing popularity of Windows and Windows CAD programs like AutoCAD Release 12 for Windows will only accelerate this trend, as the performance demands of Windows are added to the already great demands of CAD.

In this chapter, we'll discuss a number of different aspects of performance. First, we'll talk about performance versus productivity—what each is, and how they're both important. Then, we'll review hardware performance issues and AutoCAD's STATUS command, which will help you get on top of memory and disk-related performance issues with AutoCAD 386. We then discuss Release 12's "no regens" feature and the surprisingly complicated ways in which it might affect your system's performance.

Finally, we'll offer some tips for getting better performance by changing the way AutoCAD is configured, and wrap up with performance issues that are specific to workgroups. A book could be written about higher-performance hardware for AutoCAD, and another about tuning AutoCAD to get the most out of it on a specific system. In this chapter, we hit the high points of each topic.

Performance and Productivity

Bud Smith did a survey on customer satisfaction with an early version of Panaceas's TurboDLD™ line of display drivers. Users were highly satisfied with the product and the primary reason, by an overwhelming margin, was the increased speed it gave to AutoCAD. Few users had any complaints, but the main problem cited by those who did was that they wanted even more speed!

Although the TurboDLD*Lite* driver included with this book is much faster than previous versions, we probably would get similar results if we took the survey again; AutoCAD users greatly appreciate speed, and any noticeable delay is a major annoyance to them.

It's become fashionable to downplay the need for performance and to change the topic to overall productivity. We agree with the idea of broadening the discussion, but only to a point. Long-standing research by IBM and others has shown that even minor delays in response time—anything greater than three-tenths of a second between command and response—causes a major decrease in productivity.

This decrease is not due just to the cumulative sum of all the time the user spends waiting; when the system is slow to respond, the user actually works more slowly overall, even *between* the delays. People know what they want to do and expect the computer to do it; when it doesn't, they get annoyed, distracted, and less productive. So don't be fooled—while overall productivity is the most important issue, system performance will have a dramatic effect on how productive you are.

AutoCAD Power Tools is designed to help you address all facets of performance and productivity. It includes the TurboDLD*Lite* driver to increase the performance of Release 12 for DOS, and a great deal of information on how to get the most out of the new features of Release 12 and how to customize AutoCAD to make your use of it even more efficient. It even includes new interface programs to help you find files, view files, and manage drawings, all further improvements to productivity.

This chapter narrows the focus to hardware purchasing decisions and software configuration options that directly affect performance. Read through it to get a feel for the issues, and refer to it again as you make choices that affect your overall CAD environment.

Hardware

Lots of time, energy, and money go into acquiring the right hardware for AutoCAD. We're going to focus on performance-related hardware so that you'll have a general understanding of what you need to buy in order to upgrade your current system or to get the best performance from your next one. We'll also take the opportunity to discuss some possibilities for the future.

RAM

Once you have a display-list processing driver—in fact, especially when you have one—the biggest single performance enhancer you can get for your existing system usually is more RAM. Although it's possible to run AutoCAD and other "big" programs on a tight memory budget, this is false economy. When AutoCAD uses up all physical memory, it starts using disk space as "virtual memory," which is many times slower than real memory. Always be generous in your estimates of the amount of RAM you need, and then round up. If you're trying to decide whether you need more RAM, the STATUS command, described shortly, can help you decide. A quick-and-dirty indicator is the disk drive light; if it comes on frequently throughout the day as you're using AutoCAD and you notice longer delays as the day wears on, you probably need more RAM.

At about $40 a megabyte at the time of this writing, more RAM is the cheapest performance enhancement you can buy. The holdup in getting more RAM usually is the result of factors other than cost—the hassle of ordering and installing it, problems with getting approval to spend the money, or limitations on the amount of 32-bit fast RAM you can fit in your machine. So, given the benefits of additional RAM and the impediments to upgrading it, you should add as much as you can each time you buy some. Table 3.1 shows sensible minimums for different ways of using AutoCAD with small- to medium-sized drawings (less than 500KB, minimal 3D, AME, or rendering). These figures are higher than what Autodesk recommends, but fit with our experience and that of others we've talked to.

Many systems can support only a limited amount of RAM on the motherboard or on 32-bit add-in cards; on the other hand, more and more systems support up to 64MB on the motherboard. Contact the vendor of your equipment for information about the best way to add memory. When buying new systems, consider only those that can support at least 32MB of RAM on the motherboard.

Table 3.1 Suggested RAM for AutoCAD

	Release 12 for DOS	Release 12 for Windows
Straight AutoCAD, no display list	8MB	12MB
With display-list processor running	12MB	16MB
With one additional AutoCAD session	N/A	21MB
With two additional AutoCAD sessions	N/A	25MB
Other Windows programs running	N/A	+2-4M each

Hard Disk

Having a plentiful supply of RAM will help minimize AutoCAD's demand on your hard disk, but, even with adequate memory, AutoCAD still needs to load program code, drawings, and support files from the disk. Keep buying RAM as long as you can fit more in your system and as long as you see the hard disk light staying on frequently. RAM also can be used as a disk cache to speed up hard disk reads and writes, as we discuss shortly. Once you have enough RAM, you can look to the hard disk for some additional improvement in performance.

Even those who don't need a new hard disk for speed may be forced to upgrade in order to get more space; this is especially true for users of the Windows version. To run it as efficiently as possible, you should increase the size of your permanent Windows swap file to about 30MB, and specify another 30MB for AutoCAD's own drawing data swap file. All told, you will need over 100MB for DOS, Windows, AutoCAD, and the Windows and AutoCAD swap files. And, of course, your other Windows and DOS applications will add to the space requirements. Fortunately, bigger hard disks tend to be faster as well.

Disk doublers are worth looking into. DOS 6 includes disk compression; use it or a third-party program to create more room on your hard disk. But once you've installed a disk doubler and still need more disk space, which disk standard will work best for you? Let's take a quick look at the two most popular choices for high-performance systems.

IDE: INTEGRATED DRIVE ELECTRONICS

IDE is fast, cheap, and relatively standard; it's what you get these days if you don't specify something else. Local bus controllers should have the best performance; consider a caching disk controller to increase speed. Make sure that your system has one more drive bay than you think you will need over and above those needed for floppy drives, a tape backup or CD-ROM drive, and your hard disk.

SCSI: SMALL COMPUTER SYSTEMS INTERFACE

In the DOS PC world, SCSI is not quite as standard as on other platforms. Different SCSI devices and adaptors from different manufacturers sometimes aren't compatible, and you don't always get the "plug-and-play" ease of installation that SCSI was designed for. But the situation is improving, and SCSI has one significant advantage over IDE: expandability. With a single SCSI adaptor card, you can add hard disk drives, CD-ROM drives, and tape drives to your system until the cows come home (well, actually until you get to 7 devices).

You also can do something with compatible SCSI adaptors that you can't do with IDE: carry peripherals, such as a CD-ROM drive, from one system to another. If you have systems at work and home, for instance, this can be a tremendous advantage. Imagine being able to carry your whole AutoCAD environment home with you! If you standardize on a given SCSI adaptor within a workgroup, you can get this advantage among more and more people.

For now, most systems will continue to be sold with IDE, and in many cases the "fuss factor" with SCSI is still greater than it is with IDE. Stick with IDE when you need fast, simple, and standard hard drives. Consider SCSI if you need quickly expandable and flexible storage, or if you want to build toward interchangeability of devices among your own systems and those in your workgroup.

Microprocessor

With the 586 Pentium chip now shipping, there are more microprocessor choices for the AutoCAD user than ever before. Intel, in response to competition, continues to crank out faster and faster microprocessors for reasonable prices. This has been the main factor driving down the cost of high-end PCs; even an AutoCAD user can get a competent system for under $4,000.

The microprocessor is important in and of itself, and also because it is the element that a well-made system is designed around. The more advanced (and expensive) your system's microprocessor, the more likely the system is to have a large external cache, room on the motherboard for lots of RAM, a large, fast hard disk, and a local bus for video and, possibly, the hard-disk controller. At this writing, and probably until Release 13 arrives, the best advice is to get a system based on an Intel 486 running at 50 or 66MHz, or running at a slower speed with the ability to take a clock-doubling chip later.

You may get advice to go farther and buy a Pentium-ready or Pentium-based system. We discuss the upcoming changes shortly, but, for most users, we suggest waiting until a year or so after the Pentium comes out. It'll take awhile for systems and software to take much advantage of Pentium, prices should drop rapidly after the first six to 12 months, and multiprocessor-ready systems may become a better choice not too long after Pentium's arrival.

Graphics Interfaces and Boards

One of the biggest boons to PC CAD users has been the introduction of local bus video—yet another example of CAD, helped, in this case, by Windows driving the PC hardware market forward. There has been some controversy over how much benefit local bus video confers on real programs (rather than on benchmarks), and over which local bus standard, VESA or Intel's PCI, will win out. (At this writing, only the VESA standard has shipped, and sales are brisk.) But it seems clear from numerous benchmark results and the delighted response of users that local bus systems do, indeed, improve the graphics response of many programs (especially Windows), and that the VESA local bus standard, at least, is here to stay.

As an example, the system used by one of us (Smith) for running AutoCAD is a 486/25 from Bay Computer Systems, based on an Orchid Superboard motherboard with a Fahrenheit 1280/D local-bus video card plugged into a VESA VL-bus local bus slot. The local-bus version of the Fahrenheit 1280 card runs even faster than the popular nonlocal-bus version. However, the Fahrenheit 1280 is a "smart" card with graphics coprocessing based on an S3 chip set. It benefits only marginally from local bus in some operations, such as line drawing (which AutoCAD does a lot of), and much more in operations that require large data transfers in memory (which Windows does a lot of). As a result, Windows gets a greater performance boost from the local-bus capabilities of this card than does AutoCAD 386.

With both AutoCAD and Windows, the display driver is every bit as important as the graphics card itself. A fast driver can make an undistinguished graphics card really perform, and conversely, a mediocre driver will make a great graphics card look like it's stuck in first gear.

We suggest that you keep an eye on the reviews and benchmark results in magazines such as *CADalyst*, *CADENCE*, and *PC Magazine*. But also be aware that benchmarks don't tell the whole story, and realize that some manufacturers will optimize their hardware and drivers in ways that help benchmark but not real-world performance. Talk to people who know AutoCAD—other users, consultants, and dealers—about their experiences with different hardware, since AutoCAD places its own unique demands on hardware.

Hardware Futures

The Intel-based PC marketplace is about to undergo a "paradigm shift" from 32-bit, single-processor systems to 64-bit, multiprocessor and multiprocessor-ready systems. AutoCAD users, who push their systems harder than anyone, will be among the main beneficiaries. Watch out, though: There's a thin line between being on the "leading edge," where adventurous users will get workstation-like performance from cheap, PC-compatible systems, and the "bleeding edge," where overpriced and incompatible systems that can't be upgraded wait to suck thousands of dollars from the wallets of the unwary.

When the 386 was first released, the industry responded slowly and inconsistently. 32-bit memory access was achieved only by the clumsy hack of pairing 16-bit memory boards, and capacity for this fast RAM was sharply limited. IDE and standardized local bus video and disk connections took years to be developed. The first several thousand 386 chips sold had a bug that caused wrong numeric results. While some manufacturers went to great lengths to stop using the bad chips and to upgrade systems that contained them, others made few efforts to fix such problems.

Similar events could occur with the move to Intel's Pentium. If you buy the wrong system you may, for instance, be stuck with limits on the amount of RAM you can access in 64-bit chunks, which will have a great effect on the performance of AutoCAD. Worse, you could get a chip that has bugs, or that fails earlier than it should (probably on end-of-warranty day plus one).

In addition, software that takes optimal advantage of the Pentium will take time to be developed. Popular applications must be recompiled to get all of the speed boost they're capable of. (If past experience is any guide, AutoCAD should be one of the earliest programs available in a Pentium-specific version.) Though Pentium is multiprocessor-capable, a sophisticated operating system like NT or Unix may be needed to take full advantage of that capability.

Therefore, we advise caution. Don't buy for at least six months after Pentium systems are available to make sure bugs are fixed or worked around (wait a year if you want to pay anything less than top dollar), and be sure you aren't frozen out of multiprocessor-capable systems that may become available and affordable shortly after Pentium is introduced. Waiting also will give you a chance to decide if you can stick with DOS or DOS-based Windows, or need NT or Unix, with their much greater RAM and disk requirements, to get the most from the new systems. Despite all the uncertainty and potential confusion, though, these are exciting times in hardware, and you'll soon have many good opportunities to get much-improved performance at reasonable prices.

The AutoCAD STATUS Command

AutoCAD provides a somewhat obscure but powerful diagnostic utility for checking a number of statistics about your system, many of which relate to performance. We're talking, of course, about the STATUS command. It displays a convenient summary of the current drawing's size, selected system variable settings, and memory and hard disk use. It's handy for getting a quick overview of the status of the current drawing session, and is particularly helpful for troubleshooting memory and performance problems.

To start STATUS, type the command name at the Command: prompt, pick it from the Utility pull-down menu, or pick it from the INQUIRY side menu. AutoCAD flips to the text screen and displays the first part of the status report. Once you press <Enter>, AutoCAD shows an additional, memory-related portion of the report. See Figure 3.1 for an example.

```
STATUS 9857 entities in J:\SJN\SJN-S6
Model space limits are    X: 0'-0"          Y: 0'-0"  (Off)
                          X: 3'-6"          Y: 2'-6"
Model space uses          X: 0'-0"          Y: 0'-0"
                          X: 3'-6"          Y: 2'-6"
Display shows             X: 0'-1 7/64"     Y: -0'-0 51/64"
                          X: 3'-7 1/4"      Y: 2'-7 9/32"
Insertion base is         X: 0'-0"          Y: 0'-0"          Z: 0'-0"
Snap resolution is        X: 0'-0 1/8"      Y: 0'-0 1/8"
Grid spacing is           X: 0'-1"          Y: 0'-1"

Current space:            Model space
Current layer:            0
Current color:            BYLAYER -- 7 (white)
Current linetype:         BYLAYER -- CONTINUOUS
Current elevation:        0'-0"   thickness:      0'-0"
Fill on  Grid on  Ortho on  Qtext off  Snap on  Tablet off
Object snap modes:        None
Free disk (dwg/temp): 57024512/57024512 bytes
Virtual memory allocated to program: 6948 KB
Amount of program in physical memory/Total (virtual) program size: 73%
-- Press RETURN for more --
Total conventional memory: 440 KB Total extended memory: 16792 KB
Swap file size: 388 KB
Page faults: 642          Swap writes: 0          Swap reclaims: 1
```

Figure 3.1   Status report.

After the first line, which displays the number of entities in the current drawing, the Status screen for AutoCAD 386 is divided into three sections:

- X,Y values of various settings: limits, extents, display, base point, snap, and grid.

- Other drawing settings: model space/paper space; current layer, color, linetype, elevation, and thickness; on/off settings of the axis, fill, grid, ortho, qtext, snap, and tablet toggles; and current running object snap modes.

- Disk and memory use: amount of unused disk space on the current drive, percentage of AutoCAD program code in memory, total conventional and extended memory available to AutoCAD, Phar Lap DOS extender swap file size, and amount of swap file activity. Note that the memory statistics in this section only appear in AutoCAD 386. The AutoCAD for Windows STATUS command shows just the amount of free disk space.

The first two sections are useful for finding problems you or other users you support are having: mismatches between limits and extents, explicit color or linetype settings, running object snap modes, etc. But it's the lower part of the screen, which shows disk and memory use, that gives information affecting performance. Let's take a look at each statistic:

Free disk. Tells you if you're running low on hard disk space. AutoCAD Release 12, like all virtual-memory systems, requires a good deal of "elbow room" on the hard disk. Note that you can redirect the Phar Lap and AutoCAD swap and pager files to another disk drive, as described in the *Interface, Installation, and Performance Guide*.

Amount of program in physical memory/Total (virtual) program size. Indicates how much of AutoCAD's program code has been loaded into memory. If demand loading is turned off, this number will start at 100 percent. If demand loading is turned on, as it is by default in Release 12, the number will start at something much lower than that and gradually increase as you access different AutoCAD commands. At some point, the number may suddenly drop—AutoCAD, being out of RAM, started using hard disk space as additional memory. This number is also affected if you shell out (see below).

Total conventional memory/Total extended memory. The amount of conventional memory (free memory beneath the DOS 640K limit) isn't particularly critical for AutoCAD Release 12. But make sure total extended memory is roughly equal to the amount of extended memory in your computer, minus the amount you've allocated to disk caches and other programs that use extended memory. If you don't, AutoCAD may not be "seeing" all your extended memory, and performance will suffer.

Swap file size. Starts at 388KB; if it gets much larger, AutoCAD is swapping to disk, and more RAM will improve AutoCAD's performance on your computer.

Page faults / Swap writes / Swap reclaims. These are additional indicators of swap-file activity. If these numbers increase much, this indicates that more memory will give you better performance. Note that even with sufficient memory, Page faults will start out as nonzero and increase gradually, as AutoCAD loads its program code in response to the commands you use. If you have enough RAM, the number should level off once you've worked in the drawing editor for awhile. Also, shelling out will result in some swapping activity, regardless of how much extended memory you have.

Tip

If you don't see the Page faults / Swap writes / Swap reclaims line when you run STATUS, then you have the original Release 12 or Release 12c1 (the first bug fix). In that case, just refer to Swap file size as the indicator of swap-file activity (and get the Release 12c2 update, which fixes several annoying bugs).

To gauge whether you have enough extended memory, run STATUS periodically and note the memory numbers. Press <Ctrl>+Q before getting the report to send it to a printer. Press <Ctrl>+Q again when done.

As a more explicit test, load a typical medium-large or large drawing, run STATUS, draw for awhile as you normally would, and then run STATUS again at the end of the drafting session (don't shell out during this time). If the swap statistics increase very much then consider adding memory.

Note that in the DIM subcommand, STATUS does something different: It displays all the dimension variable settings.

"No Regens"

In Release 12, AutoCAD now uses a 32-bit rather than a 16-bit display list. (The precision with which drawing data is stored on disk is unchanged at 64 bits.) The good news is that you now rarely have to wait for a regen due to a pan or zoom. You can pan within a greater area beyond the edge of the screen without a regen; you can see just how big by entering the command ZOOM VMAX. And you can now zoom in by a factor of almost a million before triggering one. (A zoom of less than 100X used to do it.) The bad news is twofold: A few operations, such as regens, are actually a little slower, and the display list uses about twice as much space in memory as it did before.

The way that these changes affect AutoCAD's performance in everyday use is complicated. If your drawings or working style required a lot of regens in Release 11, you'll benefit immediately from the reduced need for them in Release 12. If they didn't, then you won't notice much of a difference, although you will be able to zoom and pan more freely than before. If you load a lot of drawings for short editing sessions, you might actually see a net performance *decrease*, since loading a drawing requires an initial regen.

While most users will see some net performance gain from the reduced number of regens, if your machine is tight on memory, the 32-bit display list could cause AutoCAD to start swapping to disk in situations where it wouldn't under Release 11. The solution, as emphasized earlier, is more RAM.

Even with "no regens," be sure to turn the REGENAUTO system variable off, as pointed out in Chapter 4, *Basic Setup and Prototypes*. This step will eliminate "surprise" regens when you change LTSCALE, alter a layer's linetype, or redefine Blocks.

Tip

In order for Release 12 to use its 32-bit display list, you must use an ADI 4.2 display-list driver that supports this feature. Otherwise, Release 12 still will use a 16-bit display list, and you won't notice any change in the frequency of regens over Release 11. All of the stock AutoCAD drivers support the 32-bit display list, but they're comparatively slow. Of course, the TurboDLD*Lite* driver included with *AutoCAD Power Tools* supports this feature.

Why You (Still) Need a Display-List Processor Under DOS

Even with "no regens," you still need a display-list processor because no matter how large your monitor is, you still need to zoom and pan often as you work in AutoCAD. The delays that accumulate as you wait for AutoCAD to redraw the screen add up to huge productivity losses, especially in large, complex drawings. Release 12 speeds up zooms, pans, and other screen redraws slightly, but a good display-list processing driver, such as TurboDLD*Lite*, will accelerate these operations by several times at least.

Release 12 for Windows has the same "no regens" feature as the DOS 386 version, but it also comes with a built-in display-list processing driver as part of the stock program. The display-list driver is one of the main reasons Release 12 for Windows has acceptable performance despite the overhead of the Windows graphical user interface. On the other hand, Release 12 for Windows with display-list processing versus Release 12/386 without it is an apples-and-oranges comparison. With its lack of Windows overhead, Release 12/386 is still the performance champ when paired with a good display-list processor.

Performance Tips for Release 12

There are a number of things you can do to increase Release 12 performance. You may not need to do much if your system is sufficiently fast, you have enough RAM for both AutoCAD and your display-list processor, and your drawings are small to medium size (less than 500K or so). But, if you're experiencing performance slowdowns in specific operations under either DOS or Windows, look in this section for tips.

RESTART AUTOCAD FOR SPEED

If AutoCAD 386 starts swapping to disk because of memory limitations, the temporary swap file used by the Phar Lap DOS extender will continue to grow; old data in the swap file doesn't get "cleaned out" automatically. The net result can be a steadily deteriorating performance, especially after you've loaded a large drawing. When this happens, exit from AutoCAD back to DOS, and then restart AutoCAD. This procedure will effectively clean out the swap file. Of course, if you need to do this very often, get more RAM.

FREEZE UNNEEDED LAYERS

Performance will increase when you freeze any layers that contain a lot of entities (e.g., dense hatching, large amounts of text, or a complex title block). The updated Layer Control dialogue box makes controlling layer settings easy. Consider freezing layers when you won't need to refer to the entities on them for awhile. Keep in mind, though, that thawing layers in order to see them again usually requires a regen, so the time you save by freezing might be offset by the time you lose with the additional regeneration.

PUT HATCHING ON A SEPARATE LAYER

With hatching on its own layer, you can freeze it without affecting other parts of your drawing.

AVOID DENSE HATCHING

Dense hatching takes a long time to regenerate and redraw. Even if you need a dense hatch in the final version of your drawing, consider substituting a less dense one, such as a simple, widely spaced, user-defined hatch, until you're nearly finished with the drawing. Try to do any hatching, even with lighter patterns, as late as possible in the process of creating the drawing.

USE QUICK TEXT

Use the QTEXT command to turn on "quick text" mode. When this mode is on, each line of text is drawn as a rectangle enclosing the approximate area occupied by the Text entity. The same caution as with freezing layers applies, though: When you want to see the actual text again, you'll have to regenerate the drawing.

USE UNFILLED SOLIDS

Solids, traces, and wide polylines are drawn unfilled—and, therefore, much faster—if you use the FILL command to turn the FILLMODE system variable off. Use this feature when your drawing contains a large number of filled entities that AutoCAD redraws slowly. Turn FILLMODE on again when you need a precise idea of what your drawing looks like.

DISPLAY ROUGHER CURVES AND LINETYPES

The VIEWRES command allows you to specify how many line segments AutoCAD will use in drawing circles and arcs on-screen. This option is called the "circle zoom percent," but it also affects the display accuracy of dashed linetypes. The default setting of 100 is already pretty performance-efficient, and you've probably noticed that, as you zoom in, circles start to look like polygons. Also, tightly spaced, dashed linetypes can appear to be continuous on the screen. These display inaccuracies don't affect the precision of your drawing or plot—only what you see on-screen. A circle zoom percent smaller than 100 will increase performance slightly, but then circles and linetypes will appear even less accurately. A number higher than 100 (up to 20,000) will improve display accuracy, but will cost some performance. Experiment with different settings on one of your average-sized drawings to determine the best trade-off.

EXPERIMENT WITH TREEDEPTH AND TREEMAX

During object selection, object snaps, and redraws, Release 12 keeps track of entities in a different way than do previous versions. The new method depends on a "spatial index," with which AutoCAD can find entities more quickly. The details of how this spatial index is structured are controlled by two new system variables: TREEDEPTH and TREEMAX. Optimizing the settings for these variables is complicated, and it depends on the types of drawings you work on and the amount of memory in your system. If you notice performance slowdowns with redraws, object selection, and object snaps, and especially if your system is tight on memory, you can try optimizing the spatial index by tuning the TREEDEPTH and TREEMAX system variables. Try a value of –3020 (note the negative sign) for 2D drawings. Release 12 includes a TREESTAT command for inspecting the current spatial index, and this command can help you decide on proper settings. See Chapter 4 of the *AutoCAD Reference Manual* for details of TREEDEPTH, TREEMAX, and TREESTAT.

USE ENDPOINT INSTEAD OF INTERSECTION OBJECT SNAP

Object snap performance is much improved in Release 12, thanks to the spatial index, but object snaps can still be too slow in very large drawings. AutoCAD has to work harder to find the intersection of two entities than it does for any other object snap. So if object snap performance slows, use other object snaps instead. ENDpoint often works just as well as INTersection and is faster.

SORT WITH CARE

The only significant disadvantage to Release 12's spatial index is that it eliminates predictability when your pick or object snap box includes two or more entities. Previous versions of AutoCAD sorted the entities based on when they were drawn, but the sorting procedure took some time and performance could suffer as a result (see Chapter 7 for details). Release 12 lets you restore the sorting for various operations, but doing so will cost you speed. Use the Entity Sort Method subdialogue of DDSELECT to control when sorting occurs; see Figure 3.2. (The Entity Sort Method dialogue is a less cryptic way of setting the SORTENTS system variable.) Leave sorting off for Object Selection, Object Snap, Redraws, and Regens unless you absolutely require sorting for one of these operations.

DON'T CLUTTER DRAWING AND SUPPORT SUBDIRECTORIES

Each time AutoCAD looks for a support file, it checks the support and drawing subdirectories (see Chapter 14 for details). These should be kept free of extraneous files, or search times will be lengthened.

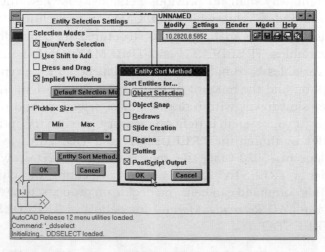

Figure 3.2   The Entity Sort Method dialogue.

KEEP YOUR HARD DISK UNFRAGMENTED

Fragmented files, with pieces scattered among different locations on your disk, can take longer to access than unfragmented files located in one contiguous area. AutoCAD, with its virtual memory management and DOS extender, tends to fragment a disk more quickly than some other programs. Use a disk defragmenter, such as the one included with DOS 6, regularly.

USE A DISK CACHE

Most DOS programs and Windows will see a real performance boost when you use a disk caching program, such as the SMARTDRV cache that comes with Windows and DOS 6. The disk cache keeps recently accessed disk information in RAM, where it can be accessed much more quickly than from disk. AutoCAD will benefit, too, as long as the memory you devote to the cache doesn't leave AutoCAD so memory starved that it has to start swapping to disk. A small cache, perhaps 64KB, is adequate for AutoCAD 386, but you'll want a much larger one, something like 2MB, with Windows. If you find yourself having to choose between a disk cache and adequate memory for AutoCAD, the usual rule applies: Buy more RAM.

Performance and Workgroups

The difficulty of balancing performance and productivity is easily seen within a workgroup. Some users are excited about computing in general and AutoCAD in particular, and spend a lot of time tuning their systems and learning new AutoCAD tricks. These users gain good performance, but their productivity can suffer if they spend more time tweaking than drawing. Other users learn as little as possible about AutoCAD or their computers, and may experience lower performance as a result but still get a lot of work done, partly due to the lack of distractions. A few find a happy medium and achieve good performance without spending too much time on doing so, resulting in good productivity.

The workgroup is where the interests of the company and the interests of the personal computer user intersect. Providing support to the members of your workgroup in getting the most performance from their systems has a double benefit. First, users will experience greater productivity when their systems run faster. Second, users have to spend less time worrying about learning to configure and tune their hardware and software setups if the work is done for them. Anyone in the group who's interested can take on the role of "performance guru," investigating performance issues and making recommendations for the group.

There are a few key things we can recommend to improve performance across a workgroup:

- Standardize your hardware and software configurations and stay away from the "bleeding edge." Avoid the temptation to try a different computer or utility program with each new purchase. Every brand of computer, graphics card, utility program, and driver has its own quirks, features, and learning curve. There's no reason to learn them all. Settle on a reasonably standard system configuration and stick with it as long as it does the job.

- Buy RAM. Buy users in your group RAM for their birthdays and major holidays. Put some in their stocking at the office holiday party. With 32-bit display lists built into Release 12, display-list processors being used to improve DOS and Windows performance, and the overall demands of Windows, dozens of megabytes of RAM per system will be needed.

- Use performance tips. Most of the tips above are relatively straightforward and can easily be implemented in a workgroup setting. You'll pick up more in your own work; share these tips with others.

Getting the best performance from AutoCAD is a big and important job. Take responsibility for at least the basics of performance at the workgroup level and watch productivity and satisfaction with CAD improve.

PART II

Power User's Guide to Release 12

4

Basic Setup and Prototypes

The next two chapters are two of the most important in this book. They describe the key things you should consider in setting up your drawings. You can modify the steps described here to meet your own needs, then put them to work. Using a standard setup procedure will save you a great deal of time and effort, and will go a long way toward ensuring consistency in your drawings.

The division between these chapters is somewhat arbitrary. This one describes setup options that you can use to create reusable prototype drawings. The next describes additional setup options that you probably will want to perform each time you start a new drawing. However, each company, workgroup, and even individual will draw the dividing line between prototype settings and drawing-specific settings differently. Once you've worked through both chapters, you can decide which setup options belong to prototype drawings and which ones need to be specified in each drawing.

Why dedicate two whole chapters to setup? Spending a relatively small amount of time on setup can save you a great deal of time later. As you create additional drawings for a project and put more work into each of them, consistency becomes increasingly more important. System variables (including dimension variables), layers, text styles, and other factors have a large influence on how your drawings look and how you work with them. If you've chosen these settings correctly in advance, you'll be much more productive and accurate than if you have to change them part way through the drawing process. The importance of setup is even greater for drawings that are reused by others; a single mistake in setting up a key drawing in a project can cost a great deal to repair or live with, as it affects the original drawing and propagates through other drawings.

Are drawing setup considerations any different between the DOS and Windows versions of Release 12? Not really, except that careful setup will be even more important to many Windows users. Part of the appeal of Windows is sharing data among different Windows programs and being able to open multiple AutoCAD sessions. These two features make drawing reuse easier and more appealing, and, thus, make consistency and careful setup even more important.

About This Chapter

This chapter describes the key basic setup options that are likely to be the same for most or all of the drawings that you do. It describes how to create one or a few prototype drawings that embody the setup choices you've made and start your drawings with the right settings made in advance.

There is little in this chapter that is new in terms of features that are in Release 12 and not in earlier releases of AutoCAD. But the interface to the features is different, since more settings are accessible now through dialogue boxes. So, to this extent, the tutorial is Release 12-specific, but the principles in it apply to past and future versions of AutoCAD as well.

Here we take a step-by-step approach to describing how to set a number of different options. In doing so, we demonstrate the variety of access methods that Release 12 uses: command-line entries, menu choices, and dialogue boxes. So, in addition to teaching you about setup, this chapter serves to demonstrate many of the basics of using AutoCAD Release 12. In later chapters, we'll describe how to enter commands in a higher-level, less detailed manner.

Third-Party Applications and Setup

You may use a third-party application that handles some setup work for you, and standards within your company or workgroup may fix other factors. But it's still important for you to understand how the pieces fit together, so you can do the right thing in new or complicated situations.

It's hard to do a good job of setup unless you really understand all the elements that go into it and how they interact. So, work through the tutorial in this chapter to learn the fundamentals of setup. Then, you'll be ready to apply direct entry of setup options and your third-party application, if any, to best advantage.

See Appendix A, Standard Libraries and System Variables

While working through this chapter, you may wish to have your *AutoCAD Reference Manual* open to Appendix A, *Standard Libraries and System Variables*. This appendix lists the initial values of system variables, and the standard fonts, hatch patterns, and linetypes available in AutoCAD. This information is especially valuable during setup. You may want to pencil in your preferred settings in the margins of Appendix A as you go through these pages.

Features Demonstrated in This Chapter

In this chapter, we describe features that relate to basic setup and creating prototype drawings. Among them are:

- The New dialogue box (new with Release 12), which makes it easy to specify a prototype drawing.

- The Drawing Aids dialogue box (redesigned for the DDRMODES command), which centralizes control of Snap, Grid, and other settings.

- Existing commands and system variables, including REGENAUTO and COORDS, which can be used during setup of an individual or prototype drawing.

- The system variable PLINEGEN (new with Release 12), which controls how linetypes are spaced around Polyline vertices.

- The DDUNITS Units Control dialogue box (new with Release 12 for the old UNITS command), which makes it easy to control linear units and specify settings for angles.

- Additional existing commands that you can use during setup, including STYLE and LINETYPE.

- The DDLMODES Layer Control dialogue box, which was radically redesigned for Release 12.

About the Example

In this chapter, we will develop a prototype drawing that we use in later chapters as the prototype for a plan of a recreation room. The rec room example will influence the choices we make for units, layer names, and so on. After reading this chapter, you should create your own prototype drawing or drawings that include the settings you need for your work, whether those settings are the same as or different from our example.

PROJECT SUBDIRECTORIES

It's important to segregate drawing files by project or task; one scheme looks like this:

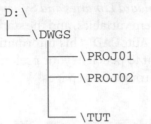

```
D:\
  └──\DWGS
         ├──\PROJ01
         ├──\PROJ02
         └──\TUT
```

We'll treat all the tutorial drawings for this book as one "project." Before you begin the first tutorial sequence, make a subdirectory that will contain all the drawing files you will create during the tutorials. Assuming you keep project drawings in subdirectories under a directory called D:\DWGS and want to call this project TUT, you would follow these steps from the DOS prompt:

1. Create a directory "branch" for your drawings.

Change to the D: drive and create a \DWGS directory if you don't have one already:

```
C:\> D:
D:\ANYWHERE> CD\
D:\> MD DWGS
```

Substitute a different drive letter or directory name if you prefer.

2. Create a project subdirectory.

Change to the \DWGS directory and create a TUT subdirectory within it:

```
D:\> CD \DWGS
D:\DWGS> MD TUT
```

In Windows, you can use the File Manager's Create Directory... command (under the File menu) instead of steps 1 and 2. Once you've created a project subdirectory and launched AutoCAD (whether in DOS or Windows), use AutoCAD's file dialogue box to navigate to the proper location. The OPEN command automatically brings up the file dialogue, but, with NEW, you have to select the New Drawing Name... button in order to bring up the file dialogue as a subdialogue (see Figure 4.1). Either way, once you've opened or created a drawing in a project subdirectory, AutoCAD uses that subdirectory as the default for subsequent file operations.

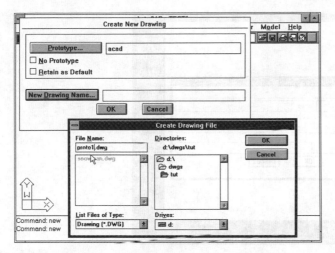

Figure 4.1 The File subdialogue of the Create New Drawing dialogue box.

Prototype Basics

About Prototypes

A prototype drawing is a template for creating other drawings. Each new drawing inherits, among other things, the system variable settings, layers, text styles, and dimension styles from its prototype. If a prototype includes AutoCAD entities (for instance, a title block), new drawings inherit those, too.

The basic idea is that it's much easier and more straightforward to use AutoCAD when the "pieces" you need are already in your drawing. A moderate amount of time spent on creating and refining prototypes and setup procedures will pay off many times over in fewer wasted hours and far less frustration. Of course, having these "pieces" predefined also helps ensure consistency in a group of drawings.

Using Prototypes

Any drawing can serve as a prototype, but, by default, AutoCAD looks for a prototype called ACAD.DWG (in Release 12, this file is usually stored in \ACAD\SUPPORT). In previous releases of AutoCAD, to specify a different one, you could start a new drawing from the Main Menu with the following syntax:

```
Enter NAME of drawing: drawing=prototype
```

The drawing name you supplied for *prototype* was then used as the prototype for the new drawing.

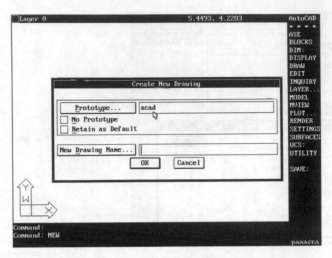

Figure 4.2 The Create New Drawing dialogue box.

With Release 12, AutoCAD makes it easier to explicitly control the use of prototypes. The NEW command's Create New Drawing dialogue box (see Figure 4.2) puts the name of the current default prototype right in front of you. You can enter a different prototype name, change the default, or specify that no prototype be used.

In the next section, we'll list some settings to consider when creating company-specific and project-specific prototypes. Use this list as a starting point, and add to or subtract from it as needed for the types of drawings you create.

Set Up a Prototype

Follow the steps below to set up basic prototype drawings that you can use for the drawings within your workgroup. If the settings are the same for all your drawings, make these changes to the AutoCAD default prototype, ACAD.DWG; otherwise, create one or more new drawings that you can use as a prototype.

Set System Variables

Start by setting system variables. The settings described in the steps below are only our suggestions; use different values if you like.

1. Set Snap and Grid on; turn blips off; set Ortho.

From the Settings menu, select Drawing Aids... (or enter DDRMODES).

The Drawing Aids dialogue box will appear (see Figure 4.3).

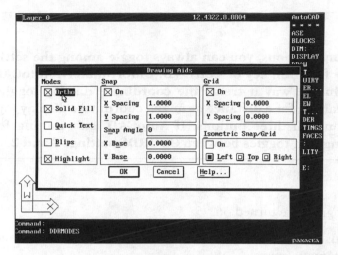

Figure 4.3 The Drawing Aids dialogue box.

Make the changes that fit your usual work.

Our suggestions: Turn Snap and Grid on (okay, you can turn them off if you're drawing contour maps); turn blips (the little markers that appear when you pick a point) off; turn Ortho on if you normally start out drawing orthogonal (horizontal or vertical) lines.

You also can modify other settings that are common to your drawings, and even enter values for X and Y spacing for Snap and Grid. (In most cases, though, you will set the spacing differently for each drawing. The next chapter describes what you need to consider in setting Snap and Grid spacing.) Use the Help... button to get quick descriptions of the options available through the dialogue box.

Pick OK when done.

2. Set coordinate display on.

You normally will want the coordinate display at the top of the screen to be updated as you move your mouse around. You also probably will want the distance and angle of the mouse pointer from the last point to be displayed when a distance or angle is requested.

```
Command: COORDS
New value for COORDS <1>: 2
```

Enter 0 to turn off coordinate updating, 1 to turn it on, or 2 to turn it on and display the relative position of the mouse pointer when a distance or angle is requested. We recommend 2.

Tip

During drawing sessions, you can always toggle among the settings with the <F6> function key or <Ctrl>+D. Unfortunately, AutoCAD is inconsistent in the way it treats the coordinate display toggle. If AutoCAD is waiting for a distance or angle, coordinate display toggle switches among all three options. If AutoCAD isn't waiting for a distance or angle, it toggles between COORDS settings 0 and 2.

3. Make sure grips are turned on.

Grips are useful for editing by direct manipulation of entities and as visible, automatic snaps.

```
Command: GRIPS
New value for GRIPS <1>: 1
```

4. Turn off automatic regens.

Despite the fewer regenerations required by Release 12, there still are many operations that can cause a regen without warning you (changing the linetype of a layer that has entities on it, for example). Unless your drawings are extremely small and simple, you'll want to turn off automatic regens. This will suppress AutoCAD's automatic regens and will cause AutoCAD to warn you before performing a regen required by a pan or zoom operation.

```
Command: REGENAUTO
ON/OFF <On>: OFF
```

With REGENAUTO turned off, you still can force a regeneration with the REGEN command.

5. Turn off text mirroring.

Usually, when you mirror a group of entities that includes text, you don't want the text to appear mirrored. To prevent this, set the MIRRTEXT system variable to 0.

```
Command: MIRRTEXT
New value for MIRRTEXT <1>: 0
```

6. Specify the way linetypes are generated around Polyline vertices.

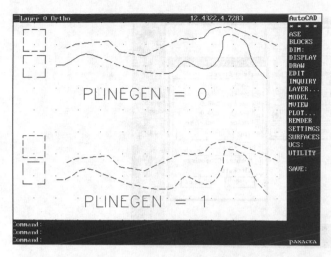

Figure 4.4   The two settings for PLINEGEN.

The new PLINEGEN system variable controls the way dashed linetypes are generated around Polyline vertices. If PLINEGEN is set to 0, each Polyline segment starts and ends with a dash. This is the way all previous versions of AutoCAD worked. If PLINEGEN is set to 1, the linetype "ignores" vertices and flows continuously from the start of the Polyline to the end (see Figure 4.4). The difference is most significant for people who draw complex Polylines with lots of short segments.

```
Command: PLINEGEN
New value for PLINEGEN <0>: 0 or 1
```

Enter 0 to retain dashes at vertices or 1 for smoothly flowing linetypes.

Set Other Options

The options described below are more likely to vary from project to project within a company, but there's a big productivity gain in having as many of them preset as possible. Consider creating a few prototype files that embody the most commonly used combinations of settings for these options.

1. Set the units you will use.

From the Settings menu, select Units Control... (or enter DDUNITS).

The Units Control dialogue box will appear. Specify the types of units and angles you will use, and the precision of each.

From the Units Control dialogue box, select Direction...

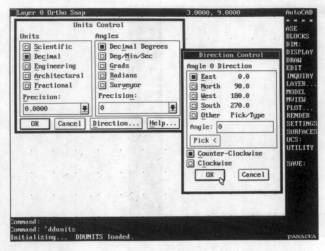

Figure 4.5   Units Control and Direction Control dialogue boxes.

The Direction Control subdialogue will appear (see Figure 4.5). Specify the *Angle 0 Direction* and whether angles are measured counter-clockwise or clockwise.

Pick OK to exit the Direction Control subdialogue.

Pick OK to exit the Units Control dialogue.

2.   Set the base text font.

In this step, we change the font used for AutoCAD's default text style (STANDARD) from TXT, which draws fast but looks ugly, to ROMANS, which draws a little more slowly but is much more attractive. If you want to see the choices, pick the Set Style… suboption from the Text option in the Draw menu. Set Style… brings up the Select Text Font icon menu (see Figure 4.6). Unfortunately, you can't use this icon menu to actually change the STANDARD style, since Select Text Font defines a new style and gives it a name based on the font you select. To change the font for STANDARD, use the STYLE command, as described here.

```
Command: STYLE
Text style name (or ?) <STANDARD>: STANDARD
```

The Select Font File dialogue will appear.

Pick ROMANS.SHX or the font file you usually use.

The default installation puts all fonts in the \ACAD\FONTS subdirectory.

Pick OK.

Press <Enter> for the rest of the prompts to leave them unchanged.

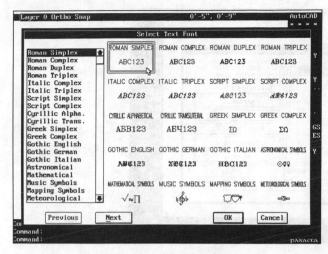

Figure 4.6   The Select Text Font icon menu.

This will specify variable height (=0); if you wish to use a fixed height, you generally will need to reset it for each drawing that has a different scale factor. We describe how to do this in the next chapter.

3. Set dimension variables and save them as a dimension style.

If you've used AutoCAD for very long, you probably have honed in on a set of dimension variables that work, more or less, for your discipline and office. It makes sense to define at least one dimension style with these settings; you might call it STANDARD, in the same way that Autodesk calls the default AutoCAD text style STANDARD.

Dimension variables and styles, along with text, are covered in more detail in Chapter 9, *Adding Dimensions and Text*. For now, you simply can save the default AutoCAD dimension variable settings as a style. In Chapter 9, we'll change the settings and redefine the style.

Choose Dimension Style... from the Settings menu (or enter DDIM).

The new Dimension Styles and Variables dialogue box will appear (see Figure 4.7).

Enter STANDARD in the Dimension Style: text box.

Press <Enter> to create the dimension style.

Pick OK.

AutoCAD will save the current dimension variables as a style called STANDARD.

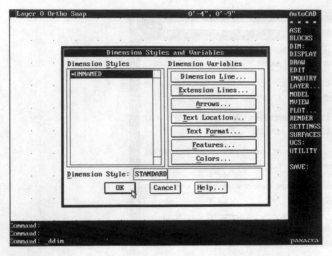

Figure 4.7   The Dimension Styles and Variables dialogue box.

4. Load the linetypes you want to have available.

The **DDLMODES, DDEMODES,** and **DDMODIFY** dialogue boxes show only linetypes that have been loaded into the current drawing; you must use the command line or side menu to load additional linetypes. This can be a time-wasting nuisance when you're in the middle of a dialogue box operation, so load all the linetypes you might need into this prototype drawing.

```
Command: LINETYPE
?/Create/Load/Set: LOAD
Linetype(s) to load: Enter the names of the linetypes you wish to
load, separated by commas.
```

Use the asterisk wildcard character, *, if you wish. Enter * by itself to get all the linetypes in the linetype file.

The linetypes included in the default linetype file, **ACAD.LIN**, are displayed in Figure 4.8.

Pick a file from the Select Linetype File dialogue box.

The default linetype file **ACAD.LIN** is located in the \ACAD\SUPPORT subdirectory. (See the *AutoCAD Customization Manual* for information on how to create custom linetypes.)

5. Create any common layers you want to have available in all drawings.

Don't get too carried away here. You don't need to put every layer you would ever use in your prototype drawing. Remember that you'll often

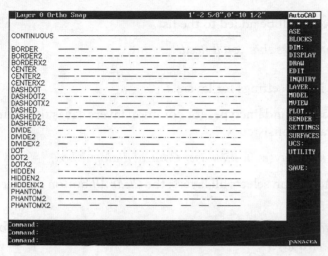

Figure 4.8   Linetypes from ACAD.LIN.

end up scrolling through the layer list in a dialogue box, so it pays to keep the list compact if you can. On the other hand, it's a good idea to set up common layers and their color and linetype settings, since this helps maintain consistency.

Pick Layer Control... from the Settings menu (or enter DDLMODES).

The Layer Control dialogue box will appear (see Figure 4.9).

Enter the names of new layers, separated by commas, in the text entry box at the bottom of the dialogue box.

Pick the New button (not OK).

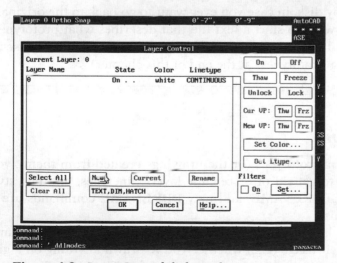

Figure 4.9   Layer Control dialogue box.

The new layers will be added to the list.

Add any other layers that you'll need.

6. Specify the initial settings for layers.

Specifying colors and linetypes for common layers saves time later on and encourages consistency.

Pick one or more layers in the Layer Control dialogue box.

The *Select All* button selects all layers; the *Clear All* button deselects all layers.

Use the buttons in the dialogue box to modify color and linetype for the group of selected layers.

Notice the list of linetypes we loaded earlier. (Now, wasn't that easier than having to interrupt the layer setup process in order to load linetypes?)

Continue selecting and assigning layers until you're finished.

SAVE YOUR PROTOTYPE

Now that you have all the settings stored, save your prototype drawing. As discussed, you can save to the default prototype name (\ACAD\SUPPORT\ACAD.DWG) or to a different name. Before you overwrite the default prototype, though, copy it to a separate subdirectory or onto a floppy disk, in case you ever want to go back to the original. You also may want to start a text file that describes what prototypes you've created, how their settings differ, and what their intended use is (see "Managing Prototypes" at the end of this chapter).

Purge and Rename

As you revise your prototypes (or the drawings created from them), you'll sometimes want to get rid of or rename layers, linetypes, and text styles. AutoCAD's PURGE, RENAME, and new DDRENAME commands are the tools for doing this.

AutoCAD calls layers, linetypes, and text styles "named objects," and it keeps track of their usage (e.g., whether you've drawn anything on a given layer or created any text using a certain text style). The PURGE command

```
Command: PURGE
Purge unused Blocks/Dimstyles/LAyers/LTypes/SHapes/STyles/All: A

No unreferenced blocks found.
Purge layer TEXT? <N>
Purge layer DIM? <N>
Purge layer HATCH? <N> Y
Purge linetype HIDDEN? <N>
Purge linetype DASHED? <N>
Purge linetype BORDER? <N>
Purge linetype BORDER2? <N> Y
Purge linetype BORDERX2? <N> Y
Purge linetype CENTER? <N>
Purge linetype CENTER2? <N>
Purge linetype CENTERX2? <N> Y
Purge linetype DASHDOT? <N>
Purge linetype DASHDOT2? <N> Y
Purge linetype DASHDOTX2? <N> Y
Purge linetype DASHED2? <N>
Purge linetype DASHEDX2? <N>
Purge linetype DIVIDE? <N> Y
Purge linetype DIVIDE2? <N> Y
Purge linetype DIVIDEX2? <N> Y
Purge linetype DOT? <N>
```

Figure 4.10 PURGE command in operation.

will let you remove any unused named objects from a drawing, but it can be used only at the beginning of an editing session, before you've made any changes to the drawing. Unfortunately, you can't use it at the end of a drawing session when you might want to clean up; you'll have to save the drawing and reload it with the OPEN command before you purge.

The easiest way to purge a drawing is from the Command: line, as follows:

```
Command: PURGE
Purge unused Blocks/Dimstyles/LAyers/LTypes/SHapes/STyles/All: specify one
```

AutoCAD will display the name of each unreferenced named object and ask if you want to purge it (see Figure 4.10). Answer Y to purge a named object; accept the default answer N to leave it defined in the drawing. (We discuss purging in greater detail in Chapter 10, *Xrefs, Blocks, and Attributes.*)

AutoCAD is less finicky about renaming than purging; you can rename named objects any time during a drawing session. The old RENAME command still is available, but the new Release 12 DDRENAME command is much easier to use, since it doesn't force you to remember the current names of all the objects you want to rename. DDRENAME brings up the Rename dialogue box shown in Figure 4.11. Simply pick each type of named object in turn, and the names of all objects of that type will appear in the list box at the right. Pick the name you want to change, enter the new name, pick the Rename To: button, and the renaming will be done.

Use the PURGE and DDRENAME commands to clean up your prototype drawings, to make changes on-the-fly while editing, and to clean up drawings as you finish them.

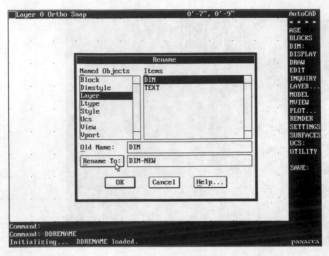

Figure 4.11   The Rename dialogue box.

More Settings

You may want to include some of the settings described in the next chapter in your prototypes. While most of these settings are probably project- or drawing-specific for most workgroups, some of them may be of general enough use in your workgroup that it's worth saving them in a prototype.

If you look carefully at the list of system variables in Appendix A of the *AutoCAD Reference Manual* (Table A.3), you'll notice that some settings are saved in the AutoCAD general configuration file, ACAD.CFG, and not in the drawing. That means that such system variables as SAVETIME and GRIPS depend on a system-wide setting, and not on a prototype drawing. These settings depend on your overall preferences and working style; once you change them, you want the changes to apply to all drawings.

Making the Most of Prototypes

Properly used, prototypes minimize the amount of time you spend on repetitive setup procedures and help ensure consistency in your drawings. These two goals are what you should aim for with your prototypes.

As with all office standards, developing prototype drawings is an evolutionary process. Once you've created one or more prototypes, you and other AutoCAD users in your office will have to try them out on real projects. Keep track of what works and what doesn't, and watch for setup changes that you find yourself repeating frequently in different drawings. The beginning of a project is an especially good time to assess and revise your general prototypes, and to create some project-specific ones.

Managing Prototypes

The only real limitation on the use of prototypes is the DOS-imposed limit of 8 characters for a filename, which sharply limits the descriptiveness of the filename. The first steps in managing prototypes are to create a subdirectory for them and to create a naming convention. The naming convention should encode whatever is important in distinguishing your different prototypes: perhaps drawing type (e.g., plan or detail), scale, and project type.

It helps if you maintain a simple text file with a file listing of prototypes and a brief description of each. Keep it in the same subdirectory with your prototype drawings, and print it out from time to time as you add prototypes.

Workgroups need a more robust and centralized prototype management strategy. If possible, prototype drawings should be stored in a subdirectory on the network server, and one person should be responsible for managing and documenting them. You might want to develop a prototype documentation form or database that includes fields for system variables and other settings. Appendix A in the *AutoCAD Reference Manual* is a good source for figuring out what to include.

5

Drawing-Specific Setup

This chapter continues the topic of setup started in the previous chapter. It covers setup options that you are more likely to change with each new drawing. Combine the information in this chapter with the previous one to create your own prototype drawings and standard setup procedure that will save you time, effort, and mistakes in your work.

As mentioned in the last chapter, the division between what we will cover in this chapter and what was covered in the previous one is somewhat arbitrary. You may wish to reset some of the options covered in the previous chapter in each new drawing. And you may wish to include some of the options we describe in this chapter in company-wide, workgroup-wide, or project-specific prototype drawings. Again, you will have to fine-tune your own approach to setup, using the information here as a starting point.

About This Chapter

This chapter describes setup options that are likely to vary with each drawing, or at least with each group of related drawings, that you do. It includes detailed descriptions of the different options you should consider as part of setup. Most of the commands described in this chapter are not new to Release 12, so, unlike the previous chapter, this one takes a high-level approach to describing how to set various options. We describe the settings and commands needed to modify them, but do not give a blow-by-blow description covering every command prompt.

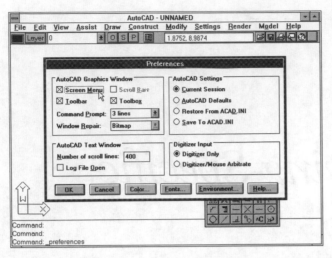

Figure 5.1   Turning on side menus in Release 12 for Windows.

The one thing we do describe step by step is MVSETUP, an AutoLISP routine included with AutoCAD that automates some factors of setup. MVSETUP uses the side menu, which we have not done much with in the book so far. Once you've gone through the tutorials in the previous chapter and the one for MVSETUP, you'll be familiar with the most important interface techniques for AutoCAD Release 12, as well as the most important setup options.

Tip

The default screen configuration for Windows does not show the side menu, but you need it available for MVSETUP. To turn on the side menu, select Preferences... from the File menu and click on Screen Menu in the Preferences dialogue box (see Figure 5.1). If you want to keep the screen menu turned on in future AutoCAD sessions, click on Save to ACAD.INI before picking OK.

Features Demonstrated in This Chapter

The drawing-specific setup features described in this chapter are:

- Text and dimension styles
- Title blocks

- Drawing-scale related features, such as limits, zoom to limits, Snap and Grid size, text height, linetype scale, and dimension scale
- The MVSETUP AutoLISP routine

About the Example

In this chapter, we add settings to the prototype drawing developed in the last chapter. In later chapters, this prototype will be used as a starting point for the drawing of a recreation room. This will influence the choices we make for drawing scale, units, and so on. (In your own work, choose settings that match your discipline's standards, local codes, and office and workgroup standards.) For this chapter's tutorial you can use the RRCH05.DWG file on the *AutoCAD Power Tools* disk as a starting point.

Before You Start Drawing

Start with a Paper Sketch

If you're making a drawing that's based on an existing paper drawing, you can use that as a model for determining your scale and other settings. But if not, it helps to start the drafting process with old-fashioned paper and pencil. Draw a rough schematic sketch or two of what your drawings will look like. In fact, a good draftsperson often will "cartoon" an entire set of drawings before turning on the computer, because it's quicker and easier to draw a sketch by hand than on the computer. Most work on the computer, especially within AutoCAD, has to be carefully thought out and executed exactly. Few of us can temporarily switch to a free-form, experimental mode of using AutoCAD while initially thinking through a drawing.

Paper and pencil, on the other hand, are appropriate for a quick and dirty sketch that you can easily erase, overwrite, or discard. Take advantage of these habits and use pencil and paper for your initial sketch. The sketch can help you answer a number of questions, perhaps the most important of which is, "Does it fit?" Will the drawing fit easily on a piece of paper or will it crowd the border, forcing you to spend time later squeezing in notes and geometry?

Using paper and pencil first is even more important at the start of a project than it is for a single drawing. Sketches will help you divide the project drawings into groups that can use the same units, scale factors, and so on. Sketch the most important drawings and any that are distinctly different in content, size, or scale from the others. Use an approximate count and listing of sheets to guide you through drawing creation and plotting.

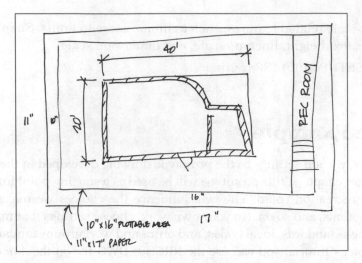

Figure 5.2   Sketch of the recreation room example.

A paper sketch of the recreation room that we'll use in the sample drawing is shown in Figure 5.2. It's truly a hand-drawn sketch done without benefit of so much as a ruler, but it gives us a good start on our AutoCAD drawing.

Set Up Your Drawing

With our paper sketch in hand, let's go over the drawing-specific setup options that you should consider.

Set General Options

The following options describe common steps in setup that you probably will perform differently in different drawings.

Create a new drawing. Start your drawing-specific setup by creating a new drawing with the NEW command. In the New dialogue box, specify the prototype you created in the last chapter as your prototype drawing. If you'll be creating more than one drawing from this prototype, click on Retain as Default before picking OK. If you choose to give your new drawing a name at this point, be sure to pick New Drawing Name... to make sure you create the drawing in the right subdirectory (see the "Project Subdirectories" sidebar in the previous chapter).

Set units. If you haven't already stored the proper units setting in your prototype, now is the time to choose your units. The previous chapter describes how to do this with the DDUNITS command.

Text Styles. You may use additional text fonts besides the basic ROMANS font we set in the previous chapter. If you choose to use variable height text styles, you can set them up now. If you prefer fixed height styles, you need to determine the scale of your drawing first, as we describe later in this chapter.

Command: STYLE will allow you to create new styles and change the fonts and other characteristics of existing styles. See Appendix A of the *AutoCAD Reference Manual* for a list of fonts that come with AutoCAD.

Menu Choice: Choosing Text from the Draw menu will bring up a choice of text-related commands. The Set Style... suboption displays examples of the different styles available and automatically sets up new styles based on the font names.

Tip

Release 12 includes over a dozen PostScript fonts, and even if you don't have a PostScript output device, you might consider using these new fonts. Release 12 will print PostScript fonts on any plotter or printer, but with one limitation: For "bold" fonts, it won't fill in the outlines of the letters. You must use the PSOUT command and a PostScript device in order to get filled-in fonts.

Release 12's PostScript font choices include two "hand-lettered" fonts and a variety of other choices (see Figure 5.3). If you use any of the PostScript fonts, be aware of one inconsistency: Because of the way text heights are measured in the publishing world, the "height" of PostScript text is not the actual character height, as it is for a regular AutoCAD font and in manual drafting. (See Chapter 9 for details.)

Dimension Styles. As discussed in the previous chapter, dimension variables and styles are an important part of setup. Some dimension variables should be set in your prototype drawings, but others may be project-or drawing-specific. If that's the case, now is the time to set them. You also might want to create additional dimension styles besides the STANDARD style we saved in the previous chapter. Dimension variables and styles, along with text, are covered in more detail in Chapter 9, and we'll defer an in-depth discussion until then. The one dimension variable that is certain to change from drawing to drawing is DIMSCALE. DIMSCALE should match your drawing scale, as we discuss later in this chapter.

Command: Chapter 9 describes the many dimension variables and how to manage them. The DDIM command will bring up the Dimension Styles and Variables dialogue box.

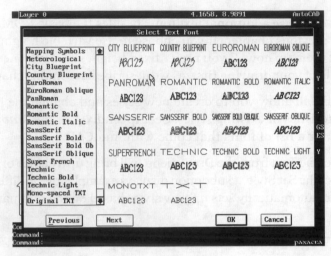

Figure 5.3 AutoCAD's PostScript fonts.

Menu Choice: Choosing Dimension Style... from the Settings menu will bring up the Dimension Styles and Variables dialogue box.

Title Block. If you know the sheet size and title block configuration at this stage of the game, create a title block. In most instances, you will want to draw the title block at full scale (1=1), WBLOCK it out to a separate file, and then INSERT or XREF it back into one or more drawings at the appropriate scale. We cover these procedures in Chapter 10. If you use paper space, the MVSETUP routine will draw a title block for you. We go through this approach in Chapter 11.

Command: Use appropriate drawing and editing commands to draw the title block. Set Limits to the full sheet size (e.g., lower left = 0,0 and upper right = 36,24) and ZOOM All before starting to draw the title block. Once you've drawn the title block, use the WBLOCK command to write it out as a separate drawing for later insertion or external referencing (see Chapter 10).

Menu Choice: Most drawing, editing, and file-saving commands can be accessed from the menus; the WBLOCK command is not included in pull-down menus, but can be accessed from the Blocks side menu.

Determine the Drawing Scale

Several of the options you should consider during setup are related to drawing scale, which tends to be the same for some or all of the drawings within a project. Creating as many drawings as possible at the same scale makes it easier to understand what's going on in a set of drawings, even if it results in wasted space in some plots. Sketching key drawings in advance, as suggested earlier in this chapter, will help you determine the right scale factors. Then, you can create a group of project-specific prototype drawings with the scales already set.

The first thing to determine when deciding on the drawing scale is the sheet size or sizes you will use for plots. This is usually determined by some combination of sheet sizes used in your discipline and standards used within countries, offices, workgroups, and projects. Remember to take into account that, depending on your plotter, the maximum plottable area may be less than the full size of the paper. You also have to consider the title block and margin requirements.

Next, compare the paper size to the real-world size of the objects being drawn, plus room for dimensions, annotations, etc. You must take into account the shape of the object and its orientation on the paper. Again, a pencil-and-paper sketch done in advance can help you better estimate the impact of these factors. The length or width of the real-world object (whichever is harder to fit onto the paper) versus the part of the length or width of the plotting paper available for the object itself, independent of supporting text and dimensions, will help you determine the best drawing scale to use.

To make this determination, divide the largest dimension of the object by the largest dimension of the paper. This number gives the greatest scale factor at which you could cram the object onto the paper. Then choose a slightly smaller scale factor that allows the object to comfortably fit on the paper. Table 5.1 below gives some standard architectural drawing scales and matching scale factors.

Table 5.1   Standard Drawing Scales and Scale Factors

Drawing Scales	Drawing Scale Factor
$\frac{1}{16}"=1'\text{-}0"$	192
$\frac{1}{8}"=1'\text{-}0"$	96
$\frac{3}{16}"=1'\text{-}0"$	64
$\frac{1}{4}"=1'\text{-}0"$	48
$\frac{3}{8}"=1'\text{-}0"$	32
$\frac{1}{2}"=1'\text{-}0"$	24
$\frac{3}{4}"=1'\text{-}0"$	16
$1"=1'\text{-}0"$	12
$1\frac{1}{2}"=1'\text{-}0"$	8
$3"=1'\text{-}0"$	4

For example, let's say that you want to fit a series of drawings onto 11" × 17" paper. Let's also say the plottable area is 10" × 16" or, since we want to use the paper in landscape mode (largest dimension is horizontal), 16" × 10". The ratio of length to width is then 1.6 to 1. Now, let's put some floor plans on this paper. The largest of the floors is about 40' long by 20' wide; a ratio of 2 to 1. Since this ratio of the floor's length to its width is greater than the ratio of the paper's length to its width, the harder dimension to fit on paper will be the length of the floor plan.

To figure out a drawing scale, we divide the length of the plan (40') by the length of the paper (16") and come up with a result of 30. This result is the maximum drawing scale factor that will allow you to squeeze the plan onto the paper. Now, let's look at our table of standard scales and find one with a drawing scale factor larger than 30 (since a larger scale factor corresponds to a smaller drawing scale). A drawing scale of 1/2" = 1' has a drawing scale factor of 24, which is not enough; a drawing scale of 1/4" = 1' has a scale factor of 48, which is plenty. Our 40' × 20' room will be 10" across by 5" tall on our 16" by 10" drawable area, leaving room for dimensions, notes, and our company's title block. So, we choose the drawing scale of 1/4" = 1', and note that the scale factor is 48. (The drawing scale factor will be used as we proceed with setup below.)

Set Drawing-Scale-Specific Options

The drawing scale affects many setup options. You may want to create a prototype drawing for each of the drawing scales that you use frequently.

Limits. Set the limits to the paper size times the drawing scale factor. For instance, if your paper size is 17" × 11" and your drawing scale factor is 48, set the upper-right corner of the limits to 816",528" (or 68',44'). If your plotter requires a margin, then you might choose to use the plottable area rather than the actual paper size.

Command: LIMITS will prompt you for the lower-left and upper-right limits.

Menu Choice: Choosing Drawing Limits from the Settings menu will start the LIMITS command.

Zoom. Once you set the limits, zoom out a bit beyond them so you can see the whole drawing area at once.

Command: Enter ZOOM All, then ZOOM .9X to give yourself a little extra room to work.

Menu Choice: You can choose Zoom from the View menu, then choose the All suboption; but there's no way to zoom by a scale factor from the menus.

View. Save the current view so that you can return to it easily with VIEW Restore. Call the view something short but descriptive, such as FULL.

Command: Enter VIEW Save, and type the name of the view.

Menu Choice: Choose the Named View... suboption from the Set View option under the View menu. Use the New... button to define a new view.

Snap and **Grid.** Use the Drawing Aids dialogue box or commands to set Snap and Grid spacing. You can set a Grid spacing that makes sense for the geometry you're entering (such as 5' for a floor plan or 12" for a detail), or you can set it so that the grid points are 1 plotted inch apart. This latter option helps you stay oriented to the "paper world" and helps prevent you from getting too carried away with detail too fine to plot. To set grid spacing to 1 plotted inch, simply set the grid spacing for both X and Y to your drawing scale factor. In this case, the drawing scale factor is 48, so we set the spacing to 48" (or 4').

Snap spacing should be set to something that makes sense for the scale you're working on, such as 6" or 1' for a floor plan or 1" for a detail. It will take some practice and experience to determine the best values for your work, and you'll change the snap spacing as you draw anyway, so don't worry about getting exactly the "right" value.

Commands: Enter GRID and the Grid spacing to set the horizontal and vertical spacing to the same value. Likewise, Enter SNAP and the Snap spacing to use an equal horizontal and vertical Snap spacing. The Aspect suboption of GRID and SNAP allows you to set the horizontal and vertical spacing separately, but this isn't common.

The command DDRMODES brings up the Drawing Aids dialogue box that allows you to turn on Snap and Grid and set spacing all at once.

Menu Choice: Choose Drawing Aids... from the Settings menu to bring up the Drawing Aids dialogue box that allows you to turn on Snap and Grid and set spacing all at once.

Text style height. If you want to use different text heights with a text style, set up the style with a height of 0; AutoCAD will then prompt you for the height each time you enter text in that style. If you intend to use only one height with a style, figure out how high you want the text to be when plotted and use that size to calculate a fixed height for the STYLE command. To calculate the height, simply multiply the desired plotted height by the drawing scale factor. For instance, if you want your plotted text to be 1/8" high, and the drawing scale factor for your drawing is 48, multiply 1/8" times 48 for a result of 6".

Command: STYLE, then specify the style you want. Enter the height using the above formula or specify 0.

Menu Choice: Choose Text from the Draw menu, then Set Style... from the Text submenu. After you specify the font, AutoCAD will create a new style with it and prompt you for the height. Enter it using the above formula or specify 0.

Linetype scale. You may have to experiment with this to get things to look good on a plot, but usually half the drawing scale factor works well. For instance, if your drawing scale is 1/4"=1', your drawing scale factor is 48. Divide this by 2 for a linetype scale of 24.

Command: LTSCALE, then enter the scale factor you want. Calculate it using the above formula.

Menu Choice: There is no pull-down menu choice for changing this variable.

Dimension scale. In most cases, you should set DIMSCALE to the drawing scale factor. For instance, if your drawing scale is 1/4"=1', use a DIMSCALE of 48. Once you've set the DIMSCALE, you need to resave any dimension styles you created earlier. (See Chapter 9 for more details.)

Command: DIMSCALE, then enter the drawing scale factor.

Menu Choice: Choose Dimension Style. . . from the Settings menu. Choose any of the buttons in the Dimension Variables box (e.g., Dimension Line...), and then enter the drawing scale factor next to the prompt, Feature Scaling:.

PLOT ONE TO THROW AWAY

Once you have worked through all the setup steps, you may want to try doing a sample plot to see how things look. Use the RECTANG command and other commands to create a drawing that's a rough outline of your final drawing. Use a couple of different linetypes, text and dimension styles, and so on. Then use the Plot Preview option, described in Chapter 1, to make sure that the screen representation of your plot looks the way you want it to. Make any changes that are indicated by the appearance of the preview, then do a real plot. This will clue you in to any fine-tuning that your setup needs before you start drawing.

Paper Space Setup

You need to do paper space setup only if you will be using paper space. Paper space is useful for certain purposes, but it does have an overhead that must be taken into account before you use it in a drawing. Use paper space to:

- Show a 3D model from different points of view.

- Show a 2D or 3D model with different zoom resolutions; for instance, an overall plan and a detailed area of that plan on the same sheet.

- Show a 2D or 3D model with different layer freeze/thaw settings to make different parts of it show up in different viewports.

Avoid using paper space for assembling detail sheets or for creating a "paste-up sheet" of externally referenced drawings or inserted blocks. The overhead of paper space makes it inefficient for this purpose. If your drawing fits the criteria for using paper space, see Chapter 11 for more information, including how to do paper space setup.

The MVSETUP Routine

The MVSETUP routine is an AutoLISP application that automates some factors of setup. You can use MVSETUP with paper space enabled (TILEMODE=0) or disabled (TILEMODE=1). If you use it with paper space disabled, which is what we'll describe below, it performs a partial setup in model space. MVSETUP has some additional features for paper space setup, which we'll cover in Chapter 11.

Here are the setup options you can specify with MVSETUP with paper space disabled:

- Units
- Scale
- Paper size

Based on these factors, MVSETUP sets up the following:

- AutoCAD Units
- Drawing Limits
- Border or title block

Next, we describe in detail how to use MVSETUP to specify these options.

Run MVSETUP

MVSETUP uses the side menu to offer choices for setting up units, scale, and paper size. It also sets the drawing limits appropriately based on the choices you make for these options. You must choose your options carefully in order to get through the whole routine. (If you do "fall out" of the routine, simply restart it.) See Figure 5.4 for what the series of side menus looks like if you choose architectural units. MVSETUP offers similar choices for other types of units.

1. Make sure that paper space is disabled.

`Command: TILEMODE 1`

If you are in paper space, AutoCAD will turn it off and regenerate your drawing.

2. Start MVSETUP with TILEMODE set to 1.

Choose Layout from the View menu, then MV Setup or enter MVSETUP.

`Paperspace/Modelspace is disabled. The pre-R11 setup will be`
`invoked unless it is enabled. Enable Paper/Modelspace? <Y>: N`

This prompt is encouraging you to turn paper space on, but we'll save that for Chapter 11.

`TILEMODE is set to 1; cannot set up paperspace/modelspace`
`viewports unless TILEMODE is set to 0. Release 10 setup:`
`Select the Units from the screen menu:`

This prompt is telling you that the model space setup is being run. It then prompts you to set the units.

3. Use the side menu to set the unit type.

In the side menu, pick one of the choices below UNIT TYPE.

Pick one of the choices (some are abbreviated): scientfc, decimal, enginrng, archtect, metric. Don't pick UNITS or DDUNITS first; these options will cancel MVSETUP.

4. Use the side menu to set the scale.

A number of choices of scale will appear, depending on the unit type you picked in the previous step.

`Select the Scale from the screen menu:` *In the side menu, pick a SCALE.*

MVSETUP uses this factor to calculate Limits after the next step. Unfortunately, it doesn't set DIMSCALE or LTSCALE for you.

5. Use the side menu to set the sheet size.

`Select the Paper size from the screen menu:` *Pick a sheet size or OTHER... to enter the width and height of the sheet separately. Pick VERTCAL> if you want to change the sheet orientation to vertical; HORZNTL> to change it back.*

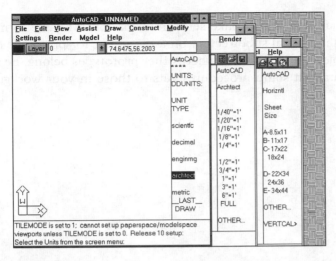

Figure 5.4   Side menu contents for all three steps of
MVSETUP routine with architectural units chosen.

A box will appear on the screen showing the outline of the paper size you
have chosen. The limits will be set appropriately for the sheet size and scale
you have chosen.

Organizing Setup

Project-Specific Setup

If you work on large, complex projects, you'll find that you and your coworkers
have many setup options that are standard to the project. This becomes
especially apparent as you decide the drawing scale or scales that you will use
within the project. We suggest that you at least do trial runs on some of the key
drawings in the project. The start of a project is one of the best times to revisit
your setup procedures, prototypes, and so on, and see if they need to be revised.

Drawing-Specific Setup for Workgroups

As with basic setup (covered in the previous chapter), setup efforts that are
worthwhile for individual users are even more so for workgroups. Take the
time to do a complete job of setup: Create multiple prototype files where they
make sense, and outline setup procedures to cover options that aren't
embedded in the prototypes. Revisit your prototype set and procedures
regularly to keep them complete and up to date; encourage others in your
workgroup to take the time to give you ideas, problem reports, and so on.

For a workgroup, you must make setup information available to many people. Besides the central subdirectory on a file server for prototype files, there may be project subdirectories where other prototypes belong. Be sure that information about setup procedures gets to those in your workgroup who need it.

CHAPTER

6

Creating New Geometry

This chapter describes some of the changes in Release 12 that influence how you create new geometry. Like the previous two chapters, which covered different aspects of setup, this chapter and the next one, *Selecting and Editing*, are closely related. Of course, in using AutoCAD, you don't actually create all your new geometry before you begin editing it. Instead, you continually switch back and forth between drawing new entities and editing existing ones. Nonetheless, thinking about these two closely related activities separately makes sense when you're trying to master a new version of AutoCAD, especially a version with as many new features and changes as Release 12.

About This Chapter

For new users, learning how to create new geometry is easier under Release 12 than under previous releases. More options are presented in menus and dialogue boxes, and on-line help explains much of what you need to know about the choices. Layer control is improved in both interface and functionality. Object snaps and routines for common construction tasks such as rectangles and parallel lines are more accessible. These changes make training and learning easier. If you're a new user, working through this chapter will help you get off to a good start with the basic process of drawing with the new release.

For the more experienced user, the advantages of Release 12 for creating new geometry may not be as obvious. The redesigned DDLMODES dialogue box includes more options and is better for working on multiple layers, but it

101

requires an extra pick or two for single layer operations. The dialogue boxes, in general, are slower than command-line operations in terms of raw speed, but, depending on the task at hand, dialogue boxes still can be more efficient, even for AutoCAD experts. And you always can stick with the old command-line commands when they're more efficient for you.

The cursor object snap menu is a clear win for experienced users. Also, users who haven't discovered the DLINE and RECTANG AutoLISP programs in previous versions of AutoCAD will appreciate having these routines easily accessible from the Draw menu.

Work through this chapter for maximum exposure to Release 12's new features in the minimum amount of time, and learn how to get the most out of the improvements for creating new geometry in Release 12.

Features Demonstrated in This Chapter

We assume that you know the basics of creating new geometry from previous AutoCAD releases. Therefore, we will now focus on features that are new or that have new interfaces under Release 12. The new or easier-to-access features demonstrated in this chapter include the following:

- The Layer Control dialogue box is substantially revised in Release 12; working with multiple layers is more efficient, but you'll have to get used to the new approaches for modifying single layers. We use the DDLMODES dialogue here to create a realistic set of layers for a drawing.

- Two newly integrated commands, RECTANG and DLINE, enhance the Draw menu. We use these commands to draw a slab and walls.

- The Entity Creation Modes dialogue box allows you to easily change such settings as color, layer, linetype, and style. We discuss this dialogue and suggest when (and when not) to use it.

- Point filters are now accessible via the cursor menu, and we show how to use them in conjunction with object snaps to locate points without drawing construction lines.

- The Geometry Calculator, new with Release 12, includes dozens of functions for locating points and calculating distances. We use several of the general-purpose functions to help with placing door and window openings.

- The new DDOSNAP dialogue box makes it easier to change running object snaps and the aperture size, as shown in an example using midpoint osnap.

- The object snap cursor menu is an easy productivity enhancer. We emphasize it throughout the chapter, along with drawing efficiently with Snap.

About the Example

We will use the prototype and drawing-specific settings we developed in the previous two chapters as the starting point for a drawing of a recreation room. Our example won't teach you much about architecture, but it will allow us to demonstrate the new techniques in a realistic example that makes sense to all readers, even those who don't draw buildings. We'll use RRPROTO.DWG file from the *AutoCAD Power Tools* disk as our prototype, so copy this file to your tutorial subdirectory.

Create a New Drawing From a Prototype

We'll use a simple prototype based on the specifications we discussed in the last two chapters as the basis for our drawing, which is called RRPROTO and can be found on the disk included with *AutoCAD Power Tools* (see Figure 6.1).

Create a new drawing, RECROOM, using RRPROTO from the *AutoCAD Power Tools* disk as the prototype.

Pick New... from the File menu.

Pick Prototype....

Locate and select the RRPROTO.DWG file.

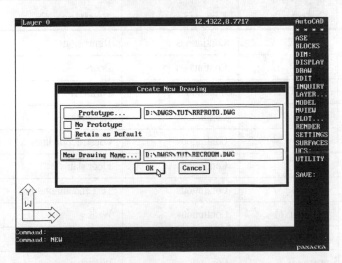

Figure 6.1 New dialogue box with RRPROTO prototype selected.

Name your new drawing RECROOM, make sure you've selected the proper subdirectory in which to save it, and then pick OK.

Create Layers with Colors and Linetypes

Like many of AutoCAD's dialogue boxes, the DDLMODES (Dynamic Dialogue Layer Modes) Layer Control dialogue was redesigned for Release 12. The changes are more than cosmetic, so, even if you're familiar with the Release 11 Layer Control dialogue, it will pay to familiarize yourself with the new layout and functionality.

To demonstrate and practice layer control, we'll create a simple set of layers for our recreation room drawing. We'll assign linetypes and colors to layers and let entities inherit these properties from the layers they're on. The revamped Layer Control dialogue box is well suited for creating and working with groups of layers, as we'll do here.

For this drawing, we'll use the layers shown in Table 6.1, three of which are already included in the prototype.

Follow the instructions below to create and set the properties for these layers:

1. Start the Layer Control dialogue box.

        Command: DDLMODES
        or
        Pick Layer Control... from the Settings menu.

Table 6.1   Layers Used in the Rec Room Drawing

Layer	Color	Linetype	Entities
DIM	yellow (2)	Continuous	Dimensions
DOOR	blue (5)	Continuous	Doors
FURNITURE	green (3)	Continuous	Furniture
HATCH	red (1)	Continuous	Hatching
SCRATCH	16	Continuous	Construction lines
SLAB	white (7)	Continuous	Floor slab
TEXT	cyan (4)	Continuous	Text and annotations
WALL	magenta (6)	Continuous	Walls
WALLFUT	magenta (6)	Dashed	Future walls
WINDOW	green (3)	Continuous	Windows

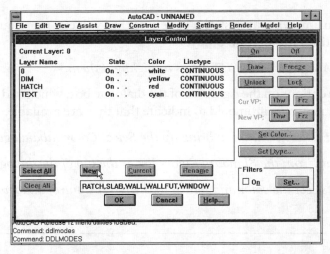

Figure 6.2   Creating a group of layers with the Layer
Control dialogue box.

2. Create the new layers.

*In the Layer Name edit box near the bottom of the screen, type the new
layer names listed in Table 6.1. Separate the names with commas, not
spaces, as shown in Figure 6.2.*

Although you might be tempted to pick OK, don't do it yet. OK will
close the dialogue box without creating any layers.

Pick the New button to create the layers
or
Press <Alt>+W to select New, then <Enter> to create the layer.

3. Specify layer colors and linetypes.

Unlike the Release 11 Layer Control dialogue, Release 12 requires you
to select a layer before you change its settings. Although this extra step

---

Tip

The quick way to select a button from the keyboard takes two steps:

1) Highlight the button by holding down the <Alt> key (which takes
you out of any text box that you've been typing in) and pressing
the letter within the button's name that's underlined.

2) Select the button by pressing <spacebar> or <Enter>.

---

might seem annoying at first, the benefit is that you can more quickly change settings for a group of layers.

Pick the WALL and WALLFUT layers to highlight them.

Most of the options on the right side of the dialogue box, which had been grayed out, now appear in bold to indicate that they are available.

Pick the Set Color... button to bring up the Select Color subdialogue.

Pick magenta from the Standard Colors list at the top of the dialogue.

Pick OK to select the color and return to the Layer Control dialogue.

Tip

When you plot, Release 12 lets you specify pen assignments for all 255 colors shown in the Select Color subdialogue. This is a useful feature when you need all those colors (e.g., for rendering), but it's overkill for most drafting. You usually don't want to have to slog through assigning all 255 colors before plotting, so stick to the first 15 or so colors unless you have a good reason to use more. (See Chapter 11, *Paper Space and Plotting*, for more information about plotting.)

Pick the WALL layer so that it's no longer highlighted. WALLFUT should be the only highlighted layer.

Pick the Set Ltype... button to bring up the Select Linetype subdialogue.

Pick the DASHED linetype from the list of linetypes. (See Figure 6.3.)

Don't pick the word DASHED; you must pick on the picture of the linetype at the left. (Use the Previous and Next buttons to page up and down through long lists of linetypes; unfortunately, the Select Linetypes dialogue doesn't have scroll bars.)

Pick OK to select the linetype and return to the Layer Control dialogue.

Pick the Clear All button to unhighlight WALLFUT.

Repeat the process of picking a layer and assigning its color for each of the layers listed in Table 6.1.

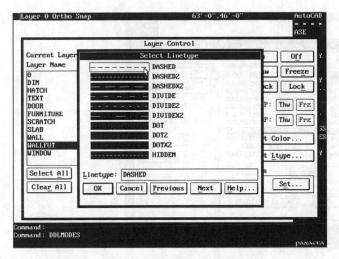

Figure 6.3 Assigning a linetype to a layer.

4. Make the SLAB layer current.

We're going to lay out the rec room slab first, so let's set the SLAB layer current.

Pick the Clear All button to deselect all the layers.

Pick the SLAB layer to select it.

Pick the Current button to make SLAB the current layer.

Note that the Current button is only available when a single, unfrozen layer is highlighted.

Figure 6.4 shows the layer settings as they should appear when you're finished with the Layer Control dialogue.

 Tip

When you create new layers with the Layer Control dialogue box, AutoCAD doesn't immediately re-sort the list; it simply adds the new layers to the end of the list. To see the sorted list, pick OK to close the Layer Control dialogue, and then hit <Return> to repeat the DDLMODES command.

Note that the MAXSORT system variable controls when AutoCAD sorts layers, filenames, and other lists. If the list has more than MAXSORT items (250 by default), then AutoCAD assumes that sorting will take too long and doesn't bother.

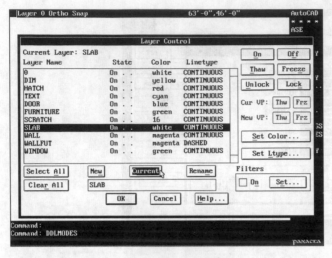

Figure 6.4   Layer Control dialogue box with rec room drawing settings.

RECTANG Command

The RECTANG command is now fully integrated into AutoCAD and is available on the Draw pull-down menu. RECTANG draws a Polyline rectangle based on two corner points you supply. We'll use it first to draw the concrete slab for our rec room. Because the slab will determine where all the other rec room geometry goes, we'll lay it out with Snap set to 1'. This will make it easy to precisely pick points later on without needing an object snap for every pick.

1. Make sure Snap is turned on and set to 1'.

Command: SNAP
or
Pick Drawing Aids... from the Settings menu.
Snap spacing or ON/OFF/Aspect/Rotate/Style<*current*>: 1'

2. Draw a 40' x 20' rectangle on the SLAB layer.

Command: RECTANG
or
Pick Rectangle from the Draw menu.

You'll be prompted for two diagonally opposite corners of the rectangle. You can pick or type points; in this case, we'll type a relative distance for the second corner.

First Corner: *Pick or type the point 12',12'*
Second Corner: @40',20'

Figure 6.5 shows the rectangular slab.

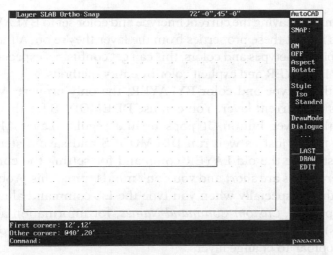

Figure 6.5 Rectangular slab drawn with the RECTANG command.

Changing Layers and Other Current Properties

AutoCAD keeps track of the current layer, linetype, and color and applies them to each entity you create. As in previous versions, Release 12 lets you change the current properties from the command line with the LAYER, LINETYPE, and COLOR commands, or from the Entity Creation Modes dialogue box. This dialogue, shown in Figure 6.6, is accessed by the DDEMODES (Dynamic Dialogue Entity Modes) command or Entity Modes... on the Settings menu. Which method should you use?

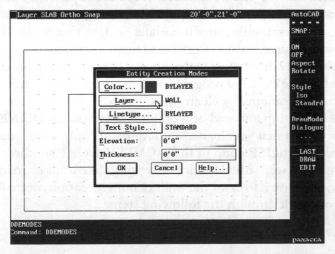

Figure 6.6 The DDEMODES Entity Creation Modes dialogue.

First, we recommend leaving the current linetype and color set to BYLAYER, which lets entities inherit these properties from the layer they're on. Although you can assign explicit linetypes and colors, this can get confusing, especially if you mix the color BYLAYER and explicit color by entity methods.

If you stick with linetype and color BYLAYER, the only property you'll need to change is the current layer. You can use DDEMODES for this, but when you pick the Layer button, it pops up the regular Layer Modes dialogue, so you might just as well run DDLMODES and save a step. Of course, you can still use the old LAYER command for setting the current layer. If your layer names are short and you don't mind typing, this probably is the fastest method, especially when you type the LA command alias for LAYER (see Chapter 15, *Custom Command Names*, for information about command aliases). In AutoCAD for Windows, you can use the drop-down layer list on the toolbar to change layers.

The Entity Creation Modes dialogue still is useful for those times when you want to check all your current properties. The Text Style… button is handy for changing the current style, and the Elevation and Thickness edit boxes will be useful for 3D work.

Release 12 has two new dialogue box commands that are similar to DDEMODES, but that let you change the properties of entities you've already drawn: DDCHPROP and DDMODIFY. We'll cover these dialogues in Chapter 8, *Modifying Properties and Hatching*.

DLINE Command

Like RECTANG, DLINE was a bonus routine in previous versions of AutoCAD and is now integrated into the pull-down menu. It's available as a suboption of Line, the first command on the Draw menu. DLINE has quite a few options, and you might decide to research some of these later on. Don't bother looking in the *AutoCAD Reference Manual*, because DLINE isn't there. Like many of the useful enhancements in Release 12, it's covered in the *AutoCAD Extras Manual* instead.

DLINE is a double-line drawing program, and not a bad one; it can draw curved double lines, automatically clean up "L" and "T" intersections, and add "caps" to the beginning and end of a double-line segment. DLINE is a large AutoLISP program that gets loaded into AutoCAD only when you run it. You can find the AutoLISP code in the \ACAD\SUPPORT subdirectory. The DLINE command is well suited for drawing things like walls or roads. In the tutorial below, we'll use it to draw the walls of our recreation room. Refer to Figure 6.7 as you work through the following steps:

1. Make the WALL layer current.

Use the DDLMODES or LAYER command to set WALL current.

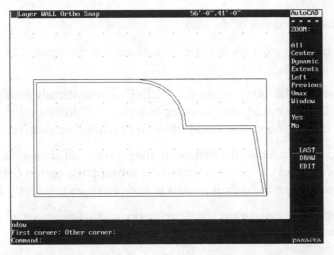

Figure 6.7 The rec room exterior walls drawn with the DLINE command.

2. Start the DLINE command.

   ```
   Command: DLINE
   ```
   or
   Pick Line from the Draw menu, then pick Double Lines from the cascading menu.

   You'll see a copyright notice and a prompt that includes the various options for the DLINE command.

3. Set the width between the double line segments.

   ```
   Break/Caps/Dragline/Offset/Snap/Undo/Width/<start point>: W
   New DLINE width <default>: 6
   ```

4. Specify an offset from center line.

   The points you will pick to draw the walls make up an imaginary path called the "dragline." By default, DLINE centers the double lines on the dragline. But in our case, it's more convenient to pick points along the outside face of the wall. Therefore, we want the dragline to define the right side of the wall (since we'll be going counter-clockwise).

   ```
   Break/Caps/Dragline/Offset/Snap/Undo/Width/<start point>: D
   Set dragline position to Left/Center/Right/<0">: R
   ```

5. Draw the first four segments.

   ```
   Break/Caps/Dragline/Offset/Snap/Undo/Width/<start point>:
   ```

Pick the lower-left corner of the slab.

```
Entity found is not an arc or line, or is not parallel to
the current UCS.
```

You can ignore the error message. DLINE automatically looks for other lines that it should trim in order to form a "T" intersection. The message is telling you that it found the slab Polyline, but didn't trim it.

Now that you have selected the first point, the prompt will change slightly. The options Arc and CLose are added to the prompt; the option Offset is removed from it; and the default, <start point>, changes to <next point>.

```
Arc/Break/CAps/CLose/Dragline/Snap/Undo/Width/<next point>:
```
Pick the lower-right corner of the slab.

We don't want our rec room to be too "boxy," so let's add a skewed wall partway along the east side.

```
Arc/Break/Caps/CLose/Dragline/Snap/Undo/Width/<next
point>: @-2',12'
```

You can use any of AutoCAD's point entry methods with DLINE. Use the *distance<angle* format to draw the next segment. We'll leave the northeast corner of the slab open for a small outside patio.

```
Arc/Break/Caps/CLose/Dragline/Snap/Undo/Width/<next
point>: @12'<180
```

6. Draw a curved segment.

DLINE's Arc option lets you draw curved double lines. Let's try it.

```
Arc/Break/CAps/CLose/Dragline/Snap/Undo/Width/<next
point>: A
```

The prompt changes to include CEnter and Endpoint arc options, which are similar to what you'll find in the ARC or PLINE command. We want a 90-degree arc (a quarter circle) that bulges outward and is tangent to the north edge of the slab.

```
Break/CAps/CEnter/CLose/Dragline/Endpoint/Line/Snap/
Undo/Width/<second point>: CE
Center point: @8'<180
Angle/Length of chord/<Endpoint>: A
Included angle: 90
```

7. Finish off the wall with straight segments.

Tip

Unlike the RECTANG command, DLINE leaves its lines as separate line segments. You can use the PEDIT command to group them into a Polyline for offsetting or other purposes.

The Line option returns to drawing straight double lines.

```
Break/CAps/CEnter/CLose/Dragline/Endpoint/Line/Snap/Undo/
Width/<second point>: L
Arc/Break/CAps/CLose/Dragline/Snap/Undo/Width/<next point>:
```

Pick the upper-left corner of the slab.

Finally, use the CLose option to complete the exterior walls.

```
Arc/Break/CAps/CLose/Dragline/Snap/Undo/Width/<next point>: CL
```

DLINE draws the final double-line segment back to the beginning point.

Figure 6.7 shows the resulting room outline. Notice that the corners are cleaned up automatically. If you don't get the walls right the first time, use the UNDO command to back up and start again.

Point Filters

Point filters allow you to use the coordinates of existing points to help specify new ones. Point filters are indispensible for creating 3D geometry, but they're also valuable in 2D drawings. You use point filters together with object snaps to locate points without having to draw construction lines. As with object snaps, the benefits are greatest when working on complex drawings or drawings with geometry that doesn't fit neatly onto a Snap grid.

Although point filters aren't new to Release 12, they have a new place of prominence thanks to the Filters cascading menu on the cursor menu (see Figure 6.8).

Tip

Unfortunately, the cursor menu that comes with Release 12 for Windows doesn't include point filters or the Geometry Calculator. If you're using Release 12 for Windows, simply type the point filters instead. You can add point filters to the cursor menu by customizing ACAD.MNU (see Chapter 17, *Menus*).

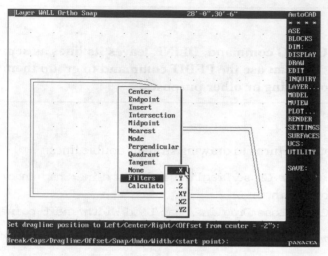

Figure 6.8   Filters option on the cursor menu.

In the example below, we use point filters to locate the corner of an interior wall so that it aligns with the end of the curved wall (refer to Figure 6.9).

1. Turn off the SLAB layer.

Since we won't be needing to refer to the slab for awhile, use DDLMODES or the LAYER command to turn off SLAB.

2. Turn off Snap, since we'll use point filters to ensure precision.

Press the <F9> key or <Ctrl>+B.

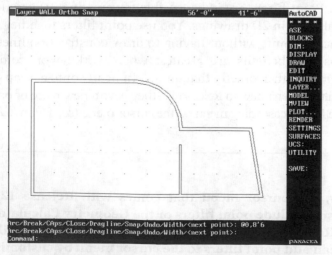

Figure 6.9   An interior wall placed with point filters.

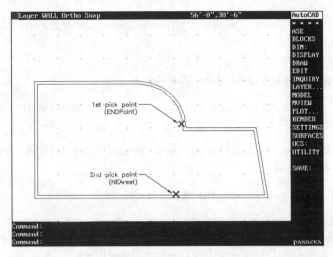

Figure 6.10 Pick points for locating the interior wall with point filters.

3. Start DLINE again; change the width to 4" and dragline to the left.

```
Command: DLINE
Break/Caps/Dragline/Offset/Snap/Undo/Width/<start point>: W
New DLINE width <6">: 4
Break/Caps/Dragline/Offset/Snap/Undo/Width/<start point>: D
Set dragline position to Left/Center/Right/<-3">: L
```

4. Use point filters to locate the lower-left corner of the interior wall.

```
Break/Caps/Dragline/Offset/Snap/Undo/Width/<start point>:
```

Hit the third button on your digitizer puck (or hold down the <Shift> key and press the second mouse button) to bring up the cursor menu. Pick Filters and then .X. If you're using Release 12 for Windows, simply type .X.

```
of:
```

By choosing .X, you're telling AutoCAD to use only the x-coordinate of the next point you pick. The of: is AutoCAD's way of asking "x-coordinate of what?"

Pop up the cursor menu again and pick Endpoint. Pick the inside arc of the curved wall, near the lower end. (See Figure 6.10.)

```
of (need YZ):
```

Now AutoCAD needs to know the remaining two coordinates of the point. Since we're working in 2D, we need to be concerned only with the y-coordinate, which is defined by the inside face of the exterior wall.

Use NEArest object snap to pick any point on the inside of the south wall. (See Figure 6.10.)

5. Finish the wall, which should be 8'–6" long.

```
Arc/Break/CAps/CLose/Dragline/Snap/Undo/Width/<next
point>: @0,8'6
```

```
Arc/Break/CAps/CLose/Dragline/Snap/Undo/Width/<next
point>: <Enter>
```

DLINE will add a cap to the end of the wall.

By using point filters, you can ensure precision as you lay out new geometry. While point filters require quite a few picks, in most cases, they're more efficient than drawing and then erasing construction lines.

Using the Geometry Calculator

The Geometry Calculator is brand new in Release 12. It combines a powerful set of functions for doing arithmetic, point, and vector calculations with a command-line interface that would make a Unix shell programmer proud. The Geometry Calculator (CAL) puts a lot of power at your disposal, but that power is available only to the extent that you're willing to memorize or look up a new set of functions and keywords besides those you've already learned to use with AutoCAD. CAL is an ADS program and, like DLINE, it's documented in the *AutoCAD Extras Manual.*

1. Start the Geometry Calculator.

```
Command: CAL
```
or
Pick Calculator from the cursor menu or the Assist pull-down menu.

The Geometry Calculator loads and displays its `>> Expression:` prompt.

Tip

As mentioned in Chapter 1, *Introducing Release 12,* **you can "preselect" the Calculator menu choice by moving the mouse cursor to a point about 1/4" above the bottom of the drawing area before popping up the cursor menu.**

2. Try some arithmetic.

```
>> Expression: 2+2
4
```

Calculate the area of a 3'–7" diameter circle using the formula pi*(d/2)².

```
Command: <Enter> to repeat CAL
>> Expression: PI*(3'7/2)^2
Error: Invalid feet'-inches" format.
```

Oops; unlike AutoCAD, CAL complains when you leave off the inch mark. Try again.

```
>> Expression: PI*(3'7"/2)^2
1452.2
```

3. Convert between units.

When you use a feet and inches distance in CAL, it gives its answer in inches, but you can convert it to feet (or another linear unit) with the cvunit() function. Conversions are fairly easy once you know the syntax of the function. If you enter the expression without the proper parameters, AutoCAD will respond with an error message that lists the correct parameters—a kind of low-budget, on-line help.

```
>> Expression: CVUNIT
>> Error: Use CVUNIT(value, from_units, to_units):
>> Expression: CVUNIT(66, INCH, FOOT)
5.5
```

You usually can guess unit names that AutoCAD will recognize. For instance, "inches," "inch," or "in" will work, as will "feet," "foot," or "ft." (See the ACAD.UNT file in your \ACAD\SUPPORT directory for a complete list of units.)

A more common use for cvunit() is to convert between different systems of measurement. Calculate the length of our rec room in meters.

```
Command: <Enter> to repeat CAL
>> Expression: CVUNIT(40, feet, meter)
12.192
```

While CAL makes a handy calculator, its real advantage is in feeding values to AutoCAD commands. In our rec room example, we'll use CAL to locate the edges of door and window openings. (Refer to Figure 6.14 as you work through this part of the tutorial.)

4. Draw the large window opening in the skewed wall.

We want the ends of this window to be 12" from the inside corners of the wall, so use CAL's pld( ) function to find the right points. pld( ) stands for Point along a Line a specified Distance from the first endpoint, and it's similar to the plt( ) function we tried in Chapter 1, *Introducing Release 12.*

```
Command: LINE
From point: 'CAL
```

If you type 'CAL, be sure to include the apostrophe so that the Geometry Calculator starts transparently.

```
>> Expression: PLD(END,END,12)
>> Select entity for END snap: Pick near one end of the wall line.
>> Select entity for END snap: Pick near the other end of the
same line.
```

(END,END,12) tells CAL to prompt you for two endpoints, and then to find the point 12" from the first end you pick. (See Figure 6.11.)

```
To point: use perpendicular object snap to draw the other end of the line.
To point: <Enter>
```

To draw the other side of the opening, repeat this sequence, but reverse the order in which you pick the endpoints. The result should look like Figure 6.12.

5. Draw the door opening 8" away from the interior wall.

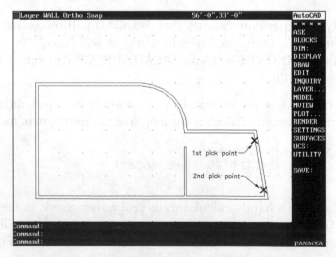

Figure 6.11   Pick points for locating a window opening with CAL.

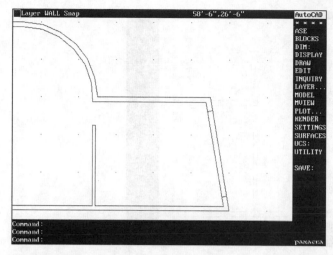

Figure 6.12 The first window opening drawn with CAL.

First turn on Snap and set it to 6", since this will make picking the outside of the wall easier.

```
Command: SNAP
Snap spacing or ON/OFF/Aspect/Rotate/Style <1'-0">: 6
```

Now draw the east side of the door opening.

```
Command: LINE
From point: 'CAL
>> Expression: INT-[8,0]
>> Select entity for INT snap: Pick the intersection of the
interior and exterior walls.
```

INT-[8,0] tells CAL to prompt you for an intersection and then find the point 8" to the left of that intersection. You always must enclose points and vectors in square brackets for CAL. (See Figure 6.13.)

```
To point: with Snap and Ortho on, simply move one 6" increment
down to draw the other end of the line.
To point: <Enter>
```

Use the COPY or OFFSET command to create the other side of the opening, 3' away (see Figure 6.14).

6. Draw other openings.

Use INT+[x,y] and PLD(END,END, *distance*) to draw other openings like those shown in Figure 6.14. Practice makes perfect with CAL, and these functions are worth learning if your work often requires finding points that are located with respect to existing geometry.

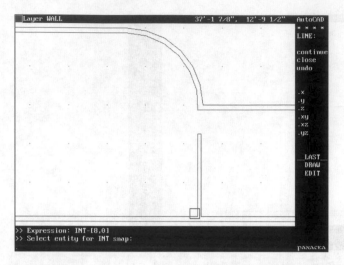

Figure 6.13   Finding one side of a door opening with CAL.

Tip

Because of the way the Geometry Calculator ADS program works with AutoLISP, you can't use CAL when you're in the middle of another AutoLISP program. For instance, if you try to enter CAL when the DLINE LISP routine is prompting you for a point, you'll get a "Can't reenter AutoLISP" error. It is possible to build CAL expressions into AutoLISP programs and to store and retrieve AutoLISP variable values. (See the _AutoCAD Extras Manual_ for details.)

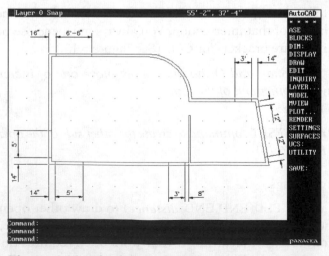

Figure 6.14   The door and window openings placed with CAL.

Snap and Object Snaps

So far, we've used Snap, single object snaps, point filters, and the Geometry Calculator to ensure precision in the points we've picked. It's important to use these features to maintain precision, even if your plotted output doesn't require high accuracy. Geometry that looks right but is inexact creates a "sloppy" drawing that becomes harder and harder to edit and dimension.

Snaps to the current Snap grid are the most efficient to use, because they are "automatic" and require no extra keystrokes or menu picks. The two keys to using Snap are toggling it on and off frequently and periodically adjusting the Snap spacing to match your current "working resolution." When you need to select entities that aren't on the current Snap grid, just toggle Snap off with the <F9> key (but remember to toggle it back on when you resume picking points). As you zoom in and out on your drawing, you'll find that you also need to adjust the Snap spacing to finer and coarser values. The "best" Snap values should become apparent as you experiment with your particular kinds of drawings.

These two techniques should help you use Snap efficiently and make you more productive. But even so, many times the point you need isn't on the current Snap grid and it may not be worth changing the Snap spacing for that one point. In these cases, object snaps, with or without point filters or the Geometry Calculator, are the way to go.

Tip

The geometry in some types of drawings, such as maps and civil engineering plans, doesn't really match any Snap grid spacing. For these types of work, you still can use Snap to keep notes and other annotations lined up.

Running Object Snap

Running object snaps were available in previous versions of AutoCAD, but some users weren't aware of this feature. The OSNAP command lets you set one or more object snap modes so that they stay in effect for multiple picks. This is useful whenever you anticipate using the same snap modes repeatedly.

You probably won't have as much need for running object snaps in Release 12, since the cursor menu makes single osnaps faster to access. But there still will be times when running object snaps come in handy, and

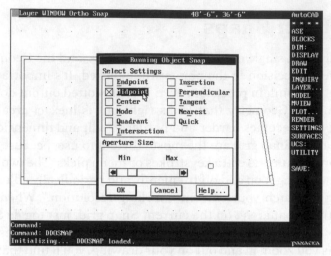

Figure 6.15 Running Object Snap dialogue box.

Release 12 makes them easier to access in the new Running Object Snap dialogue box. You can start it by entering 'DDOSNAP from the command line (it's a transparent command) or by choosing Object Snap... from the Settings menu. (See Figure 6.15.)

The dialogue box allows you to quickly see what the settings are and toggle them on and off. As a bonus, it lets you adjust the size of the object snap aperture, which can be very helpful in crowded drawings. There's no extra work or surprises here; just check the mode or modes you want and click OK. When you're finished with running object snaps, pop up the Running Object Snap dialogue again and clear all the check marks.

To finish off the basic plan for the recreation room, we'll use a running object snap mode to draw lines representing the windows. Refer to Figure 6.16 as you work through the following sequence.

1. Turn off Snap and make the WINDOW layer current.

Use <F9> to toggle Snap off.

Set WINDOW current with DDLMODES or LAYER.

2. Set running object snap to midpoint and reduce the aperture size.

```
Command: DDOSNAP
```
or
Pick Object Snap... from the Settings menu.

Check the box next to Midpoint and move the slider under Aperture Size so that it's about a quarter of the distance from the left (see Figure 6.15).

Tip

There's one subtle difference between single and running object snaps. With single object snaps, AutoCAD gives you an error message if it doesn't find a suitable object snap location. When this happens, you can reselect the object snap and point. With running object snaps, there's no error message; AutoCAD just uses the point you picked, even though it doesn't meet the current running object snap criterion. This discrepancy can cause subtle errors in your drawing, so be careful when picking with running object snaps.

The smaller aperture will make it easier to pick the short window opening lines.

3. Draw the window lines.

Use the LINE command to draw lines between the midpoints of the 6" window opening lines (see Figure 6.12).

4. Turn off the running object snap mode and reset the aperture.

Command: DDOSNAP

Clear the Midpoint check box and move the slider in the Aperture Size area back to the middle.

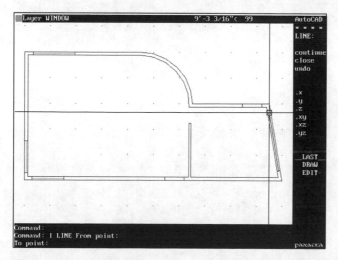

Figure 6.16   Windows drawn with the midpoint object snap mode.

Workgroups and Creating New Geometry

Although the members of your workgroup should already know how to create geometry, there's a real danger of getting stuck in a rut. All of us tend to rely on old and familiar ways of doing things, and it will take some effort to get everyone to take advantage of all the new or newly integrated features presented in this chapter.

Most users will quickly learn what they need to know about the Layer Control dialogue box, but the dialogue is a "busy" one and you may want to emphasize some of the finer points. Osnaps and the cursor menu should be immediately obvious once each person finds the right puck or mouse button.

Point out the RECTANG and DLINE commands if your workgroup hasn't discovered them yet, and go over the DLINE options that apply to your work. This might be a good time to review point filters and running object snaps with your workgroup members if they haven't mastered these features yet. Also, emphasize the use of Snap if it's appropriate to your types of drawings.

The tallest order will be making the Geometry Calculator a regular part of your workgroup's regimen. Because of its primitive interface and large number of functions, many users will find CAL overwhelming. Demonstrate a few useful functions and consider developing a "short list" of the functions that your workgroup is most likely to find useful.

We'll run into the problem of getting "old" users familiar with new features again, especially in the next chapter. While every situation is different, taking the time to explore new features yourself, then using persistence and creativity to make sure others in your workgroup are exposed to them, will pay off greatly in the long run.

7

Selecting and Editing

The biggest change in your hour-by-hour use of AutoCAD under Release 12 will come from the enhancements to editing and selecting entities. The old editing and selection methods still are available, but there are plenty of new ones in addition. In fact, there are so many ways to select and change entities in Release 12 that the only problem is figuring out which methods to use.

This chapter and the previous one, *Creating New Geometry*, are closely related. While the previous chapter covers making new entities, this one deals with changing entities once you've drawn them. Since even the most methodical among us continually move back and forth between these activities, you'll find yourself intermixing the features described in these two chapters.

About This Chapter

New users should find editing easier under Release 12. The new noun/verb editing style, which allows the user to make a selection and then specify the command to act on it, is more natural for many users and will make AutoCAD easier for them to learn. Grips are a new feature that will be familiar to those who have experience with an illustration package or other graphics software. On the other hand, AutoCAD's implementation of noun/verb and grip editing is different from the methods used in some other programs. If you're new to AutoCAD, this chapter will help you sort out the differences.

Experienced AutoCAD users are likely to have the opposite problem: integrating new and very different editing methods into their current working style. Many of the new selection and editing features require a "mental readjustment," and in a few cases, the new feature isn't worth the trouble for an experienced user.

Most of the features described in this chapter are worth the trouble of rethinking old habits, though. Grip editing, in which you grab hold of an entity and then modify it interactively without having to start a command, is powerful but full of subtleties. The new selection set options, including Fence and ALL, are welcome additions to AutoCAD's already impressive array of methods for selecting entities. Layer locking is a tremendous boon, especially for users who work in crowded drawings.

This chapter describes the wide range of new selection and editing options in Release 12, and focuses on those we think carry the greatest benefit for existing AutoCAD users. After working through the chapter, you should be well on your way to developing an editing style that takes advantage of Release 12 and fits your type of work.

Features Demonstrated in This Chapter

This chapter demonstrates features that are used to select and modify existing geometry and that are new, or have changed significantly in Release 12. We assume that you know the basics of building a selection set and editing from previous releases or other training on AutoCAD. The features demonstrated in this chapter include the following:

- Noun/verb editing promises greater consistency with other graphics packages, but limits on what you can select first make this new style of editing too restrictive for many users. We demonstrate its strengths and weaknesses.

- New selection methods let you control how AutoCAD responds when you select entities individually or as a group. We present the new possibilities, discuss how to change them with the new **DDSELECT** dialogue box, and then pick some favorites.

- Additional selection set options make picking entities in crowded drawings easier. We demonstrate the new options and suggest some ways to apply them.

- The new FILTER dialogue box is a powerful but complex tool for selecting entities based on their characteristics rather than their position on the screen. We show one way to use entity filters.

- Layer locking is a welcome new feature for anyone who has ever wanted to keep layers turned on but immune to editing changes. We use this feature to select the right entities more efficiently.

- Grips are the most radical change to Release 12's editing abilities; we show you how to get the most out of them and how to take advantage of some of the finer points.

Of all the new features in Release 12, the new selection and editing options, taken as a group, will require the most work to learn to take advantage of. It's worth the effort. Most CAD users spend the bulk of their time editing existing geometry, and many editing operations are repetitive. As a result, small improvements in selecting and editing efficiency can add up to big productivity gains. Use the tutorial in this chapter to learn about the new options, and begin thinking about how you can best use them in your current work.

About the Example

In this chapter, we pick up the RECROOM drawing as we left it in the previous chapter, with walls, door and window openings, and a slab. We first add a few chairs and then use them to experiment with the new selection methods in Release 12. Next we bring in a more extensive furniture collection from another drawing and try the new selection set options, layer locking, and entity filters. Finally, we use grips to modify and create several objects.

If you don't have an up-to-date version of RECROOM as of the previous chapter, you can use the RRCH07.DWG file on the *AutoCAD Power Tools* disk as a starting point. You'll definitely need the RRFURN.DWG file from the disk, so copy it to your tutorial subdirectory before starting.

Selecting Entities

Release 12 has something for everyone in the entity selection department. Some of the new features are designed to appeal to new AutoCAD users who have experience with other graphics software. Other features will make everyone, including long-time AutoCAD users, more productive. We cover a lot of ground in this section, but, by the end of it, you should have a clear picture of what your options are and which choices are likely to serve you best.

Noun/Verb Editing

Noun/verb editing is fundamentally simple: It means choosing an entity or set of entities (the "noun") first, then entering a command (the "verb") that modifies them. Verb/noun editing, the style that's always been available in AutoCAD, is the opposite: You enter a command first, then choose the entity or set of entities you want it to operate on. Autodesk added noun/verb editing to Release 12 because many other graphics programs use the noun/verb sequence and some new users find it more intuitive. Let's try it.

1. Load RECROOM.DWG.

Use your drawing from the previous chapter, or copy RRCH07.DWG from the *AutoCAD Power Tools* disk.

2. Make the FURNITURE layer current and make sure the PICKFIRST system variable is turned on.

Use the DDLMODES or LAYER command to make FURNITURE current.

```
Command: PICKFIRST
New value for PICKFIRST <default>: 1
```

PICKFIRST controls whether or not you can do noun/verb editing.

3. Draw a chair.

Use the PLINE or RECTANG command to draw a shape that represents a chair.

Don't get too carried away, since we'll be erasing it later.

4. Select the chair.

Pick the chair without entering a command first.

Notice that it highlights and displays small blue boxes.

5. Make multiple copies of the chair.

Enter the COPY command.

```
Command: COPY
Select objects: 1 found
```

AutoCAD automatically uses the preselected entity (See Figure 7.1).

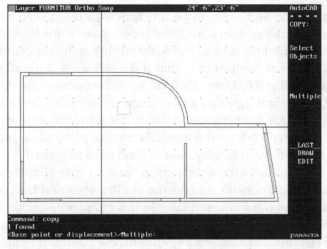

Figure 7.1 Copying noun/verb style.

```
<Base point or displacement>/Multiple: M
Base point: Pick a point.
Second point of displacement: Pick another point.
```

Continue copying until you've created about a dozen chairs.

6. Try using other editing commands noun/verb style.

Experiment with simple commands such as MOVE and ERASE. Also try TRIM and BREAK. For extra credit, see if you can master STRETCH.

In AutoCAD, noun/verb editing doesn't replace verb/noun editing, but is available alongside it when the PICKFIRST system variable is set to 1. Verb/noun editing is always available; noun/verb is an option that you can turn on if you wish, then use as needed. There's little harm in leaving noun/verb editing turned on, but if you prefer that it be off, simply set PICKFIRST to 0. Table 7.1 summarizes the options.

Table 7.1   Verb/Noun and Noun/Verb Editing

	Verb/Noun (Traditional)	Noun/Verb (Release 12 only)
PICKFIRST=1 (default)	*Available for all commands*	*Available for some commands*
PICKFIRST=0	*Available for all commands*	*Not available*

At first glance, there doesn't seem to be much new to noun/verb editing (other than a different order of operation), but it does have some limitations and characteristics that make it a less than ideal editing style, especially for experienced users. The first limitation is that it doesn't work with all commands. If you tried to use TRIM or BREAK in the sequence above, you noticed that AutoCAD simply ignored any existing noun/verb selection set. See Chapter 2 of the *AutoCAD Reference Manual* for a breakdown of what commands work and don't work with noun/verb editing. Also, when picking groups of entities for noun/verb editing, you're limited to Release 12's built-in AUto selection set option (which we'll cover later in this chapter); you can't use any of the explicit options such as the old Previous and Last or the new Fence and WPolygon (also covered later in this chapter).

One other possible source of confusion is the relationship of noun/verb editing to grips. Selecting entities before you enter a command can be a prelude to either editing noun/verb style or editing with grips. This suggests that the two are linked, but, in fact, you can turn each one on and off separately, and you can use one while completely ignoring the other. Grips are a major topic later in this chapter.

The bottom line is that noun/verb editing will help many new users feel more comfortable in AutoCAD, and there's nothing wrong with using it for simple editing with common commands such as COPY and ERASE. Most experienced AutoCAD users will want to stick with verb/noun editing because of the greater flexibility and consistency they get with the old approach. By supplementing verb/noun editing with grip editing, you'll get the best of both worlds and avoid the confusion of dealing with two opposite ways of using editing commands.

DDSELECT and New Selection Methods

Noun/verb editing is just the tip of the new selection method iceberg in Release 12. AutoCAD includes three other new PICK... system variables, in addition to PICKFIRST:

- PICKAUTO activates a "running AUto" selection set option (the AutoCAD manuals call this feature "implied windowing").

- PICKADD controls whether each selection replaces or adds to the currently selected entities.

- PICKDRAG determines whether you specify selection windows with two picks or with a pick-drag-release sequence.

The variety of new options can be pretty confusing at first, but Release 12's Entity Selection Settings (DDSELECT) dialogue box, shown in Figure 7.2, provides a convenient way to try them out, as we'll do now.

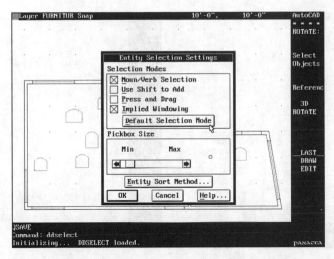

Figure 7.2 The Entity Selection Settings dialogue box.

1. Make sure you have a group of chairs to experiment with.

If necessary, use COPY Multiple to create more chairs.

2. Pop up the Entity Selection Methods dialogue box.

Command: DDSELECT

or

Pick Selection Settings... from the Settings menu.

3. Start with the default Release 12 settings.

Pick the Default Selection Mode button, and then pick OK.

This button ensures that you're starting with the default settings: Noun/Verb Selection and Implied Windowing turned on; Use Shift to Add and Press and Drag turned off.

4. Try implied windowing (PICKAUTO).

Pick a chair.

The entity highlights.

Pick below and to the left of a group of chairs.

The pickbox changes to a window.

Move the cursor up and to the right until your selection window encloses a group of chairs, and then pick again (see Figure 7.3).

AutoCAD selects the entities inside the window.

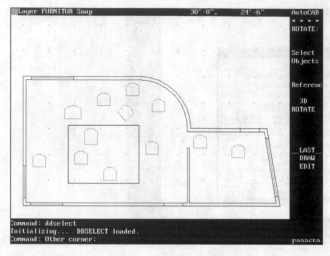

Figure 7.3 Using implied windowing to select entities.

Pick below and to the right of another group of chairs, but this time move the cursor to the left and pick again.

When you specify a selection window by moving to the left, AutoCAD uses Crossing (i.e, everything inside of or cutting through the box). The selection window is shown dashed to remind you of this (see Figure 7.4).

Hold down the <Shift> key and pick some more entities, either individually or with an implied window.

<Shift>+pick removes entities from the selection set.

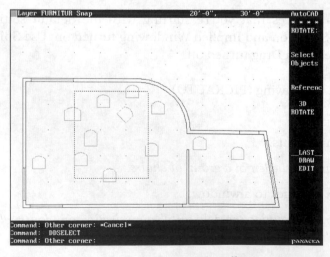

Figure 7.4 Implied windowing also allows a Crossing window.

5. Try the Use Shift to Add option (PICKADD).

Cancel (<Ctrl>+C) twice from the keyboard to clear the selection set and grips.

Pop up the Entity Selection Methods dialogue box again and check the box next to Use Shift to Add.

Repeat the sequence in step 4: Select a single chair, a group of chairs with a window to the right, and a group of chairs with a window to the left.

Notice that this time each selection replaces, rather than adds to, the previous one. The blue grip boxes still appear on all entities, but only the most recently selected set is highlighted.

Hold down the <Shift> key and pick more entities.

Now AutoCAD adds entities to the selection set.

6. Try Press and Drag (PICKDRAG).

Cancel (<Ctrl>+C) twice from the keyboard to clear the selection set and grips.

Pop up the Entity Selection Methods dialogue box again and check the box next to Press and Drag.

Repeat the sequence in step 4.

If you're used to AutoCAD's pick-release-pick-release sequence for specifying selection windows, you'll think implied windowing doesn't work any more.

Try a selection window again, but this time press and hold down the pick button when you choose the first corner. Move to the opposite corner of the selection window while holding the button down, and then release the button.

Specify a few more selection windows with Press and Drag.

Notice that when both Press and Drag and Use Shift to Add are turned on, you can quickly clear the current selection set by picking and releasing on a blank spot in the drawing.

7. Return to the default Release 12 settings.

Pop up the Entity Selection Methods dialogue box and pick the Default Selection Mode button.

Although we experimented with Implied Windowing, Use Shift to Add, and Press and Drag in noun/verb mode, they work the same for verb/noun editing. As you can see, each feature lets you fine-tune how you select entities in Release 12. Chapter 2 of the *AutoCAD Reference Manual* describes the new selection modes in detail, and their operation should be fairly obvious from the previous tutorial. All you need to do is decide which settings to use.

Tip

We didn't try turning Implied Windowing off, because turning it off (i.e., setting PICKAUTO to 0) doesn't really work. With PICKAUTO set to 0, implied windowing shuts off for one pick in verb/noun editing mode, but, after that, it mysteriously turns back on. Noun/ verb mode isn't affected by PICKAUTO at all. Fortunately, implied windowing is so useful that most users won't want to turn it off.

Use Shift to Add and Press and Drag are "Mac-like" features. As with noun/ verb editing, they're most likely to appeal to people who have used illustration and other graphics software. Those sorts of programs tend to be used for less complicated drawings in which users will manipulate single objects or small groups of objects. Use Shift to Add makes sense for that style of working, especially when it's combined with noun/verb and grip editing. Conversely, incrementally building a complex selection set makes more sense with the complicated graphics that AutoCAD traditionally has been reserved for, so experienced AutoCAD users probably will want to leave the Use Shift to Add feature turned off.

Implied Windowing, on the other hand, is for everyone. It's simply the old AUto selection set option, but now available automatically whenever you select entities. This "automatic AUto" is one of the biggest time-savers in Release 12, since it saves you the trouble of entering Window, Crossing, or AUto every time you use a selection window.

The only downside to Implied Windowing is that occasionally, when you intend to pick a single entity, you'll just miss it and end up in the middle of specifying a selection window. The easiest way to recover from this misstep is to pick the same spot again in order to finish the selection window without selecting anything. The Press and Drag feature performs this "error recovery" automatically, but because Press and Drag doesn't apply consistently in Release 12 (for instance, you still must define zoom windows with two picks, even when Press and Drag is turned on), you might not want to bother with it.

The Entity Selection Settings dialogue also lets you change the pickbox size and specify when Release 12 should sort entities (we'll discuss entity sorting later in this chapter). Table 7.2 translates the choices in the Entity

Selection Settings dialogue box to the settings of the corresponding system variables. Use the table to help decide the best settings for you. To summarize:

- There's no harm in leaving Noun/Verb Selection on unless it conflicts with the way you use grip editing.

- Leave Use Shift to Add off unless you're more accustomed to working with other software that favors that approach.

- Likewise with Press and Drag.

- Leave Implied Windowing on, especially since turning it off doesn't really work anyway.

All the PICK... system variable settings are stored in your configuration file. Once you change them in one drawing, therefore, the new settings apply globally until you change them again.

 Tip

Don't confuse Pickbox Size in the Entity Selection Settings dialogue box with Aperture Size in the Running Object Snap dialogue that we covered in the the previous chapter. Pickbox Size (i.e., the PICKBOX system variable) controls the size of the little square target you use to pick individual entities. Aperture Size (i.e., the APERTURE system variable) controls the size of the object snap target. AutoCAD's defaults are 3 pixels for PICKBOX and 10 pixels for APERTURE.

Table 7.2 Entity Selection Settings Options vs. Relevant System Variables with Defaults Starred

	System Variable	Unchecked	Checked
Noun/Verb Selection	PICKFIRST	0	1*
Use Shift to Add	PICKADD	1*	0
Press and Drag	PICKDRAG	0*	1
Implied Windowing	PICKAUTO	0	1*
Pickbox Size	PICKBOX	0-32,767 pixels (3 by default)	

New Verb/Noun Selection Options

With all the hype about noun/verb editing, you might think that Autodesk had forgotten about its faithful verb/noun crowd. Not so—there are four new selection set options that you can use at Release 12's Select objects: prompt, just as you use Window, Crossing, Previous, Last, and the other selection set options from Release 11 and before. As we pointed out earlier, these options are available only during regular verb/noun editing.

The new selection options are:

- WPolygon (Windowed Polygon) and CPolygon (Crossing Polygon).

  These options work just like the Window and Crossing options, but the shape doesn't have to be a rectangle; it can be a polygon with any number of sides.

- Fence.

  This option was "borrowed" from Autodesk's arch-rival Intergraph. It's something like a cross between the Crossing option and the PLINE command. You just pick a series of points that defines a temporary polyline, and AutoCAD selects everything cut by the polyline. Unlike Crossing and CPolygon, Fence doesn't select anything "inside" the fence line.

- ALL.

  This option selects all the entities in the drawing. ALL is simple, powerful, and, as the tip below explains, potentially dangerous.

Tip

Be careful with the ALL option. When you enter an editing command and then specify ALL, even entities on layers that are turned off will be affected by the editing operation. That means that ALL lets you edit entities you can't see! Because of this, it's usually wise to turn all layers on before using ALL. Layers that are frozen or locked are not affected by editing operations with ALL.

The new options extend AutoCAD's selection set possibilities in useful ways, especially when you're trying to select entities in a crowded drawing. In order to create a moderately crowded drawing quickly, we're going to insert a proposed furniture layout sent by our interior decorator. We'll cover Blocks in Chapter 10, *Xrefs, Blocks, and Attributes*, but for now, simply follow the instructions.

1. Use WPolygon to erase the chairs you drew.

```
Command: ERASE
Select objects: ?
*Invalid selection*
Expects a point or Window/Last/Crossing/BOX/ALL/
Fence/WPolygon/CPolygon
/Add/Remove/Multiple/Previous/Undo/AUto/SIngle
```

If you enter an invalid selection set option, AutoCAD displays the 15 valid options. Enter 'HELP or '? to get more information about the options.

```
Select objects: WP
```
or
Pick Select Objects and then WPolygon from the side menu, or
Pick WP on the tablet menu.

You can use the side or tablet menu to access most selection set options, but typing probably is the most efficient method.

`First polygon point:` *Pick a point below and to the left of all the chairs.*
`Undo/<Endpoint of line>:` *Continue picking points to define a polygon that encloses all the chairs (see Figure 7.5).*

```
Undo/<Endpoint of line>: <Enter>
12 found
```

CPolygon works the same way, but like the Crossing option, it selects everything inside of or cutting through the polygon.

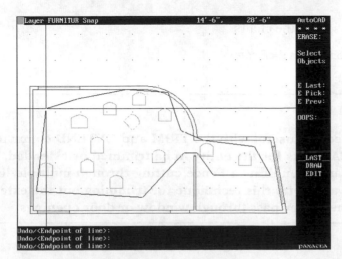

Figure 7.5 Selecting entities with WPolygon.

2. Insert the furniture layout.

```
Command: DDINSERT
```
or

Pick Insert... from the Draw menu.

The Insert dialogue appears.

Pick the File... button.

AutoCAD's standard file dialogue appears.

Locate the RECFURN drawing in your tutorial subdirectory or on the AutoCAD Power Tools disk.

Check the Explode box.

Pick OK.

Pick the lower-left corner of the rec room.

Make sure you use Snap or an object snap to ensure precision.

Accept default values for the remaining prompts.

3. Use Fence to erase some of the patio chairs.

```
Command: ERASE
Select objects: F
First fence point: Pick the first point of a fence line (see Figure 7.6).
Undo/<Endpoint of line>: Pick additional points defining a fence line.
Undo/<Endpoint of line>: <Enter>
3 found
```

AutoCAD selects the chairs.

```
Select objects: <Enter>
```

Tip

Fence is especially useful with the TRIM and EXTEND commands. When AutoCAD asks for the entity to be trimmed or extended, you can enter F and then draw a Fence cutting through multiple lines. You might want to try this technique for trimming out the exterior wall lines where they pass through window or door openings.

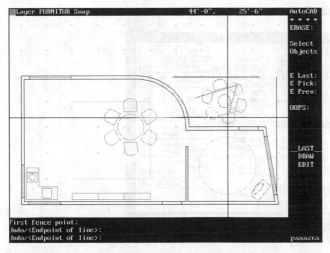

Figure 7.6   Selecting entities with Fence.

Layer Locking

Another new Release 12 feature that will benefit those who work on crowded drawings is layer locking. The concept is simple: Layer locking lets you leave entities visible but immune to editing. The implementation is simple, too; layers now have a lock/unlock status, along with their on/off and freeze/thaw status. AutoCAD editing commands will ignore any entities on locked layers, but you still can object snap to those entities. You can toggle the lock/unlock status for layers using the DDLMODES Modify Layer dialogue box or the LAYER command. We demonstrate both methods in the following sequence.

1. Lock the RUG layer.

We want to move some of the furniture around without affecting the location of the rugs.

`Command: DDLMODES`

Pick the RUG layer, and then pick the Lock button to lock it (see Figure 7.7).

2. Move the inside table and chairs closer to the curved wall.

`Command: MOVE`
`Select objects:` *use implied windowing to draw a crossing window (i.e, to the left) that encloses the rug, table, and chairs in the main room (see Figure 7.8).*

AutoCAD reports 8 entities found, 1 on a locked layer.

Move the table and chairs a couple of feet closer to the curved wall.

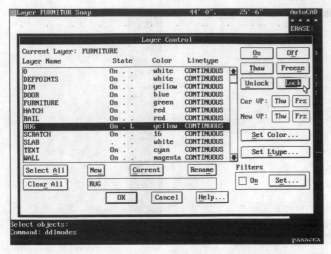

Figure 7.7   Locking the RUG layer.

3. Unlock and turn on all layers.

```
Command: LAYER
?/Make/Set/New/ON/OFF/Color/Ltype/Freeze/Thaw/LOck/
Unlock: U
```

Notice the new LOck and Unlock options for the Layer command.

```
Layer name(s) to Unlock: *
```

While you're at it, turn on all layers.

```
?/Make/Set/New/ON/OFF/Color/Ltype/Freeze/Thaw/LOck/
Unlock: ON
```

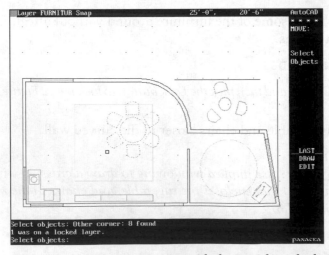

Figure 7.8   Selecting entities with the RUG layer locked.

```
Layer name(s) to turn On: *
?/Make/Set/New/ON/OFF/Color/Ltype/Freeze/Thaw/LOck/
Unlock: <Enter>
```

Selection Set Filters

Although the 15 selection set options in Release 12 give you lots of choices for picking entities, sometimes it's more efficient to select a group of objects using some qualities they share, rather than pointing at them on the screen. Selection set filters are a powerful technique for creating selection sets based on entity properties such as layer name, linetype, text style, or entity type. The Entity Selection Filters dialogue box, which is brought up by the FILTER command, lets you create and apply these selection set filters.

The FILTER command is another of the Release 12 "extra" programs, and it's documented in Chapter 4 of the *AutoCAD Extras Manual*. Despite its dialogue box interface, FILTER can be tricky to figure out at first. A filter is actually a one-line criterion or specification such as "Layer = FOO" or "Text Style Name = FANCY." A single filter works fine in many situations, but sometimes you need to use a more elaborate filter list to find the entities you're after. As an example, we'll explode all the Polylines on the FURNI-TURE layer.

1. Enter the EXPLODE command and then start FILTER.

```
Command: EXPLODE
```
or
Pick Explode... from the Modify menu.

```
Select objects: 'FILTER
```
or
Pick Object Filters... from the Assist menu.

The Entity Selection Filters dialogue box appears (see Figure 7.9).

2. Specify Polyline as the type of entity we want to select.

Pull down the pop-up list beneath the words Select Filter by clicking on the down arrow.

Scroll down and pick Polyline.

The word Polyline will appear, highlighted, next to the down arrow.

Pick the Add to List button.

3. Specify FURNITURE as the layer.

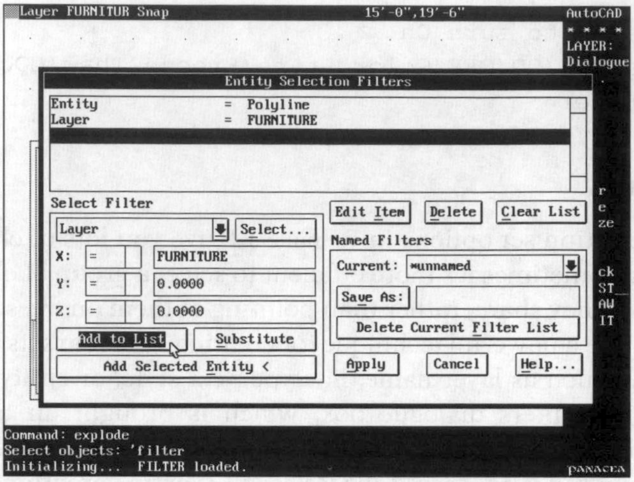

Figure 7.9   A filter list.

Pick Layer from the pop-up list.

Pick the Select... button and choose the FURNITURE layer.

Pick the Add to List button.

4. Apply the filter.

Now that we've specified the filter list (see Figure 7.9), we can apply it to our EXPLODE selection set.

Pick Apply.

```
Applying filter to selection.
Select objects: ALL
54 found
42 were filtered out.
```

AutoCAD selects only the entities that match the filter criteria.

```
Select objects: <Enter>
Exiting filtered selection. 12 found
Select objects:<Enter>
```

AutoCAD explodes all the Polylines.

5. Undo.

Nice trick, but on second thought, we might not want all those little line segments in our drawing. Restore them to Polylines.

```
Command: U
```

FILTER also can be used in a sort of noun/verb mode. To do this, enter FILTER at the Command: prompt, build the filtered selection set, start the editing command, and then type P for Previous.

You can get even more elaborate than our two-line filter list with relational and grouping operators (less than, greater than, OR, XOR, etc.), but simple filters will do the job in many cases. If you find yourself reusing complex filter lists, it's time to start saving and recalling them with the Named Filters section of the Entity Selection Filters dialogue. (See Chapter 4 of the *AutoCAD Extras Manual* for details.)

Tip

You might be tempted to use selection set filters to grab all the entities of a certain color or linetype. Keep in mind, though, that if you let entities inherit their color and linetype from the layers they reside on (as we suggested in the previous chapter), then AutoCAD stores the entity color and linetype names as "BYLAYER." As a result, a filter of "Color = red" won't find anything. You need to filter by layer name instead. If you have more than one layer that uses a certain color or linetype, use the OR operator.

Entity Sorting

In Release 12, selecting entities and snapping to them are noticeably faster in medium- to large-sized drawings because of a change in the way AutoCAD searches for objects. Release 12 uses a more efficient "spatial index" method for finding entities, and this method improves object selection and object snap performance.

There is one downside to spatial indexing, though: It also eliminates predictability when your pick or object snap box includes more than one entity. In previous versions of AutoCAD, you could always be sure of selecting the most recently drawn entity whenever there was any ambiguity, but no longer; Release 12 sometimes will grab the most recent entity, and sometimes not. As a result, you'll need to pick more carefully now whenever two entities overlap or lie close to one another.

If you really need the old Release 11 predictability and are willing to sacrifice some speed, you can turn on entity sorting in the Entity Sort Method dialogue box. Entity Sort Method is a subdialogue of the Entity Selection Settings dialogue described earlier in this section (see Figure 7.10). Simply check the boxes next to Object Selection and/or Object Snap

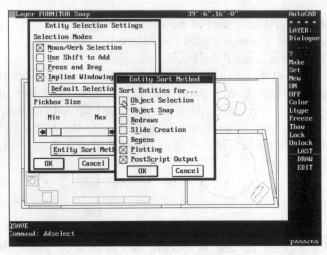

Figure 7.10   The Entity Sort Method dialogue box.

to tell AutoCAD to sort entities before selecting and/or snapping to objects. The Entity Sort Method dialogue controls the new SORTENTS system variable.

Editing with Grips

Most of the new Release 12 features discussed in this chapter are incremental changes to capabilities that existed in AutoCAD Release 11. Even noun/verb editing is a modest modification, in the sense that you're still performing the same old editing operations, but in reverse order. Grips, on the other hand, bring a whole new editing approach to Release 12. Grip editing lets you grab entities, and then stretch, move, rotate, mirror, scale, and copy them by pulling on their grips or "handles."

As with several of the previously mentioned new editing and selection features in Release 12, the idea for grips came from other graphics software packages. Grip editing is more interactive and fluid than traditional AutoCAD command-oriented editing, and thus is well suited to creating illustrations, where ease of manipulation is more important than high precision. But grip editing turns out to be valuable for CAD, too, even when maintaining precision is vital. AutoCAD's implementation of grips lets you use the traditional tools such as Snap and object snaps to edit accurately, and even adds two new techniques that are unique to grip editing.

Throughout this section, we assume that the PICKADD system variable is turned on (i.e., Use Shift to Add is off), as we left it in the section on DDSELECT. If you prefer to keep PICKADD off, some of the rules for when to hold down the <Shift> key will be reversed.

Basic Grip Editing

Grip editing is a "deep" subject in the sense that there are lots of possibilities and subtleties to discover, but don't let that overwhelm you. The basic grip editing methods are simple and obvious, and once you've mastered them, you can explore more complex approaches. In this chapter, we'll build a repertoire of useful techniques that will demonstrate the power and flexibility of grips. After you've worked through the tutorials, experimentation and the first part of Chapter 6 in the *AutoCAD Reference Manual* will answer any remaining questions you might have about grips.

Let's start with a simple example: stretching circles and lines.

1. Make sure grip editing and all layers are turned on. Set Snap to 3".

   ```
   Command: GRIPS
   New value for GRIPS <default>: 1
   ```

   The **GRIPS** system variable controls whether or not you can do grip editing.

   Turn on all layers if you haven't already.

   Set Snap to 3".

2. Stretch the patio table.

   Select the circle located on the patio at the upper right of the drawing.

   AutoCAD highlights the circle and displays its grips.

   Pick on any of the four quadrant grips.

   The grip becomes solid and turns color (red by default) to indicate that it's the "hot" grip you'll be using to manipulate the circle. Note that AutoCAD displays "STRETCH" on the status and command lines (see Figure 7.11).

   Move the cursor about 6" away from the original grip location and pick.

   Your patio table is now about a foot larger in diameter.

   This time, pick on the grip at the center of the circle.

   Now AutoCAD moves the circle rather than changes its radius. Note, however, that the command line still says "STRETCH."

   Pick again to place the circle anywhere else on the patio.

This first example demonstrates the basic sequence for all grip editing:

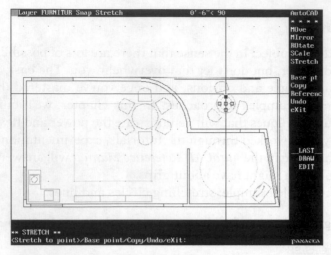

Figure 7.11   Grip editing a circle.

- Make a selection.

  Select one or more entities as if you were going to do noun/verb editing.

- Get a grip.

  Instead of entering an editing command, pick on one of the grips.

- Let go.

  Move the cursor to a new location and then pick.

There are many variations on this theme, but all of them are based on this "select-pick-pick" framework. In the remainder of this section, we'll explore a few of the more useful variations.

Grip Editing Lines and Visible Object Snaps

Circles make good examples for learning the basics of grip editing, but more often you'll be grip editing lines. In addition, you'll be using other grip editing modes besides STRETCH, and you'll want to use the "visible object snap" feature of grips to ensure precision without having to explicitly specify an object snap. The next sequence demonstrates these ideas.

1. Stretch and move the line representing the fence railing at the north edge of the patio.

   Make sure Ortho is on.

   Select the horizontal line near the north edge of the patio.

   Lines have a midpoint and two endpoint grips.

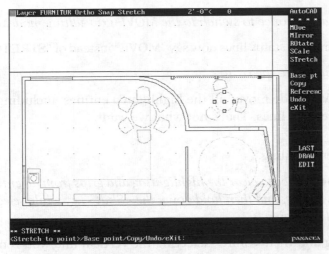

Figure 7.12 Stretching a line with grips.

Pick the right endpoint grip and use it to stretch the line farther to the right. As you stretch the line, toggle Ortho off and on (<F8> or <Ctrl>+O) to see the effects of Ortho on grip editing.

Notice that even though the circle is still highlighted and displaying grips, only the line stretches (Figure 7.12). The STRETCH mode of grip editing affects only the entity with the hot grip.

Pick on the midpoint grip and use it to move the line a few inches to the left.

The midpoint grip of a line, like the center grip of a circle, is used to move the entity. Think of it as enclosing the entire entity in a stretch window.

2. Try moving the fence railing line at the east edge of the patio.

Grips also act like "visible object snaps." Use this feature to connect the two parts of the fence railing.

Select the vertical line at the east edge of the patio in order to display its grips. Experiment with visible object snaps by moving your cursor until it just grazes one of the grip boxes.

Grips act like tiny magnets: They "capture" the cursor as soon as it touches the edge of the grip box.

Pick on the right endpoint grip of the horizontal line again.

This time we want to move, rather than stretch, the line to the right, but we want to do it using the endpoint grip.

Press the spacebar once to switch to the MOVE grip editing mode.

The command and status lines now say "MOVE" instead of "STRETCH".

Move your cursor to the right.

Oops—MOVE mode moves all the highlighted entities, including the circle and vertical lines. That's not what we want.

3. Move the fence railing.

Press <Ctrl>+C twice to clear the highlighting and grips from all entities. Select the two lines, and then hold down the <Shift> key while selecting the vertical line again.

By selecting and then <Shift>-selecting the vertical line, you remove its highlighting but leave its grips.

Pick on the right endpoint grip of the horizontal line again. Press the spacebar to switch to the MOVE grip editing mode.

Now only the horizontal line moves, since it's the only highlighted entity.

Move your cursor to the right until the endpoint of the vertical line captures it, and then pick (see Figure 7.13).

Voilà—you've mastered visible object snaps.

Because grips are used for editing entities and for object snapping, Release 12 distinguishes between three grip "states": warm, hot, and cold (see Figure 7.14). When you first select an entity for grip editing, its grips are "warm;"

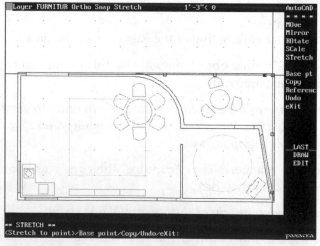

Figure 7.13 Using grips as visible object snaps.

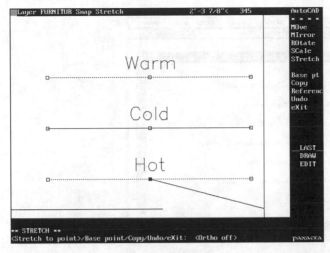

Figure 7.14 Warm, cold, and hot grips.

that is, they appear as open squares and the entity they sit on is highlighted. Warm grips make an entity subject to grip editing and available for object snapping. If you <Shift>+pick an entity with grips, its grips turn "cold;" the entity is no longer highlighted, but the open square grips remain. Cold grips are used only for object snapping, and entities with cold grips aren't affected by grip editing operations (since they aren't highlighted). A "hot" grip is simply a warm grip that you've picked in order to begin a grip editing operation. Hot grips appear as solid squares.

If all these rules seem overwhelming, just spend a few minutes picking, <Shift>+picking, and editing with grips.

Tip

An alternative to <Shift>+picking is <Ctrl>+C. The first <Ctrl>+C deselects all the currently highlighted entities, and the second <Ctrl>+C removes their grips. Unfortunately, you're limited to the keyboard with this technique; pressing the cancel button on your digitizer puck doesn't work for this operation.

Other Grip Modes and Options

So far, we've experimented with two grip editing modes: STRETCH and MOVE. These two are likely to be the modes you use most often, but Release 12 provides three others: ROTATE, SCALE, and MIRROR. You switch among the modes by pressing the spacebar (or <Enter>), as we did in the

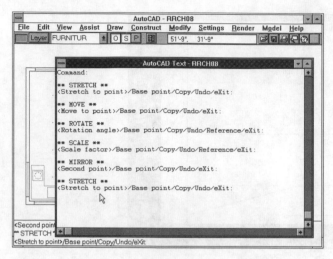

Figure 7.15   The five grip editing modes.

previous tutorial sequence. The modes are arranged in a loop, so that pressing the spacebar from MIRROR mode returns you to STRETCH mode (see Figure 7.15).

Why isn't there a COPY mode? Instead of a separate *mode*, grip editing provides a Copy *option* for each of the other five modes: STRETCH with Copy, MOVE with Copy, etc. This approach is very different from standard AutoCAD editing, where COPY is a distinct command. It's also much more flexible, since it effectively gives you 10 different editing operations for the price of five. Even better, you can make as many copies as you want with Copy mode; it's like the Multiple option of the old COPY command.

There are two ways to activate the Copy option. One method appears in the prompt for each grip mode (see Figure 7.15): Type C before you pick the destination point for a grip. The other method is to hold down the <Shift> key as you pick the destination point. (Don't hold down the <Shift> key as you're picking a grip to make it hot. That procedure is reserved for multiple hot grips, which we'll discuss in a moment.)

As you can see in Figure 7.15, all five grip editing modes have Basepoint and Undo options in addition to Copy. Basepoint lets you specify a point other than the hot grip as the "from" point. Undo works with Copy mode: When you've made one or more copies, Undo gets rid of the last one. Finally, the ROTATE and SCALE grip editing modes have a Reference option. Reference works the same for these modes as it does for the old ROTATE and SCALE commands.

Take a moment to experiment with the five grip editing modes and some of their options, especially Copy. For instance, try creating a rotated and mirrored copy of one of the patio chairs. As you experiment, think about the types of editing you usually do and see which grip editing techniques are best for your work.

Grips and Precision

Grips make for a wonderfully interactive approach to editing, but it's easy to use grips in an imprecise way that results in sloppy drawings that become difficult to edit, dimension, and hatch later on. Thus, it's just as important to think about precision when you're doing grip editing as when you're using AutoCAD's traditional editing commands.

All the usual AutoCAD methods for maintaining precision also work with grip editing. You can use Snap, object snaps (including the cursor menu), and .XYZ point filters to locate precise points. Ortho mode is helpful when you want to stretch or move orthogonally. You can type absolute or relative coordinates when you want to move a grip to a known point or by a known distance.

Grip editing adds two other possibilities. As we just saw, all grips act as visible object snaps, which often spares you the trouble of specifying an osnap explicitly. The other possibility is unique to the Copy option, and it works something like the **ARRAY** command. Remember that holding down the <Shift> key while you pick the destination point for a grip is one way to activate the Copy option. If you *continue* to hold down the <Shift> key while picking additional points, AutoCAD enforces a temporary snap grid whose spacing (or angle) is based on the first destination point you picked.

Like so many of the grip editing rules, the temporary snap grid is easier to use than it is to explain. We'll demonstrate it in an example at the end of this section, but you might want to experiment now with this technique using the MOVE and ROTATE grip editing modes.

Multiple Hot Grips

So far, we've been working with one hot grip at a time. Although you can do a lot with one grip, in some situations you'll want to use two or more hot grips. A common example is when you're stretching a rectangle or double-line arrangement. Fortunately, Release 12 includes this capability and it's tied to—you guessed it—the <Shift> key. When you hold down <Shift> while picking a grip to make it hot, AutoCAD lets you pick additional grips to make them hot as well. Once you're finished picking grips, you release the <Shift> key and then repick any of the hot grips to start the grip editing operation. Let's use multiple hot grips to shorten the interior wall by 6".

1. Select all three lines that make up the wall.

   Press <Ctrl>+C twice to make sure all grips are cleared.

   Zoom in fairly close on the north end of the interior wall.

   Use an implied window to select the two vertical lines and horizontal cap.

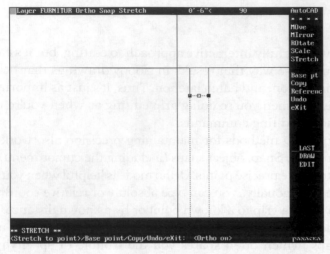

Figure 7.16   Stretching with multiple hot grips.

2. Make the two endpoint grips on the wall hot.

Hold down the <Shift> key while picking one grip. Continue to hold down <Shift> as you pick the other grip.

Both grips should now be hot.

3. Grab one of the hot grips.

Release the <Shift> key and then repick either of the hot grips (see Figure 7.16).

4. Type in a 6" displacement.

```
**STRETCH**
<Stretch to point>/Base point/Copy/Undo/eXit: @0,-6
```

The end of the wall stretches 6" to the south.

By now, you're probably wondering how you'll remember all these different uses for <Shift>. We'll summarize them at the end of this chapter, but just remember that, with grips, it's all in the timing:

- <Shift> while picking a grip to allow multiple hot grips.

- <Shift> while picking a grip destination point to activate the Copy option.

- <Shift> after picking the first grip destination point to enforce a temporary snap grid.

Creating New Entities with Grips

We've emphasized using grips to change existing geometry, but with the Copy option, grips also are good for creating new entities. In our final grips tutorial, we'll demonstrate this by creating a sectional sofa. This simple example also will allow us to exercise some of the other grips features we've discussed in this section. As with other examples that describe how to use AutoCAD features that include direct manipulation, it takes many steps to describe actions that will seem simple once you get used to them. Refer to Figure 7.20 as you work through this tutorial.

1. Draw a square 2' on a side in the upper-left corner of the main room.

   Make sure the FURNITURE layer is current, and zoom to the upper-left quadrant of the rec room.

   ```
   Command: RECTANG
   or
   ```
   Pick Rectangle from the Draw menu.
   ```
   First corner: Pick a point inside and near the upper-left corner of
   the room.
   Other corner: : @2',-2'
   ```

   A square will appear (see Figure 7.17).

2. Use grips to make three equally spaced copies of the square.

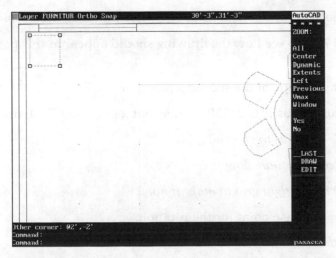

Figure 7.17 The RECROOM drawing with a square in the corner with grips.

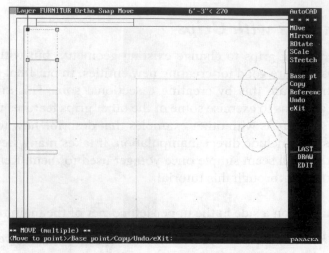

Figure 7.18   Three equally spaced copies of the original square.

Pick anywhere on the square to make grips appear (see Figure 7.17).

Pick on the upper-left grip to make it hot.

Press the spacebar to switch to MOVE mode.

Hold down the <Shift> key to activate the Copy option.

Move your cursor down until it's captured by the grip at the lower-left corner of the square. Pick while still holding down the <Shift> key.

The first copy appears.

Continue holding <Shift> and make two more equally spaced copies.

See Figure 7.18 to see how the drawing should appear at this point.

3. Make a rotated copy of the second square.

We could just as easily use **COPY** mode, but let's try **ROTATE** instead.

Press <Ctrl>+C twice to clear all grips.

Select the second square down.

Pick on the upper-right grip to make it hot.

This will be the base point for the rotation.

Press spacebar twice to switch to ROTATE mode.

Hold down the <Shift> key to activate the Copy option.

With Ortho on, point anywhere to the left of the hot grip to specify a

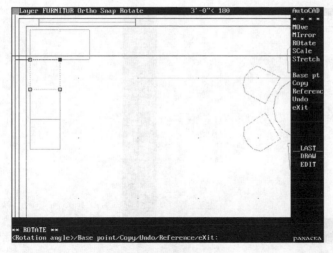

Figure 7.19 Rotating with grips.

rotation angle of 180 degrees. Pick while holding down <Shift> (see Figure 7.19).

4. Stretch the new section.

Press <Ctrl>+C twice to clear all grips.

Select the new square.

We need to make two endpoint grips hot.

Hold down the <Shift> key while picking the upper-right grip. Continue to hold down <Shift> as you pick the lower-right grip.

Both grips should now be hot.

Release the <Shift> key and then repick either of the hot grips.

With Ortho on, stretch the square about two feet to the right.

Figure 7.20 shows the completed sofa.

Configuring Grips

There are five new system variables that allow you to control whether or not grips appear and what they look like. These are Enable Grips (the default), Enable Grips within Blocks, Grip Colors/Unselected, Grip Colors/Selected, and Grip Size, All the variables are available in the Grips dialogue box.

You can bring up the Grips dialogue box in one of two ways: by entering the command DDGRIPS or by choosing Grips… from the Settings menu (see Figure 7.21).

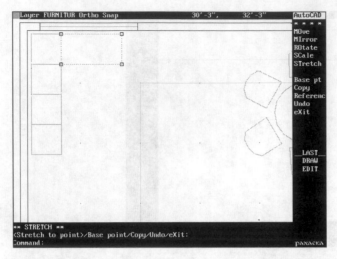

Figure 7.20   The sectional sofa created with grips.

The default settings shown in Figure 7.21 work fine for most purposes. The only setting that you might want to toggle occasionally is Enable Grips Within Blocks. When this setting is turned off, AutoCAD displays a single grip on each Block (at the Block's insertion point). When the setting is turned on, AutoCAD displays grips on all the internal geometry in a Block. In general, you should leave the setting off, since displaying a lot of grips on complex Blocks will slow down AutoCAD. Occasionally, though, it's useful to turn on Enable Grips Within Blocks so that grips on the Block geometry can be used as visible object snaps or to move Block Attributes. Table 7.3 summarizes the Grips dialogue box settings and shows their system variable equivalents.

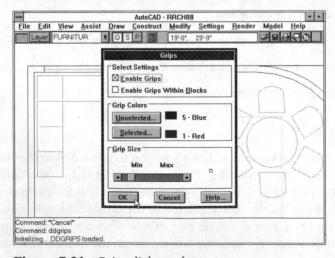

Figure 7.21   Grips dialogue box.

Table 7.3   Grips Dialogue Box Options vs. Relevant System Variables with Defaults Starred

	System Variable	Unchecked	Checked
Enable Grips	GRIPS	0	1*
Enable Grips Within Blocks	GRIPBLOCK	0*	1
Grip Colors Unselected	GRIPCOLOR	Color 1-255 (5 by default)	
Grip Colors Selected	GRIPHOT	Color 1-255 (1 by default)	
Grip Size	GRIPSIZE	0-255 pixels (3 by default)	

Tip

As long as either the GRIPS or PICKFIRST (i.e., Noun/Verb Selection) system variable is turned on, Release 12 displays a small pickbox on the crosshairs. This pickbox is a reminder that you can select objects for grip or noun/verb editing without entering a command first.

The Shifty Shift Key

Now that we've covered grip editing and PICKADD (i.e., Use Shift to Add), this is a good time to review the many uses for the <Shift> key in Release 12. The possibilities are summarized below:

Selecting with PICKADD =1

- Selecting for verb/noun editing: Remove entities from selection set

- Selecting for noun/verb or grip editing:
  First <Shift>+pick: Remove entities from selection set
  Second <Shift>+pick: Remove grips from entities

Selecting with PICKADD = 0

- Selecting for verb/noun, noun/verb, or grip editing: Toggle entities into/out of selection set

Grip editing (PICKADD = 1 or 0)

- While picking a grip to make it hot: Multiple hot grips
- While picking first destination point: Activate Copy option
- After picking first destination point: Enforce temporary snap grid

Selecting, Editing, and Workgroups

Most of the workgroup issues that are raised by the features covered in this chapter simply are amplifications of the issues faced by an individual. Which features are worth learning and using? How much practice will it take to make them part of each user's repertoire? How do you schedule each user's learning and practice activities so they don't create a productivity hit in the middle of a project?

As described in the previous chapter, the challenge is to get workgroup members to set aside old and comfortable habits long enough to acquaint themselves with new features. Implied windowing ("running AUto"), grips, and layer locking will be the three "biggies" for most users, so make sure your group is aware of them. If these features are being used in a haphazard way across the workgroup, you'll want to organize training or at least some brief demo sessions to get everyone up to speed. Grips, in particular, deserve some training or coaching time, since many experienced AutoCAD users will be unfamiliar with editing by direct manipulation.

The only tools management issue raised in this chapter is with selection filters. Some workgroups or projects will benefit from a standard set of predefined filters that everyone can use. Experiment with selection filters on some of your more complex drawings to see whether filters benefit your work. If so, develop and test a set of common filters, and then distribute the FILTER.NFL file to everyone in the workgroup. At the very least, show others how to filter a selection based on layer or block name, since these simple filters can be useful to anyone.

Some of the new selection features (for instance, noun/verb editing) may be more trouble to integrate into your workgroup's regimen than they're worth. Be realistic about what people can absorb, and focus on those new features that genuinely increase the efficiency of selecting and editing. By managing the training and learning process in this way, you'll bring to your group the advantages of the new features with as small a productivity loss as possible.

8

Modifying Properties and Hatching

Many of the enhancements to AutoCAD in Release 12 are based on its improved user interface. In some cases, the interface simply makes it easier to use previously existing functionality; in other cases, new features are integrated with easier access to existing features in a way that makes a big difference in power, as well as ease of use. In this chapter, we describe changes to modifying entity properties and to hatching, two sets of features that exemplify these two different kinds of usefulness.

This chapter brings together themes that have been introduced in previous chapters. All of the features described in this chapter use the new dialogue box interface. The importance of drawing setup is underscored once again by how easy the new dialogue boxes make it to modify the layer, linetype, text style, or other properties of an entity—if the desired property is already loaded into your drawing. Some of the new object selection features covered in the previous chapter are used again in this one.

About This Chapter

In previous releases of AutoCAD, changing entity properties required choosing between two seemingly similar commands (CHANGE and CHPROP), and either command demanded a lot of typing. The process was error-prone and not especially friendly. AutoCAD now provides two dialogue boxes, DDMODIFY and DDCHPROP, that make changing properties for individual or groups of entities much easier.

159

Hatching was a serious problem in earlier releases. Making a fully enclosed hatching border often was tedious, and getting the hatch parameters just right was a difficult job. Release 12's BHATCH dialogue box removes most of the hassle and almost makes hatching a pleasure. As a bonus, the "boundary finding" portion of BHATCH is available as a separate BPOLY command that can be used for, among other purposes, calculating areas and perimeters of complex areas or creating boundaries for PostScript fills.

The entity property and hatching improvements in Release 12 make AutoCAD much easier for new users to learn. Windows and illustration program users also may start to see something different. While in other chapters, AutoCAD might seem frustratingly different from other graphics software, the degree of control given by the features in this chapter is unique to AutoCAD and a few other highly specialized programs. You may find yourself wishing for some of the capabilities described here when using other programs.

Experienced users also will find the hatching and property modification enhancements very worthwhile. While the experienced user is more likely to choose the command line for making specific, detailed changes, he or she is still well served by the new dialogue boxes; they're another tool in the arsenal (and, especially in the case of hatching, a very valuable one), rather than a big change to accustomed ways of working. This chapter shows you the different options offered by the new functionality and demonstrates techniques that will help you get the most out of it.

Features Demonstrated in This Chapter

Release 12 introduces new ways of changing entity properties and powerful new hatching features that are described here. The features demonstrated in this chapter include the following:

- The DDCHPROP Change Properties dialogue box gives you a point-and-click interface for changing the properties of a single entity or a selection set.

- When you need to make more detailed modifications to a single entity, the DDMODIFY Modify Entities dialogue box affords even greater control than DDCHPROP. It handles the same properties as Change Properties, plus others which vary depending on the kind of entity you're modifying.

- If you do much hatching, Release 12 will be worthwhile for its hatching features alone. In this chapter, we demonstrate the key features of the new BHATCH Boundary Hatch dialogue box.

- The BHATCH function that automatically creates hatching boundaries has been broken out into a stand-alone BPOLY Polyline Creation dialogue. This feature makes it easy to create a polyline that traces a boundary which includes parts of several entities.

About the Example

In this chapter, we modify the RECROOM drawing assembled in the previous chapters. We modify properties of some of the objects and add hatching to the walls and patio slab. If you don't have an up-to-date version of RECROOM as of the previous chapter, you can use the RRCH08.DWG file on the *AutoCAD Power Tools* disk as a starting point.

Modifying Entity Properties

The CHANGE command has long been one of AutoCAD's most powerful, but most perplexing, features. Because it allows you to change almost any characteristic of any entity, CHANGE behaves differently depending on what entity or entities you select. Also, the characteristics you most often would want to change are hidden in a Properties subcommand. In Version 2.5 (a.k.a. Release 7), Autodesk segregated the CHANGE Properties features in a separate CHPROP command. While CHPROP made the process of changing entity properties more straightforward, it still required that you remember and type the names of layers, linetypes, and colors.

 ### *Tip*

Release 12 adds back the CHANGE Properties Elev subcommand that was removed in Release 11.

Release 12 adds two new commands—DDCHPROP and DDMODIFY—that provide the functionality of CHPROP and CHANGE, but in easy to use dialogue boxes (see Figure 8.1). The new dialogues are similar to each other and to the DDEMODES Entity Creation Modes dialogue box described in Chapter 6. The difference is that, while the Entity Creation Modes dialogue box sets the current properties that apply to entities as you draw them, the dialogues described here modify existing entities.

The ease-of-use factor is the same for all these dialogue boxes: If you have the right properties—layers, linetypes, text styles—already created and loaded

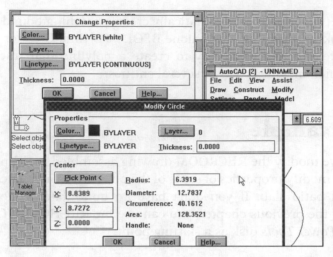

Figure 8.1   The Change Properties and Modify Entities dialogues.

into your drawing, using them is easy. But if you have to cancel the current dialogue box operation in order to create or load properties, your work will grind to a halt. So take the time, before you start a new drawing, to do a thorough job of setup, and these dialogue boxes will be truly easy to use.

DDCHPROP is a dialogue box version of the old CHPROP command (which is a subset of the CHANGE command). Like CHPROP, DDCHPROP lets you change the properties that are common to all types of entities: color, layer, linetype, and thickness.

DDMODIFY incorporates the functionality of the LIST command in a dialogue box. Like LIST, it works only on one entity at a time; but unlike LIST, it allows you to modify most of the characteristics it displays directly in an interactive dialogue box. The things you can modify include all the ones controlled by Change Properties plus others, right down to the points, angles, and other characteristics that define the entity. The dialogue box's appearance and contents differ depending on the kind of entity you've selected.

Change Properties and Modify Entities share some capabilities, but each of them is best suited to a different task. Use the Change Properties dialogue when you want to make general changes to one or more entities. Use the Modify Entities dialogue when you want to list or modify only a single entity and need to be able to see or change all of the entity's characteristics.

Both DDCHPROP and DDMODIFY are implemented as separate AutoLISP programs with dialogue interfaces written in Dialogue Control Language (DCL), but DDCHPROP is documented in Chapter 6 of the *AutoCAD Reference Manual*, while DDMODIFY appears in Chapter 6 of the *AutoCAD Extras Manual*.

In the next two sections, we'll describe both these dialogue boxes in detail and show all the variants of the Modify Entities dialogue.

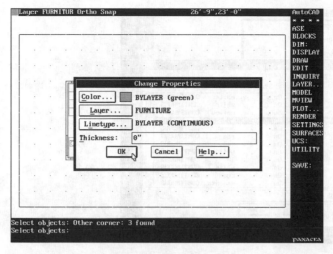

Figure 8.2 The Change Properties dialogue box.

The Change Properties Dialogue

There's not much to explain about the Change Properties dialogue box, other than that it saves you a lot of typing—and mistyping—over the CHPROP command. Figure 8.2 shows the Change Properties dialogue, which resembles Entity Creation Modes.

Let's take a quick look at the options you can access from the Change Properties dialogue box:

Color. Brings up the Select Color dialogue, including all the usual color choices, BYLAYER, and BYBLOCK. As discussed in Chapter 6, most users will want to stick with BYLAYER and avoid assigning explicit colors to cntitics.

Tip

Release 12 lets you click and drag a dialogue box title bar in order to move the dialogue box around on the screen. Change Properties is one of the few dialogue boxes with which you might actually want to take advantage of this feature. Because Change Properties is fairly compact, you can slide it over to the side when you want to see the underlying entities as you modify them.

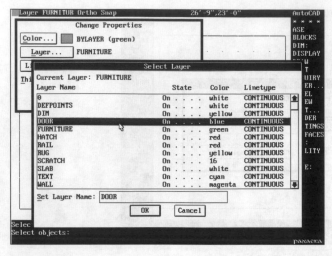

Figure 8.3   Change Properties dialogue with Select Layer subdialogue.

Layer. Brings up the Select Layer dialogue (see Figure 8.3). Select Layer is a subset of the full Layer Control dialogue box, and it lets you select from only the currently defined layers. If you decide you need to create a new layer or change the properties of an existing one, you'll need to use DDLMODES instead. But Select Layer does show you a list of currently defined layers and their properties, and it lets you assign entities to any layer, including one that's frozen or locked.

Linetype. Brings up the Select Linetype dialogue (see Figure 8.4). As with Select Layer, you're limited to already-defined properties. Only the currently

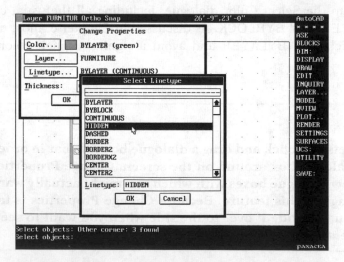

Figure 8.4   Change Properties dialogue with Select Linetype subdialogue.

selected linetype displays graphically, above the list of names, so you have to click on each name to see what the linetype looks like.

As with color, you should be careful about assigning explicit linetypes to entities, since you'll be giving up the ability to use layers to control linetypes for those entities. Stick with linetype BYLAYER unless you have a good reason to do otherwise.

Thickness. Allows you to type in a new 3D-extrusion thickness, which we'll discuss in Chapter 12.

Change Properties Tutorial

In this brief tutorial, we'll use DDCHPROP to move the interior wall lines to the WALLFUT layer, as shown in Figure 8.5.

1. Load RECROOM.DWG.

Use your drawing from the previous chapter, or copy RRCH08.DWG from the *AutoCAD Power Tools* disk.

2. Bring up the Change Properties dialogue box with the three Lines making up the interior wall.

```
Command: DDCHPROP
```
or
Pick Change from the Modify menu, then Properties from the submenu.
```
Select objects: Select the three interior wall Lines.
```

Use a crossing implied window (i.e., pick to the right of the wall, then move the cursor to the left in order to specify a crossing box that includes all three Lines).

Press <Enter> to complete the selection of objects.

The Change Properties dialogue will appear.

3. Change their layer to WALLFUT.

Pick the Layer... button.

The Select Layer dialogue box will appear (see Figure 8.5).

Pick the WALLFUT layer.

Pick OK (or double-click on WALLFUT) to exit the Select Layer subdialogue.

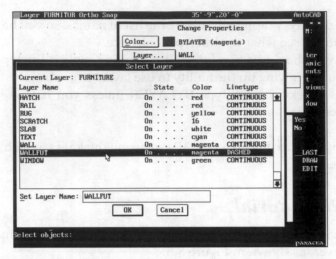

Figure 8.5   Using the Change Properties dialogue to change wall layers.

You'll be returned to the Change Properties dialogue.

Pick OK to exit the Change Properties dialogue.

The Modify Entities Dialogue

DDMODIFY is like a combination of the CHANGE and LIST commands, bundled into a family of Modify Entities dialogue boxes. The Modify Entities dialogues allow you to change the same things as the Change Properties dialogue, but for only one entity at a time. Why give up the flexibility of handling multiple entities? Because like the CHANGE command, DDMODIFY allows you to alter other characteristics besides color, layer, linetype, and thickness, and most of the additional characteristics are specific to individual entities.

DDMODIFY also displays entity statistics, such as the length of a line segment, in addition to allowing you to make changes. Because of the different statistics and characteristics for each entity type, the name and capabilities of the dialogue box vary with the entity you've selected. For instance, if you pick a Line to modify, the dialogue box is called Modify Line; if you pick a Block, it's called Modify Block Insertion.

In this section, we'll describe the characteristics common to all Modify Entities dialogues and experiment with one version, Modify Circle. Then, we'll describe the capabilities offered by each version of the dialogue box and suggest ways to apply them to RECROOM or other drawings.

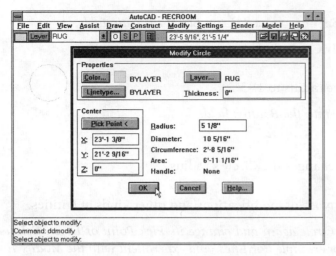

Figure 8.6 The Modify Circle dialogue box.

A Quick Tour

Figure 8.6 shows the Modify Circle dialogue box, the version of Modify Entities that appears when you enter DDMODIFY and select a Circle.

You should recognize the Properties section of the dialogue box, since it contains exactly the same fields as the Change Properties dialogue. For a more detailed description of this group of options, see the description of Change Properties on page 159. The Properties section is the same in all Modify Entities dialogues.

The lower portion of all Modify Entities dialogues contains fields showing the points, other defining characteristics, and statistics for the type of entity you selected. In the case of Modify Circle, the center of the Circle is the only defining point. To the right of the point coordinates is the one other defining characteristic of a circle—its radius—and some geometric statistics. Most Modify Entities dialogues will contain more than one defining point and, of course, the statistics will change with the type of entity, but the basic layout is always the same.

Modify Entities Tutorial

Now that we've seen the basic layout of a Modify Entities dialogue, we'll use DDMODIFY to change the radius of the patio table, as shown in Figure 8.6.

1. Bring up the Modify Circle dialogue box by selecting the patio table.

```
Command: DDMODIFY
```
or
Pick Entity... from the Modify menu.

`Select object to modify:` *Select the patio table.*

The Modify Circle dialogue appears.

2. Change the radius to 1'–3".

Enter 1'-3" into the Radius: field.

Pick OK.

AutoCAD changes the Circle's radius.

3. Try other types of modifications and other kinds of entities.

Select the Circle again and change its Pick Point or Layer. Select other entities, for example Polylines, and experiment with the Modify Entities dialogues for them.

Versions of the Modify Entities Dialogue

In this section, we'll briefly list the capabilities of each version of the Modify Entities dialogue box—Modify Arc, Modify Circle, and so on—and show a picture of each one. Together, this information will show you what DDMODIFY can do and when you might want to use it.

We've arranged the different versions of the Modify Entity dialogue boxes into "families" of similar entity types. Each family has similar characteristics and, thus, similar fields in the dialogue boxes. For more information on each version of the Modify Entity dialogue boxes, see the *AutoCAD Extras Manual.*

COMMON AREAS IN MODIFY ENTITIES DIALOGUE BOXES

Properties. The Properties area appears at the top of each Modify Entities dialogue box. The fields in it are the same as in the Change Properties dialogue box and are described in the section on Change Properties earlier in this chapter.

Handle. The handle of the entity selected is displayed in each of the Modify Entities dialogue boxes. The handle is the identifier used by AutoCAD to track the entity and is accessible through AutoLISP or ADS. Some third-party applications use handles for purposes such as linking entities to external databases.

Pick Point <. This is a button that appears at least once in most of the Modify Entities dialogue boxes, above the X, Y, and Z coordinates of each point you're allowed to change. When you pick a Pick Point < button, the dialogue box disappears temporarily and you're prompted to pick a point in the drawing. The dialogue box then reappears with the X, Y, and Z coordinates filled in with the coordinates of the point you chose.

Changing points from a Modify Entities dialogue usually isn't the most efficient way to edit an entity, but it occasionally comes in handy, especially for 3D drawing.

Geometric Entities

This section describes the Modify Entity dialogues that apply to basic geometric entities: Arcs, Circles, Lines, Points, Polylines, Solids, and Traces.

MODIFY ARC

The Modify Arc dialogue box (see Figure 8.7) displays the following:

- The Properties area and Handle field, described above.

- The Center area, to pick or enter the X, Y, and Z coordinates of the Arc's center.

- The Radius, Start Angle, and End Angle fields.

- Statistics: Total Angle and Arc Length.

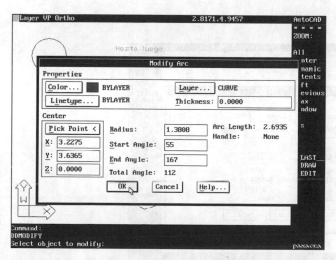

Figure 8.7 The Modify Arc dialogue box.

Tip

The Modify Arc dialogue is useful when you want to fine-tune the radius, start angle, and end angle of an existing arc.

MODIFY CIRCLE

The Modify Circle dialogue box (see Figure 8.8) displays the following:

- The Properties area and Handle field, described above.

- The Center area, to pick or enter the X, Y, and Z coordinates of the Circle's center.

- The Radius field.

- Statistics: Diameter, Circumference, and Area.

MODIFY LINE

The Modify Line dialogue box (see Figure 8.9) displays the following:

- The Properties area and Handle field, described above.

- The From Point and To Point areas, to pick or enter the X, Y, and Z coordinates of the Line's starting and ending points.

- Statistics: Delta XYZ, Length, and Angle for the Line.

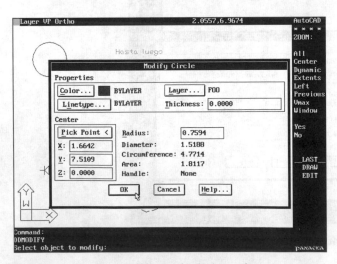

Figure 8.8   The Modify Circle dialogue box.

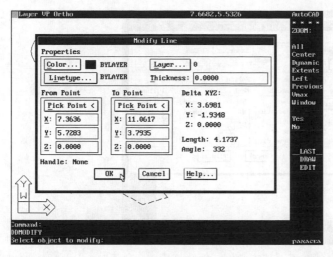

Figure 8.9　The Modify Line dialogue box.

MODIFY POINT

The Modify Point dialogue box (see Figure 8.10) displays the following:

- The Properties area and Handle field, described above.

- The Location area, to pick or enter the X, Y, and Z coordinates of the Point.

MODIFY POLYLINE

The Modify Polyline dialogue box (see Figure 8.11) displays the following:

- The Properties area and Handle field, described above.

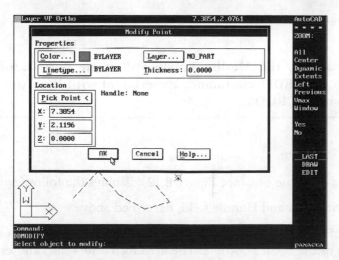

Figure 8.10　The Modify Point dialogue box.

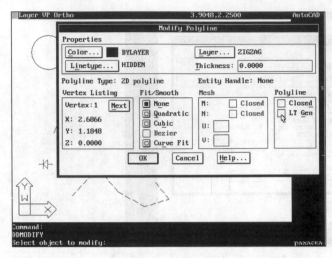

Figure 8.11   The Modify Polyline dialogue box.

- The Fit/Smooth area, in which you can specify the type of curve fitting: None, Quadratic, Cubic, Bezier, or ordinary Curve Fit.

- The Mesh area, grayed out if the entity is not a polygon mesh, in which you can specify mesh properties: M , N closed, U, V.

- The Polyline area, grayed out if the entity is not an ordinary 2D Polyline, with checkboxes to specify a Closed polygon and the LT Gen, or linetype generation style (checked=uniform, unchecked=vertex to vertex).

- Statistics: Polyline Type; Vertex Listing area that displays (but doesn't let you modify) vertices one by one as you click on Next.

 Tip

In many situations, the Modify Polyline dialogue is a friendlier alternative to the PEDIT command. Experiment with it on some of the Polylines in RECROOM.

MODIFY SOLID

The Modify Solid dialogue box (see Figure 8.12) displays the following:

- The Properties area and Handle field, described above.

- Areas for Point 1, 2, 3, and 4, allowing you to pick or enter the X and Y coordinates of the Solid's corners. The area for Point 4 also allows you to pick or enter the Z coordinate for the Solid.

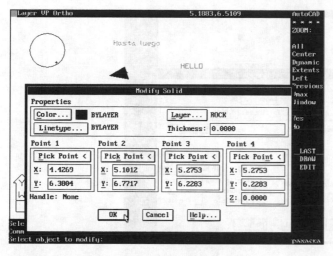

Figure 8.12   The Modify Solid dialogue box.

MODIFY TRACE

The Modify Trace dialogue box (see Figure 8.13) displays the following:

- The Properties area and Handle field, described above.

- Areas for Point 1, 2, 3, and 4, allowing you to pick or enter the X and Y coordinates of the Trace's corners. The area for Point 4 also allows you to pick or enter the Z coordinate for the Trace segment.

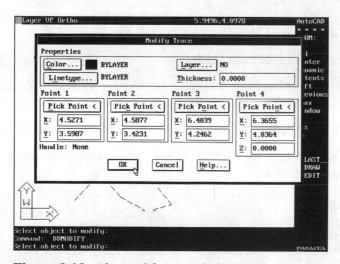

Figure 8.13   The Modify Trace dialogue box.

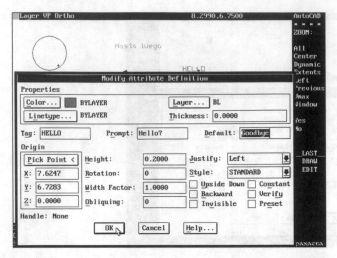

Figure 8.14 The Modify Attribute Definition dialogue box.

Textual Entities

This section describes the Modify Entity dialogues that apply to textual entities: Attribute Definitions, Dimensions, and Text.

MODIFY ATTRIBUTE DEFINITION

The Modify Attribute Definition dialogue box (see Figure 8.14) displays the following:

- The Properties area and Handle field, described above.

- The Tag, Prompt, and Default fields.

- The Origin area, to allow you to pick or enter the X, Y, and Z coordinates of the Attribute Definition's location.

- The Height, Rotation, Width Factor, Obliquing, Justify, and Style fields.

- Statistics: Check boxes for Upside Down, Backward, Invisible, Constant, Verify, and Preset.

MODIFY DIMENSION

The Modify Dimension dialogue box (see Figure 8.15) displays the following:

- The Properties area and Handle field, described above.

- Statistics: Dimension Type, Dimension Text, and Dimension Style.

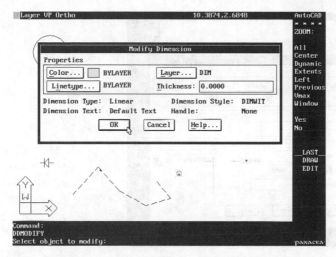

Figure 8.15   The Modify Dimension dialogue box.

MODIFY TEXT

The Modify Text dialogue box (see Figure 8.16) displays the following:

- The Properties area and Handle field, described above.

- The Text field.

- The Origin area, to allow you to pick or enter the X, Y, and Z coordinates of the Text's location.

- The Height, Rotation, Width Factor, Obliquing, Justify, and Style fields.

- Statistics: Check boxes for Upside Down and Backward.

 Tip

Because there are so many Attribute Definition characteristics you can change, the Modify Attribute Definition dialogue is one of the most useful Modify Entities dialogue boxes. Besides using it to fine-tune Attribute Definitions, you can create new Attribute Definitions from similar existing ones quickly. Make a copy of an existing Attribute Definition, enter DDMODIFY and select the copy, and then change the attribute tag, prompt, and any other characteristic that should be different from the original.

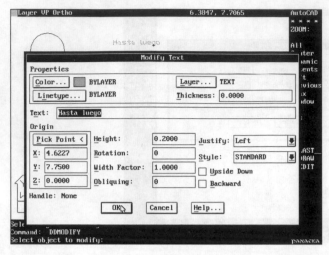

Figure 8.16   The Modify Text dialogue box.

Grouped Entities

This section describes the Modify Entity dialogues that apply to grouped entities: Blocks, External References (Xrefs), and Shapes.

MODIFY BLOCK INSERTION

The Modify Block Insertion dialogue box (see Figure 8.17) displays the following:

- The Properties area and Handle field, described above.

- Statistics: the Block Name.

- The At area, to allow you to pick or enter the X, Y, and Z coordinates of the Block's insertion point.

- The X-scale, Y-scale, Z-scale, Rotation, Columns, Rows, Col Spacing, and Row Spacing fields.

Tip

Like Modify Attribute Definition, the Modify Text dialogue box is useful because it gathers the many characteristics you can change in one place. It's especially handy for changing text justification and for altering the width factor in order to squeeze a piece of Text into a smaller space.

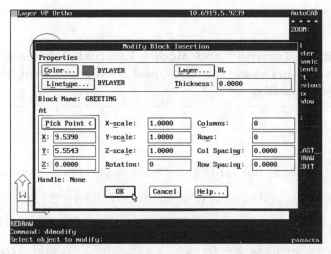

Figure 8.17 The Modify Block Insertion dialogue box.

MODIFY EXTERNAL REFERENCE

The Modify External Reference dialogue box (Figure 8.18) displays the following:

- The Propertics area and Handle field, described above.

- Statistics: the Xref Name and Path.

- The At area, to allow you to pick or enter the X, Y, and Z coordinates of the Xref's insertion point.

- The X-scale, Y-scale, Z-scale, Rotation, Columns, Rows, Col Spacing, and Row Spacing fields.

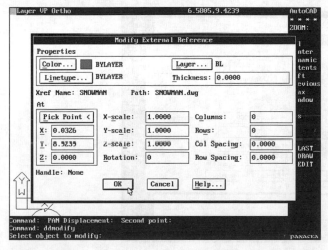

Figure 8.18 The Modify External Reference dialogue box.

Tip

The Modify Block Insertion and Modify External Reference dialogues make it easy to change the X-, Y-, and Z-scale factors of Blocks and Xrefs independently.

MODIFY SHAPE

The Modify Shape dialogue box (see Figure 8.19) displays the following:

- The Properties area and Handle field, described above.

- Statistics: the Shape name.

- The Origin area, to allow you to pick or enter the X, Y, and Z coordinates of the Shape's location.

- The Size, Rotation, Width Factor, and Obliquing fields.

3D & Paper Space Entities

This section describes the Modify Entity dialogues that apply to 3D-only and paper space entities: 3D Faces and Viewports.

MODIFY 3D FACE

The Modify 3D Face dialogue box (see Figure 8.20) displays the following:

- The Properties area and Handle field, described above.

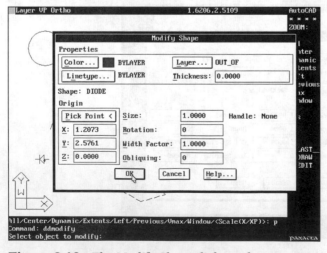

Figure 8.19 The Modify Shape dialogue box.

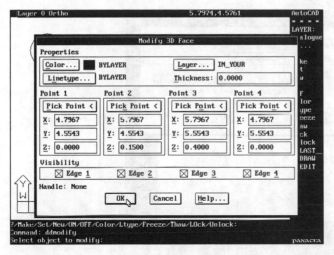

Figure 8.20   The Modify 3D Face dialogue box.

- Areas for Point 1, 2, 3, and 4, allowing you to pick or enter the X, Y, and Z coordinates of the face's corners.

- Statistics: Visibility check boxes for Edges 1, 2, 3, and 4.

Tip

The Modify 3D Face dialogue is extremely useful for anyone who works with 3D Faces. It gives you an interactive way to set the visibility of each edge and to move Face vertices in 3D space.

MODIFY VIEWPORT

The Modify Viewport dialogue box (see Figure 8.21) displays the following:

- The Properties area and Handle field, described above.

- Statistics: the View Center area displays the X, Y, and Z coordinates of the center of the view; VPort ID, Width, Height, and Status.

Summary

DDMODIFY isn't perfect. It allows you to change some things (a string of text) but not other similar ones (dimension text). And there are some out-and-out glitches: For instance, some of the point coordinate and distance fields are too short for some numbers, so you'll occasionally see truncated values. But these limitations and problems are minor compared with the flexibility and ease of

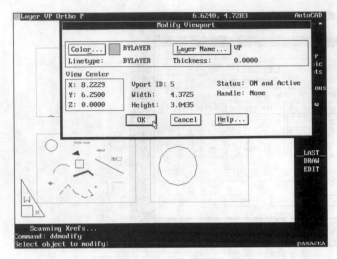

Figure 8.21   The Modify Viewport dialogue box.

use you get with DDMODIFY. Try using it instead of the LIST command for inspecting entities, and get in the habit of using it for fine-tuning the characteristics of Text, Attribute Definition, and Polyline entities.

Hatching and Boundary Polylines

For most users, the Boundary Hatch dialogue box (see Figure 8.22) will be one of the top time—and aggravation—savers in Release 12. BHATCH makes AutoCAD's hatching functionality more interactive and powerful and,

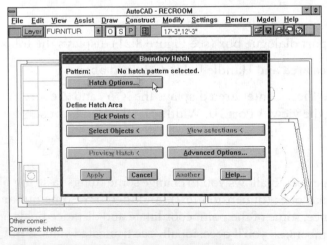

Figure 8.22   The Boundary Hatch dialogue box.

thus, much easier for beginners and experts to use. All of the improvements are wrapped up in a well-designed dialogue box interface that actually makes it fun to experiment with hatches.

The BPOLY command for creating boundary polylines is an interesting feature borrowed from BHATCH. BPOLY is covered at the end of this section.

When to Hatch

Before you get too carried away with the new hatching features, stop to think about when you should add hatching to your drawings. In most cases, it's best to defer hatching until late in the drafting process if you can.

There are two reasons for hatching late in the game—one practical, the other psychological. The practical reason is that if you hatch early, all too often you'll spend a lot of time rehatching later. Although hatches are easier to apply in Release 12, they aren't any more "intelligent" about their borders once you've created them. Hatches still aren't attached to any entity or group of entities, so any change to the borders of the area they fill will require rehatching. Thus, ideally, you want to save hatching until after you've made modifications to the boundary geometry. Of course, you can't always foresee changes, and sometimes project requirements will force you to hatch preliminary geometry.

The other reason for delaying hatching is psychological. As with desktop publishing, it's easy in CAD to spend hours fiddling with the "look" of a document or drawing, while losing sight of the overall purpose and schedule. By making hatching easier to experiment with, Release 12 lets you try different patterns and approaches easily, but this ease of use actually can be detrimental if you get too carried away with it. Keep in mind that hatching is supposed to clarify certain parts of a drawing; it isn't an end in itself. To sum up, no one is going to be happy with a late project, even if it's perfectly hatched.

The "right" time to hatch can be different for each discipline, office, project, and perhaps even drawing. In this book, we're covering hatching just before dimensions and text, but you even may want to save hatching until after you've dimensioned and annotated your drawings. In any case, use "hatch late rather than early" as your rule of thumb.

A Quick Tour

Before we examine the Boundary Hatch dialogue box in detail, let's get a feel for how it works by hatching a section of the walls.

1. Make the HATCH layer current and start BHATCH.

Use the DDLMODES or LAYER command to make HATCH the current layer.

```
Command: BHATCH
```

or

Pick Hatch... from the Draw menu.

The Boundary Hatch dialogue box will appear.

2. Set the hatch options as follows:

- Pattern type: User-Defined Pattern
- Angle: 45
- Spacing: 3"
- Hatching Style: Normal

Pick Hatch Options...

The Hatch Options subdialogue box will appear.

Figure 8.23 shows the dialogue box with the options set as specified above.

3. Pick a point in the curved wall to define the hatch area.

Pick Pick Points <.

The dialogue box temporarily disappears and you're prompted to pick a point.

```
Select internal point:
```
Pick a point between the two arcs representing the curved wall.

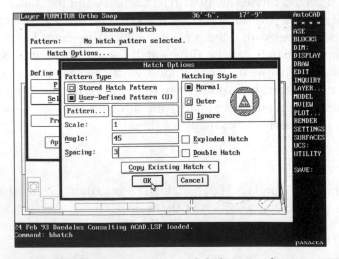

Figure 8.23 Hatch Options subdialogue with options set for hatching walls.

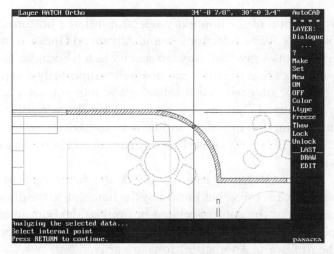

Figure 8.24 Hatch pick point and preview.

Make sure you pick *between* the arcs rather than on one of them. You'll probably need to turn Snap off. (See Figure 8.24.)

AutoCAD analyzes the area around the point you picked and finds the nearest completely closed boundary.

```
Select internal point: <Enter>
```

4. Preview the hatch.

Pick Preview Hatch <.

AutoCAD displays a temporary hatch pattern based on the options you set in step 2. (See Figure 8.24.)

Press <Enter> to return to the Boundary Hatch dialogue box.

5. Apply the hatch.

Pick Apply.

The Boundary Hatch dialogue closes, and AutoCAD makes the hatching a permanent part of the drawing.

The Boundary Hatch Dialogue Box

Although it might not be obvious at first glance, the Boundary Hatch dialogue box is divided into four conceptual pieces. The first one is Hatch Options... You can specify options at almost any point in the process, but it's simplest to do it first and then work your way down the dialogue box.

The next area is made up of the boundary selection-related buttons, Pick Points <, Select Objects <, View selections <, and Advanced Options.... Pick Points < and Select Objects < give two ways to specify hatch boundaries (the angle bracket, <, indicates that the dialogue box will temporarily disappear to let you pick points or objects). View selections < lets you look at the current boundary. Advanced Options... is for tweaking the way BHATCH hunts for boundaries. You don't need to bother with the Advanced Options subdialogue unless BHATCH has trouble locating the correct boundary lines in your drawings.

The third part, Preview Hatch <, lets you check the hatch options and location to make sure they're correct before adding the hatching to the drawing.

The fourth area includes the control-related buttons at the bottom of the dialogue box: Apply, Cancel, Another, and Help... Until a boundary selection has been made, the Apply and Another buttons are grayed out.

We've gathered some tips and tricks for each button below. The Advanced Options subdialogue is described in exhaustive detail in Chapter 12 of the *AutoCAD Reference Manual*.

HATCH OPTIONS...

This button brings up the Hatch Options subdialogue (see Figure 8.23). If you choose the Stored Hatch Pattern radio button, you must type in a pattern name, or, more conveniently, pick the Pattern... button to bring up a subdialogue showing the stock AutoCAD hatch patterns (see below). Once you've selected a pattern, type in values for the Scale and Angle fields. The User-Defined Pattern radio button is the equivalent of the old HATCH command's U option. You simply specify an angle and spacing for straight hatch lines, and check the Double Hatch box if you want crosshatching rather than lines in one direction only.

The Hatching Style radio buttons select among three ways of treating internal hatch boundaries. These three options are the same as the N, O, and I parameters used by the old HATCH command, and the differences should be clear from the icon that appears when you pick each button.

Tip

User-defined hatch patterns are good for experimenting, since it's easy to figure out a reasonable line spacing. Stored hatch patterns often require more guesswork to determine an appropriate hatch scale.

Tip

You need to worry about the Hatching Style buttons only if you select nested boundaries. AutoCAD looks at only the boundaries you specifically designate; it ignores any internal geometry if you haven't selected it.

The Exploded Hatch check box tells BHATCH to construct the hatch as individual line segments, rather than as a single Block. Avoid using this option unless you really need to manipulate pieces of a hatch. You always can use the EXPLODE command later to explode an existing hatch.

The Copy Existing Hatch < option is one of the major hatching improvements in Release 12. Once you pick an existing Release 12 hatch, BHATCH reads the pattern, scale or spacing, and angle from the hatch Block and restores those values in the Hatch Options dialogue box fields. Before Release 12, there was no way to determine these parameters from an existing hatch; you had to use trial and crror. The only limitation of Copy Existing Hatch < is that it doesn't work with exploded or pre-Release 12 hatches.

PATTERN...

This button in the Hatch Options subdialogue brings up the Choose Hatch Pattern subdialogue (see Figure 8.25). The dialogue shows more than 50 patterns arranged alphabetically in groups of 12.

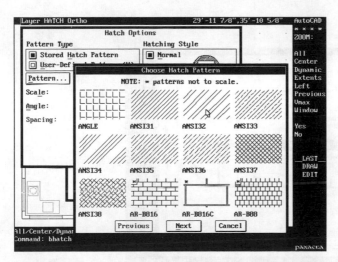

Figure 8.25 First screen of the Choose Hatch Pattern dialogue box.

Tip

The Choose Hatch Pattern subdialogue is easier than memorizing 50 hatch pattern names, but if you use a small number of patterns and already remember their names from previous versions of AutoCAD, typing the pattern name into the Hatch Options subdialogue text box usually is more efficient.

PICK POINTS <

This button is Release 12's most important improvement to hatching. Thanks to Pick Points <, you no longer have to spend all your time picking individual lines and drawing temporary hatching boundaries. Instead, you can just pick a point inside the area you want hatched. In most cases, AutoCAD will do the job of constructing a fully closed hatching boundary automatically, even when the boundary is made up of parts of different entities.

Occasionally, when picking points, you'll receive the error message "Boundary is not closed" or "Point is outside of boundary." The error dialogue will give you two options: OK and Look at it (see Figure 8.26). Use Look at it to view the boundary AutoCAD found and to try to determine where the problem lies.

"Boundary is not closed" usually means two lines don't quite meet, often because someone forgot to use Snap or object snaps when constructing the lines. It doesn't take much of a gap to cause this error, and sometimes you won't even be able to see any discontinuity. When this happens, use FILLET 0, grip editing, or some other means to join the lines precisely, then try BHATCH again.

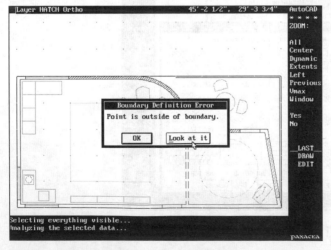

Figure 8.26   A Boundary Definition Error dialogue box.

"Point is outside of boundary" usually indicates a problem with your pick point, rather than with your geometry. AutoCAD looks for the nearest boundary, and doesn't know until after it traces around whether the point is inside or outside the boundary. To resolve this problem, pick inside of, but closer to, the boundary you want AutoCAD to find. We'll see an example in the next tutorial.

SELECT OBJECTS <

Pick Points < is one of two buttons you can use to set the boundaries that determine what will get hatched; Select Objects < is the other. Select Objects < works the same as selecting objects for the regular HATCH command: You pick a closed Polyline or a collection of entities that forms a completely closed boundary. Although you'll probably use Pick Points < most of the time, Select Objects < still is useful for those few situations where BHATCH's boundary finding procedure can't locate the boundary you're after.

VIEW SELECTIONS <

This option is selectable only when you've picked points or selected objects to identify at least one boundary for the hatch. Its only value is after you've chosen Select Objects <. Select Objects < removes the highlighting from any already selected boundaries, so, after you choose another boundary with Select Objects <, you might want to use View selections < to see the complete boundary selection set.

Tip

Be careful not to specify unreasonably small hatch pattern scales. Preview Hatch <, just like the regular HATCH command, has to generate all the hatching lines at the scale you specify. If you've chosen too small of a scale, you'll end up staring at the screen for awhile as AutoCAD draws all those closely spaced lines. If this happens, use <Ctrl>+C to abort the preview. A good strategy for honing in on a reasonable hatch scale is to start relatively large (with the drawing scale factor, for example), and gradually work smaller.

PREVIEW HATCH <

Previewing is the other major hatching improvement in Release 12. Preview Hatch < does just what the name implies: It lets you look at (and optionally adjust) hatching before you commit to adding it to your drawing. Always use this option if you're the least bit unsure of your hatch option settings. After you've previewed the hatching and confirmed that it's what you want, pick Apply or Another (described below) to add it to the drawing permanently. If you pick Cancel instead, AutoCAD will delete the temporary hatching.

APPLY, CANCEL, ANOTHER, AND HELP…

These buttons are simple. Pick Apply to apply a hatch using the current parameters; remember to use it if you've just previewed a hatch and like the result. Cancel closes the Boundary Hatch dialogue without adding hatching to your drawing. Another adds the current hatching to your drawing, and then lets you pick another boundary. It's like picking Apply and then restarting BHATCH, only much faster. Help… brings up several screenfuls of help information.

Hatching Tutorial

Now that we've looked at all the pieces of the Boundary Hatch dialogue, let's add some more hatching to the RECROOM drawing. We'll use a concrete pattern for the patio slab, and then finish off the wall hatching. Refer to Figure 8.29 as you work through this tutorial.

> **1.** Turn off the RAIL layer, start BHATCH, and specify the hatch options as follows:
>   - Pattern type: AR-CONC
>   - Scale: 48
>   - Angle: 0
>
> *Use the DDLMODES or LAYER command to turn off the RAIL layer, since it will interfere with finding the slab boundary.*
>
> Command: BHATCH
> or
> *Pick Hatch… from the Draw menu.*
>
> *Pick Hatch Options…*
>
> *Pick the Stored Hatch Pattern… radio button.*
>
> The Scale: field becomes active and the Spacing: field is grayed out.
>
> *Pick Pattern… and then Next to go to the second Choose Hatch Pattern dialogue.*
>
> *Double-click on the AR-CONC pattern.*
>
> *Enter 48 in the Scale field and 0 in the Angle field.*

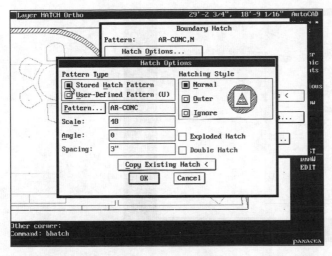

Figure 8.27 Hatch Options subdialogue with options set for hatching the patio.

Since we don't yet know a reasonable scale for AR-CONC, we'll start with the drawing scale factor (48 for a 1/4"=1'-0" drawing) and work smaller.

Figure 8.27 shows the dialogue box with the options set as specified above.

2. Pick a point inside the patio to define the outer hatching boundary.

Pick Pick Points <.

In order to force a boundary definition error, we'll pick a point too close to the table.

`Select internal point:` *Pick a point outside of but near the circle (point 1 in Figure 8.28).*

AutoCAD reports "Point is outside of boundary," as shown in Figure 8.26.

Pick Look at it from the Boundary Definition Error dialogue.

AutoCAD shows you that it found the circle rather than the edge of the patio.

`Press RETURN to continue:` *Do so.*

`Select internal point:` *This time, pick away from the table and chairs and near the edge of the patio (point 2 in Figure 8.28).*

Now AutoCAD finds the right boundary.

`Select internal point:` *<Enter>*

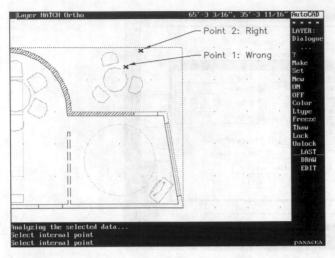

Figure 8.28   Correct and incorrect pick points.

3. Select the patio furniture in order to exclude it from being hatched.

Pick Select Objects <.

`Select objects:` *Use an implied window to select all the patio chairs and table.*

`Select objects: <Enter>`

4. Preview and adjust the hatch options.

Pick Preview Hatch <.

No hatching appears, because our hatch scale turns out to be much too large for this pattern.

Press <Enter> to end preview, and then return to the Hatch Options subdialogue. Change the hatch scale to 12.

Close the Hatch Options subdialogue and pick Preview Hatch < again.

Still a bit too large.

Change the hatch scale to 6 and preview once more.

Just right (See Figure 8.29).

Press <Enter> to return to the Boundary Hatch dialogue box.

Tip

Once you work out an appropriate scale factor for a hatch pattern, write it down. There's no reason to go through step 4 more than once per pattern. Usually, you'll want a hatch pattern to appear the same plotted size regardless of drawing scale, so write down scale factors in terms of drawing scale. For instance, in our example we found that AR-CONC looked good at a scale of 6/48, or 1/8 of the drawing scale factor.

5. Apply the hatch.

Pick Apply.

Now we'll finish hatching the walls.

6. Repeat the BHATCH command.

`Command:` *<Enter> to repeat the previous command.*

Pick Hatch Options....

Pick Copy Existing Hatch <.

`Select a hatch block.`
`Select objects:` *Pick on the wall hatching you added earlier.*
`Select objects:` *<Enter>*

AutoCAD extracts the hatch option settings and enters them into the dialogue box fields.

Pick OK.

Pick Pick Points <.

`Select internal point:` *Pick a point inside another section of wall.*

Because we've already used these hatch options in this drawing, there's no need to preview this time.

Pick Another.

AutoCAD adds the hatching and remains in the Boundary Hatch dialogue.

Repeat the process of picking a point and then picking Another, until all the walls are hatched, as shown in Figure 8.29.

Turn the RAIL layer back on when you're finished.

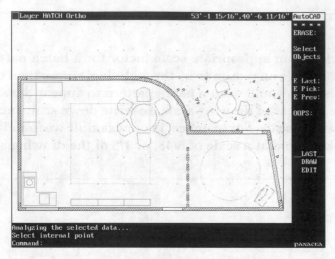

Figure 8.29 The completed patio and wall hatching.

 Tip

> In step 6, we could've picked all the internal wall points at the same time without picking Another in between, but that approach would've combined all the wall hatching defined by these points into one Block. Any change to the walls or openings would then require rehatching all the wall segments. By picking Another in between, we forced BHATCH to create individual Blocks for each section of wall hatching. This approach lets you erase and rehatch individual segments easily.

Boundary Polylines

When you use BHATCH's Pick Points < option to specify a hatching boundary, AutoCAD actually draws a temporary Polyline which gets erased when you pick Apply or Another. The BPOLY Polyline Creation dialogue box (Figure 8.30) uses this same functionality, but draws permanent Polylines. The Polyline Creation dialogue includes all the detailed boundary selection control options from Boundary Hatch's Advanced Options subdialogue, but, as with BHATCH, you'll rarely need them. Just pick the Pick Points button and select internal points as you did with BHATCH.

Tip

BPOLY is useful when you need to create a hatched "margin" starting at a boundary and extending inward or outward a certain distance. Use BPOLY to create a Polyline on the boundary, and then use OFFSET on the Polyline to make the other boundary. Once you've hatched, erase the two Polylines.

Summary

BHATCH makes the old HATCH command obsolete for most purposes. Get in the habit of using BHATCH, and take advantage of the Copy Existing Hatch <, Pick Points <, and Preview Hatch < buttons. We've covered everything most users need to know, but if you need more information, refer to Chapter 12 of the *AutoCAD Reference Manual* and the extended hatching tutorial in Chapter 3 of the *AutoCAD Tutorial Manual*.

Modifying, Hatching, and Workgroups

Unlike some of the new features we covered in the previous two chapters, none of the features in this chapter are difficult to understand or use. You shouldn't have any trouble persuading people to use BHATCH, since it will make their hatching chores so much easier. Make sure your workgroup members are familiar with all the capabilities of BHATCH, and show them how to avoid "Point is outside of boundary" errors. Take the time to experi-

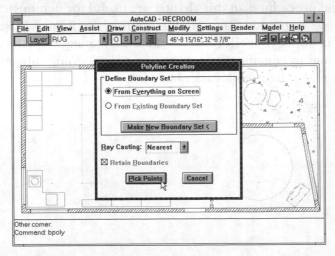

Figure 8.30   The Polyline Creation dialogue box.

ment with hatch scales for the patterns you use, and develop a sheet of hatching standards that everyone can follow. By doing this, you'll help ensure consistency and minimize the time everyone spends experimenting with different hatch options.

Point out DDCHPROP and DDMODIFY to workgroup members who haven't discovered them, and emphasize the advantages of modifying entities by pointing and clicking. Most people don't need to scrutinize every Modify Entities dialogue, but show them those that will be most helpful in your work.

One of the most important things about this chapter is that it brings you to payoff time. If you and your workgroup use a standard setup procedure for drawings, if you have a standard set of layers, and if the right text styles, linetypes, and layers are available in your drawings, you'll save a lot of work using the features described in this chapter. The consistent use of Snap and object snaps will result in drawings that are easy to modify and hatch, and that also will be easier to dimension and annotate (which we cover in the next chapter).

For those who don't follow standards and who create drawings sloppily, these same features represent payback time, rather than payoff time. Work will grind to a halt as users try to change linetypes and find the one they need unavailable; as they assign and reassign entities to layers that have no consistency from one drawing to the next; and as they struggle with hatching boundary definition errors because entities don't quite meet up where they're supposed to. Note that members of the first group probably would describe AutoCAD as relatively easy to use, and members of the latter group would call it difficult to use; but the real difference is planning and procedures, not the underlying program.

The features and procedures in this chapter are useful for demonstrating the value of setup, standards, and careful drafting techniques. Use the material in this chapter in your efforts to sell skeptical managers on the value of CAD training, and to convince wayward users of how doing things right the first time will make their work easier later on.

9

Adding Dimensions and Text

AutoCAD is one of the largest and most complex pieces of software you can run on a desktop computer. In addition, hundreds of add-on programs and millions of drawings depend on each detail of its workings. These factors have made it more and more difficult for Autodesk to change anything about AutoCAD's basic functionality without negatively affecting another part of the program, breaking a third-party application, or changing the way older drawings display and plot .

Release 12 does a great job of improving AutoCAD by adding to and enhancing, rather than actually changing, the features from previous releases. The Windows version of Release 12 is an even better example of the same approach. This chapter covers the incremental improvements to AutoCAD's dimensioning and text features.

These topics often are treated as afterthoughts by those learning CAD, since dimensions and text usually are added later in the drafting process and are subsidiary to the basic geometry. Yet, every drafter knows that accurate dimensioning and appropriate annotations are at least as important to communicating the intent of a design as are the lines, arcs, and other geometric entities. And every CAD drafter knows that dimensioning and annotating can consume a large chunk of the time spent completing a drawing. Improving your efficiency at adding text and dimensions to drawings will have a big impact on overall productivity.

About This Chapter

Dimensioning is one of the most complicated aspects of AutoCAD, thanks in part to the dozens of dimension variables ("DIMvars") that control how a dimension looks. Release 12's major improvement to dimensioning is a comprehensive Dimensioning Styles and Variables dialogue box that organizes all the DIMvars and makes them easier to tweak. This dialogue box also makes creating and using dimension styles (one of the major enhancements to Release 11) almost automatic.

Text handling has improved less quickly in recent versions of AutoCAD, and Release 12 is no exception. The one significant text improvement in Release 12—support for PostScript—won't be important to most of AutoCAD's traditional users, although it's very important in desktop publishing and other applications where PostScript reigns. Of more value to most current AutoCAD users are three AutoLISP programs for manipulating text. These routines aren't new to Release 12, but more users will discover them because they're documented in the *AutoCAD Extras Manual*, and because one of them has been integrated into the menus.

In this chapter, we pull together the changes to dimensioning and text into a coherent whole. We cover the changes in an organized fashion, and also shed light on some features, such as dimension styles and the text handling programs, that were added in Release 11, but that some users haven't yet learned to take advantage of. This chapter should help you "finish" your drawings with better results and less frustration.

Features Demonstrated in This Chapter

Release 12 introduces new ways of using dimension styles and adds the ability to use PostScript fonts. The features demonstrated in this chapter include the following:

- Several improvements to dimensioning make it easier to get your dimensions right the first time.

- The DDIM command brings up a dialogue box that makes setting up, managing, and using dimension styles much easier (see Figure 9.1). We demonstrate how to work with dimension styles and provide a link between this top-down way of working and the dozens of DIMvars that you can use to make on-the-fly adjustments.

- The AutoLISP routines ASCTEXT, CHTEXT, and PTEXT provide various ways of entering and modifying text. The new DDMODIFY command lets you change everything about a text string.

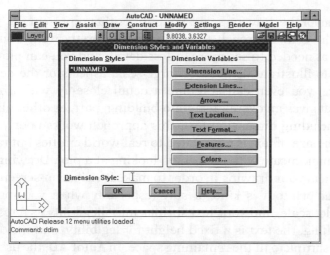

Figure 9.1 The DDIM Dimension Styles and Variables
dialogue box.

- We describe a way to get through the PostScript maze with your
  drawings improved and your sanity intact.

For any user who has struggled with dimension variables, the new dimensioning dialogue box is a significant step forward. The text handling routines, on the other hand, are mixed and work inconsistently. And the
PostScript improvements should be approached with caution and attention
to costs and benefits. Generally, we try to steer you toward the best ways to
take advantage of these changes.

About the Example

In this chapter, we add dimensions and text to the RECROOM drawing built
up in previous chapters. If you don't have an up-to-date version of RECROOM
as of the previous chapter, you can use the RRCH09.DWG file on the
AutoCAD Power Tools disk as a starting point. You also should copy
RECNOTES.TXT from the diskette to your tutorial subdirectory, since we'll
use it in the text tutorial.

Text and Dimensioning Scale and Layout

With AutoCAD, as with any other CAD program, you usually draw physical
objects—walls, bolts, roads, and so on—at their actual "real-world" size, and
then scale up text, dimensions, and other symbols that need a fixed size on

paper, independent of the drawing scale. For entities that represent the "real-world" objects, the CAD approach to scaling works pretty well. You can zoom in and out as needed to see more or less detail, and you can plot at a variety of scales to illustrate detailed or large-scale aspects of the design. With paper space, you even can combine a detail close-up with a more inclusive view that gives an overall feel for a building, part, or other object.

But for text, including dimension text, this approach works poorly. The problem is that the size of text is not related to real-world entities but rather to the need to communicate with the person looking at a plot. Drawing this kind of text 2' high in your drawing in order to make it visible on-screen and, hopefully, in your printout is kind of silly (especially when you make a change to your plot scale, and your text shrinks into illegibility as a result).

In manual drafting, the text is a fixed height for legibility, and the object being depicted is shrunk to fit the remaining space. In AutoCAD, the user has marvelous flexibility in manipulating the on-screen and printed representations of the object, but little of that kind of flexibility with text.

Paper space can help with this problem, and it gives you a lot of control over layout as well. But paper space adds a performance and organizational overhead that make it unsuitable for use all the time. There are no "magic bullets" in Release 12 that fix text scaling problems, although, for dimensioning, the presence of the new dialogue box and consistent use of dimension styles will give you a fighting chance.

The other tool that will help you keep control over text and dimensions is planning. If you're working on drawings that are similar to those you've done in the past, you have the benefit of experience and it should be easy to solve most problems before they get serious. If you're starting a new kind of drawing or set of drawings, you can work out problems in the setup phase and minimize problems later.

During setup, or later in the process when it's time to actually add text and dimensions, you may want to sketch out your drawing with dimensions and text. Or you may want to do some plot previews and check plots with single text and dimension entries to get a feel for how they'll look in the final version. (See this chapter and Chapter 11, *Paper Space and Plotting*, for information that will help you with controlling the appearance of text; see Chapters 4 and 5 for information about setup procedures that will help you get a good start.)

Dimensions

There aren't many changes to AutoCAD's dimensioning capabilities in Release 12; for the most part, you'll be drawing the same kinds of dimensions in the same way as before. The same large number of dimension variables, with their obscure names and different kinds of values, are there to offer you endless control and potentially endless confusion as well. But the addition of a DDIM dialogue box front-end for dimension styles makes the whole process a great deal easier. You no longer have to remember or look up the names of the dimension variables. They're presented in an organized way that makes it much easier, especially for the experienced user, to modify the important variables and ignore the unimportant ones. And styles are integrated with the options in a way that makes it easy to look at the details of existing styles and create new ones.

Dimensioning capabilities also are well-documented in the AutoCAD manuals. The *AutoCAD Reference Manual* has a whole chapter on dimensioning, including coverage of the new dialogue box, and the *AutoCAD Tutorial Manual* also includes a full chapter on dimensioning with both the dialogue box and command-line entry well represented.

So, what can this book offer that the manuals don't? If you've read through to this point, you no doubt know the answer: focus. Leaving exhaustive coverage to the manuals, we'll discuss the key and changed features that will make the most difference to your work. In the following sections, we'll highlight several new features that make dimensioning more powerful; describe dimension styles and how to get the most out of them; summarize the workings of the dialogue boxes and their relationship to the dimensioning variables in a series of tables; and discuss useful sets of default values for a couple of major disciplines. In the tutorials, you'll become acquainted with the many DDIM dialogue boxes and learn how to use them to create and manage dimension styles.

Dimensioning Highlights

Release 11 added many new features to dimensioning, including TEDIT and dimension styles. TEDIT, a new dimension subcommand, allows you to control the placement and even orientation of dimension text. This helps manage the appearance of dimensions, especially when there are several associative dimensions crammed into a small space. Dimension styles allow much better control over groupings of dimension variables, just as text styles do for text characteristics. Dimension variables also prevent a common problem: Any time you edit an "unstyled" dimension (for instance, with the STRETCH command), AutoCAD reformats it using the current DIMvars, which can wreak havoc on a finely tuned dimension.

While dimension styles were a great addition, many users didn't take advantage of them because of a lack of exposure or the usual inertia that keeps all of us from mastering new features. Also, setting up a useful set of dimension styles required you to sort out the dozens of DIMvars and then manage them with the DIM subcommand's primitive command-line interface.

Dimension styles and the DIMvars they control are much more approachable with the new Release 12 DDIM dialogue box. Along with the incremental improvements to dimensioning in Release 12, DDIM makes using associative dimensions and the dimension commands in AutoCAD easier and more worthwhile. The changes include:

- Visibility of dimension text as you "drag" a dimension into place.

  At last, you can see the dimension text as you decide where to put the dimension.

- The ability to dimension entities within external references and Blocks without exploding them.

  Dimensioning now works the same way for entities nested within Xrefs and Blocks as it does for other entities. This simple change removes one of the obstacles to leaving Xrefs and Blocks "whole," as we describe in the next chapter.

- Reference dimensions, also known as basic dimensions. Dimension text can be drawn with a box around it.

- Addition of automatic prefixes, as well as suffixes to dimension text.

  Previous releases let you specify a standard suffix (such as "mm") to add to dimension text. Now you can configure for a prefix, suffix, or both.

- The DDIM dialogue box.

  DDIM is your toolkit for managing DIMvars and dimension styles. Much more on it below.

- The Modify Dimensions dialogue box.

  This is one of the least capable of the DDMODIFY dialogue boxes (described in the previous chapter), but it does let you inspect the characteristics of a Dimension.

Tip

Don't forget about grips when you need to edit Dimensions. Grip editing is a great way to move dimension text around (like TEDIT, only without the overhead of entering a command—see Figure 9.2) and to stretch dimensions.

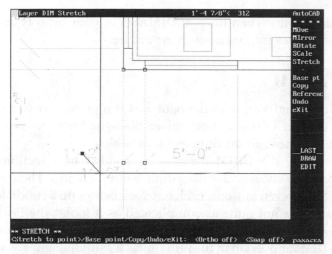

Figure 9.2   Using grips to move associative Dimension text.

Associative Dimensions

Many of the Release 12 and Release 11 improvements to dimensioning apply only to associative Dimensions—Dimensions drawn with the DIMASO DIMvar turned on. AutoCAD treats an associative Dimension as a single entity, rather than as individual lines and text. If you aren't currently using associative Dimensions, you might wonder whether they're worth the bother, especially if you experimented with them before Release 11 and found how difficult they were to edit.

Dimension styles, TEDIT, and a host of new DIMvars in Release 11 made associative Dimensions much easier to edit and control, to the point where there was little reason not to use them. The dimensioning improvements in Release 12, and especially DDIM, tip the scales even more in favor of associative dimensions. If you haven't been using them, you really owe it to yourself to start now.

A major advantage of associative dimensions is that dimension text updates automatically as you stretch the dimension with the object it's attached to. There are other advantages, though, and for some users they are more important. An associative Dimension is a single entity, which means that you have to pick only once to erase, move, or copy it. In other words, like Polylines and Blocks, associative Dimensions let you group entities that are logically related. Associative dimensions, together with dimension styles, give you the means to create families of consistent-looking dimensions, just as text styles help ensure consistent text appearance.

So, even if you tried associative dimensions in a previous release and found them difficult to work with, use this upgrade as your chance to reevaluate. Read through this chapter and use it as a guide for setting up a couple of dimension styles. Then turn on DIMASO in your prototypes and integrate dimension styles into your setup procedure.

A Quick Tour of DDIM

The Dimension Styles and Variables dialogue box is a great way to control dimension styles. It's one of the best-organized dialogue boxes in AutoCAD and allows access to almost all the dimension variables.

As Figure 9.3 shows, the DDIM dialogue is divided into sections for working with dimension styles and setting dimension variables. The Dimension Variables area has seven buttons, each of which brings up a subdialogue for setting DIMvars. (It's not quite as complicated as it looks; the Features subdialogue is a "summary" of most of the fields from the other subdialogues, and there is some DIMvar overlap in the remaining six subdialogues as well.) The only two variables you can't control from here are DIMSHO and DIMASO, which aren't saved as part of dimension styles. We'll discuss these two variables and each of the dialogues below.

Before we do that, however, let's explore how DDIM and dimension styles work. In this tutorial, we'll guide you through dimensioning the horizontal and vertical extents of the RECROOM and changing one of the dimension variables with DDIM. After that, we'll move on to a detailed tour of DDIM and leave it to you to add other dimensions.

1. Load RECROOM.

Use your drawing from the previous chapter, or copy RRCH09.DWG from the *AutoCAD Power Tools* disk. You'll want to copy RECNOTES.TXT from the disk, since we'll use it during the text tutorial later in the chapter.

2. Set the DIM layer current, turn off HATCH, set Snap to 6", and make sure STANDARD is the current dimension style.

Use the DDLMODES or LAYER command to make DIM the current layer and to turn off the HATCH layer.

The hatching would interfere with picking points and entities for dimensioning.

Turn snap on and set it to 6" with the DDRMODES or SNAP command.

```
Command: DDIM
```
or
Pick Dimension Style... from the Settings menu.

The Dimension Styles and Variables dialogue appears.

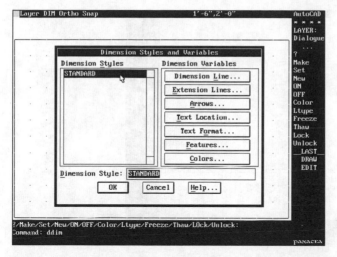

Figure 9.3   Setting the current dimension style using DDIM.

Double-click on STANDARD in the Dimension Styles listbox.

AutoCAD makes STANDARD the current dimension style and closes the dialogue box.

3. Draw a horizontal dimension below the south wall.

Under the Draw menu, pick Dimensions, then Linear, then Horizontal.

AutoCAD starts the HORIZONTAL dimensioning subcommand.

`First extension line origin or RETURN to select:` *<Enter>*
`Select line, arc, or circle:` *Pick anywhere on the horizontal line representing the outside of the front wall (see Figure 9.4).*

AutoCAD finds the endpoints of the wall.

`Dimension line location (Text/Angle):` *Pick any point with a Y coordinate of about 5'–0".*

Notice that AutoCAD displays the dimension text as you drag the dimension into place.

`Dimension text <40'>:` *<Enter>*

4. Draw a vertical dimension to the left of the west wall.

Repeat step 2, but this time, pick Vertical from the menu and pick a point on the side wall at the left of the drawing (see Figure 9.4).

Figure 9.4 shows the completed dimensions.

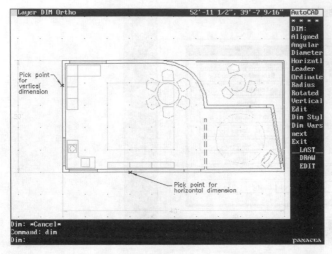

Figure 9.4   Dimensions and pick points.

5. Use DDIM to change the text color for the STANDARD dimension style.

Start DDIM again (see step 1).

The Dimension Styles and Variables dialogue shows STANDARD as the current style, so the change we make will apply to all dimensions drawn with that style.

Pick Colors....

The Colors subdialogue appears.

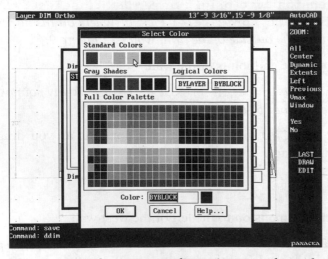

Figure 9.5   Selecting a new dimension text color with the Select Color subdialogue.

Pick on the color box to the right of Dimension Text Color (see Figure 9.5).

The Select Color subdialogue appears.

Pick cyan from the list of Standard Colors at the top.

Pick OK three times until you've closed all the dialogue boxes.

The text in both the horizontal and vertical dimensions automatically becomes cyan.

Tip

The reason for making dimension text a different color is so that you can assign it a heavier pen when plotting, while still maintaining associative dimensions. But assigning an explicit color to dimension text runs counter to our advice in Chapter 6 that you leave color BYLAYER and control entity color by changing layer colors. So, why did we do it? In Release 11, Autodesk added the ability to control the color of each part of an associative Dimension, but, unfortunately, they didn't add the same sort of control for layer (or linetype). In this instance, we've opted for better looking drawings (i.e., dimension text that stands out), even though it costs us some consistency in how we use colors and layers. Fortunately, if you do need to change the color of dimension text later, you can do it quickly by redefining the dimension style.

---

6. Add other dimensions.

Dimension a few window openings, the curved wall, and other parts of the rec room until you have a mix of different dimensions similar to what's shown in Figure 9.6.

By drawing a mix of dimensions—horizontal, vertical, text inside extension lines, text outside extension lines, radial, aligned, etc.— you'll be better able to judge the overall impact of changing dimension variables.

In the rest of this section, we'll work step by step through the DDIM dialogue and subdialogues. We've mixed description and brief tutorial instructions so that you can get hands-on experience in establishing your DIMvar settings and saving them as dimension styles.

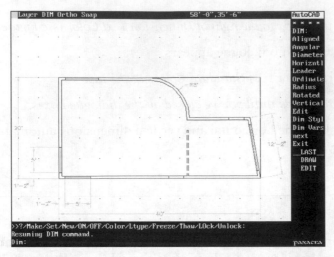

Figure 9.6   The dimensioned rec room.

Dimension Styles

Consistency in dimensioning is important not only for the "look" of your drawings, but also for making the job of creating and editing dimensions easier. A consistent set of dimension variables makes it easier for you to predict how dimensions will look when you draw them and how they'll react to editing. But it's difficult, especially when you're in an unusual or tricky situation, to remember just how you tweaked the DIMvars for a similar situation in the past. This is why dimension styles are so valuable; they can encapsulate into a single, easy to pick choice a lot of hard thinking and experimentation about how you want dimensions to look.

STYLE MANAGEMENT

Setting up new styles is an iterative process of reviewing DIMvars, changing settings, and trying out the changes. We describe the steps below. The kind of thinking and planning that goes into getting styles right is different from, and interferes with, the kind of thinking and planning that goes into cranking out dimensions efficiently. We suggest, therefore, that you set up dimension styles in your prototype drawings, whether you use one prototype for all your work or separate prototypes for different kinds of work, different projects, etc. Then you'll have at least the basics in place when you start your drawing.

Tip

Beware of one quirk with the DDIM dialogue and UNDO. If you make a change in DDIM and then use UNDO, AutoCAD correctly restores the old DIMvar settings for the dimension style you changed, but it also changes the current style name to *UNNAMED. To work around this problem, you can either use UNDO twice or pop up DDIM again and select the style to make current.

CREATING A DEFAULT DIMENSION STYLE

Creating a new dimension style is easy, but a little confusing at first. When you open the dimension dialogue in a drawing in which no style has been created, it displays only one dimension style: *UNNAMED. This is AutoCAD's way of saying that you're not currently using a dimension style; think of it as "Release 10 mode."

The first thing to do is to create a default dimension style, as we did during setup in Chapter 4. In the Dimension Style edit box, enter a suitable name, such as STANDARD. Unless this is the only thing you want to do in the dialogue, press <Enter> instead of picking OK; if you pick OK, the dialogue box disappears.

If the standard AutoCAD defaults are fine for you, no further action is needed to get STANDARD right. Most people will want to change some of the settings, though. As long as STANDARD is the currently selected style, all the changes you make will be saved immediately with the style. You don't need to save the style explicitly each time you make a change, as is true when you change DIMvars from the command line.

On the other hand, there's a potential danger in having the style updated automatically. If you get carried away in the dimension variable subdialogues, it may be difficult to restore the settings back to what they were. Remember to use the Cancel button if this happens or, if you've already picked OK, use UNDO twice.

A useful safeguard against accidentally messing up your "good" dimension styles is to create a copy before you start experimenting. For instance, once you've got STANDARD right, immediately create a second style, calling it something like TEMP. Then, use the TEMP style to experiment without changing the values in STANDARD. To create the TEMP style, make sure STANDARD is the currently selected style, type TEMP in the Dimension Style edit box, and then press <Enter>. Each time you create a new style, DDIM uses the currently selected style as a "template" for it.

Tip

Two things you can't do with DDIM are rename or delete dimension styles. Use the DDRENAME or RENAME command to rename dimension styles, and use PURGE to delete any that aren't referenced by a dimension (see Chapter 4).

ADDING MORE DIMENSION STYLES

Once you have a default dimension style and a temporary one to experiment with, think about other dimension styles you might need. If there are several types of dimensions you customarily show on drawings, set up a style for each of them. Some variations to consider include different dimension block types (ticks, arrow, dots, or custom) and different on/off settings for the extension lines. As you work through this chapter, make a note of any DDIM settings that you might want to alter for different dimensioning situations, and then decide whether they merit a separate style.

In order to create additional dimension styles, follow the same steps listed above for creating TEMP. Make sure you always select the proper template style (whether it's STANDARD or something else) before you type in the new name and press <Enter>. By doing as much of the dimension style setup work as possible before you start drawing, you'll minimize later distractions to your drawing work.

DIMASO and DIMSHO

As mentioned above, the only two variables you can't control from the DDIM dialogues are DIMASO and DIMSHO. DIMASO controls whether associative dimensioning is on; if it is, all the pieces that make up a dimension are treated as a single entity, tied to the definition points you pick when you create the Dimension entity. DIMSHO controls the dynamic recalculation of Dimension entities when they're dragged. With DIMSHO on, AutoCAD shows the Dimension as you drag it into place, which helps you position it correctly. If your computer is slow enough that you need to turn DIMSHO off, then it probably is too slow to run Release 12 effectively.

DIMASO and DIMSHO are turned on in the default AutoCAD prototype drawing, and you'll almost always want to leave them that way. On the other hand, you may find one or both DIMvars turned off in older drawings, so be sure to check them when you load a drawing that was created in a previous version of AutoCAD. You can set DIMASO and DIMSHO from the Command: or Dim: prompt—just type the name of the variable. From the

Command: prompt, you type **1** to turn them on and **0** to turn them off, while, from the Dim: prompt, you type **ON** or **OFF**. Isn't it a relief to know that the AutoCAD interface hasn't become *completely* consistent?

Using the Dimension Variables Subdialogues

All the other dimension variables are easily controlled from the dialogues. One of the few problems is that the names in the dialogues don't have a clear-cut relationship with the dimension variables. In most cases, fields in the dialogues map directly onto a corresponding DIMvar, but you can't tell the name of the DIMvar from the prompt name in the dialogue.

In other cases, many of which involve checkbox settings, the relationship between field values and DIMvars is complicated. For instance, if you use the new reference dimensions feature, the gap between the text and the surrounding box is stored as a negative value in DIMGAP; if it's a regular text gap, it's still stored in DIMGAP, but as a positive number.

But if you have the dialogue boxes, why worry about DIMvars? Because a good part of the power of AutoCAD Release 12 is the ability to move flexibly between the ease of use of the dialogue boxes and the power of the command line. You get more control over DIMvars and dimension styles at the command line, at the cost of more complication and a more cryptic interface. But, if you try to move back and forth between the command line and DDIM without understanding their relationship, you'll have a difficult time taking advantage of either. This kind of information is in the *AutoCAD Reference Manual*, but it's spread out over many pages and separate figures and tables.

To ease this problem, the sections below cover each of the dialogues. Each section contains a table that maps the dialogue's prompts and fields to the DIMvars that are affected by them. You can use these tables to move flexibly between the dialogue boxes and the command line.

In each table, we've also listed the default value for each DIMvar—it's often valuable, after experimenting, to be able to get back to the defaults—and, where applicable, recommended values for architectural and mechanical drawings. These values won't be right for all situations, but they're a useful starting point that will place you closer to the finish line than you'd be with AutoCAD's defaults.

 ## Tip

All the fields in the Dimension Line, Extension Lines, Arrows, and Text Location dialogues are combined in the Features dialogue. You can specify everything you need with the Text Format, Features, and Colors dialogues.

COMMON ELEMENTS—STYLE, SCALING, COLOR

Each of the subdialogues has a "header" area that varies little from one dialogue to the next (see Figure 9.7 for an example). This section explains the fields in the header area. The sections below, each with the name of a dialogue, explain the fields in that dialogue that are not in the header area.

Style	The current dimension style. All changes you make in the dialogues apply immediately to this style.
Feature Scaling	Value by which to multiply all dimension variables for size, distance, or offset.
Use Paper Space Scaling	Computes value for feature scaling based on model space/paper space zoom factor.
Dimension Line Color	Color to use for dimension line.

(Three of the dialogues—Dimension Line, Extension Lines, and Text Location (not Text Format, as you might expect)—also have a color-related field near the top that allows you to set the color of the feature controlled by the dialogue. Figure 9.7 includes the header section with the color setting for dimension lines, and it is described below; the other two are similar. You can access all three of the color settings at once in the Colors dialogue.)

Table 9.1 summarizes the relationship between the prompts, values, and DIMvars in the header of the Dimension Line dialogue, as well as those for the other two color settings. For instance, a value of 0.0 in DIMSCALE serves

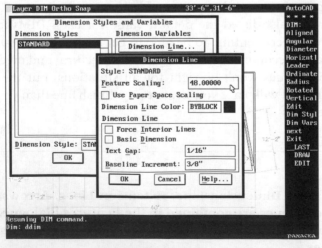

Figure 9.7 Header section of Dimension Lines dialogue.

Table 9.1 Fields Found in Header Area of Dialogues

Prompt	Default	Rec'd. Mech.	Rec'd. Arch.	DIMvar Affected	Type	Notes
Shared Header: Style	*UNNAMED	STANDARD	STANDARD	DIMSTYLE	Name	
Shared Header: Feature Scaling	1.00000	D.S.F.*	D.S.F.*	DIMSCALE	Scale	Value of 0.0 in DIMSCALE means use paper space scaling
Shared Header: Use Paper Space Scaling	☐	☐	☐	DIMSCALE	Scale	Value of 0.0 in DIMSCALE means use paper space scaling
Dimension Line Color, Extension Line Color, Dimension Text Color	BYBLOCK BYBLOCK BYBLOCK	BYBLOCK BYBLOCK = med. pen	BYBLOCK BYBLOCK = med. pen	DIMCLRD, DIMCLRE, DIMCLRT	Color number	

* D.S.F. = Drawing Scale Factor

as a flag for AutoCAD to use paper space scaling; otherwise, the value in the Feature Scaling field is stored in DIMSCALE. The various color values are each stored in an appropriate variable.

 NOTE

We already set these variables earlier in this chapter and in Chapter 5, but take a moment to make sure the values are as shown in the Rec'd Arch. column of Table 9.1.

DIMENSION LINE DIALOGUE

The Dimension Line dialogue (see Figure 9.8) includes the header section described above and a Dimension Line section that allows you to set values for DIMvars specific to dimension lines. This latter section allows you to specify several fields.

Tip

All the distance-type values displayed in the dialogues are rounded based on the current LUPREC (linear units precision) system variable setting, which you set with the DDUNITS or UNITS command (see Chapter 4). The rounding can be a problem when you're viewing or setting dimension variables; for instance, when you have linear precision set to display 16ths of an inch, the default DIMGAP— 0.09—displays as 1/16, even though it's closer to 3/32. To avoid this problem, set linear precision as high as possible (e.g., 256ths of an inch) before entering the DDIM dialogue.

Force Interior Lines	Forces dimension lines to be drawn inside the extension lines, even when text is drawn outside.
Basic Dimension	Chooses basic, or reference, dimensions— dimensions with a box drawn around them.
Text Gap	Gap between dimension text and dimension lines.
Baseline Increment	Offset for continued dimensions drawn with the Baseline command.

Table 9.2 summarizes the relationship between the Dimension Line dialogue's prompts, values, and DIMvars.

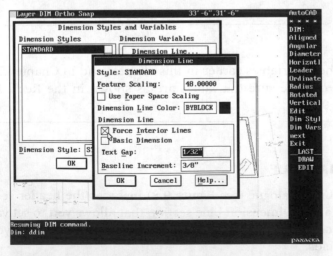

Figure 9.8   Dimension Line dialogue.

Table 9.2   Fields Specific to Dimension Line Dialogue

Prompt	Default	Rec'd. Mech.	Rec'd. Arch.	DIMvar Affected	Type	Notes
Force Interior Lines	☐	☐	☒	DIMTOFL	Switch	
Basic Dimension	☐	☐	☐	DIMGAP	Distance	If checked, stores value in Text Gap as negative# in DIMGAP
Text Gap	0.0900	0.09	1/32"	DIMGAP	Distance	
Baseline Increment	0.3800	0.32	3/8"	DIMDLI	Distance	

 NOTE

Turn on Force Interior Lines, reduce Text Gap to 1/32", and make sure Baseline Increment is set to 3/8" (see Figure 9.8).

EXTENSION LINES DIALOGUE

The Extension Lines dialogue (see Figure 9.9) includes the header section described above and an Extension Lines section that allows you to set values

 Tip

DIMGAP (along with DIMASZ) controls the amount of space AutoCAD needs between each end of the dimension text and the extension lines; a small DIMGAP helps keep text inside the dimension lines more often. We've recommended 1/32" for architectural dimensions, but you might try even smaller values, all the way down to 0. The disadvantage of a tiny DIMGAP is that it leaves less of a gap between the text and the end of the dimension line. This isn't a problem if you put text above the dimension line, as is common in architectural drafting, but it still affects leaders, including radius and diameter leaders. Experiment with different DIMGAP values, and consider setting up a separate style just for leaders.

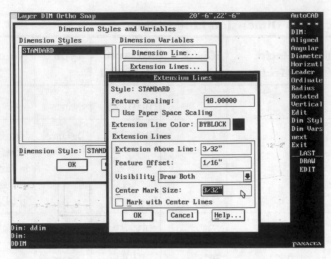

Figure 9.9 Extension Lines dialogue.

for DIMvars specific to extension lines. This latter section allows you to specify the following fields:

Extension Above Line
Distance that extension line extends beyond dimension line.

Feature Offset
Distance that extension lines are offset from dimension origin points.

Visibility
Suppresses none, either, or both extension lines.

Center Mark Size
Size of center marks for CENTER, DIAMETER, and RADIUS dimension commands; 0 for no center mark.

Mark with Center Lines
Adds center lines to center mark for CENTER, DIAMETER, and RADIUS dimension commands.

Table 9.3 summarizes the relationship between the Extension Line dialogue's prompts, values, and DIMvars.

 NOTE

Change both Extension Above Line and Center Mark Size to 3/32", and change Feature Offset to 1/16" (see Figure 9.9).

Table 9.3   Fields Specific to Extension Lines Dialogue

Prompt	Default	Rec'd. Mech.	Rec'd. Arch.	DIMvar Affected	Type	Notes
Extension Above Line	0.1800	0.1200	$\frac{3}{32}''$	DIMEXE	Distance	
Feature Offset	0.0625	0.0625	$\frac{1}{16}''$	DIMEXO	Distance	
Visibility	Draw Both	Draw Both	Draw Both	DIMSE1, DEMSE2	Switch	Switches turned on to suppress extension lines
Center Mark Size	0.0900	0.0900	$\frac{3}{32}''$	DIMCEN	Distance	0=no center mark
Mark with Center Lines	☐	☐	☐	DIMCEN	Distance	If checked, stores value in Center Mark Size as neg. # in DIMCEN

ARROWS DIALOGUE

The Arrows dialogue (see Figure 9.10) includes the header section described above and an Arrows section that allows you to set values for DIMvars specific to arrows, tick marks, and other dimension blocks. This section allows you to specify the following fields:

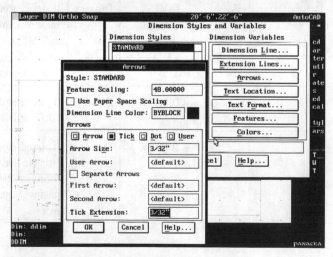

Figure 9.10   Arrows dialogue.

Arrow, Tick, Dot, User	Choose a radio button to specify the type of arrowhead to be drawn.
Arrow Size	Arrowhead or tick length.
User Arrow	Block name of a user-defined arrowhead or tick.
Separate Arrows	Specifies that different Blocks be used at each end of the dimension line.
First Arrow	Block name of first arrowhead or tick.
Second Arrow	Block name of second arrowhead or tick.
Tick Extension	How far dimension line extends past extension line.

Table 9.4 summarizes the relationship between the Arrows dialogue's prompts, values, and DIMvars.

Table 9.4   Fields Specific to Arrows Dialogue

Prompt	Default	Rec'd. Mech.	Rec'd. Arch.	DIMvar Affected	Type	Notes
Arrow	■	■	☐	DIMASZ, DIMTSZ	Distance	If picked, stores value in Arrow Size in DIMASZ, 0 in DIMTSZ
Tick	☐	☐	■	DIMTSZ, DIMASZ	Distance	If picked, stores value in Arrow Size in DIMTSZ, 0 in DIMASZ, ungrays Tick Extension
Dot	☐	☐	☐	DIMBLK	String	If picked, stores "DOT" in DIMBLK
User	☐	☐	☐	DIMBLK	String	If picked, stores string in User Arrow in DIMBLK, ungrays Separate Arrows

(continued)

Table 9.4   Fields Specific to Arrows Dialogue *(continued)*

Prompt	Default	Rec'd. Mech.	Rec'd. Arch.	DIMvar Affected	Type	Notes
Arrow Size	0.1800	0.1400	³⁄₃₂"	DIMASZ, DIMTSZ	Distance	
User Arrow	N/A	N/A	N/A	DIMBLK	String	
Separate Arrows	N/A	N/A	N/A	DIMSAH	Switch	If checked, stores On in DIMSAH, ungrays First, Second Arrows
First Arrow	N/A	N/A	N/A	DIMBLK1	String	Gray unless Separate Arrows checked
Second Arrow	N/A	N/A	N/A	DIMBLK2	String	Gray unless Separate Arrows checked
Tick Extension	N/A	N/A	³⁄₃₂"	DIMDLE	Distance	Gray unless Tick button on

 NOTE

Pick the Tick radio button, and set Arrow Size and Tick Extension to 3/32" (see Figure 9.10).

 Tip

If you like a heavy, "chiselled" tick mark, define a custom dimension block that consists of a line on a layer whose color corresponds to a heavy pen. See the *AutoCAD Reference Manual* for more information about custom dimension blocks.

TEXT LOCATION DIALOGUE

The Text Location dialogue (see Figure 9.11) includes the header section described above and a Text Position section that allows you to set values for

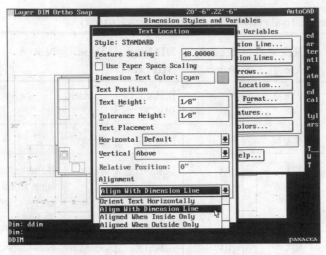

Figure 9.11   Text Location dialogue.

fields specific to the location of text. This latter section allows you to specify the following fields:

Text Height	Height, if current text style doesn't have a fixed height.
Tolerance Height	Height of dimension tolerance values.
Horizontal	Use to force text or text and arrows inside the extension lines.
Vertical	Use to place text above or below the dimension line.
Relative Position	Distance to place text above or below the dimension line.
Alignment	Use to specify when text should be aligned with dimension line.

Table 9.5 summarizes the relationship between the Text Location dialogue's prompts, values, and DIMvars.

Tip

The labels Aligned When Inside Only and Aligned When Outside Only in the Alignment listbox are reversed. Aligned When Inside Only sets DIMTIH on and DIMTOH off, which causes AutoCAD to make the text horizontal whenever it's inside the extension lines. Dimension text that falls outside the extension lines is aligned with the dimension line. Aligned When Outside Only works in the reverse way. If you're going to use one of these choices, draw several dimensions and experiment to be sure that you've got the right one.

Table 9.5   Fields Specific to Text Location Dialogue

Prompt	Default	Rec'd. Mech.	Rec'd. Arch.	DIMvar Affected	Type	Notes
Text Height	0.1800	0.14	1/8"	DIMTXT	Distance	
Tolerance Height	0.1800	0.6	1/8"	DIMTFAC	Scale	DIMTFAC = Tol. Height/Text Height; default is 1.0
Horizontal	Default	Default	Default	DIMTIX, DIMSOXD	Switch	Default: Off/Off Force Text Inside: On/Off Text, Arrows Inside: On/On
Vertical	Centered	Above	Above	DIMTAD	Switch	Centered: Off Above: On, uses DIMTXT for distance Relative: Off, ungrays Relative Position, uses DIMTVP for placement
Relative Position	N/A	N/A	N/A	DIMTVP	Scale	DIMTVP=Rel. Pos. Text Height; default is 0.0
Alignment	Orient Horizontally	Aligned When Outside Only	Align With Dimension Line	DIMTIH, DIMTOH	Switch	Orient H: On, On Align w/Dim Line: Off, Off ...Inside Only: On, Off ...Outside Only: Off, On

 NOTE

Change Text Height and Tolerance Height to 1/8". Set Vertical to Above and Alignment to Align With Dimension Line (see Figure 9.11).

TEXT FORMAT DIALOGUE

The Text Format dialogue (see Figure 9.12) includes the header section described above and four sections—Basic Units, Zero Suppression, Tolerances, and Alternate Units—that allow you to set values for DIMvars specific to the format of text. (But the text color is set in the Text Location dialogue, described above, or the Colors dialogue, described below.)

Basic Units.   The Basic Units section controls the basic "look and feel" of the main dimension text.

Length Scaling	Value by which to multiply the actual AutoCAD length to arrive at default dimension text.
Scale in Paper Space Only	Applies length scaling value only to dimensions in paper space.
Round Off	Value to round off to.
Text Prefix	String to insert in front of default dimension text.
Text Suffix	String to insert following default dimension text.

Zero Suppression.   The Zero Suppression section controls when zeroes in dimension text are suppressed.

0 Feet	Suppresses foot values of zero.
0 Inches	Suppresses inch values of zero.
Leading	Suppresses leading zeroes (for units other than architectural).
Trailing	Suppresses trailing zeroes (for units other than architectural).

Tolerances.   The Tolerances section controls "plus or minus" and "upper bound / lower bound" type tolerances.

None, Variance, Limits	Choose a radio button to specify the type of tolerances to append to dimensions.
Upper Value	Value for upper bound variance.
Lower Value	Value for lower bound variance.

Alternate Units. The Alternate Units section controls the display of additional text showing the dimension in a different system of measurement.

Show Alternate Units?	Enables display of alternate units in brackets after dimension text.
Decimal Places	Number of digits to show after decimal point.
Scaling	Value by which to multiply the actual AutoCAD length to come up with default alternate dimension text.
Suffix	String to insert following alternate value; usually, a measuring unit.

Table 9.6 summarizes the relationship between the Text Format dialogue's prompts, values, and DIMvars.

Table 9.6   Fields Specific to Text Format Dialogue

Prompt	Default	Rec'd. Mech.	Rec'd. Arch.	DIMvar Affected	Type	Notes
Length Scaling	1.0000	1.0000	1.0000	DIMLFAC	Scale	Multiplies dimension text by DIMLFAC
Scale in Paper Space Only	☐	☐	☐	DIMLFAC	Scale	If checked, stores value in Length Scaling as neg. # in DIMLFAC
Round Off	0.0000	0.0000	0	DIMRND	Scaled distance	
Text Prefix	none	none	none	DIMPOST	String	
Text Suffix	none	none	none	DIMPOST	String	
0 Feet	☒	N/A	☒	DIMZIN	Integer	DIMZIN = 0 if both are checked DIMZIN = 1 if neither are checked
0 Inches	☒	N/A	☐	DIMZIN	Integer	DIMZIN = 2 if only Inches is checked DIMZIN = 3 if only Feet is checked

(continued)

Table 9.6   Fields Specific to Text Format Dialogue   *(continued)*

Prompt	Default	Rec'd. Mech.	Rec'd. Arch.	DIMvar Affected	Type	Notes
Leading	☐	☐	N/A	DIMZIN	Integer	If checked, adds 4 to DIMZIN
Trailing	☐	☐	N/A	DIMZIN	Integer	If checked, adds 8 to DIMZIN
None	■	■	■	DIMTOL, DIMLIM	Switch	If picked, turns DIMLIM and DIMTOL off
Variance	☐	☐	☐	DIMTOL, DIMLIM	Switch	If picked, turns DIMLIM off, DIMTOL on
Limits	☐	☐	☐	DIMTOL, DIMTM	Switch	If picked, turns DIMLIM on, DIMTOL off
Upper Value	0.0	N/A	N/A	DIMTP	Scaled distance	If DIMTOL on, value is used as positive tolerance; if DIMLIM on, value is used to calculate upper limit
Lower Value	0.0	N/A	N/A	DIMTM	Scaled distance	If DIMTOL on, value is used as negative tolerance; if DIMLIM on, value is used to calculate lower limit
Show Alternate Units?	☐	☐	☐	DIMALT	Switch	If checked, stores On in DIMALT, ungrays Decimal Places, Scaling, Suffix
Decimal Places	2	N/A	N/A	DIMALTD	Integer	
Scaling	25.40000	N/A	N/A	DIMALTF	Scale	Default converts inches to mm
Suffix	none	N/A	N/A	DIMAPOST	String	

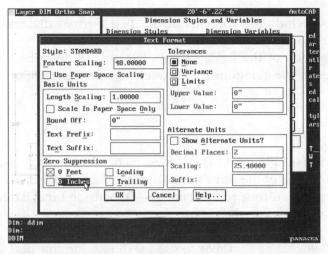

Figure 9.12 Text Format dialogue.

 NOTE

Under Zero Suppression, turn off 0 Inches. Leave all the other fields as is (see Figure 9.12).

FEATURES DIALOGUE

The Features dialogue (see Figure 9.13) includes the header section described above and several sections that include the contents of the Dimension Line, Arrows, and Text Position dialogues (see above). The Features

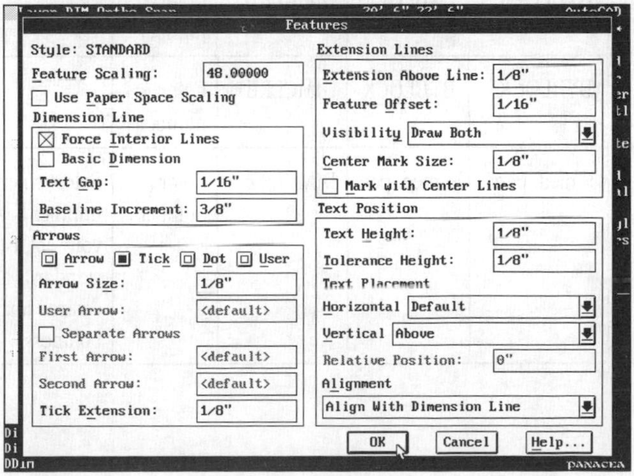

Figure 9.13 Features dialogue.

dialogue does not include the contents of the Text Format dialogue (see above) or Colors dialogue (see below).

The specifics of each of the fields in the dialogue are described in the sections above, as is the relationship between the prompts, values, and DIMvars.

COLORS DIALOGUE

The Colors dialogue (see Figure 9.14) includes the header section described above and fields for each of the three color DIMvars. Each color also can be set in the appropriate feature-specific dialogue—Dimension Line, Extension Lines, or Text Location—described above.

Dimension Line Color   Color to use for dimension line and arrow or tick.

Extension Line Color   Color to use for extension line.

Dimension Text Color   Color to use for dimension text.

Table 9.7 summarizes the relationship between the Colors dialogue's prompts, values, and DIMvars.

Table 9.7   Fields Specific to Colors Dialogue

Prompt	Default	Rec'd. Mech.	Rec'd. Arch.	DIMvar Affected	Type	Notes
Dimension Line Color	BYBLOCK	BYBLOCK	BYBLOCK	DIMCLRD	Color number	
Extension Line Color	BYBLOCK	BYBLOCK	BYBLOCK	DIMCLRE	Color number	
Dimension Text Color	BYBLOCK	= med. pen	= med. pen	DIMCLRT	Color number	Select color number based on your color-to-pen standards and desired text boldness

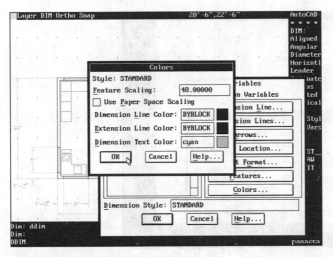

Figure 9.14   Colors dialogue.

 NOTE

We've already changed Dimension Text Color, so there's nothing more to do in this dialogue. Click on OK to close the Color subdialogue, and then OK again to close DDIM and save all changes to the STANDARD dimension styles. Notice that AutoCAD updates all the dimensions, including the radius dimension, which looks rather strange with the DIMvar settings appropriate to linear architectural dimensions. As mentioned earlier, the best approach is to set up a different style or two for leaders and radius dimensions.

THE MODIFY DIMENSIONS DIALOGUE

DDMODIFY (see Chapter 8) allows you to change the properties of a single Dimension entity, and it also displays some statistics about the Dimension. But you also can change properties for one or more entities with the DDCHPROP command, so the only time you need to use DDMODIFY is when you want to see the statistics. You can view (but not change) the dimension type, text, style, and handle. (See Figure 9.15 for an example.)

 Tip

To change the dimension style of one or more existing associative Dimensions, make the style you want to change to current, and then run the DIM UPDATE subcommand. DIM UPDATE is available from the Modify menu: pick Edit Dimensions, and then Update Dimension.

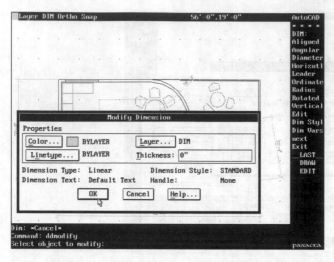

Figure 9.15   The Modify Dimensions dialogue box.

Summary

Dimension styles are a powerful tool for making your dimension work easier while maintaining consistency. The new DDIM dialogue provides a complete "control panel" for creating and managing dimension styles; use it first to set up a group of styles that meet your needs, and then continue to use it to select or inspect dimension styles as you work.

Text

The basic functionality for creating and editing text that isn't part of dimensions hasn't improved much in Release 12. Adding or modifying a lot of text in your drawings is still a big chore, but there are three included AutoLISP programs—ASCTEXT, CHTEXT, and PTEXT—that can ease the burden in some cases. These programs aren't new, but one of them has been added to the pull-down menu, and all of them are now documented in the *AutoCAD Extras Manual*. In addition, the new DDMODIFY command and revised DDEMODES dialogue have some useful text-handling capabilities.

The one major text change in Release 12 is the ability to use PostScript fonts in AutoCAD text styles. This feature greatly increases the number of fonts available for use in AutoCAD, and helps people with PostScript printers produce better-looking output.

In this section, we describe how to use the text utility programs and PostScript fonts. We'll also take this opportunity to introduce the new APPLOAD command for loading AutoLISP and ADS programs. The tutorials show examples of how you can take advantage of these features.

Loading AutoLISP Routines

Release 12 includes a new command called APPLOAD, which you can use to search for and load AutoLISP and ADS programs. The simple dialogue box interface makes it easier for beginners to use AutoCAD's sample routines or programs from CAD magazines or BBSs. But APPLOAD also is useful for experienced users, because it lets you build up a list of commonly used programs, and then load them in future AutoCAD sessions just by pointing and clicking (see Figure 9.16).

Assuming you've mastered the Release 12 file dialogue box from previous chapters, APPLOAD is easy to use. Start APPLOAD by typing the command name or by picking Applications... from the File menu. Then, just click on File... and locate the AutoLISP (.LSP) or ADS (.EXP or .EXE) file you want to add to the list. Click on the Load button to load the program into memory. If you need more details, see Chapter 1 of the *AutoCAD Extras Manual*.

Tip

APPLOAD uses a text file called APPLOAD.DFS to store the name of each AutoLISP and ADS program you load, so that the same programs are directly available in a future session. APPLOAD always stores APPLOAD.DFS in the current directory, which can be a problem if you start AutoCAD from a lot of different directories, as many DOS users do. Every time you start from a new directory, you must rebuild the APPLOAD list and, after awhile, you end up with a bunch of APPLOAD.DFS files on your hard disk, each of them slightly different.

One workaround, although it isn't very elegant, is to load most of the routines you're likely to want in one session, then copy the APPLOAD.DFS file from that directory into all the other directories you start AutoCAD from. A better solution is available on the CompuServe ACAD forum, where Autodesk has uploaded an improved version of APPLOAD that stores APPLOAD.DFS in one central place.

AutoLISP Routines for Text

AutoCAD still treats each line of text as a separate entity, which can make editing text slow and cumbersome. The ASCTEXT, CHTEXT, and PTEXT AutoLISP programs are designed to help in those situations. Use ASCTEXT to import an ASCII, or "plain text," file you've created in an outside editing

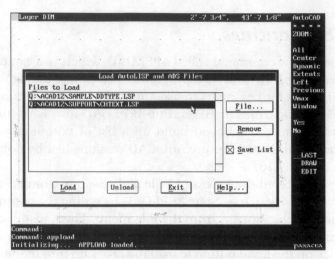

Figure 9.16   The APPLOAD Load AutoLISP and ADS
Files dialogue box.

program. Use CHTEXT for either line-at-a-time or "mass" editing of multiple
text strings. Use PTEXT to edit multiple lines of text as "paragraphs."

These routines are described in detail in the *AutoCAD Extras Manual*. We'll
summarize the features and operation of each command and then use two of
them in the tutorial at the end of this section.

ASCTEXT.LSP

ASCTEXT is a simple but useful utility for adding text from an ASCII file to
your drawing. ASCTEXT helps you overcome AutoCAD's limited text-editing
capabilities by letting you use any ASCII text editor to create and edit text.
This approach is usually much more efficient than the DTEXT and DDEDIT
commands for working with large blocks of text, such as general notes or
materials lists. The outside editor you use can be any stand-alone or memory-
resident text-editing utility, such as DOS EDIT, Sidekick, or Windows
Notepad.

The one thing to remember with ASCTEXT is that you must set the desired
text style (and layer) before running it. ASCTEXT lets you change many
things about the text when you import it, but the current style isn't one of
them. The easiest way to change the current text style is with the DDEMODES
Entity Creation Modes dialogue (see Chapter 6).

Once you've selected the current text style and layer, start ASCTEXT by
typing it at the Command: prompt or selecting Text and then Import Text
from the Draw menu. Select an ASCII file from the standard AutoCAD file
dialogue box. Respond to the prompts in order to specify how ASCTEXT
should place the text in the drawing.

Tip

If you want to preview an ASCII text file inside an AutoCAD dialogue box, use the DDTYPE sample routine located in the \ACAD\SAMPLE subdirectory. As Figure 9.16 shows, you can use APPLOAD to load DDTYPE.

ASCTEXT will let you import all the lines or just a range of lines from a file; but, since you can't preview the text before placement, you'd best know the contents well, or bring them in once, figure out the lines you really want, delete the text, and reimport only the lines you need. You can specify some text characteristics like height and justification, and you can set up columns of text for tables or a long sequence of general notes. See the "Commands for Entering Text" section below for a summary of features.

When you need to make major changes to the text after importing it, it may be more efficient to delete the text, edit the original ASCII file in your text editor, and reimport; editing text in place, even with the new commands, can be slow and error-prone. But, if you've done a lot of formatting to the text in AutoCAD, you may have to edit the text in place, so put off fancy formatting until late in the process of creating your drawing.

Windows Tip

The Windows multitasking feature makes it easy to edit and import text without leaving AutoCAD. You can keep a text editor such as Notepad running in one window while Release 12 for Windows is running in another. Switch to the Notepad window to enter or edit text, then switch back to the AutoCAD window for importing text with ASCTEXT.

CHTEXT.LSP

Think of this routine as a souped-up CHANGE command for Text entities. CHTEXT lets you edit one or more lines of text, and you can make modifications either one line at a time or on the whole group at once. CHTEXT can change the style or height of a group of Text entities, search for and replace strings within multiple lines of text, alter the justification of text, and do many other things besides. One of its uses is fine-tuning the characteristics of text imported with the ASCTEXT command.

Figure 9.17   A sample editing session with CHTEXT.

To use CHTEXT.LSP, you must load it into AutoCAD first. (See above for a description of how to load an AutoLISP routine.) Once the routine is loaded, type CHT to start it (not CHTEXT) and select the Text entities you want to edit. You don't have to worry about removing Lines or other types of entities from the selection set—CHTEXT knows to ignore them. Once you've specified a selection set, use the command line prompts, "Commands for Entering Text" section, and the *AutoCAD Extras Manual* to guide you through the options. Figure 9.17 shows a sample editing session with CHTEXT.

DDMODIFY.LSP (AND .DCL)

As discussed in Chapter 8, Modify Text is one of DDMODIFY's most flexible dialogues (see Figure 9.18). It puts most of the functionality of CHTEXT in a dialogue box, but it works only on one Text entity at a time. (See Chapter 8 for a description of DDMODIFY and the Modify Text dialogue box.)

PTEXT.LSP (AND .ADS)

This is a promising-sounding routine for editing text strings as "paragraphs" rather than as single lines. Unfortunately, it's awkward to use and prone to quirkiness. PTEXT lets you pick multiple lines of text, define a line length, and then add or remove characters with automatic word wrapping. The control characters for editing are similar to those used by the once-ubiquitous WordStar word processor, but there are enough differences to confuse even WordStar fans. It might be worth overcoming the difficult interface, except that PTEXT often just doesn't work correctly.

If you're still not deterred, you can load PTEXT.LSP from the

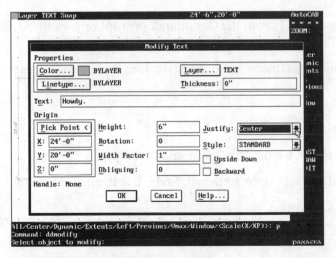

Figure 9.18 The Modify Text dialogue box.

\ACAD\SAMPLE directory and try it out. (See the *AutoCAD Extras Manual* for instructions and a table of control characters.)

 Tip

If you need to do much "paragraph-style" editing in AutoCAD, a better choice than PTEXT is one of the third-party text editing utilities. Among these are two shareware programs by Walt Craig: AutoEd and WCEdit, both available on CompuServe's ACAD forum. WCEdit is a full-blown programmer's editor that includes AutoCAD text-editing features (see Chapter 14 for more details). AutoEd is a simpler editor for non-programmers.

SUMMARY OF TEXT-RELATED COMMANDS AND ROUTINES

With all the commands and sample routines available for entering and editing text, it can be difficult to figure out which command is most appropriate for a given task. The following sections briefly summarize the capabilities of AutoCAD commands for entering and editing text.

COMMANDS FOR ENTERING TEXT

DTEXT

Description: Create Text entity or entities.

To start: Enter DTEXT from the Command: prompt or pick the Dynamic option in the Text submenu under the Draw menu.

Options: Justification (many options), Style, Height, Location, Text string.

TEXT

Description: Create Text entity.

To start: Enter TEXT from the Command: prompt.

Options: Justification (many options), Style, Location, Text string.

Tip: Use DTEXT instead.

ASCTEXT.LSP

Description: Imports ASCII text from an external file.

To start: Enter ASCTEXT from the Command: prompt or pick the Import Text option in the Text submenu under the Draw menu.

Options: Start point, Height, Rotation angle, Distance between lines, Underscore/overscore each line, Change text case, Set up columns.

COMMANDS FOR EDITING TEXT

DDEDIT

Description: Edit content of Text entity.

To start: Enter DDEDIT from the Command: prompt.

Options: Change content only.

Tip: Use CHTEXT to drive DDEDIT through multiple lines of text or to search and replace.

DDMODIFY.LSP

Description: Modify one Text entity.

To start: Enter DDMODIFY from the Command: prompt or pick Entity… from the Modify menu.

Options: Properties (Color, Layer, Linetype, Thickness), Text, Location, Height, Rotation, Width, Obliquing, Justification, Style, Upside Down, Backward.

Tip #1: set Width to .85 to squeeze in more text without adversely affecting appearance.   #2: Use this dialogue to experiment with how you want text to look in your drawing before entering multiple lines.

CHTEXT.LSP

Description: Modify one or more lines of text.

To start: Load the application, then enter CHT (not CHTEXT) from the Command: prompt.

Options: Height, Justification, Location, Rotation, Style, Text, Undo, Width.

Tip #1: Use CHTEXT to drive DDEDIT through multiple lines of text. #2: Use DDMODIFY, instead, for single lines of text.

CHANGE (Text Entity)

Description: CHANGE Text entity.

To start: Enter CHANGE from the Command: prompt or pick Change from the Modify menu.

Options: Properties (Color, Elevation, Layer, Linetype, Thickness), Location, Text Style, Height, Rotation Angle, Text String.

Tip: Modify properties with DDMODIFY instead.

PTEXT.LSP

Description: Edit text as paragraphs.

To start: Load the application, then enter PTEXT or PT from the Command: prompt.

Options: Justification, Text String, Location.

Tip: Use a third-party utility instead.

DDTYPE.LSP

Description: Display an ASCII file in a dialogue box.

To start: Load the application, then enter DDTYPE from the Command: prompt.

Options: None.

A Word About PostScript Fonts

Release 12 adds a number of PostScript-related capabilities to AutoCAD, most notably the ability to import from and export to PostScript files. These features allow a great deal of flexibility for those doing presentations and desktop publishing. They can be useful for importing artwork (e.g., for a logo) into a drawing, or for including drawings in PostScript documents. However, taking full advantage of these features requires a PostScript printer or other output device. Also, there are many complexities with using PostScript images, and getting the images to appear and plot correctly can be a challenge.

There is one PostScript-related capability, however, that any AutoCAD user can take advantage of: the ability to include PostScript fonts in AutoCAD drawings. Text drawn using some of the PostScript fonts included in AutoCAD is shown in Figure 9.19.

There are some problems and limitations that can trip up the unwary, though. In the publishing world from which PostScript came, text height is measured differently than it is in the drafting world. In order to make PostScript font text match regular AutoCAD font text, you need to specify a height about one third larger than you normally would. For example, where you would use 0.125" for ROMANS.SHX, try 0.165" for the CIBT____.PFB hand-lettered PostScript font.

AutoCAD is able to plot PostScript fonts on non-PostScript devices, such as a pen plotter or LaserJet printer, but with one limitation. On a non-PostScript device, the fonts will appear as outlines only; they won't be filled in. In order to get filled fonts, you must use the PSOUT command and send the resulting file to a PostScript device.

Figure 9.19   Text drawn using some of AutoCAD's PostScript fonts.

Even with a PostScript device, there can be problems. If the printer doesn't have the font you want to use (a likely occurrence with obscure fonts, such as those included with AutoCAD) or if AutoCAD's font mapping table isn't set up correctly, your PostScript plots will appear with Courier text in them.

Tip

To change the font mapping table, you must edit the file ACAD.PSF. See Chapter 14 in the *AutoCAD Reference Manual* and Chapter 10 in the *AutoCAD Customization Manual* for more information on this and other aspects of using PostScript with AutoCAD.

Despite the limitations, you still might want to use PostScript fonts with non-PostScript devices in two situations: when you want a "hand-lettered look" to your text, and when the PostScript font outlines are adequate for title blocks and such. Release 12 includes two fonts (City Blueprint and Country Blueprint) that mimic hand-drawn lettering in an upright and an oblique style. In most cases, the lack of outline filling isn't a problem with these fonts, because the "outlines" are so close together that they merge (see Figure 9.19). The remaining fonts sometimes are appropriate for large, fancy titles when you want to show outlined rather than solid letters.

Release 12's PostScript fonts are defined in .PFB files stored in the \ACAD\FONTS directory. You can use these files directly when defining a new text style, but if you intend to create much text with a PostScript font, it's best to compile the font into a standard AutoCAD shape file (.SHX). AutoCAD generates compiled font text more quickly than it does uncompiled font text. Compiling a PostScript font is a simple matter of running the COMPILE command, which is available on the File menu.

One word of caution, however, about a copyright issue that has not been emphasized enough. If you compile a third-party PostScript font (i.e., one that doesn't come with Release 12), in most cases, you cannot legally give the .SHX files to other Release 12 users. In particular, you can't buy a bunch of Type 1 PostScript fonts, compile them, and distribute the resulting .SHX files around your company.

Since we've spent so much time in this book talking about how important it is to centralize and make available shared resources, we want to emphasize that you can't do this with PostScript fonts, whether in their original or compiled form. Be careful with the fonts you compile, and don't accept .SHX files from others unless you know that the files are free of copyright restrictions.

FONTS AND PERFORMANCE

As mentioned in Chapter 4, *Basic Setup and Prototypes*, it's important to use the "right" fonts in your drawings. Simpler fonts regenerate, redraw, and plot faster than complicated ones. But the simplest font, TXT, is embarrassingly ugly. ROMANS is a good compromise.

The same performance concern holds, only more so, for PostScript fonts, since they tend to be more elaborate. Compiling the fonts, as recommended above, helps minimize the performance loss. Among PostScript fonts, the hand-lettered fonts mentioned above look good and are reasonably fast to use, especially in compiled versions.

If performance really starts to suffer in drawings with lots of text, you can use the QTEXT command to turn on quick text mode. This mode draws an enclosing rectangle where text normally appears. You also can set the option in the DDRMODES Drawing Aids dialogue.

Text Tutorial

Now that we've reviewed the text and PostScript options, we'll experiment with a few of them by adding some text to the RECROOM drawing. Refer to Figure 9.24 as you work through the tutorial.

1. Change to the TEXT layer and make sure Snap is set to 6".

Use the DDLMODES or LAYER command to make TEXT the current layer.

Snap should be set to 6".

2. Add the text-handling programs to the APPLOAD list.

```
Command: APPLOAD
```
or
Pick Applications... under the File menu.

The Load AutoLISP and ADS Files dialogue appears.

Use the File... button to add CHTEXT, DDTYPE, and, if you like, PTEXT to the Files to Load list (see Figure 9.20).

Figure 9.16 shows the completed list.

Pick Exit to leave APPLOAD.

We'll actually load the programs we need later.

3. Compile the City Blueprint (CIBT) PostScript font.

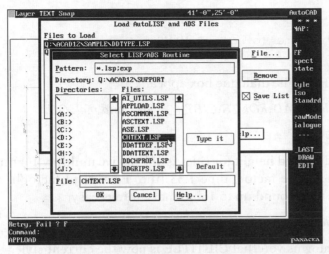

Figure 9.20 Adding CHTEXT to the APPLOAD list.

Command: COMPILE

or

Pick Compile... from the File menu.

The Select Shape or Font File dialogue appears (see Figure 9.21).

Select the file \ACAD\FONTS\CIBT____.PFB and pick OK.

AutoCAD compiles the font and creates CIBT____.SHX.

4. Create a text style for the drawing title using the CIBT____.SHX font file.

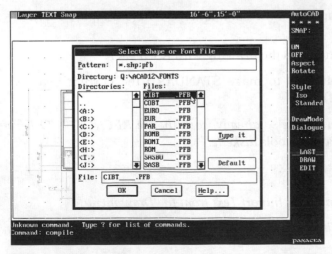

Figure 9.21 Compiling the City Blueprint PostScript font.

```
Command: STYLE
Text style name (or ?) <ROMANS>: CIBTITLE
New style.
```

The Select Font File dialogue box appears.

Select the file \ACAD\FONTS\CIBT____.SHX and pick OK.

```
Height <0'-0">: 16"
```

Our desired plotted height for titles is 1/4", so we multiply 1/4 time 48 (the drawing scale factor) time 1.33 (the "PostScript factor") to get 15.96", and then round up to 16" to make things easy.

Accept the defaults for the remaining prompts.

AutoCAD informs you that CIBTITLE is now the current style.

5. Put the title: RECREATION ROOM under the recreation room.

```
Command: DTEXT
or
```
Pick Text... from the Draw menu, then pick the Dynamic option.
```
Justify/Style/<Start point>: J
Align/Fit/Center/Middle/Right/TL/TC/TR/ML/MC/MR/BL/
BC/BR: C
Center point: Pick or type the point 32',2'.
Rotation angle <0>: <Enter>
Text: RECREATION ROOM<Enter>
Text: <Enter>
```

The title appears in the hand-lettered font (see Figure 9.24).

6. Add some notes to the drawing with ASCTEXT.

Use **DDEMODES** to make **STANDARD** the current text style (see Figure 9.22).

If you haven't done so already, copy the file RECNOTES.TXT from the AutoCAD Power Tools *diskette.*

```
Command: ASCTEXT
or
```
Pick Text and then Import Text from the Draw menu.

From the File to Read dialogue, select RECNOTES.TXT, and then pick OK.

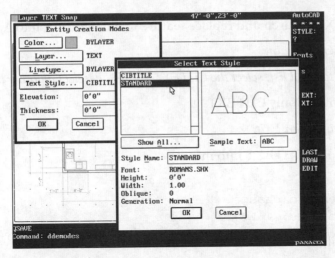

Figure 9.22 Setting the current style with DDEMODES.

Start point or Center/Middle/Right/?: *Pick or type 12',41'
as the starting point for text.*
Height *<default>*: 6"
Change text options? <N>: *<Enter>*

ASCTEXT imports the text from RECNOTES.TXT.

If you find the number of lines of text is too large to fit in one column, you can set up multiple text columns by answering Yes to the Change text options? prompt.

Figure 9.23 shows the completed notes.

Figure 9.23 Notes entered with the ASCTEXT routine.

7. Use CHTEXT's search and replace feature to change March to April.

Start APPLOAD again.

In the Files to Load list, select the CHTEXT line and deselect all other lines.

We want to load only CHTEXT.

Pick Load and then Exit.

AutoCAD loads CHTEXT into memory.

```
Command: CHT
Select text to change.
Select objects: ALL
```

CHTEXT filters out entities that aren't Text.

```
Select objects: <Enter>
10 text entities found.
Height/Justification/Location/Rotation/Style/Text/
Undo/Width: T
Search and replace text. Individually/Retype/
<Globally>: <Enter>
```

Changing text globally works like search and replace in a word processor.

```
Match string : March
New string : April
Changed 3 text lines.
```

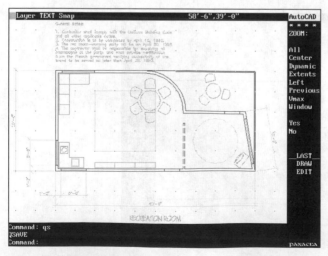

Figure 9.24 RECROOM with the completed text

CHTEXT changes the three instances of March to April.

```
Height/Justification/Location/Rotation/Style/Text/Undo/
Width: <Enter>
```

Figure 9.24 shows the revised notes and title.

Turn all layers back on before saving your drawing.

Dimensions, Text, PostScript, and Workgroups

For both dimensions and text, styles and standards are key. You should include in your prototype(s) a set of dimension styles and text styles that cover the majority of the needs of your workgroup. This will save all users a great deal of time and effort. Chapter 4, *Basic Setup and Prototypes*, contains more detailed information on how to include styles in prototypes. Make sure your workgroup members understand the value and use of associative dimensions and dimension styles, and help everyone develop a consistent approach to using them.

There are two PostScript issues you should be careful of. The first is font licensing. Most font licensing agreements prohibit you from making .SHX files compiled from PostScript fonts purchased by one user available to other users. This can get trickier than you think. For instance, it would seem that the PostScript fonts included in Release 12 could be freely shared around your workgroup or company, whether "as is" or compiled into .SHX files. But the license for versions of AutoCAD prior to Release 12 doesn't include these PostScript fonts, so you need to be careful about distributing compiled versions of even the standard Release 12 PostScript fonts. Plus, the font files could easily find their way to contractors or others who need to take drawing files offsite. So, it's easy to commit license violations if you're not careful. Think about this problem before you start using lots of fancy fonts; it may be best to stick with the stock non-PostScript fonts if your drawings will be shared by many users.

The second PostScript-related concern is a productivity issue. PostScript can be a tremendous time sink. Getting the right fonts on your system and your PostScript printers, doing check prints to make sure the font really looks right, and being locked into PostScript printers for faithful output are some of the issues that cause problems, even if your PostScript use is limited to fonts. Creating PostScript files so you can import them, exporting to PostScript, and modifying the result—all of these are opportunities to spend tremendous amounts of time doing things that, at first, seem simple.

A professional desktop publisher has spent about as much time becoming an expert as a top-notch AutoCAD user, and getting even so-so results takes a lot of work. Save PostScript for when you really need it and, when you do, designate one person in your workgroup or company to become the internal PostScript consultant to everyone. (You already may have a "presentations expert" who can add PostScript to his or her repertoire.) He or she can be responsible for fine-tuning the appearance of documents and creating PostScript elements that can be imported by others.

This person can serve as a test pilot who spares others from expending a lot of time and ending up with poor results. If the workload grows beyond what can be handled by one person, you'll have a sense of the kind of training and experience needed to get good results throughout your workgroup. Then, you can accurately plan and budget for the expenditure of time and money that will be needed to get the results you want.

10

Xrefs, Blocks, and Attributes

As the amount of data in and related to drawings increases, the drawing capabilities of AutoCAD become a proportionately smaller part of the picture. Of greater and greater importance is the need to see the drawing as an element in a database, which connects to other data elements and is itself included in other drawings. Release 12 makes managing these elements easier.

The fastest way to get a specific drawing done may still be to start with a blank screen, a paper sketch, and an early deadline. But projects get done faster with reuse of drawing elements, and if new projects can leverage off earlier ones, productivity can increase greatly. So can the place of CAD as a central element in the business of a company, and not just as a technical exercise. The appropriate use of external references and Blocks improves productivity and reduces errors and frustration. Attaching data to Blocks by means of Attributes can further increase the usefulness of drawings outside the drafting arena.

About This Chapter

Xrefs, Blocks, and Attributes aren't new to Release 12, but the interface to all of them has been improved with dialogue boxes, and several improvements add much needed flexibility to external references. Users who share Xrefs over a network will be especially well-served by the changes.

The two major changes to Xrefs are better simultaneous access and more control over layer settings. You now can externally reference a drawing while someone else is modifying it. This feature is a nod to how things are done in the real world, with constant, interrelated changes occurring, and it removes one of the big limitations to using Xrefs over a network. In Release 12, you also get better control over the color, linetype, on/off, and freeze/ thaw settings for layers in externally referenced drawings. Both of these changes make it easier to use external references instead of simply copying geometry into multiple drawings.

Another improvement is that entities nested inside of Blocks and Xrefs can now be dimensioned. Again, this change adds to the flexibility of Blocks and Xrefs, so that you can more often leave them whole rather than exploding them.

This chapter is designed to provide a context for external references, Blocks, and Attributes, so that you can understand their application, rather than just the mechanics of the commands. We describe the new and revised features in enough detail for you to master them, but we focus on when and how to put them to use.

Improving the techniques and sophistication you bring to organizing drawings with Xrefs and Blocks is at least as important as improving your drafting skills. You can get only so fast at drawing lines and circles (or with a third-party application, wall assemblies and pipes). You can always improve the management of your drawings and drawing-related data, though, and skillful data management is what makes the difference between marginally successful CAD and truly productive CAD.

Features Demonstrated in This Chapter

Release 12 introduces new interfaces to existing commands for Xrefs, Blocks, and Attributes. Also, the DDMODIFY Modify Entities command works for all three of these kinds of entities, and as usual, AutoCAD includes a few AutoLISP programs that solve some problems for each. Among the features demonstrated and discussed in this chapter are the following:

- For Xrefs: soft locks; maintaining local specifications for layer colors and linetypes; the XREFCLIP AutoLISP program for clipping Xrefs in paper space.

- For Blocks: new dialogues for inserting and modifying Blocks; the XPLODE.LSP AutoLISP program, which gives you finer control over exploding a Block.

- For Attributes: dialogue boxes for creating, editing, and modifying Attribute Definitions, and for entering and extracting Attribute values; the ATTREDEF AutoLISP program, which makes it easier to add Attributes to a Block Definition.

These capabilities are an important step toward managing and reusing CAD data rather than re-creating the wheel (or screw, nut, rocket ship, etc.) every time one is needed. They also make it easier to manage textual data in the drawing. These changes can bring on a new attitude toward CAD drawing and data management that will ultimately reduce workloads, frustration, and missed deadlines. We recommend that you spend time becoming adept with the features described in this chapter.

About the Example

In this chapter, we add to the RECROOM drawing a title block composed of two parts: an externally referenced file containing the linework and constant text, and a Block containing Attributes. If you don't have an up-to-date version of RECROOM as of the previous chapter, you can use the RRCH10.DWG file on the *AutoCAD Power Tools* disk as a starting point. Also, copy the file RECTB.DWG from the disk; you'll need it during the Xref tutorial.

AutoCAD As a Publishing Program

In a desktop publishing program, a document is often like a bulletin board to which various pieces from other programs are pinned. The document itself has little data; instead, it contains formatting information about where the pieces reside, how text (imported from another program) flows from one column or page to another, and so on. The actual data resides in documents that "belong" to word processing, illustration, and other kinds of programs. Various kinds of links allow the desktop publishing document to be updated as the pieces it "contains" are updated from within the other programs.

AutoCAD can increasingly be used in a similar way. Although most of the pieces in a drawing are created in AutoCAD, any given drawing may not contain much "original" data. Instead, it can be a collection of external references and Blocks; the important contents of the drawing itself are the arrangement of the pieces, dimensioning, added text, and other elements that have more to do with visual communication than with geometry.

Blocks can also contain variable text Attributes that indicate the characteristics of that particular insertion of the Block: identification number, brand, etc. This data can be used for a variety of purposes and can be exported to other programs for further manipulation or report extraction.

Paper space is a refinement of the "CAD as bulletin board" theme. When using Paper space, you are doing desktop publishing just as much as CAD. In fact, this "model" approach is a clever way of separating the concerns of creating accurate geometry from those of creating a useful presentation. We'll discuss this aspect more in the next chapter, which includes coverage of paper space.

So, AutoCAD is used in three ways: as a tool for creating accurate geometrical representations; as a front end for the entry and manipulation of text data about entities; and as a repository and publishing tool for geometry and graphical elements created in AutoCAD itself and in other programs. Most of the information in previous chapters has focused on the use of AutoCAD as a tool for creating accurate geometry; this chapter focuses on its use as an entry point and storage engine for text data and as a repository for geometric and graphical elements. Each of these uses deserves separate attention as you plan and execute your drawings.

Users of Release 12 for Windows will get a major advantage in working with external references and Blocks. The ability of the Windows version to keep several AutoCAD files open simultaneously makes it easy to search files for elements you need.

External References

External references (Xrefs) were among the most important new features in Release 11. Release 12, through the mechanisms described below, improves the flexibility and ease of use of Xrefs.

Xrefs and Blocks share two benefits: They save drawing work up front, and they save maintenance work over time. The first benefit, saving work up front, is achieved as soon as you insert a Block or attach an Xref more than once. The second, saving maintenance work over time, occurs only as time passes, and changes to a single Block or Xref allow you to automatically update numerous drawings. So in using either Xrefs or Blocks, there is one key goal: keeping the original data in a single place and leaving all the Xrefs or Blocks that refer to it "whole" (i.e., not exploding them).

Both Xrefs and Blocks have their place in any drawing management strategy, but Xrefs have the following advantages over Blocks:

- Xrefs are automatically updated as their source drawings change. This eliminates the need to specifically update Block Definitions in all the drawings that use a given Block.

- Xref geometry is not actually copied into your drawing file; it's merely "borrowed" from the external file and held in memory. Thus, Xrefs can save a lot of disk space.

The Release 12 changes to Xref capabilities make it easier to edit a drawing with external references while the referenced files are being updated (soft locks); to maintain layer settings in the local drawing without changing the referenced one (the VISRETAIN system variable); to modify characteristics of Xrefs (Modify External Reference dialogue); to use part of an externally referenced drawing, rather than the whole thing (XREFCLIP); and to dimension nested entities inside Xrefs. Taken together, these improvements increase the number of situations in which you can use external references.

Using Soft Locks

Soft locks are easy to understand because they remove a former problem, rather than add new functionality. The problem in previous versions was that drawing files were locked when in use, which limited how you could use them as Xrefs over a network. Some degree of locking is crucial on a network, since you don't want two people to be allowed to edit the same file at the same time; the first person to save would have his or her changes overwritten by the last one. But what if one of the users wants only read access to a file? He or she should be able to have that kind of access, even while someone else has write access to it, and this is what soft locks allow.

Instead of a "hard lock" that denies file access to all except to the person who's actually editing a file, a soft lock allows a file to be externally referenced, which is a form of read access even while the file is being edited. This makes a difference during three operations: attaching, reloading, and binding. The XREF command and the Attach, Reload, and Bind options are available in the File menu, as well as from the command line (see Figure 10.1).

Attaching is the default option for the XREF command; it creates the reference to the external drawing. Reloading "refreshes" the Xref so that the

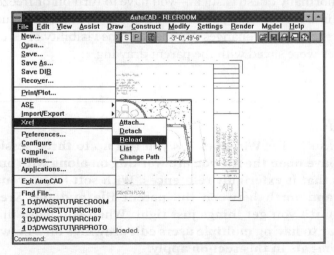

Figure 10.1 The Xref option of the File menu.

Tip

The one concern that soft locks raise is that someone might be making important changes to an externally referenced drawing while you're referring to it. To prevent surprises, reload Xrefs before you do any major creation or editing of geometry that is dependent on objects in external references. A good habit is to reload at the end of an editing session, just before you close a drawing, so that you'll be alerted to any changes that happened during your editing session.

most current version of the referenced drawing is loaded into memory. Xrefs are refreshed automatically when a drawing is loaded, and on command during editing.

Binding an Xref is the process of making an external reference a permanent part of your drawing by turning it into a Block. This procedure removes the pointer to the external file, copies the file into the current drawing as a Block Definition, and inserts it where the Xref was. Binding also constructs new names for symbols, such as layers, that had been in the referenced drawing, and adds them to your drawing.

The VISRETAIN System Variable

The VISRETAIN system variable was added to Release 11 as a way of giving some control over layers in external references. Normally, AutoCAD reads layer settings from the external references each time you load a drawing containing Xrefs. Because of this, turning off or freezing an externally referenced layer normally doesn't "stick"—you have to turn off or freeze the layer again each time you load the parent drawing. With VISRETAIN turned on in Release 11, though, any changes you made to the visibility of layers in external references were saved with the parent drawing.

Windows Tip

Because Release 12 for Windows lets you run up to three sessions, you can now have open the file you are working on along with one or two drawings that it externally references. With soft locks, you can switch back and forth between the parent file and the Xref(s), editing them until you get things just right. When you work in this way, it's similar to having multiple users edit drawings on a network, so all the comments in this section apply.

Tip

In general, you want to avoid binding Xrefs, since it cuts the link to the external drawings. However, you *should* bind all Xrefs when you need to create an archival set of AutoCAD drawings (do this on a copy of the drawings, so that you can still work on the "live," unbound drawings later if necessary). By binding, you ensure that the archived drawings don't accidentally change when someone modifies an externally referenced drawing. Also, you ensure that AutoCAD can "find" all the pieces of a drawing, even after you move them to a diskette or tape.

In Release 12, VISRETAIN extends this control to layer colors and linetypes. This enhancement is important when you use an Xref in multiple drawings and want the linetype or plotted lineweight to be different in some of them.

You might think that VISRETAIN=1 would always be the preferred setting, but that isn't so. Sometimes, you want to control layer visibility, color, and linetype by setting them in an externally referenced drawing (so that changes to these settings automatically appear in all drawings that reference it). Other times, you want to control the settings from each individual parent drawing. There isn't one "right" way to do it; you'll have to analyze the drawing management needs of your office and projects. You'll probably come up with a preferred approach for most projects, at which time you can set VISRETAIN in your prototype drawings

The Layer Control dialogue box (see Figure 10.2) shows only the "local" settings for layer control. If you want to know what the settings are in the externally referenced file, you'll have to open it and examine them directly.

The Modify External Reference Dialogue

The DDMODIFY Modify External Reference dialogue, which we described in Chapter 8, allows you to control many of the characteristics of an Xref (see Figure 10.3). Two additional comments are in order here:

Tip

Earlier versions of the *AutoCAD Reference Manual* list the values of VISRETAIN backward in the System Variables table in Appendix A. VISRETAIN=0 (the default) means that the layer settings in the external file always control; VISRETAIN=1 means that layer setting changes in the parent file are retained.

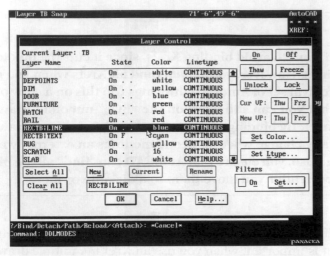

Figure 10.2   Layer Control dialogue box with externally referenced files.

- When VISRETAIN is set to 0 (the default), any changes you make to color or linetype in the Properties area will last for only the current drawing session.

- With the Columns, Rows, Col Spacing, and Row Spacing fields, you can create a rectangular array out of an Xref, and the array will act like a single entity. This is like the MINSERT command for Blocks.

The XREFCLIP AutoLISP Program

This AutoLISP application allows you to clip an external reference; that is, select only a specified rectangular area of the externally referenced file to display. XREFCLIP isn't quite as clever as you might first think, though. It does the clipping by entering paper space (that is, setting TILEMODE to 0) and putting the external reference in a viewport. It then uses the built-in clipping capability of a viewport to clip the Xref.

WHY NOT XREFCLIP?

There's some performance and conceptual overhead to using paper space (see the next chapter), so you may not want to use XREFCLIP unless you're already committed to paper space for the drawing. Also, the viewport must be rectangular, which does not always allow you to get just the part of the external drawing that you want. In order to clip an oddly shaped area, you'd have to edit the externally referenced drawing or create a complicated assembly of abutting viewports.

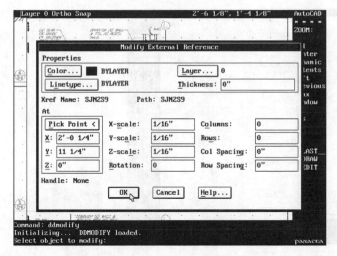

Figure 10.3 Modify External Reference dialogue box.

If you have to go to all that trouble, you may want to really do things right and break down the original drawing into the pieces you need. Here are some suggested steps for doing so:

1. Create a new drawing containing just the geometry you need from the drawing you were going to externally reference.

2. Modify the drawing you were going to externally reference, so that it has an Xref to the newly extracted geometry.

3. Put an external reference to the newly extracted geometry in your own drawing.

This process is depicted in Figure 10.4. It gives you the external reference you need for your own drawing, without the need for clipping or paper space, and sufficiently preserves the original drawing so that external references to it will still work. Also, it's quite possible that the newly created drawing will be needed again by others, amortizing the effort you put into creating it.

USING XREFCLIP

Having given you some reasons not to use XREFCLIP and a suggestion for how to avoid it, we now admit that it may be just what you need in some cases. If your drawing needs paper space anyway, or circumstances prevent you from modifying the Xref, XREFCLIP may be the way to go. To use it, follow these steps:

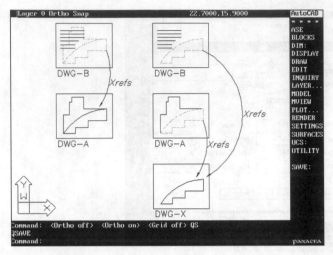

Figure 10.4   One file with external references to another versus two files with external references to a third.

1. Load the **XREFCLIP.LSP** file from the **\ACAD\SAMPLE** subdirectory.

Instructions for loading AutoLISP files with the new **APPLOAD** dialogue box are given in the "Loading AutoLISP Routines" section of Chapter 9.

2. Start the application.

```
Command: XREFCLIP
or
XC
```

3. Follow the prompts in the application.

You will be asked to enable paper space; to name the drawing you want to reference; to enter the name of a new layer to put it on; to specify the clipping rectangle; and to specify a ratio of paper space units to model space units (this ratio will determine the scale of the Xref). Finally, you'll be asked for an insertion point; the clipped, externally referenced geometry then appears in your drawing.

See the *AutoCAD Extras Manual* for more detailed instructions.

Xref Tutorial

Title blocks are one common use for Xrefs, and are a good way to get acquainted with them if you haven't already. At the beginning of a job, you can create a simple title block and reference it in each project drawing. When it comes time to plot the final drawings, you can embellish the title block with fancy fonts and logos, and it will automatically be updated in each project drawing. This approach not only saves you the time of revising a title block in many drawings, but it also saves lots of regen and redraw time by dispensing with complicated title block geometry until you need it.

The one complication is that Xrefs, unlike Blocks, can't contain Attribute Definitions (described later in this chapter). You can't create an externally referenced title block that contains variable text for the sheet number, name, and other information that changes from sheet to sheet. A good compromise, then, is to use an Xref for the unchanging part of the title block (linework, project name, company logo, etc.) and a Block with Attributes for the variaable text.

In the following tutorial, we'll attach the externally referenced part of the title block, and then at the end of the chapter we'll add the Block with Attributes. Chapter 5 of the *AutoCAD Tutorial Manual* also includes a tutorial on Xrefs, and those users who didn't learn about them in Release 11 will find it helpful.

1. Load RECROOM.

Use your drawing from the previous chapter, or copy RRCH10.DWG from the *AutoCAD Power Tools* disk.

Also copy RECTB.DWG (the title block) from the *AutoCAD Power Tools* disk to your tutorial subdirectory.

2. Create a new layer called TB.

Use the DDLMODES or LAYER command to make a new layer called TB and set it current. Leave its color as #7 and linetype as Continuous.

3. Attach the file RECTB.DWG as an external reference.

Make sure you've copied RECTB.DWG from the *AutoCAD Power Tools* disk into your tutorial subdirectory.

Erase the rectangular border around the drawing; our title block includes trim marks.

```
Command: XREF
?/Bind/Detach/Path/Reload/<Attach>: <Enter>
Xref to Attach: RECTB
```
or
Pick Xref from the File menu, then Attach... from the submenu.
In the Select File to Attach dialogue, pick the RECTB.DWG file.
```
Insertion point: 0,0
```

```
X- scale factor <1> / Corner / XYZ: 48
Y- scale factor (default=X): <Enter>
```

The title block was drawn at full scale (i.e., 1=1), so we scale it up by the drawing scale factor, which is 48 for a 1/4" = 1' drawing.

```
Rotation angle <0>: <Enter>
```

The drawing title block will appear. (See Figure 10.5.)

4. Modify some layers and set VISRETAIN.

```
Command: DDLMODES
```

AutoCAD displays the Layer Control dialogue. Notice that the externally referenced layer names contain the filename and a vertical bar (i.e, the DOS "pipe" symbol) before the actual layer name (see Figure 10.2).

Freeze RECTB\TEXT and change the color of RECTB\LINE to blue (5).

```
Command: VISRETAIN
New value for VISRETAIN <0>: 1
```

We'll turn VISRETAIN off again in a moment, but let's see what effect it has.

5. Save RECROOM, open RECTB, and add a circle.

Use the QSAVE command to save RECROOM.

Open RECTB.

Add a circle for the architect's registration stamp, as shown in Figure 10.6.

6. Return to RECROOM and reset VISRETAIN.

Save RECTB and open RECROOM.

The title block text is still frozen and the linework remains blue because we set VISRETAIN. In this instance, we probably want to leave VISRETAIN off.

```
Command: VISRETAIN
New value for VISRETAIN <1>: 0
```

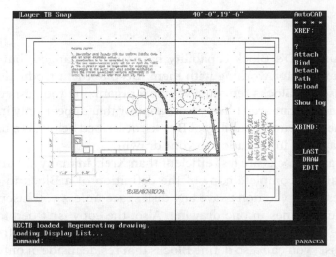

Figure 10.5 The externally referenced title block.

Now reload the Xref.

```
Command: XREF
?/Bind/Detach/Path/Reload/<Attach>: R
Xref(s) to reload: *
```
or
Pick Xref from the File menu, then Reload from the submenu.

AutoCAD displays the revised title block, as shown in Figure 10.6.

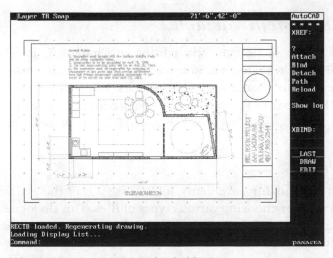

Figure 10.6 The revised title block.

Blocks

In Release 12, AutoCAD's Block capability hasn't been changed, but new dialogues are available for working with them. Despite the introduction of Xrefs with Release 11, Blocks remain a valuable organizing tool, especially for small components that aren't likely to change or that appear only in one drawing. Also, the Attribute capability of Blocks, described below, is a useful way to tie nongraphical information to your drawing.

On the other hand, Blocks are less efficient than Xrefs in many situations. AutoCAD maintains a complete copy of the definition of a Block in each drawing that uses it, so you don't save any disk space unless you insert the same Block multiple times in one drawing. Also, the copy isn't tied to the original, separate drawing file (assuming that the Block was inserted from a drawing file on disk; you can also define Blocks that reside inside of only one drawing). As a result, Blocks aren't updated automatically when the original changes.

As with Xrefs, the goal in using Blocks is to leave them whole and not to resort to exploding them. The changes and additions to Block capabilities in Release 12 support this goal. Dialogue box front ends make it easier to insert Blocks (DDINSERT) and modify them (DDMODIFY). The GRIPBLOCK system variable allows you to control whether one or many grips appear on Blocks, and the ability to dimension entities nested inside Blocks eliminates one excuse for exploding them. When you finally give up, the XPLODE AutoLISP routine gives you more control over the properties taken on by the entities that get created from the exploded Block.

The GRIPBLOCK System Variable

As we described in the section on grip editing in Chapter 7, Release 12 provides the GRIPBLOCK system variable so that you can decide how many visible object snap points should appear on Blocks. In general, you should leave GRIPBLOCK set to 0, but if you do a lot of grip editing and need to snap to Block geometry, temporarily set it to 1. Figure 10.7 shows the difference.

The Insert Dialogue

One of the most helpful improvements to Release 12 is the redesigned standard file dialogue for choosing various types of files. This dialogue, with different names and sometimes a slightly different layout, shows up over and over again with different commands. From a philosophical point of view, the file dialogue underscores the increasing degree to which an AutoCAD user's job is data management as well as geometry creation; from a practical point of view, it just makes things easier.

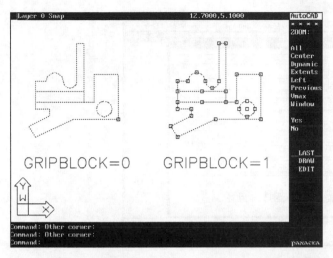

Figure 10.7   GRIPBLOCK set to 0 versus GRIPBLOCK set to 1.

The DDINSERT dialogue box for inserting Blocks is a good example. It combines the ability to locate drawing files on disk with the ability to select from a list of Blocks already defined in the current drawing. Unlike the INSERT command, DDINSERT attempts to clarify the subtle distinction between inserting an already defined Block and inserting an outside drawing, so that it becomes a defined Block.

Once you've found the Block you want, DDINSERT lets you specify the insertion point, scale, and rotation, either by entering parameters or by picking on the screen. You can even explode the Block on insertion if needed.

To start the Insert dialogue (see Figure 10.8), enter the command DDINSERT or pick Insert... off the Draw menu. The fields in the dialogue are as follows:

- The Select Block Name is where you specify a Block to be inserted. The Block... button brings up a list of Blocks already defined in the current file. The File... button, on the other hand, is for inserting an outside drawing.

- The Options area has three subareas and a checkbox that controls access to them. If Specify Parameters on Screen is checked, the subareas are grayed out and you specify the insertion factors by picking and typing at the Command: prompt, just as you do with the INSERT command.

- If Specify Parameters on Screen is not checked, you can specify the insertion point, scale, and rotation angle in the dialogue box. As with other dialogue boxes, the scale factors are displayed in (rounded) units of measurement, rather than dimensionless, unrounded scale factors, as they should be.

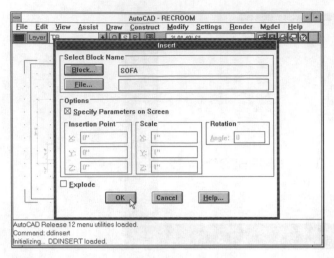

Figure 10.8   Insert dialogue box.

- The Explode checkbox specifies that the Block will be exploded on insertion. If you want to explode the Block but want finer control over how it's done, don't check this box; bring the Block in whole and use the XPLODE command described below.

The Modify Block Insertion Dialogue

The DDMODIFY Modify Block Insertion dialogue box should be familiar, since it's almost identical to the Modify External Reference dialogue mentioned earlier. Modify Block Insertion allows you to control most of the characteristics of a Block (see Figure 10.9). See Chapter 8 for more information about DDMODIFY, but two additional comments are in order here:

- The X-scale, Y-scale, and Z-scale fields are handy when you need to change one scale factor independently of the others, or when you want to make an unequally scaled Block equally scaled.

- The Columns, Rows, Col Spacing, and Row Spacing fields are the equivalent of using the MINSERT (multiple Block insert) command. These fields create a rectangular array that AutoCAD treats as a single entity.

The XPLODE AutoLISP Program

This AutoLISP application allows you more detailed control over the process of exploding a Block (converting it into its component parts and adding them to the drawing as separate entities). Despite the advantages of keeping both external references and Blocks whole whenever possible, you sometimes do have to explode a Block, and this routine makes it easier to do so in a way that makes sense.

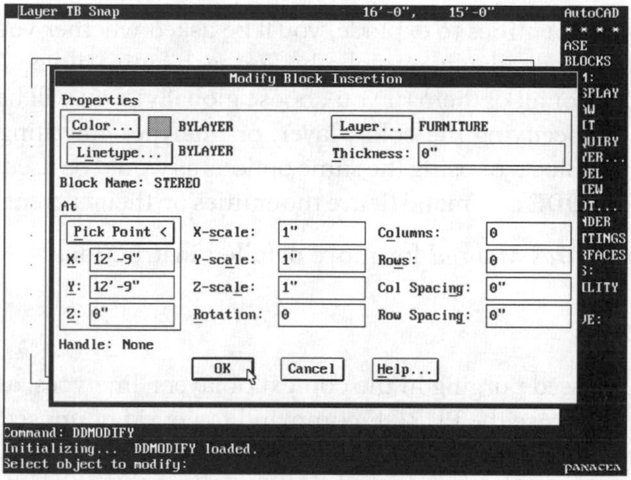

Figure 10.9 Modify Block dialogue box.

The normal AutoCAD **EXPLODE** command is used to explode equally scaled Blocks or Polylines. It leaves all the component entities with the layer, color, and linetype with which they were originally drawn. These properties may not always be desirable.

XPLODE allows you to specify the color, layer, and linetype of each entity in an exploded Block, or of all of them as a group. Alternatively, you can specify that the entities inherit these quantities from the Block Definition. One other advantage that XPLODE has over EXPLODE is that it can explode mirrored Blocks (Blocks with X-, Y-, and Z-scale factors of equal magnitude but unequal sign; for instance, 3, −3, and 3).

USING XPLODE

1. Make sure that any colors, layers, or linetypes that you want the entities from the exploded Block to assume are already present in your drawing.

2. Load the **XPLODE.LSP** file.

Instructions for loading AutoLISP files with **APPLOAD** are given in Chapter 9.

3. Start the application.

```
Command: XPLODE
or
XP
```

4. Follow the prompts in the application.

After selecting the entities to explode, you'll be asked whether you want to explode them individually or globally. For each entity (if you choose individually) or for all of them (if you choose globally), you will be given the options of specifying the color, layer, or linetype; inheriting them from the parent Block; or using the same options as would be used by the AutoCAD EXPLODE command (leave the entities on their current layer).

See the *AutoCAD Extras Manual* for more detailed instructions.

Purging for Experts

In Chapter 4, we discussed purging in the context of layers, linetypes, and text styles. More often, you'll use the PURGE command to get rid of unused Block Definitions, since they can increase the size of a drawing and slow regens a lot. Now that we've discussed Block management, this is a good time to talk about some of the more advanced aspects of the PURGE command.

AutoCAD keeps track of Blocks, layers, and other so-called named objects within each drawing in special storage areas called symbol tables. There are nine symbol tables in every Release 12 drawing, as shown in the following list:

BLOCK	Blocks (also Xrefs)
DIMSTYLE	Dimension styles
LAYER	Layers
LTYPE	Linetypes
STYLE	Text styles
UCS	Named User Coordinate Systems
VIEW	Named views
VPORT	Named viewport configurations
APPID	Registered applications using Extended Entity Data

The Block table is like a collection of recipes for making each of the defined Blocks; AutoCAD calls each recipe a Block Definition. When you insert a Block, AutoCAD creates an entity called an Insert (or Block Insert), which is essentially just a pointer to the recipe. Similarly, you can think of dimension styles, layers, linetypes, and text styles as specifications for how to show entities with those properties.

If a table entry (i.e., a Block Definition, dimension style, layer, etc.) is used by at least one entity, then that table entry is said to be referenced. If a table entry isn't used (e.g., you create a new layer but haven't drawn anything on it

---

Tip

The TABLES.LSP program in the \ACAD\SAMPLE subdirectory will let you peek at what's in each table.

Tip

You can't purge an external reference, since an Xref is, by definition, always referenced. To get rid of an Xref in a drawing use the XREF Detach subcommand. XREF Detach is equivalent to deleting all insertions of, and then purging, a Block.

yet, or you insert a Block and then erase it), then the table entry is unreferenced. Each table entry takes up a certain amount of disk space and regeneration time, and in the case of Blocks, both can be quite substantial. So it's worthwhile to use PURGE to delete unreferenced table entries.

PURGE will not delete any Block Inserts or other entities in your drawing; it lets you get rid of only *unreferenced* Block Definitions, layers, linetypes, etc. The only way you can do much harm with PURGE is if you delete all instances of a complex Block, purge the Block Definition, and then decide later that you want to use that Block. If you're worried about that, just make sure you WBLOCK out the Block Definition before purging it from the current drawing.

PURGE works only one level at a time, so if you have nested Blocks or other named objects unique to Blocks you're purging, it can take several iterations of PURGE to clean everything out. Unfortunately, you have to reload the drawing between each purge session, as described in Chapter 4. See the Tip below for a more elegant method.

Tip

Purging can be quite tedious if there are lots of unreferenced table entries and/or several levels of nesting. Here's a quick and thorough way to purge a drawing of all unreferenced entries:

```
Command: WBLOCK
Filename: Enter current drawing name.
A drawing with this name already exists.
Do you want to replace it? <N>: Y
Block name: *
Command: QUIT
or
OPEN
Really want to discard all changes to drawing? Y
```

This technique writes out the current drawing to disk, leaving behind any unreferenced entries. One caution, though: Because of a bug in Release 12, you will lose any changes you've made to externally referenced layer settings, even if VISRETAIN is turned on.

Blocks Tutorial

The following simple tutorial focuses on the new DDINSERT dialogue. If you're not completely familiar with Blocks from previous releases of AutoCAD, work through Chapter 4 of the *AutoCAD Tutorial Manual*, which covers Blocks and Attributes.

1. Make FURNITURE the current layer.

Set FURNITURE as the current layer.

2. Create a Block using the sectional sofa.

```
Command: BLOCK
```
or
Pick Block on the Construct menu.

If we wanted to write out the sofa as a separate .DWG file for use as a Block in other drawings, we would use the WBLOCK command, instead.

```
Block name (or ?): SOFA
Insertion base point: Specify ENDpoint object snap.
```
or
Pick the upper right corner of the sofa.

```
Select objects: Pick the rectangles that make up the sofa.
Select objects: <Enter>
```

The sofa will disappear from the drawing, but is now defined as a Block. *Do not* type OOPS to bring back the individual entities! This would defeat the whole purpose of creating a Block.

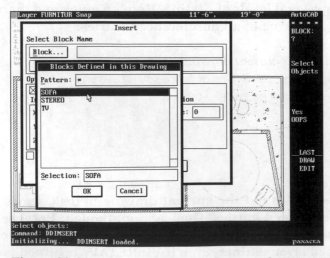

Figure 10.10 Selecting a Block to insert with DDINSERT.

3. Insert the sofa Block back into the upper left corner of the room.

> Command: DDINSERT
> The Insert dialogue will appear.
> *Pick the Block... button.*

The Blocks Defined in this Drawing subdialogue will appear. See Figure 10.10.

If we had used WBLOCK in step 1, we would pick the File... button here, instead.

Pick SOFA, then pick OK.

You will be returned to the Insert dialogue.

Check the Specify Parameters on Screen checkbox.

The Insertion Point, Scale, and Rotation areas will be grayed out.

Pick OK.

The sofa's outline will appear at the crosshairs.

Insertion point: *Pick near the inside corner of the room.*

Press <Enter> to accept the default values for the remaining prompts.

The sofa will appear in the drawing. If you want to modify the insertion, enter **DDMODIFY** and pick the sofa.

4. Insert the sofa Block again, but this time in the smaller room, and mirrored with a Y-scale factor of −1.

> Command: DDINSERT

The Insert dialogue will appear. You will use the same Block and file as before.

Clear the Specify Parameters on Screen checkbox.

The Insertion Point, Scale, and Rotation areas will be ungrayed.

In the Insertion Point area, enter: 38' for X:, and 12'–8" for Y:.

In the Scale area, enter: −1 for Y:

Pick OK.

The sofa will appear mirrored in the lower left-hand corner of the smaller room (see Figure 10.11).

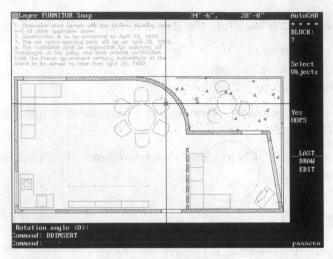

Figure 10.11   RECROOM with two sofas.

Attributes

Attributes, like Blocks, are unchanged in Release 12, but easier to use than before. Dialogue box interfaces for most Attribute-related functions make it much easier to create Attributes, change them, and keep the values in them updated. In fact, it's now fairly easy for a non-AutoCAD user to learn enough to keep the Attributes values updated, though the cost of an AutoCAD license is high enough to make companies think twice before choosing this option.

For overall data management, the new AutoCAD SQL Interface (ASI) may be a superior choice in the future, because it allows AutoCAD to directly read and write database files. This capability lets AutoCAD share data with other non-CAD applications, just as Xrefs let different users share the same drawing data. For instance, using an application developed with ASI, an AutoCAD drafter could modify a drawing without even being aware that his or her actions were updating Paradox database tables used by other depart-

Tip

As of this writing, ASI and ASE (the sample application that comes with Release 12) haven't yet gained a lot of acceptance by developers or users, and there is still some question about the direction and future of ASI. There are several good third-party toolkits for developing database links with AutoCAD, though, including AutoTOOL dB from Robert McNeel & Associates for xBASE links, and PDB-ACAD from CADology Limited for Paradox links.

ments. Likewise, changes to the database tables made by data entry people would automatically affect the drawing. Attributes can't do this because Attribute data can be easily exported, but there isn't a standard way to bring Attribute data back into AutoCAD. But until custom solutions using ASI are developed for your specialty, Attributes are a good interim solution.

With Release 12, you can now use a dialogue box to create Attribute Definitions (DDATTDEF). Once you've inserted a Block containing Attributes, other dialogues let you modify the values (DDMODIFY), edit them (DDATTE), and extract them (DDATTEXT). This section describes the new and revised dialogues, and demonstrates how to use them to finish our title block.

The Attribute Definition Dialogue Box

Like other Release 12 dialogues, the DDATTDEF Attribute Definition dialogue box simply makes previously existing functionality more accessible. In this case, that's a big plus, because the old ATTDEF command was awkward and somewhat hard to follow. With the dialogue, it's all right in front of you.

In combination with the DDMODIFY Modify Attribute Definition dialogue, the DDATTDEF dialogue box makes it easy to define and modify Attribute Definitions. To start the Attribute Definition dialogue, enter the command DDATTDEF or Pick Text, then Attributes, then Define... from the Draw menu. The dialogue shown in Figure 10.12 will appear. The fields in the Attribute Definition dialogue are as follows:

- The Mode area makes all the previously obscure Attribute control options easier to fathom. They are:

  Invisible. If set, the Attribute is not displayed in your drawing. You can still see the value when editing Attributes (see below), and can override the setting of this option with the ATTDISP command.

  Constant. If set, the value in the Value field is used for the Attribute; no value is prompted for when the Block is inserted or in the Edit Attributes dialogue (see Figure 10.15).

Tip

Before you start defining Attributes with DDATTDEF or ATTDEF, consider what order you want Attributes to appear in when you fill in their values. AutoCAD displays the prompts in the order you create the Attribute Definitions. You can use WBLOCK or BLOCK later to reorder, but often it's easier to define them in the right order in the first place.

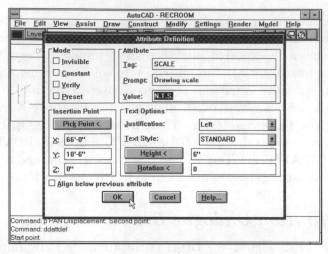

Figure 10.12   Attribute Definition dialogue box.

Verify.   If set, you are asked to verify the Attribute value at insertion.

Preset.   Same as Constant, but you can change the value in the Edit Attributes dialogue.

- The Attribute area allows you to enter the Attribute's Tag, or field name; Prompt for data entry; and Value, used as a default, constant, or preset value. The tag name you enter will be converted to all uppercase letters; use an underscore, LIKE_THIS, to separate words. Up to 23 characters of the prompt and 32 characters of the value can be displayed in the Edit Attributes dialogue box (Figure 10.15).

- The Insertion Point area allows you to pick or specify the insertion point for the prompt when a Block is inserted. A checkbox allows you to automatically align the current prompt below the one for the previous Attribute.

- The Text Options area allows you to control the Justification, Text Style, Height, and Rotation angle of the tag and value. Picking a text style with a defined height disables the Height option. Picking the Align justification option disables Height and Rotation; picking the Fit option disables Rotation only.

The Modify Attribute Definition Dialogue Box

The DDMODIFY Modify Attribute Definition dialogue box is similar to the DDATTDEF dialogue, except that it's arranged somewhat differently and contains a few additional property and text-related fields (see Figure 10.13).

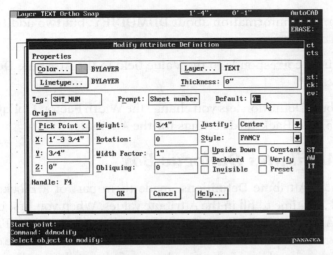

Figure 10.13 Modify Attribute Definition dialogue box.

 Tip

You may not be aware that the DDEDIT command, which you normally use to edit ordinary text, also works on Attribute Definitions. If you want to change only the tag, prompt, or default of an Attribute Definition, DDEDIT is a bit faster and brings up an Edit Attribute Definition dialogue that's less "busy" than Modify Attribute Definition (see Figure 10.14).

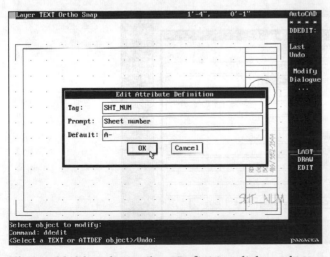

Figure 10.14 Edit Attribute Definition dialogue box.

See Chapter 8 for more information about DDMODIFY, but two additional comments are in order here:

- The Default field corresponds to the Value field in the Attribute Definition dialogue.

- Modify Attribute Definition lets you change the Width Factor, Obliquing, Upside Down, and Backward settings for the Attribute.

The Enter/Edit Attributes Dialogue Box

Once you've created Attribute Definitions, made them part of a Block, and inserted the Block, it's time to fill in the Attribute values. When you first insert the Block, AutoCAD pops up the Enter Attributes dialogue box if the ATTDIA (ATTribute DIAlogue) system variable is set to 1. If ATTDIA is 0, Attribute entry takes place at the command line. Later on when you edit attribute values with the DDATTE command, AutoCAD uses the same dialogue but calls it Edit Attributes (see Figure 10.15). DDATTE, which is also available by picking Text, then Attributes, then Edit... from the Draw menu, always brings up a dialogue box, no matter what ATTDIA is set to. Use the ATTEDIT command if you want command-line editing and the option to globally edit Attribute values. The Edit Attributes dialogue has the following features:

- The Block name is displayed.

- The Prompt you specified for each Attribute Definition is displayed, up to 23 characters in length.

- The current value for each Attribute is displayed. As with all text entry fields, you can scroll through long entries with the cursor movement keys.

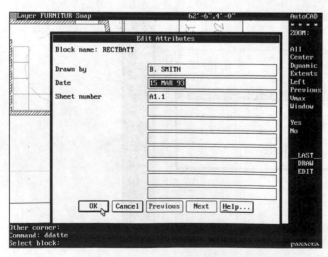

Figure 10.15   Enter/Edit Attributes dialogue box.

- The OK and Cancel dialogue buttons allow you to accept or throw out changes at any point. Unfortunately, the <Enter> key doesn't act like OK in this dialogue; you have to actually pick on (or tab) to the OK button.

- If there are more than 10 editable Attributes for the Block, the Next button becomes available. Once the Next button has been used, the Previous button becomes available, allowing you to move back and forth through long lists of Attributes.

- The Help button brings up help for the DDATTE command.

The Attribute Extraction Dialogue Box

The DDATTEXT Attribute Extraction dialogue box is a dialogue box version of the ATTEXT command. Both commands are used to extract Attribute values to a comma delimited or space delimited file, which many database and spreadsheet programs can import. As pointed out earlier in this section, exchanging Attribute values with other programs is a one-way street; AutoCAD by itself can't import Attribute values after you've manipulated them in a database. Nonetheless, the one-way export can still be useful in some situations.

One word of caution: File interchange is not something that's easy to do in a hurry. The interaction between the program in which the data is created and the one in which it's processed usually causes some amount of confusion and rework on one side or the other. If you're considering using this functionality, start early with some experiments on extracting, reading in, and manipulating the data. This will give you a better chance of finding and

---

 ## Tip

One way to manipulate and reformat extracted files, which is not discussed in the AutoCAD documentation, is to use a word processor. Word processors are easy to use and they allow you to see and edit many records at once. The best format for word processor manipulation is the tab delimited format, which is not one of AutoCAD's export options. It's relatively easy to convert a comma delimited or space delimited file to a tab delimited one within the word processor, though. If you use a monospaced font and set tabs far apart so that the fields line up in regular columns, this can be a productive way to manipulate data before outputting it to another kind of program. You can also use your word processor's mail-merge feature for reports, inventory lists, etc.

---

solving any problems early on. Look in the documentation for both AutoCAD and the program(s) you plan to use the data in, to learn more about how file transfer is handled.

Before you can extract attributes, you need to create an ASCII template file that tells AutoCAD what Attributes to look for, what precisely to extract, and how to display it in the extract file. See Chapter 10 of the *AutoCAD Reference Manual* for details.

Let's take a quick look at the options available in the Attribute Extraction dialogue box. To start it, enter the command DDATTEXT or Pick Text, then Attributes, then Extract... from the Draw menu; the dialogue box in Figure 10.16 will appear.

The fields in the dialogue box are:

- The File Format area allows you to specify the output file format that will be used:

  A Comma Delimited File (CDF) puts commas between fields; it is the most common output format and is easily used by dBASE, other xBASE-compatible programs, BASIC, and word processors.

  A Space Delimited File (SDF) sets fields to a fixed length and adds spaces to any values that don't fill up the whole length, which can make the extract file much larger. This format is easily used by dBASE, other xBASE-compatible programs, FORTRAN, COBOL, and word processors.

  A Drawing Interchange File (DXF), using a version of AutoCAD's Drawing Interchange File format, is most likely of interest if you're doing AutoLISP or ADS programming. It is documented in the *AutoCAD Customization Manual*.

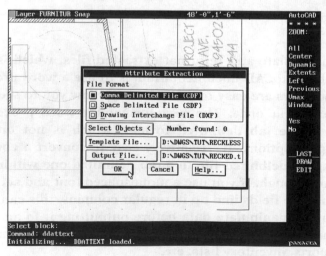

Figure 10.16 Attribute Extraction dialogue box.

- The Select Objects < button allows you to pick objects for Attribute extraction. Suggestion: Use the new ALL selection set option (see Chapter 7) to easily specify all Blocks with Attributes.

- The Template File button allows you to select the template file you've created.

- The Output File button allows you to name the output file to which AutoCAD will write all the extracted values.

ATTREDEF—Block and Attribute Redefinition Program

ATTREDEF is an AutoLISP program that overcomes an annoying problem. Normally, you can change all insertions of a Block by redefining it, but as the *AutoCAD Reference Manual* warns, redefinition doesn't work properly if you've added or changed Attribute Definitions. ATTREDEF works around this limitation.

Start by inserting the Block you want to change somewhere off to the side of your drawing. Make sure you insert the Block at a known point (e.g., use Snap or object snap), since you'll need to pick this same point when you redefine the Block. Explode it and then add or modify Attribute Definitions and any other geometry. Start ATTREDEF and type in the name of the Block you want to redefine. Select the entities you want to include in the Block (including any new Attributes you've created, and excluding any you want to remove), and then specify a base point for the Block.

Once you've performed these steps, ATTREDEF will correctly add, move, or delete Attributes in every instance of the redefined Block. Any new Attributes will take on the default value you specified when creating the Attribute Definition. You may have to edit some of these values, but at least everything will be in the right place.

USING ATTREDEF

1. Create the revised Block geometry you want to use, as described above. Make sure that any new Attributes are appropriate for all copies of the Block, and that you specify reasonable default values to minimize subsequent attribute editing time.

2. Load the ATTREDEF.LSP file from the \ACAD\SAMPLE directory.

Instructions for loading AutoLISP files with APPLOAD are given in Chapter 9.

3. Start the application.

```
Command: ATTREDEF
```

4. Follow the prompts in the application.

You will be asked to enter the name of the Block you wish to redefine, to select the objects for the new Block, and to specify a base point for the new Block.

ATTREDEF is documented briefly in the *AutoCAD Extras Manual*.

Attribute Tutorial

In the final tutorial for this chapter, we complete the title block begun in the Xref section. Here, we create Attribute Definitions for several title block fields, make a Block out of them, and then insert the Block and fill in the Attribute values. As we mentioned in the Block tutorial, you should work through Chapter 4 of the *AutoCAD Tutorial Manual* if you haven't used Attributes in previous versions of AutoCAD.

1. Save RECROOM, and open RECTB.

Use the QSAVE command to save RECROOM.

Open RECTB.

We'll use RECTB as a visual reference while creating the Attribute Definitions.

2. Create a sheet number Attribute Definition.

Make TEXT the current layer.

```
Command: DDATTDEF
or
```
Pick Text, then Attributes, then Define... from the Draw menu.

The Attribute Definition dialogue will appear.

Enter the following values in the Attribute area:

```
Tag: SHT NUM
Prompt: Sheet number
Value: A-
```
In the Insertion Point area, pick the Pick Point < button.

Pick the point 1'–3 3/4", 3/4".

Enter the following values in the Text Options area:

```
Justification: Center
Text Style: FANCY
Height: 3/4"
Rotation: 0
```

The contents of the dialogue box should look like that shown in Figure 10.17.

Pick the OK button.

3. Create two more Attribute Definitions: "drawn by" and "date."

Repeat step 2 twice with the following values:

```
Tag:                DRAWN_BY            DATE
Prompt:             Drawn by           Date
Value:              ME                 XX/XX/XX
Insertion Point:    1'-4 1/2", 2 1/4"  1'-4 1/2", 1 7/8"
Justification:      Right              Right
Text Style:         STANDARD           STANDARD
Height:             1/8"               1/8"
Rotation:           0                  0
```

4. WBLOCK the Attributes to a separate RECTBATT.DWG file.

```
Command: WBLOCK
```

The Create Drawing File dialogue appears.

Enter RECTBATT in the File Name field.

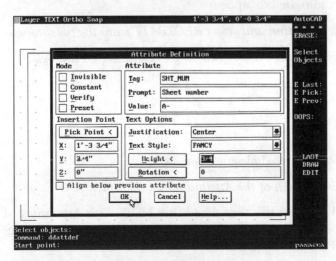

Figure 10.17 Attribute Definition Dialogue.

```
Block name: <Enter>

Insertion base point: 0,0
Select objects:  Pick the three Attribute Definitions in the order you
want their prompts to appear.
Select objects: <Enter>
```

AutoCAD creates RECTBATT.DWG.

5. Open RECROOM and discard changes to RECTB.

Open RECROOM. Discard changes to RECTB, since we were just using it to lay out the Attribute Definitions.

6. Make TB the current layer and turn ATTDIA on.

Set the TB layer current.

```
Command: ATTDIA
New value for ATTDIA <default>: 1
```

If you prefer to always use the dialogue box to fill in attributes when you insert a Block, turn on ATTDIA in your prototype.

7. Insert RECTBATT and fill in the attributes.

```
Command: DDNSERT
or
```
Pick Insert from the Draw menu.

The Insert dialogue box appears.

Pick the File... button and select RECTBATT from the file dialogue box.

Pick OK twice to close Select Drawing File and Insert dialogues.

```
Insertion point: 0,0
X-scale factor <1> / Corner / XYZ: 48
Y-scale factor (default=X): <Enter>
Rotation angle <0>: <Enter>
```

The Enter Attributes dialogue appears.

Enter values for each of the Attributes and then pick OK.

Figure 10.18 shows the completed title block with Attributes. If you want to experiment more, use DDATTE to edit the attribute values and ATTREDEF to add an Attribute to the title block.

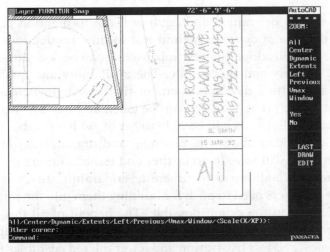

Figure 10.18 Title block with Attributes.

Entity Reuse and Workgroups

Xrefs, Blocks, and Attributes are AutoCAD features that represent the tip of a large iceberg. The iceberg is a different approach to AutoCAD: a primary focus on its use as a data management tool, rather than a tool for drafting lines and circles.

In this approach, planning is vital. The mottos are "enter things once" and "avoid duplication." The idea is that neither geometry nor data should be entered multiple times or stored in multiple places. Ideally, geometry and text data are created once, then reused via pointers many times within a project.

Without planning and coordination, such an approach can be problematic or even disastrous. For instance, if many drawings contain external references to a particular detail and that detail is changed without sufficient forethought, some of the drawings that depend on it could change when they're not supposed to. Other, more subtle problems can occur. If conventions aren't created and followed, a drawing with many Blocks inserted from other drawings can end up looking inconsistent because of different layer properties used in the different Blocks. Users, such as outside contractors who don't have constant access to shared drawings, can end up with subtle differences between their drawings and those created by people who are on the same network.

But a data-management-oriented approach is a significant benefit to most companies that use AutoCAD, and this approach is becoming a practical necessity on complex projects. The cost and time needed to manage proliferating drawing files becomes a strong productivity hit as more and more old work accumulates. The increasing cost of hiring more and more drafters, each of whom needs to be trained and equipped, not to mention paid, is unacceptable in this age of downsizing and just-in-time production. Most companies eventually will adopt this new approach; it can be done either late and haphazardly or early and thoroughly. The availability and quality of AutoCAD's tools for putting data management first has, with Release 12, reached the point where proactive steps can be taken and made to work.

Smaller firms and individuals will be able to get by with a few hours per project devoted to thinking about the planning and organization of data files. Larger companies will have to go farther and establish more rigorous rules and procedures. In addition to documenting and training users in these procedures, CAD managers need to push for building them into the software through customization to the extent possible. The benefit of all this extra work is faster turnaround of projects, more work from the same number of people and machines, and less frustration and fewer missed deadlines for all concerned.

The first step is to learn to get the most out of the AutoCAD features covered in this chapter. Once you've mastered the tools, try to do more with them in each project you take on. One good early step is to develop a Block and Xref library, and then produce a document describing its contents (with pictures!) and how to use it. In doing something like this, you will no doubt also start to address issues of prototype drawings, layer naming, layout standards, and more.

Further steps will follow naturally from this one. If you make it a goal to minimize duplication and maximize reuse of geometry and other data within each project, organization will start to go up and costs to go down. If not, frustration and lost time will only increase as the complexity of AutoCAD and its third-party tools, as well as the number of drafters and the amount of drawing data stored on hard disks around your company, continue to grow.

11

Paper Space and Plotting

Throughout Part II we've emphasized the importance of maintaining drawing precision and using a "data management" approach with CAD. These two practices will make your drawings easier and more efficient to work with on the computer, but the proof is still in the plotting. Until someone invents an E-size, flexible monitor that contractors can roll up and toss on the dashboards of their pickup trucks, we'll be confronted with the challenge of getting good-looking plotted output in a timely manner.

One of Release 11's most important changes was the addition of paper space, which made it possible to use AutoCAD as a kind of desktop publishing program for designs. Paper space increased AutoCAD's plot layout flexibility for both 3D and 2D drawings. Release 12's plotting improvements are of a different nature; they don't introduce any new conceptual leaps the way that paper space does. Instead, they're aimed at nuts-and-bolts issues such as specifying plot parameters, switching among output devices, and catching plot problems on the monitor, rather than at the plotter. In other words, Release 12 makes it faster and easier to get what's on your screen onto paper.

About This Chapter

In this chapter, we discuss two distinct but related features: paper space and plotting. We cover paper space and the setup procedures for it, plus the all-important question of when to take the plunge into paper space. The powerful but crowded new Plot Configuration dialogue box (Figure 11.1) is one of the star attractions of Release 12; we take you on a tour of it and discuss ways to put it to good use. Finally, we'll also mention several other less obvious Release 12 enhancements to plotting and paper space, as described below.

You certainly don't need to use paper space in order to take advantage of the plotting enhancements in Release 12 (in fact, we'll give you some reasons to *avoid* paper space). But both sets of features relate to the important business of getting hard-copy output, and studying them together will help you understand your options.

Features Demonstrated in This Chapter

The "new" features in this chapter straddle Release 11 and Release 12, but all of them concern getting plotted output:

- Paper space how-to: when to use it and when not to use it; paper space setup with MVSETUP and other commands; the Modify Viewports dialogue box.

- The Plot Configuration dialogue: how to use the new PLOT command, configuring new output devices, setting and saving plot parameters, and previewing plots on screen.

- Other plotting enhancements: better handling of the UNDO buffer and AutoLISP, new system variables for plotting, and freeplotting.

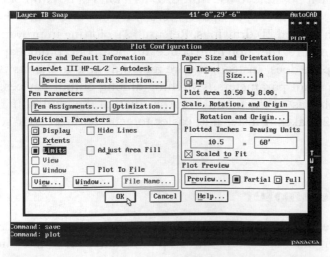

Figure 11.1   The new Plot Configuration dialogue box.

About the Example

In this chapter, we set up paper space and use it to show several different views of our rec room drawing. We then plot the drawing to a file. If you don't have an up-to-date version of RECROOM as of the previous chapter, you can use the RRCH11.DWG file on the *AutoCAD Power Tools* disk as a starting point. Also, copy MVSETUP.LSP from the diskette to your \ACAD\SUPPORT subdirectory, but make a backup of the stock AutoCAD version of this file first. The *AutoCAD Power Tools* version of Autodesk's MVSETUP.LSP fixes several paper space setup bugs, which we'll discuss in the next section.

Getting the Most Out of Paper Space

Although paper space dates back to Release 11, many users are still unfamiliar with it. As with dimension styles, the conceptual shift that was required to use it effectively, coupled with a relatively primitive interface, prevented many Release 11 users from becoming comfortable with paper space.

On the other hand, some users embraced paper space *too* eagerly, and started using it in situations for which it wasn't designed. Paper space is practically a necessity for presenting 3D models, but it should be used more sparingly with 2D drawings. Paper space can impose a severe performance penalty when it's used improperly, and the additional work needed to arrange paper space views just doesn't buy you anything in many drawings.

In this section, we'll show you a realistic example of when and how to use paper space with 2D drawings. By working through the tutorial, you'll not only understand the basic steps required to set up paper space properly, but you'll also gain an insight into when you should bother.

When to Use Paper Space

In Chapter 5, *Drawing-Specific Setup*, we discussed the three main reasons for using paper space:

- When you want to show a 3D model from different points of view (e.g., top, side, and front).

- When you want to show a model with different zoom resolutions (for instance, an overall plan and a larger-scale detail of part of the plan on the same sheet).

- When you want to show a model with different layer freeze/thaw settings to make different parts of it show up in different viewports (for example, a floor plan and a reflected ceiling plan, which you've drawn on top of one another).

Here the word "model" just means whatever geometry you've drawn in AutoCAD; it doesn't necessarily refer to a 3D representation of an object.

As discussed in the previous chapter, paper space also can be beneficial when you want to visually "clip" a small area out of a drawing. As you'll see in the tutorial, paper space viewports act like window openings, allowing you to mask everything outside of a rectangle. The XREFCLIP program, also described in Chapter 10, helps automate this process.

When Not to Use Paper Space

By contrast, here are the drawbacks to paper space, along with their implications for how you should use paper space:

- Every zoom and pan in paper space requires a regeneration. Unlike model space (the "normal" space where you draw most things), paper space doesn't have a virtual screen, which means that AutoCAD remembers only the current view. Every time you want to zoom in or out or pan in paper space, AutoCAD has to recalculate (i.e, regen) the paper space entities in the drawing. Thus, you should use paper space in a way that keeps zooms and pans to an absolute minimum.

- Switching between model space and paper space also requires a regeneration. As a result, you'll want to develop a paper space working style that reduces the amount of switching back and forth.

- Arranging the model space views inside paper space viewports can be time-consuming. To minimize this problem, use Snap and ZOOM intelligently, and lay out viewports in an efficient manner. XREFCLIP also can help, if the geometry you want to show is part of an external reference.

As you can see, the big problem with paper space is the potential for an enormous number of regens. If your drawing is small (and your computer is fast), this may not be a big deal, but it doesn't take a very large drawing before the regen delays begin to seriously hurt your productivity.

In most cases, you shouldn't use paper space for assembling a group of independent details or other drawings on one sheet. Paper space doesn't offer any benefit for this sort of "paste-up" work, unless you need to clip an area out of a larger drawing. Instead, when you need to paste up a detail sheet, create a drawing containing just a border in model space, and xref or insert each independent detail into it.

Tip

If you have a mixed-scale detail sheet, create the parent drawing at full scale (i.e., 1=1). Then xref or insert each detail at the inverse of its drawing scale factor. For instance, insert a 1" = 1'– 0" (drawing scale factor = 12) detail at 1/12, and insert a 3/4" = 1'– 0" (drawing scale factor = 16) at 1/16.

This technique is based on a simplified version of the general rule for inserting one drawing into another of a different scale: Use an insertion scale equal to the parent drawing's scale factor divided by the Xref's or Block's scale factor. For instance, to insert a 3/4" = 1'– 0" detail into a 1/4" = 1'– 0" plan (drawing scale factor = 48), use a scale factor of 48/16 (or 3). If all this division makes you dizzy, make up a little chart with the drawing and insertion scale factors you commonly use and post it near your computer.

Paper Space Setup and MVSETUP

When paper space does make sense for a drawing, setting it up and using it correctly are what make the difference between it being a productive tool or a huge time-sink. The interface for paper space hasn't really improved in Release 12, and some of the factors that go into using it efficiently are subtle.

There are two ways to set up paper space. One is to use the individual commands added to Release 11 for working in paper space: TILEMODE, MVIEW, MSPACE, PSPACE, VPLAYER, and the ZOOM XP option. These commands give you a great deal of control, but they're all command-line driven, and figuring out the right way to use all of them isn't always easy. The other approach to paper setup is MVSETUP.LSP. This routine, which we used in Chapter 5 for model space setup, has a lot of paper space-specific options, and is a good introduction to paper space. Among its talents are the ability to create ready-made viewports, draw title blocks, zoom to the right scale, and align entities in different but related viewports. MVSETUP is command-line driven also, but it walks you through the process of setting up in paper space.

Tip

MVSETUP is a huge and unwieldy AutoLISP program, and along with its benefits come a number of nasty bugs. The *AutoCAD Power Tools* disk includes an updated MVSETUP.LSP that fixes the ones we've encountered. Make a backup of MVSETUP.LSP in your \ACAD\SAMPLE subdirectory, and then replace it with the *AutoCAD Power Tools* version.

In practice, you'll probably end up using a mixture of MVSETUP and individual commands for paper space setup. Next, we present one such "hybrid" approach that works reasonably well for 2D drawings. After working through the steps, we'll outline an overall approach to paper space setup.

Paper Space Setup Tutorial

In this tutorial, we'll use paper space to create an alternate way of viewing and plotting our rec room drawing: as four different views on a D-size sheet. The four views will show a regular floor plan, a simplified foundation plan, a detailed view of the patio, and the general notes. Refer to Figure 11.10 as you work through the tutorial. Refer to Chapter 2 of the *AutoCAD Extras Manual* for more details about MVSETUP.

CREATING THE TITLE BLOCK AND FIRST VIEWPORT WITH MVSETUP

1. Load RECROOM.DWG and make sure you've copied MVSETUP.LSP to your support directory.

   Use your drawing from the previous chapter, or copy RRCH11.DWG from the *AutoCAD Power Tools* disk.

   Also, make sure you're using the *AutoCAD Power Tools* version of MVSETUP.LSP, as described in the Tip above.

2. Determine the size of the viewport we'll need.

   In order to view model space geometry from paper space, you have to create paper space viewports. MVSETUP includes an option for doing this, but it's useful to know beforehand approximately how big the viewport should be.

   We want the viewport to just fit around the floor plan and dimensions, but not include the title and general notes text. Use the distance command to determine how large this is (see Figure 11.2).

   ```
   Command: DIST
   First point: Pick a point below and to the left of the dimensions.
   Second point: Pick above and to the right of the floor plan.
   Delta X = 55'-0", Delta Y = 30'-0", Delta Z = 0'-0"
   ```

   AutoCAD reports that this rectangular area is 55' × 30'. Since in paper space everything is measured in paper units, we divide it by our drawing scale factor, 48" (or 4') to get 13 3/4" × 7 1/2". We'll use these numbers in step 6 below.

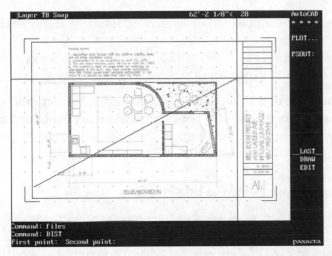

Figure 11.2 Measuring the future viewport size with DIST.

3. Start MVSETUP and enable paper space.

    Command: MVSETUP
    or
Pick Layout, then MV Setup from the View menu.

If you have not already enabled paper space, the following prompt will appear:

    Paperspace/Modelspace is disabled. The pre-R11 setup will be
    invoked unless it is enabled. Enable Paper/Modelspace? <Y>:
    <Enter>

When we encountered this prompt in Chapter 5, we answered No and used the model space setup options. This time, we chose to enable paper space.

AutoCAD switches to paper space, which at this time is a blank screen. Note the paper space "drafting triangle" icon at the lower left corner of the drawing area, and the "P" on the status line (or the selected P button on the Windows toolbar). In order to switch manually to paper space, you'd type TILEMODE 0. TILEMODE 1 returns you to model space.

Tip

If you're running Release 12 for Windows and get an error message, then you've encountered one of the MVSETUP.LSP bugs. Copy the version from the *AutoCAD Power Tools* disk and start again.

```
Entering Paper space. Use MVIEW to insert Model space viewports.
Regenerating drawing.
MVSetup, Version 1.15, (c) 1990-1992 by Autodesk, Inc.
Align/Create/Scale viewports/Options/Title block/Undo:
```

Undo undoes, one at a time, and in reverse order, the actions you've performed so far in MVSETUP. The other options are explained in the steps below. You should use them in the following order: Options, Title block, Create, Scale viewports, Align.

4. Set paper space options for the title block.

```
Align/Create/Scale viewports/Options/Title block/Undo: O
Set Layer/LImits/Units/Xref: L
Layer name for title block or for current layer: PSTB
```

The Layer option puts the paper space title block on its own layer.

```
Set Layer/LImits/Units/Xref: LI
Set drawing limits? <N>: Y
```

LImits tells MVSETUP to reset limits to the title block extents when it's done.

```
Set Layer/LImits/Units/Xref: X
Xref Attach or Insert title block? <Insert>: X
```

Xref causes MVSETUP to attach the title block as an external reference, rather than insert it as a Block.

```
Set Layer/LImits/Units/Xref: <Enter>
```

5. Insert the title block.

```
Align/Create/Scale viewports/Options/Title block/Undo: T
Delete objects/Origin/Undo/<Insert title block>: <Enter>
```

MVSETUP displays a list of title block options (see Figure 11.3). Select #13 (Generic D-size Sheet).

```
Add/Delete/Redisplay/<Number of entry to load>: 13
```

AutoCAD draws the title block.

```
Create a drawing named gs24x36.dwg? <Y>: <Enter>
```

MVSETUP writes the title block out to disk and then attaches it as an external reference.

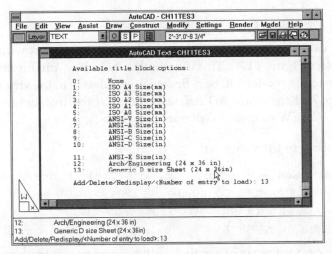

Figure 11.3 MVSETUP's title block options.

CREATING VIEWPORTS

6. Create the first viewport.

In order to view model space geometry, you have to create paper space viewports. MVSETUP includes an option for doing this, or you can use the MVIEW ("make a paper space viewport" command).

First set Snap to 1/4".

```
Align/Create/Scale viewports/Options/Title block/Undo: 'SNAP
>>Snap spacing or ON/OFF/Aspect/Rotate/Style <default>: 1/4
```
or use DDRMODES to change the Snap spacing.

Now create a single 13 3/4" × 7 1/2" viewport at 3",3".

```
Align/Create/Scale viewports/Options/Title block/Undo: C
Delete objects/Undo/<Create viewports>: <Enter>
Available Mview viewport layout options:
    0:  None
    1:  Single
    2:  Std. Engineering
    3:  Array of Viewports
Redisplay/<Number of entry to load>: 1
Bounding area for viewports. Default/<First point >:
```

Pick or type 3",3".

```
Other point: @13.75,7.5
```

These were the numbers we calculated in step 2.

MVSETUP uses the MVIEW command to create a viewport with our model in it (see Figure 11.4). This is actually a "window" on our model; any changes to the model will be reflected immediately in the viewport. See Chapter 7 of the *AutoCAD Reference Manual* for instructions on how to use MVIEW to create viewports.

7. Scale the model in the viewport.

```
Align/Create/Scale viewports/Options/Title block/Undo: S
Select the viewports to scale:
Select objects: Pick the viewport's border.
Select objects: <Enter>
```

In paper space, viewports are actual entities, and you select them as you would select a rectangle.

```
Enter the ratio of paper space units to model space units...
Number of paper space units. <1.0>: 1
Number of model space units. <1.0>: 48
```

Tip

If you're running AutoCAD 386 Release 12c2 and get an error message at this step, then you've encountered one of the MVSETUP.LSP bugs. Copy the version from the *AutoCAD Power Tools* disk and start again.

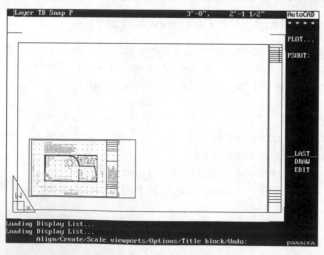

Figure 11.4 A paper space viewport.

Answering these prompts sets the relative zoom factor, a ratio between the paper space scale (usually 1) and the model scale (in this case, 1/4" = 1', or 1 = 48). To do this outside of MVSETUP, you'd enter ZOOM 1/48XP. Figure 11.5 shows the completed viewport.

8. Exit MVSETUP.

```
Align/Create/Scale viewports/Options/Title block/
Undo: <Enter>
```

As you can see, there are quite a few steps involved just to get one viewport set up correctly. Now we can take advantage of the fact that viewports are entities, and create three more of them quickly. Although MVSETUP includes an option to create arrays of viewports, it doesn't give us the control we need in this situation.

9. Create a special layer for the paper space viewport entities.

Because paper space viewports are entities, they reside on a layer, like any other entity. It's best to put them on their own layer, for reasons you'll see later.

Create a new layer called VPB and assign it color 8.

Use the DDCHPROP command to change the viewport's layer to VPB.

10. Pan the model so that the right part of it shows up in the viewport.

First, move "inside" the model space viewport. The commands MSPACE

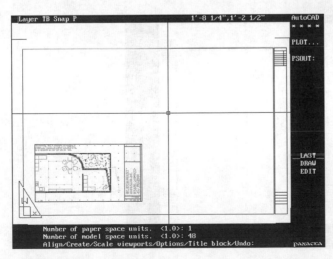

Figure 11.5 A paper space viewport zoomed to the right scale.

and PSPACE toggle you between paper space and the model space viewports displayed in paper space. Don't confuse the MSPACE/PSPACE toggle with the TILEMODE 1/0 toggle. MSPACE/PSPACE leaves paper space on the screen, but moves in and out of the viewports. TILEMODE 1/0 changes the entire screen between model space and paper space (and also causes a regen). Try setting TILEMODE to 1 and then back to 0 and you'll see the difference.

```
Command: MSPACE
```

The paper space "drafting triangle" icon goes away, and your crosshairs are now constrained inside the viewport (see Figure 11.6).

```
Command: PAN
```

Pan until the floor plan and dimensions just fit in the viewport, as shown in Figure 11.6.

11. Return to paper space and array the viewports.

```
Command: PSPACE
```

The paper space icon reappears and your crosshairs are now free to move all the way across the screen.

Create a 2x2 array with a row spacing of 9 1/2" and a column spacing of 15 3/4" (the viewport size, plus a 2" gap).

```
Command: ARRAY
Select objects: L
```

L selects the last entity drawn, i.e., the viewport.

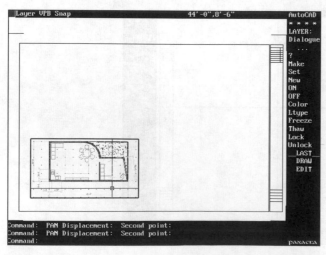

Figure 11.6 The floor plan after being panned into position.

Tip

MS is a command alias for MSPACE, and PS is an alias for PSPACE.

```
Select objects: <Enter>
Rectangular or Polar array (R/P) <R>: <Enter>
Number of rows (—) <1>: 2
Number of columns (||||) <1>: 2
Unit cell or distance between rows (—): 9.5
Distance between columns (||||): 15.75
Regenerating drawing.
```

AutoCAD creates the three additional viewports; see Figure 11.7.

12. Return to model space and zoom and pan so that you have a 1/2" = 1'–0" view of the patio in the lower left viewport.

```
Command: MS
```

Make sure your crosshairs are in the lower left viewport. If not, move to that viewport and pick in order to make it current.

This time, we'll use the ZOOM command instead of MVSETUP.

```
Command: ZOOM
All/Center/Dynamic/Extents/Left/Previous/Vmax/Window/
<Scale(X/XP)>: 1/24XP
```

XP ("times paper space") was a new ZOOM command option added in Release 11 to address paper space/model space scaling. As discussed above, you'll usually want to zoom with an XP factor of 1 divided by the desired scale factor for the viewport. Since we want a 1/2" = 1'–0" view of the patio (drawing scale factor = 24), we chose 1/24 XP.

```
Command: PAN
```

Pan around until you can see most of the patio, as shown in Figure 11.7.

Windows Tip

In AutoCAD for Windows, you can toggle between paper space and model space by clicking on the P in the toolbar.

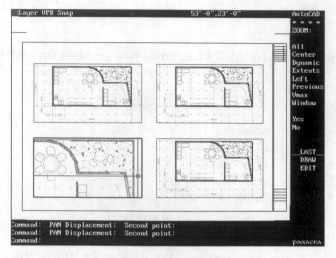

Figure 11.7   The four viewports with the patio close-up at lower left.

13. Reduce the size of the upper left viewport so that only the general notes show.

Move your cursor to the upper left viewport and pick in order to make it current.

Pan around until you can see the general notes text.

Besides being arrayed, paper space viewports can be copied, erased, and stretched. Use grip editing or the STRETCH and MOVE commands to resize the upper left viewport so that only the notes show.

`Command: PS`

You must be in paper space to select and edit the viewport.

Select the viewport border, pick one of its grips, and then stretch to make it smaller. Repeat until your drawing looks something like Figure 11.8.

Now all the viewports are in place and zoomed and panned properly. All that remains is to set the layers in each one. You can't use the LAYER on/off and freeze/thaw settings command for this purpose, because they affect the model; i.e., any changes to these settings will appear in all paper space viewports. Instead, Release 11 added a new VPLAYER ("viewport layer") command modeled after layer, and added some new settings to the DDLMODES dialogue. DDLMODES is good for making changes to a single viewport; VPLAYER is better when you want to apply changes to more than one viewport.

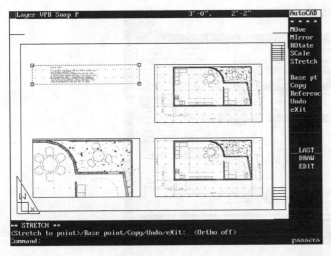

Figure 11.8   The general notes viewport made smaller.

SETTING VIEWPORT LAYERS

14. Freeze the HATCH and DIM layers in the lower left viewport.

The hatching will be the wrong scale in the patio close-up, and we don't want to see half of the dimension line, so we'll use DDLMODES to freeze these two layers in that viewport only.

Command: MS

Move your cursor to the lower left viewport and pick in order to make it current.

You must be in the model space viewport where you want to make the layer changes.

Command: DDLMODES

The Layer Control dialogue appears.

Select the DIM and HATCH layers.

Pick on the Frz button to the right of Cur VP: (not New VP: Frz, and not Freeze).

C (frozen in Current viewport) appears in the State information for each layer (see Figure 11.9).

Pick OK to put away the Layer Control dialogue.

Note that AutoCAD doesn't immediately display the changes. All changes to the viewport freeze/thaw status of layers require a regeneration.

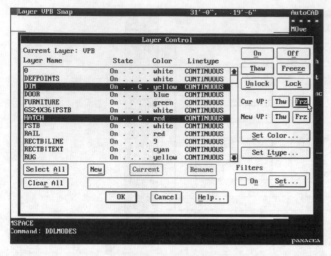

Figure 11.9   Freezing layers in a single viewport.

Because REGENAUTO is off, AutoCAD displays Regen queued to remind you it's waiting for the next regen before it makes the necessary change. If you want to see the change immediately, type REGEN; otherwise just wait until you've made all the layer changes.

15. Freeze all layers except DIM, SLAB, and WALL in the upper right viewport.

We want to show the foundation plan in the upper right viewport. Although we could use DDLMODES again, this is a good opportunity to introduce the VPLAYER command. Using VPLAYER is much like using the LAYER command.

Move your cursor to the upper right viewport and pick in order to make it current.

```
Command: VPLAYER
```

We'll freeze everything and then thaw the layers we want.

```
?/Freeze/Thaw/Reset/Newfrz/Vpvisdflt: F
Layer(s) to Freeze: *
All/Select/<Current>: <Enter>
```

You can select one or more viewports, or apply the change to all of them, but we just want to change the current viewport.

Now thaw the three layers we're interested in.

```
?/Freeze/Thaw/Reset/Newfrz/Vpvisdflt: T
Layer(s) to Thaw: SLAB,WALL,DIM
```

```
All/Select/<Current>: <Enter>
?/Freeze/Thaw/Reset/Newfrz/Vpvisdflt: <Enter>
Regenerating drawing.
```

VPLAYER doesn't observe REGENAUTO, so you're stuck with this regen. See Chapter 8 of the *AutoCAD Reference Manual* for more information about VPLAYER and freezing layers in viewports. Figure 11.10 shows the drawing with layers frozen in the lower left and upper right viewports.

16. Turn off the viewport borders and add titles.

Before plotting, you'll often want to turn off viewport borders. Since we put the viewports on their own layer, this is easy to do.

Use the DDLMODES or LAYER command to turn off the VPB layer.

The viewport borders disappear. Note that you'll have to turn them back on if you need to select viewports for more editing or layer changes.

Return to paper space.

```
Command: PS
```

Add titles if you wish. Be sure to use actual plotted text height now, since the text will appear in paper space.

The completed paper space setup is shown in Figure 11.10.

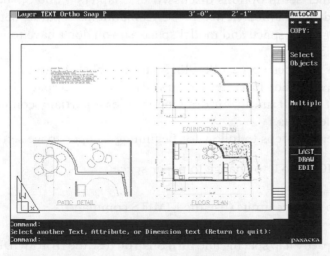

Figure 11.10 The viewports with some layers frozen and titles added.

Tip

It's possible to add dimensions and annotations in paper space as well, but we recommend against it in most situations for two reasons. First, it's difficult to dimension or annotate without zooming a lot, and every paper space zoom requires a regen. Second, dimensions added in paper space aren't associated with points in model space, so you lose one of the advantages of associative dimensions.

General Paper Space Setup

We've taken you through one approach to setup. As you can see, there are a lot of things to attend to, and MVSETUP covers only some of the steps. Paper space setup is ripe for customization, so if you're going to use it much, look for a third-party application that helps automate it, or develop your own custom scripts or AutoLISP programs, using Part III of this book as a guide.

In general, paper space setup involves the three parts we divided the tutorial into:

- Change to paper space with the TILEMODE command and create a title block or border.

- Create viewports (on their own layer) and zoom and pan the model inside them.

- Set viewport layers.

Along with these paper space-specific requirements, you'll need to attend to some of the other setup options discussed in Chapters 4 and 5, such as limits, Snap, Grid, and named views. AutoCAD maintains separate settings for these items in paper space and model space, so you don't have to worry about their conflicting.

You can create a paper space title block and establish Snap and other settings any time, including just after you first set up in model space. In most cases, you'll want to wait until your drawing is at least partially completed before creating viewports.

Here are the general steps to follow for beginning a paper space setup:

1. Set TILEMODE to 0 to change to paper space.

2. Set the paper space limits (use the LIMITS command).

3. Set paper space Snap spacing and turn Snap on (use the DDRMODES or SNAP command, or the Drawing Aids... option of the Settings menu).

4. Optional: Set paper space Grid spacing and turn Grid on (use the DDRMODES or GRID command, or the Drawing Aids... option of the Settings menu).

5. If you haven't already done so in MVSETUP, create a border or title block. (This can be an Xref, an inserted Block, or new geometry that you draw.)

6. Set TILEMODE back to 1 to return to model space.

Once you've done the initial paper space setup and created most or all of the geometry for your drawing, you're ready to complete the paper space setup:

1. Set TILEMODE to 0 to change to paper space.

2. Create paper space viewports (use the MVIEW command).

3. Zoom and pan the model in viewports (use the ZOOM XP and PAN commands).

4. Arrange layer settings (use the VPLAYER command and DDLMODES Layer Control dialogue box).

5. Set hidden line removal in any 3D viewports (use the Hideplot option of the MVIEW command; see Chapter 7 of the *AutoCAD Reference Manual*).

6. Plot from paper space.

7. Set TILEMODE back to 1 to return to model space.

Tip

Save your paper space plot area as a named view so that you can plot it easily. This step can cut down on regens, since you can plot a paper space named view even when TILEMODE=1 (i.e., when the screen displays model space).

The Modify Viewport Dialogue

Unlike other Modify Entity dialogues described in this book, the Modify Viewport dialogue (see Figure 11.11) doesn't let you do much. It allows you to change the color and layer of the viewport. It also displays several statistics—information fields that you can't change from within the dialogue box. The Linetype (always BYLAYER), Thickness (always 0), centerpoint of the view, width and height of the viewport, status, and viewport ID and handle are all displayed. Use this dialogue to quickly change the color and/or layer of a viewport or to view the statistical fields.

Plotting Improvements

For many users, the Plot Configuration dialogue box alone was reason enough to upgrade to Release 12. Multiple output devices, plot previewing, saved plot parameters, and a more usable interface promised to save all users a great deal of time, paper, and money by making it easier to plot and by reducing plotting errors.

For the Windows version of Release 12, the Plot menu entry on the AutoCAD 386 Release 12 File menu is referred to as Print/Plot. This is for two reasons: Windows users are used to seeing a Print command on the File menu; and many more AutoCAD plots will be sent to printers, rather than to plotters, now that AutoCAD simultaneously supports more configurations and supports PostScript better. But the results of choosing the options are the same in either case: The Plot Configuration dialogue box (Figure 11.12) appears. You also can bring up the dialogue box from the root menu in the side-screen menu area or by entering PLOT at the command line.

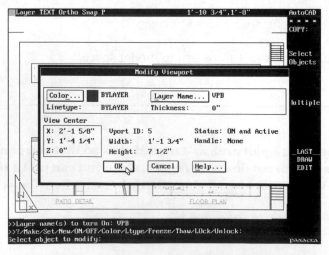

Figure 11.11 Modify Viewport dialogue box.

Tip

The first shipping version of AutoCAD 386 Release 12, as well as the Release 12c1 update, contained a number of easy to stumble upon plotting and plot driver bugs. If you encounter plotting problems, make sure you have the Release 12c2 update, which fixes most of these bugs. Release 12c1 for Windows is roughly equivalent to Release 12c2 386 in terms of bug fixes.

Configuring New Output Devices

Release 12 does away with the Release 11 (and previous versions) distinction between plotters and printers. Everything is now treated as a "plotter," and you can configure for up to 29 different plotters at once. You still have to use the primitive, old CONFIG text screen menu to configure plotters and other devices. In this example, we'll add a PostScript plotter to the list of output devices. You can delete this device at the end of the chapter if you wish.

```
Command: CONFIG
```
or
Pick Configure from the File menu.

AutoCAD displays your current configuration, and once you press <Enter>, the text screen Configuration Menu appears.

```
Enter selection <0>: 5 (Configure plotter)
```

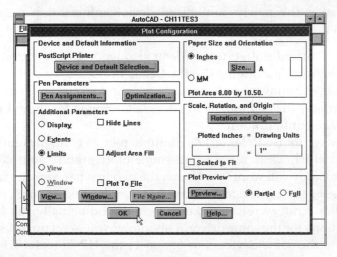

Figure 11.12 Plot Configuration dialogue box.

AutoCAD lists your current plotter and then shows the Plotter Configuration Menu.

```
Plotter Configuration Menu
    0.   Exit to Configuration Menu
    1.   Add a plotter configuration
    2.   Delete a plotter configuration
    3.   Change a plotter configuration
    4.   Rename a plotter configuration
Enter selection, 0 to 4 <0>: 1
```

A list of available plotter drivers appears.

```
Select device number or ? to repeat list <1>:
```
Enter the number corresponding to PostScript device ADI 4.2.

AutoCAD then asks a number of driver-specific and general plotting questions (see Figure 11.13).

Press <Enter> to accept the default values until you get to the following prompt.

```
Do you want to change anything? (No/Yes/File) <N>:
```
<Enter>
```
Enter a description for this plotter: PostScript Plotter
```

The Plotter Configuration Menu returns.

Press <Enter> twice.

If you answer N to the following question, all configuration changes you have just made will be discarded.

```
Keep configuration changes? <Y>:
```
<Enter>

AutoCAD adds the newly configured device information to your ACAD.CFG file.

As you saw, the Plotter Configuration Menu also lets you delete, change, and rename existing configurations. Use the Delete option at the end of this chapter if you want to remove the plotter configuration we just created. See the *AutoCAD Interface, Installation, and Performance Guide* for more information about device configuration.

There are two ways to use Release 12's multiple plotter configurations to great advantage, which we'll refer to as single-plotter and multiplotter strategies. You probably will want to intermix the two in whatever way takes greatest advantage of the 29 devices you can have configured at once.

The single-plotter strategy relies on knowing that you actually can have several configurations for the same driver. This allows you to set up different ways of plotting to the same device. For instance, the HP LaserJet III can handle either letter-size or legal-size paper. You can handle this at plot time

```
┌─────────────────────────────────────────────────────────────┐
│■            AutoCAD Text - CH11TES3                    ▼ ▲│
├─────────────────────────────────────────────────────────────┤
│Select device number or ? to repeat list <1>: 12           ▲│
│                                                            ░│
│Supported models:                                           ░│
│                                                            ░│
│   1.  300 dpi                                              ░│
│   2.  1270 dpi                                             ░│
│   3.  2540 dpi                                             ░│
│                                                            ░│
│Enter selection, 1 to 3 <1>:                                ░│
│                                                            ░│
│Do you want color output? <N>                               ░│
│                                                            ░│
│Some PostScript devices require a special ^Z (control-Z) character│
│at the end of the file.                                     ░│
│                                                            ░│
│Do you wish to append a ^Z? <N>                             ░│
│                                                            ░│
│Is your PostScript device connected to a <S>erial, or <P>arallel port? <S> p│
│Enter parallel port name for plotter or . for none <LPT1>:  ░│
│                                                            ░│
│Plot optimization level = 1                                 ░│
│Plot will NOT be written to a selected file                 ░│
│Sizes are in Inches and the style is portrait               ░│
│Plot origin is at (0.00,0.00)                               ░│
│Plotting area is 8.00 wide by 10.50 high (A size)           ░│
│Plot is NOT rotated                                         ░│
│Area fill will NOT be adjusted for pen width                ░│
│Hidden lines will NOT be removed                            ░│
│Plot will be scaled to fit available area                   ░│
│                                                            ░│
│Do you want to change anything? (No/Yes/File) <N>:          ░│
│                                                            ░│
│Enter a description for this plotter: PostScript Printer    ░│
│Your current plotter is: System Printer ADI 4.2 - by Autodesk, Inc│
│                                                          ▷ ▼│
└─────────────────────────────────────────────────────────────┘
```

Figure 11.13 Part of the CONFIG sequence for adding a PostScript printer.

by making a change in the Change Device Requirements... option of the Device and Default Selection subdialogue (see Figure 11.14). But you also can create two different configurations for the LaserJet, one for each type of paper. Each configuration will appear, with the name you supply during the CONFIG sequence, in your list of output devices.

The multiplotter strategy simply means adding at least one configuration for every plotter you're likely to use, whether it's in-house or at a service bureau. These might include several different printers connected to the network, one or more in-house plotters, and a couple of service bureau configurations. Also, don't forget about output file formats. Release 12 can

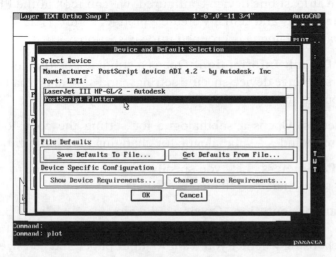

Figure 11.14 The Device and Default Selection subdialogue.

plot to a variety of plotter and raster file formats, including ADI, PCX, GIF, and TIF, but getting these formats set up correctly can be tricky, so experiment before the deadline comes.

As with the other setup considerations discussed throughout the book, this one is designed to increase the capabilities available to you and avoid last-minute problems. The information you need to set up a given plotter, printer, or file format might not be available on short notice; by doing the setup work early, you ensure that you have the greatest possible number of choices when you need them.

Tip

AutoCAD stores plotter configuration information in the ACAD.CFG file, along with configuration settings for your graphics and pointing devices and a host of other miscellaneous settings. Unfortunately, it's difficult to share this file, so don't expect to be able to configure one computer and then copy the ACAD.CFG file to all the others. Keep careful notes when you configure, so that you can reproduce the same configuration on other computers. If you use AutoCAD for Windows, capture the configuration session to a log file and print it out. If you have a lot of machines to configure, write a configuration script to automate the process (see Chapter 16 for information about scripts).

The Plot Dialogue Box

Now that we have at least one device configured, we can look at the PLOT dialogue box more closely and actually create a plot. As Figure 11.12 shows, the Plot Configuration dialogue is grouped into six sections:

- **Device and Default Information.** Opens a subdialogue that lets you select plotters, change device-specific settings, and save and recall Plot Configuration Parameters (.PCP) files.

- **Pen Parameters.** Opens a subdialogue for setting the color-to-pen mapping. Also includes a subdialogue for changing pen optimization.

- **Additional Parameters.** Lets you specify what to plot, where to send it, and a few additional miscellaneous settings.

- **Paper Size and Orientation.** Opens a subdialogue with a list of paper sizes and orientations for your output device. Also includes radio buttons for choosing whether you want to input paper and pen sizes in inches or millimeters.

- **Scale, Rotation, and Origin.** Gives two ways of specifying the plot scale. Also includes a subdialogue for rotating the plot on the sheet and changing the plot origin.

- **Plot Preview.** Lets you choose to do a quick, partial preview or more involved, full preview.

Most of the settings in the Plot Configuration dialogue are borrowed from the old, text-screen version of the PLOT command; they're just easier to interactively change from the dialogue box. Instead of rehashing the PLOT command, we'll review the new features and offer some ideas for using them to make your plotting life more productive. Chapter 13 of the *AutoCAD Reference Manual* covers AutoCAD plotting in detail.

Tip

The old, text-screen PLOT command is still available, and in fact, Release 12 switches to it automatically if a script or AutoLISP program is running. If you want to see the text-screen version rather than the dialogue, set the new system variable CMDDIA ("command dialogue") to 0 before running the PLOT command. Set it back to 1 in order to restore the Plot Configuration dialogue. One use for setting CMDDIA to 0 is when you want to determine the prompts for a plot script. See Chapter 16, *Scripts*, for more information about scripts and plotting.

SELECTING DEVICES

The Device and Default Selection subdialogue (see Figure 11.14) is where you select from the output devices you've configured and look at or modify any device-specific settings (such as number of copies or paper tray). Also hidden away in this subdialogue are the Save Defaults to File... and Get Defaults from File... buttons for saving and retrieving Plot Configuration Parameters (.PCP) files.

PCP files let you take a snapshot of the current plot settings and save them in an ASCII file. Later on, you can recall these same settings by loading the file. PCP files are a tremendous tool for automating plot setup and ensuring plot consistency; they can save most of the time and aggravation that many users spend trying to remember what plot settings they used on a project three months ago. PCP files are documented in Chapter 2 of the *AutoCAD Customization Manual*. Figure 11.15 shows the beginning of a sample .PCP file.

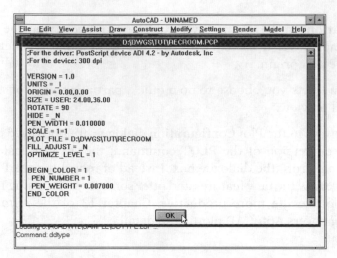

Figure 11.15 A sample Plot Configuration Parameters file.

 NOTE

Select the PostScript Plotter device you added earlier.

ASSIGNING PENS

Assigning pen parameters (see Figure 11.16) is a bit easier now, since you can assign to multiple colors at once. It's also more flexible; you now can specify values for up to 255 colors, although you should save this flexibility for when you need it. You don't want to be worrying about assigning parameters to 255 colors when a plotting deadline is bearing down on you. Use .PCP files to save company-wide or project-specific pen parameter configurations.

 NOTE

Assign Pen No. or Width to the first 15 colors, using a scheme similar to the one shown in Figure 11.16, or your own office's conventions.

CHOOSING WHAT TO PLOT

Nothing new here. Click the radio button of your choice. Choose the View... or Window... button first in order to pick a named view or plot window. Pick the Plot To File checkbox and then the File... button in order to specify a plot file.

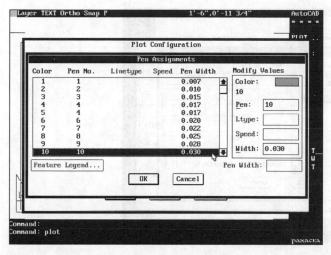

Figure 11.16 The Pen Assignments subdialogue.

Tip

Some plotters are controlled by the Pen No. field, while others are controlled by the Width field. Check your plotter documentation and the *AutoCAD Interface, Installation, and Performance Guide*. If you're more familiar with specifying pen widths in millimeters, choose the MM radio button in the Paper Size and Orientation area of the main Plot Configuration dialogue before entering the Pen Assignments subdialogue. Remember to change back to Inches (assuming that's what you normally use) when you're done assigning pens.

NOTE

Pick Limits and Plot To File. Pick the File... button and use the drawing name (RECROOM) as the plot filename.

SELECTING PAPER SIZES

The enhancements here (see Figure 11.17) are more standard paper sizes for most devices, and up to five user-defined sizes (instead of one, as in Release 11).

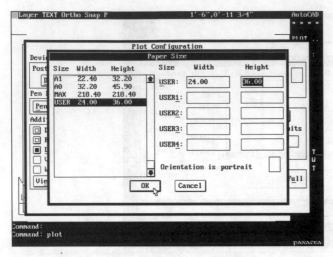

Figure 11.17   The Paper Size subdialogue.

 NOTE

The default D-size sheet is 22" × 34", which is smaller than the "architectural D" of 24" × 36". Specify a Width of 24 and a Height of 36 in the User: row.

SPECIFYING ROTATION AND SCALE

When you choose Scaled to Fit, AutoCAD now displays the scale it calculates. When you uncheck this box, you can enter values into the Plotted Inches = Drawing Units text fields. The Plot Rotation and Origin subdialogue (Figure 11.18) is a simple way to specify these settings.

 NOTE

Uncheck the Scaled to Fit box and enter 1 = 1 for the plot scale, since we're plotting from paper space. Leave the rotation and origin alone for now.

PREVIEWING

AutoCAD finally lets you preview plots! Release 12 offers two types of previews, a quick "see whether it fits" Partial preview (Figure 11.19), and a "show all the geometry" Full preview (Figure 11.20). Partial preview allows you to see how the scale, rotation, and origin interact with the paper size and orientation. Note that plot rotation is indicated by a small triangle. It's in the

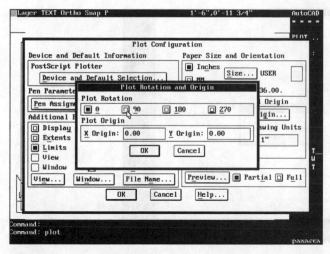

Figure 11.18 The Plot Rotation and Origin subdialogue.

lower left corner for 0 degrees rotation, upper left for 90 degrees, and so on. You can quickly catch a lot of plotting problems by looking at this preview. Get in the habit of using it before every plot.

Full preview takes longer, because AutoCAD has to generate all of the geometry, but it gives you a better idea of where specific parts of your drawing will land on the paper. Do a full preview when you're not sure whether your drawing has "slipped off the edge" of the paper.

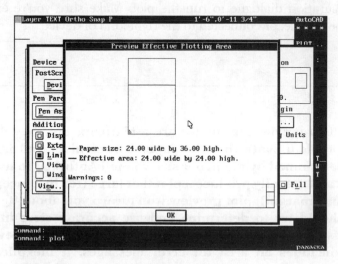

Figure 11.19 Partial preview.

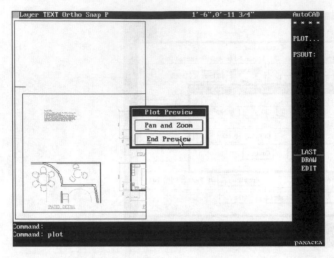

Figure 11.20 Full preview.

 NOTE

Use both preview modes to check your settings. Try changing the plot scale, paper size, and rotation angle a few times in order to note the effect on previewing. You should find that you need to rotate the plot 90 degrees in order to fit it on the paper. Once you've got things right, return to the Device and Default Selection subdialogue and use the Save Defaults to File... button to save your current plot parameters to a .PCP file. Finally, pick the OK button in the main Plot Configuration dialogue to run the plot. Make sure you're either configured to plot to a file, or connected to the right kind of device.

Tip

Release 12's two previewing modes are a big help, but they don't solve every problem. Note that the paper border displayed in the previews is determined by the paper size you tell AutoCAD to use. If your plotter can't actually produce a plot that large (for instance, if it requires a small margin), plot preview won't warn you about it. As a result, you should try to determine and use accurate sizes in the Paper Size subdialogue. Also, although the partial preview subdialogue includes an area for error messages, it inexplicably doesn't report the most common error: a plot that's slightly too large for the paper. If you have any doubts, do a full preview and check to be sure that all your geometry appears in the plot area.

Other Plotting Enhancements

There are several enhancements to plotting in Release 12 that don't appear in the Plot Configuration dialogue, but that can make life easier on users, AutoLISP programmers, and network administrators. We'll mention each of them in this section.

AutoLISP, Undo Buffer Preserved

In previous releases, plotting disabled AutoLISP and emptied the Undo buffer (so that you couldn't undo anything after plotting). AutoLISP now remains active during plotting, which means that customizers can write LISP programs to automate plotting. This feature, along with .PCP files, extends the control available over plotting; previously, the only way to automate plotting was with scripts. See Chapters 16 and 19 for suggestions on automating plotting with scripts and AutoLISP.

Because Release 12 preserves the Undo buffer when you plot, you now have one less worry when plotting. If you don't realize until after plotting that you've made a horrible editing mistake, you can still use Undo to get rid of it.

PLOTID and PLOTTER

Release 12 includes two new system variables that store the name of the current output device: PLOTTER and PLOTID. Both are intended for use in scripts and AutoLISP programs, when you want to automatically select an output device.

The PLOTTER system variable is an integer ranging from 0 to 28 that represents configured output devices 1 through 29. PLOTTER numbers are assigned based on the order in which you configure your devices; the first one is 0, the second one is 1, and so on (programmers do this just to aggravate us normal folk). If you delete an output device from the list, the numbers of the plotters after it in the list are changed to fill in the gap. As a result, you have to be careful when selecting a plotter by number in scripts and LISP programs. If your script uses a valid but incorrect number, the results probably will be interesting but not very useful.

PLOTID, on the other hand, is the name of the currently selected output device, as you typed it when you created the configuration. Since you have more control over PLOTID, it's usually the best one to use in scripts and AutoLISP programs. Just be sure you specify unique and consistent names when you configure output devices. Chapter 16 shows how to use PLOTID in plot scripts.

Freeplotting

Freeplotting is a special "mode" for starting up AutoCAD solely to plot a drawing. The advantages of freeplotting are that it doesn't consume a network license, and it doesn't regenerate the drawing or create temporary files on the hard disk. If you run AutoCAD on a network where the program files are located on the server, freeplotting can be a big help because it lets people plot without buying additional AutoCAD licenses. The disadvantage is that you can't change anything, including layer settings, while freeplotting.

To start up AutoCAD in freeplotting mode, enter the following:

```
C:\>ACADR12 -P <SCRIPT.SCR>
```

The parameter in angle brackets, *<SCRIPT.SCR>*, is optional; enter it to designate a plot script to use. Although you can use scripts in freeplotting mode, you can't run an AutoLISP program.

Most heavy users of AutoCAD won't use freeplotting much; the slightly increased speed is not worth the hassle of having to restart AutoCAD with freeplotting off if you suddenly realize that you need to make a change.

Paper Space, Plotting, and Workgroups

Release 11's paper space and the plotting improvements in Release 12 offer a lot of opportunities for getting the most out of the resources available to your workgroup. High-quality plots that take advantage of AutoCAD's plot composition abilities (when appropriate) and are cranked out on schedule get a lot of positive attention; the high costs and missed deadlines that result from poor plotting practices get a lot of negative attention. So, it's worth devoting some time to getting the most out of the new features.

You will need to reevaluate your approach to automating plotting as users move up to Release 12 (or if you haven't automated it yet, now is the time). Plot Configuration Parameters files are your simplest tools for making plotting easy and almost automatic. Develop and document a set of standard .PCP files for your workgroup, and make sure everyone knows how to retrieve and create .PCP files. Scripts are still useful when you want to automate the entire plot process, rather than use the Plot Configuration dialogue. You'll need to revise existing plot scripts, though, to account for the additional PLOT command prompts and to take advantage of the PLOTID system variable. AutoLISP provides additional control, but developing a robust plotting application with LISP and DCL is not for the faint of heart.

Three of the major topics discussed in this chapter differ in the degree to which they are amenable to organization. Plotter and printer setup is something that you want to standardize as much as possible. Everyone on your network should have a complete and consistent set of plotter drivers and configurations. Consider setting up multiple configurations for each device if that approach helps minimize the time people spend fiddling with plotter settings.

Paper space is a more difficult call. If your company hasn't yet used it much, you'll have to experiment with it a bit to find out where it's appropriate. If you find useful applications for it, work at developing a streamlined approach to using paper space that you can communicate to your workgroup members. Stress the importance of proper paper space setup and of using it in a way that minimizes its performance overhead. People are almost certain to need training in how to use paper space effectively; it's not the sort of thing that someone learns to use well by haphazard experimentation or by being under the gun.

Plot Preview, on the other hand, is something that most users will pretty much figure out for themselves. If you see a lot of wasted plots with obvious mistakes on them, you can take the opportunity to make sure that users understand Plot Preview and what to look for in the on-screen representation before plotting. Other than that, just emphasize efficient use of the Plot Configuration dialogue. And finally, get the AutoCAD 386 Release 12c2 update if you haven't already; it will minimize the time people spend scratching their heads over plotting and driver bugs.

12

Introduction to 3D

3D gets much of the attention in CAD advertising and the computer press, but it's no secret that most people still use AutoCAD and other CAD programs primarily for 2D drafting. While the prospect of developing a single three-dimensional project model from which drawings are extracted is appealing, there are practical impediments to working in this way, and few users have overcome the obstacles yet. Nonetheless, it's becoming more common to develop 3D models with AutoCAD for the purpose of examining design options or making presentations.

Release 10 was AutoCAD's "3D release;" before that, the program offered limited capabilities for constructing and viewing 3D models. Since Release 10, Autodesk has continued to move the program forward in the direction of full 3D work. Release 11 added paper space, a simple SHADE command, and the Advanced Modeling Extension (AME) option. Paper space provides a much more flexible way of viewing and plotting 3D models. The SHADE command helps you visualize 3D models better by shading opaque surfaces. AME lets mechanical engineers and others work with solid entities, rather than just surfaces and edges. Release 11 included a limited function "AME Lite" designed to introduce users to AME and encourage them to purchase the $500 AME option.

Release 12's major 3D enhancement is the new Render module, which sometimes is referred to as "AVE" (the Advanced Visualization Extension). AutoCAD Render includes most of the rendering capabilities of Autodesk's AutoShade program, including numerous lighting and surface finish and texture options. AutoCAD Render lacks Autodesk's Renderman, a powerful photo-realistic rendering engine that is available with AutoShade.

311

Release 12 no longer includes the AME Lite "teaser" that came with Release 11, but comes with the Region Modeler instead. The Region Modeler is a 2D version of AME: It lets you create and manipulate two-dimensional regions that can be extruded into three-dimensional solids.

Despite the substantial 3D improvements in Releases 10, 11, and 12, constructing and presenting 3D models is still a daunting task, especially when the subject being modeled is something as complex as a building. In part, the difficulties are the result of having to learn a radically new way to create drawings. Also, some seemingly simple tasks, such as punching a door opening through a wall, are still tedious multistep processes in AutoCAD. Some third-party applications will help flatten the learning curve and automate tedious tasks, but the job of using 3D efficiently is still a challenging one.

In the near future, most AutoCAD users will continue to spend the bulk of their time creating 2D drawings, but many users will benefit by becoming familiar with some basic 3D techniques. As third-party applications improve their 3D support and using AutoCAD for 3D applications becomes more common, users who are already acquainted with the basics will be ready to take advantage of 3D CAD.

Most users will get a solid payoff by learning a subset of AutoCAD's 3D capabilities, and by using those capabilities for some or all of the following:

- As a design aid for gross visualization.

- As a design aid for solving specific problems, such as how (or whether) objects fit together in 3D space.

- For on-screen presentations of concepts or completed design work.

- For simple printed presentations of concepts or completed design work.

If you start out with smaller, simpler applications of 3D, you should become familiar with working in 3D while solving problems in your daily work. As your experience grows, you'll be able to take advantage of a wider range of 3D capabilities in AutoCAD, third-party add-ons to AutoCAD, and the increasing number of 3D symbol libraries from manufacturers and third-party developers.

If you try to go much farther, especially in the beginning, you're likely to encounter obstacles and spend a lot of time without necessarily reaping much benefit. The potential pitfalls include hardware that isn't up to the job, getting lost in details that aren't appropriate for 3D, and inadequate 3D support from your third-party applications.

It's possible to overcome all these problems, but doing so is an evolutionary process that takes time and experience. Some users find the benefits of using 3D for a large part of their work to be worth the problems, while others do not. Rendering, in particular, can take up a great deal of your time in learning and in waiting on your machine before producing many benefits. Also, many users find that getting the results they want, especially for presentations, requires coupling AutoCAD with other programs, such as 3D Studio. The results can be spectacular, but the learning curve can be spectacularly long, also.

About This Chapter

In this chapter, we introduce a useful subset of AutoCAD's 3D capabilities to those who haven't ventured much beyond 2D work in the past. This is the most useful approach for 2D-oriented AutoCAD users and covers 3D in a way that can fit in a chapter, rather than taking up a whole separate book. Those who already are familiar with 3D probably will know most of what we cover here, and probably will have experience with additional programs used for 3D-specific work, as well.

Our example here, as in the rest of the book, is a simple architectural one. Houses and buildings have the advantage of being meaningful to anyone who lives and works in them, and they present 3D problems that are general in nature. However, 3D techniques tend to be more specialized than 2D ones. For example, some disciplines can make due with wireframe representations, while other disciplines are concerned primarily with surfaces.

Mechanical engineers usually are interested in the solid properties of their models and may need to delve into AME. We don't cover AME (nor Region Modeler) in this book. Refer to the *Advanced Modeling Extension Reference Manual*, the *AutoCAD Extras Manual* (for information on Region Modeler), and other third-party books.

Because this chapter is intended as an introduction to 3D, we cover AutoCAD Render only briefly and use the simpler SHADE command for showing shaded surfaces. We discuss the differences between SHADE and Render, and we demonstrate Render briefly at the end of the chapter. The *AutoCAD Render Reference Manual* is a good source of information for those who want to delve more deeply into rendering, and it includes an extensive tutorial.

Features Demonstrated in This Chapter

This chapter demonstrates 3D basics and shows off some of the new Release 12 dialogue boxes that make working in 3D a bit easier. The chapter is not as strictly focused on Release 12 as earlier chapters, because working in 3D is still new ground for most users. We discuss the following features and capabilities:

- Quickly setting up model space viewports in order to create a 3D workspace comprising multiple, simultaneous views of a 3D model.

- Establishing a different viewpoint in each viewport with the new DDVPOINT dialogue box.

- Extruding 2D entities into 3D by adding thickness.

- Covering areas with 3D Faces so that they'll appear as surfaces.

- Shading a 3D model to give a quick feel for its real-world appearance.

- Rendering a 3D model in order to have more control over lighting and surfaces than is available with simple shading.

About the Example

In this chapter, we create a model space viewport layout for our RECROOM drawing, use extrusion and 3D Faces to add surfaces to it, shade it, and finally, render it to the screen. If you don't have an up-to-date version of RECROOM as of the previous chapter, you can use the RRCH12.DWG file on the *AutoCAD Power Tools* disk as a starting point.

Using Viewports in Model Space

AutoCAD supports two types of viewports: the paper space viewports we used in the previous chapter and model space viewports. Paper space viewports, like paper space itself, are used primarily for plot layout and other presentation needs, whether for 2D or 3D drawings. Model space viewports are for creating a workspace in which you can construct 3D models effectively.

Model space viewports are more limited than paper space viewports, but they impose less of a conceptual and performance overhead. Model space viewports carve AutoCAD's drawing area into an assemblage of "tiled" windows, each of which can show the 3D model from a different point of view. The viewports are tiled in the sense that they abut one another and fill the drawing area. Unlike paper space viewports, model space viewports aren't entities, and you can't move or stretch them. Also, you can't plot a group of model space viewports together; for that, you need to use paper space. Finally, you can't change layer visibility in individual model space viewports; there's nothing like paper space's VPLAYER for model space.

Model space viewports subdivide already limited screen real estate, but they're indispensable for 3D work. You can't see where things are in 3D space without them! Even with viewports, it can be hard to figure out what's going

Tip

Viewports can have 3D performance advantages, as well. The HIDE and SHADE commands work more quickly in small viewports. If your display driver supports rendering in a viewport, you can render in a viewport rather than to the full screen. The rendering process will go faster, and you'll be able to look at the rendering alongside the views in other viewports.

on, but at least with them you have a fighting chance. Your brain is pretty good at taking multiple 2D views and assembling them into a 3D image; viewports give it the opportunity to do so.

Use model space viewports to set up multiple views, differing only in the viewpoint from which you look at the model (e.g., top, side, and isometric). The different viewpoints make it much easier to create geometry in the proper place in 3D space and to see the overall effects of editing changes.

In the following sections, we'll discuss how to create and use tiled model space viewports. Then, a tutorial section will show how to set up viewports and viewpoints for our RECROOM drawing.

Before Using Viewports

Before you set up your viewports, consider the fact that working in 3D usually requires a lot of regenerations. Smart drafters learn to avoid regens in 2D work, but the techniques for doing so don't always work in 3D. Every viewpoint change requires a regen, and 3D work often involves these viewpoint changes, especially during setup. You'll want to arrange your model so that regens are as short as possible. Take these steps before you start setting up viewports:

Clean up	Make any needed changes in the drawing that you've been putting off. It can be hard to see what's going on in quarter-screen viewports; having the drawing in good shape will help.
Freeze layers	You should freeze layers that contain text, dimensions, hatching, title blocks, or anything else that isn't part of your 3D model. As discussed in Chapter 3, *Performance*, AutoCAD ignores geometry on frozen layers during regens. Use the DDLMODES or LAYER command to freeze unneeded layers, then thaw them when you need them again for 2D work.

Turn on UCS icon   The UCS icon indicates the orientation (and, optionally, the origin) of the User Coordinate System that's currently in use. The icon will help you stay oriented and prevent you from having to change viewpoints in order to find out "where" you are in 3D space. The command-line sequence UCSICON ON will turn on the UCS icon.

Setting Up Viewports

In the previous chapter, we used MVSETUP to create a paper space viewport and ARRAY to make three more of them. We also mentioned the MVIEW command as an alternative way to create paper space viewports. Setting up model space viewports proceeds in a different way, and is based in the VPORTS command. VPORTS includes options for dividing and joining viewports, saving and restoring viewport configurations, and returning to a single viewport.

For creating a viewport layout, the easiest approach is to use the Tiled Viewport Layout icon menu, which is available from the View menu: Pick View, then Layout, then Tiled Vports... . This icon menu (which looks like a dialogue box—see Figure 12.1) lets you choose from a dozen preset viewport configurations. When you pick one of the configurations, AutoCAD runs the VPORTS command and selects the options necessary to create the configuration.

The "Four: Equal" configuration is a reasonable choice for general 3D work, especially on a small to medium-size screen where smaller viewports make it difficult to make out details of your model. You can work in any of the four equally sized viewports, although you might end up settling on one as your primary working view. One of the upper viewports is a good choice because it's closer to the menus.

Some users prefer a configuration with one large working viewport and two or three small viewports along the left or right side of the screen (e.g., the "Four: Left" configuration in Figure 12.1). The large viewport gives you more room in which to work and the smaller ones act as reference viewports.

Once you've created a viewport configuration and set of viewpoints you like, you can use the VPORTS Save option to give the configuration a name. This procedure is similar to saving a named view; it lets you return to a desired screen arrangement (with VPORTS Restore) quickly. See Chapter 7 of the *AutoCAD Reference Manual* for more information about the VPORTS command.

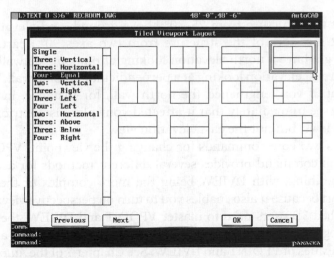

Figure 12.1 The Tiled Viewport Layout icon menu.

Tip

Model space viewport configurations don't directly affect paper space; any viewport setup you do in one space is independent of the other space. There is one handy exception: If you create a model space viewport configuration you'd like to use as the starting point for a paper space viewport layout, you can "import" the configuration with the MVIEW command's Restore option. This technique is useful when you want to plot several 3D views that you've already arranged in model space.

Establishing Viewpoints

When you first create multiple viewports, AutoCAD puts the same view into all of them—a sensible default, but not particularly useful. You need to change each view to a viewpoint that's useful in itself and that coordinates well with the others. Then you have to pan and zoom until the viewport shows the portion of the model you're interested in seeing.

In most cases, you'll use some variation on orthographic projection views (top, front, and side), plus an isometric view. The isometric view usually provides the best overall feel for how the object looks in three dimensions, but the orthographic views often are more convenient for drawing and editing. (Note: We use "isometric" in the more general sense of a nonorthographic view.)

For instance, on an architectural project, a useful arrangement of four views might be a plan view, looking straight down; an isometric view, looking down at the structure from 25–30° above ground; and elevations, views looking at the sides of the structure from two axes 90° apart. For instance, you might have a north elevation looking at one outside wall of a structure, and an east elevation looking at a perpendicular outside wall. With this arrangement, if you lengthened the north wall, for instance, in plan view, you would see immediately that it affected your plan, isometric, and north elevation views, but not the east elevation view.

AutoCAD offers two core commands for changing the viewpoint: VPOINT and DVIEW. Each command provides several different methods for accomplishing the same thing, with DVIEW being the more complex of the two commands (in part because it also enables you to turn on perspective viewing). While accomplished 3D users need to master VPOINT and DVIEW, the new DDVPOINT dialogue in Release 12 is adequate for many users' needs and it avoids the complexities of VPOINT and DVIEW. See Chapter 7 of the *AutoCAD Reference Manual* for more information about VPOINT and DVIEW.

The DDVPOINT Dialogue

The Viewpoint Presets dialogue box (see Figure 12.2), makes it easy to set up and experiment with multiple views. (Not only that, it's a good example of sophisticated dialogue box design and programming.) To bring this dialogue up, enter the command DDVPOINT, or from the View menu, pick Set View, then Viewpoint, and finally, Presets....

Unlike some other AutoCAD dialogues, this one does even more than a quick glance might indicate. For some reason, DDVPOINT isn't described in the AutoCAD Release 12 documentation. Since some of its functionality

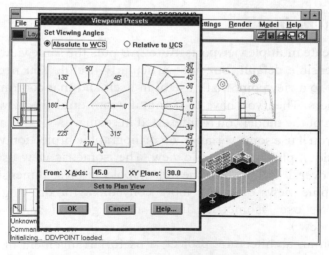

Figure 12.2   The Viewpoint Presets dialogue box.

might not immediately be obvious, we'll cover it in some detail. We'll also demonstrate the use of this dialogue in the tutorial below.

You define a viewpoint in the Viewpoint Presets dialogue by specifying two angles: rotation from the X axis in the XY plane, and rotation up out of the X plane. These two rotations define a direction from which the eye looks back at the drawing's origin point (0,0,0). DDVPOINT, like VPOINT, creates parallel projection views, so the eye is assumed to be infinitely far away (i.e., no perspective).

SET VIEWING ANGLES

The Set Viewing Angles section at the top of the dialogue allows you to tell AutoCAD whether to treat the viewing angles as Absolute (i.e., in relation to the World Coordinate System, or WCS) or Relative (in relation to the User Coordinate System, or UCS). The User Coordinate System is AutoCAD's way of letting you create, draw, and edit in other coordinate systems. In this chapter, we'll do all our work in the World Coordinate System; see Chapter 9 of the *AutoCAD Reference Manual* for more information about UCSs.

FROM X AXIS

This section sets the angle of the viewpoint from the X axis. This setting takes effect only when the From XY Plane setting (described below) is anything other than 90° or –90° (i.e., when you aren't looking from a direction directly perpendicular to the XY plane). Assuming the From XY Plane setting is something other than 90° or –90°, changing From X Axis has the effect of rotating your eye around the object. Imagine flying a helicopter in a circle while maintaining the same altitude and keeping your eye fixed on one point on the ground. The default value for From X Axis is 270°, which usually translates to a "front" view of your model once you change the From XY Plane setting.

The From X Axis section consists of two related parts: the entry area, in which you can key in an angle, and the "square with a donut hole," in which you can pick the angle interactively. At any time, the current angle is shown by a number in the entry area and also by the direction of one of the line segment pointers (the other pointer shows what the setting was when you started DDVPOINT).

This interactive area is worth experimenting with. If you pick in the area between the outer square and the inner circle, the angle is set to the nearest multiple of 45°: 45°, 90°, 135°, and so forth. But if you pick in the area inside the circle, the angle is set based on exactly where you pick, to within one-tenth of a degree. In either case, the number in the entry box and the line segment in the center both change to show the angle you have selected, and changing one updates the other.

FROM XY PLANE

This section sets the angle of the viewpoint from the 2D XY plane—what anyone but an architect would call the elevation. The effect of changing this angle is the same as changing altitude in the helicopter: You see the landscape from a steeper or flatter angle.

Like the From X Axis section, the From XY Plane section consists of two related parts: the entry area, in which you can key in an angle, and the "half of a pineapple slice," in which you can pick the angle interactively. At any time, the current angle is shown by a number in the entry area and also by the direction of the line segment at the center of the interactive area.

Similar to the From X Axis area, picking between the two semicircles selects a nice, round angle: 0°, 10°, 30°, 45°, etc. Picking inside the inner semicircle selects an exact angle to a precision of one-tenth of a degree. The number in the entry box and the line segment in the center both change to show the angle you have selected, and changing one updates the other.

SET TO PLAN VIEW

This button resets the angles to 270° from the X axis and 90° from the XY plane (i.e., AutoCAD's default plan view).

3D Setup Tutorial

In this tutorial, we'll create four equal-size model space viewports in the RECROOM drawing, and then set the viewpoint in each viewport to a different angle. These are preparatory steps before we make a simple 3D model from the recreation room and then shade it in the next tutorial.

Before you convert a 2D drawing to 3D, it's a good idea to save it with a different name so that you don't have to worry about corrupting your 2D version. This approach breaks the associativity between the 2D drawing and 3D model, but when you're starting out with 3D CAD, it's a safer route.

1. Load RECROOM.DWG and save it as RECROOM3.DWG.

Use your drawing from the previous chapter, or copy RRCH12.DWG from the *AutoCAD Power Tools* disk.

Also copy RECFURN3.DWG from the AutoCAD Power Tools *disk.*

You'll need RECFURN3 in the second tutorial.

Start AutoCAD and open RECROOM.DWG.

Use the SAVEAS command to save the drawing as RECROOM3.DWG.

This step creates a new drawing for our 3D work and leaves the original 2D drawing unharmed.

2. Leave paper space.

```
Command: TILEMODE
New value for TILEMODE <default>: 1
Regenerating drawing.
```

This command sequence turns off paper space and returns you to model space.

3. Make sure the UCS icon is turned on.

```
Command: UCSICON
ON/OFF/All/Noorigin/ORigin <default>: ON
```

The UCS icon will appear in the lower left corner of the drawing window.

4. Freeze all unneeded layers—all except RUG, SCRATCH, SLAB, WALL, and WALLFUT.

Pick Layer Control... from the Settings menu.

Select the RUG layer and make it current.

Select the WALLFUT layer and change its linetype to Continuous.

Dashed linetypes don't look very good in 3D.

Pick the Select All button.

Pick the RUG, SCRATCH, SLAB, WALL, and WALLFUT layers to deselect them.

Pick the Freeze button.

Pick OK.

The drawing will appear with only the slab, walls, and rugs. We'll need the SCRATCH layer in a later tutorial.

5. Create a model space viewport configuration with four identically sized viewports .

Zoom in on the plan.

Zoom so that you leave a small margin around the slab.

Pick Layout from the View menu.

Pick Tiled Vports... from the Layout submenu.

Pick the fourth choice, four equal-size viewports, from the Tiled Viewport Layout icon menu.

The drawing will appear identically in four different viewports. See Figure 12.3.

6. Bring up the Viewpoint Presets dialogue for the lower right viewport.

Pick in the lower right viewport to make it current.

```
Command: DDVPOINT
```
or
Pick Set View from the View menu.
Pick Viewpoint from the Set View submenu.
Pick Presets... from the Viewpoint submenu.

The Viewpoint Presets dialogue will appear over the drawing; see Figure 12.4.

7. Set the viewpoint in the lower right viewport to an isometric view, 45° from the X axis, 30° from the XY plane.

Pick 45° in the X Axis area on the left.

Pick 30° in the XY Plane area on the right.

Check the contents of the entry boxes to make sure you picked the angles correctly.

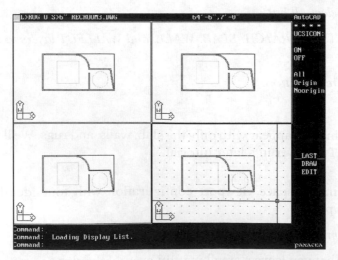

Figure 12.3 Four equal viewports showing RECROOM with most layers frozen.

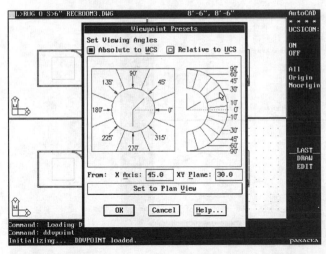

Figure 12.4   Setting the viewpoint with DDVPOINT.

Pick OK.

The viewing plane will be rotated and tilted.

8. Set the viewpoint in the lower left viewport to a north elevation: 90° from the X axis, 0° from the XY plane.

Pick in the lower left viewport to highlight it.

`Command:` *<Enter> to repeat DDVPOINT.*

Pick 90° in the X Axis area on the left.

Pick 0° in the XY Plane area on the right.

Pick OK.

The viewing plane will be turned and laid flat; you won't see much yet, because you're looking "edge-on" at a 2D drawing.

Zoom to a comfortable level.

When you change viewpoints, AutoCAD does the equivalent of a ZOOM Extents. In order to leave a small margin around the elevation view, you can ZOOM .9X, and then ZOOM Window if necessary.

9. Set the viewpoint in the upper left viewport to an east elevation: 0° from the X axis, 0° from the XY plane.

Pick in the upper left viewport to highlight it.

`Command:` `DDVPOINT`

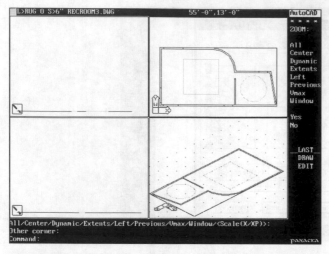

Figure 12.5 The RECROOM drawing from four different viewpoints.

> *Pick 0° in the X Axis area on the left.*
>
> *Pick 0° in the XY Plane area on the right.*
>
> *Pick OK.*
>
> Once again, you won't see much yet.
>
> *Zoom to a comfortable level.*
>
> See Figure 12.5 for the appearance of the drawing after these steps.

10. Save the viewport configuration, and then save the drawing.

```
Command: VPORTS
Save/Restore/Delete/Join/SIngle/?/2/<3>/4: S
?/Name for new viewport configuration: 4EQ
```

This step makes it easy to return to the current viewport configuration.

> *Save the drawing at this point.*

From 2D to 3D

Once you've set up viewports and viewpoints, you're ready to add the third dimension to your drawing. There are many ways to create 3D models, from simple extrusion of lines to complicated generation of 3D meshes. In some cases, it's easiest to modify a 2D drawing, while in other situations, building the 3D model from scratch makes more sense.

In this chapter, we'll explore two of the simpler methods for creating a 3D model from a 2D drawing: extruding existing 2D entities (by adding thickness to them) and "pasting" 3D Faces over areas and onto extruded entities. These techniques are comparatively simple to learn and can be used in many situations. They let you work in familiar 2D views without requiring UCS changes.

Extrusion is the simplest method for creating a 3D model from 2D entities. AutoCAD lets you assign a "thickness" (architects would call it a height) to most types of entities. The thickness makes the entity "pop up" from the plane it was drawn in, and the resulting surface works well for hiding, shading, and rendering. A common application for extrusion is to create 3D walls.

Extrusion is fine for simple shapes, but its limitations become obvious as you work with more complicated objects, such as walls with openings in them. You might think you could just draw closed Polylines to create solid areas, but that doesn't work; unfortunately, AutoCAD doesn't treat closed Polylines as surfaces. Circles are treated as surfaces—if you shade them, they "fill in" with the appropriate color. But triangles, squares, and more complicated closed shapes are treated as one-dimensional lines. If you shade them, nothing happens to the enclosed areas. 3D Faces are the simplest solution to this problem. 3D Faces are quadrilateral or triangular surfaces with which you can build up more complex surfaces.

We'll discuss extrusion and 3D Faces, and then demonstrate in a tutorial some simple ways of using them. This introduction to 3D construction will get you started, but don't expect excellent results or complete mastery right away. Efficient 3D drawing takes many hours of experimenting, training courses or additional books, and additional third-party software. Nonetheless, you can benefit from 3D in the short term if you limit your goals and learn how to use simple techniques creatively.

Adding Thickness to Entities

Adding thickness to entities, also known as "extruding" them, is easy and immediately rewarding. If you're working with a drawing that's well-suited to this kind of treatment, you may be able to generate an acceptable 3D version of your model with just a few commands.

CHPROP, DDCHPROP, and DDMODIFY are the AutoCAD commands for adding thickness to existing entities. Chapter 8, *Modifying Properties and Hatching*, discusses these commands and offers suggestions on when to use each one. To summarize, use CHPROP and DDCHPROP for changing the thickness (or other properties) of multiple entities. CHPROP is the quick, keyboard-oriented command; DDCHPROP puts CHPROP's functionality in a friendly dialogue box interface. Use DDMODIFY when you want to change the thickness or other characteristics of a single entity, and you want to be able to see all the characteristics at a glance. Figure 12.6 shows how you

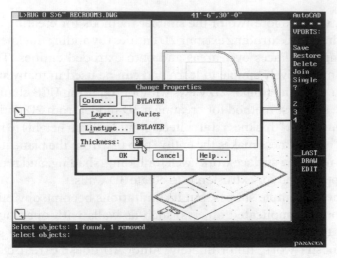

Figure 12.6 Changing thickness with DDCHPROP.

change the thickness of a group of entities with DDCHPROP. Figure 12.7 shows the DDMODIFY command being used to extrude a Line.

Adding thickness to entities and then shading them is a quick and satisfying way to give your drawing a 3D appearance, but as discussed earlier, this approach is limited. You can't easily create fully closed volumes (e.g., walls will appear hollow, with no cap on top) or cut away pieces of the extruded surfaces (e.g. door and window openings). To perform these sorts of tasks, you'll need to resort to 3D Faces.

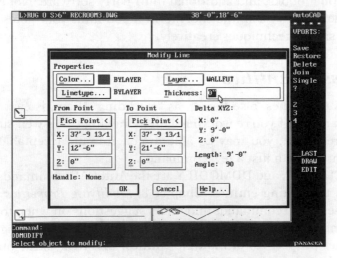

Figure 12.7 Changing thickness with DDMODIFY.

Tip

An alternative to extruding entities after you've drawn them is to use the ELEV command. ELEV allows you to set the ELEVATION and THICKNESS system variables, which determine the base elevation and thickness for entities as you draw them. In some situations, using ELEV is more efficient, since it lets you create extruded entities as you go. On the other hand, you need to keep a close watch on the ELEV settings, especially if you're working in a single 2D view. It's easy to create entities at the wrong elevation or with the wrong thickness if you aren't careful. See Chapter 8 of the *AutoCAD Reference Manual* for more information about ELEV.

3D Faces

A 3D Face is a quadrilateral or triangle that AutoCAD treats as a surface for the purposes of hiding, shading, and rendering. You use 3D Faces to cover polygonal areas or volumes. A 3D Face resembles a 2D Solid entity, but 3D Faces need not lie in a plane; their corners can be situated anywhere in 3D space. This capability gives 3D Faces a lot of flexibility, but it also means that you have to specify each point carefully. Also, because 3D Faces must be 4- or 3-sided, covering a complex area or volume can be a tedious task (third-party applications are a big help here).

The easiest way to use 3D Faces is to "paste" them on existing entities by snapping to intersections and typing in relative coordinates when necessary. In the next tutorial, we'll use this technique to create a rug that shades properly and a wall opening.

Tip

AutoCAD normally displays all edges of each 3D Face, but you can tell the program to make one or more edges invisible. This capability is useful when you build up a surface out of 3D Face "tiles" and want to hide the lines where the tiles abut. The DDMODIFY command is one way to make 3D Face edges invisible. See Chapter 5 of the *AutoCAD Reference Manual* for more information about hidden edges.

Hidden Line Removal

By default, AutoCAD displays 3D models in a wireframe view—one in which edges are displayed and surfaces are transparent. The resulting "x-ray vision" view can be helpful, but it gets confusing as your model grows more complex. Often, you'll want to view a model in a more realistic way: with hidden lines removed or surfaces made opaque.

We'll discuss shading and rendering options in the next section of the chapter. Hidden line removal is a more primitive way to create semirealistic views. The view is still of edges only (i.e., no surface shading), but portions of entities that are behind other surfaces (such as extruded lines or 3D Faces) disappear. The advantages of hidden line removal are that it's simple and, in Release 12, relatively fast. You just type HIDE and wait for the results—there are no options to worry about. The hidden-line view is only temporary; type REGEN to restore the normal view.

Tip

If there are layers you don't want included in a hidden-line view, be sure to freeze them rather than turn them off. The HIDE command ignores entities on frozen layers, but it does consider entities on layers that are turned off. For instance, a 3D Face on a layer that's been turned off will obscure anything behind it, even though the face itself won't appear. The results can be confusing, to say the least.

Fine-Tuning the 3D Image

One of the problems with generating a 3D model is that many 2D representations don't resemble 3D objects. For instance, the convention of representing a door in a floor plan by a line and an arc doesn't cut it in 3D. Using bare AutoCAD to generate a doorway and a door to fit in it that look anything like reality is a great deal of work.

Third-party applications can hide a lot of the painful details of working in 3D, with built-in support for such common objects as doors, windows, mechanical components, and so on. At a certain point, however, you'll probably need to resort to stock AutoCAD commands for fine-tuning the 3D appearance of your model. At this point, you might find that the package has enabled you to get in over your head. In some cases, you can create a complex 3D drawing quickly, but modifying it to come up with a useful end product can be tricky and time-consuming.

These kinds of problems—and even the solutions have their own problems—make 3D work a real time-sink, especially when you're starting out. You can spend a great deal of time and end up with something that still doesn't look all that great. Try for "pretty good" results within a reasonable time period before pushing for even better results.

Solving these kinds of problems is what separates the experienced 3D user from the novice. Initially, you'll learn to solve problems; then you'll begin to learn which ones you can avoid by doing things differently in your original 2D drawing, by using third-party extensions to AutoCAD, and by using other software packages. Or you'll set a level of expertise that you want to achieve and a level of quality that you're willing to accept, and limit your investment of time and energy appropriately.

3D Construction Tutorial

In this tutorial, we'll extrude the walls, create 3D Faces for the slab and square rug, and import some 3D furniture.

1. Extrude the walls to a height of 8'.

```
Command: DDCHPROP
Select objects: Select all of the wall lines.
```

Use a window to select everything, and then deselect the slab and two rugs by holding down the <Shift> key and picking these three entities.

In the Thickness: edit box, type 8'.

The walls will become 8' tall, as is apparent in all the viewports except the plan view in the upper right. See Figure 12.8.

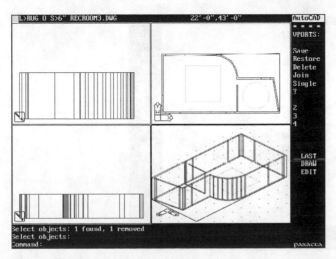

Figure 12.8 RECROOM with extruded walls.

2. Hide and then shade the model.

Pick in the lower right viewport to make it current.

Hiding and shading usually works best in an isometric view.

```
Command: HIDE
```
or
Pick Hide from the Render menu.

```
Regenerating drawing..
Hiding lines: done 100%
```

After several seconds, a hidden-line view appears in the viewport. Notice that the walls appear "empty" on top, and that they have no true openings (see Figure 12.9).

```
Command: SHADE
```
or
Pick Shade from the Render menu.

```
Regenerating drawing..
Shading complete.
```

This time, a shaded surface view appears in the viewport. We'll discuss shading in the next section, but for now, notice that the slab and square rug don't shade (see Figure 12.9).

Unless you have a fondness for magenta walls, you might want to change the color assigned to the WALL layer. This is a good opportunity to experiment with all those colors your graphics card can dis-

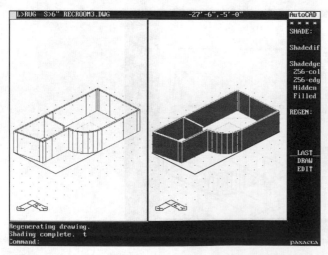

Figure 12.9   HIDE versus SHADE.

play. Once you've changed the color of the WALL layer, run SHADE again to see the results.

3. Replace the Polyline representing the rug with a 3D Face so that it shades correctly.

First, you should move the Polyline to the SCRATCH layer so that you can erase it more easily later.

Pick in the upper right viewport to make it current.

Use CHPROP or DDCHPROP to change the square rug Polyline to the SCRATCH layer.

Now create the 3D Face:

Set Snap to 6" and turn Ortho on.

```
Command: 3DFACE
```
or
Pick 3D Surfaces from the Draw menu.
Pick 3D Face from the 3D Surfaces submenu.

```
First  point:  Pick the upper left corner of the square rug.
Second point:  Pick the upper right corner of the square rug.
Third  point:  Pick the lower right corner of the square rug.
Fourth point:  Pick the lower left corner of the square rug.
Third point: <Enter>
```

The additional Third point: Prompt gives you the opportunity to draw another 3D Face starting from the last edge of the previous face.

A 3D face appears, with its edges coinciding with the Polyline.

Run SHADE again and note that the rug now shades correctly.

4. Repeat step 3 for the slab.

Make SLAB the current layer.

Change the slab Polyline to the SCRATCH layer.

Start the 3DFACE command and trace over the slab edge.

5. Create a door opening in the wall next to the patio.

As mentioned earlier, extruded entities don't work well when you need to cut a notch or hole (such as a door or window opening) in a surface. 3D Faces are one approach to this task. As an example, we'll construct

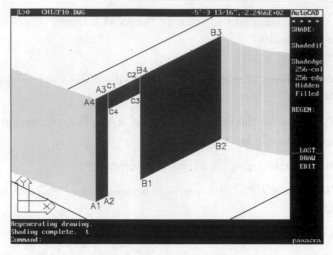

Figure 12.10   Three 3D Faces and the pick points for creating them.

a doorway in the wall between the patio and small TV room. The doorway will require three 3D Faces on each side of the wall: one face on either side of the doorway, and one above it (see Figure 12.10).

Use CHPROP or DDCHPROP to change the four Lines representing the wall and door opening to the SCRATCH layer.

These four Lines appear just north of the round rug.

Pick in the lower right viewport to make it current.

Set running object snap to ENDPoint:

```
Command: OSNAP
Object snap nodes: ENDP
```

ENDPoint helps ensure that you pick the right point in 3D space.

Now draw the first face:

```
Command: 3DFACE
First point: Pick the point labeled A1 in Figure 12.10.
Second point: Pick point A2.
Third point: Pick point A3.
Fourth point: Pick point A4.
Third point: <Enter>
```

These four points define the tall, narrow face to the east of the doorway.

Repeat the 3D Face sequence to draw the wide panel to the west of the opening:

Start the 3DFACE command and pick the four points labeled B1, B2, B3, and B4 in Figure 12.10.

Now use a combination of object snaps and relative coordinates to draw the header above the doorway:

```
Command: 3DFACE
First point: Pick the point labeled C1 (= A3) in Figure 12.10.
Second point: Pick point C2 (= B4).
Third point: @0,0,-1'4
```

These coordinates define point C3, 1'–4" below (i.e., in the negative Z direction from) point C2.

```
Fourth point: PERP
to: Pick near point C4.
Third point: <Enter>
```

If you temporarily turn off the SCRATCH layer and then run SHADE, the outside of the wall should look similar to Figure 12.10.

6. Repeat step 5 for the inside face of the wall, and then view the results.

Use DDVPOINT to change the viewpoint in the lower right viewport to 225° from the X axis, 30° from the XY plane.

The new viewpoint will make it easier to pick points on the inside face of the wall.

Repeat the procedure in step 5 to draw three faces on the inside of the wall.

Use DDVPOINT to change the viewpoint in the lower right viewport back to 45° from the X axis, 30° from the XY plane.

Set running object snap back to NONE:

```
Command: OSNAP
Object snap nodes: NONE
```

Freeze the SCRATCH layer.

Run SHADE.

You should be able to see the round rug through the door opening you created.

7. Import the 3D furniture layout.

Drawing 3D furniture from scratch is even more tedious than punching openings into walls. We'll assume that the interior decorator came to our rescue again with a simplified 3D furniture layout. This isn't quite as facetious as it sounds; many furniture manufacturers provide 3D (and 2D) renditions of their products on diskette.

```
Command: DDINSERT
```

The Insert dialogue appears.

Pick the File... button.

Locate the RECFURN3 drawing in your tutorial subdirectory or on the AutoCAD Power Tools *disk.*

Pick OK.

Pick the lower left corner of the rec room.

Make sure you use Snap or an object snap to ensure precision.

Accept default values for the remaining prompts.

8. Hide and Shade once more.

Repeat step 2 above and view the results.

If you want to explore further, try changing viewpoints and then hide or shade again (see Figure 12.11). For the most impressive results, return to a single viewport (type VPORTS SI) and hide or shade an isometric view.

As you can see, even simple 3D work can require a lot of steps. Of course,

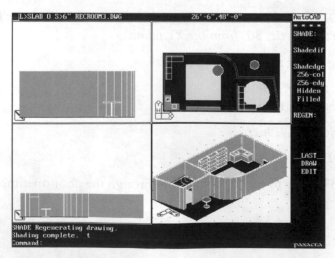

Figure 12.11 All four views of RECROOM shaded.

Tip

Once you create 3D views you like, you can use MSLIDE to make AutoCAD slides out of them and VSLIDE to view the slides later. By linking the slides together in a script, you can create a slide show. See Chapter 16, *Scripts,* **for details.**

you'll become more efficient as you gain more experience, and third-party applications can streamline many tasks. Chapter 7 of the *AutoCAD Tutorial Manual* contains an extended tutorial on 3D modeling that covers many additional 3D construction and editing techniques.

Shading and Rendering

In AutoCAD, "shading" and "rendering" refer to two superficially similar ways of showing opaque surfaces in drawings. These terms often are used interchangeably in everyday conversation, but in this book we use AutoCAD's distinction. "Shading" means "producing an image with the AutoCAD SHADE command," and "rendering" means "producing an image with the AutoCAD RENDER command."

The previous tutorial showed how SHADE works. In this section, we compare SHADE and RENDER, discuss some of the finer points of each, and then briefly demonstrate both in a tutorial section.

Shading

The SHADE command was added in Release 11 as a simple way of showing 3D models more realistically in AutoCAD. SHADE obscures hidden lines, as does HIDE, but it also "paints" extruded entities, 3D Faces, and other surfaces so that the model looks like more than an assemblage of wire edges. Assuming that your graphics card and driver support at least 256 colors, SHADE also uses a simple lighting scheme that helps make the model look more realistic. SHADE employs a combination of ambient light and a single directed light source, pointing from the viewpoint toward the origin. You can control the percentage of ambient light versus direct light (i.e., "diffuse reflection"), but you can't add other lights or define surface qualities other than color.

The advantages of shading are that it's easy and comparatively quick, with consistent, if unspectacular, results. The disadvantages of shading are that it doesn't produce a particularly attractive image and that the shaded image can't be printed.

SHADE is one of the few commands in AutoCAD that has no additional parameters; just enter SHADE (or pick Shade from the Render menu) and the current viewport will be shaded. You can exercise limited control over shading by setting the SHADEDGE and SHADEDIF system variables (described below) before running SHADE. Only the following entities will be affected by the SHADE command:

- Circles, which define surfaces as well as edges.

- Entities that have been assigned an extrusion thickness.

- 3D Faces.

- Polygon meshes and polyface meshes (see Chapter 5 of the *AutoCAD Reference Manual*).

- Wide Polylines, Solids, and Traces (SHADE fills these entities in the same way they appear in plan view).

As with HIDE, the effects of the SHADE command are temporary; the next regen restores the wireframe view.

SHADEDGE

The SHADEDGE system variable controls how the SHADE command displays edges and surfaces. The settings range from 0 to 3. Most users will want to stick with 0 or 1, which use the lighting effects described above. 1 is a good all-around setting: Shaded surfaces are displayed with lighting effects, and edges appear highlighted in the background color (usually black or white) so that they stand out better.

The 0 setting is like 1, except that edges aren't highlighted. The lack of edge highlighting looks better with some models, but in others it causes the surfaces to merge into a formless blob. Experiment to find out which setting is more appropriate for your models. The 0 and 1 settings require that your graphics card and driver support at least 256 colors.

The highest setting, 3, works like 1, except that no lighting effects are used. As a result, every surface is uniformly bright, which doesn't look very realistic. A SHADEDGE setting of 2 causes SHADE to perform a simulated hidden line removal. This setting isn't very useful, except on monochrome screens.

SHADEDIF

The SHADEDIF system variable determines the relative contributions of diffuse reflection (from direct light) and ambient light to each surface's appearance. SHADEDIF is meaningful only when SHADEDGE is set to 0 or 1. By default, SHADEDIF is set to 70, which means that diffuse reflection from direct light contributes 70% and ambient light contributes 30% to each surface's appearance.

Increasing SHADEDIF increases direct light and decreases ambient light, which increases contrast but also makes the entire image appear darker. Decreasing SHADEDIF makes ambient light more predominant, which lightens the entire scene but also makes surfaces appear more uniformly lit. The plates in the middle of the *AutoCAD Render Reference Manual* show an example of high versus low ambient light.

Resolution, Colors, and Performance

Display resolution, number of available colors, and performance considerations are significant issues in shading, and vital issues in rendering. As mentioned above, a display mode that supports fewer than 256 colors limits what the SHADE command can do. With most graphics cards and drivers, you can reduce resolution in exchange for more colors. On the other hand, if you reduce the resolution too low, the shaded or rendered image won't be very useful or impressive.

A plain VGA video card with 256KB of video memory is limited to 320 x 200 resolution with 256 colors. Most graphics cards come with at least 512KB of video memory, which buys you 256 colors at 640 x 480 or 800 x 600 resolution. It takes 1MB of video memory to display 256 colors at 1024 x 768 resolution. With 1MB, your graphics card also may be able to display 32,000-plus colors or even "true color," 64,000-plus colors, in 640 x 480 resolution. Try different settings to get 256 colors for shading and the largest number of colors for rendering (without resolution becoming too low). Note that your AutoCAD driver also must support the mode you want to use.

Performance is an even more significant issue for 3D than it is for 2D AutoCAD, if only because of the additional regens required in 3D work. Generating a shaded image or hidden-line view takes longer than a regen, and rendering can take many times longer. Part of the appeal of 3D is generating these images, so one way or another, you'll be spending time waiting on your computer. Because of these factors, many of the system speedup options that help make your AutoCAD system more responsive become absolutely vital for efficient 3D work. See Chapter 3, *Performance*, for a discussion of some of the options.

As resolution and the number of colors increase, so do shading and rendering times. These times can become prohibitively long as your 3D models grow in complexity. Shading or rendering in a smaller viewport will help. Also, consider using a lower resolution mode as you experiment, and then switching to a higher resolution mode for final presentations.

Rendering

While the SHADE command is perfectly adequate for viewing many 3D models, it's inadequate for people who want more realistic 3D images or who want to output these images to color printers and plotters. AutoCAD Render adds the ability to define multiple light sources and different surface qualities, and to create rendered hardcopy on a variety of output devices.

On the other hand, rendering can become as complicated as shading is simple. Remember that AutoCAD Render used to be an entire stand-alone program (AutoShade), and as a result, it adds its own learning curve and set of commands. For those who need rendering capability, having it built into Release 12 certainly is convenient. Just be sure that you have the need, the hardware, and the time to master AutoCAD Render.

An image created with simple shading, rather than true rendering, may be just as effective in communicating as an overdone rendered image. A shaded image certainly is less expensive to generate. Also, bear in mind that effective rendering is as much art as technique. Just as AutoCAD won't magically turn someone into a good drafter or architect, AutoCAD Render won't ensure that your images are beautiful or compelling.

AutoCAD Render adds three qualities that you can't get with simple shading. Together, these qualities make for more realistic representations:

Color	In a simple shaded image, surfaces are one color at all points. In real life, color varies depending on the intentensity of light and the color characteristics of the light itself.
Texture	The smoothness or roughness of an object has a great effect on how an object looks.
Light and shadow	Light can bounce around a lot between objects before it reaches the viewer. Secondary and tertiary reflections and shadows that obscure them add a lot of the visual subtlety we perceive in reality.

Simple Rendering in AutoCAD

Despite the inherent complexities of rendering, getting a moderate amount of benefit from it doesn't have to be a big deal. You can use it as a fancy SHADE command, if only to compare the results and get hard-copy output. Start with a simple model you've shaded successfully, and then apply the RENDER command to it. In the DOS version of AutoCAD, unless your rendering driver supports rendering in a viewport, AutoCAD will clear the screen and create the rendered image in its own, blank screen. Because there will be only a single light source and no textures or other rendering-specific parameters, the rendered image won't be all that impressive, but it can be printed.

Tip

AutoCAD treats the display and print drivers for rendering separately from the normal video and plotter drivers. To make matters more confusing, some drivers combine the rendering and normal functionality in one driver. Among these are Autodesk's VGA and super VGA driver, SVADI, and the TurboDLD™ *Lite* driver included with this book. In other cases, you might have a completely separate driver for rendering.

The first time you run Render, AutoCAD will ask you to select a rendering display and rendering hard-copy driver. In most cases, you can accept the defaults in order to get started. Use the Information... button in the Rendering Preferences dialogue to check your current configuration. See Chapter 6 of the *AutoCAD Interface, Installation, and Performance Guide* for more details about rendering drivers and configuration.

In Release 12 for Windows, you can render to a separate window instead of to the regular AutoCAD window. Also, you can do other work while rendering proceeds in the background. And you can keep multiple rendered images open and on-screen at once. If you do much rendering, these features are valuable; you may well find it worthwhile to upgrade from AutoCAD DOS 386 to AutoCAD for Windows just to take advantage of them.

A few key rendering notes:

- To get better results without a lot of extra work, choose Smooth Shading from the Rendering Preferences dialogue box. To bring up this dialogue, pick Preferences... from the Render menu or enter the RPREF command.

- To print, bring up the Rendering Preferences dialogue and pick Hard copy as the destination. If you have not yet configured a destination for rendering to hard copy, you will have to do so before printing.

- The Rendering Preferences dialogue also gives you a choice of Quick Rendering or Full Rendering. Use the Shade command for a high-level check of fit, Quick Rendering for a status check as you work on perfecting the image, and Full Rendering for final rendering and for producing hard copy.

- AutoCAD Render is not a "photo-realist" rendering program. Its rendering algorithms are adequate for some purposes, but it doesn't offer capabilities, such as ray tracing, that provide really fancy results. For that, you'll need to invest in additional software, training time, and probably hardware, as well. Rendering professionals often have at least two powerful systems at hand—one for preparing models and one devoted to generating the rendered images, which can take hours.

Shading and Rendering Tutorial

1. Change back to a single viewport.

Pick in the lower right viewport to make it current.

Use the Tiled Viewport Layout icon menu or VPORTS command to return to a single viewport.

2. Shade with SHADEDGE set to 1 and SHADEDIF set to 70.

```
Command: SHADEDGE
New value for SHADEDGE <default>: 1
Command: SHADEDIF
New value for SHADEDIF <default>: 70
```

The settings for these two variables are stored with the drawing and affect shading in all viewports.

Run SHADE.

Note the results, and especially the lighting effects. If your graphics card and driver support at least 256 colors, surfaces pointing away from the viewer are darker, and surfaces that most directly face the viewer appear brighter. If your system supports fewer colors, you're likely to see some strange color schemes. See Figure 12.12.

3. Try other SHADEDGE and SHADEDIF settings.

Try setting SHADEDGE to 0 and reshading. Note the absence of edges. Try SHADEDGE = 3 if your system supports fewer than 256 colors.

Try smaller and larger settings of SHADEDIF (e.g., 30 and 90) and note the differences in lighting.

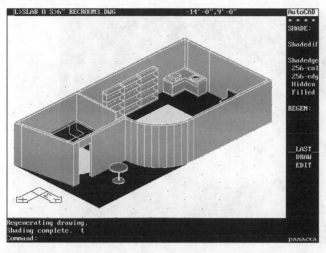

Figure 12.12 RECROOM shaded.

4. Perform a quick render with no smooth shading.

Command: RPREF
or
Pick Preferences... from the Render menu.

In the Render Preferences dialogue, set Rendering Type to Quick Render and make sure Smooth Shading is turned off.

Command: RENDER
or
Pick Render from the Render menu.

```
Using current view.
Default scene selected.
Projecting objects into view plane.
Processing face: 416
Applying parallel projection.
Calculate extents for faces.
Sorting 794 triangles by depth.
Checking 794 triangles for obscuration.
Comparing 794 triangles.
Calculate shading and assign colors.
Outputting triangles.
```

As you can see, AutoCAD Render has a lot of work to do, even to create a comparatively simple image.

The viewport will be rendered to the full screen or in a viewport, depending on your rendering display driver. The image may appear at

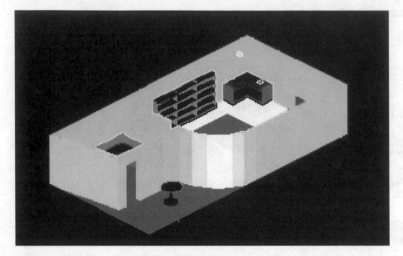

Figure 12.13   RECROOM rendered (at low resolution).

a lower resolution than it did with SHADE; again, this depends on your display driver (and graphics card). You should be able to see some improvement versus the SHADE command in the more subtle variation in the colors of the surfaces in the curved section of the wall.

5. Perform a full render with smooth shading.

Command: RPREF

In the Render Preferences dialogue, set Rendering Type to Full Render and turn on Smooth Shading.

Command: RENDER

See Figure 12.13 for a rendered example.

This tutorial has been an admittedly cursory introduction to AutoCAD Render. Hopefully, it will help you decide whether rendering would be useful in your work. If so, the tutorial in Chapter 2 of the *AutoCAD Render Reference Manual* will help you become better acquainted with the rendering capabilities built into Release 12.

3D and Workgroups

3D CAD most often is reserved for preparing presentations and for occasional studies of "fit and finish." The goal of working in 3D all the time, with a central 3D model serving as the source of all 2D drawings, is a fine one, but most companies lack the software, hardware, and user expertise to make it a reality right now. It makes sense for most workgroups to continue doing the bulk of their work in 2D (or "2½ D," i.e., extruding walls and other simple entities). As opportunities to take advantage of 3D arise, the more advanced members of the workgroup can begin exploring 3D CAD and building their expertise.

Start simply with extrusion and 3D Faces, and choose limited, reasonable tasks. Look for third-party applications that automate 3D construction and editing tasks for your discipline. Also look for 3D Block libraries from manufacturers of components you use. Make sure these resources are available (legally, of course) to all the members in the workgroup who need them.

Stick with simple shading and hidden-line removal, unless you really need rendering. If you can convince yourself that rendering capabilities would benefit your workgroup, be realistic about the hardware, software, and time demands of doing a decent job. Note that it may be more effective to use a third-party rendering package, rather than the one that comes with Release 12.

Make sure at least one person in your workgroup has enough artistic sensibility to guide the group in a realistic direction. Appoint one or two experienced users to investigate and experiment with rendering, and keep careful track of the costs in time and money. These figures will give you a good baseline for calculating the cost of extending 3D and rendering use to a larger portion of your workgroup.

3D CAD and rendering are subjects that can benefit from consulting help and additional training. This is especially true for people who are approaching the subjects for the first time. A good consultant should be able to help you assess what kind of results you can reasonably expect, how long the learning curve will be, what tools are available, and how to proceed. Effective training will minimize the time users spend floundering around in unfamiliar territory.

PART III

Customizing AutoCAD

13

Customization Overview

Customizability is AutoCAD's most important feature and the fount of its immense popularity. Other CAD programs match many of AutoCAD's drawing and editing features, but none offer its combination of customization options and selection of custom third-party applications. Among the many possibilities: You can write scripts to automate repetitive tasks, modify any of AutoCAD's menus, and develop AutoLISP programs for your common drawing tasks. You can even develop AutoCAD applications and utilities, and then distribute them as shareware or commercial software.

With Release 12, your range of choices is even wider—and possibly more confusing—than before. Release 12 includes four completely new programming interfaces—DIESEL, Dialogue Control Language (DCL), AutoCAD SQL Interface (ASI), and the Render API—and a host of enhancements to menu programming, AutoLISP, and ADS. In particular, the new programmable dialogue box interface raises the stakes for anyone who customizes AutoCAD.

About This Part of the Book

This part of the book, Part III, will lead you through this maze of options, whether you're new to AutoCAD customization or a veteran at menu macros and AutoLISP. Each chapter presents the fundamentals of one AutoCAD customization interface and gives you the information you need to start solving real-world customization problems. Along the way, you develop and refine genuinely useful programs that can become part of your AutoCAD environment.

347

Our approach in this part of the book is to present you with condensed and digested information about customizing AutoCAD. Rather than burden you with every detail and subtlety (which would require several books this size), we've consolidated the information so that you can become proficient more quickly. With this approach, you spend less time learning how to customize and more time actually customizing.

You can skip around among these chapters as much as you like, but you should be aware of some interdependencies. Start by reading this chapter and at least skimming the next one before you start to customize. Chapter 15, *Custom Command Names*, and Chapter 16, *Scripts*, can be read separately or together; they are both easy to do and can save you a great deal of time. Knowing scripts is a useful precursor to writing menu macros (Chapter 17).

The remaining customization techniques are more involved and tend to depend on knowledge of preceding approaches. The subject of menus, in general, is somewhat complex, though less so if you focus on pop-up menus and the cursor menu. Knowing about menus is a necessity in order to do much with DIESEL (Chapter 18). Learning DIESEL is a great way to start learning AutoLISP (Chapter 19), and you need to know AutoLISP to do anything useful with Programmable Dialogue Boxes (Chapter 20).

As surprising as it may sound to those who never bother looking at software manuals, Autodesk's documentation for customizing AutoCAD is quite useful. This is especially true in Release 12: The *AutoLISP Programmer's Reference Manual* has been reorganized in a more sensible way, and the new *AutoCAD Customization Manual* is very helpful. This book will give you a toehold on customization with ACAD.PGP, scripts, menus, DIESEL, AutoLISP, and programmable dialogue boxes. Once you understand the fundamentals and have a few examples under your belt, the AutoCAD manuals will be useful as references and for going beyond what we discuss here.

About This Chapter

This chapter describes AutoCAD Release 12's customization options in a general way. Just as important, it gives you a framework for deciding how much you need to customize and which interfaces to use. By understanding the strengths, weaknesses, and learning demands of each customization interface, you'll be able to discern which you need to learn and which you can ignore.

How Much Should You Customize?

Not only was AutoCAD designed to be customized, it *requires* customization before it becomes a productive tool. Although many people use AutoCAD as it comes "out of the box"—Autodesk's surveys show that about half of its customers do so—for most kinds of work, this is an inefficient way to draw or design. Watch a drafter lay out a ceiling tile grid or draw a reinforced concrete beam with bare AutoCAD, and you'll understand the need for customization. AutoCAD provides the basic drawing, editing, and viewing tools, but it's up to you to build it into a full–fledged and efficient application for your type of work.

Fortunately, you have lots of help, and not just from this book. AutoCAD has given rise to hundreds of general–purpose and discipline–specific third-party applications, not to mention thousands of freeware and shareware programs. In most cases, you're far better off going as far as you can with off–the–shelf applications and customization components, rather than developing your own application from scratch. Your customization work is then reduced to tying the pieces together and doing custom work to add capabilities that you can't find elsewhere. The trick, then, is finding the right applications and understanding what parts you need to develop on your own.

Commercial Applications

For most companies, commercial third-party applications are the way to go. Figure 13.1 shows one example: Allegro Basic from Robert McNeel & Associates. Third-party developers make their living by selling applications for use inside AutoCAD, so they can invest the time needed to create full–featured, robust applications, and then amortize that effort over many customers. Competent third-party developers also will have the resources to both document and update the applications they sell; these two tasks often don't get done for in–house customization.

On the other hand, third-party developers won't understand your customization needs as thoroughly as you or a consultant will. Given the large number of applications available for AutoCAD, though, you'll probably be able to find one that covers the bulk of your customization needs. That will free you to spend more time using AutoCAD for billable work. You'll still have the pleasure of customizing the things not addressed by your third-party application.

Autodesk includes a guide to third-party applications and related resources with Release 12: *The AutoCAD Resource Guide*. Use this guide as a starting point to research applications for your discipline. The reviews and advertisements in *CADalyst* and *CADENCE* magazines are a good source of up–to–date information. Talk to colleagues in your profession and members

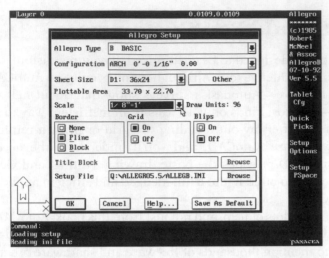

Figure 13.1 Allegro Basic, a third-party application.

of your local user group about the applications they've used. Many AutoCAD dealers sell third-party applications and can supply you with brochures, demo diskettes, user references, and perhaps a product demonstration.

Most users will find it worthwhile to do some small-scale customization to their AutoCAD environment, which probably already includes one or more third-party pieces. But few users need to develop a complete application of their own. There are a few situations in which it's reasonable to consider developing your own application:

- Your company is big enough that development costs can be spread over a large number of users.

- Your use of AutoCAD is so unique that no one sells a competent third-party application for it.

- You need complete control of your application.

- You enjoy programming and are willing to do AutoCAD customization as a hobby.

Don't be in a hurry to put yourself in any of these categories, though. Developing even a modest application will require hundreds or even thousands of hours. If your time is worth anything at all, those hours will buy a lot of commercial software.

If you do decide to develop a discipline–specific application, consider building it on top of a general–purpose commercial application, such as Robert McNeel & Associates' Allegro Basic, LANDCADD's Cadpanion, or Softdesk's Productivity Tools. General–purpose applications address the customization needs common to many disciplines (drawing setup, layer and

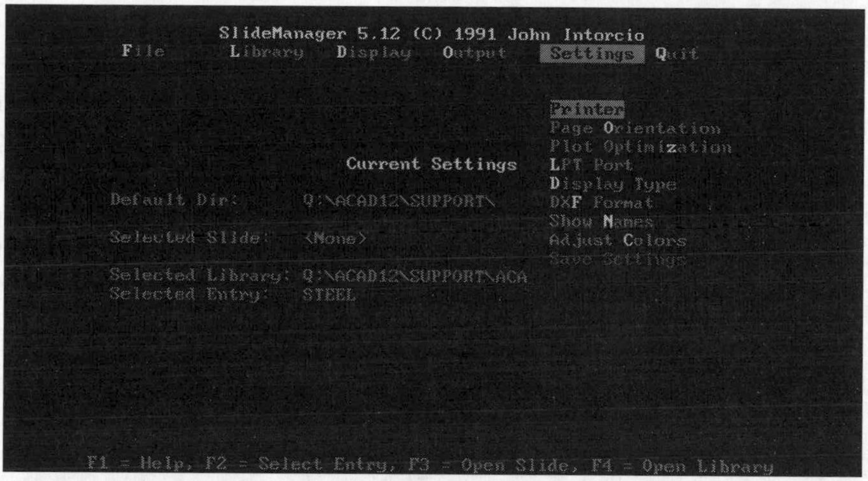

Figure 13.2   A shareware utility program: SlideManager.

scale management, improved text handling, etc.), and thus they'll free you to concentrate on your discipline–specific customization needs.

Shareware and Freeware Customization

Whether you go commercial or roll your own, there's a huge stash of inexpensive and free AutoCAD customization available to supplement your AutoCAD system. Figure 13.2 shows one example: John Intorcio's SlideManager, a shareware utility for managing slides and slide libraries (see Chapter 16, *Scripts*, for more information). Many users who develop AutoLISP and ADS programs, menu macros, hatch patterns, text fonts, and other miscellaneous utilities offer them to others free or for a nominal shareware fee. Incorporating these components into your commercial or home–grown application will extend its power and save you development time.

The only problem is finding the right pieces. The data libraries in CompuServe's ACAD forum are probably the largest single repository of freeware and shareware custom software for AutoCAD. Other resources include local BBSs, user groups, and *CADalyst* and *CADENCE* magazines. Of course, the usual shareware and freeware rules apply: Send in the registration fee for any shareware you use, include copyright notices if you incorporate freeware into work that you distribute, and don't violate an author's copyright.

If you decide to share or sell your own customization efforts, these same resources can be your distribution mechanism.

Who Should Customize?

The job of customizing AutoCAD usually falls to the CAD manager or another "CAD wizard" in the office. Customization doesn't require programming experience, but it does demand a solid understanding of AutoCAD, natural curiosity accompanied by a willingness to learn, and a desire to tweak things. Most people who customize AutoCAD are self–taught, and with this book's help, you should have no trouble gaining the necessary skills. Also, AutoCAD's customization interfaces range from simple to complex, so it's easy to create useful enhancements no matter what your level of experience.

Of course, in an office of more than one person, it makes sense to coordinate the customization efforts. We discuss this issue further in the "Customization and Workgroups" section at the end of the chapter.

If you don't have in–house customization talent, consider hiring an AutoCAD consultant. Although a consultant's hourly rate will be higher than yours, a competent consultant will work much more quickly than you can, and will have lots of off–the–shelf customization components from previous programming projects. Always insist on documentation and unencrypted source code for any custom work.

What Should You Customize?

As discussed above, look for a good third-party application that covers most of your company's needs, and then concentrate your efforts on those discipline– or office–specific needs that aren't addressed by the application.

Identify the AutoCAD tasks you do most often and think about how you might automate them. Drawing setup, layer manipulation, dimensioning, and plotting usually are good candidates (although your third-party application should address at least the first two to some degree). Here are some other ideas:

- Consider the types of components you draw most often—would a parametric routine help you draw them more quickly?

- Are there certain kinds of "mass editing," like updating title blocks for a group of drawings, that you do often—would automating this process save you time?

- Does your office have CAD standards that no one follows because the standards are too numerous or obscure—would building those standards into AutoCAD so that they're automatically enforced save grief?

- Are there commands you often use that have long names or are buried deeply in the menu structure — would rearranging the menus or renaming commands with one- or two-letter command aliases save you menu picks and keystrokes?

- Do you build similar kinds of sheets, perhaps of typical details, again and again—could this procedure be streamlined?

- Do you spend a lot of time entering text for general notes or numbers for tables—would importing this data from a word processor or spreadsheet help?

In short, there are always plenty of opportunities for customization. Be observant, keep a list of customization needs, and develop a reasonable plan and schedule for meeting them.

Once you've identified customization needs, the fun begins. Before actually beginning to customize, you need to decide which of AutoCAD's customization interfaces is best suited to each problem.

AutoCAD's Customization Interfaces

Depending on how you count, AutoCAD Release 12 provides about 20 different customization interfaces! Don't be overwhelmed—you're already familiar with some of them, and others you'll probably never need to know. The interfaces are listed in Table 13.1 and described, by group, in subsequent sections.

Table 13.1   AutoCAD's Customization Interfaces

	Interface	**File Type**	**Difficulty**	**Documented In**
Drawings:	Prototype drawings	*.DWG	Simple	*Ref. Manual*
	Blocks and Xrefs	*.DWG	Simple	*Ref. Manual*
Drawing Elements:	Linetypes	*.LIN	Simple	*Custom. Manual*
	Hatch patterns	*.PAT	Moderate	*Custom. Manual*
	Fonts and Shapes	*.SHP/*.SHX	Moderate	*Custom. Manual*
Aliases:	Command aliases	ACAD.PGP	Simple	*Custom. Manual*
	External commands	ACAD.PGP	Simple	*Custom. Manual*
Script Languages:	Scripts	*.SCR	Simple	*Custom. Manual*
	Menu macros	*.MNU/.MNX	Moderate	*Custom. Manual*

(continued)

Table 13.1   AutoCAD's Customization Interfaces (continued)

	Interface	File Type	Difficulty	Documented In
Progr. Languages:	DIESEL	*.MNU/.LSP	Moderate	*Custom. Manual*
	AutoLISP	*.LSP/.MNL	Mod./Complex	*AutoLISP Prog. Ref.*
	ADS	*.C/.H/.EXP	Complex	*ADS Prog. Ref.*
Extension APIs:	ASE/ASI/LISP SQL	*.C/.LSP	Complex	*ASE Manual*
	AME API	*.C/.LSP	Mod./Complex	*AME Ref. Manual*
	Render API	*.C/.LSP	Mod./Complex	*Render Ref. Manual*
Interface:	Help	*.HLP/.HDX	Simple	*Custom. Manual*
	Programmable Dialogue Boxes	*.DCL/.LSP/.C	Mod./Complex	*Custom. Manual*
Miscellaneous:	Plot Configuration Parameters files	*.PCP	Simple	*Custom. Manual*
	PostScript	ACAD.PSF, FONTMAP.PS	Moderate	*Custom. Manual*
	Windows DDE	*.LSP/C	Mod./Complex	*Using AutoCAD for Windows*

Customization through Drawings

The simplest method of customization is using drawings as the basis for, or as components in, other drawings. Every time you modify AutoCAD's default prototype drawing (ACAD.DWG) or create new prototypes, you're customizing settings for a family of future drawings. Similarly, Blocks and Xrefs allow you to develop a library of custom components that can be reused and redefined. We covered prototype drawings in Chapters 4 and 5, and Blocks and Xrefs in Chapter 10, so review those chapters if you need more information.

Although prototypes, Blocks, and Xrefs are simple to create and use, they aren't always easy to locate. Third-party drawing viewers and managers are a big help, since they let you browse through and locate drawings quickly. The DWGDB file finder and SirlinVIEW/Lite drawing viewer included on the *AutoCAD Power Tools* disk are two useful tools for this purpose.

An organizational scheme for your office's commonly used drawings is as important as the drawings themselves. Often, it's useful to develop a menu "front end" that gives ready access to prototype and component drawings. Chapter 8 of the *AutoCAD Tutorial Manual* shows one method for doing this that uses an icon menu.

Drawing Elements

Three kinds of AutoCAD drawing elements can be customized: linetypes, hatch patterns, and fonts and Shapes. (An AutoCAD Shape is a primitive sort of Xref that isn't much used anymore. Shapes and fonts are often grouped together because they are both defined as a series of vectors.) You can supplement AutoCAD's default dash–dot linetypes with custom linetypes of your own invention by editing ACAD.LIN. Likewise, you can create custom hatch patterns to supplement the ones defined in ACAD.PAT. Finally, you can define custom AutoCAD fonts and Shapes by editing .SHP (SHaPe) files and then compiling them into .SHX files with the Release 12 COMPILE command.

Creating custom linetypes is a simple and fast process that's well covered at the beginning of Chapter 4 of the *AutoCAD Customization Manual*. Developing custom hatch patterns and fonts is covered in Chapters 4 and 5 of the same manual. Hatch patterns and fonts aren't difficult to create, but it's usually a tedious and fussy process. Most people are better off acquiring high–quality and inexpensive (or free) third-party hatch patterns and fonts.

Chapter 17 of this book (*Menus*) includes a useful tip on how to customize the BHATCH command's Choose Hatch Pattern subdialogue. By reordering or adding to the patterns in this dialogue, you can make it easier to use.

Aliases

Despite Release 12's improved interface, typing still is the most efficient method of executing many AutoCAD and DOS commands. With keyboard input, "shorter is better," and AutoCAD provides two methods for defining shorthand names: command aliases and external commands. Command aliases are simply shortened names (usually one, two, or three letters) for AutoCAD commands. External commands allow you to launch DOS programs and operating system commands from the AutoCAD Command: prompt.

AutoCAD ships with a few predefined command aliases and external commands, but it's useful to build a complete set for the AutoCAD and DOS commands you use most often. Command aliases and external commands reside in the ACAD.PGP file, and we show you the simple techniques for editing this file in Chapter 15, *Custom Command Names*.

Script Languages

In programming parlance, a script language is an incredibly fast and incredibly dumb automatic typist. Script languages are a means of replaying often–repeated keystroke sequences, and AutoCAD provides two such languages: scripts proper and menu macros. Scripts execute a series of standard AutoCAD commands that you store in an .SCR file and then launch with the AutoCAD SCRIPT command. AutoCAD scripts are akin to simple DOS batch files or word processing program macros. AutoCAD menu macros resemble scripts in format and function, but menu macros are more direct and obvious to the user because they are launched by menu labels.

Scripts are useful for automating any procedure you do over and over again in exactly the same way: restoring a particular group of layer settings, plotting a batch of drawings, or displaying a group of AutoCAD slides, for example. We cover how to create scripts and show several useful applications for them in Chapter 16.

Menus are the "glue" that holds most AutoCAD customization together. Menus are part script language and part user interface, and we cover both aspects in Chapter 17. Menus also can include DIESEL and AutoLISP expressions, and we demonstrate how to enhance menus with DIESEL and AutoLISP in Chapters 18 and 19.

Programming Languages

Programming languages, unlike a script language, permit decision–making (*if–then–else*) and looping (*repeat* and *while*). The program's code sometimes interacts with the AutoCAD command line in the same way a script does, but more often the code is performing calculations and carrying out actions on the drawing database behind the scenes. As a result, programming languages allow for programs that are not only fast, but also flexible and robust. Release 12 supports three programming languages: Direct Interpretively Evaluated String Expression Language (DIESEL), AutoLISP, and the AutoCAD Development System (ADS).

DIESEL, which is new to Release 12, is for customizing AutoCAD's status line and for building smarter menu macros and labels. DIESEL enables you to create menu labels that change based on the drawing's current status. It also can be used in menu macros that calculate values or perform different actions, depending on system variable settings. DIESEL is a simplified subset of AutoLISP functions with a slightly different syntax, and because of this, it's also a good training ground for AutoLISP. We devote Chapter 18 to DIESEL.

AutoLISP is AutoCAD's most popular programming language for everyone except experienced C programmers. With AutoLISP, you can perform tasks as simple as setting a layer current or as complex as creating entire drawings based on a few user–supplied parameters. AutoLISP code usually lives in .LSP files or menu macros. Autodesk uses AutoLISP to create many of its most useful commands, including DLINE and DDMODIFY. The possibilities are nearly endless, and the only obstacle is learning enough of AutoLISP's programming conventions to start modifying existing programs and creating your own. In Chapter 19, we review the fundamentals of AutoLISP and then show you how to begin developing practical programs.

Although AutoLISP suffices for most people's needs, ADS provides more rapid program execution, more flexible file input and output, and lower-level system access. ADS lets experienced programmers write routines in C source code (or borrow C code from existing programs) and then compile them into special executable programs for use in AutoCAD's drawing editor. ADS typically is used by third-party developers to write programs that do a lot of "number crunching" or that need to read and write binary files (Paradox or dBASE databases, for instance). Many of AutoCAD's own enhancements, including AME, ASE, AutoCAD Render, and the Geometry Calculator, are ADS applications written by Autodesk programmers. Unless you know C, and until you begin writing programs that push the limits of AutoLISP, you usually don't need to worry about ADS. ADS, the C programming language, and specific C programming environments are big, complicated topics we don't cover in this book; see the *ADS Programmer's Reference Manual* to get started.

Extension APIs

With each new AutoCAD extension comes a new set of commands and characteristics that programmers might want to control. As a result, Autodesk has added application programming interfaces (or APIs) for the AutoCAD Modeling Extension (AME), AutoCAD Render, and the AutoCAD SOL Interface (ASI). The APIs are a melange of ADS and AutoLISP programming functions, and usually require an intimate understanding of the extension and the programming language. We don't cover the AME or Render APIs here, but see the *Advanced Modeling Extension Reference Manual* and *Render Reference Manual* if you're interested in customizing these aspects of AutoCAD.

Windows Tip

Release 12 for Windows includes an ADS interface to Visual Basic. This interface provides a somewhat easier method of using ADS. See Chapter 8 of the *Using AutoCAD for Windows Manual* for more information.

Tip

ASI requires ADS (that is, C) programming knowledge and tools. As a gesture to AutoLISP programmers, Autodesk provides an application called LISP SQL on the Release 12 Bonus CD. LISP SQL is a small set of AutoLISP functions that mimic the corresponding ADS C functions that make up ASI. LISP SQL isn't easy to master, but with a bit of determination, you can read and write external database files from AutoLISP. The *AutoCAD SQL Extension Manual* gives more details about ASI, and is required reading for C or AutoLISP programmers who want to use ASI in their programs.

If you want to experiment with LISP SQL, be aware that the version of LISP SQL on the Bonus CD contains a significant bug. Download the revised version (LSPSQL.ZIP) from the ACAD forum on CompuServe.

The AutoCAD SQL Extension (ASE) serves as an example of how an AutoCAD API can be used. ASE is an Autodesk-designed sample application built with ASI, and it shows one way of linking AutoCAD drawing entities to external databases.

Interface

A program's user interface is as important as its functional capabilities, and the same is true of your customization. Release 12 lets you modify and extend three aspects of its interface: on–line help, menus, and dialogue boxes.

On–line help is finally helpful in Release 12, thanks to the search capability and Help dialogue box. AutoCAD DOS 386 stores help topics and text in an ASCII file called ACAD.HLP. It isn't difficult to add custom help screens for your own AutoCAD enhancements, or to modify the existing descriptions to fit your own knowledge and procedures. Chapter 2 of the *AutoCAD Customization Manual* tells you in two short pages how to edit ACAD.HLP.

Windows Tip

AutoCAD for Windows uses a much more sophisticated help facility than AutoCAD 386, but, unfortunately, it's not directly customizable in the way ACAD.HLP is. You can, however, attach annotations to help topics. See Chapter 2 of the *Using AutoCAD for Windows Manual*.

As mentioned above, menu macros are part script language and part user interface, and both parts are addressed in Chapter 17, "Menus."

Release 12's new programmable dialogue box (PDB) facility is the most significant customization change for AutoLISP and ADS programmers in this release, and the trickiest enhancement to master, as well. Creating custom dialogue boxes involves two activities: designing the dialogue box's visual layout, and specifying how the dialogue box will interact with the user and with its underlying AutoLISP or ADS program. You control a dialogue box's appearance by writing Dialogue Control Language (.DCL) files that designate the location and attributes of each area, or *tile*, in the dialogue. You control a PDB's behavior and consequences by writing AutoLISP or ADS programs that include the new Release 12 dialogue–handling functions. Chapter 20, *Programmable Dialogue Boxes*, shows you how to build PDBs and control them from AutoLISP.

Miscellaneous

But wait! There's more! Three customization interfaces don't quite fit into any of the above categories: Plot Configuration Parameters (.PCP) files; PostScript import/export, fonts, and fills; and Windows Dynamic Data Exchange (DDE). We discussed .PCP files in Chapter 11, *Paper Space and Plotting*. Chapter 10 of the *AutoCAD Customization Manual* contains information about PostScript customization.

DDE is a method by which Windows programs can communicate with and control one another. With DDE, you can exchange data between AutoCAD Release 12 for Windows and a Windows spreadsheet, database management system, word processor, or other program. DDE is likely to drive a whole new generation of AutoCAD applications that work together with other Windows programs.

Developing a simple link between AutoCAD and another Windows program isn't tremendously difficult, but doing something useful and user-friendly with that link usually requires a lot of programming. You need to have an intimate understanding of AutoCAD, the other Windows application, and either AutoLISP and C to make a robust and useful link. We don't discuss DDE in detail in this book. Chapter 7 of the *Using AutoCAD for Windows Manual* covers DDE and using it with AutoLISP. Chapters 8 and 9 of that manual include information on using DDE with Visual Basic ADS and C ADS.

Where to Go from Here

With AutoCAD customization, as with anything interesting, it's easy to focus so narrowly on a few trees that you lose sight of the forest. Always keep your customization goals in mind, and plan your learning and work to serve them.

Don't get stuck on one customization interface (e.g., AutoLISP) and neglect others that might accomplish a given task more simply (e.g., a script or DIESEL). Also, be reasonable about what you can learn and implement, given the other demands on your time. Look for third-party applications or consulting help on major programming projects.

Following are customization strategies for three types of people: an ordinary AutoCAD user, a workgroup manager, and a consultant. Use these profiles to help plan your own strategy.

User

Users should understand the following customization interfaces as a minimum:

- Blocks, Xrefs, and prototype drawings. All users should be conversant with using prototypes to streamline drawing setup. Likewise, users should be very familiar with Blocks and Xrefs and their uses as custom components.

- Scripts. Scripts are simple but powerful, and all users should know how to use them to automate repetitive tasks.

- .PCP files. Plot Configuration Parameters files are simple to save and recall from the PLOT dialogue box. Users should also know how to modify .PCP files with a text editor.

All users should start with a third-party application that covers most of their general-purpose and discipline-specific customization needs. Supplement the application with the tools from this book, even if you don't work through the remaining customization chapters. We recommend Chapter 16, *Scripts*, for everyone, though.

More ambitious users can take on additional customization tasks, such as modifying ACAD.PGP, writing simple menu macros, and incorporating AutoLISP programs from other sources into menus.

Workgroup Manager

Workgroup managers and anyone else who's responsible for other AutoCAD users should understand the following customization interfaces (in addition to the ones mentioned for users):

- ACAD.PGP. Workgroup managers should create a custom ACAD.PGP with command aliases and external commands that are tuned for the group.

- Menus. A custom menu is the central component of any customized AutoCAD system, so workgroup managers need to understand at least the basics of modifying menus.

- DIESEL. Workgroup managers should know enough DIESEL to use it in menu labels and simple macros.

- A little LISP. Most shareware and freeware routines are written in AutoLISP, so workgroup managers should know enough LISP to modify existing routines.

Workgroup managers have to keep the "big picture" in view at all times. They need to focus on consistency, standards, training, identifying needs, and gathering and disseminating tools, rather than on being full-time programmers. They need to understand enough about each customization interface to know which ones are worth learning more about and to decide which ones to apply to a given customization problem. This knowledge also will help the workgroup manager make intelligent decisions when selecting third-party applications or hiring and managing consultants. The workgroup sections in this book will help with all these tasks.

Workgroup managers with more interest and experience in customization also may want to delve more deeply into AutoLISP and start creating custom dialogue boxes.

Consultant

Consultants need to be intimately familiar with everything listed under user and workgroup manager, plus the following:

- Solid AutoLISP. Consultants should be able to create robust LISP programs from scratch.

- Programmable dialogue boxes. Clients will come to expect dialogue box-driven interfaces for custom programs, so consultants need to learn how to supply them.

Clients who pay money for customization have a right to expect programs with good error trapping and decent interfaces. Consultants who provide these services will need to continue to improve their skills, which, for Release 12, means mastering DIESEL and programmable dialogue boxes as well as some basics of user interface design.

Usually, consultants will burn up a lot of unbillable hours the first time they use a new customization interface or develop a new customization approach. To make this initial investment worthwhile, a consultant needs to be able to amortize that effort over several clients. Thus, consultants, more than anyone else, need to think about reusability when developing custom tools. Depending on the clients they serve, some consultants may need to go farther and begin using ADS, Windows-specific customization methods, or links to external databases.

Customization and Workgroups

Centralizing and coordinating customization is crucial to a workgroup's AutoCAD efficiency. Those great LISP routines and custom menus won't do the workgroup much good if they're hidden on one member's hard disk. Your support job will be a nightmare, especially at upgrade time, if each user has a differently customized menu and a unique support file subdirectory structure.

Finding a golden mean between despotism and anarchy is key. Someone should be in charge of all customization for a company, but each workgroup in a large office might have its own customization expert who is responsible for the workgroup's unique needs. Together, the company and workgroup customization experts will have to develop a scheme for incorporating both general and workgroup–specific enhancements into everyone's AutoCAD system.

If a company values the dedication of its AutoCAD users, it's important that the customization managers not stifle the interest and creativity of those users who might want to contribute custom menu macros or LISP routines. Customization is one of the most rewarding aspects of using AutoCAD, and involving interested employees in it can improve the morale, cohesiveness, and productivity of a workgroup. There should be a mechanism for evaluating contributions and incorporating those that will be useful to the workgroup or company. Equally important, customization managers need to manage the time others spend tweaking AutoCAD, so that the benefits are worth the efforts.

We discuss workgroup issues specific to ACAD.PGP, scripts, menus, DIE-SEL, AutoLISP, and programmable dialogue boxes at the end of the chapters devoted to each of these topics. Use these sections to guide your workgroup customization.

Summary

Customization is the key to AutoCAD productivity, but Release 12's customization interfaces offer an overwhelming variety of choices. The challenge is in identifying and acquainting yourself with the ones that you need. Use existing commercial, shareware, and freeware third-party programs whenever you can. Supplement and tie together these off–the–shelf components with your own custom programs and menus. In the coming chapters, we'll show you the tools and tricks for building a custom AutoCAD environment that's tuned to your office's CAD needs.

14

Getting Ready to Customize

Before you start customizing, you need to do two things: understand AutoCAD's "in the box" customization, and set up an efficient customization environment on your system. It also helps to think about how you'll transfer your custom files to future AutoCAD updates or versions, and how you can streamline the process of upgrading your custom menus, programs, and other files for each new AutoCAD release. Finally, if your customizing efforts will be shared among members of a workgroup, you want to develop a distribution mechanism that ensures everyone's files are always "in synch." This chapter covers these four requirements.

If you've never customized AutoCAD before, you're probably anxious to dive in and start customizing right away—thinking about logistics at this stage of the game might seem tedious. If that's the case for you, then scan this chapter quickly and make sure you can launch a text editor from AutoCAD (as described in the tutorial later in the chapter). Once you've done that, you can continue on to the next chapter and begin modifying your ACAD.PGP file. Return to this chapter and read it more carefully once you've worked through a few more chapters and gotten some of the flavor and satisfaction of customizing AutoCAD to your liking.

If you have customized AutoCAD before, you've probably begun to experience some of the problems that arise in creating, using, and maintaining the changes and additions you've made to your work environment. In some cases, a lack of planning can cause your improvements to seem to be more trouble than they're worth. This chapter will help you solve these problems and free you to make further improvements that work well together.

AutoCAD's "In the Box" Customization

AutoCAD isn't a blank slate waiting for you to create its custom personality from scratch. Many of the files you need for customization already exist; they're called AutoCAD's support files. The location, structure, and interaction of these files are considerably more complicated in Release 12, so you need to understand AutoCAD's support file framework before doing major surgery on the files.

In the previous chapter, we took great pains to distinguish between bare AutoCAD and an efficient CAD system comprising AutoCAD, custom applications, and additional custom programs. In reality, the distinction isn't so clear-cut. AutoCAD comes loaded with custom menus and programs. In fact, some of its most useful commands, such as CHTEXT and DDCHPROP, are custom programs that have been added to the Release 12 menus. You'll want to know more about these files in case you need to modify them. In addition, Release 12 includes other hidden treasures in the SAMPLE subdirectory and on the new Bonus CD.

AutoCAD's Subdirectory Structure

The Release 12 installation program creates fifteen subdirectories on your hard disk (assuming you performed a full installation). The directory structure follows:

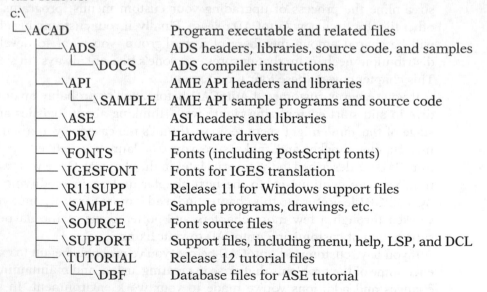

```
c:\
 └─\ACAD                    Program executable and related files
      ├──\ADS               ADS headers, libraries, source code, and samples
      │    └─\DOCS          ADS compiler instructions
      ├──\API               AME API headers and libraries
      │    └─\SAMPLE        AME API sample programs and source code
      ├── \ASE              ASI headers and libraries
      ├── \DRV              Hardware drivers
      ├── \FONTS            Fonts (including PostScript fonts)
      ├── \IGESFONT         Fonts for IGES translation
      ├── \R11SUPP          Release 11 for Windows support files
      ├── \SAMPLE           Sample programs, drawings, etc.
      ├── \SOURCE           Font source files
      ├── \SUPPORT          Support files, including menu, help, LSP, and DCL
      └── \TUTORIAL         Release 12 tutorial files
           └─\DBF           Database files for ASE tutorial
```

(\ACAD\API and \ACAD\API\SAMPLE will be present only if you purchased AME.)

\ACAD\SUPPORT holds most of AutoCAD's modifiable support files, and it's the place where you'll find many of the files you customize. \ACAD\SAMPLE also contains some useful programs and customization examples. Source files for AutoCAD's many fonts are stored in \ACAD\SOURCE, so that's where you'll look if you want to customize AutoCAD fonts. ADS programmers will need some of the files in \ACAD\ADS for compiling their ADS programs.

After creating subdirectories and copying files, the installation program then creates a batch file in the root directory called ACADR12.BAT for launching AutoCAD. This batch file ensures that several crucial DOS environment variables are set; without these variables, AutoCAD won't be able to locate its support files, drivers, and fonts. A typical ACADR12.BAT looks like this:

```
SET ACAD=C:\ACAD\SUPPORT;C:\ACAD\FONTS;C:\ACAD\ADS
SET ACADCFG=C:\ACAD
SET ACADDRV=C:\ACAD\DRV
C:\ACAD\ACAD %1 %2
```

The most important of these variables for customization purposes is the first one. The ACAD= environment variable tells AutoCAD where to search for its support files, which include Blocks and Xrefs, scripts, menus, fonts, AutoLISP and ADS programs, and DCL files. As we'll discuss later, AutoCAD also looks in the current subdirectory, drawing subdirectory, and ACAD.EXE program subdirectory, but ACAD= is the primary mechanism for directing AutoCAD to its support files.

The second line tells AutoCAD where to look for its configuration file, ACAD.CFG, and the third line tells it where to look for drivers. The fourth line starts the program; both of the parameters represented by %1 and %2 are optional. The first parameter specifies a drawing for AutoCAD to load on startup, and the second specifies a script file for AutoCAD to run once the drawing is loaded.

Tip

Unless you regularly use one of the nine sample ADS programs in \ACAD\ADS (which is unlikely), you can remove C:\ACAD\ADS from your ACAD= search path. All the ADS programs required by Release 12 are located in \ACAD and \ACAD\SUPPORT.

AutoCAD's Standard Support Files

The \ACAD\SUPPORT subdirectory contains over 90 support files, and some of the 50+ files in the \ACAD subdirectory also can be considered support files. The following list contains the most important files to know about when you customize AutoCAD. The files with names in bold are the ones you are most likely to want to customize.

\ACAD

ACADAPP.ADS	List of ADS applications AutoCAD loads automatically
ACADAPP.EXP	Contains code for BHATCH, DDIM, etc.

\ACAD\SUPPORT

Dialogue definitions (see Chapter 20, Programmable Dialogue Boxes):

ACAD.DCL	Dialogues for core commands
BASE.DCL	Dialogue prototypes and subassemblies
*.DCL	Dialogues for other commands

Prototype (see Chapters 4 and 5):

ACAD.DWG	Default prototype drawing

Utility programs (see Chapter 16, Scripts):

DXFIX.*	Translate DXF files to Release 10
SLIDELIB.EXE	Compile slides into slide libraries

Help:

ACAD.HLP	Help text
ACAD.HDX	Help index (created by AutoCAD)

Linetypes:

ACAD.LIN	Linetype definitions

AutoLISP programs (see Chapter 19, AutoLISP):

ACADR12.LSP	Functions loaded during AutoCAD startup
AI_UTILS.LSP	Miscellaneous utility functions
*.LSP	Other commands

Menu (see Chapter 17, Menus):

ACAD.MNU	Menu source
ACAD.MNX	Compiled menu
ACAD.MNL	LISP code associated with menu

Hatch patterns:

ACAD.PAT	Hatch patterns

Additional commands (see Chapter 15, Custom Command Names):

ACAD.PGP	External commands and command aliases

Slides (see Chapter 16, Scripts):
  ACAD.SLB   Slide library for AutoCAD icon menus

AutoCAD's Sample Programs and Bonus CD

Autodesk has included sample (or bonus) routines with AutoCAD for several
releases, but because both the programs and their documentation were well
hidden until recently, many users don't know about them. The Release 12
\ACAD\SAMPLE subdirectory includes over 60 sample programs and drawings, a few of which are quite useful. Some of these programs are documented in the *AutoCAD Extras Manual*. In addition, Autodesk now ships a
Bonus CD containing over 250 MB of samples (along with demos and some
sales hype). If you have a CD-ROM drive, or know someone who does, some
of the CD samples might be worth copying to your hard disk and including in
your customization bag of tricks. The following sample programs are by no
means the only potentially useful ones. Browse the sample subdirectory or
the Bonus CD if you'd like to see what else is available.

Selected AutoCAD Release 12 Sample Programs
(All files are located in \ACAD\SAMPLE.)

Dialogue box samples:
DDTYPE.DCL/.LSP   List ASCII files in a dialogue
DLGTEST.DCL/.LSP   Test dialogues you develop

Tablet overlay drawing:
TABLETAC.DWG   Stock AutoCAD tablet overlay

Handy AutoLISP programs:
ALIAS.LSP   List command aliases in ACAD.PGP
ATTREDEF.LSP   Redefine Blocks with changed attribute
                          definitions
DELLAYER.LSP   Delete all entities on a layer
XDATA.LSP   Attach and display extended entity data
XREFCLIP.LSP   Attach and clip Xrefs

Selected Programs from the AutoCAD Release 12 Bonus CD

\ASE\LISPSQL   AutoLISP version of ASI
\DOSUTILS\SLDMGR   SlideManager shareware program
\LISP\MODEMACR   Program for testing DIESEL custom status lines
\LISP\TUTOR   AutoLISP tutorials
\TOOLKITS\SDK1   AutoCAD customization Software
\TOOLKITS\SDK2   Development Kit (SDK)

Tip

If you want ready access to the AutoLISP progams and dialogue boxes in \ACAD\SAMPLE, you can add the subdirectory to your ACAD= environment variable:

```
SET ACAD=C:\ACAD\SUPPORT;C:\ACAD\FONTS;
C:\ACAD\ADS;C:\ACAD\SAMPLE
```

(The complete SET statement should be on a single line in your batch file.)

The Release 12 Initialization Sequence

Anyone who customizes AutoCAD should understand what goes on "under the hood" as AutoCAD launches and then loads drawings. These initialization sequences depend on several files you can customize. Once you understand the files and when they're loaded, you can exercise control over what happens each time AutoCAD creates a new drawing or opens an existing one.

The initialization sequence is more involved in Release 12 than it was in prior versions, thanks in part to the addition of menu LISP (.MNL) files. Also, the sequence is less obvious because there's no longer a text screen Main Menu to mark the hiatus between ending one drawing and starting another. DOS and Windows versions of Release 12 both follow the same steps.

An outline of the initialization sequence follows. Some of the terminology may be unfamiliar if you're not acquainted with AutoLISP, but for now, just note the filenames and the order in which they're loaded. Let's look at the sequence in more detail.

Each time AutoCAD launches from DOS:
> Read \ACAD.ADS and load \ACADAPP.EXP
> (plus any other ADS programs listed in ACAD.ADS).

Each time a drawing is loaded:

1. Load ACAD.PGP.

2. Load a custom ACAD.LSP file, if one exists.

3. Load ACAD.MNX.

4. Load ACAD.MNL.

5. Load ACADR12.LSP.

6. Execute any S::STARTUP function defined in ACAD.LSP or ACAD.MNL.

When you launch AutoCAD from DOS, AutoCAD always looks for a file called ACAD.ADS. This is an ASCII text file containing the names of ADS applications (i.e., C programs written to work with AutoCAD). If AutoCAD finds ACAD.ADS, it loads the listed ADS programs into memory for later use. Stock AutoCAD contains but one program name in ACAD.ADS: ACADAPP.EXP. This ADS application contains the code for some of the new Release 12 commands such as BHATCH and DDIM, and defines a few new functions used by AutoLISP.

Note that this step occurs only once at the beginning of an entire AutoCAD session. That's because ADS programs "survive" through drawing loads, unlike AutoLISP programs and other support files, which are cleared out of memory each time you finish with a drawing. Thus the remaining steps occur each time you create or open a drawing.

1. Load ACAD.PGP.

AutoCAD's ProGram Parameters file defines AutoCAD command aliases, as well as external DOS commands you can run directly from the Command: prompt.

Release 12's stock ACAD.PGP contains a few external commands, a limited number of AutoCAD command aliases, and a whole slew of AME aliases. Turn to Chapter 15, *Custom Command Names*, for instructions on how to create a more efficient .PGP file.

2. Load a custom ACAD.LSP file, if one exists.

ACAD.LSP is AutoCAD's storehouse for AutoLISP programs that you or your third-party application want to have loaded into memory for every drawing session. Unlike ACAD.ADS, ACAD.LSP doesn't contain just names: It includes actual LISP code. We discuss ACAD.LSP in Chapters 18 and 19.

Since stock AutoCAD doesn't use an ACAD.LSP file, this step doesn't occur until you or your third-party application have created such a file.

3. Load ACAD.MNX.

AutoCAD reads the menu name from the drawing you're opening (or from the prototype drawing if you're creating a new drawing) and loads the appropriate menu. The finer points of menu names and compilation are covered in Chapter 17, *Menus*.

The default menu name is ACAD, and ACAD.MNX defines the standard pull–down, side screen, tablet, button, and icon menus you see in Release 12.

Tip

If AutoCAD reports "Unknown command" when you try to run a stock command, then ACADR12.LSP probably isn't getting loaded. This problem often occurs with third-party applications that haven't been updated for Release 12. One workaround is to create a menu LISP file for your third-party application's menu. For instance, if your application uses the menu \AUTOFOO\FOO.MNX, create a new .MNL file by copying \ACAD\SUPPORT\ACAD.MNL to \AUTOFOO\FOO.MNL.

4. Load ACAD.MNL.

After loading the menu, AutoCAD looks for a file with the same name and an extension of .MNL (MeNu Lisp). .MNL files are new to Release 12, and they're simply ordinary AutoLISP files containing LISP code that is associated with a menu file. See Chapter 19, *AutoLISP*, for more details.

Release 12's stock ACAD.MNL defines 12 miscellaneous functions and commands used by the standard menu.

5. Load ACADR12.LSP.

This is the tricky part. ACADR12.LSP isn't built into the Release 12 initialization sequence in the way that ACAD.ADS, ACAD.LSP, ACAD.MNX, and ACAD.MNL are. Those four files have "magic names": AutoCAD *always* looks for them (or at least for their extensions—you can designate a different menu name, but its extension still will be .MNX). AutoCAD loads ACADR12.LSP only because ACAD.MNL tells it to do so.

ACADR12.LSP is an important file because it includes code that instructs AutoCAD how to load two dozen Release 12 commands, including DDMODIFY, FILTER, DLINE, and PLUD. In addition, it defines numerous functions required by AME, the Region Modeler, and ASE. We tell you more about ACADR12.LSP and its nifty (autoload) function in Chapter 19, *AutoLISP*.

Warning

ACAD.MNL includes AutoLISP code to gray out menu choices for ASE and AME. This code can conflict with custom menus. See Chapter 17, *Menus*, for more information and a workaround.

6. Execute any S::STARTUP function defined in ACAD.LSP or ACAD.MNL

When AutoCAD loads ACAD.LSP in step 2 and ACAD.MNL in step 4, the drawing editor isn't yet fully "awake." In other words, AutoCAD isn't yet ready to accept regular commands that you might want to feed it in ACAD.LSP or ACAD.MNL. S::STARTUP addresses this difficulty. If there's a function called S::STARTUP in ACAD.LSP or ACAD.MNL, AutoCAD executes the function at the end of the initialization sequence, at which point the drawing editor is ready to accept commands. Chapter 19, *AutoLISP*, discusses the details.

Stock AutoCAD doesn't come with an ACAD.LSP file and doesn't define S::STARTUP in its ACAD.MNL file, so there's no S::STARTUP to execute until you or your third-party application create one.

Customization Documentation

Autodesk rearranged and, of course, expanded its documentation for Release 12. Although the number and bulk of its nine manuals are overwhelming at first, the documentation now is much more useful for those who customize AutoCAD. There are five manuals of potential interest to customizers: the *AutoCAD Customization Manual*, *AutoCAD Extras Manual*, *AutoLISP Programmer's Reference Manual*, *AutoCAD Development System Programmer's Reference Manual*, and *AutoCAD Reference Manual*.

The *AutoCAD Customization Manual* is new with Release 12. Much of it comprises information that in previous versions resided in appendices of the *AutoCAD Reference Manual* (e.g., ACAD.PGP, linetypes, and custom menus). There are useful overviews of customization basics and of AutoCAD's various programming interfaces. The *AutoCAD Customization Manual* also documents the new DIESEL, programmable dialogue box, and PostScript customization interfaces. Finally, two appendices list AutoCAD's system variables and commands, so that you don't have to break out the *AutoCAD Reference Manual* to look up this information. This is the manual to browse first, and to keep at hand as you customize.

The *AutoCAD Extras Manual* is new as well. It's primarily a reference for AutoCAD's "extra" commands: those that Autodesk implemented as ADS applications or AutoLISP programs. It's also useful for customization, because it documents some of the sample programs you might want to add to your AutoCAD working environment. See Appendix A of the manual, *Command/Application Summary*, for a list of what's covered.

The *AutoLISP Programmer's Reference Manual* has been reorganized for Release 12, and the result is a much more usable reference. Since this manual is a reference rather than a teaching guide, it still requires a preexisting understanding of LISP or programming language concepts. A welcome addition to this manual is Appendix B, *DXF Group Codes*. You'll see examples of how to use these codes in Chapter 19, *AutoLISP*.

The *AutoCAD Development System Programmer's Reference Manual* does for ADS what the *AutoLISP Programmer's Reference Manual* does for AutoLISP. The *ADS Reference* won't teach you how to program with C and ADS, but it will clue you in on the ADS library and suggest programming techniques. Even if you have no interest in ADS programming, you might want to glance at Chapter 5 of the manual: It documents the sample ADS programs in the \ACAD\ADS\ subdirectory.

Finally, don't forget the *AutoCAD Reference Manual*. Customizing AutoCAD requires thorough understanding of how the drawing editor behaves, and the *AutoCAD Reference Manual* is your guide to that behavior. Customizers need to pay particular attention to Appendix B, *Upgrading from an Older Version*, including the "Features to be Dropped in the Next Release" section. This information can clue you in on potential customization conflicts when you upgrade AutoCAD, and will help you avoid incompatibilities with future releases.

Support File Organization

We pointed out earlier that ACAD= defines the support file search path, but this path isn't the only place where AutoCAD looks for support files. In fact, AutoCAD conducts a fourfold search in the following order:

1. The current subdirectory (i.e., the directory that was current when AutoCAD was loaded).

2. The subdirectory where the current drawing resides (which might be the same as the current subdirectory).

3. The support file search path defined by the ACAD= environment variable.

4. The subdirectory containing the AutoCAD executable program ACAD.EXE (\ACAD or its equivalent on your system).

Most users don't concern themselves with these details; they simply keep all support files somewhere in the stock ACAD= search path, or perhaps add a subdirectory or two containing Blocks and custom AutoLISP programs to the end of the ACAD= path. On the other hand, the details become significant when you start to customize. By understanding the search order, you can avoid support file conflicts and set up efficient production and customization development environments. We explain below how to take advantage of the search order to avoid conflicts.

Organizing Your Custom Support Files

A common approach to customizing AutoCAD's existing support files is to edit the stock Release 12 files located in \ACAD\SUPPORT. Some users also copy their custom programs to this subdirectory. This method works, but it turns upgrade time into a nightmare, and in general, makes managing your custom AutoCAD environment difficult. When you upgrade AutoCAD, even by installing a bug fix release, you're forced to sift through dozens of support files in the existing \ACAD\SUPPORT directory in order to extract the modified or added files.

Warning

If, despite our advice, you decide to edit the original files in \ACAD\SUPPORT, always make a backup of the originals before you edit them.

Spare yourself this tedium by creating separate subdirectories for modified or added support files. There are several workable organizational schemes for segregating custom support files. In the beginning, you'll probably have only one custom support subdirectory, but as the number and sophistication of your custom support files grow, you may decide to divvy them up. In either case, the basic decision is whether to create a custom subdirectory underneath the \ACAD program directory (\ACAD\CUSTOM, say), or to create the custom subdirectory independent of the \ACAD program directory structure (\ACUSTOM, perhaps).

An \ACAD\CUSTOM directory sits close to the other AutoCAD files, which sometimes is convenient. Also, if you have more than one version of AutoCAD on your hard disk at a time, this approach lets you maintain separate customization directories for each version. This is especially beneficial when you are doing a major upgrade and keeping old and new versions on your hard disk for the 90 days allowed by Autodesk. Since some support files, especially menus and the help file, will undergo significant revision with each new major AutoCAD release, organizing by AutoCAD version makes sense for some files.

A separate \ACUSTOM custom directory has the advantage of being completely segregated from your AutoCAD program files. When you upgrade, you can "prune" the entire \ACAD subdirectory without fear of wiping out any custom files. \ACUSTOM also makes sense for support files that don't change much from version to version of AutoCAD (e.g., ACAD.LIN and ACAD.PAT).

We tend to use the \ACUSTOM approach ourselves, largely for ease of upgrading. Either approach works, and if you see no compelling reason to use one over the other, pick the method that feels right based on how your hard disk is organized. Just make sure that your custom directories are part of your regular backup regimen. The following table shows two schemes you can use as examples:

Simple Scheme:

\ACAD	\CUSTOM	All custom files

Complex, Hybrid Scheme:

\ACAD11	\CUSTOM	R.11 menus, etc.
\ACAD12	\CUSTOM	R.12 menus, ACAD.MNL, ACADR12.LSP,etc.
\ACUSTOM	\LISP	Common AutoLISP programs
	\ADS	Common ADS programs
	\FONTS	Common fonts
	\SCRIPTS	Common scripts
	\UTILS	Common utility programs

Once you've chosen a scheme, you need to add your custom subdirectory or subdirectories to the ACAD= search path. Do this by editing ACADR12.BAT (or other batch files you use to launch AutoCAD) and adding your subdirectories to the *beginning* of the path:

```
SET ACAD=C:\ACAD\CUSTOM;C:\ACAD\SUPPORT;
C:\ACAD\FONTS;C:\ACAD\ADS
```

Tip

If you see an "Out of environment space" error message when loading your AutoCAD batch file, then you need to make the DOS environment larger. You do this by adding a SHELL= line to your CONFIG.SYS file. For example:

```
SHELL=C:\DOS\COMMAND.COM C:\DOS\ /E:1024 /P
```

expands the environment to 1024 bytes. See your DOS manual for details.

AutoCAD uses the first version of a given support file that it finds, so putting your custom subdirectory first is crucial whenever there are duplicate support files on your disk. Since AutoCAD searches the ACAD= subdirectories in order, it will find your custom versions of any files that also are located in \ACAD\SUPPORT before it finds the stock version, and will use yours. Thus, by taking advantage of AutoCAD's support file search order, you can leave the standard support files as they are, and still ensure that AutoCAD will find and use your custom versions.

Tip

You might want to create a development subdirectory where you can experiment without fear of damaging the "good" versions of support files. Create a directory such as \ACUSTOM\TEST, and before you edit a support file, copy it there. Change to that directory and then launch AutoCAD. Since AutoCAD always looks for support files in the current subdirectory first, it will find your test version instead of the one in your custom subdirectory or the \ACAD\SUPPORT subdirectory. Once you've finished editing the file, you can either copy the revised version back to its proper location or delete it if you don't want to retain the changes.

In the following chapters, we use \ACUSTOM as our custom support file subdirectory and \ACUSTOM\TEST as our subdirectory for testing changes. If you choose a different scheme, substitute the appropriate path name for your system.

Custom Support Files and Third-Party Applications

Third-party applications can complicate the support file picture, since most of them have their own support subdirectories and need to add at least one subdirectory to the ACAD= search path. Some third-party applications require their own versions of common support files such as ACAD.PGP, ACAD.PAT, ACAD.LIN, and ACAD.LSP. A well-behaved application will supply its own set of these files or merge the changes with your existing support files, rather than overwrite the latter.

Unfortunately, there aren't any infallible rules for integrating AutoCAD's, a third-party application's, and your own custom support files. Check your third-party application's manuals for guidelines, or ask the developer. Compare the contents of any duplicated files. Often, AutoCAD support files supplied with a third-party application will be supersets of the stock AutoCAD versions. If not, you may need to create your own superset of files that contains everything you want from the third-party application and from stock AutoCAD. This is especially likely when you try to integrate a third-party application that hasn't been updated for the current release of AutoCAD.

Tip

Autodesk's Software Development Kit (SDK) includes application integration guidelines that provide guidance on making sure your customization works with other applications. The SDK is included on the Release 12 Bonus CD.

In general, though, try to apply the same approach as you do with stock AutoCAD. Leave the third-party application's files alone whenever you can, and copy any of the files you want to change to your custom support subdirectory. Put your custom subdirectory at the front of the ACAD= search path, followed by your third-party application's subdirectories, followed by the stock AutoCAD subdirectories. For instance, if your third-party application requires that its \AUTOFOO subdirectory be on the AutoCAD search path, then arrange your ACAD= path something like this:

```
SET ACAD=C:\ACUSTOM\;C:\AUTOFOO;
C:\ACAD\SUPPORT;C:\ACAD\FONTS;C:\ACAD\ADS
```

With third-party applications, as with stock AutoCAD, the key is understanding AutoCAD's support file search order. By arranging the ACAD= path correctly, you'll eliminate support file conflicts and minimize upgrade hassles.

Warning

Be careful not to launch AutoCAD when any of the AutoCAD support subdirectories are current. Remember that AutoCAD always looks first in the current directory for support files, so if you start AutoCAD from a support subdirectory, AutoCAD will use any support files it contains and ignore your custom versions in other directories.

Planning for Upgrades

Upgrading AutoCAD alone is complex, and adding third-party applications, ADI drivers, and your own custom programs to the equation only compounds the complexity. There's no way to make it all happen painlessly and automatically, but you can minimize the hassles by keeping upgrade time in mind as you customize. Don't forget that you'll also be upgrading some of your custom files many times between AutoCAD releases. You want to keep track of these incremental changes so that you can see at a glance what you've changed.

Documenting Changes

First, segregate your custom files as we suggested earlier in the chapter. Also, keep notes about what files you've changed, when you changed them, and what the changes were. You can set up an electronic log for this information, but there's nothing wrong with a low-tech notebook and pencil, if that approach works best for you.

One possibility is to use a three-ring binder with a page for each file you customize. Note the date, customizer, and modification for each change you make. If the changes are extensive, print out a portion of the modified file, highlight the changes, and insert it behind the log sheet for that file. Figure 14.1 shows a sample log sheet you can use as an example. The key is to make the process of logging changes simple and quick; if your system is too elaborate or time-consuming, you won't use it.

By segregating your custom files and keeping a log of changes, you'll make the task of reconciling custom support files with new versions of AutoCAD much more manageable.

Another technique for minimizing upgrade hassles is to customize "one version ahead." Of course this is difficult, since Autodesk doesn't divulge much about upcoming releases until they're imminent, but they do try to clue us in on important forthcoming changes. As mentioned earlier in the chapter, Appendix B of the *AutoCAD Reference Manual* includes a "Features to be Dropped in the Next Release" section. This should be the first section you read before you start customizing for a new release of AutoCAD. Of course, you should avoid using any features that will be dropped, but also search through your existing custom files for any references to obsolete features. It's easier to resolve these impending incompatibilities before the next release crashes into them.

Upgrade Time

When that fateful day does arrive, gather your wits, your patience, and your custom modifications log. Print out a list of your custom files, in case you've forgotten to log some of them. Then print out a list of the new AutoCAD version's support files. For each of your custom files that duplicates a stock AutoCAD support file, you have to determine what the differences are and whether they're significant. If the files are small, you can simply print out both versions. For long files such as menus, comparing complete listings may not be practical; you may need to browse the file or experiment with its operation to get a feel for the changes.

When you've compared files, decide what you need to do for each pair. You'll either keep your custom version, substitute the new AutoCAD version, or "graft" parts of one file into the other. Practically speaking, the biggest

File:		\ACUSTOM\ACAD.LSP
AutoCAD version:		R.12
Third-party app:		AutoFoo v. 2.2

Date	By	Modification
6 Nov 92	MM	Added S::STARTUP w/(autoload) for custom programs
8 Nov 92	MM	Added error handler
20 Nov 92	MM	Redefined PLOT
23 Nov 92	MM	Revised PLOT redefinition
27 Nov 92	MM	Revised PLOT definition (again!) — see printout
15 Dec 92	JR	Redefined OPEN and NEW — see printout
11 Feb 93	MM	Added more (autoload)s to S::STARTUP

Figure 14.1   Sample customization log sheet.

reconciliation job usually is the menu. Menus are large, messy files, and Autodesk seems to perform a major rearrangement of them with every release. We discuss strategies for making custom menus more easily upgradeable in Chapter 17, *Menus*.

Once again, third-party applications complicate the picture further. Unfortunately, third-party developers often don't ship upgraded applications until months after Autodesk releases a new version of AutoCAD. As a result, your choices are to hold off on upgrading anything until your third-party application is ready or to reconcile the old third-party application with the new AutoCAD support files yourself. Waiting is a prudent strategy, but it may not be practical if your projects require use of the new version of AutoCAD. Even if your firm isn't under any contractual obligations that require the new version, you might decide that the benefit of using the new AutoCAD release earlier is worth the cost of reconciling incompatibilities.

If you decide it's worth trying to make your older third-party application work with a new version of AutoCAD, first talk to the developer and make sure the job is possible. You don't want to spend hours editing a menu only to learn that an encrypted AutoLISP or compiled ADS program is incompatible with the new AutoCAD release and won't allow some vital part of the menu to work properly.

Assuming you get some assurance of the feasibility of the task, it's usually wise to do a minimal reconciliation. Third-party application menus are heavily customized, and reconciling them completely with a new AutoCAD menu could take many, many hours. Instead, simply add any new AutoCAD commands to the menus and resolve any incompatibilities. The goal is to make available in one set of menus the commands for your third-party application and all the AutoCAD commands and new features you need. It's not your job to fully integrate and optimize the third-party application—let the developer do that.

Preparing for Customization

If you're feeling overwhelmed by all these things to think about before you start customizing, relax. If you're new to customization, your immediate concern should be your text editor and loading it from AutoCAD. Treat the preceding parts of this chapter as background information and don't get stuck on the details. You can revisit this chapter once you've gained some experience with menu and AutoLISP programming.

If you're comfortable launching a text editor from AutoCAD, you can skip the rest of this chapter and proceed to the next one.

Choosing a Text Editor

The activity of customizing consists primarily of editing ASCII text files. To do this efficiently, you need a good text editor, preferably one that loads quickly, doesn't demand much memory, and saves files in ASCII (i.e., "nondocument") format by default. Editors with these qualities usually are called "programmers' editors" to distinguish them from large, memory–hungry word processing programs, such as WordPerfect or Microsoft Word. Word processors are designed with sophisticated formatting in mind, while programmers' editors are more efficient for AutoCAD customization and other programming tasks.

There are plenty of good, inexpensive programmers' editors available, including a number of shareware programs. If you plan to do much customization or other programming, you should invest in one. Two commercial editors that work well with AutoCAD are Symantec's Norton Editor and Borland's Brief.

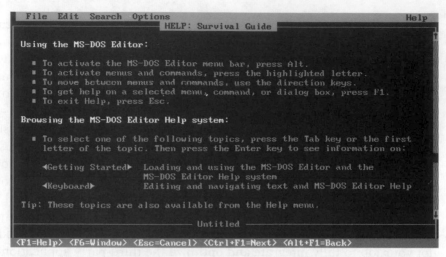

Figure 14.2   EDIT with its on-line Survival Guide.

For heavy-duty AutoCAD customizers, one of the best editors is ELSA's WCEDIT. WCEDIT, originally developed by Walt Craig, is an ADS application that runs inside AutoCAD 386. It loads almost instantaneously and it contains quite a few specialized features for AutoLISP programming. On the other hand, WCEDIT can't run outside of AutoCAD, so it's not a substitute for a general-purpose editor if you do other kinds of programming. But the best feature of WCEDIT is that it's free: The graphics card maker ELSA provides the editor gratis in order to make people aware of its other products. You can download WCEDIT from CompuServe's ACAD forum (see Appendix B for instructions on accessing the ACAD forum). Once you've downloaded WCEDIT, you have to call ELSA, give them some information about yourself, and obtain a registration number.

Finally, EDIT, the no-frills text editor that comes with DOS 5 and 6, is an acceptable choice for simple customization (see Figure 14.2). EDIT is limited as a programmers' editor, especially since it won't let you load more than one file at a time. Nonetheless, it's quite serviceable for editing scripts, menus, and short AutoLISP programs, and it has the advantage of being available on any machine running DOS 5 or 6.

Users of AutoCAD for Windows can run their favorite DOS editor from Windows or use a Windows-specific editor. Windows comes with two editors: Notepad and Write. Notepad is similar to EDIT—it's a no-frills ASCII editor—but it can't open files larger than about 50K. This limitation makes Notepad inadequate for editing menus, most of which are much larger than 50K (See Figure 14.3).

Windows Write is a simple word processor with some formatting options. Write can load menus and other large files, but by default it saves files in a unique, non-ASCII format. You can make a choice in the Save dialogue to

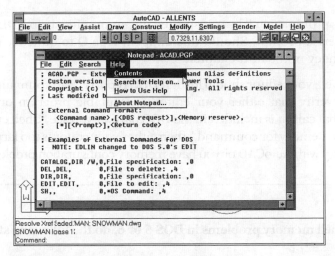

Figure 14.3 The Windows Notepad.

save in ASCII format. When you open an ASCII file, Write asks "Text document: Do you want to convert this document to Write format?" Click on the No Conversion button to leave the file in ASCII format.

Besides Notepad and Write, there are other editors available for Windows. In particular, the programmers' editors that come with Windows programming languages from Borland, Microsoft, and other companies work well for customizing AutoCAD for Windows.

We'll use EDIT for the customization examples and screen shots in the chapters that follow. Substitute your own editor if you have a better one. In either case, we expect you to know how to load and save a file and copy text with your editor. If you choose to use EDIT but are unfamiliar with it, browse through the on-line Survival Guide that pops up when you hit <Enter> after starting EDIT.

Running a Text Editor from AutoCAD

Once you've selected a text editor, you just need to make sure you can launch it from AutoCAD. This procedure requires shelling out of AutoCAD temporarily to DOS (unless you're using an ADS–based editor such as WCEDIT). Use the following tutorial to familiarize yourself with the process.

1. Shell out of AutoCAD and start your text editor.

```
Command: SHELL
OS Command: EDIT (or substitute your editor's name)
```

For now you must enter SH or SHELL before typing EDIT. AutoCAD's stock ACAD.PGP file confusingly defines EDIT as a command alias for the old DOS line editor EDLIN. If you type EDIT at the AutoCAD

Command: prompt, you'll be transported unceremoniously to EDLIN's cryptic asterisk prompt. Should this happen, type Q to quit. We'll fix this inelegancy in the next chapter.

If all goes well, your editor should load. If DOS reports "Bad command or filename," verify that either your editor's executable program or the batch file that calls it is included in the DOS path. If you see "Shell error: insufficient memory for command," then either your editor is too large to fit in memory with AutoCAD or you have memory configuration problems.

Tip

To diagnose shell memory problems in DOS 5 or 6, do the following steps:
```
Command: SHELL
OS Command: <Enter>
C:\ACUSTOM\TEST\>> MEM
```
Note the amount of memory reported by DOS, and check your editor's documentation to see whether that is sufficient. If it isn't, you can either switch to a different editor, try freeing up more of DOS's 640 KB of low memory, or use SHROOM, the SHell ROOM expander that comes with AutoCAD. SHROOM.COM and its documentation file, SHROOM.DOC, are located in the \ACAD\SAMPLE subdirectory.

---

2. Create a sample script.

Once you've successfully loaded your text editor, test it by creating a sample script. We cover scripts in detail in Chapter 16, but for now, just type carefully the text shown in Figure 14.4. Include the blank lines, but don't leave any trailing spaces at the end of lines or additional blank lines at the end of the file.

Save the file as ASTERISK.SCR and then exit your text editor.

 NOTE

In most scripts, including our example, you want there to be a carriage return at the end of the last line of the script (Polar MIDp @ 4 135 in the example). Some editors, such as EDIT and Brief, add an extra carriage return automatically, while others don't. Thus, if you're using EDIT, don't press <Enter> at the end of the last line. If you're using a different editor, you probably will need to press <Enter> at the end of this line. If you're in doubt, try it both ways. See Chapter 16, *Scripts*, for more information.

```
ZOOM 0,0 12,9
LINE 5,4 6,4
                              (leave a blank line here)

ARRAY Last
                              (leave a blank line here)
Polar MIDp @ 4 135            (see the note in step 2)
```

Figure 14.4   A sample script file.

3. Test the script.

You should be back in the AutoCAD drawing editor (if you returned to a DOS prompt, type EXIT). Now execute the script.

```
Command: SCRIPT
Script file: ASTERISK
```
Type or pick from the file dialogue.

If all goes well, AutoCAD should draw an asterisk in the middle of the screen (see Figure 14.5). If you see strange characters on the command line, then your editor probably saved the script file with special formatting, rather than as a plain ASCII text file. Use a different editor or figure out how to save ASCII files with your current one. If AutoCAD appears as if it tried to run the script, but got confused and stalled somewhere, then you probably mistyped something.

Once you've worked out any text editor problems so that you can successfully edit ASCII files from AutoCAD, you're ready to start customizing!

Customizing for Workgroups

The customization planning issues for workgroups are essentially the same as for individual users: Understand and take advantage of AutoCAD's initialization sequence, organize your support files, and plan for upgrades. With workgroups, though, these issues take on additional importance. If you waste a day struggling with a new AutoCAD release because you didn't properly integrate your custom files with it, you can just chalk it up to experience. The stakes are quite a bit higher when you waste a day for many people and frazzle the nerves of everyone in your workgroup.

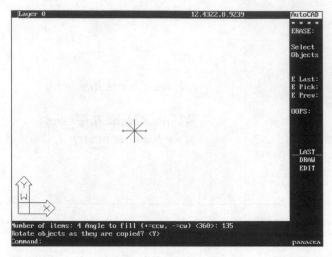

Figure 14.5   The sample script in action.

Perhaps the greatest workgroup customization challenge is keeping everyone's files in synch. Networks provide an obvious solution, as long as everyone uses one set of AutoCAD program and support files on the server. For a variety of reasons, including AutoCAD's history of network glitches, this approach isn't always possible or desirable.

If AutoCAD and its support files reside locally on each workstation, it's imperative that you have a scheme for updating everyone's files at the same time. If your workgroup is connected with a network, you can keep a master set of support subdirectories on the server and copy them to each workstation as needed. If not, you'll have to use "sneaker–net" with floppies or tapes. In either case, DOS disk management utilities, such as XTree Gold, are useful tools. These utilities, among their many benefits, make it easier to copy large groups of files while maintaining subdirectory structures. You also can use DOS's XCOPY command, although it's less forgiving.

Be cognizant of some people's desires to do their own customization. Savvy users will collect their own favorite AutoLISP programs or want to use a set of command aliases that their fingers have memorized. As discussed in the previous chapter, your company needs to decide how far (or whether) to accommodate these desires. Of course, you can "just say no," but doing so can sap a workgroup's productivity and inspire animosity.

A more enlightened approach is to provide a simple means for members of your workgroup to add their own custom files without mucking up the standard workgroup ones. Create a special subdirectory for user customization on each workstation, and add that subdirectory to the front of the ACAD= search path. Note that there will be times when users have to reconcile their own custom files with revised workgroup versions.

Finally, don't spring major support file changes on your workgroup without warning them. If you've just spent a day customizing a group of files, it's easy to forget that the impact of your clever changes may not be obvious to other people who don't even know what the files are called. Notify workgroup members by memo or e-mail *before* you activate the modifications, and if the changes are significant enough, gather everyone for a quick demo of what to expect.

Summary

Efficient customization requires understanding the location and operation of AutoCAD's stock support files, and then establishing a strategy for developing and using custom support files. Your strategy should take into account the process of upgrading AutoCAD and third-party applications, and should address keeping support files for the workgroup or office in synch.

In subsequent chapters, we'll implement our own advice by means of \ACUSTOM and \ACUSTOM\TEST subdirectories. We'll also offer additional advice on how to customize specific files efficiently.

15

Custom Command Names

AutoCAD's ProGram Parameters file (ACAD.PGP) is the best place to start customizing, because it provides two eminently useful but simple ways to streamline the keyboard interface: 1) "command aliases," your own names for AutoCAD commands, and 2) "external commands," names and parameters for launching DOS operating system commands, programs, or batch files from the drawing editor.

About This Chapter

In this chapter, we'll cover both forms of customization—command aliases and external commands—and develop an improved ACAD.PGP that will make AutoCAD's keyboard interface more efficient and easier on your fingers. If you're working through the chapter, make sure you can launch a text editor from AutoCAD, as described in the previous chapter.

If you don't want to bother modifying ACAD.PGP yourself, copy the custom one from the book's diskettes into your AutoCAD custom support file subdirectory (\ACUSTOM\ or an equivalent (see the "Support File Organization" section in the previous chapter). You should print out the file and keep it near your workstation until you're familar with the aliases and external commands.

Command Aliases

Many computer programs include a "macro" capability, whereby you can assign a command or series of commands to a shorter sequence of keystrokes. AutoCAD's command aliases offer a simple form of this capability.

Using Command Aliases

The first tutorial demonstrates how command aliases work, for users who aren't yet familiar with them. If you're already using aliases, you can skip to the next section.

1. Change to the \ACUSTOM\TEST subdirectory and start AutoCAD.

If you haven't already done so, create the subdirectories \ACUSTOM and \ACUSTOM\TEST\, and modify your AutoCAD batch file so that \ACUSTOM is on the ACAD= search path.

See the "Support File Organization" section in the previous chapter for more information.

Change to \ACUSTOM\TEST and launch AutoCAD.

2. Try some of the command aliases defined in the stock ACAD.PGP.

```
Command: L
LINE
```

AutoCAD translates the command alias L into LINE.

```
From point:
```
draw several line segments

When you're finished drawing lines, try M for move and E for ERASE.

How about COPY?

```
Command: C
CIRCLE 3P/2P/TTR/<Center point>:
```

Oops—C is defined as CIRCLE instead. Cancel and try again with CP.

```
Command: CP
COPY
Select objects:
```

Tip

The \ACAD\SAMPLE\ALIAS.LSP routine will list your currently defined aliases. You can use the APPLOAD command to run and load ALIAS. See Chapter 9, *Adding Dimensions and Text,* for information about APPLOAD.

Default Command Aliases

Now we'll take a look at how AutoCAD's default aliases are defined in ACAD.PGP.

1. Copy \ACAD\SUPPORT\ACAD.PGP to \ACUSTOM\TEST.

Use Release 12's redesigned FILES command to copy ACAD.PGP to your development subdirectory (see Figure 15.1).

```
Command: FILES
```
or
Pick Utilities... from the File menu.
Pick the Copy File... button.

Watch the dialogue box labels carefully: Copy file... first displays a Source File subdialogue from which you choose an existing file. Once you've selected a file, click on OK—*don't* type the new name in the Source File dialogue. After you click OK, AutoCAD displays the Destination File subdialogue for you to select the new directory and type the new name.

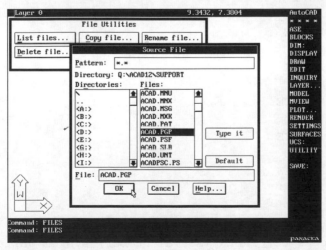

Figure 15.1 Copying ACAD.PGP with the FILES command.

2. Browse through ACAD.PGP.

Launch your text editor and open ACAD.PGP.

With **DOS's EDIT**, the sequence goes like this:

```
Command: SHELL
OS Command: EDIT ACAD.PGP
```

Page through the file, noting the different sections.

Lines that begin with a semicolon are *comments*—notes added by the customizer to document or clarify something. AutoCAD ignores comment lines when it loads ACAD.PGP. Blank lines are just for visual layout—AutoCAD ignores those, as well.

All but the first 15 or so lines are dedicated to command aliases (we'll return to those first 15 lines later). The following section defines aliases for standard AutoCAD commands. The remainder of ACAD.PGP contains aliases for AME and Region Modeler.

```
; Command alias format:
;    <Alias>,*<Full command name>

; Sample aliases for AutoCAD commands
; These examples reflect the most frequently used commands.
; Each alias uses a small amount of memory, so don't go
; overboard on systems with tight memory.

A,        *ARC
C,        *CIRCLE
CP,       *COPY
DV,       *DVIEW
E,        *ERASE
L,        *LINE
LA,       *LAYER
M,        *MOVE
MS,       *MSPACE
P,        *PAN
PS,       *PSPACE
PL,       *PLINE
R,        *REDRAW
Z,        *ZOOM

3DLINE, *LINE

; easy access to _PKSER (serial number) system variable
SERIAL, *_PKSER
```

Tip

Aliases for transparent commands can be used transparently, as well. Try it with the Z (for ZOOM) alias: Start the line command, pick a point, then type 'Z.

As you can see, the format for defining command aliases is simply:

```
<alias>,    *<AutoCAD command name>
```

You simply type the alias, a comma, any number of spaces, an asterisk, and finally the AutoCAD command that the alias should call. The spaces are for appearance only: It's easier to scan a list of aliased commands if the AutoCAD command names are aligned.

Custom Command Aliases

Now we'll customize the AutoCAD command aliases.

1. Modify the CIRCLE and COPY aliases.

If you haven't done so already, launch your text editor and load ACAD.PGP.

Most people use COPY a lot more often than CIRCLE, so let's revise these aliases so that they're a bit more sensible.

Change the CIRCLE and COPY lines so that they read as follows:

```
...
A,      *ARC
CI,     *CIRCLE
C,      *COPY
DV,     *DVIEW
...
```

Save ACAD.PGP and then exit your editor.

2. Test the changes.

```
Command: C
CIRCLE 3P/2P/TTR/<Center point>:
```

AutoCAD still runs the CIRCLE command. That's because AutoCAD reads the ACAD.PGP at the beginning of the drawing load sequence, and

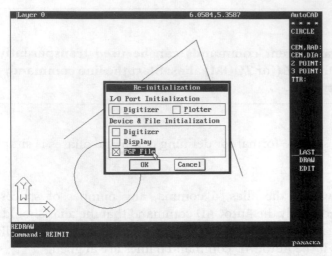

Figure 15.2   Use REINIT to force AutoCAD to reread ACAD.PGP.

then stores its contents in memory (see the section on the Release 12 initialization sequence in the previous chapter). To force AutoCAD to reread ACAD.PGP, use the REINIT command, as shown in Figure 15.2.

Tip

Keyboard jockeys can type RE–INIT 16 (note the hyphen in RE–INIT) instead of using the REINIT dialogue box. RE–INIT with the hyphen calls the RE-INIT system variable, and 16 is the numerical "bit" that tells AutoCAD to reinitialize the ACAD.PGP file. See the "System Variables" section of Appendix A in the *AutoCAD Customization Manual* for details.

```
Command: C
COPY
Select objects:
```

Now when you type **C**, AutoCAD executes COPY, as any right-thinking CAD program should. Be sure to test CI also.

3. Add and modify other aliases.

Once you've tested your modifications, edit ACAD.PGP again, but this time add other command aliases for the AutoCAD commands you use most often. Of course, you can change or delete existing aliases, as well.

Warning

Always **test each and every modification you make to support files thoroughly, even with something as obvious as command aliases. You'll be amazed at how often a trivial change will break a support file because you left out a comma, mistyped a word, or just forgot an obscure but important customization rule.**

Make the modifications shown in italics in the following listing, or substitute your own preferences.

Save the file, return to AutoCAD, run REINIT, and test all your modifications.

You might want to print out ACAD.PGP to guide you in your testing.

```
...
; Custom AutoCAD Power Tools aliases:

A,        *ARRAY
AE,       *DDATTE
BH,       *BHATCH
BR,       *BREAK
CI,       *CIRCLE
C,        *COPY
CH,       *CHANGE
CHP,      *DDCHPROP
DS,       *DIST
DT,       *DTEXT
DV,       *DVIEW
E,        *ERASE
ED,       *DDEDIT
F,        *FILLET
I,        *INSERT
L,        *LINE
LA,       *LAYER
LM,       *DDLMODES
LS,       *LIST
M,        *MOVE
MD,       *DDMODIFY
MI,       *MIRROR
MS,       *MSPACE
O,        *OFFSET
OS,       *DDOSNAP
```

(continued)

```
P,        *PAN
PE,       *PEDIT
PL,       *PLINE
PS,       *PSPACE
QS,       *QSAVE
R,        *REDRAW
RO,       *ROTATE
S,        *STRETCH
SN,       *SNAP
T,        *TRIM
TM,       *TILEMODE
V,        *DDVIEW
VP,       *VPOINT
X,        *EXTEND
Z,        *ZOOM


3DLINE, *LINE

; easy access to _PKSER (serial number) system variable
SERIAL, *_PKSER

; NOTE: AME aliases were removed.
; Copy them from \ACAD\SUPPORT\ACAD.PGP if you want them.
```

Tip

We removed the AME and Region Modeler aliases from ACAD.PGP, because they do take up a small amount of load time and memory. Of course, if you use AME or Region Modeler, you should leave these aliases in.

Notice that none of the aliases include command suboptions (e.g., LAYER Set or ZOOM Previous). Unfortunately, AutoCAD won't allow suboptions—it's simply a design limitation of command aliases. Menu macros and AutoLISP programs aren't saddled with this constraint, so you can use them for more elaborate "aliases." Chapter 17, *Menus,* shows how to make a COPY Multiple macro.

On the other hand, menu macros and AutoLISP are considerably more complicated than command aliases. Despite their limitations, aliases are a great tool for making the keyboard interface more efficient, and they take little time to implement and test.

External Commands

ACAD.PGP's other purpose—its *only* purpose until Release 11—is defining new AutoCAD command names that launch DOS commands, programs, and batch files. When you run an external command, AutoCAD *shells out* to DOS, temporarily suspending the drawing editor until you return from your DOS operation or program.

Windows Tip

Although you can define and launch external commands in AutoCAD for Windows, it's usually more productive to launch DOS programs from Program Manager. Instead of using SHELL, simply open a DOS window from Program Manager. That way, you can switch back and forth between AutoCAD and the DOS program with <Alt>+<Tab>. For DOS programs you run frequently, create a program definition in Program Manager with the File New... menu choice.

Using External Commands

The simplest way to run an external program from DOS is to use AutoCAD's SH or SHELL command. (In fact, SH and SHELL are external program commands themselves, as we'll see shortly.) When you type SH or SHELL, AutoCAD replaces its customary Command: prompt with an OS Command: prompt. You can respond either by typing an operating system command (including a program or batch file) or by pressing <Enter>. If you type a command, AutoCAD passes it on to DOS, which tries to locate and execute it in the usual manner. When the DOS command finishes, control returns immediately to AutoCAD, and you're back at the Command: prompt. If, instead, you press <Enter> at the OS Command: prompt, AutoCAD hands control over to DOS, which issues its customary prompt, only with an extra ">" appended as a cue that you're shelled out:

```
C:\ACUSTOM\TEST\>>
```

From this prompt, you can execute as many DOS commands as you wish—DOS remains in control. To return to AutoCAD, type EXIT at the DOS prompt.

Warning

Be careful about manipulating files while you're shelled out. AutoCAD creates temporary files (most of which contain dollar signs), and if you mess with these, you're likely to crash AutoCAD. Refer to SHELL in Chapter 4, *Utility Commands and Services,* **in the** *AutoCAD Reference Manual* **for other warnings. It's always prudent to save your drawing before shelling out, just in case anything goes awry.**

Default External Commands

While SHELL provides a simple means for running any DOS command or program, it's convenient to automate the process of launching the programs that you shell to frequently. Autodesk has done this for you with several common DOS commands, such as DIR and TYPE. Try the TYPE external command.

1. Use TYPE to display the contents of ACAD.PGP.

```
Command: TYPE
File to type: ACAD.PGP
```

The contents of your custom ACAD.PGP should race by.

2. Use your text editor to look more closely at the external commands in ACAD.PGP.

Shell out with SH, run your text editor, and load ACAD.PGP.

The stock external command section is at the top of the file, as shown below:

```
; External Command format:
;    <Command name>,[<DOS request>],<Memory reserve>,
```

Tip

AutoCAD hangs onto about 120 KB of memory when you shell out. If the program you want to run needs a lot of memory, it may not execute when you try to run it from the shell. If you encounter this problem, see the "Running a Text Editor" from the AutoCAD section in the previous chapter for suggestions for freeing up more memory.

```
;       [*][<Prompt>],<Return code>

; Examples of External Commands for DOS
    CATALOG,DIR /W,           0,File specification: ,0
    DEL,DEL,                  0,File to delete: ,4
    DIR,DIR,                  0,File specification: ,0
    EDIT,EDLIN,               0,File to edit: ,4
    SH,,                      0,*OS Command: ,4
    SHELL,,                   0,*OS Command: ,4
    TYPE,TYPE,                0,File to list: ,0
...
```

The syntax for external commands is shown in the comment lines at the beginning of the above list of commands. This syntax is slightly more involved than it was for aliases: Instead of two fields (alias and AutoCAD commands separated by a comma) external commands require five fields separated by commas. As with aliases, the extra spaces are merely cosmetic. [Square brackets] indicate optional fields, but all four commas have to be there. The five fields function as follows:

1. <Command name>:

This field defines the name you type at the AutoCAD Command: prompt in order to launch the external program. Note that this name often will be the same as the actual DOS command name (e.g., DEL, DIR, and TYPE).

2. [<DOS request>]:

This field is the name of the DOS operating system command, program, or batch file you want to launch. AutoCAD feeds this field, followed by your response to the <Prompt>, to DOS. If this field is omitted, as it is for the SH and SHELL external command definitions, then only your response to the <Prompt> gets fed to DOS.

3. <Memory reserve>:

This field is a throwback to the days when AutoCAD tried to do everything in DOS's lower 640 KB. You still need a number here for compatibility purposes, but it doesn't matter what the number is.

4. [*][<Prompt>]:

This field defines the prompt the user sees after entering the external command name. Whatever the user types in response to the prompt is tacked onto the <DOS request> field and fed to DOS. Precede the prompt with an asterisk if a user's response is allowed to contain spaces; otherwise, AutoCAD will treat the spacebar like the <Enter> key, as it normally does. You may want to use the asterisk for all commands so that spaces in responses are treated consistently. You can omit the prompt if the <DOS request> doesn't require additional input.

5. <Return code>:

This field is a number that tells AutoCAD what to do when the external command is finished and AutoCAD receives control again. 0 means always return to the text screen, while 4 means return to whichever screen was current (graphics or text) when the user entered the external command name. Use 0 when the external command will be writing something of interest to the screen and then immediately returning control to AutoCAD (e.g., DIR). Use 4 in all other cases. (There are two other return codes, but they're almost never used).

Custom External Commands

The most important modification you can make to ACAD.PGP's external commands is to add your text editor. Because you'll be launching your text editor many, many times as you customize, you want to be able to load it with a minimum number of keystrokes.

1. Change the EDIT external program.

Assuming you use DOS 5 or 6, you should change the EDIT external command's <DOS request> so that it calls EDIT rather than the pathetic line editor EDLIN.

If you haven't done so already, launch your text editor and load ACAD.PGP.

Change the <DOS request> field so that the line looks like this:

```
EDIT,EDIT,      0,File to edit: ,4
```

Save ACAD.PGP, return to AutoCAD, REINIT, and test.

You now should be able to launch EDIT directly from the Command: prompt, without typing SHELL or SH first.

2. Add your own text editor as an external program.

If you're using a text editor other than EDIT, add a new external command definition for it.

Launch EDIT, open ACAD.PGP, and add an external command definition for your text editor.

For instance, if you use the Norton Editor, add the following line (location doesn't matter, but for now, put it just below the existing external commands):

```
NE,NE,          0,*File to edit: ,4
```

Note the asterisk before the prompt—like most programmers' editors, the Norton Editor allows more than one argument, so the asterisk is there to let you type spaces without AutoCAD treating them as <Enter>s.

Save ACAD.PGP, return to AutoCAD, REINIT, and test.

3. Add other external programs.

Although your text editor is the only crucial external command you need to add, there might be other DOS commands or programs that you run frequently and that merit their own line in ACAD.PGP. On the other hand, there's no need to go crazy trying to define every DOS command you ever will want to run from AutoCAD: You can use SHELL for external programs that you run less frequently.

Add the external command definitions shown in italics below, or add others of your choosing.

The following list shows, in italics, the custom external commands from the ACAD.PGP contained on the *AutoCAD Power Tools* diskette. We've added external commands for three handy DOS commands and for LIST (Vernon Bucrg's excellent shareware ASCII file listing program, available on most BBSs and from the IBMSW forum on CompuServe). Use these additions as examples for your own modifications to ACAD.PGP.

Save ACAD.PGP, return to AutoCAD, REINIT, and test.

```
DIR,DIR,        0,File specification: ,0
EDIT,EDIT,      0,File to edit: ,4
SH,,            0,*OS Command: ,4
SHELL,,         0,*OS Command: ,4
TYPE,TYPE,      0,File to list: ,0
```

(continued)

```
;   Additional AutoCAD Power Tools external commands
;    Text editors and viewer:
;    (Delete lines for programs you don't own;
;     add a line for your text editor)
;    - Borland's Brief -
B,B,                0,*File to edit: ,4
;    - Symantec's Norton Editor -
NE,NE,              0,*File to edit: ,4
;    - Vernon Buerg's LIST -
LISTF,LIST,         0,File(s) to list: ,4
;   Handy DOS commands:
;    - DIR sorted by date -
DIRD,DIR /OD/P,     0,,0
;    - DIR sorted by extension -
DIRE,DIR /OE/P,     0,,0
;    - Display DOS environment -
DOSSETS,SET,        0,,0
...
```

Warning

Be careful not to duplicate a regular AutoCAD command name when you create external commands. For instance, in defining an external command for Vernon Buerg's LIST, you might be tempted to use LIST as its AutoCAD command name. That won't work, since LIST also is the name of the AutoCAD command for listing entities, and AutoCAD internal commands always take precedence. For this reason, we used LISTF (for LIST File) instead.

Tip

Use DOS batch files to make the same synonyms available at the DOS prompt as in AutoCAD. In the subdirectory that holds your DOS files, create batch files with the same name as your external commands, but ending with .BAT. The file should contain a single line that's the same as the second field in your external command specification. In DOS 5 or later, you can do the same thing more easily with the DOSKEY command. By making synonyms the same inside and outside of AutoCAD, shortcuts you spend time creating and learning for AutoCAD will benefit you at the DOS prompt, and vice versa.

Finishing Up

Edit your test version of ACAD.PGP to your satisfaction, and test each of the command names to make sure they work properly. If you choose to copy the custom ACAD.PGP from the *AutoCAD Power Tools* diskette, delete any external commands that refer to programs you don't have loaded on your computer, and make sure you've added a line for your text editor. You also should check whether your third-party application requires any ACAD.PGP external commands. If it does, you'll need to type or paste in these commands.

Once everything works, use the Rename file... option of the FILES command to move the revised ACAD.PGP file up to your \ACUSTOM subdirectory (see Figure 15.3).

Warning

Avoid leaving duplicates of your support files in the \ACUSTOM\TEST subdirectory. If you let files build up in \ACUSTOM\TEST, you'll eventually end up testing with a mish–mash of obsolete, current, and "not quite finished" support files spread between \ACUSTOM and \ACUSTOM\TEST. Reserve \ACUSTOM\TEST for the support files you're currently working on, and either move or delete those files when you finish an editing session.

Chapter 3 of the *AutoCAD Customization Manual* covers the ACAD.PGP file in somewhat more detail. We've covered just about everything you need to know, though—there isn't that much to it!

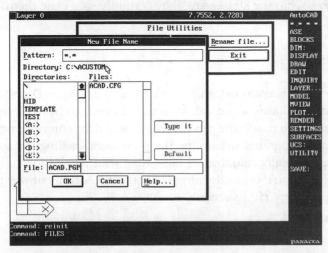

Figure 15.3 Moving ACAD.PGP with the FILES command.

Custom Command Names and Workgroups

As with other customization options, the benefits of creating custom command names are multiplied many times over a workgroup. Custom command names not only improve productivity, they raise the base level of users' AutoCAD expertise and DOS survival skills within a workgroup.

The only real challenge with using custom command names in a workgroup is coming up with names that everyone can live with. Each of us has our own idea about what the "right" alias for a command or external program is (witness C and CP in the stock AutoCAD ACAD.PGP). Try to gain a consensus among your workgroup members, since maintaining different ACAD.PGP files for different people adds support and upgrade headaches. On the other hand, command names shouldn't become a battleground. If some users are insistent about their own names, let them modify aliases in their own version of ACAD.PGP, but warn them that they'll have to remodify the file each time the workgroup version is upgraded.

As workgroup members become accustomed to using aliases and external commands, they'll undoubtedly discover other commands that deserve them. Your own experiences and a little bit of observation of other people can be your guide. Take a moment now and then to think about the commands you type frequently (or would've typed if their names were shorter). Watch other users unobtrusively for a few minutes to see what commands they type. Add new entries for these commands to ACAD.PGP. Within a short time, you'll converge on a set of aliases and external commands that matches your group's work style.

After you modify the ACAD.PGP file, always print out the new version. Keep a copy in your customization log and office CAD manual. Also, it's a good idea to highlight the changes and tack a copy on each person's monitor or digitizer. If people don't know what the aliases are, they certainly won't use them.

Summary

ACAD.PGP is the easiest way to customize the keyboard interface. Despite their limitations, command aliases will create a more efficient AutoCAD interface, especially for experienced users who rely on the keyboard for entering common commands. External programs streamline the process of shelling out to DOS programs, and are especially valuable for launching your text editor.

In the next chapter, you'll take advantage of your text editor's new external command definition for writing scripts.

16

Scripts

In Chapter 13, *Customization Overview*, we defined script languages as incredibly fast and incredibly dumb automatic typists. AutoCAD scripts certainly fit that description: They're nothing more than a way of storing keystrokes in an ASCII text file and then executing those keystrokes one or more times in one or more drawings.

Scripts are Autodesk's gift to those who are customization–phobic. Scripts are simple to understand and create, and unlike most of the other AutoCAD customization interfaces, they don't require modifications to the stock support files. That means you can write and use scripts without fear of messing up some other part of your AutoCAD support environment. Simplicity and self-sufficiency make scripts the one customization interface that every AutoCAD user should understand.

Scripts are useful whenever you perform the exact same sequence of actions more than a couple of times. Besides plotting, common applications include restoring a group of layer settings, establishing system variable settings, and binding all Xrefs in or purging a batch of drawings. In addition, scripts are well suited for displaying slide shows: sequences of snapshots of your drawings.

The disadvantage of scripts is that they offer limited capabilities and control. Scripts can't make decisions (e.g., *if...then...else*), delve deeply into entities or the drawing editor environment, or do much with the interface. Scripts are like having the world's dumbest but fastest–typing AutoCAD user at your keyboard.

About This Chapter

In this chapter, we cover how to write and run scripts, but the focus is on useful applications of scripts. We introduce scripts with a simple example that creates new layers. The remainder of the chapter comprises three sets of tutorials that show how to use scripts to set layers and dimension variables, to plot, and to run slide shows. These tutorials demonstrate the power of scripts and some of their subtleties.

Scripts, and hence this chapter, are for everyone, so we recommend that you work through the chapter if you're not yet familiar with scripts. Even if you're already comfortable with scripts, scan the chapter for ideas, tips, and warnings.

Introduction to Scripts

The best way to master scripts is to write a few of them, so let's dive right in. Suppose you're an architect and you find yourself frequently creating a group of layers for three different types of walls in remodeling projects: existing, to be demolished, and new, as follows:

	Layer Name	Color	Linetype
Existing walls:	WALL-EXIST	CYAN (4)	CONTINUOUS
Walls to be demolished:	WALL-DEMO	RED (1)	DASHED
New walls:	WALL-NEW	MAGENTA (6)	CONTINUOUS

You could add these layers to a prototype drawing, as we described in Chapter 4, *Basic Setup and Prototypes*, but then every drawing would carry the layers around, even if they weren't required for that drawing. Instead, let's write a script that creates the layers and sets their colors and linetypes on-the-fly.

1. Change to \ACUSTOM\TEST and run through the layer creation sequence.

   Change to the \ACUSTOM\TEST subdirectory and start AutoCAD.

   Using the keyboard only, go through the steps you'd use to create three layers with the colors and linetypes as shown above. Write down each keystroke.

You can't use menus or dialogue boxes such as DDLMODES when developing scripts, because scripts can't control them; everything must be typed at the Command: prompt. Don't be surprised if this takes you a few tries.

2. Create the new script WALLNEW.SCR.

Launch your text editor and create a new file called WALLNEW.SCR.

The procedures for launching a text editor from AutoCAD are described in Chapters 14 and 15.

Transcribe the keystrokes you wrote down, using a space or a carriage return for each time you hit the spacebar or <Enter> key.

Press <Enter> at the end of the last line of the script unless your editor automatically adds one (see the Warning below).

The results should be similar to the WALLNEW.SCR script file shown below:

```
LAYER New WALL-EXIST,WALL-DEMO,WALL-NEW
Color CYAN WALL-EXIST
Color RED WALL-DEMO
Color MAGENTA WALL-NEW
Ltype DASHED WALL-DEMO
```

(see the Warning below)

Save WALLNEW.SCR and return to AutoCAD.

Warning

Some editors, including DOS's EDIT and Borland's Brief, have an annoying habit of adding an extra <Enter> to the end of files. This behavior can drive you crazy trying to figure out why your AutoCAD scripts don't run the way you wrote them. Unfortunately, you just have to be aware of the problem and press <Enter> at the end of the script one time less than you normally would. If the damage is already done and you're using EDIT, press <Ctrl>+<End> to move to the end of the file, and then backspace until you get to the last actual text character in the script.

---

3. Test the script.

Since you already created the WALL-* layers in the current drawing to

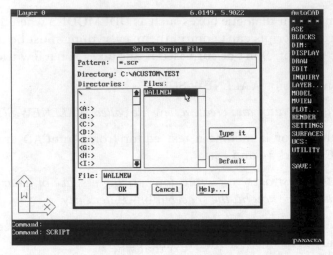

Figure 16.1 Running the WALLNEW script.

establish the script sequence, you need to start a new drawing before testing the script. You frequently will run into this kind of consideration when writing and testing scripts.

Start a new drawing, discarding changes to the current one.

Now run the script with the **SCRIPT** command.

```
Command: SCRIPT
Script file: WALLNEW
```

(type or pick from the file dialogue—see Figure 16.1)

Assuming you typed carefully, the script should execute the **LAYER** command, create the new layers, set each of their colors, and assign a dashed linetype to WALL-DEMO. If not, reopen WALLNEW.SCR in your text editor, correct any errors, start a new drawing, and test again.

In scripts, both spaces and carriage returns act like <Enter>, just as they do at the AutoCAD Command: prompt. The choice of whether to use a space or an <Enter> is arbitrary. You'll want to keep the lines of scripts to a reasonable length, but the first two lines of the script could just as well have been formatted "vertically;" that is, with LAYER on one line, New on the next line, and so on. Choose a formatting style that makes sense to you.

Warning

Don't add spaces to the ends of lines to act as <Enter>s. Most editors don't provide any visual cue that the extra spaces are there, and you're likely to become confused when you go back to edit the script later and have forgotten about the additional spaces. Always add blank lines rather than trailing spaces.

There's one small glitch in our first script: It leaves you in the LAYER command, rather than back at the Command: prompt. This problem highlights the trickiest aspect of scripts: You have to account for *every* keystroke, and especially every <Enter>, required by the command sequence you're scripting. Remember that when you start the LAYER command interactively, it remains active until you type an extra <Enter>. Our script needs to include that additional <Enter>.

4. Add one more carriage return to WALLNEW.SCR.

Edit the script and add one more <Enter> to the end of the script.

Remember to account for whether your editor adds a final <Enter>.

Save, return to AutoCAD, start a new drawing, and test the change.

The script should now leave the Command: prompt, rather than the LAYER command, current when it finishes.

Tip

The choice of upper- or lowercase letters is arbitrary as well, but it's a good idea to adopt a convention and stick to it. In this book, we use uppercase letters in scripts for those characters that you would have to type if you were carrying out the same sequence interactively at the Command: prompt. Lowercase letters are ones that "fill out" command suboption names (e.g., the New suboption of LAYER). Technically, you could leave out all the letters we show in lowercase and the script would still run. We suggest leaving them in, though, since they make the action of the script clearer to someone (including yourself) who is looking at or editing it.

Setting Layers and Dimension Variables with Scripts

Now that you're familiar with creating and running scripts, we'll move on to some more useful examples. In this pair of tutorials, we'll develop scripts that change the settings of existing layers and establish dimension variable settings and save them to a dimension style.

Layer Settings with Scripts

This tutorial builds on our WALL-* layers example and demonstrates a common application of scripts: restoring layer settings. Suppose you frequently find yourself establishing the layer settings shown below in preparation for drawing new walls. Our WALLSET script will automate this task.

Layer Name	Setting
WALL-NEW	On and current
WALL-EXIST	On but Locked
WALL-DEMO	Off

1. Draw some lines on each of the WALL-* layers.

Use AutoCAD's DLINE command to draw a few double lines on each of the three WALL- layers.*

The lines will be needed for testing.

2. Run through the layer setting sequence and transcribe it into WALLSET.SCR.

As in the first tutorial, you start by stepping through the sequence you want to automate and writing down each keystroke.

Using the keyboard only, go through the steps you'd use to set the three layers as shown above.

Watch those <Enter>s.

Transcribe the keystrokes into a new file called WALLSET.SCR.

Our version is shown in the WALLSET.SCR script file below:

```
LAYER Thaw WALL-* On WALL-* Unlock WALL-*
```

```
Set WALL-NEW
Lock WALL-EXIST
Off WALL-DEMO
```
(leave a blank line here)

Leave a blank line at the end of the file to act as a final <Enter> that ends the LAYER command.

Perhaps your version didn't include the Thaw, On, and Unlock subcommands? Although these steps are unnecessary in the context of the current layer settings on our test drawing, you can't depend on these settings. Perhaps the next time you want to run the script, WALL-NEW will be locked and WALL-EXIST will be turned off. The first line of the script assumes the worst and thaws, turns on, and unlocks all WALL-layers. These steps establish a "baseline" from which your script will always run correctly. It takes a bit of practice to "customize defensively" in this way, but doing so will make your scripts more robust and useful.

Warning

Note that our script sets WALL-NEW as the current layer *before* turning off WALL-DEMO. Performing these steps in the opposite order would work most of the time, but if WALL-DEMO happened to be the current layer when we ran the script, then AutoCAD's "Really want to turn the current layer off?" prompt would crash the script.

---

3. Test the script.

Turn off all the WALL-* layers.

Run the WALLNEW script.

Make sure the Command: prompt is current when the script ends.

Check the layer settings with DDLMODES or the LAYER command's question mark suboption.

WALLNEW.SCR is a simple example of a layer setting script. With real drawings, you're likely to include many more layers in scripts. Don't forget that you can use wildcard characters to specify similarly named layers (see Chapter 4 of the *AutoCAD Reference Manual*). Layer scripts are especially handy as an alternative to the VISRETAIN system variable for restoring the settings of externally referenced layers.

Dimension Styles with Scripts

In Chapter 9, *Adding Dimensions and Text,* we emphasized the importance of establishing consistent dimension variable settings and saving them as dimension styles. Ideally, your third-party application should help automate this process, but scripts provide a good "quick and dirty" approach. This tutorial presents a typical DIMVAR script and shows how to use the EX-PERT system variable to make your scripts more robust.

Assume you want a way to set all the dimension variables to the baseline architectural settings shown in the tables throughout Chapter 9. If you took the time to set all these DIMVARS from the command line (i.e., not with the DDIM dialogue), wrote down the keystrokes, and then transcribed them into a script file, you'd get something like the DIMSET.SCR script file below:

```
; NOTE: This version contains a bug!
;*DIMSET.SCR: script to set dimension variables
; and save them as the dim style STANDARD.
; Last modified by MM, 20 Feb 93
DIM
DIMALT 0 DIMALTD 2 DIMALTF 25.4 DIMAPOST .
DIMASO 1 DIMASZ 0
DIMBLK . DIMBLK1 . DIMBLK2 .
DIMCEN -3/32
...                              (other DIMVAR settings here)
DIMTOL 0 DIMTSZ 3/32 DIMTVP 0 DIMTXT 1/8
DIMZIN 0
;Save these settings as STANDARD dim style:
SAVE STANDARD
;Exit back to the Command: prompt:
EXIT
;end of script
```

Tip

Beginning with Release 12, AutoCAD allows comments in scripts. As in the ACAD.PGP file, comment lines must begin with a semicolon. Unlike ACAD.PGP, though, extra blank lines are *not* permitted in scripts—remember that AutoCAD treats each blank line in scripts as an <Enter>. Use comment lines to document the name, purpose, and date of each script, and to clarify parts of the script whose function might not be obvious. It's also helpful to put a comment line at the end of each script, since doing so will make trailing blank lines obvious.

This script will work fine *most* of the time, but it contains a subtle bug: If a dimension style called STANDARD already exists, the script will crash at the SAVE STANDARD line. At this point, AutoCAD will warn "That name is already in use, redefine it? <N>." Our script, completely oblivious of the warning, will merrily continue typing EXIT, AutoCAD will stubbornly keep prompting and waiting for a Yes or No, and the dimension style won't be saved.

Fortunately, AutoCAD provides a way around this program function: the EXPERT system variable. EXPERT normally is set to 0, but setting it from 1 up through 5 suppresses progressively more of AutoCAD's "Are you sure...?" prompts. In effect, an EXPERT value of 5 lets a script or AutoLISP program tell AutoCAD "don't bother me, I know what I'm doing." (See Appendix A of the *AutoCAD Customization Manual* for more information about EXPERT.)

Let's fix the bug and then actually run the script.

1. Type in or copy the script DIMSET.SCR.

Type the script as shown below in the fixed DIMSET.SCR script file:

Alternatively, you can copy DIMSET.SCR from the *AutoCAD Power Tools* diskette.

```
;*DIMSET.SCR: script to set dimension variables
; and save them as the dim style STANDARD.
; Last modified by MM, 20 Feb 93
;Set EXPERT sysvar in case STANDARD already exists:
EXPERT 5
DIM
DIMALT 0 DIMALTD 2 DIMALTF 25.4 DIMAPOST .
DIMASO 1 DIMASZ 0
DIMBLK . DIMBLK1 . DIMBLK2 .
DIMCEN -3/32
DIMCLRD BYBLOCK DIMCLRE BYBLOCK DIMCLRT 4
DIMDLE 1/16 DIMDLI 3/8
DIMEXE 1/16 DIMEXO 1/16
DIMGAP 1/16
DIMLFAC 1 DIMLIM 0
DIMPOST .
DIMRND 0
DIMSAH 0 DIMSCALE 1 DIMSE1 0 DIMSE2 0
DIMSHO 1 DIMSOXD 0
DIMTAD 1 DIMTFAC 1 DIMTIH 0 DIMTIX 0
DIMTM 0 DIMTP 0 DIMTOFL 1 DIMTOH 0
DIMTOL 0 DIMTSZ 3/32 DIMTVP 0 DIMTXT 1/8
DIMZIN 0
```

```
;Save these settings as STANDARD dim style:
SAVE STANDARD
;Exit back to the Command: prompt:
EXIT
;Restore EXPERT sysvar:
EXPERT 0
;end of script
```

2. Test the script.

Set UNITS to architectural.

Run DIMSET.SCR.

Make sure that the script doesn't stall and that it exits properly back to the Command: prompt. Use the DIM STATUS subcommand to check the variable settings.

Run DIMSET.SCR again.

The second run tests to make sure that the EXPERT part of the script works.

Warning

It's *very important* that your scripts always set EXPERT back to 0 before they terminate. Otherwise AutoCAD will continue to suppress its "Are you sure...?" prompts, which could be confusing, not to mention dangerous, for the user.

Slide Shows

You've probably encountered situations where you needed to show a client or coworker a series of views of one or more drawings, and then spent time fumbling with trying to load the right drawings and zoom to the right locations. AutoCAD slides and scripts offer a more polished approach.

The method is simple: You use AutoCAD's MSLIDE command to capture snapshots of the drawings and views you want to display, and then arrange them into an appealing sequence, using a script and the VSLIDE command as your "slide tray."

Simple Slide Shows

To show how this works, we'll make three slides from AutoCAD's SITE-3D sample drawing. If you opted to install sample files with AutoCAD, SITE-3D.DWG will be located in your \ACAD\SAMPLE subdirectory. If you didn't install the samples, select a drawing of your own. It doesn't need to be a 3D drawing: A slide show displaying plan and detail views of a project can be compelling as well, and technical audiences may find them more informative than "pretty 3D pictures."

1. Copy and load SITE-3D.DWG.

Copy \ACAD\SAMPLE\SITE-3D.DWG to \ACUSTOM\TEST\.

Use the AutoCAD FILES command or DOS's COPY. Substitute your own drawing if you prefer.

Start AutoCAD and load the drawing.

If you're using SITE-3D, you should see a house on a hilly site from four different points of view, arranged in paper space (Figure 16.2).

2. Create three slides.

Make sure you're in paper space, and then use MSLIDE to create a slide called SITE-3D1 from the current screen (if you're not familiar with the MSLIDE command, see Chapter 14 of the *AutoCAD Reference Manual*). If you like, you can run HIDE first in the upper-two viewports in order to make the picture clearer.

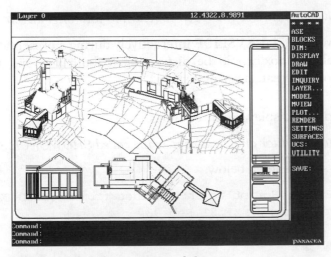

Figure 16.2   The SITE-3D1 slide view.

```
Command: HIDE
Regenerating drawing.
Hiding lines...
Command: MSLIDE
Slide file: SITE-3D1
```

AutoCAD captures the current drawing display to SITE-3D1.SLD (see Figure 16.2). Note that if TILEMODE=0 but your crosshairs are in model space, the slide will show only the current model space viewport.

Leave paper space (set TILEMODE = 1) and create two more slides by changing your viewpoint, zooming, and panning. Call the slides SITE-3D2 and SITE-3D3.

The views we chose are shown in Figures 16.3 and 16.4. We got SITE-3D2 by zooming in on the single view of the house and running HIDE. SITE-3D3 is the same view, but we ran SHADE (AutoCAD's quick shade) instead of HIDE. The SHADEDGE variable was set to 1; see Chapter 12 for more information on shading.

If you used your own drawing rather than SITE-3D, select three different views of it and make a slide for each.

3. Preview the three slides.

Now that you have three new slide files (.SLDs) on your hard disk, use the VSLIDE command to review them and make sure they're what you want.

```
COMMAND: VSLIDE
Slide File: SITE-3D1
```

View each slide in turn. Use REDRAW to return to your original screen.

Of course, you could use VSLIDE interactively during a presentation, but the dialogue box would be distracting to both you and your audience, so let's create a script instead.

4. Create a script to display the three slides.

Launch your text editor and create a new file called SHOWONCE.SCR.

Type in the script shown below.

```
;*SHOWONCE.SCR: Script to show slides from SITE-3D.DWG.
; Last modified by MM, 21 Feb 93
VSLIDE SITE-3D1
DELAY 3000
VSLIDE SITE-3D2
```

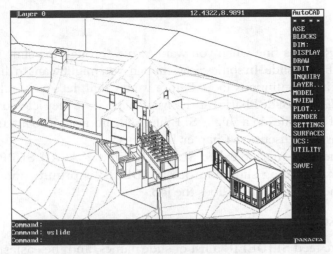

Figure 16.3 The SITE-3D2 slide view.

```
DELAY 1500
VSLIDE SITE-3D3
;end of script
```

The script is simply a sequence of VSLIDE/DELAY pairs. DELAY adds a pause so that your audience has time to peruse the preceding slide. The number after DELAY is in milliseconds (roughly), so a delay of 3000 lasts about three seconds.

Save SHOWONCE.SCR, return to AutoCAD, and test the script.

Figure 16.4 The SITE-3D3 slide view.

Slide Libraries

SHOWONCE.SCR works fine when you want to run through the slide show once and stop at the last slide. In some cases, though, you might want to display a series of slides in a continuous loop. Before we try that, let's assemble the slides into a *slide library*. Slide libaries are convenient because they let you store a large number of .SLD files in a single .SLB file. Slide libraries also are useful for icon menus, as we'll discuss in Chapter 17, *Menus*.

AutoCAD includes a program called SLIDELIB (in the \ACAD\SUPPORT subdirectory) for compiling slide libraries. SLIDELIB is primitive in both interface and functionality, but it does the job.

1. Create a listing of the slides to be compiled.

You need to feed SLIDELIB a list of slide names, and the easiest way to do this is by creating a file containing the filenames. You can type the names, or, more conveniently, use the DOS DIR command's /B switch. DIR /B creates a "bare" listing of filenames without file sizes, dates, etc. (Note that the /B switch was added in DOS 5.0.) Shell out to DOS and use DIR /B to create a listing called SITE-3D.LST.

```
C:\ACUSTOM\TEST\>>DIR SITE-3D*.SLD /B > SITE-3D.LST
```

DOS creates SITE-3D.LST.

If your DOS version is prior to 5.0, create SITE-3D.LST in your text editor. Simply type the three slide filenames, one to a line.

2. Compile the slide library.

```
C:\ACUSTOM\TEST\>> \ACAD\SAMPLE\SLIDELIB SITE-3D.SLB <
SITE-3D.LST
```

This command feeds the filename list to the SLIDELIB program and creates the new slide library SITE-3D.SLB. (See Chapter 7 of the *AutoCAD Customization Manual* for more information and warnings about SLIDELIB.)

Looping Slide Shows

Now that we've compiled the slide library, we'll modify the script to read the slides from the library, and we'll add a "loop" at the end.

1. Create SHOWLOOP.SCR and run it.

Copy SHOWONCE.SCR to SHOWLOOP.SCR.

Tip

If you work with slide libraries much, use John Intorcio's shareware program SlideManager. For only $25, you get a menu-driven interface and a host of features not included in SLIDELIB, including the ability to add slides to existing libraries and decompile slide libraries back to individual slides. SlideManager comes on the Release 12 Bonus CD (\DOSUTILS\SLDMGR). A more recent version is available as SLIDEM.EXE in the ACAD forum on CompuServe. John Intorcio also has written HyperSlide, a shareware utility that lets you build stand-alone, interactive presentations with slides and external DOS programs.

Open SHOWLOOP.SCR in your text editor and make the changes indicated in italics as shown below:

```
;*SHOWLOOP.SCR: Script to show slides from SITE-3D.DWG
; in a loop.
; Last modified by MM, 21 Feb 93
VSLIDE SITE-3D(SITE-3D1)
DELAY 3000
VSLIDE SITE-3D(SITE-3D2)
DELAY 1500
VSLIDE SITE-3D(SITE-3D3)
DELAY 4000
RSCRIPT
;end of script
```

As you can see, the syntax for viewing a slide from a slide library is simply *SLB-name(slide-name)*. RSCRIPT, an AutoCAD command unique to scripts, rewinds the script and plays it again from the top, in an infinite loop.

2. Run SHOWLOOP.SCR.

```
Command: SCRIPT
Script name: SHOWLOOP
```

AutoCAD displays the slides in a continuous loop.

Hit the <backspace> key to stop any script, and type RESUME to pick up again where it left off.

Plotting with Scripts

Plotting is where scripts really shine. Release 12's plot dialogue box and PCP (Plot Configuration Parameters) files have improved the plotting situation markedly, but scripts still are the preferred method for some plotting chores. In this section, you'll learn how to automate plotting for individual drawings, groups of drawings, and entire subdirectories.

Writing plot scripts is a finicky business—even more so than writing other scripts—because each plotter driver asks a slightly different series of questions. For this section, we use Autodesk's Release 12 HP-GL/2 driver configured for a LaserJet III. In order to ensure that the test scripts work on your system, create a new plotter configuration with Autodesk's HP-GL/2 driver:

Follow the steps in the "Configuring New Output Devices" tutorial in Chapter 11, Paper Space and Plotting.

Instead of selecting the PostScript driver, select the driver labeled:

`Hewlett-Packard (HP-GL/2) ADI 4.2 — by Autodesk`

Then select choice 1, LaserJet III.

Accept the defaults for the remaining plotter configuration prompts until AutoCAD asks for a description.

`Enter a description for this plotter:`

Type in the following description:

`HP LaserJet III HP-GL/2 - Autodesk`

Return to the drawing editor, saving your configuration changes.

Always make a note of the name you type in response to AutoCAD's "Enter a description for this plotter:" prompt, since you'll need to know it later.

Plotting Individual Drawings

The Release 12 PLOT dialogue is an excellent tool for interactively changing plot settings, but once you've found the right settings for a group of drawings, a plot script often is more efficient.

As with other scripts, the first task is writing down the command line keystrokes you'd use to plot. When a script calls the PLOT command, AutoCAD doesn't pop up the Plot Configuration dialogue, but substitutes the old command-line version instead. In order to see what the script will "see," you need to set the CMDDIA and FILEDIA system variables to 0 (see Chapter 11 of this book or Appendix A of the *AutoCAD Customization Manual* for more information about CMDDIA and FILEDIA). Remember to set CMDDIA and FILEDIA back to 1 when you're finished writing down the plot sequence.

1. Set CMDDIA and FILEDIA to 0 and run through the plot sequence.

```
Command: CMDDIA
New value for CMDDIA <default>: 0
Command: FILEDIA
New value for FILEDIA <default>: 0
```

Using the keyboard only, go through the steps you'd use to plot, including establishing all the proper plot settings.

Remember to set the correct plotter first.

2. Create the new script PLOTLJF.SCR.

Launch your text editor and create a new file called PLOTLJF.SCR.

Transcribe the keystrokes into PLOTLJF.SCR.

Our version follows; we've transcribed almost every one of AutoCAD's plot sequence prompts as comment lines. This is a tedious procedure, but it makes the action of the script much clearer, and it will save you time when you need to debug or otherwise edit the script later.

Notice in particular the sequence for setting the pen assignments. The C1, C2, ... commands at the beginning of each line aren't strictly necessary, but they make the script easier for humans to decipher. Of course your pen width standards will be different from the ones shown in our script. Substitute your own pen standards if you prefer.

```
;*PLOTLJF.SCR: script to plot current drawing to Fit
; on LaserJet III.
; Last modified by MM, 20 Fcb 93
PLOT
;"What to plot - Display, Extents, Limits, View, or Window:"
Limits
;"Do you want to change anything? (No/Yes/File/Save) <N>:"
Yes
;"Do you want to change plotters? <N>:"
Yes
;Enter selection (number or description):
HP LaserJet III HP-GL/2 - Autodesk
;"What to plot - Display, Extents, Limits, View, or Window:"
Limits
;"Do you want to change anything? (No/Yes/File/Save) <N>:"
Yes
```

```
;"Do you want to change plotters? <N>:"
No
;"How many copies of this plot would you like? <1>:"
1
;"Select paper tray currently installed, 1 to 4 <2>:"
2
;"Do you want to change any of the above {pen} parameters? <N>:"
Yes
;Color #, Pen #, Plotter linetype, Line width:
C1 7 0 0.003
C2 7 0 0.003
C3 7 0 0.007
C4 7 0 0.007
C5 7 0 0.007
C6 7 0 0.010
C7 7 0 0.010
C8 7 0 0.010
C9 7 0 0.010
C10 7 0 0.010
C11 7 0 0.010
C12 7 0 0.014
C13 7 0 0.014
C14 7 0 0.014
C15 7 0 0.014
;Exit pen parameters:
X
;"Write the plot to a file? <N>:"
No
;"Size units (Inches or Millimeters) <I>:"
Inches
;"Plot origin in Inches <0.00,0.00>:"
0,0
;"Enter the Size or Width,Height (in Inches) <A>:"
A
;"Rotate plot clockwise 0/90/180/270 degrees <0>:"
0
;"Remove hidden lines? <N>:"
No
;"Plotted Inches=Drawing Units or Fit or ? <F>:"
Fit
;"Press RETURN to continue or S to Stop for hardware setup"

;end of script
```

Warning

Another variable that affects plot sequence prompts is whether or not you plot to a file. If you plot to a file, the "Press RETURN to continue or S to Stop for hardware setup" prompt won't appear.

3. Test the script.

Run the script on the current drawing or on one of your own drawings.

PLOTLJF.SCR does a competent job, but it's awfully long. We can simplify it by loading most of the settings from a Plot Configuration Parameters (.PCP) file. (See Chapter 11 of this book or Chapter 2 of the *AutoCAD Customization Manual* for information about PCP files.) In addition, we'll use a different technique for setting the plotter.

4. Save the current plot settings to PLOTLJF.PCP.

The PLOT dialogue box is the easiest way to do this.

```
Command: CMDDIA
New value for CMDDIA <default>: 1
Command: PLOT
```

The Plot Configuration dialogue box appears.

Pick Device and Default Selection... and then Save Defaults to File....

Tip

In these examples, we're plotting to Fit, which is appropriate for doing a reduced plot on a LaserJet, but, of course, you'll usually want to plot at a specific scale on larger plotters. You could hard-code a plot scale into the script, but then you'd need a different script for each scale. A smarter method is to let AutoCAD determine the drawing scale (and hence plot scale) for you. The Geometry Calculator's GETVAR function will do the trick, assuming your drawing scale factor is stored in DIMSCALE or another system variable:

```
;"Plotted Inches=Drawing Units or Fit or ? <F>:"
'CAL
1/GETVAR(DIMSCALE)
```

Save the current settings to PLOTLJF.PCP (see Figure 16.5).

Return to the main Plot Configuration dialogue and then pick Cancel.

We don't want to plot yet.

The file PLOTLJF.PCP now resides in the current directory. If you've never looked at a PCP file, open this one in your text editor and browse through it.

5. Modify and test PLOTLJF2.SCR.

Copy PLOTLJF.SCR to PLOTLJF2.SCR.

We'll leave PLOTLJF.SCR alone so that you can work with it later if you wish.

Make the changes to the plot script as shown below in italics.

If you prefer, you can copy PLOTLJF2.SCR from the *AutoCAD Power Tools* diskette instead of typing the changes.

Test and revise the script until it functions properly with your plotter configuration.

```
;*PLOTLJF2.SCR: script to plot current drawing to Fit
; on LaserJet III - 2nd version.
; NOTE: requires PLOTLJF.PCP
; Last modified by MM, 20 Feb 93
;Set plotter
PLOTID
HP LaserJet
PLOT
;"What to plot - Display, Extents, Limits, View, or Window:"
Limits
;"Do you want to change anything? (No/Yes/File/Save) <N>:"
File
;"Enter plot configuration filename <UNNAMED>:"
PLOTLJF.PCP
;"Do you want to change anything? (No/Yes/File/Save) <N>:"
No
;"Press RETURN to continue or S to Stop for hardware setup"

;end of script
```

The first part of the script sets the LaserJet driver current by means of the Release 12 PLOTID system variable. Note that "HP LaserJet III"

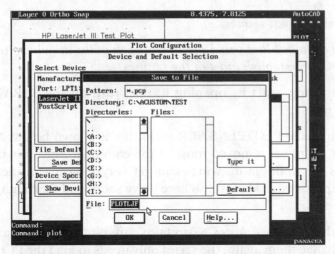

Figure 16.5 Saving plot settings to a PCP file.

isn't a magic name for the driver—it's just the first part of the description we gave when we used CONFIG to add this driver (see above). This same name appears in the "Device and Default Selection" subdialogue we used in step 4. See Chapter 11, *Paper Space and Plotting*, for more information about the PLOTID system variable.

Plotting Multiple Drawings

Often, you'll use scripts to plot a batch of drawings. Scripts are the perfect tool for this job because they can "survive" across different drawing sessions. Every other AutoCAD customization interface, including AutoLISP and ADS, halts operation when you change drawings, but scripts keep right on running.

In this tutorial, we'll use PLOTLJF2.SCR as the basis for a new script, PLOTPLNS.SCR, that plots three drawings in a row.

1. Create three drawings.

   Create a sample drawing called PLAN1.DWG.

   Draw a few lines so that something shows up when you plot.

   Create a layer called SCRATCH and draw some additional lines.

   SCRATCH is assumed to be a construction layer containing entities that you don't want to plot.

   Repeat these steps to create two other sample drawings called PLAN2.DWG and PLAN3.DWG.

2. Step through the plot sequence.

Go through the procedure you'd use to plot each of the drawings (using PLOTLJF.PCP to establish most of the settings).

For each drawing, start by opening it, then turn off the SCRATCH layer, then plot.

Our version of the PLOTPLNS.SCR script file is shown below. Note that in this script we removed most of the comment lines this time. Plot scripts for multiple drawings can get very long if you include every prompt, as we did before, so here we've sacrificed thoroughness for conciseness.

Also note that, because AutoCAD retains any plot settings changes until you change them again, the script only needs to load the PCP file once, before plotting PLAN1.DWG.

Test and revise the script until it plots all three drawings properly.

```
;*PLOTPLNS.SCR: script to plot PLAN1, PLAN2, & PLAN3
; to Fit on LaserJet III.
; NOTE: requires PLOTLJF.PCP
; Last modified by MM, 20 Feb 93
PLOTID
HP LaserJet
OPEN PLAN1 LAYER Set 0 OFf *SCRATCH*
PLOT Limits File PLOTLJF.PCP No
;"Yes" responds to "Really want to discard all changes...?"
OPEN Yes PLAN2 LAYER Set 0 OFf *SCRATCH*
PLOT Limits No
OPEN Yes PLAN3 LAYER Set 0 OFf *SCRATCH*
PLOT Limits No

;end of script
```

PLOTPLNS.SCR is a good example of the power of scripts. It automates the tedious procedure of opening and plotting a group of drawings. A script such as this one really pays off when you plot the same batch of project drawings repeatedly.

Batch Plotting from DOS

In other situations, you'll want to batch plot a list of drawings that changes from time to time. You could edit PLOTPLNS.SCR each time, adding and removing sections as needed, but there's a more efficient way. The DOS FOR command and AutoCAD's ability to accept a script name when you launch the program are the two keys. In this tutorial, we'll develop a script that plots all or some of the drawings in the current subdirectory.

So far, we've been starting all our scripts from inside the drawing editor, but, in fact, we could use any of them when starting AutoCAD from DOS. Recall from Chapter 14, *Getting Ready to Customize*, that the AutoCAD batch file contains two replaceable parameters after the program call: ACAD %1 %2 (see your DOS manual if you're not familiar with replaceable parameters). The first parameter is an optional drawing name for AutoCAD to load, and the second parameter is an optional script name to execute immediately. In other words, the syntax is:

ACADR12 *dwgname scrname*

Specifically,

ACADR12 MYDETAIL PLOTLJF

would load MYDETAIL.DWG, run our PLOTLJF script, and leave AutoCAD at the Command: prompt.

ACADR12 X PLOTPLNS

would start AutoCAD and plot the three plan drawings. The drawing name "X" could be anything: It's just a place keeper, since the PLOTPLNS script loads each drawing explicitly.

In order to batch plot any group of drawings, use the DOS FOR command to launch AutoCAD repeatedly, substituting a different drawing name each time. This technique requires that the script file exit AutoCAD and return to DOS when it's done, so that FOR can regain control and launch AutoCAD again with the next drawing. To make this happen, you simply need to add a QUIT Yes to the end of the script, as shown on the following pages.

1. Create DPLOTLJF.SCR.

Use PLOTLJF2.SCR as the basis for a new script called DPLOTLJF.SCR. The "D" is our way of denoting a script that returns to DOS.

Exit AutoCAD and copy PLOTLJF2.DWG to DPLOTLJF.SCR.

Make the modifications shown below, and delete the extraneous sections.

```
;*DPLOTLJF.SCR: script to plot one or more drawings
; to Fit on LaserJet III, and then return to DOS.
; To batch plot, call from DOS with a command like this:
; FOR %F IN (*.DWG) DO CALL ACADR12 %F DPLOTLJF
; NOTE: requires PLOTLJF.PCP
; Last modified by MM, 20 Feb 93
```

```
PLOTID
HP LaserJet
LAYER Set 0 OFf *SCRATCH*

PLOT Limits File PLOTLJF.PCP No

;"Yes" responds to "Really want to discard all changes...?"
QUIT Yes
```

Note that this script doesn't contain OPEN, because we'll be feeding the drawing name to AutoCAD when we run the script.

2. From DOS, test the script.

```
C:\ACUSTOM\TEST\> FOR %F IN (*.DWG) DO CALL ACADR12 %F
DPLOTLJF
```

(Note: Type the complete FOR statement on one line.)

AutoCAD should load and plot each of the drawings in the current subdirectory in turn.

When DOS parses the FOR statement, it assembles a list of files that matches the file specification in parentheses, and then one by one with each file, executes everything after DO, substituting the current file's name for %F. The word CALL is important, since ACADR12 is a batch file rather than an executable .EXE or .COM file. See your DOS manual for more information about FOR and CALL.

3. Return CMDDIA and FILEDIA to 1.

Now that we're finished experimenting with plot scripts, you should load AutoCAD and set the CMDDIA and FILEDIA system variables back to 0.

```
Command: CMDDIA
New value for CMDDIA <default>: 1
Command: FILEDIA
New value for FILEDIA <default>: 1
```

Tip

You can use this "plot a whole subdirectory" technique at the end of a project to create a laser–printed archive of the project drawings.

As the comment lines indicate, you can batch plot any group of drawings that can be specified with DOS wildcards. Here are two other examples:

```
FOR %F IN (D:\PROJ06\S-?PLAN.DWG) DO CALL ACADR12 %F
DPLOTLJF

FOR %F IN (PLAN1.DWG PLAN2.DWG PLAN3.DWG) DO CALL ACADR12
%F DPLOTLJF
```

Also, although DPLOTLJF.SCR's forté is batch plotting, it will work fine for plotting a single drawing from DOS:

```
ACADR12 MYPLAN DPLOTLJF
```

Warning

If you use FOR in a batch file, you have to double each of the percent signs:

```
FOR %%F IN (*.DWG) DO CALL ACADR12 %%F DPLOTLJF
```

As you can see, there are plenty of script plotting possibilities, accompanied by quite a few niggling details. The details are worth mastering, though, since plotting with scripts can save you lots of time and tedious plot-queuing. There's nothing quite so satisfying as starting a script and then going home while your computer labors long into the night cranking out dozens of plots.

Tip

Third-party script generation programs are an alternative to the DOS FOR command. Script generators take a script you've written for one drawing and "expand" it to act on the group of drawings you select. One of their advantages over FOR is speed: They don't have to exit back to DOS and reload AutoCAD for each drawing. A good script generation program is David A. Roman's shareware program SCR, available from the ACAD forum on CompuServe.

Tip

In Release 12 for the first time, AutoLISP can call the PLOT command. This new feature is appealing, because LISP can provide more intelligent control than a script can. Unfortunately, there are several serious limitations to plotting from AutoLISP, and developing a robust AutoLISP plotting program is a complex project. For many people's needs, scripts remain the best choice for automating plotting.

Warning

AutoCAD Release 12 and 12c1 (the initial release and first bug fix) contained a number of annoying plotting bugs, several of which involved PCP files. If you encounter problems, check to be sure that you have Release 12c2 (or later) by selecting About... from the File pull-down menu.

Finishing Up

You'll want to save any of the scripts from this chapter that would be useful to you. You can move them to the \ACUSTOM directory or create a separate subdirectory, such as \ACUSTOM\SCR, just for scripts. The *AutoCAD Power Tools* disk contains versions of the longer scripts: DIMSET.SCR, PLOTLJF.SCR, PLOT2LJF.SCR, and DPLOTLJF.SCR. If any of these are useful to you, copy them from the diskette. You'll need to modify the dimension variable settings and plot prompt sequences to match your dimensioning conventions and output device.

Delete or move SITE-3D and all the other files you created from it. \ACUSTOM\TEST should be empty when you're finished moving and deleting files.

If you use output devices other than the LaserJet III, run through the plot sequence for each additional device and note the prompt sequence. Then create a "template" script that contains the prompts as comments and your most common responses. With the template scripts completed, you'll be able to create project- or drawing-specific scripts quickly when a plotting deadline is bearing down on you.

Tip

To avoid file clutter, keep only general-purpose scripts in \ACUSTOM or \ACUSTOM\SCR. Many scripts will be project- or even drawing-specific, so keep them in project subdirectories. If a script for one project seems like it might be useful for others, copy it to the \ACUSTOM\SCR subdirectory and tell others about it as well.

Chapter 7 of the *AutoCAD Customization Manual* covers scripts and slide shows, but we've covered almost everything in that chapter, and then some.

Scripts and Workgroups

The most important script issue for workgroups is getting everyone to use them. No one should have any problem running scripts (assuming everyone knows where the scripts are and what they do), but you should encourage other group members to create their own. Don't forget that some workgroup members might not be familiar with using a text editor, so you may have to walk them through the rudiments of EDIT. At that point, they should be able to work through some of the tutorials in this chapter.

Most AutoCAD users who started with Release 11 or earlier should be able to learn to create and modify scripts on their own. But newer users who cut their teeth on Release 12 for DOS or, especially, Release 12 for Windows may have a hard time doing so. This is because Release 12 makes it so easy to do things via menus and dialogue boxes that few new users will learn all of the keyboard commands needed to run AutoCAD most efficiently and to create scripts. This is another reason to centralize the creation and maintenance of the most widely needed scripts.

Develop a mechanism for sharing scripts, and make \ACUSTOM\SCR the locus of that sharing. As mentioned in the previous section, develop template scripts for each output device, so that others can create plot scripts by simply changing the answers to a few prompts. You should periodically print a list of scripts along with a brief description of each and distribute it to the workgroup. It also helps to develop a naming scheme for scripts, particularly plot scripts, since they tend to multiply quickly.

When adding plotter configurations in workgroups, always use identical names for the same driver. Otherwise, you won't be able to set the device automatically with PLOTID.

Summary

Scripts are simple but versatile tools for automating anything you do repeatedly in an identical way, including setting layers and system variables, plotting, and showing slides. Scripts are especially valuable for batch plotting a group of drawings.

In the next chapter you'll use what you've learned about automating procedures with scripts to create menu macros.

17
Menus

From the user's point of view, AutoCAD Release 12 boasts six menu interfaces—pull-down, cursor, side-screen, icon, button, and tablet—and every one of them is customizable. Menu customization is a combination of laying out the structure of the menus and defining command sequences to be performed by each menu choice. You do this by editing ASCII menu definition files, such as the stock ACAD.MNU file that comes with AutoCAD.

Custom menus are used to improve AutoCAD's interface for specific disciplines or offices, and to create menu macros—custom "miniprograms"—that execute when you pick a menu label. Menu macros also are used to load and execute more elaborate programs written in AutoLISP and ADS. These capabilities are used heavily by third-party programs.

The ability to modify AutoCAD's menus is at the heart of the program's customizability. It also can be a complicated task. While there is quite a bit to learn, you can take on small tasks first, then build up to bigger ones. Developing some expertise at menu customization will greatly improve your ability to make AutoCAD work well for you.

About This Chapter

In this book, our focus will be on customizing the pull-down and cursor menus. These menus offer the best combination of ease of customization and flexibility. Many of the customization enhancements in Release 12 are aimed at improving AutoCAD's pull-down menus, and it's clear from Release 12 for

Windows and other trends that pull-downs are becoming AutoCAD's primary menu interface. The other menu interfaces remain useful for some types of applications, and we'll cover the basics of how and when to customize them.

In this chapter, we demonstrate how to create two useful menu additions: a custom pull-down menu page and a custom cursor menu that pops up when you press the second mouse button while holding down the <Ctrl> key. We also describe the icon, side-screen, and tablet menus, and discuss the strengths and weaknesses of each interface. Chapter 6 of the *AutoCAD Customization Manual* covers all of the menu interfaces in a reference format, and Chapter 8 of the *AutoCAD Tutorial Manual* includes tutorials on adding to existing side-screen and pull-down menus and building an icon menu from scratch.

A Menu Customization Primer

Customizing menus involves defining the labels that will appear at each location in the menu and writing script-like command sequences that instruct AutoCAD what to do when the user picks each label. Both of these menu components reside in an ASCII format .MNU file. In this section, we'll review the structure and content of AutoCAD's default menu file, ACAD.MNU, and then discuss the syntax you'll use to modify it. ACAD.MNU usually is located in the \ACAD\SUPPORT subdirectory.

AutoCAD actually relies on two types of menu files: the ASCII .MNU source file and the compiled binary .MNX file. The .MNU file is the human-readable one that you edit with your text editor. AutoCAD automatically recompiles the .MNU file into the .MNX binary version whenever you edit the former.

Tip

How does AutoCAD know when to recompile the .MNU file? Every AutoCAD drawing stores the name (but not the contents) of the menu file that was in use when the drawing was last saved. When you load a drawing, AutoCAD reads this name—ACAD by default—and searches the support file search path, as described in Chapter 14, for the menu (the same thing happens when you load a menu with the MENU command). Once AutoCAD finds ACAD.MNU, it checks the DOS file date and time and compares it with the date and time for ACAD.MNX. If ACAD.MNX is newer, AutoCAD assumes that ACAD.MNU hasn't been changed since the last recompile and simply loads ACAD.MNX into memory. If ACAD.MNU is newer, AutoCAD assumes that the source file has been changed and creates a new .MNX by recompiling.

The Six Menu Section Types

A single .MNU file defines all of the AutoCAD menus: pull-down, side-screen, tablet, etc. An .MNU file is divided into six types of sections, as shown in Table 17.1. Some of the section types, such as ***POP*n*, include more than one instance: ***POP0, ***POP1, ***POP2, etc. Each instance defines a different part of the menu interface: a different pull-down menu "slot," a different tablet menu area, and so on. Other section types, such as ***SCREEN, appear only once. You might want to take a moment now to load \ACAD\SUPPORT\ACAD.MNU into your text editor and browse through it. It's a long file, about 100K in size; in order to get a feel for the overall structure, search for the three asterisks (***) indicating the beginning of a new section. Don't make any changes just yet.

Table 17.1 The Six Types of Menu Sections

.MNU Section Type	Defines the action and appearance of...
***BUTTONS*n* (*n* = 1 — 4)	Pointing device buttons
***AUX*n* (*n* = 1 — 4)	System pointing device buttons (not applicable to DOS 386 version)
***POP*n* (*n* = 0 — 16)	Cursor menu (*n* = 0) and pull-down menus (*n* = 1 — 16)
***ICON	Icon menus
***SCREEN	Side-screen menus
***TABLET*n* (*n* = 1 — 4)	Tablet menus

The easiest way to start learning menu customization is to look at samples, so we'll take a quick tour of the six menu section types contained in ACAD.MNU and then review general menu syntax.

BUTTON MENUS

The ***BUTTONS*n* sections of ACAD.MNU define the operation of puck, mouse, or stylus buttons. Release 12 adds support for three alternate pointing device button menus, which the user accesses by picking a button while holding down <Shift>, <Ctrl>, or <Ctrl> + <Shift> keys. The primary button menu (***BUTTONS1), along with comments describing each line, is shown below.

```
***BUTTONS1
;                              <Enter>
$p0=*                          Pops up the cursor menu
^C^C                           Cancel
^B                             Toggle Snap
^O                             Toggle Ortho
^G                             Toggle Grid
^D                             Toggle Coords
^E                             Toggle Isometric plane
^T                             Toggle Tablet
```

The first line below the ***BUTTONS1 section label actually is assigned to the *second* button on your pointing device; AutoCAD reserves the first button for selecting objects and pointing on the screen, and doesn't let you redefine it. The actual menu macro assigned to the second button is simply a semicolon, which acts like <Enter> in menus. Note that this convention is inconsistent with script files and ACAD.PGP (and AutoLISP), where a semi-colon begins a comment line.

Each subsequent line defines the next button. Most of the button assignments in ACAD.MNU use the special <Ctrl> key character (^) to define a toggle. The exception is the macro assigned to the third button: $p0=*. This is the magic sequence that tells AutoCAD to pop up the cursor menu. $*menu_type=something* is a general instruction to AutoCAD to do something with the menu represented by *menu_type*. In this case, $p0 refers to the cursor menu, and * simply means "make it appear on the screen." We'll show another example of this peculiar syntax in the icon menu section below.

The default ACAD.MNU defines only the second through tenth buttons of the primary button menu (***BUTTONS1) and the second button of the <Shift> alternate (***BUTTONS2) menu, so there's room for expansion, whether you have a two-button mouse or a 16-button puck. For instance, with a two-button device, you can define custom actions for the second button in combination with the <Ctrl> and <Shift>+<Ctrl> keys. With a 16-button device, you can define actions for the eleventh through fifteenth buttons, plus all the <Shift>, <Ctrl>, and <Shift>+<Ctrl> combinations.

AUXILIARY POINTING DEVICE MENUS

The four auxiliary pointing device button menus (***AUX*n*) work like button menus, but are assigned to the system pointing device (usually a mouse) on AutoCAD platforms, such as Windows, SUN SPARCstation, and Apple Macintosh. A system pointing device is the device recognized by the operating system for pointing and clicking operations. Although it might seem that an ordinary mouse connected to your system would be the DOS "system pointing device," this isn't so. DOS wasn't designed with a pointing device in mind, and it's up to applications to use it as they see fit. Since DOS doesn't recognize a system pointing device, AutoCAD 386 ignores the ***AUX*n* menu sections and uses ***BUTTONS*n* instead.

In AutoCAD for Windows, the situation is more complicated. If you configure AutoCAD for System Pointing Device (i.e., whatever device you use to navigate in Windows), then AutoCAD will get button definitions from the ***AUX*n* menu sections. This will be true even if your Windows system pointing device happens to be a digitizer. If you configure for a specific digitizer instead, AutoCAD will get button definitions from the ***BUTTONS*n* sections. The default ACAD.MNU defines the ***AUX*n* and ***BUTTONS*n* menu sections identically, so that no matter what device you use, the buttons will act the same. It's usually best to maintain the ***BUTTONS*n* and ***AUX*n* sections in this way.

POP-UP MENUS

The ***POP*n* sections of ACAD.MNU define the operation of AutoCAD's pull-down and cursor menus. These types of menus are sometimes called "pop-up" menus to distinguish them from Lotus 1-2-3-style moving-bar menus or AutoCAD's side-screen menu, and hence the name POP. The improvements to pop-up menus in Release 12 are substantial: In addition to the new cursor menu, there are now cascading submenus and the ability to gray out or put check marks next to pop-up menu labels. Release 12 also lets you define as many as 16 pull-down menus (instead of only 10), although, depending on your display driver resolution, it may be difficult to squeeze more than 10 labels in the menu bar. ACAD.MNU defines pull-down menus ***POP1 through ***POP9; ***POP2 is shown below:

```
***POP2
[Assist]
[Help!]'?
[Cancel]^C^C^C
[- -]
[Undo]_U
[Redo]^C^C_redo
[- -]
[Object Filters...]'filter
[->Object Snap]
 [Center]_center
 [Endpoint]_endp
 [Insert]_ins
 [Intersection]_int
```

```
      [Midpoint]_mid
      [Nearest]_nea
      [Node]_nod
      [Perpendicular]_per
      [Quadrant]_qua
      [Tangent]_tan
      [<-None]_non
   [--]
   [->Inquiry]
      [List]^C^C_list
      [Status]'_status
      [--]
      [Area]^C^C_area
      [Distance]^C^C'_dist
      [<-ID Point]'_id
   [--]
   [Calculator]'cal
```

Each line in the ***POP2 menu section contains a label in square brackets, followed by the menu macro. The label defines what the user sees, and the macro defines what the menu pick does. This two-part definition also appears in other menu sections, including the ***ICON and ***SCREEN sections.

The one new label feature demonstrated in ***POP2 is cascading submenus. A right-pointing ([->*xxx*]) or left-pointing ([<-*yyy*]) "arrow" at the beginning of a menu label tells AutoCAD to begin or end a submenu. Compare the Assist menu, shown in Figure 17.1, with the ***POP2 listing shown above, to see how the submenu arrows are used.

Windows Tip

AutoCAD for Windows and other non-DOS platforms provide one other menu label feature: underlined accelerator and mnemonic keys. An accelerator key is a letter you press while holding down the <Alt> key in order to pull down a menu; for example, <Alt>+F pulls down the File menu. A mnemonic key is a letter you press while a menu is pulled down in order to select one of the menu choices; for example, R selects Preferences when the File menu is pulled down. Accelerator and mnemonic keys are defined in exactly the same way: You precede the menu label text with a forward slash (/) followed by the appropriate letter, like this: [/FFile] or [/rPreferences]. See the ACAD.MNU file that comes with AutoCAD for Windows for other examples.

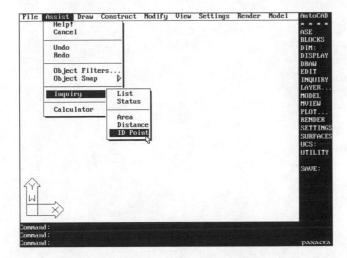

Figure 17.1   The default POP2 menu in action.

The menu macros are pretty much what you would type at the Command: prompt in order to run the command or activate the object snap shown in the menu label. The main additions are apostrophes (') before any transparent commands (so that you can run them while in the middle of another command) and ^Cs before commands that cannot be executed transparently, so that any pending command is cancelled.

The one other mysterious character is the underscore (_) before each command or option name. Autodesk added this feature to Release 12 to make it easier for them to translate AutoCAD into other languages. The underscore tells foreign-language versions of AutoCAD that the command is in English, rather than in the native language. This feature works only for core AutoCAD commands; it doesn't apply to LISP routines such as DDINSERT. As a result, it can be tricky to figure out when to use the underscore. Unless your menus will be used with foreign-language versions of AutoCAD, it's easiest to omit the underscores when writing your own menu macros.

The new cursor menu is defined exactly like a pull-down menu, in a new menu section called ***POP0 shown below. The only distinction is that its main label, [Osnap], doesn't appear on the cursor menu when you pop it (a label must be included in the menu definition, though, for compatibility with the other ***POP*n* sections). The usual way to pop up the cursor menu is by calling it with a button, as described above.

```
***POP0
[Osnap]
[Center]_center
[Endpoint]_endp
```

```
[Insert]_ins
[Intersection]_int
[Midpoint]_mid
[Nearest]_nea
[Node]_nod
[Perpendicular]_per
[Quadrant]_qua
[Tangent]_tan
[None]_non
[->Filters]
[.X].X
[.Y].Y
[.Z].Z
[.XY].XY
[.XZ].XZ
[<-.YZ].YZ
[Calculator]'cal
```

Pop-up menus were added to AutoCAD Release 9, and their capabilities and organization have gradually improved to the point where many users and developers prefer them over the side-screen and tablet menus. This will become even truer as AutoCAD attracts more users who have more experience with Windows and other graphical user interfaces than with early versions of AutoCAD. We suggest you use the pull-down and cursor menus as your primary menu customization areas. Put often used commands or options on alternate button menus, and use the tenth pull-down menu slot as a central area for handy menu macros and calling up custom LISP programs. We'll show some examples in this chapter's tutorials.

ICON MENUS

The ***ICON section of ACAD.MNU defines icon menus that use AutoCAD slides to present an array of options (see Figure 17.2). Icon menus look a lot like dialogue boxes, but they're easier to create and customize (in part because they're much more limited than programmable dialogues). There is only one ***ICON menu section, but it contains subsections beginning with **sublabels corresponding to each individual icon menu. Shown below are portions of two icon menus—**icon_3DObjects and **icon_fonts1—from ACAD.MNU.

```
***icon
...
**icon_3DObjects
[3D Objects]
```

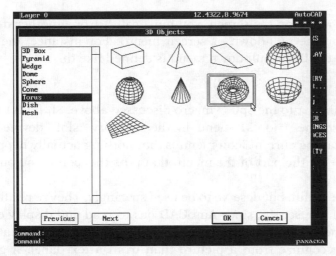

Figure 17.2 The 3D Objects icon menu.

```
[acad(box3d,3D Box)]^C^Cai_box
[acad(Pyramid)]^C^Cai_pyramid
[acad(Wedge)]^C^Cai_wedge
[acad(Dome)]^C^Cai_dome
[acad(Sphere)]^C^Cai_sphere
[acad(Cone)]^C^Cai_cone
[acad(Torus)]^C^Cai_torus
[acad(Dish)]^C^Cai_dish
[acad(Mesh)]^C^Cai_mesh


**icon_fonts1
[Select Text Font]
[acad(romans,Roman Simplex)]'_style romans romans
[acad(romanc,Roman Complex)]'_style romanc romanc
[acad(romand,Roman Duplex)]'_style romand romand
[acad(romant,Roman Triplex)]'_style romant romant
[acad(italicc,Italic Complex)]'_style italicc italicc
...
```

Icon menu item labels are more complicated than other menu item labels, because they identify the slide to be displayed along with an optional label for the listbox at the left side of the icon menu (see Figure 17.2). The general format is:

```
[slide_library_name(slide_name,list_box_label)]
```

Icon menu macros work the same as macros in the ***POP*n* or any other menu section: Once the user picks an icon (or its label in the listbox), AutoCAD executes the menu macro statements after the label. In order to bring up an icon menu on the screen, you must call it from another menu choice (usually on the pull-down or screen menu). For instance, the Set Style... choice on the Draw pull-down menu is defined like this:

```
[Set Style...]$I=fonts1 $I=*
```

This macro is similar to the $p0=* macro discussed above. $I=fonts1 tells AutoCAD to stash the **fonts1 menu in the memory "slot" devoted to remembering what the current icon menu is, but nothing actually happens on-screen yet. $I=* is the part of the macro that puts the icon menu on the screen.

Icon menus are useful, but deserve to be used sparingly. They're relatively slow to appear on the screen, since AutoCAD has to read and display each slide. Save icon menus for when you need to display a list of choices that are much easier to recognize from a picture than from a text label. A good example is when you're developing a menu for inserting a collection of similar Blocks: Rather than use an indecipherable pull-down menu with choices Widget1, Widget2, Widget3, etc., create an icon menu showing each of the widgets.

Chapter 16, *Scripts*, describes how to create slides and slide libraries that can be used in your icon menus. Chapter 8 of the *AutoCAD Tutorial manual* includes a short but useful tutorial on how to create an icon menu for Block libraries.

Tip

The BHATCH command's Choose Hatch Pattern subdialogue (see Chapter 8, *Modifying Properties and Hatching*) looks like an icon menu, but actually is a dynamically constructed dialogue box. When you call up this dialogue, AutoCAD reads pattern names from the ACAD.PAT file and looks for matching slides in ACAD.SLB. Adding a custom pattern to the Choose Hatch Pattern subdialogue requires two steps. First, add the hatch pattern definition to ACAD.PAT (see Chapter 4 of the *AutoCAD Customization Manual*). Second, use MSLIDE to create a slide showing the hatch pattern and give the slide the same name as the pattern (see Chapter 16 of this book, *Scripts*, for details). The only trick is adding this new slide to ACAD.SLB so that BHATCH will find it. AutoCAD's SLIDELIB program isn't able to add slides to existing libraries; instead, you can use John Intorcio's shareware SlideManager program, as described in Chapter 16.

SCREEN MENUS

The ***SCREEN section of ACAD.MNU defines the many menus that display in AutoCAD's menu area at the right side of the screen. Before pull-down menus were added to AutoCAD in Release 9, the side-screen menus were the only menus that appeared on the screen, as opposed to the tablet or button menus, and hence the name SCREEN. As with the ***ICON menu section, ***SCREEN comprises subsections or menu "pages," each of which begins with a **sublabel*. Shown below is the main screen menu page (labeled **S) from the ***SCREEN section in ACAD.MNU.

```
***SCREEN
**S
[AutoCAD]^C^C^P(ai_rootmenus) ^P
[* * * *]$S=OSNAPB
[ASE]^C^C^P(ai_aseinit_chk) ^P
[BLOCKS]$S=X $S=BL
[DIM:]^C^C_DIM
[DISPLAY]$S=X $S=DS
[DRAW]$S=X $S=DR
[EDIT]$S=X $S=ED
[INQUIRY]$S=X $S=INQ
[LAYER...]$S=LAYER '_DDLMODES
[MODEL]$S=X $S=SOLIDS
[MVIEW]$S=MVIEW
[PLOT...]^C^C_PLOT
[RENDER]$S=X $S=RENDER
[SETTINGS]$S=X $S=SET
[SURFACES]$S=X $S=3D
[UCS:]^C^C_UCS
[UTILITY]$S=X $S=UT
[SAVE:]^C^C_QSAVE
```

Screen menu item labels work like ***POP*n* section labels, except that there's room for only eight characters on most displays, so the labels need to be kept short. Most of the menu macros in the **S menu simply call other screen menus, often in pairs (you can tile and overlay pieces of screen menu to create hybrid screen menus).

Tip

Release 12 includes a new system variable called MENUCTL, which enables automatic, context-sensitive side-screen menu swapping. When MENUCTL is set to 1, each time you enter a command, AutoCAD looks for a ***sublabel*** menu section that matches the name of the command. This feature can be useful for reminding beginners of the selection set, osnap, or other options available with a command. On the other hand, if you use a custom menu that wasn't written with MENUCTL in mind, you may find your screen menu pages "flying away" at inopportune moments. In that case, you'll want to keep MENUCTL set to 0. The stock menu LISP file (ACAD.MNL) includes a line near the end that turns MENUCTL on: (setvar "MENUCTL" 1). If you use this menu LISP file and want MENUCTL to remain off, simply change the 1 to a 0.**

The main item of interest in **S is the AutoLISP code contained in the first and third lines. The (ai_rootmenus) and (ai_aseinit_chk) functions are defined in ACAD.MNL and ACADR12.LSP, the two LISP files that load each time you start AutoCAD or load a drawing. The content of these functions isn't as important as the fact that you can incorporate LISP code in menu macros. We'll show a simple example of this technique later in the chapter. The ^Ps flanking the LISP functions are for cosmetic purposes: They toggle menu echoing on and off so that the user doesn't see LISP code on the command line.

Side-screen menus used to be the primary menu interface for most people, and they do have one advantage over pull-down menus: The side-screen menu bar "stays put," rather than disappearing each time you pick a command. Most of the advantages are now with pull-down menus, though: cascading submenus, no eight-character label limitation, dynamic menu labels through graying out and check marks, and, not the least important, easier customizability. The menu swapping defined in the ***SCREEN menu section of ACAD.MNU is intricate and easy to mess up, while the ***POP*n* sections are more modular and easier to modify without fear of trashing the entire menu interface. We suggest you begin or complete the transition to pull-down and cursor menus. If you insist on sticking with side-screen menus, perhaps for context-sensitive menu swapping with MENUCTL, Chapter 6 of the *AutoCAD Customization Manual* describes ***SCREEN menu syntax in detail.

Tip

Once you wean yourself from the side-screen menu, you can turn it off and regain the screen real estate for your drawing. Use AutoCAD's CONFIG command and answer NO to the question "Do you want a screen menu area?" In Windows, the default configuration doesn't display the side-screen menu; use PREFERENCES to turn it back on.

TABLET MENUS

The ***TABLET*n* sections of ACAD.MNU define the four tablet areas into which the stock AutoCAD digitizer template is divided. Shown below is part of the ***TABLET4 menu section from ACAD.MNU (***TABLET4 defines the bottom quarter of the template).

```
***TABLET4
...
^C^C_TIME
'_ID
'_STATUS
^C^C_LIST
'_HELP
'_HELP
;
'_DDEMODES
'_DDEMODES
'DDOSNAP
;
_NONE
_CENTER
_ENDPOINT
_INS
_INTERSEC
_MIDPOINT
_NEAREST
_NODE
_PERPEND
_QUADRANT
_TANGENT
;
^C^C_QSAVE
^C^C_SAVEAS
...
```

Tablet menus are useful for presenting a large number of options at once, without requiring the user to search through menus for a command. On the other hand, they're less than ideal for in-house customization. Keeping tablet menus up to date requires more work, because you have to revise and replot the digitizer overlay in addition to editing the .MNU file. Also, some people in your office might use a mouse instead of a digitizer, in which case they won't have access to the tablet menus. Most offices will be best served by sticking with the stock AutoCAD tablet menus and concentrating their customization efforts on the other menu interfaces.

 Tip

Our argument against customizing the tablet menus isn't an argument against digitizers. Many users prefer the "absolute positioning" and greater pointing accuracy of a digitizer over a mouse, even if they don't use the tablet for picking commands or tracing ("absolute positioning" means that one spot on the tablet always maps to the same spot on the screen). Another advantage of tablets is the additional buttons available with digitizer pucks. On the other hand, some users are more comfortable with mice. There is no "best" pointing device for AutoCAD, and the personal preference of the user should be your guide in equipping each workstation.

General Menu Syntax

Many of the details of menu syntax should be apparent from the ACAD.MNU examples above. Chapter 6 of the *AutoCAD Customization Manual* includes a compact but complete reference to menu syntax. Rather than repeat the information from that chapter, we'll summarize the most important points here, and then move on to making some useful modifications to ACAD.MNU.

MENU STRUCTURE

- Begin menu sections with ***section_name.

   See Table 17.1 above for a summary of section names.

- Begin submenu sections with **submenu_name.

   You decide on the names for submenus. Submenus can be used in any menu section, but they're necessary only when you need to swap different menu "pages" into a section. Swapping is most common for icon, screen, and sometimes cursor menus. Put a blank line between submenus.

- Enclose labels in [square brackets].

Menu item labels can be used in any menu section, but, of course, they appear on screen only for the ***POP*n*, ***ICON, and ***SCREEN menus. Look at the conventions used in the stock AutoCAD menu labels (capitalization, an ellipsis to indicate a dialogue box, etc.), and try to mimic those when you create custom labels.

- Put comments in separate menu "sections" called ***COMMENT.

Because a semicolon acts like <Enter> in menus, AutoCAD provides this different mechanism for including comments in menus. See ACAD.MNU for examples.

- Break long lines with a +.

If your menu macro gets too long, you can split it into two or more lines by adding a + to all but the last line of the macro.

- Be careful with blank lines.

Blank lines usually *are* significant in .MNU files. They act as terminators in ***POP*n* menus (i.e., AutoCAD ignores anything below the blank line for that menu), but serve as blank labels in ***SCREEN menus.

MENU MACRO BASICS

- Type command sequences as you would at the Command: prompt.

Simple menu macros are similar to scripts: Jot down the command sequence you want to put into a macro, and then transcribe it into the .MNU file.

- Use a space or semicolon for each <Enter>.

 Tip

You can call dialogue box commands from a menu macro, but the macro will pause indefinitely until the user picks OK or Cancel to put away the dialogue. At that point, the menu macro regains control and can continue with other commands if necessary.

Tip

Technically, a semicolon in a menu macro acts like one press of the <Enter> key, and a space acts like one press of the spacebar. In practice, these actions are almost always equivalent. The main exception is when you use a text-oriented command, such as TEXT or ATTEDIT, in a menu macro. In these cases, a space can act like a literal space in a text string.

You don't need to put a space or semicolon at the end of a menu macro; AutoCAD automatically tags an extra <Enter> onto the end of each macro, unless the macro ends with a special character such as \ or + (see below). Be on the lookout for trailing spaces at the ends of lines; each one will act like another press of the spacebar.

- Begin transparent commands in macros with an apostrophe (').

Menu macros that can run in the middle of another command (e.g., 'ZOOM Previous) should include the apostrophe.

- Begin macros that are not transparent with ^c^c.

Menu macros that can't run in the middle of another command (e.g., ^c^cLINE) should begin with ^c^c to cancel any pending command and subcommand.

GETTING USER INPUT

- Use a backslash (\) to pause for user input.

Include one backslash for each pause. For example:

```
[Break at Int]^c^cBREAK \First INT \@
```

This macro lets the user break an entity in two at an intersection with another entity. It requires one pause to select the entity and a second pause to pick the intersection point. The @ sign at the end of the macro is the standard AutoCAD way of specifying the last point selected (BREAK requires two break points, and, for this macro, we want them to be the same point).

- Use SELECT and then Previous to provide flexible object selection.

Normally, object selection would be a problem in menu macros, since you don't know in advance how many pauses the user will require in order to complete object selection. To overcome this problem, the SELECT command receives special treatment in menu macros: Follow it by a single backslash, and AutoCAD will remain paused until the user hits <Enter> to end object selection. At that point, your menu macro can execute a command and then supply Previous (or simply P) to retrieve the selection set. Here's an example that puts COPY Multiple in a menu macro:

```
[Copy Multiple]^c^cSELECT \COPY Previous ;Multiple
```

Tip

Note the two <Enter>s required after Previous in the [Copy Multiple] macro. The first <Enter> (represented by the space) sends the Previous selection option to the Command: prompt, and the second <Enter> (represented by the semicolon) ends object selection. As in scripts, you have to count your <Enter>s carefully. In this book, we use a space for a single <Enter> and a semicolon for each additional <Enter>, since multiple spaces are difficult to make out in printed listings.

Warning

In order to maintain compatibility with pre-Release 12 menus, menu macros don't provide implied windowing, no matter how the PICKAUTO system variable is set. To make matters worse, adding AUto after SELECT in a menu macro doesn't properly enable the Auto selection method in Release 12.

POPPING AND SWAPPING

- Use $menu_type=*$ to display a pull-down, cursor, or icon menu.

  $p0=*$ pops up the cursor menu, $pn=*$ pops up pull-down menu number n, and $i=*$ displays the current icon menu.

- Use $menu_type=submenu_name$ to swap menus.

  You can swap menus in any menu area, including the ***POP*n* and ***BUTTON*n* sections, but in most cases, you'll want to limit swapping to icon, screen, and cursor menus. $s=*submenu_name* displays the **submenu_name submenu in the side-screen menu area. $i=*submenu_name* makes *submenu_name* the current icon menu (add $i=* after $i=*submenu_name* in order to display the icon menu).

OTHER SPECIAL CHARACTERS

AutoCAD refers to the square brackets, ^C, backslash, semicolon, space, plus sign, and several other characters that receive special treatment as "special characters." Chapter 6 of the *AutoCAD Customization Manual* includes a table describing all the special characters. Following are a few of the more useful ones.

- Use ^B, ^G, and ^O to toggle Snap, Grid, and Ortho, respectively.

  Menu macros normally can't mimic pressing the function keys, so you can use the keyboard <Ctrl> key equivalents instead.

- Use an underscore (_) before commands and suboptions if you need to ensure compatibility with foreign-language versions of AutoCAD.

- Place LISP functions and other menu macro code you don't want to have echoed on the command line between ^Ps.

  ^P helps keep the command line "clean" so that users aren't confused by extraneous messages.

Tip

To be precise, ^P toggles the current menu echoing state, which is controlled by the MENUECHO system variable. MENUECHO is set to 0 every time you load a drawing, and contrary to common sense, a setting of 0 means *do* echo menu macro code on the command line. Thus, the first ^P in a macro toggles menu echoing off, and the second one toggles it back on. Appendix A in both the *AutoCAD Customization Manual* and *AutoCAD Reference Manual* describes other possible settings for MENUECHO.

SPECIAL PULL-DOWN AND CURSOR MENU LABEL FEATURES

AutoCAD includes several special characters for enhancing pull-down and cursor menu labels. A complete list is given in Chapter 6 of the *AutoCAD Customization Manual*.

- Use [->*xxx*] to indicate the parent of a cascading submenu and [<-*yyy*] to mark the last child of the submenu.

  Each right "arrow" must be matched by a corresponding left "arrow." If the submenu is the last child of a last child (for instance, in the Draw pull-down menu, Extract... is the last child of Attributes, which is itself the last child of Text), you need two left "arrows": [<-<-Extract...] ^C^Cddattext.

- Use two dashes in a menu label to draw a separator line: [--]

  This feature is handy for grouping menu items.

- Use a tilde at the beginning of a label to gray out and disable that menu choice: [~No Can Do].

  This feature alone isn't very valuable, since you'll usually want to disable a menu choice only under certain conditions. The most effective way to do this is to combine the tilde with DIESEL, as described in the next chapter.

- Use an exclamation point and period at the beginning of a label to put a check mark next to that menu choice [!.Checked].

Tip

Chapter 6 of the *AutoCAD Customization Manual* describes another method for graying out and checking menu labels. This method, called "referencing," uses a syntax similar to the $menu\_type$=* syntax for popping up a menu. For instance, $p1.6=~ grays out the sixth item on the first pull-down menu, and $p0.1=!. puts a check mark next to the first item on the cursor menu. While this method seems easier than using DIESEL to construct dynamic menu labels, it's difficult to maintain because it refers to an absolute position in the menu (rather than to a specific label). If you add or remove items from a menu and forget to update the referencing code, you'll suddenly find the wrong labels being checked or grayed out.

This approach is even harder to maintain if you use it in LISP programs outside of the .MNU file. Unfortunately, this is what Autodesk did in the ACAD.MNL and ACADR12.LSP files. If you use a custom menu and discover that items on the first and ninth pull-down menus are mysteriously being grayed out, the culprits are the (ai_asegrey) and (ai_amegrey) functions. To eliminate this problem, comment out the lines (ai_asegrey "~") in ACAD.MNL and (ai_amegrey "~") in ACADR12.LSP by placing a semicolon at the beginning of the line.

As with the tilde, you'll usually want to combine this feature with DIESEL in order to create a "dynamic" label that is checked under certain conditions and not checked under others.

- In AutoCAD for Windows, use /*letter* at the beginning of a label to define an underlined accelerator or mnemonic key.

Menu Customization Techniques

In Release 12, the stock ACAD.MNU has evolved to the point where it covers most AutoCAD commands in a reasonably consistent and thorough way, but you'll still want to modify it, if only to add custom menu macros or LISP routines that help speed your work. In some cases, it's worth going further and reorganizing the stock menus to make them more efficient for your company's or workgroup's approach to using AutoCAD. In this chapter's tutorials, we'll use the "add on" approach to enhance the pull-down and cursor menus. You can use these additions as the basis of your own menu customization.

Before you actually start customizing a menu, take the time to plan how your menus should be organized. Make a list of your additions or changes, and then sketch out menu pages that are organized in a sensible way. For many people, it makes sense to segregate custom macros in a separate, unused pull-down menu such as ***POP10 or one of the alternate ***BUTTON*n* menus. These are good places to add custom menu macros, since they won't interfere with the other menus and they're easy to paste from one .MNU file to another. Group similar choices together using cascading submenus and separator lines. Make the menu labels consistent, and avoid using all uppercase letters, which are harder to read.

Tip

Figure out some way to keep track of your modifications, since you'll need to reconcile them with new menu files at upgrade time. In practice, no one ever has the time or inclination to completely document menu customization, but at least try to log *where* you made changes, if not the specifics of those changes, so that you can find them again. One approach is to jot down the menu area, submenu, and label of each macro you modify. Another possibility is to print out ACAD.MNU and then highlight lines as you change them.

The technique for customizing menus is simple. Always keep a backup copy of the original ACAD.MNU in case you mess something up. While shelled out of AutoCAD, load the .MNU file into your text editor and add or modify a menu macro. Save the file, return to AutoCAD, and reload the menu with the MENU command in order to force AutoCAD to recompile it. Test the macro to make sure it works as you expected, and if not, edit, save, recompile, and test again.

Warning

Release 12's .MNU file is much more compact than in previous versions, but at just under 100KB, it's still too large for some text editors, including the Windows Notepad. If your editor reports that ACAD.MNU is too large to load, you'll have to use EDIT or another text editor with a larger capacity. In Windows, you can use Windows Write, but be sure to save ACAD.MNU in standard ASCII text format (i.e., answer NO to the prompt "Do you want to convert this file to Write format?").

Third-Party Application Considerations

Most third-party applications rely heavily on custom menus, so before you start customizing, you'll need to take into account any special requirements or limitations imposed by your applications. The first concern is whether or not the developer of your application includes the menu source file (.MNU) with the program files. Most developers do, but a few still view their menu macros as proprietary information and include only the compiled .MNX file with the program. There are menu decompilers available, but using them may violate your license agreement. In general, you'll want to avoid third-party applications that don't include menu source files.

Next, you need to determine what menus the application uses and how they're structured. Application menus often have names other than ACAD.MNU, and some applications use more than one menu. An application menu might be a slightly modified version of the stock ACAD.MNU, or it might be completely different. Locate and make a note of any unused menu areas, especially unused ***POP*n* sections so that you can determine where to put your custom macros.

Once you've done your research, you can proceed with customization in the same way as for ACAD.MNU. If more than one menu file is used, develop and test the changes in one menu and then paste the changes into the other files.

Adding a Custom Pull-Down Menu

In this tutorial, we'll create a custom pull-down menu in the unoccupied tenth menu slot (***POP10), as shown in Figure 17.4. This menu can serve as the basis for future customization as you add menu macros and LISP routines.

1. Copy ACAD.MNU to your test customization directory.

Change to your \ACUSTOM\TEST subdirectory.

Copy AutoCAD's stock ACAD.MNU (usually located in \ACAD\SUPPORT) to \ACUSTOM\TEST.

The original \ACAD\SUPPORT\ACAD.MNU will remain as your backup.

Start AutoCAD.

2. Add the ***POP10 menu section and the [Copy Multiple] and [Break at Int] menu macros from above to ACAD.MNU.

Launch your text editor and open ACAD.MNU.

*Use your editor's search function to find ***ICON.*

The ***ICON section comes right after ***POP9, so we'll insert ***POP10 between the two.

Add the menu code shown in italics below:

```
...
    [<-Unload Modeler]^C^C^P(ai_unloadame) ^P
***Comment
    Custom AutoCAD Power Tools pull-down menu:
***POP10
[APTCust]
[Copy Multiple]^c^c_SELECT \_COPY _Previous ;+
_Multiple
[Break at Int]^c^c_BREAK \_First _INT \@
***ICON
**poly
...
```

Watch out for trailing spaces.

Save ACAD.MNU, return to AutoCAD, and reload the menu with the MENU command (see Figure 17.3).

AutoCAD recompiles the menu.

Test the new menu macros.

Tip

In this book, we use the same uppercase/lowercase convention for menu macros as we do for scripts: uppercase for letters you would have to type if you were carrying out the operation at the command line, and lowercase for other letters. We also use lowercase for special characters, such as ^c, and for LISP code. These conventions are slightly different from Autodesk's, but different parts of the stock ACAD.MNU are inconsistent with one another anyway.

3. Add a macro that loads and executes CHTEXT.LSP (see Chapter 9 for information about CHTEXT).

One of the most common uses of custom menus is for loading and running LISP or ADS programs. Although Release 12 includes APPLOAD for loading programs, a menu pick is usually easier and faster for commonly used programs.

Loading LISP routines requires a small amount of AutoLISP code. For now, just type the code in carefully; we'll explain it more fully in Chapter 19.

Reload ACAD.MNU into your text editor, search for ***POP10, and add the new macro code shown in italics below:

```
***Comment
  Custom AutoCAD Power Tools pull-down menu:
***POP10
```

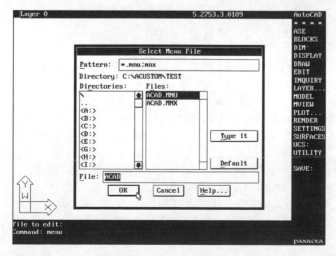

Figure 17.3   Reloading ACAD.MNU.

```
[APTCust]
[Copy Multiple]^c^c_SELECT \_COPY _Previous ;+
_Multiple
[Break at Int]^c^c_BREAK \_First _INT \@
[ChText]^c^c^p(load "CHTEXT") ^pCHT
***ICON
...
```

Save ACAD.MNU, return to AutoCAD, reload the menu, and test.

The LISP function (load) loads an .LSP file into memory; since
\ACAD\SUPPORT\CHTEXT.LSP is located in AutoCAD's support file
search path, AutoCAD can find it without your specifying the path.
After the routine is loaded into memory, CHT executes the command.

Note that there's a small inefficiency in this macro, since it reloads the
routine each time you pick the menu choice. In Chapter 19, we'll show
how to prevent this multiple loading.

4. Add a Layer cascading submenu.

Layer manipulation is an area that's always ripe for customization.
We'll add a Layer submenu that includes macros for turning on all
layers, turning off all but the current layer, and turning the HATCH
layer on and off.

*Edit ACAD.MNU once more and add the new macro code shown in
italics below:*

```
***Comment
  Custom AutoCAD Power Tools pull-down menu:
***POP10
[APTCust]
[Copy Multiple]^c^c_SELECT \_COPY _Previous ;+
_Multiple
[Break at Int]^c^c_BREAK \_First _INT \@
[ChText]^c^c^p(load "CHTEXT") ^pCHT
[--]
[->Layer]
  [* On]'_LAYER _ON * ;
  [Isolate Current]'_EXPERT 0 '_LAYER _OFf * No ;
  [HATCH Off]'_LAYER _OFf HATCH ;
  [<-HATCH On]'_LAYER _ON HATCH ;
***ICON
...
```

Warning

You might discover a bug with the [HATCH Off] macro. If HATCH happens to be the current layer, the macro will stall at the "Really want to turn the current layer off?" prompt. We could have the macro set EXPERT to 1 and then back to 0 in order to get around this problem, but then the macro would let the user turn the current layer off without warning, which is even more undesirable. For now, we'll leave the macro as it is, since the bug doesn't really harm anything. In the next chapter, we'll use DIESEL to gray out the choice while HATCH is the current layer.

Tip

Depending on the speed of your computer, menu compile times can be substantial. If you spend a lot of time customizing menus, it pays to develop new menu code in a small test menu that contains only the sections you're currently working on. Copy the relevant sections from ACAD.MNU to a different menu file, such as TEST.MNU, work out the changes and additions, and then replace the appropriate parts of ACAD.MNU with the revised code.

If you use this approach, be aware of one quirk: Cursor menus (***POP0) won't appear if your TEST.MNU file doesn't contain at least one other ***POP*n* menu section. Always copy at least a portion of ***POP1 to avoid this problem.

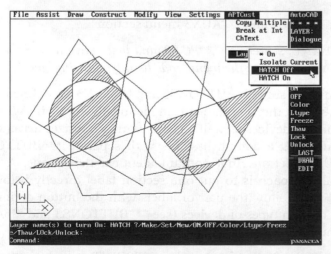

Figure 17.4 The completed custom pull-down menu.

Note the separator line ([– –]) to divide the three editing macros from the Layer submenu. Also note that each layer macro requires two <Enter>s at the end: one to finish the current subcommand, and one to finish the LAYER command.

Save ACAD.MNU, return to AutoCAD, reload the menu, and test.

You should make a layer called HATCH and draw some geometry on it in order to test the macros.

Figure 17.4 shows the completed menu.

The [Isolate Current] macro takes advantage of the fact that AutoCAD warns you before turning the current layer off. The macro first sets the EXPERT system variable to 0 to ensure that AutoCAD does issue the warning, and then tries to turn all layers (*) off. When AutoCAD prompts "Really want to turn the current layer off?," the macro answers No, which then leaves only the current layer on.

Adding Alternate Button and Cursor Menus

The previous tutorial should have given you a good idea of how you can start building a custom pull-down menu. The alternate button menus (***BUT-TONS2 through ***BUTTONS4) are other useful menu areas for customization, especially when you combine them with custom cursor menus. In this next tutorial, we'll create a custom ***BUTTONS3 menu that calls up an editing menu at the cursor when you pick the second button while holding down the <Ctrl> key. Refer to Figure 17.5 as you work through this tutorial.

1. Add ***BUTTONS3 and ***AUX3 menu sections.

*Edit ACAD.MNU, search for ***POP0, and just above it, add the italic lines shown at the top of the menu code listing following step 1.*

We want to make sure ***BUTTONS3 and ***AUX3 are defined in the same way, so that the alternate button menu will work with Windows system pointing devices as well as with regular digitizer drivers. The stock ACAD.MNU accomplishes this with separate ***BUTTONS*n* and ***AUX*n* sections that contain identical definitions. A more economical approach is to put one section label directly below the other, and then follow the pair of labels with the button definitions that apply to both types of devices (see ***BUTTONS3 and ***AUX3 in the menu code listing following step 1).

The macro $p0=p0edit $p0=* makes **P0EDIT (which we'll define next) the current cursor submenu and then pops it up on-screen. Note the similarity to the syntax for loading and displaying an icon menu. Since there's only one cursor menu section (***POP0), you must define submenus, as in ***ICON, in order to make different versions of the menu appear.

```
...
***AUX2
$p0=*
***Comment
 Custom AutoCAD Power Tools button menu
***BUTTONS3
***AUX3
$p0=p0edit $p0=*
***POP0
[Osnap]
[Center]_center
[Endpoint]_endp
[Insert]_ins
[Intersection]_int
[Midpoint]_mid
[Nearest]_nea
[Node]_nod
[Perpendicular]_per
[Quadrant]_qua
[Tangent] tan
[None]_non
[->Filters]
  [.X].X
  [.Y].Y
  [.Z].Z
  [.XY].XY
  [.XZ].XZ
  [<-.YZ].YZ
[Calculator]'cal
***Comment
 Custom AutoCAD Power Tools cursor menu
**PUEDIT
[Cursor Edit Menu]
[Copy]^c^c_COPY
[Erase]^c^c_ERASE
[Move]^c^c_MOVE
[Rotate]^c^c_ROTATE
```

```
[--]
[Break]^c^c_BREAK
[Extend]^c^c_EXTEND
[Trim]^c^c_TRIM
***POP1
[File]
...
```

2. Add the **P0EDIT cursor submenu.

Below the default ***POP0 menu, add the new submenu label **P0EDIT, a menu title, and some simple editing macros, as shown in italics at the bottom of the menu code listing following step 1.

The menu title [Cursor Edit Menu] doesn't actually appear on the cursor menu, so you can put anything in it.

3. Save, recompile, and test.

Save ACAD.MNU, return to AutoCAD, reload the menu, and test.

To test the new cursor menu, hold down the <Ctrl> key and press the second mouse or puck button.

Try to access the old osnaps cursor menu by pressing the third button or <Shift> plus the second button.

Oops; we defined <Ctrl>+button 2 so that it made **P0EDIT the current cursor menu, but we didn't provide a way to swap the original osnaps menu back in.

4. Create a **P0OSNAP submenu label for the stock cursor menu, and put a $p0=p0osnap submenu call before each $p0=*.

$p0=* appears four times (once each in ***BUTTONS1, ***BUT-TONS2, ***AUX1, and ***AUX2). To make life a bit easier, let's consolidate ***BUTTONS1 with ***AUX1 and ***BUTTONS2 with ***AUX2, so that there's less duplication.

Move the ***AUX1 label just below ***BUTTONS1, and move ***AUX2 below ***BUTTONS2, as shown below. Delete the menu macro code that was in the ***AUX1 and ***AUX2 sections.

Add **P0OSNAP on a new line just below ***POP0.

```
...
***BUTTONS1
```

```
***AUX1
;
$p0=p0osnap $p0=*
^C^C
^B
^O
^G
^D
^E
^T

***BUTTONS2
***AUX2
$p0=p0osnap $p0=*
***Comment
  Custom AutoCAD Power Tools button menu
***BUTTONS3
***AUX3
$p0=p0edit $p0-*
***POP0
**P0OSNAP
[Osnap]
[Center]_center
[Endpoint]_endp
[Insert]_ins
...
```

The default cursor menu now has a submenu name.

Add $p0=p0osnap *in front of the two* $p0=* *lines.*

These additions ensure that the cursor osnaps menu gets reloaded. The listing above shows the changes in italics.

Save ACAD.MNU, return to AutoCAD, reload the menu, and test.

You should now be able to access both the cursor menus: osnaps and edit. The completed cursor edit menu is shown in Figure 17.5.

The new alternate button and cursor menus work equally well with a two-button mouse or a many-button puck, but if you have the latter, you might want to extend the idea to take advantage of your additional buttons. Define the other buttons to perform your most common commands (such as LINE or COPY), or use them to call up additional cursor menus. The resulting interface can be very efficient, since it minimizes the cursor movement required for operating menus.

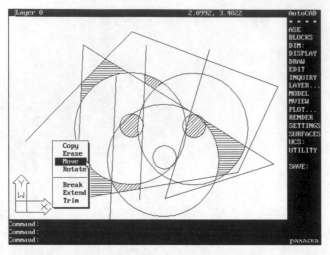

Figure 17.5   The completed cursor edit menu.

Finishing Up

Once you've tested all the new menus thoroughly, move ACAD.MNU *and* ACAD.MNX to your \ACUSTOM directory so that they become the standard menu files. Take a moment to jot down or highlight the changes you made so that you'll have something to jog your memory at upgrade time.

As mentioned earlier, Chapter 6 of the *AutoCAD Customization Manual* contains reference material on menu customization, so refer to it for a detailed treatment of some of the finer points we skipped over.

Menu Customization and Workgroups

Menus are one of the most important aspects of workgroup customization. Unlike scripts and the ACAD.PGP file, a menu file is a large, relatively messy affair with lots of interconnections. Thus, it's important that your workgroup standardizes its menus, so that the menu interface is consistent and menu updates require no more than copying a revised .MNU or .MNX file to each workstation.

Develop a standard custom menu using ACAD.MNU or your third-party application's menu as a starting point. Ask other workgroup members for their favorite menu macros and LISP routines, and try to incorporate these into the menus. People will be a lot less likely to mess with the menu file if you put what they want in it in the first place. One way to help prevent unauthorized editing of menu files is to distribute only the compiled .MNX file, but don't rely solely on restrictive measures for enforcing consistency. Try to provide a menu that users will *want* to use as is.

Documenting menu customization is especially important when you head up a workgroup. At upgrade time, you're likely to be the one called upon to transfer menu customization to the new release. No one will be very happy if they have to wait weeks while you try to ferret out and transfer all your menu changes to the new version, or if their first experiences with it are marred by bugs caused by poorly implemented additions.

You should pay some attention to the user interface concerns raised by your customization. Look for good examples in AutoCAD and Windows. Keep menu labels as short as you can while still maintaining recognizability. Be consistent in your changes. Consider trying your changes out on a couple of people before springing them on a large group.

If you keep your additions isolated in complete, self-contained add-on menus, you have a fair degree of flexibility and even room for error. But if you start to reorganize the existing menus of AutoCAD or your third-party application, be much more careful. Changing things that people have gotten used to is a big deal and shouldn't be done lightly; you probably shouldn't make more than one such set of changes per release of AutoCAD. Test any such changes thoroughly before rolling them out to your group.

There are a couple of menu training issues as well. Remember that alternate button menus are new to Release 12, and many users won't be familiar with them (especially since the stock ACAD.MNU doesn't really take advantage of them). If you customize the alternate button menus, you'll probably have to spend a few minutes showing others in your workgroup how to use them with the <Shift>, <Ctrl>, and <Shift>+<Ctrl> keys. Also, take the time to show off new menu macros once you've added them. The use of these clever macros may not be readily apparent to others, especially if they aren't aware of the power of menu customization.

Summary

A custom menu should be the focal point for all your customization. First, menu customization provides a way to make the AutoCAD interface more efficient and friendly for your style of working. Second, menu macros, like scripts, can automate tasks that require a lot of keystrokes. And third, menus are good for launching LISP and ADS programs from the CAD magazines, CompuServe, and other sources.

In the next two chapters, we'll come back to menu customization as we look at ways of enhancing menus with DIESEL and incorporating AutoLISP code into menu macros.

18

DIESEL

DIESEL is Release 12's new programming language for customizing the AutoCAD status line and creating smarter menu labels and macros. DIESEL is a "bare-bones" language based on a LISP-like syntax. It comprises just 28 functions, and all program data and expressions are treated as text strings. These qualities make DIESEL easy for AutoLISP programmers to master, and they also make it a good "training ground" for those who don't know LISP yet. You can learn some of the fundamentals of LISP while actually doing useful customization!

DIESEL's primary usefulness to most customizers comes from its ability to control menu labels and to be included in menu macro code. With DIESEL you can design menu labels that respond dynamically to system variable settings. You also can write more flexible menu macros that make decisions and calculations based on system variable values.

About This Chapter

In this chapter, we discuss DIESEL and demonstrate how to use it to create more sophisticated and useful menus. We also describe how to design a custom status line with DIESEL. In addition, this chapter serves as an introduction to AutoLISP and to "real" programming for those who are new to it. We'll use a small amount of LISP in our custom status line example, but more importantly, many concepts in this chapter will carry over into the AutoLISP chapter.

Chapter 8 of the *AutoCAD Customization Manual* covers DIESEL in detail, and includes a number of examples of custom status lines and menu code. The last part of that chapter contains a catalogue of DIESEL string functions, which will serve as your primary reference to DIESEL as you extend your use of it.

A DIESEL Primer

According to the *AutoCAD Customization Manual*, DIESEL stands for Direct Interpretively Evaluated String Expression Language. Rumor has it, though, that the acronym was originally conceived as *Dumb* Interpretively Evaluated String Expression Language—"dumb" in the sense that the language has limited capabilities and doesn't go very fast. In this case, dumbness is a virtue, since it means that the language is easy to learn and use. And DIESEL is plenty fast for the small jobs it's normally called on to do.

Expressions and Strings

The rest of the acronym—Interpretively Evaluated String Expression Language—means two things. First, AutoCAD must *evaluate* DIESEL program statements, or *expressions*, each time they're to be executed. Programmers call languages that use this method *interpreted* languages, and distinguish them from *compiled* languages, in which a compiler translates the program statements into binary gibberish called machine code. AutoLISP and ordinary BASIC are examples of other interpreted languages. Most implementations of Pascal and C (including Autodesk's C-based ADS) are compiled languages.

Second, DIESEL handles nothing but text *strings*. Most programming languages, including AutoLISP, work with different *data types* such as integers, decimal numbers, individual ASCII characters, and strings. DIESEL, being dumb, knows only about strings, and everything that goes into or comes out of a DIESEL expression must be a string. This limitation isn't quite as restrictive as it sounds, since DIESEL will deal with numbers by turning them into strings that work just fine for most purposes.

Functions and Syntax

All DIESEL expressions are composed of *functions*, which are like little sausage grinders that take strings in one end, do something with them, and then spit different strings out the other end. This process is shown schematically in Figure 18.1. The strings that go in one end are called *arguments*. The "do something with them" procedure is called *evaluating* the DIESEL func-

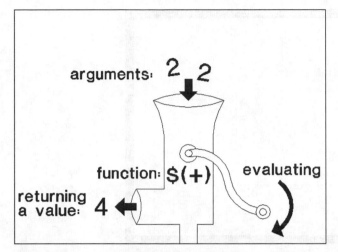

Figure 18.1   The DIESEL function as sausage grinder.

tion. The process of spitting a new string out the other end is called *returning a value*. It helps to know these terms, because they're used a lot by programmers and by the AutoCAD manuals. Also, these concepts—especially evaluating a function and returning a value—form the basis of an understanding of AutoLISP.

A DIESEL function looks something like this:

```
$(function,argument1,argument2...)
```

The function and its arguments are enclosed in parentheses, and the function name always comes first, as is true with AutoLISP functions. DIESEL functions, though, are preceded by a dollar sign in order to distinguish them from LISP. Commas separate the function from the arguments and the arguments from one another.

This syntax will seem odd at first (even to LISP programmers, who will leave out the dollar sign and commas), but it'll seem obvious once you use it a few times.

Experimenting with DIESEL Functions

To get a feel for how DIESEL functions work, try the following tutorial (see Figure 18.2).

1. Copy DIESEL.LSP to your customization development directory and start AutoCAD.

Copy DIESEL.LSP from the AutoCAD Power Tools disk to your \ACUSTOM\TEST directory.

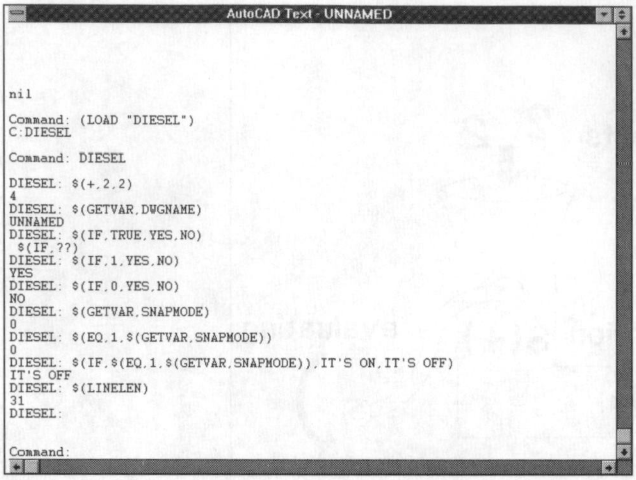

Figure 18.2 A sample session with DIESEL.LSP.

DIESEL.LSP is a simple AutoLISP program for testing DIESEL expressions from the AutoCAD Command: prompt. DIESEL.LSP comes from Chapter 8 of the *AutoCAD Customization Manual*.

Launch AutoCAD.

2. Load DIESEL.LSP.

```
Command: (LOAD "DIESEL")
```

As mentioned in the previous chapter, (load) is an AutoLISP function for loading an .LSP file into memory. We'll discuss LISP functions in the next chapter.

DIESEL.LSP defines a new AutoCAD command called DIESEL that replaces the Command: prompt with a DIESEL: prompt and evaluates DIESEL expressions that you type.

3. Run the DIESEL command and try a couple of functions.

```
Command: DIESEL
DIESEL: $(+,2,2)
4
```

In this example, + is the DIESEL function for adding two numbers, and the two 2s are the arguments. Note that even for mathematical functions, the operation comes before the arguments.

Obviously, this is a pretty strange way to add two numbers, and it's made even stranger by the fact that DIESEL will evaluate the numbers as strings (but still return the right answer). In most cases, you'll be using functions other than mathematical ones. For example:

```
DIESEL: $(GETVAR,DWGNAME)
UNNAMED
```

$(getvar) is the DIESEL function for reading the value of an AutoCAD system variable. Think of it as the inverse of the SETVAR command. DWGNAME is the AutoCAD system variable that holds the current drawing name, and in this example we haven't yet named the drawing, so DIESEL returns "UNNAMED." You'll be using $(getvar) a lot in your DIESEL code.

4. See what happens when you type something wrong.

```
DIESEL: $(IF,TRUE,YES,NO)
 $(IF,??)
```

DIESEL has a simple but limited error reporting capability—it spits out question marks indicating where it's confused. In this case, it's trying to tell you that it doesn't understand one of the arguments. If you look up the syntax for the $(if) function in the *AutoCAD Customization Manual*, you'll see that DIESEL expects a number for the first argument.

```
DIESEL: $(IF,1,YES,NO)
YES
DIESEL: $(IF,0,YES,NO)
NO
```

$(if) tests the first argument, and if it's not 0, returns the second argument. If the first argument is 0, $(if) returns the third argument instead. This is a regular if...then...else programming construct, but disguised in DIESEL's odd syntax: $(if,*test*,*then*,*else*). This example will become more useful once we use a "nested function"—a function inside a function—for the first argument, as you'll see in the next step.

5. Try a nested function.

```
DIESEL: $(GETVAR,SNAPMODE)
0
DIESEL: $(EQ,1,$(GETVAR,SNAPMODE))
0
```

The first example uses the $(getvar) function to check the SNAPMODE system variable (which is set to 0 when Snap is off, and 1 when Snap is on). The second example returns the same answer, but for a different reason. $(getvar) was nested inside the $(eq) function, which tests whether its two arguments are equal, and returns 1 (true) if they are, and 0 (false) if they aren't. In this case, SNAPMODE was 0, and 0 does not equal 1, so the $(eq) function returned 0. Now use the $(eq) function to do something moderately useful.

```
DIESEL: $(IF,(EQ,1,$(GETVAR,SNAPMODE)),IT'S ON,IT'S OFF)
IT'S OFF
```

This time, we nested everything from before inside the $(if) function, and used the function to report on the current Snap status.

6. Check your maximum custom status line length and then exit DIESEL.

```
DIESEL: $(LINELEN)
34
DIESEL: <Enter>
Command:
```

$(linelen) is a DIESEL function that returns the maximum length of the customizable status line area on the current system. Note that this particular function doesn't take any arguments, since it gets the information it needs from AutoCAD itself. The number returned by $(linelen) will depend on your display driver, display resolution, and platform. With stock VGA drivers, it turns out to be 34 for AutoCAD 386 and 31 for AutoCAD for Windows (TurboDLD*Lite*™ gives you at least 43 characters). Keep these numbers in mind when you create custom status lines with DIESEL.

Tip

Notice that we typed all DIESEL expressions in as continuous strings, without any intervening spaces. In some cases, you can insert spaces after commas to improve readability, but the rules for when you can and when you can't insert a space will seem obscure at first. We recommend that, for now, you omit spaces except where you explicitly want DIESEL to leave a blank space in a menu or status line label (see the custom status line tutorial below for an example).

A DIESEL Function Minicatalogue

Learning a new programming language is, in many ways, like learning a spoken language. You need to know something about the basic syntax, but you also need some vocabulary, or functions, in order to get anything done. Figuring out *which* words or functions you need to know right away can be a big problem. Few people would start learning a foreign language by reading a dictionary or thesaurus, but that's how most programmer's reference manuals (and some books) present computer languages.

The problem isn't quite so acute with DIESEL, since it only has 28 functions, but still it makes sense to focus on a few "workhorse" functions at first. Later, you can build up your repertoire as you run into situations that aren't covered by the basic functions.

In this section, we present a minicatalogue of eight functions that will get you started using DIESEL in menus. Once you've mastered these functions, use the complete listing in Chapter 8 of the *AutoCAD Customization Manual* as your guide to the rest of them.

ARITHMETIC FUNCTIONS

- `$(+,val1,val2)`

- `$(−,val1,val2)`

- `$(*,val1,val2)`

- `$(/,val1,val2)`

These four functions perform the four basic arithmetic operations. Each function takes two (or more) numbers as arguments and returns the result of the operation applied to those numbers. Example:

```
$(*,0.5,0.25)
```

returns 0.125.

GET SYSTEM VARIABLE VALUE FUNCTION

- `$(getvar,varname)`

$(getvar) returns the value of the AutoCAD system variable varname. Example:

```
$(getvar,CLAYER)
```

returns the name of the current layer.

EQUALITY FUNCTION

- $(eq, *val1*, *val2*)

$(eq) tests whether its two arguments are identical (equal) and returns 1 if they are and 0 if they aren't. The arguments can be strings or numbers, but DIESEL converts any numbers to strings. Example:

    $(eq,HATCH,$(getvar,CLAYER))

returns 1 if HATCH is the current layer, and 0 otherwise.

IF FUNCTION

- $(if, *test*, *then*, *else*)

$(if) inspects the value returned by *test,* and if it's not 0, takes any actions indicated in the *then* branch and returns the value returned by it. If test is 0, $(if) takes any actions indicated in the *else* branch and returns the value returned by it. Example:

    $(if,$(eq,HATCH,$(getvar,CLAYER)),Y,N)

returns Y if HATCH is the current layer, and N otherwise.

DATE FUNCTION

- $(edtime, *julian_time*, *picture*)

$(edtime) formats a date according to a specification "picture." The *julian_time* argument is a time expressed in Julian format, and often comes from the DATE system variable (which stores the current system date and time). The *picture* argument consists of special codes, such as HH for hour, MON for month expressed in three-letter format, and YY for year expressed in two-number format. See the *AutoCAD Customization Manual* for a complete table of picture options. Example:

    $(edtime,$(getvar,DATE),DD MON YY - HH:MM)

returns 15 Mar 94 – 00:03 at 12:03 am on March 15th, 1994.

Tip

$(edtime)'s date formatting capabilities are very good, especially when compared with AutoLISP, which doesn't have any built-in date functions. You might use $(edtime) in a simple menu macro that stamps the date and time on the current drawing. In addition, LISP programmers can use $(edtime) (or any other DIESEL function) in AutoLISP programs. See the *AutoCAD Customization Manual* for date stamp and LISP examples.

DIESEL Techniques

So far, we've only experimented with DIESEL functions, but we haven't seen how they're actually put to use. There are two different procedures, depending on whether you're incorporating DIESEL expressions into menus or using them to define a custom status line.

DIESEL in Menus

DIESEL expressions can show up in .MNU files in both menu labels and menu macros. In menu labels, DIESEL expressions are used to create dynamic labels that can change as system variables change. For instance, you might create a pull-down menu that displays the current layer, linetype, and other settings. More frequently, you'll use DIESEL to gray out or put check marks next to menu labels. For example, you could set up a menu for toggling system variables, such as Snap, Ortho, and Grid, and show check marks next to the names of variables that are currently turned on (see Figure 18.3 for a simple example). In a similar way, you can use DIESEL to gray out menu choices that aren't appropriate in the current context. The menu tutorial below shows examples of checking and graying out with DIESEL.

In menu macros, DIESEL is used to create smarter macros that can read values from system variables and perform different actions, depending on these values. The $(if) function lets you write macros that choose between two courses of action, and $(getvar) is often used along with other functions in macros that feed strings to AutoCAD commands. Examples of both techniques appear below.

To include DIESEL code in .MNU files, you simply type it using the syntax described above. Expressions inside square brackets affect menu labels. DIESEL expressions in macros need to be preceded by $m=, which is the signal to AutoCAD that what follows is DIESEL, rather than normal macro code. The examples will clarify these conventions.

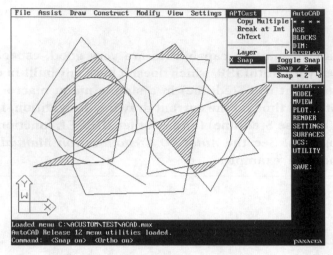

Figure 18.3 The completed Snap submenu (Render and Model menus removed for clarity).

Tip

If you do much with DIESEL in menu macros, you'll encounter situations where it would be handy to store and retrieve your own variables, rather than rely solely on the standard AutoCAD system variables. The USER*xn* system variables are useful for this purpose. There are 15 USER*xn* variables, divided into three groups of five: string (USERS*n*), integer (USERI*n*), and real (USERR*n*); *n* = 1 to 5. You can stash your own variables in any of these slots and then extract them with $(getvar). Be careful, though; some third-party applications use the USER*xn* variables, and if you overwrite their values, the application might not work correctly. Also note that the USERS*n* string variables aren't saved in the drawing.

DIESEL on the Status Line: MODEMACRO

The original idea for DIESEL came from the desire to make the status line customizable. It's ironic, then, that creating a custom status line is more convoluted than using DIESEL in menus. Release 12 added a new system variable called MODEMACRO, and this variable can hold a DIESEL expression that instructs AutoCAD what to display on the portion of the status line to the left of the coordinate readout. All well and good, but useful MODEMACRO DIESEL expressions tend to be fairly long, and typing them in at the Command: prompt would be tedious at best. To make matters worse, MODEMACRO is reset each time you load a drawing; it isn't saved in the drawing, in ACAD.CFG, or anywhere.

So, how do you "load" a DIESEL expression into MODEMACRO automatically? In most cases, you type the expression into a separate .LSP file and then load it from ACAD.LSP. We'll show you how to do this in the custom status line tutorial below, and explain some of the details more thoroughly in Chapter 19, *AutoLISP*.

Windows Tip

If you use AutoCAD for Windows, you'll probably not want to customize the status line. A custom status line replaces some of the most useful tools on the toolbar: the DDLMODES Layer button, the layer drop-down list, and the Snap, Ortho, and paper space toggles.

Debugging

In DIESEL, as in any other programming language, debugging is half the battle. The DIESEL.LSP utility we used above is a useful debugging tool, and you should use it as you experiment with new functions. Release 12 also provides the MACROTRACE system variable, which lets you see how and when AutoCAD evaluates DIESEL expressions. MACROTRACE is set to 0 by default, but when you set it to 1, AutoCAD echoes all DIESEL evaluation to the command line. The result can be a very busy command line, especially if MODEMACRO contains a DIESEL expression. In most cases, you should set MODEMACRO to a null string (by typing in MODEMACRO followed by a period) before turning on MACROTRACE.

The MENUECHO system variable is another useful DIESEL debugging tool. If you set it to 8, AutoCAD displays both the input and output of all DIESEL expressions that are part of menu macros (unlike MACROTRACE, MENUECHO=8 ignores DIESEL in menu labels and MODEMACRO). By seeing both the input and output, you often can figure out more readily what's going wrong with your macros.

DIESEL displays its error messages wherever the expression results would normally be displayed: in a menu label, at the command line for a menu macro, or on the status line. This can look fairly weird, so debugging your DIESEL expressions thoroughly before putting them into use, or especially before sharing them with others, is a good idea. The end of Chapter 8 of the *AutoCAD Customization Manual* lists the error messages and meanings.

Third-Party Application Considerations

Some third-party applications include DIESEL expressions in their Release 12 menus, and some may use MODEMACRO to define a custom status line. The only significant compatibility concern is with ACAD.LSP. If your third-party application adds statements to (or worse, uses its own) ACAD.LSP and you want a custom status line, then you'll have to combine your code for loading a MODEMACRO string with the third-party application's code. Chapter 19, *AutoLISP*, discusses ACAD.LSP and third-party applications in more detail.

DIESEL Tutorials

The tutorials below demonstrate how to use DIESEL to customize menus and the status line. The first tutorial uses DIESEL to create "smart" menu labels and menu macros that rely on system variable values. The second tutorial shows how to create a custom status line that displays the current drawing name and Snap spacing.

Adding DIESEL to Menus

In this tutorial, we'll enhance the ***POP10 pull-down menu page we created in the previous chapter by adding DIESEL to one of the menu labels and creating a Snap submenu, as shown in Figure 18.3.

1. Copy ACAD.MNU from \ACUSTOM to \ACUSTOM\TEST.

Change to your \ACUSTOM\TEST subdirectory and copy ACAD.MNU from \ACUSTOM.

If you don't have a current version of ACAD.MNU as of the end of the previous chapter, copy ACADCH18.MNU from the *AutoCAD Power Tools* diskette and rename it ACAD.MNU.

Start AutoCAD.

2. Modify the [Hatch Off] label so that it's grayed out whenever HATCH is the current layer.

In the previous chapter, we mentioned that the [Hatch Off] macro didn't work when HATCH was the current layer. By graying out the label when HATCH is current, we'll let the user know when the menu choice is inappropriate. In addition, AutoCAD disables a menu choice when the label is grayed out.

Shell out to your text editor, load ACAD.MNU, and search for ***POP10.

Add the menu code shown below in italics to the [Hatch Off] label. Save ACAD.MNU, return to AutoCAD, and test the change by making a new layer called HATCH.

```
***POP10
[APTCust]
[Copy Multiple]^c^c_SELECT \_COPY _Previous ;_Multiple
[Break at Int]^c^c_BREAK \_First _INT \@
[ChText]^c^c^p(load "CHTEXT") ^pCHT
[- -]
[->Layer]
  [* On]'_LAYER _ON * ;
  [Isolate Current]'_EXPERT 0 '_LAYER _OFf * _No ;
  [$(if,$(eq,HATCH,$(getvar,CLAYER)),~)HATCH  Off]'_LAYER +
OFf HATCH ;
  [<-HATCH On]'_LAYER _ON HATCH ;
```

Menu code for graying out or checking a menu label always goes after the opening bracket and before the label text. In this example, the $(if) expression returns "~" if HATCH is the current layer, and nothing if any other layer is current. Thus, if HATCH is current, AutoCAD reads the menu label as "~HATCH" and grays it out. If not, AutoCAD displays the label normally.

Note that when we use + to continue the menu macro on the next line, the macro text, unlike the labels, must be flush left. We show the labels indented in order to make the submenu structure clearer (this is optional). Unfortunately, we can't do the same thing with the macro, since AutoCAD will treat any additional spaces inside a menu macro as <Enter>s.

3. Add a Snap submenu with a choice for toggling Snap on and off.

We'll add a Snap cascading submenu beneath the Layer submenu.

Add the menu code shown below in italics. Save the file and test the new [Toggle Snap] option.

```
   . . .
[- -]
[->Layer]
  [* On]'_LAYER _ON * ;
  [Isolate Current]'_EXPERT 0 '_LAYER _OFf * _No ;
```

```
 [$(if,$(eq,HATCH,$(getvar,CLAYER)),~)HATCH Off]'_LAYER +
OFf HATCH ;
 [<-HATCH On]'_LAYER _ON HATCH ;
[->$(if,$(eq,1,$(getvar,SNAPMODE)),!.)Snap]
 [Toggle Snap]'_SNAP  $m=$(if,$(eq,1,$(getvar,SNAPMODE)),+
OFf,ON)
```

The Snap menu label serves as the heading for the submenu, but it also displays a check mark when Snap is turned on. The DIESEL code preceding the label is very similar to what we used for [Hatch Off], except that it queries the SNAPMODE system variable (0 = Snap off; 1 = Snap on) and concatenates "!." rather than "~" with the menu label when SNAPMODE is 1. "!." is the menu label code for a check mark (some display drivers, including TurboDLD*Lite*™, show the check mark as an X).

The [Toggle Snap] macro runs the SNAP command and then uses DIESEL to feed either OFf or ON to the command, depending on the current state of SNAPMODE.

4. Add macros for doubling and halving the Snap spacing.

In Part II, we emphasized Snap as a means of maintaining precision while minimizing picks. We also pointed out that effective use of Snap requires changing the spacing frequently as you work. To make this job easier, we'll add two macros that let you double or halve the current Snap spacing with a menu pick.

Add the menu code shown below in italics. Save ACAD.MNU and test both new Snap submenu options.

```
...
[->$(if,$(eq,1,$(getvar,SNAPMODE)),!.)Snap]
 [Toggle Snap]'_SNAP  $m=$(if,$(eq,1,$(getvar,SNAPMODE)),+
OFf,ON)
 [Snap / 2]'_SNAP $m=$(/,$(getvar,SNAPUNIT),2.0)
 [<-Snap * 2]'_SNAP $m=$(*,$(getvar,SNAPUNIT),2.0)
```

The DIESEL code for these macros should seem straightforward; it divides or multiplies the SNAPUNIT system variable (which holds the current Snap spacing) by 2. In the next step, we'll show that there are some hidden subtleties, but the version shown above will work fine for most people.

5. Streamline the Snap submenu's DIESEL code and modify it to account for unequal snap spacings.

The [Snap / 2] and [Snap * 2] macros have one undesirable character-istic that will affect people who use unequal Snap spacings. SNAPUNIT actually stores a pair of numbers representing the X and Y spacings. The macros shown in step 4 look at just the X value of SNAPUNIT, divide or multiply it by 2, and then feed the answer to the SNAP command. The result is that these macros will always leave you with an equal X and Y Snap spacing.

To make a smarter macro, we have to extract the X and Y spacings from SNAPUNIT and divide or multiply each of them by 2. Doing this requires the DIESEL $(index) function, which selects an item in a comma-delimited list. $(index), like many computer functions, starts counting at 0 rather than 1. Below, the improved version of the Snap submenu shows how to modify the macros so that they deal properly with unequal snap spacings.

```
...
[->$(if,$(getvar,SNAPMODE),!.)Snap]
  [Toggle Snap]'_SNAPMODE $m=$(if,$(getvar,SNAPMODE),0,1)
  [Snap / 2]'_SNAP _Aspect +
$m=$(/,$(index,0,$(getvar,SNAPUNIT)),2.0) +
$m=$(/,$(index,1,$(getvar,SNAPUNIT)),2.0)
  [<-Snap * 2]'_SNAP _Aspect +
$m=$(*,$(index,0,$(getvar,SNAPUNIT)),2.0) +
$m=$(*,$(index,1,$(getvar,SNAPUNIT)),2.0)
```

Make the modifications shown above in italics. Save ACAD.MNU and test all the Snap submenu options.

In the above Snap submenu, we've also made two other minor changes. First, in the [Snap] label we've changed

```
$(if,$(eq,1,$(getvar,SNAPMODE)),!.)
```

to

```
$(if,$(getvar,SNAPMODE),!.).
```

There's no need to test whether the value of SNAPMODE is equal to 1 when we can use the value of SNAPMODE (which must be either 0 or 1) directly.

The other minor change is to have the [Toggle Snap] macro set the SNAPMODE system variable to 0 or 1, rather than run the SNAP command and supply ON or OFf. There's no practical difference between these two methods, but the system variable approach is common among programmers, and it sometimes makes for a cleaner command line.

Tip

You might wonder why we didn't make a similar modification to the [Snap / 2] and [Snap * 2] macros by substituting SNAPUNIT for SNAP at the beginning of the macro. The reason involves another subtlety. The SNAP command automatically turns on Snap when you set the spacing, while the SNAPUNIT system variable does not. We assume that anyone changing the Snap spacing wants Snap on, and the SNAP command does both things, while the system variable approach would require calling both SNAPUNIT and SNAPMODE.

The finished Snap submenu is shown above in Figure 18.3.

Don't worry if the last set of modifications weren't entirely clear or seemed overly subtle. We included them to show a more refined approach, but also to point out that with all your customization, you need to decide when you reach the "good enough" stage. For most people, the goal is not to create a full-blown, professional application that accounts for every conceivable possibility. Rather, you should aim to develop menu macros and other custom components that work and are reasonably robust for your needs. If your workgroup or company never uses unequal Snap spacings, then the menu code shown above in step 4 is every bit as good as that shown in step 5. And if you save an hour by stopping at the step 4 version, that'll leave you more time to do other useful customization or maybe even billable work!

Creating a Custom Status Line

In this tutorial, we'll create a custom status line that shows the current drawing name and Snap spacing, in addition to the other information normally displayed by AutoCAD (see Figure 18.4 on page 485).

1. Experiment with some simple MODEMACRO settings.

To get a feel for how MODEMACRO works, type a few DIESEL expressions at the command line.

```
Command: MODEMACRO
New value for MODEMACRO, or . for none <default>:
$(GETVAR,SNAPUNIT)
Command: SNAP
Snap spacing or ON/OFF/Aspect/Rotate/Style <1.0000>: A
Horizontal spacing <1.0000>: .5
Vertical spacing <1.0000>: .25
```

AutoCAD now displays the X and Y Snap spacings on the status line. Note that the status line updates dynamically as you change the Snap spacing.

Use the DDUNITS or UNITS command to change to architectural units.

Notice that the status line still displays the Snap spacing in decimal units. We'll show how to fix this problem in step 3.

2. Try displaying the current time on the status line.

```
Command: MODEMACRO
New value for MODEMACRO, or . for none <default>:
$(edtime,$(getvar,DATE),HH:MM:SS)
```

AutoCAD displays the system time, but note that the clock is stopped. Try changing layers or toggling Snap and you'll see the time update. AutoCAD "refreshes" the status line only at certain predefined operations, such as mode toggles and layer changes, so **MODEMACRO** isn't much good as a status line clock.

Restore the default status line.

```
Command: MODEMACRO
New value for MODEMACRO, or . for none <default>: .
```

The period resets **MODEMACRO** to a null string, which tells AutoCAD to use its normal status line.

3. Create a **MODEMACRO** status line with the current layer, Ortho, and Snap settings.

Now we'll start building up a more useful custom status line. As mentioned in the previous section, the most practical way to do this is to use a separate .LSP file.

Create a new text file called MODEMAC.LSP and type in the code shown below.

```
;MODEMAC.LSP: AutoCAD Power Tools custom status line

(setvar "MODEMACRO" (strcat
  "$(getvar,CLAYER)"
  "$(if,$(getvar,ORTHOMODE), O, )"
  "$(if,$(getvar,SNAPMODE), S)"
))
```

Type the text, parentheses, and quotation marks carefully. We've indented the three DIESEL expression lines for clarity.

Save MODEMAC.LSP, return to AutoCAD, and then load it from the command line.

At the end of the tutorial, we'll set up MODEMAC.LSP so that it loads automatically from ACAD.LSP, but while we're testing, it's easier to load it explicitly.

```
Command: (LOAD "MODEMAC")
```

The status line now displays the current layer, Ortho, and Snap settings in a format similar to AutoCAD's default status line.

(setvar) is the AutoLISP function for setting an AutoCAD system variable; it's similar to the SETVAR command, except that you have to enclose the system variable name in quotation marks. (strcat) stands for "string concatenate," and it's the LISP function for making one big string out of smaller pieces. In this case, the pieces are individual DIESEL expressions. Each expression is enclosed in quotation marks because, unlike DIESEL, AutoLISP isn't limited to dealing with strings. LISP knows about other data types, and the quotation marks tell it explicitly that these DIESEL expressions are strings.

Test the custom status line by toggling Ortho and Snap and by changing layers.

If you see question marks or other odd characters on the status line, go back into MODEMAC.LSP and check your typing. When you return to AutoCAD, reload MODEMAC.LSP with the LISP (load) function.

4. Add the Snap spacing to MODEMAC.LSP.

Edit MODEMAC.LSP, and add the code shown below in italics. Return to AutoCAD, reload MODEMAC, and test.

```
;MODEMAC.LSP: AutoCAD Power Tools custom status line

(setvar "MODEMACRO" (strcat
  "L>"
  "$(getvar,CLAYER)"
  "$(if,$(getvar,ORTHOMODE), O, )"
  "$(if,$(getvar,SNAPMODE), S>"
    "$(rtos,$(index,0,$(getvar,SNAPUNIT))), )"
))
```

Be sure to remove the close parenthesis from the end of the "$(if,$(getvar,SNAPMODE), S" line. We've added a greater-than sign after the S in order to separate the S from the spacing. Also, we've added "L>" to the beginning of MODEMACRO in order to inform the user that the first piece of information is the current layer name. As you build a more complex and densely packed status line, these little cues help distinguish each piece of information.

Try several different UNITS settings.

AutoCAD displays the Snap spacing in the current units.

The most important change is the new line that begins "$(rtos...). We could just use $(getvar,SNAPUNIT) to display both the X and Y Snap spacing, as we did from the command line in step 1. While this approach would be easier, it takes up more of our precious status line space, so we've decided to just display the X spacing (since most people use equal X and Y spacings, anyway).

To display the X spacing, we extract the first value from the SNAPUNIT X,Y pair with $(index,0...), as we did in the [Snap /2] macro, and then convert it with the DIESEL $(rtos) function. As in AutoLISP, "rtos" stands for Real TO String, and is used to convert a real (i.e., decimal) number to a text string. This might seem like an unnecessary conversion in DIESEL, but it's helpful because $(rtos) also formats the number according to the current units settings. $(rtos) also can accept mode and precision arguments to alter the way it formats numbers; see Chapter 8 of the *AutoCAD Customization Manual* for details.

5. Create an ACAD.LSP file that loads MODEMAC.LSP automatically.

ACAD.LSP is something like AutoCAD's AUTOEXEC.BAT: It gets loaded every time AutoCAD opens a drawing (including when you first launch AutoCAD). We won't worry too much about the specifics of the code right now; just type it in with the usual attention to parentheses and quotation marks.

Create a new text file called ACAD.LSP and type in the code shown below.

```
; AutoCAD Power Tools ACAD.LSP - Chapter 18: DIESEL

(defun s::startup ()
  (load "MODEMAC")
  (princ)
)
```

As you can see, the main "action" of ACAD.LSP is to load MODEMAC, just as we were doing as we tested it. (defun) and (princ) are AutoLISP functions we'll describe in the next chapter, and S::STARTUP is a magic name that you'll also learn about then.

Save ACAD.LSP, return to AutoCAD. Test by starting a new drawing or loading an existing one.

AutoCAD should now automatically load MODEMAC.LSP and display the custom status line each time you load a drawing.

6. Add the current drawing name to the status line.

You might think that adding the drawing name to the status line would be a simple task, since AutoCAD stores the name in the DWGNAME system variable. Unfortunately, the job is complicated by the fact that DWGNAME often (but not always) includes the drawing path. The obvious problem is that a long path could eat up most of the command line (or even get truncated so that you didn't see the actual drawing name). To make matters worse, extracting just the eight-letter drawing name from the DWGNAME system variable requires taking into account that it might or might not be prefixed by the path.

If this sounds tricky, that's because it is. Even Autodesk got it wrong in their sample MODEMACRO status line in Chapter 8 of the *AutoCAD Customization Manual*. Nonetheless, we think the enhancement is useful enough to be worth struggling through, and it will give you a sense of how elaborate DIESEL expressions can become.

Edit MODEMAC.LSP and add the eight new lines of code shown below in italics. Return to AutoCAD and test by starting a new, unnamed drawing and then loading one or two existing drawings.

```
;MODEMAC.LSP: AutoCAD Power Tools custom status line

(setvar "MODEMACRO" (strcat
  "L>"
  "$(getvar,CLAYER)"
  "$(if,$(getvar,ORTHOMODE), O, )"
```

Warning

Some third-party applications require certain statements in ACAD.LSP in order to initialize properly. See the next chapter for tips on integrating your ACAD.LSP with third-party applications.

```
"$(if,$(getvar,SNAPMODE), S>"
  "$(rtos,$(index,0,$(getvar,SNAPUNIT))), )"
"$(if,$(eq,$(getvar,DWGPREFIX),"
  "$(substr,$(getvar,DWGNAME),1,"
  "$(strlen,$(getvar,DWGPREFIX)))),"
    " $(substr,$(getvar,DWGNAME),$(+,1,"
      "$(strlen,$(getvar,DWGPREFIX)))),"
    " $(getvar,DWGNAME)"
  ")"
  ".DWG"
))
```

The drawing name code relies on comparing DWGNAME with the DWGPREFIX system variable, which always contains only the drawing path. The idea is that if the first part of DWGNAME matches DWGPREFIX, then DWGNAME must contain the full path, and we need to extract the name from the end of DWGNAME. If the first part of DWGNAME doesn't match DWGPREFIX, then we assume that DWGNAME contains only the name without the path, and use it as is.

Warning

There's one inconsistency that even our complicated MODEMACRO can't get around, and that's when you type a relative rather than absolute path when loading a drawing. For instance, if the current directory is \DWGS\HERE and you open \DWGS\HERE\THERE\ MYPLAN.DWG by typing THERE\MYPLAN, the status line will display the entire relative path (THERE\MYPLAN.DWG), if it will fit.

The DIESEL code uses two new functions: $(substr) and $(strlen). The $(substr) function extracts a substring from a string, and $(strlen) calculates the number of characters in a string. Together, these functions cut up and compare strings. If you're interested in the details of how the drawing name code works, try using DIESEL.LSP to test parts of it.

7. Finish up MODEMAC.LSP.

AutoCAD's stock status line displays a P when you're in paper space, so we'd better include that functionality.

Edit MODEMAC.LSP and add the two new lines of code shown below in italics. Return to AutoCAD, reload MODEMAC, and test by setting TILEMODE to 0, making a viewport with MVIEW and changing to model space, and then setting TILEMODE back to 1.

```
;MODEMAC.LSP: AutoCAD Power Tools custom status line

(setvar "MODEMACRO" (strcat
  "L>"
  "$(getvar,CLAYER)"
  "$(if,$(getvar,ORTHOMODE), O, )"
  "$(if,$(getvar,SNAPMODE), S>"
    "$(rtos,$(index,0,$(getvar,SNAPUNIT))), )"
  "$(if,$(and,$(=,$(getvar,TILEMODE),0),"
    "$(=,$(getvar,CVPORT),1)), P)"
  "$(if,$(eq,$(getvar,DWGPREFIX),"
    "$(substr,$(getvar,DWGNAME),1,"
    "$(strlen,$(getvar,DWGPREFIX)))),"
      " $(substr,$(getvar,DWGNAME),$(+,1,"
      "$(strlen,$(getvar,DWGPREFIX)))),"
      " $(getvar,DWGNAME)"
  ")"
  ".DWG"
))
```

The "P" should display only while TILEMODE is 0 and your crosshairs extend all the way across the screen.

Two things must be true in order for you to be in paper space: TILEMODE must be 0, and the current viewport (stored in the CVPORT system variable) must be 1. The new DIESEL expression uses the $(and) function to test whether both of these things are true, and if they are, it shows "P" on the status line.

Figure 18.4 shows the completed status line in action.

As you can see, creating useful custom status lines is not a trivial process, in part because of the length limitation on the customizable area. MODEMACRO is a good test of your DIESEL skills, but you might want to save it until you've built up your repertoire by adding DIESEL expressions to menu labels and macros.

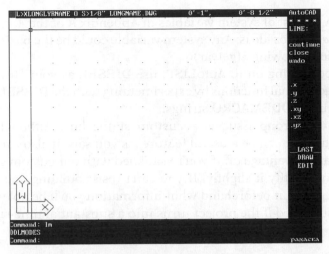

L>XLONGLYRNAME 0 S>1/8" LONGNAME.DWG   0'-1",   0'-8 1/2"   AutoCAD
* * * *
LINE:

continue
close
undo

.x
.y
.z
.xy
.xz
.yz

LAST
DRAW
EDIT

Command: ln
DDLMODES
Command: PANACEA

Figure 18.4   The custom status line in action.

Tip

The Release 12 Bonus CD includes a useful dialogue box driven utility in the \LISP\MODEMACRO subdirectory for testing, saving, and loading MODEMACRO strings.

Finishing Up

Once you've tested the menu changes and custom status line, move ACAD.MNU, ACAD.MNX, ACAD.LSP, and MODEMAC.LSP to your \ACUSTOM directory, so that they become the standard support files. Make a note of your changes, especially the ones to ACAD.MNU.

As mentioned earlier, Chapter 8 of the *AutoCAD Customization Manual* documents DIESEL, and besides the function and syntax documentation, it includes a number of useful examples. As you become more comfortable with DIESEL, look at other functions in the "Catalogue of DIESEL String Functions" section at the end of that chapter.

DIESEL and Workgroups

Most of the workgroup issues raised by DIESEL are the same ones mentioned at the end of the previous chapter on custom menus. Use DIESEL to extend the usefulness and responsiveness of your workgroup menu. Think of ways to use DIESEL to create menu enhancements such as our Snap submenu. Review the list of system variables in Appendix A of the *AutoCAD Customization Manual* for ideas: Any system variable could be the basis for a DIESEL expression involving $(getvar).

Also, if you'll be moving on to AutoLISP, use DIESEL as your "training ground." Master additional functions by experimenting with the DIESEL.LSP program or creating MODEMACRO strings.

The one new workgroup issue is a custom status line. Although the customizable status line can be a useful feature, as you saw, it also can be a complex one to take advantage of. If you're satisfied with our custom status line, use it as is or modify it slightly. If you can't resist building one from scratch, fine, but plan out beforehand what information you'll be able to fit in, and don't be surprised if the project turns into a substantial time-sink.

Summary

DIESEL is a wonderful new tool for improving menus and getting a leg up on LISP. Its strengths are its comparative simplicity and the ability to do some things (such as menu label and status line customization) that are difficult or impossible with AutoLISP. On the other hand, DIESEL works best and is easiest to debug with short, less complex expressions. DIESEL has many limitations, and it's no match for LISP when you need to write real programs. Also, DIESEL's interface to LISP is rather poor; it can't directly read AutoLISP variables.

When you hit the customization wall with DIESEL, it's time to jump over to AutoLISP, and that's the subject of the next chapter. Fortunately, the path will look familiar in many ways.

19

AutoLISP

AutoLISP is AutoCAD's "workhorse" programming language, because it combines flexibility with relative accessibility. Despite the advent of ADS in Release 11, AutoLISP remains the language of choice for most AutoCAD customization, because it's much easier to learn and use and almost as powerful for most people's purposes.

You can get started with AutoLISP by using it in menu macros, in the same way in which we used DIESEL expresssions in the last chapter. But AutoLISP can do much more. With it, you can write programs that extend AutoCAD's capabilities in a wide range of ways. You can develop robust utility programs that streamline often-repeated command sequences and that look just like core AutoCAD commands. You can create discipline-specific parametric programs that draw components based on parameters supplied by the user or taken from a database. You even can automate drawing start-up procedures such as updating title block data.

A number of AutoCAD's most useful commands, including DDMODIFY, DLINE, and CHTEXT, are written in AutoLISP, and most of the code that makes up third-party application software is still AutoLISP (although more and more application code is being written in ADS, especially where computational speed is important). In addition, there are thousands of shareware and freeware utilities written in LISP. In fact, AutoLISP can be thought of as the "engine" that has driven the entire industry that's grown up around AutoCAD.

AutoLISP is good for any customization job that requires more muscle than is available with scripts or menu macros (including DIESEL). Scripts and menu macros work well for rote command sequences, and DIESEL adds limited decision-making and calculation abilities to menu macros. But if you use these features for long, you'll soon bump up against their limitations. AutoLISP is appropriate when your custom commands need the capability to do more complex decision-making, more involved arithmetic, and more robust interaction with the user. LISP also is the way to go when you need to use variables to store, manipulate, and retrieve values.

AutoLISP's disadvantages depend upon your perspective. It's considerably more complex than scripts or menus, so the learning curve for it is longer. AutoLISP is a relatively simple and forgiving programming language, though, and it doesn't take too much effort to begin modifying existing programs or writing your own short but useful utlities. For programmers at the other end of the customization spectrum, AutoLISP has two obvious limitations: LISP is slow compared to ADS, and its file input/output capabilities are constrained to sequential access of text files. These limitations won't affect most people who do in-house customization, and we reserve a more detailed discussion for the end of the chapter.

About This Chapter

This chapter introduces AutoLISP, clarifies some of the finer points that can be confusing at first, and then presents some useful applications. Our goal is not to cover every aspect of AutoLISP, which we obviously can't do in one chapter, but to get you started using LISP and give you enough background to understand and use the *AutoLISP Programmer's Reference Manual*. Once you have a basic understanding of AutoLISP, it will serve you well as you expand your knowledge of LISP.

This chapter presents a lot of information. If you're new to LISP (and especially if you're new to programming), start by reading through the chapter quickly for a general understanding. After you've gone through the tutorials and perhaps worked on a few small LISP programs, come back to the conceptual and descriptive portions of the chapter; they'll make more sense once you have a context in which to place them. After that, you'll be ready to proceed with more complicated tasks, using this chapter and the *AutoLISP Programmer's Reference Manual* for reference.

An AutoLISP Primer

LISP (the "LISt Processing" or "LISt Programming" language) was developed by John McCarthy at MIT's Artificial Intelligence Project in the late 1950s. LISP quickly became the preferred language of artificial intelligence research because of its flexibility and elegance. In the mid-1980s, Autodesk chose XLISP, a LISP interpreter by David Betz, as the basis for its new AutoLISP customization language, which debuted in Version 2.18.

Why did Autodesk choose LISP, with its roots in mathematical logic and its branches in the rarefied air of AI research, as the basis of AutoCAD's primary programming language? The *AutoLISP Programmer's Reference Manual* lists several reasons, but perhaps the most compelling reasons are the ones that first drew AI researchers to LISP: flexibility and elegance. LISP is flexible in the sense that it deals well with heterogeneous collections of objects, which are what AutoCAD stores and manipulates. LISP is elegant in the sense that its data and procedures ("program code") have the same form. These qualities will become apparent as you work with AutoLISP.

Variables and Expressions

AutoLISP began life in AutoCAD Version 2.0 as a more limited feature called "variables and expressions," and those two terms describe AutoLISP in a nutshell. As in DIESEL, AutoLISP program statements are called *expressions*, and they comprise functions and the data on which the functions operate. An important distinction between DIESEL and AutoLISP, though, is that LISP recognizes data types other than text strings.

As in any programming language, AutoLISP *variables* are symbols you use to store numbers, strings, or other data. Like AutoCAD's system variables, AutoLISP variables keep track of different values that the program might want to use for various purposes. The difference is that system variables have fixed names and purposes, while LISP variables can have almost any name and purpose you decide upon. This is one of the reasons AutoLISP is so much more flexible than DIESEL: DIESEL is limited to AutoCAD's system variables, while LISP can operate on variables that you name and manipulate as you wish.

Tip

In LISP, variables are often called *symbols*, expressions are called *symbolic expressions*, and LISP itself is referred to as a *symbol manipulation language*. A symbol (or variable) is said to be *bound* to its value. Although the terminology may seem strange at first, it's helpful to be acquainted with it, because the *AutoLISP Programmer's Reference Manual* and other books sometimes will use it.

Functions and Arguments

AutoLISP *functions* are very similar to DIESEL functions (in fact, many of them even have the same name). Functions are fed strings, numbers, variables, and other data in the form of *arguments*, and then, these functions send back, or *return*, other values. Refer to the "Functions and Syntax" section of Chapter 18, *DIESEL*, if you're unfamiliar with this process.

A prototypical LISP function looks like this:

```
(function argument1 argument2 ...)
```

For example, a function that returns the distance between two points looks like this:

```
(distance point1 point2)
```

As in DIESEL, the AutoLISP function and its arguments are enclosed in parentheses, and the function name always comes first. In AutoLISP, though, there's no dollar sign preceding the open parenthesis, and spaces, rather than commas, are used as delimiters.

A function that's built into AutoLISP is called a *Subr* (short for "subroutine") and is distinguished from functions that you or another programmer define. AutoLISP includes about 170 Subrs, but fortunately you can get started writing useful programs with a small subset of these.

Much of the power of AutoLISP comes from the ability it gives you to define your own functions with the (defun), or "define function," function. We'll describe (defun) and show examples later in the chapter.

Data Types

Unlike DIESEL, AutoLISP recognizes 10 different data types, as described in Table 19.1. LISP functions (or Subrs) expect their arguments to be of a specific type, and if you feed them anything else, they complain with a "bad argument type" error message. For instance, the (+) function requires integer or real-number arguments, while (substr) requires a text string. You'll see the "bad argument type" error message a lot as you begin writing AutoLISP programs, so get in the habit of paying attention to data types, especially the data types of the variables you define. The syntax for each function, given in the *AutoLISP Programmer's Reference Manual*, will tell you what types of arguments the function expects.

Most of the data types listed in Table 19.1 are part of XLISP and other implementations of LISP, but a few are unique to AutoLISP. Of special note are entity names and selection sets, since these are the data types your AutoLISP programs will use to manipulate AutoCAD entities.

Table 19.1 The 10 AutoLISP Data Types

Data type	Description	Examples
String	Text	"Hello, world." "foo"
Integer	Whole number	3 – 47 0
Real number	Decimal number	3.0 – 47.0 0.0 365.25
Symbol	Variable name	foo myvar point1 i
List	Collection of atoms or other lists	(1 2 3) ("Yes" "No")
Entity name	Single AutoCAD entity	<Entity name: 600000044>
Selection set	Collection of AutoCAD entities	<Selection set: 3>
Subr	Built-in function	getvar setq findfile
External Subr	Function defined by ADS program	acad_strlsort c:bhatch
File descriptor	External file opened by AutoLISP	<File: #5269e>

ENTITY NAMES

Every AutoCAD drawing is actually a database whose "records" are drawing entities. When AutoLISP programs refer to an AutoCAD entity, they must use a special hexadecimal numeric label called an "entity name," which is similar to a record number in a database. AutoCAD assigns entity names automatically, and they can change between drawing sessions. AutoLISP provides 11 functions, most of which start with (ent...), for obtaining and using entity names.

SELECTION SETS

AutoLISP programs, like AutoCAD users, often find it convenient to operate on groups of entities, or selection sets. To make this possible, AutoLISP includes a special selection set data type and functions unique to it. There are six selection set functions, all of which begin with (ss...).

Atoms, Lists, and Dotted Pairs

Although AutoLISP recognizes 10 different data types, a more fundamental categorization is between atoms and lists. Everything in LISP is one or the other. An *atom* is the indivisible unit in LISP. A *list* is simply a collection of atoms gathered between parentheses. Here are some atoms:

```
2    "Hello, world."   1.4141   foo   +   car
```

and here are some lists:

```
(1.0 2.54 0.0)    ("Flip" "Flop" "Fly")
(+ 2 2)    ((left right) (top bottom))
(cdr (assoc 8 (entget (car (entsel)))))
```

Of fundamental importance is the fact that LISP lists can be nested. Nesting can indicate the structure of data lists, as in the ((left right) (top bottom)) example, but more often nesting is used to feed the value returned by one function as data to the function at the next higher level, as in the last example. We nested DIESEL functions in the same way, but you'll find that AutoLISP programs are nested much more deeply.

LISP uses a special kind of list called a *dotted pair* that turns out to be very common in AutoLISP programs. Dotted pairs are similar to a normal two-atom list, except that AutoLISP displays them with a period between the two atoms:

```
(A B)                    ordinary list
(A . B)                  dotted pair
```

The period in the middle indicates that a dotted pair is treated in a unique way by LISP. Dotted pairs appear, among other places, in entity data lists (see below).

The (command) Connection

AutoLISP and AutoCAD can be thought of as two separate programs that exchange information. One of the most common ways for AutoLISP to talk to AutoCAD is with the (command) function. (command) feeds its arguments to the AutoCAD Command: prompt, just as if you'd typed them interactively or from a script. The difference is that (command) expressions can include variables and other expressions, which make AutoLISP's (command) function much more flexible than scripts.

The simplest way to use (command) is to feed it strings, like so:

```
(command "LINE" "1,1" "2.5,4.5")
```

Of course in this case you could accomplish the same result as easily with a script, but most (command) expressions are more elaborate than this one.

Chapters 2 and 4 of the *AutoLISP Programmer's Reference Manual* describe the rules for using (command). We'll present some practical examples later in this chapter.

Entity Data

The entity names described above uniquely identify entities, but often an AutoLISP program needs to know more about an entity than just its name. An entity's type, layer, defining points, and other characteristics are called "entity data," and these data are like the additional field values in a database record. Shown below are the entity data for two common entities. Note that the entity data are lists composed of sublists, and that many of the sublists are stored as dotted pairs. In each sublist, the first number is called the *DXF group code*, and it functions like a database field name: 0 is the field describing the entity's type, 1 is the field describing its layer, and so on. Note that different types of entities contain different numbers and types of DXF groups.

A Line:

```
((-1 . <Entity name: 600000aa>) ;entity name
 (0 . "LINE")                   ;entity type
 (8 . "WALL")                   ;layer
 (10 5.90241 5.74441 0.0)       ;beginning point
 (11 11.163 6.6243 0.0)         ;ending point
 (210 0.0 0.0 1.0)              ;extrusion direction
)
```

A Text String:

```
((-1 . <Entity name: 600000cc>) ;entity name
 (0 . "TEXT")                   ;entity type
 (8 . "NOTES")                  ;layer
 (10 1.34661 4.41201 0.0)       ;insertion point
 (40 . 0.2)                     ;height
 (1 . "Hello, world.")          ;text string
 (50 . 0.0)                     ;rotation angle
 (41 . 1.0)                     ;width factor
 (51 . 0.0)                     ;obliquing angle
 (7 . "STANDARD")               ;text style
 (71 . 0)                       ;backward and upside-down flags
 (72 . 0)                       ;horizontal alignment
 (11 0.0 0.0 0.0)               ;alignment point
 (210 0.0 0.0 1.0)              ;extrusion direction
 (73 . 0)                       ;vertical alignment
)
```

AutoLISP provides the (entget) function for extracting and the (entmod) function for modifying entity data based on an entity name. Chapter 3 of the *AutoLISP Programmer's Reference Manual* describes entity names and data in detail, and it's worth your while to review this information as you become more familiar with AutoLISP. The "Entity Data Functions" section includes a useful LISP program that prints the entity data for the last entity drawn.

 Tip

Appendix B of the *AutoLISP Programmer's Reference Manual* documents the DXF group codes for each type of entity.

Symbol Table Access

An AutoCAD drawing contains more than just entities; it also includes *symbol tables* that store layers, text and dimension styles, named views, Block Definitions, and other "named objects." See the "Purging for Experts" section of Chapter 10, *Xrefs, Blocks, and Attributes*, for a complete list of these symbol tables.

AutoLISP programs sometimes need to search through symbol tables in order to extract or modify data for named objects. For instance, a program might want to check whether a certain layer exists or to redefine a particular Block Definition. The data describing a symbol table entry looks much like an entity data list, as shown below.

A Layer:
```
((0 . "LAYER")            ;table entry type
 (2 . "JUNK")             ;layer name
 (70 . 64)                ;referenced, freeze/thaw, and
                          ; lock/unlock status
 (62 . 2)                 ;color
 (6 . "CONTINUOUS")       ;linetype
)
```

A Text Style:
```
((0 . "STYLE")            ;table entry type
 (2 . "STANDARD")         ;style name
 (70 . 0)                 ;referenced and vertical status
 (40 . 0.0)               ;text height
 (41 . 1.0)               ;width factor
```

```
(50 . 0.0)              ;obliquing angle
(71 . 0)                ;backward and upside-down flags
(42 . 0.2)              ;last height used
(3 . "txt")             ;primary font filename
(4 . "")                ;big-font filename
)
```

AutoLISP provides functions for searching (tblsearch) and stepping through (tblnext) symbol tables, as described in Chapter 3 of the *AutoLISP Programmer's Reference Manual*. The TABLES.LSP sample program (located in \ACAD\SAMPLE) uses these functions to display the contents of all nine symbol tables.

Tip
Don't confuse AutoCAD symbol tables with AutoLISP symbols. Symbol tables are "bookkeeping" areas in AutoCAD drawing files. Symbols are AutoLISP program variables that are stored in memory.

Experimenting with AutoLISP Functions

To get a feel for how AutoLISP functions work, try the following tutorial and compare the input and results to the similar steps in Chapter 18, *DIESEL*. Figure 19.1 shows part of the tutorial sequence as it would appear on the AutoCAD text screen.

```
                     AutoCAD Text - UNNAMED
4
Command: (GETVAR "DWGNAME")
"UNNAMED"

Command: (+ DOG CAT)
error: bad argument type
(+ DOG CAT)
*Cancel*

Command: (SETVAR "DWGNAME" "MYPLAN")
error: AutoCAD rejected function
(SETVAR "DWGNAME" "MYPLAN")
*Cancel*

Command: (LOAD "CHTEXT"

1> )

        c:CHText loaded.  Start command with CHT.
Command: (GETVAR "SNAPMODE")
0

Command: (EQUAL 0 (GETVAR "SNAPMODE"))
T

Command: (EQUAL 1 (GETVAR "SNAPMODE"))
nil

Command: (IF (EQUAL 1 (GETVAR "SNAPMODE")) "IT'S ON" "IT'S OFF")
"IT'S OFF"

Command: (SETQ INT1 4)
```

Figure 19.1   A sample session with AutoLISP.

1. Start AutoCAD and try a couple of functions.

We don't need to run a special program to get AutoCAD to recognize AutoLISP expressions (as we had to with DIESEL). The opening parenthesis warns AutoCAD that what follows is LISP rather than a normal command.

```
Command: (+ 2 2)
4
Command: (GETVAR "DWGNAME")
"UNNAMED"
```

Every LISP expression returns a value, which AutoCAD displays on the line below after you press <Enter>.

2. See what happens when you type something wrong.

```
Command: (+ DOG CAT)
error: bad argument type
(+ DOG CAT)
*Cancel*
```

When AutoLISP detects an error, it reports an error message, the expression in which the error was detected, and then *Cancel*.

```
Command: (SETVAR "DWGNAME" "MYPLAN")
error: AutoCAD rejected function
(SETVAR "DWGNAME" "MYPLAN")
*Cancel*
```

In this instance, AutoLISP is telling you that AutoCAD refused to accept your instruction—in this case, because the DWGNAME system variable is read-only.

```
Command: (LOAD "CHTEXT"
1>
```

If you omit a parenthesis—easy to do in any form of LISP—or quotation mark, AutoLISP responds with the prompt $n>$, where n indicates the number of missing close parentheses (and/or quotation marks). Depending on what you left off and where, you may be able to just type it in. Type the closing parenthesis:

```
1>)
c:CHText loaded. Start command with CHT.
```

In other cases, you have to cancel with <Ctrl>+C and try again.

3. Try a nested function.

```
Command: (GETVAR "SNAPMODE")
0
Command: (EQUAL 0 (GETVAR "SNAPMODE"))
T
Command: (EQUAL 1 (GETVAR "SNAPMODE"))
nil
```

This example demonstrates another important difference between LISP and DIESEL. In DIESEL, false and true were represented by 0 and non-zero (usually 1). In LISP, false and true are represented by nil and non-nil. LISP treats anything other than the atom nil as true, and by convention, the uppercase letter "T" often is used.

```
Command: (IF (EQUAL 1 (GETVAR "SNAPMODE"))
"IT'S ON" "IT'S OFF")
"IT'S OFF"
```

4. Experiment with variables and getting user input.

```
Command: (SETQ INT1 4)
4
Command: (SETQ INT2 7)
7
```

(setq) is LISP's function for assigning a value to a variable. These steps stored the integers 4 and 7 in the variables int1 and int2, respectively. Note that (setq) returns the value of the variable. Now add the two variables:

```
Command: (+ INT1 INT2)
11
```

LISP returns the sum.

Try prompting the user for a point and storing it in a variable:

```
Command: (SETQ PT1 (GETPOINT "PICK A POINT:"))
PICK A POINT: do so
(8.0 3.0 0.0)
```

(getpoint) waits for the user to pick a point and then returns the point's X, Y, and Z coordinates as a list. Your point's coordinates will be different, of course.

```
Command: (SETQ PT2 (GETPOINT "PICK ANOTHER POINT:"))
PICK ANOTHER POINT: do so
(12.5 6.25 0.0)
```

Again, the point you pick will have different coordinates. Now use the (command) function to draw a line between the points.

```
Command: (COMMAND "LINE" PT1 PT2 "")
Command: nil
```

AutoCAD draws a line between the points. The final pair of quotation marks acts like <Enter> and ends the LINE command. The subsequent nil comes from LISP; (command) always returns nil.

5. Experiment with an entity name and entity data.

Many AutoLISP programs work with entity names and entity data. The steps required to do so will seem strange at first, but they'll become natural as you work with AutoLISP more.

Make a new layer called WALL and draw a line.

Use the (entsel) function to store the line's entity name in the variable ename:

```
Command: (SETQ ENAME (ENTSEL))
Select object: pick the line
(<Entity name: 600004ea> (8.75 1.5 0.0))
```

(entsel) (ENTity SELect) returns a list containing the entity name of the line and the coordinates you used to pick it (your entity name and point will be different). Use (car) to extract the entity name from the list:

```
Command: (SETQ ENAME (CAR ENAME))
<Entity name: 600004ea>
```

(car) returns the first element in a list. Now extract the line's entity data with (entget) and save it in the variable edata:

```
Command: (SETQ EDATA (ENTGET ENAME))
((-1 . <Entity name: 600004ea>) (0 . "LINE") (8 . "WALL")
(10 8.25 1.0 0.0) (11 12.5 5.5 0.0) (210 0.0 0.0 1.0))
```

(entget) (ENTity data GET) returns the entity's data as a nested list (compare the entity data for a Line and a string of Text shown earlier in this chapter).

Your LISP program might be interested in the entity's layer. Use (assoc) to extract the dotted pair that begins with DXF group code 8 (the layer code):

```
Command: (SETQ ELYR (ASSOC 8 EDATA))
(8 . "WALL")
```

(assoc) looks for a sublist that begins with the first argument (8 in this case) and returns the sublist.

Now use (cdr) to obtain just the layer name, without the group code:

```
Command: (SETQ ELYR (CDR (ELYR)))
"WALL"
```

(cdr) is the complement to (car); (cdr) returns everything in a list *except* the first element. In a dotted pair, the only thing besides the first element is the second element, so (cdr) returns just that element.

You can query a variable's value from the AutoCAD Command: prompt by typing the variable's name preceded by an exclamation point:

```
Command: !ELYR
"WALL"
```

An AutoLISP Function Minicatalogue

In this section, we present a minicatalogue of 32 functions that will get you started using AutoLISP in menus and separate programs. Optional arguments are shown in [square brackets]. Refer to the listings and reference in Chapter 4 of the *AutoLISP Programmer's Manual* for more information about these and other functions.

ARITHMETIC FUNCTIONS

- (+ *num1 num2*)
- (− *num1 num2*)
- (* *num1 num2*)
- (/ *num1 num2*)

These four functions perform the four basic arithmetic operations. Each function takes two (or more) numbers as arguments and returns the result of the operation applied to those numbers. Example:

```
(+ 0.5 0.25)
```

returns 0.75.

Warning

The division function (/) performs integer division when both of its arguments are integers. This means that (/ 10 4) returns 2, not 2.5. If you want to prevent values from being truncated in this way, just make sure that at least one of the arguments is a decimal number: (/ 10.0 4) returns 2.5.

SYSTEM VARIABLE FUNCTIONS

- (getvar *varname*)

- (setvar *varname new_value*)

(getvar) and (setvar) get and set the value of AutoCAD system variables. Both functions return the value of *varname*. Example:

```
(setvar CLAYER "WALL")
```

makes WALL the current layer (if it exists) and returns the string "WALL."

EQUALITY FUNCTION

- (equal *val1 val2*)

(equal) tests whether its two arguments are equal, and returns T if they are and nil if they aren't. The arguments aren't limited to integers or real numbers; they can be, for example, strings or lists. Example:

```
(equal "WALL" (getvar CLAYER))
```

returns T if WALL is the current layer, and nil otherwise.

Tip

AutoLISP includes three "equal to" Subrs: (=), (eq), and (equal). (equal) is the most flexible and least confusing function for beginners. Avoid using (eq) until you understand what it means in LISP for a variable to be *bound* to an object.

ASSIGNMENT FUNCTION

- `(setq varname value)`

(setq) (SET Quote) assigns *value* to the variable *varname*. It returns *value*. Example:

`(setq myvar 1.414)`

Tip

(setq) is different from the (set) function, which you shouldn't use until you have a deeper understanding of LISP. Briefly, the q for Quote in (setq) tells LISP not to evaluate the variable name, but to accept it as is. If you accidentally type (set) rather than (setq), you'll most likely see a "bad argument type" error.

COMMAND FUNCTION

- `(command acad_commands...)`

(command) feeds all its arguments to AutoCAD, which attempts to carry them out as if you'd typed them at the Command: prompt. Use two quotation marks for <Enter> and use the symbol *pause* to pause for user input. Example:

`(command "LINE" "0,0" pt1 pause "")`

draws a line from 0,0 to pt1 (assumed to be a point variable) to a point the user picks, and then ends the LINE command.

Tip

(command) without any arguments acts like <Ctrl>+C.

USER INPUT FUNCTIONS

- `(getpoint [basepoint] [prompt])`
- `(getcorner basepoint [prompt])`

(getpoint) and (getcorner) both obtain a point from the user. They display the *prompt*, wait for the user to pick (or type the coordinates of) a point, and then return the point as a list of three real numbers. *basepoint* is a reference point; (getpoint) shows a rubberband line from *basepoint*, while (getcorner) shows a box, as if you were selecting objects or zooming with a window. Example:

```
(setq pt1 (getpoint "Where do you want it?"))
```

prompts the user, waits for a point, and then stores it in variable pt1.

- (getstring *[spaces_allowed] [prompt]*)

(getstring) obtains a text string that the user types. If the [spaces_allowed] argument is present and non-nil, the spacebar is treated as a space in the string, rather than as <Enter>. Example:

```
(setq uname (getstring T "State your name:"))
```

prompts the user, waits for a string, and then stores it in the variable uname. Because of the T argument, the string can contain spaces.

- (getdist *[basepoint] [prompt]*)

- (getangle *[basepoint] [prompt]*)

(getdist) and (getangle) obtain a distance and an angle, respectively, from the user. They work similarly to (getpoint), except that they return a single number rather than a list of coordinates. (getangle) returns the angle in radians rather than degrees. Example:

```
(setq ds1 (getdist "How long?: "))
```

prompts the user, waits for a distance, and then stores it in variable ds1.

Tip
180 degrees equals π (approximately 3.14) radians. To convert from radians to degrees, use (*/* (* *radians* 180) pi). To convert from degrees to radians, use (*/* (* *degrees* pi) 180). The symbol pi is predefined in AutoLISP.

GEOMETRIC FUNCTIONS

- (distance *point1 point2*)

(distance) returns the distance between two points. Example:

```
(distance '(0 0 0) (getvar "LASTPOINT"))
```

returns the distance between the drawing origin and the last point the user picked.

- (angle *point1 point2*)

(angle) returns the angle in radians between two points. The angle is measured from the X axis of the current UCS. Example:

```
(angle '(0 0 0) (getvar "LASTPOINT"))
```

returns the angle of an imaginary line running from the drawing origin to the last point the user selected.

- (polar *basepoint angle distance*)

(polar) returns the point located at *angle* and *distance* from the *basepoint*. *angle* is in radians. Example:

```
(polar '(1.0 1.25 0.0) (/ pi 4) 2.5)
```

returns the point located at an angle of 45 degrees (= π/4 radians) and the distance of 2.5 units from the point (1.0,1.25).

 Tip

In the above examples, the single quotation mark is required before the point lists. As LISP evaluates an expression, it assumes that the first element in a list is a function. The single quotation mark tells LISP not to treat the list as a function, but to pass it on to the next higher-level function as is. Or, in LISP-speak, "quote inhibits evaluation." If we'd left out the quote, AutoLISP would think 1.0 was supposed to be a function name and report "bad function."

It takes some time to understand quoting in LISP. For now, just remember to use (setq) rather than (set), and to put a single quotation mark before point lists.

LIST-HANDLING FUNCTIONS

- (car *list*)

(car) returns the first element of a list. Example:

```
(car '(1.0 2.25 0.0))
```

returns 1.0.

- (cdr *list*)

(cdr) returns all but the first element of a list. If *list* is an ordinary list, (cdr) returns a list stripped of its first element, but if *list* is a dotted pair, (cdr) returns the second item as a separate element (i.e., not in a list). Examples:

```
(cdr '(1.0 2.25 0.0))
```

returns (2.25 0.0), but:

```
(cdr '(40 . 2.25)
```

returns 2.25 without parentheses.

Tip

(car) and (cdr) are acronyms for "Contents of the Address part of the Register" and "Contents of the Decrement part of the Register." These odd terms refer to hardware features of an ancient IBM computer on which LISP was first implemented.

- (cadr *list*)

(cadr) returns the second element of a list. Example:

```
(cadr '("Fee" "Fie" "Foe" "Fum"))
```

returns "Fie."

- (assoc *search_for list*)

(assoc) searches a so-called *association list* for a sublist beginning with the value *search_for* and, if it finds a match, returns the sublist. Association lists are of the form ((*key1 . value1*) (*key2 . value2*) (*key3 . value3*) ...). An entity data list is one common type of association list (see the entity data for a Line and a string of Text shown earlier in this chapter). Example:

```
(assoc 8 '((0 . "LINE") (8 . "WALL")))
```

returns (8 . "WALL").

- (list *element1 element2* ...)

(list) assembles a list out of individual elements. Example:

```
(list 1.25 6.5 0.0)
```

returns (1.25 6.5 0.0), which could be supplied as a point to the (command) function.

SCREEN OUTPUT FUNCTIONS

- (princ *what_to_display*)

(princ) displays *what_to_display* on the command line. *what_to_display* can be a string or other expression (including a variable name). Literal strings must be included in quotation marks and usually should start with "\n," a special code that causes AutoCAD to begin a new line before displaying the string.

```
(princ "\nThis is a test.")
```

starts a new line below the Command: prompt and displays "This is a test."

Tip

AutoLISP includes other screen output functions, including (print) and (prompt), but (princ) is the most appropriate and flexible function for beginners.

CONDITIONAL FUNCTIONS

- (if *test then else*)

(if) inspects the value returned by *test*, and if it's non-nil, evaluates the *then* expression. If *test* is nil, (if) evaluates the *else* expression instead. *then* and *else* are limited to a single expression each. Example:

```
(if (equal "WALL" (getvar CLAYER))
  (command "DLINE")
  (command "LINE")
)
```

runs DLINE if WALL is the current layer, and runs LINE otherwise.

Tip

If you want to include more than one expression for *then* or *else*, wrap all the expressions inside the function (progn). See (progn) in the *AutoLISP Programmer's Reference Manual* for details.

- (cond *(test1 do1)* *(test2 do2)* (T *do_else*)...)

(cond) (CONDitional) is like a "super-if": It lets you have as many tests as you like. If *test1* is non-nil, then (cond) evaluates *do1*. If *test1* is nil but *test2* is non-nil, then (cond) evaluates *do2*. *do1*, *do2*, etc. can be one or more expressions. Often a (cond) expression will end with the test T, which always is non-nil, and thus acts like an *else*. The only trick is keeping track of all the parentheses. Example:

```
(cond
  ((equal "WALL" (getvar CLAYER))
    (command "DLINE")
  )
  ((equal "ROAD" (getvar CLAYER))
    (command "ARC")
  )
  (T
    (command "LINE")
  )
)
```

runs DLINE if WALL is the current layer, ARC if ROAD is the current layer, and LINE otherwise.

- (while *test do_again*)

(while) checks whether *test* is non-nil, and if so, evaluates *do_again*, which can be one or more expressions. After *do_again*, (while) checks *test* again, and if it's still non-nil, reevaluates *do_again*. This loop continues until *test* is nil, so make sure that an expression inside the loop changes *test* to nil at some point. Example:

```
(while (not (equal password "SWORDFISH"))
  (setq password
    (getstring "What's the password?:"))
)
```

repeatedly prompts the user for a password until SWORDFISH is typed.

ENTITY DATA AND SELECTION SET FUNCTIONS

- (entsel *[prompt]*)

(entsel) (ENTity SELect) obtains an entity that the user picks. It returns a list containing two elements: the entity name and point used to select the entity. Example:

```
(setq ent1 (entsel "Select an entity: "))
```

- `(entget` *entity_name*`)`

(entget) (ENTity data GET) returns the entity data associated with *entity_name*. The entity data are returned as a nested list. Example:

```
(entget (car (entsel "Select an entity: ")))
```

returns the entity data for a selected entity in a form similar to that in the entity data for a Line and a string of Text shown earlier in this chapter.

- `(ssget)`

(ssget) (Selection Set GET) obtains a selection set from the user. It returns a selection set in a form that can be used by AutoCAD commands. Example:

```
(setq ss1 (ssget "Select objects: "))
(command "ERASE" ss1 "")
```

mimics AutoCAD's ERASE command.

Tip

(ssget) has many other capabilities, including the ability to select entities based on their characteristics (layer, entity type, Block name, etc.). See Chapter 4 of the *AutoLISP Programmer's Reference Manual* for details.

DEFINE FUNCTION FUNCTION

- `(defun` *func_name* `(`*[arguments]* `/` *[local_vars]*`)`
  expressions...
  `)`

(defun) (DEfine FUNction) allows you to create your own LISP functions and AutoCAD-like commands. *func_name* is the name of the new function. If it begins with C:, then the function acts like an AutoCAD command and can be typed at the Command: prompt (C: stands for "Command:" and has nothing to do with DOS drive letter designations). If *func_name* does not begin with C:, then the new function acts like a LISP Subr.

arguments are one or more arguments that your LISP-like function requires (C: functions can't use arguments). *local_vars* are a list of variable names used in the new function. The variables listed here remain *local* to the function, which means that they can't conflict with variables of the same name that other functions might happen to use. Any variable names used by the program but not listed in *local_vars* are global. This means that they retain their value even when the function isn't running. It also means that there's the possibility of a conflict if another LISP function happens to rely on a global variable of the same name.

expressions... are the program statements that make up the function. Example:

```
(defun C:TEXTEDIT (/ oteval en ed etype)
  expressions...
)
```

defines a new AutoCAD command-like function called TEXTEDIT and defines the variables oteval, en, ed, and etype as local. *expressions...* stands for the actual program statements (as in the completed TEXTEDIT routine shown at the end of the chapter).

LOAD FUNCTION

- `(load LSPname)`

(load) loads the file *LSPname*.LSP into memory. (load) searches the normal AutoCAD search path (see Chapter 14, *Getting Ready to Customize*, for details). Example:

```
(load "CHTEXT")
```

AutoLISP Techniques

Most AutoLISP code appears in separate .LSP or .MNL files, but you also can include LISP expressions in menu macros (though not in menu labels). In this section, we discuss the different ways of using LISP and some techniques for debugging.

AutoLISP in Menus

Before DIESEL, menu customizers relied solely on AutoLISP to create more powerful menu macros. In fact, we even used a bit of LISP in our [ChText] macro in Chapter 17, *Menus*. Adding LISP to menus is a good way to get started, because you can create useful macros with only a few functions and it's a natural step from DIESEL. Including LISP expressions in menu macros is simply a matter of typing them into the .MNU file. The open parenthesis tells AutoCAD to hand off the expression to AutoLISP, and once LISP has performed the necessary computations, it feeds the answer back to AutoCAD. We'll show examples of using LISP in menus later in the chapter.

When should you use AutoLISP expressions in menus and when should you stick with DIESEL? In many cases, the choice is arbitrary, and seasoned LISP programmers will favor AutoLISP, while those who learned DIESEL first will lean toward it. There is a reason to use DIESEL when you can, though, especially for macros that can be executed transparently (such as our Snap macros from Chapter 18, *DIESEL*).

AutoLISP is not *reentrant*, which means that LISP expressions in a menu macro can't be used when another LISP program is running. If you're running Autodesk's DLINE.LSP, for instance, and you pick a menu choice that contains LISP code, AutoLISP will report "can't reenter AutoLISP." DIESEL doesn't have this problem. On the other hand, AutoLISP is much more powerful than DIESEL, and there will be situations where you won't have any choice about which to use. We'll show an example in an upcoming tutorial.

Once you become comfortable with incorporating LISP code in menu macros, it's easy to generate long and involved menu macros that span several lines and include deeply nested expressions (the Release 11 ACAD.MNU contains several choice examples). The resulting macros may work well, but they're difficult to decipher and debug, and they can make your .MNU files huge. The Release 11 ACAD.MNU was over 200 Kb—twice as large as the one that comes with Release 12!

Release 12 helps address this problem with a new kind of .LSP file called .MNL (MeNu Lisp). An .MNL file can contain AutoLISP expressions and function definitions. In fact, it's no different from an ordinary .LSP file, except that the .MNL extension is a "magic" one. Before AutoCAD loads a menu, it looks for an .MNL file with the same name, and if it finds one, loads that first. (See Chapter 14, *Getting Ready to Customize*, for more information on AutoCAD's load sequence.) By segregating long segments of LISP code in an .MNL file, you'll keep your .MNU file more manageable and make debugging easier. AutoCAD includes a stock ACAD.MNL that defines about a dozen LISP functions used by ACAD.MNU. We'll add a new function to ACAD.MNL in one of the forthcoming tutorials.

AutoLISP in .LSP Files

.LSP (and .MNL) files can contain three types of things: function definitions, stand-alone expressions, and comments. (The LISP routine developed in this chapter's final tutorial, shown in the completed TEXTEDIT routine at the end of this chapter, contains all three). Most .LSP files begin with a series of comment lines describing the name, purpose, and author of the file, along with any other general comments, such as copyright information or instructions on how to use the file. Comments in LISP begin with a semicolon, as they do in scripts and ACAD.PGP.

The bulk of most .LSP files comprises one or more function definitions wrapped inside (defun ...)s. When you load the .LSP file, each (defun ...) defines a new function in memory, but doesn't actually evaluate (or "execute") it. As mentioned earlier, if the function name (the first argument after defun) starts with "C:," then the function is defined as a command that the user can type just like an AutoCAD command. If the function name doesn't start with "C:," then the function acts like one of AutoLISP's built-in Subrs, and can be used by LISP programs.

In some cases, .LSP files will contain LISP expressions outside of (defun)s. AutoLISP evaluates these expressions immediately when the file loads. You can get as fancy as you wish, mixing multiple (defun)s and stand-alone expressions in a single .LSP file. When you're starting out with LISP, though, you'll usually want to keep it simple: In each .LSP file, use (defun) to define a single function whose name starts with "C:." As you develop your LISP skills, you'll learn how to take advantage of more elaborate approaches.

Release 12 includes a large number of .LSP files in the \ACAD\SUPPORT and \ACAD\SAMPLE directories. While these files are worth perusing once you're up to speed on AutoLISP, they're not the best examples for beginners. Autodesk's .LSP files contain a lot of error trapping and other complex code. While the techniques this code demonstrates are valuable, they're likely to confuse users who are new to LISP. Instead, look for shorter samples in the CAD magazines and on CompuServe or BBSs.

Debugging and Developing Efficiently

Debugging AutoLISP programs is often more involved than debugging menu macros or DIESEL, if only because LISP programs tend to be longer and more complex. Also, the debugging tools included with AutoLISP are exceedingly primitive.

As with all full-fledged programming languages, the most effective way to write programs couples careful planning with a step-wise approach to building and revising the program. Don't expect to sit down at the keyboard, type several dozen lines of LISP code, and end up with a working (or easily debuggable) program. Instead, invest some time planning each program before you start writing code. As with planning how to organize and create a drawing, a moderate amount of time spent up front can save lots of time later on.

Begin by outlining the program with pencil and paper. Write down the input your program will require and the output it will produce (often a drawn or modified object). Then list the variables your program will need. Finally, describe the steps the program will go through in order to achieve its

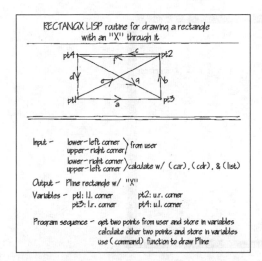

Figure 19.2 Planning a LISP program.

results. Use this outline as your roadmap as you develop the program (see Figure 19.2 for an example). If you're unsure of any of the steps, try them out in isolation first. It's much easier to see and correct problems in small code fragments than to do it in larger programs.

Once you start developing and debugging, make sure the (*error*) function is set to nil (type (setq *error* nil) at the command line). (*error*) is a magic name that LISP programs can use to define an *error handler*—a short program that runs when something goes wrong. Many third-party applications define an error handler when they initialize. Error handlers make for more robust LISP programs, but they get in the way when you're debugging. If you or your third-party application has an error handler defined, AutoLISP will display only a brief error message, with no indication of where in your LISP code the problem occurred. This minimalist approach is good for keeping the AutoCAD interface clean, but when you're developing and debugging, you need the additional "traceback" of scrolling LISP code (see Figure 19.3). By setting *error* to nil, you temporarily disable the error handler and ensure that LISP displays the traceback.

The first expression in the traceback pinpoints where AutoLISP choked on your program. The next expression shows where the bad expression was nested. The next expression shows where that expression was nested, and so on. A deeply nested LISP program can result in some very long tracebacks that scroll off the screen, which is unfortunate, because you usually want to see the information at the beginning of the traceback, not the end. Sometimes, you can catch the beginning of the traceback by pressing the flipscreen key very quickly followed by the <Pause> key. Other times, you may need to turn on printer echoing with <Ctrl>+Q, or to modify your program so that the problem code is less deeply nested.

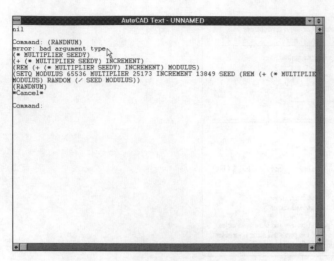

```
                      AutoCAD Text - UNNAMED
nil

Command: (RANDNUM)
error: bad argument type
(* MULTIPLIER SEEDY)
(+ (* MULTIPLIER SEEDY) INCREMENT)
(REM (+ (* MULTIPLIER SEEDY) INCREMENT) MODULUS)
(SETQ MODULUS 65536 MULTIPLIER 25173 INCREMENT 13849 SEED (REM (+ (* MULTIPLIE
MODULUS) RANDOM (/ SEED MODULUS))
(RANDNUM)
*Cancel*

Command:
```

Figure 19.3 LISP traceback after an error.

The simplest debugging method is to type questionable expressions at the AutoCAD Command: prompt and see what they return. Assuming you can isolate the problem to one or two lines of code, start by typing the most deeply nested function and seeing what it returns. Then work your way outward, one nesting level at a time, until AutoLISP complains. At that point, the error message should give you a clue about what's going wrong and, with the assistance of Appendix C in the *AutoLISP Programmer's Reference Manual*, you should be able to figure out and correct the problem.

Of course, this approach gets tedious quickly, but it's helpful when you're learning. As you become more proficient, you'll get better at spotting where the problem lies, and at that point, you won't have to be quite so methodical. A variation on the "type the code fragment" method is to isolate the offending code fragment in a separate .LSP file, such as TEST.LSP. When you enter (load "TEST") at the AutoCAD Command: prompt, TEST.LSP will do the "typing" for you. By modifying and then reloading TEST.LSP several times, you should be able to isolate the problem.

As you gain experience at interpreting AutoLISP's error messages, your debugging will focus on variables and their values and types. By inspecting variable values after an AutoLISP program crashes, you often can pinpoint where the problem is. You can check the value of a global variable by typing an exclamation point followed by the variable name at the command line, as we did in the tutorial above. While you're developing and debugging, leave all variables global, and then define them as local once you've fully debugged the program. See the next section and the tutorials for more information about declaring variables as local.

Sometimes, you need to supplement the exclamation point method with temporary (princ *varname*) statements in the .LSP file. (princ *varname*) will print out the current value of the variable *varname* on the command line. This is especially helpful when you want to see how a variable's value changes throughout a program or during a program loop.

There are many other approaches to debugging and several third-party development tools to help. Whichever methods and tools you use, though, don't neglect the initial "thinking" stage of program development. No debugging method is fast enough to compensate for incomplete planning.

Chapter 5 of the *AutoLISP Programmer's Reference Manual* contains a section called "Good Programming Techniques" that contains additional tips.

Third-Party Application Considerations

The primary concerns with third-party applications are compatibility issues among them on the one hand, and ACAD.LSP and global variable names on the other. In addition, you might want to modify AutoLISP programs supplied by third-party developers.

Third-party applications sometimes use ACAD.LSP as the repository for code they want to make sure always gets loaded. Usually, you can just add your own code to the third-party application's ACAD.LSP (or vice versa), but you must watch out for conflicts with the "magic" S::STARTUP function. As discussed in Chapter 14, *Getting Ready to Customize*, AutoCAD looks for an S::STARTUP function definition when it loads ACAD.LSP and *menuname*.MNL. If AutoCAD finds (defun S::STARTUP ...), it stores the function definition in memory and then executes it at the end of the drawing editor initialization sequence. In the previous chapter, we used S::STARTUP to load our MODEMACRO status line. There can be only one S::STARTUP function definition, and some third-party applications define one, so you may have to paste together code from your S::STARTUP function and code from your third-party application's S::STARTUP.

Another potential problem is global variable names. If two different AutoLISP programs use the same name for a global variable, the last one that assigns a value to that variable wins. This means that your program could end up trying to use a variable whose value has been changed by some other LISP program. This conflict will lead to either wrong results—often hard to catch until they've caused other problems—or a "bad argument type" error.

Conflicting variable name problems can be very hard to track down, so the best approach is to program defensively. Unless you really need a variable to be global, declare it as local by putting it in the defun argument list—see the tutorials below for examples. When you do need to use global variables, try to come up with unique names. You might prefix all global variables with your initials and an underscore character (mm_width, mm_lastpt, etc.) or with an unusual character (#width, #lastpt, etc.).

Occasionally, you might want to modify or build on LISP routines that come with your third-party applications. Doing so can be difficult because many developers encrypt their code. If the unencrypted source code is included, make modifications carefully, because other programs and menus may depend on the routine you're changing. Also, be aware of copyright considerations. If you've incorporated code from your third-party application into your own custom LISP program, you normally can't distribute that program to others.

AutoLISP Tutorials

The tutorials below demonstrate three ways of using AutoLISP: adding short LISP expressions to menu macros, creating a new command by modifying an existing LISP program in an .MNL file, and writing a "stand-alone" LISP program. The tutorials build in complexity, and by the third tutorial, you'll be using AutoLISP in a moderately sophisticated way.

Adding AutoLISP to Menus

In this tutorial, we'll enhance the ***POP10 pull-down menu page we created in the previous two chapters. We'll modify the [ChText] macro and add a new layer macro, as shown in step 3 below.

1. Copy your custom ACAD.MNU and the stock ACAD.MNL to \ACUSTOM\TEST.

Change to your \ACUSTOM\TEST subdirectory and copy ACAD.MNU from \ACUSTOM.

If you don't have a current version of ACAD.MNU as of the end of the previous chapter, copy ACADCH19.MNU from the *AutoCAD Power Tools* disk and rename it ACAD.MNU.

Copy ACAD.MNL from \ACAD\SUPPORT.

Later in the tutorial, we'll modify the .MNL file.

Start AutoCAD.

2. Modify the [ChText] menu macro so that CHTEXT.LSP loads only once per drawing session.

*Load ACAD.MNU into your text editor and search for ***POP10.*

When we created this macro in Chapter 17, *Menus*, we noted that it reloads CHTEXT.LSP every time you pick the menu choice. It's more efficient to load the .LSP file only once per drawing session.

Add (if (not C:CHT) before and an additional close parenthesis after (load "CHTEXT"), as shown in italics in the menu macros in step 3.

If CHTEXT.LSP hasn't been loaded yet, the function name C:CHT will be undefined (i.e., nil), whereas if CHTEXT.LSP has already been loaded in the current drawing session, C:CHT will be defined (i.e., non-nil). Thus, (not C:CHT) returns T if CHTEXT.LSP hasn't been loaded, and nil if it has. By wrapping (load "CHTEXT") inside the (if) function, we ensure that it gets evaluated only when CHTEXT.LSP hasn't been loaded.

Tip

Another way of loading LISP programs only when they're needed is to use the (autoload) function defined in ACADR12.LSP. If you look at the end of ACADR12.LSP (located in the \ACAD\SUPPORT directory), you'll see that Release 12 uses (autoload) to load many of its own LISP routines. For instance:

```
(autoload "ASCTEXT" '("ASCTEXT"))
```

tells AutoCAD to load ASCTEXT.LSP if necessary and execute the command ASCTEXT whenever ASCTEXT is typed (whether from the command line or from a menu macro). The general syntax is:

```
(autoload "LSP_name" '("command_name"))
```

In many cases, the two names are the same, but occasionally not:

```
(autoload "CHTEXT" '("CHT"))
```

The (autoload) approach works especially well for users who prefer typing rather than selecting from menus. You can copy ACADR12.LSP to your \ACUSTOM subdirectory and add your own (autoload)s to it.

---

3. Add a macro for setting the current layer by selecting an entity.

Add the [Set Current] macro shown below in italics.

This macro looks nasty because of the deep nesting, but if you trace its action from the inside out, as we did in the command-line tutorial earlier in the chapter, you'll see how it works.

Note the pause and <Enter> at the end of the macro. To see why these are needed, you might first test the macro without the backslash and semicolon, with just the backslash, and with just the semicolon. The backslash is required in order to make the menu macro pause for you to select an entity. You might think that AutoCAD would be smart enough to pause when it gets to the (entsel) function, but it isn't. The semicolon is required in order to exit the LAYER command. We mentioned in Chapter 17, *Menus*, that AutoCAD normally adds an <Enter> after a macro, except when the macro ends with a special character (such as the backslash). The trailing semicolon forces AutoCAD to add the <Enter> anyway.

```
***Comment
 Custom AutoCAD Power Tools pull-down menu:

***POP10
[APTCust]
[Copy Multiple]^c^c_SELECT \_COPY _Previous ;_Multiple
[Break at Int]^c^c_BREAK \_First _INT \@
[ChText]^c^c^p(if (not C:CHT) (load "CHTEXT")) ^pCHT
[- -]
[->Layer]
 Set Current]'_LAYER _Set ^p(cdr (assoc 8 (entget +
(car (entsel)))))) ^p\;
 [* On]'_LAYER _ON * ;
 [Isolate Current]'_EXPERT 0 '_LAYER _OFf * _No ;
 [$(if,$(eq,HATCH,$(getvar,CLAYER)),~)HATCH Off]+
 '_LAYER _OFf HATCH ;
 [<-HATCH On]'_LAYER _ON HATCH ;
...
```

Using AutoLISP in .MNL Files

Often, the easiest way to develop useful AutoLISP programs is to modify existing ones, and we'll use this approach to create a new command called RECTANGX that draws a Polyline rectangle with an X through it. You might use this command to draw floor openings (or treasure maps).

This example also shows how to incorporate LISP programs in an .MNL file. We could create RECTANGX in a separate .LSP file, but it often makes sense to put short programs that are tied closely to the menu in an .MNL file instead. AutoCAD's RECTANG command is defined as a LISP program in ACAD.MNL and then called from the Draw menu. We'll copy the AutoLISP code that defines the C:RECTANG function, modify it to create the new function C:RECTANGX, and then add a menu choice to ***POP10.

1. Load ACAD.MNL and look at C:RECTANG.

Load ACAD.MNL into your text editor and search for "rectang."

Return to AutoCAD and run RECTANG by selecting Rectangle from the Draw menu.

Compare the program prompts and operation to the code below.

C:RECTANG is a fairly simple function, and like most functions it consists of four parts: set up, get input, do the job, and clean up. C:RECTANG is shown below, with comments added to indicate these four sections.

```
(defun c:rectang ( / cmde pt1 pt2)
;*Set up————————————————————
  (setq m:err *error* *error* *merr*
     cmde (getvar "CMDECHO")
  )
  (setvar "CMDECHO" 0)
;*Get input————————————
  (setq pt1 (getpoint "\nFirst corner: ")
     pt2 (getcorner pt1 "\nOther corner: ")
  )
;*Do the job———————————————
  (command "_.PLINE" pt1 "_non" (list (car pt1) (cadr pt2))
            pt2 "_non" (list (car pt2) (cadr pt1))
          "_C"
  )
;*Clean up——————————————
  (setvar "CMDECHO" cmde)
  (setq *error* m:err m:err nil)
  (princ)
)
```

The "set up" section swaps its own error handler and sets the CMDECHO (CoMmanD ECHO) system variable to 0 after saving the old values of CMDECHO and the error handler. Don't worry about the error handler business for now. Setting CMDECHO to 0 suppresses command-line echoing and makes for a cleaner interface.

The "get input" section simply gets two points from the user and stores their values in the variables pt1 and pt2.

The "do the job" section uses the (command) function to start the PLINE command, then feeds it four points, and finally, closes the

Polyline. The lower-right and upper-left corners of the rectangle are calculated while the PLINE command is running. The (car) and (cadr) functions extract the X and Y values, respectively, from pt1 and pt2, and the (list) function assembles the two values into a point list. This is a common technique for calculating points based on the coordinates of other points. The final (command) argument, "_C," closes the Polyline, just as you would if you were drawing it interactively.

There are two subtleties to note in the (command) function sequence. First, the PLINE command name is preceded by both an underscore and a period. As described in Chapter 17, *Menus,* the underscore tells foreign-language versions of AutoCAD that the command name is in English. The period tells AutoCAD to use the stock AutoCAD PLINE command, even if someone has redefined PLINE to work differently (LISP lets you redefine AutoCAD commands). Second, the lower-right and upper-left corner points are preceded by "_non" (the NONe object snap mode). NONe ensures that if a running object snap mode is set, AutoCAD doesn't accidentally snap to a point that would distort the rectangle. If you remove the two instances of "_non," set osnap to endpoint, and then try drawing rectangles in a crowded drawing, you'll see the problem that NONe prevents.

The "clean up" section resets CMDECHO and the error handler to the values they had when the RECTANG command started. The final (princ) is the standard way of ensuring that the routine exits "quietly," i.e., without printing anything extraneous on the command line.

2. Make a copy of the RECTANG function.

Copy everything from (defun c:rectang... to the matching close parenthesis 16 lines below (i.e., everything in the C:RECTANG function shown above in step 1).

Copy it just below the matching close parenthesis, leaving a blank line.

Our RECTANGX will be similar to RECTANG except that, instead of using Close after drawing the third segment of the rectangle, RECTANGX will draw the fourth segment explicitly, followed by two diagonals connected at the top (see Figure 19.2). Because we'll be using each of the points twice, it makes sense to calculate the lower-right and upper-left corner points and assign them to new variables pt3 and pt4.

3. Make the following modifications to the copy, as shown below.

- Change the function name to C:RECTANGX.

  We use uppercase for C: function names, but you can stick with lowercase if you like.

- Add pt3 and pt4 to the list of local variables.

  pt3 and pt4 are the lower-right and upper-left corner points.

- Add lines that calculate the variables pt3 and pt4.

  These calculations are the same ones used by RECTANG inside the (command) function.

- Modify the (command) function arguments as shown.

  Now all of the arguments are simply point variable names, preceded by the NONe osnap mode where appropriate. Don't forget to remove the "_C."

```
(defun C:RECTANGX ( / cmde pt1 pt2 pt3 pt4)
  (setq m:err *error* *error* *merr*
      cmde (getvar "CMDECHO")
  )
  (setvar "CMDECHO" 0)
  (setq pt1 (getpoint "\nFirst corner: ")
      pt2 (getcorner pt1 "\nOther corner: ")
      pt3 (list (car pt1) (cadr pt2))
      pt4 (list (car pt2) (cadr pt1))
  )
  (command "_.PLINE" pt1 "_NON" pt3 pt2 "_NON" pt4 pt1
              pt2 "_NON" pt4 "_NON" pt3 "")
  )
  (setvar "CMDECHO" cmde)
  (setq *error* m:err m:err nil)
  (princ)
)
```

4. Save ACAD.MNL and test.

Save ACAD.MNL and return to the AutoCAD drawing editor. Force AutoCAD to reload ACAD.MNL by reloading ACAD.MNU with the MENU command.

Everytime you load a menu, AutoCAD loads its associated .MNL file (if any), so this is an easy way to reload ACAD.MNL. If you prefer, you can load it explicitly from the command line: (LOAD "ACAD.MNL").

Test the command by entering RECTANGX at the command line.

If you typed carefully, you should be able to draw rectangles with Xs in them (see Figure 19.4). If you encounter any errors, edit ACAD.MNL, check your typing carefully against the new RECTANGX function shown above in step 3, save and reload ACAD.MNL, and test again.

5. Add RECTANGX to your ***POP10 menu.

Once RECTANGX is working properly, you'll want to add it to the menu.

*Edit ACAD.MNU, and add a new macro at the beginning of your ***POP10, as shown below.*

The new macro simply cancels anything in progress and executes RECTANGX. We don't need to worry about loading RECTANGX into memory (as we did with CHTEXT), since it automatically gets loaded with ACAD.MNL.

Save ACAD.MNU, return to the drawing editor, reload the menu, and test.

Figure 19.4 shows the modified menu.

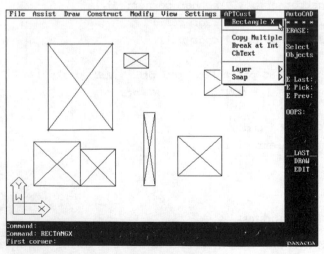

Figure 19.4 RECTANGX in action.

```
***Comment
  Custom AutoCAD Power Tools pull-down menu:

***POP10
[APTCust]
[Rectangle X]^c^cRECTANGX
[--]
[Copy Multiple]^c^c_SELECT \_COPY _Previous ;_Multiple
[Break at Int]^c^c_BREAK \_First _INT \@
[ChText]^c^c^p(if (not C:CHT) (load "CHTEXT")) ^pCHT
[--]
[->Layer]
...
```

Tip

Including LISP programs in an .MNL file (or ACAD.LSP) is a handy feature, but don't get carried away with it. AutoCAD reloads the .MNL file and ACAD.LSP every time you open or create a drawing, and the more code you dump in these files, the longer AutoCAD's drawing initialization procedure will take. Most LISP programs, especially longer ones, should go in separate .LSP files and be loaded from the menu, as we did with [ChText].

Creating "Stand-Alone" AutoLISP Programs

Once you've modified a few existing AutoLISP programs, you'll probably want to start creating your own. In this tutorial, we develop a simple text editing utility that wraps the DDEDIT, DDATTE, and DIM NEWTEXT commands into a single command called TEXTEDIT. This utility prevents you from having to think about whether the text you want to change is ordinary text, an attribute in a Block, or part of an associative Dimension. The program is useful in itself, but the tutorial also demonstrates how to build a LISP routine in step fashion.

1. Plan out the program.

Outline the program input, output, and steps, as described in the "Debugging and Developing Efficiently" section found on page 510.

See Figure 19.5 for our plan.

2. Develop the initial routine.

For the first pass, we won't worry about DIM NEWTEXT or making the command repeat automatically. We can add those refinements later.

Create a new ASCII text file called TEXTEDIT.LSP, and enter the text shown below.

As always, watch your typing and punctuation carefully.

```
;  TEXTEDIT.LSP: routine to edit Text or Attributes
;  with a single command.
(defun C:TEXTEDIT ()
  ;get entity name:
  (setq en (entsel "\nSelect Text or Attribute: "))
  (setq ed (entget (car en))                ;get entity data
  (setq etype (cdr (assoc 0 ed)))           ;extract entity type
  (cond
    ((equal etype "TEXT")                   ;it's Text
      (command "_.DDEDIT" en "")
    )
    ((equal etype "INSERT")                 ;it's a Block Insert
      (command "_.DDATTE" en)
    )
    (T (prompt "\nEntity is not Text or Block."))
  )
  (princ)
)
```

The program starts out with a short comment that we'll expand later. Next comes the (defun) function and C:TEXTEDIT function name. For now, we leave the argument list empty. As mentioned above, this makes all variables global, which is helpful during debugging. At the end, we'll come back and make the variables local.

The object of the three (setq ...) lines is to determine the type of entity the user picked. These three lines get an entity from the user and store its name in the variable en ("Entity Name"), read its entity data into the variable ed ("Entity Data"), and extract its entity type from the data. The entity type is always stored in DXF group code 0, so (assoc 0 ed) locates that group, (cdr) extracts only the group value, and (setq) sets the variable name etype ("Entity TYPE") to this value.

The rest of the program is a conditional statement with three possible conditions: (1) The entity is a Text string, (2) The entity is a Block

TEXTEDIT LISP routine for editing Text, Attributes,
and Dimensions with one command
_____

Input —   entity name (from user)
           entity type (extract from entity data — DXF group 0)

Output —   Modified Text, Dim text, or Block attributes
           (use DDEDIT, DDATTE, or DIM NEWTEXT command)

Variables — en: entity name
            ed: entity data
            etype: entity type

Program sequence — ▲ get entity from user (Text, Dimension, or
                        Block w/ attributes, hopefully)

                   ▲ extract entity data and store in <u>ed</u> var.

                   ▲ extract entity type and store in <u>etype</u> var.

                   ▲ conditional—

                       → if etype=TEXT, run DDEDIT

                       → if etype=INSERT, run DDATTE

                       → if etype=DIMENSION, run DIM NEWTEXT

                       → otherwise, print error message

Figure 19.5 Outline for TEXTEDIT.LSP.

Insert, or (3) the entity is neither of the above. In cases 1 and 2, the program runs the DDEDIT or DDATTE command, respectively, and feeds it the entity name, which AutoCAD commands treat exactly as if the user had picked the entity directly. Note that case 1 requires <Enter> as the last argument to (command), because the DDEDIT command stays active until you hit <Enter>. The final case, which starts with (T ...), simply tells the user that the entity isn't an appropriate one.

Like most AutoLISP programs, TEXTEDIT ends with (princ) and a closing parenthesis to match the opening one before defun.

Save TEXTEDIT.LSP, return to AutoCAD, and test the program on a text string and a Block with an attribute.

```
Command: (LOAD "TEXTEDIT")
C:TEXTEDIT
```

C:TEXTEDIT is AutoLISP's way of telling you that the program has been loaded into memory.

```
Command: TEXTEDIT
Select Text or Attribute: do so
```

AutoCAD should pop up the Edit Text or Edit Attributes dialogue box.

Edit the Text or Attribute and click on OK.

Repeat the command and try the other type of entity. Also try picking on an entity that is neither Text nor a Block, to make sure the error message works.

If anything doesn't work, reload TEXTEDIT.LSP and compare your version with the first pass at TEXTEDIT.LSP shown earlier in this tutorial step. Correct and test until the program performs properly.

3. Add a (while) loop that makes the command repeat.

Reload TEXTEDIT.LSP and make the following changes, as shown below in italics:

- Enclose the (cond) statement in a (while) loop.

  (while en ...) tests whether the user actually selected an entity.

- Move the (setq ed...) and (setq etype) lines inside the (while) loop.

  Since the routine will now process multiple entities, these two steps must be performed after each entity is selected. Also note that we've enclosed both assignment statements inside one (setq ...), as Autodesk did with its C:RECTANG routine shown in step 1 of the previous tutorial. This approach is slightly more efficient than using two separate (setq)s and, more importantly, it makes the code look cleaner.

- Add another (entsel) line at the end of the (while) loop.

  This line prompts the user for the second and subsequent entities. Don't forget the closing parenthesis to match the opening one before "while."

```
; TEXTEDIT.LSP: routine to edit Text or Attributes
; with a single command.

(defun C:TEXTEDIT ()
   ;get entity name:
   (setq en (entsel "\nSelect Text or Attribute: "))
   (while en                      ;while there's an entity...
      (setq ed (entget (car en))       ;get entity data
            etype (cdr (assoc 0 ed))   ;extract entity type
      )
      (cond
        ((equal etype "TEXT")          ;it's Text
          (command "_.DDEDIT" en "")
        )
        ((equal etype "INSERT")        ;it's a Block Insert
          (command "_.DDATTE" en)
        )
        (T (princ "\nEntity is not Text or Block."))
      )
```

```
      ;get next entity name:
      (setq en (entsel
            "\nSelect another <Return to quit>: "))
   )
   (princ)
)
```

With the first entity, TEXTEDIT works the same as before. Once the program has processed the first entity, though, it prompts the user for another one. The program then returns to the top of the (while) loop and tests whether an entity was selected (i.e., whether the variable en is non-nil). If so, the statements inside the loop run again with the new entity. Once the user hits <Enter> instead of picking an entity, the variable en will be nil and AutoLISP will exit the loop.

Save TEXTEDIT.LSP, return to AutoCAD, and retest the program on a text string, a Block with an attribute, and other types of entities.

4. Add code to handle Associative Dimension text.

Experiment with the DIM NEWTEXT command.

Draw several dimensions and use DIM NEWTEXT to change the dimension text. Note the curious sequence: You type in the new text first, and then select one or more entities. Also, if you're not familiar with DIM1, try it in lieu of DIM. DIM1 lets you run a single dimensioning command, and then returns immediately to the Command: prompt. DIM1 often is used in menu macros and AutoLISP programs.

Reload TEXTEDIT.LSP and make the following changes:

• Change the opening comment and user prompts to reflect the new addition.

Note that we've put the user prompts on separate lines in order to avoid excessively long lines or word wrapping. You can split an AutoLISP expression into multiple lines, as long as you don't split the line in the middle of a text string.

• Add code for saving, setting, and restoring the TEXTEVAL system variable.

When you use commands such as TEXT or DIM NEWTEXT in AutoLISP, you usually have to set the TEXTEVAL system variable to 1. If you leave it at 0, AutoCAD accepts literally whatever AutoLISP feeds it, including special symbols such as pause. You'll know something is wrong, because you'll see backslashes, parentheses, or other strange characters in your text strings. TEXTEVAL = 1 tells AutoCAD to be on the lookout for these special symbols and to treat them appropriately.

- Add a new case inside (cond) for etype = "DIMENSION."

Make sure you add it above the (T ...) condition, otherwise AutoCAD will never get to it. This block of code is similar to the Text and Block cases. The first difference is that we have to prompt the user at the command line, since DIM NEWTEXT doesn't use a dialogue box. Also, because of the sequence in which NEWTEXT works, we have to include a pause to get command line input from the user (similar to a backslash in menus), and then feed NEWTEXT the entity name.

Save TEXTEDIT.LSP, return to AutoCAD, and retest using text, Blocks, and Associative Dimensions.

```
; TEXTEDIT.LSP: routine to edit Text, Attributes,
; and Dimensions with a single command.
(defun C:TEXTEDIT ()
  (setq en (entsel
         "\nSelect Text, Attribute, or Dimension text: ")
      oteval (getvar "TEXTEVAL")           ;save old value
  )
(setvar "TEXTEVAL" 1)        ;req'd for DIM NEWTEXT

  (while en                    ;while there's an entity
    (setq ed (entget (car en))        ;get entity data
         etype (cdr (assoc 0 ed))  ;extract entity type
    )
    (cond
      ((equal etype "TEXT")          ;it's Text
        (command "_.DDEDIT" en  "")
      )
      ((equal etype "INSERT")        ;it's a Block Insert
        (command "_.DDATTE" en)
      )
      ((equal etype "DIMENSION")   ;it's an Assoc. Dim.
        (princ "\nEnter new dimension text: ")
        (command "_.DIM1" "_NEWTEXT" pause en "")
      )
      (T (princ
        "\nEntity is not Text, Block, or Dimension."))
    )
```

```
;get next entity name:
(setq en (entsel
      "\nSelect another <Return to quit>: "))
)

(setvar "TEXTEVAL" oteval)        ;restore TEXTEVAL value
(princ)
)
```

5. Finish up the routine by defining local variables and adding a load message.

Reload TEXTEDIT.LSP and make the following changes:

- Add a comment line with version, date, and name information.

  You'll find yourself revising LISP programs, and it's always useful to see which version you're working with.

- Declare all variables as local.

  None of our variables need to be global, and as mentioned earlier, it's always best to keep them local when you can. Scan through the routine looking for (setq)s, and copy each variable name to the argument list. Make sure you put local variables *after* the forward slash.

- Add a load message at the end.

  It's good practice to inform the user of what was loaded and how to run it. By putting a prompt message outside the (defun) statement, we ensure that AutoLISP evaluates it only once, when the .LSP file is loaded.

Save TEXTEDIT.LSP, return to AutoCAD, and retest one last time.

```
; TEXTEDIT.LSP: routine to edit Text, Attributes,
; and Dimensions with a single command.
; Version 1.0  11 May 93  by Mark Middlebrook

(defun C:TEXTEDIT (/ oteval en ed etype)
   (setq en (entsel
         "\nSelect Text, Attribute, or Dimension text: ")
         oteval (getvar "TEXTEVAL")        ;save old value
   )
   (setvar "TEXTEVAL" 1)        ;req'd for DIM NEWTEXT

   (while en                    ;while there's an entity...
      (setq ed (entget (car en)))        ;get entity data
```

```
              etype (cdr (assoc 0 ed))    ;extract entity type
          )
          (cond
            ((equal etype "TEXT")          ;it's Text
              (command "_.DDEDIT" en "")
            )
            ((equal etype "INSERT")        ;it's a Block Insert
              (command "_.DDATTE" en)
            )
            ((equal etype "DIMENSION")        ;it's an Assoc. Dim.
              (princ "\nEnter new dimension text: ")
              (command "_.DIM1" "_NEWTEXT" pause en "")
            )
            (T (princ
                "\nEntity is not Text, Block, or Dimension."))
          )
          ;get next entity name:
          (setq en (entsel
              "\nSelect another <Return to quit>: "))
        )
        (setvar "TEXTEVAL" oteval)  ;restore TEXTEVAL value
      (princ)
  )

(princ "\nTEXTEDIT.LSP loaded. TEXTEDIT runs it.")
(princ)
```

Tip

Always retest your LISP program after any changes, no matter how inconsequential they seem. It's surprisingly easy to make simple mistakes, such as leaving out a semicolon before a comment. These kinds of mistakes are pretty embarrassing when you deliver a program to your workgroup or client and it won't even load properly.

6. Add TEXTEDIT to the ***POP10 menu.

Load ACAD.MNU into your text editor and add the [Text Edit] macro shown below.

This macro works the same as [ChText].

Save ACAD.MNU, reload it, and test.

```
***Comment
  Custom AutoCAD Power Tools pull-down menu:

***POP10
[APTCust]
[Rectangle X]^c^cRECTANGX
[- -]
[Copy Multiple]^c^c_SELECT \_COPY _Previous ;_Multiple
[Break at Int]^c^c_BREAK \_First _INT \@
[ChText]^c^c^p(if (not C:CHT) (load "CHTEXT")) ^pCHT
[Text Edit]^c^c^p(if (not C:TEXTEDIT)
(load "TEXTEDIT")) +^pTEXTEDIT
[- -]
[->Layer]
...
```

We've covered a lot of ground in the TEXTEDIT tutorial. Hopefully, it's given you a sense of how to plan, develop, and refine an AutoLISP program, and if nothing else, you can use TEXTEDIT to streamline text editing. The *AutoCAD Power Tools* disk includes a version of TEXTEDIT.LSP with several small enhancements, including detection of Block Inserts without Attributes and the ability to select the last entity by typing L.

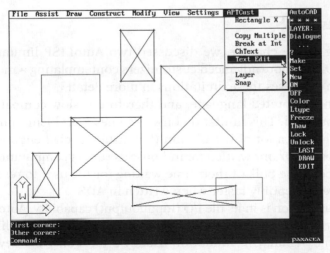

Figure 19.6 The completed menu (Render and Model menus removed for clarity).

Finishing Up

Once you've tested the menu changes and custom status line, move ACAD.MNU, ACAD.MNX, ACAD.MNL, and TEXTEDIT.LSP to your \ACUSTOM directory so that they become the standard support files. Make a note of your changes, especially the ones to ACAD.MNU and ACAD.MNL.

The AutoLISP Programmer's Reference Manual

The *AutoLISP Programmer's Reference Manual* will be your bible as you progress with LISP. Acquaint yourself with its structure and content, and refer to it any time you want to use a new function or learn about a new topic. Appendix E contains an extended tutorial that uses a not very useful example, but does teach you a lot about developing parametric programs. The tutorial also shows how to use a dialogue box to get user input for the program.

The first three chapters of the *AutoLISP Programmer's Reference Manual* present important conceptual information that will help deepen your understanding of AutoLISP. The Synopsis of Functions at the beginning of Chapter 4 groups all the AutoLISP Subrs by functional topic, so it's easy to find out, for example, which Subrs you might use on text strings. Appendix B is a welcome addition in Release 12: It documents all the DXF group codes, and you'll refer to it often as you use the entity and table access functions. Finally, don't forget to look at Appendix D when you can't decipher an AutoLISP error message.

AutoLISP Versus ADS

In the beginning of the chapter, we discussed two AutoLISP limitations: speed and file I/O. For more advanced customizers contemplating a move to ADS, this section discusses these limitations in more detail.

AutoLISP is an interpreted language, and therefore is slow compared to ADS, which is compiled. This limitation only becomes a problem in heavy-duty programs that do a lot of calculation (for instance, civil engineering applications). Most programs written for in-house use aren't computationally intensive; they spend the bulk of their time waiting for the user to respond, and thus won't be perceptibly faster when written in ADS.

LISP's second limitation is in its file I/O (input/output) capability. AutoLISP provides only for reading and writing ASCII files sequentially, one line or character at a time. Again, this limitation usually affects only the developers of high-end applications that require more flexible access to text and binary files.

In short, AutoLISP provides plenty of power and speed for most users and CAD managers. If your customization work reaches a level of sophistication that requires ADS, you'll know it. At that point most people are better off looking for an ADS-based third-party application that addresses their needs or hiring a competent consultant who has extensive experience with C and ADS.

AutoLISP and Workgroups

AutoLISP is a powerful tool for workgroup customization, but you'll need to decide how far to go with it. Someone in the workgroup should know enough to incorporate simple LISP expressions in menu macros and to make minor modifications to existing programs. Beyond that, you or another workgroup member may have enough interest in programming and LISP to go further. Having the capability to create short custom programs as the need arises can improve your workgroup's productivity dramatically. Keep in mind, though, that writing LISP programs efficiently takes some practice and experience. Be reasonable about what you can accomplish, and consider investing in training or self-study.

Also be aware that in-house programming can be a big time-sink, especially for someone who enjoys the challenge and creativity of programming. You might find yourself spending hours or even days writing programs that are available more economically elsewhere. Remember that your goal is not to write a complete third-party application from scratch, but to build on commercial, shareware, and freeware programs.

Make sure your workgroup has a standard ACAD.LSP and ACAD.MNL, and keep these files lean so that drawing load times aren't lengthened. Use menu macros like the ones we developed for CHGTEXT.LSP and TEXTEDIT.LSP in order to load custom LISP programs only when they're needed.

All workgroup members should be familiar with the (load) function and APPLOAD command, in case they want to try out a LISP routine from a magazine or BBS. (APPLOAD is described in the *AutoCAD Extras Manual* and in Chapter 9 of this book, *Adding Dimensions and Text.*) As with menu macros, make users aware of the power of AutoLISP so that they're open to the possibility of customizing repetitive tasks. Of course, you'll need to decide how to make that possibility a reality once they come to you with dozens of ideas for new LISP routines.

Some users make a habit of gathering routines from magazines, CompuServe, BBSs, and other sources. This behavior usually is worth encouraging, but it needs to be managed. Your workgroup or office should have a mechanism for evaluating LISP offerings and deciding whether to incorporate them for everyone. Users can keep those routines that don't make the cut on their own systems and use APPLOAD to launch them.

Summary

AutoLISP is the customization language of choice when you bump up against the limits of scripts, menu macros, and DIESEL. AutoLISP is a full-fledged programming language, but one that's comparatively easy to begin using. Mastery of LISP takes considerable experience, but by using AutoLISP to enhance menus, modify existing programs, and develop short programs, you can take advantage of LISP's power with a minimum of time investment.

20

Programmable Dialogue Boxes

The new Programmable Dialogue Box (PDB) facility is the most important customization improvement in Release 12. It answers a long-time wish of AutoLISP and ADS programmers: to be able to create custom dialogue boxes similar to the ones built into AutoCAD, such as DDLMODES and the file dialogue box. Programmable dialogue boxes will allow Autodesk and its developers to create a more modern and consistent interface.

PDBs also answer an Autodesk wish: to be able to port AutoCAD to different platforms more easily, while retaining the "look and feel" of each platform's native interface. Autodesk designed this facility so that dialogue boxes can be designed once, then used on all AutoCAD platforms. The version of AutoCAD for each platform knows how to display its dialogue boxes in a way that conforms to the interface standards for that platform: Release 12 for Windows dialogue boxes look like standard Windows dialogues, Release 12 for Sun SPARCstation dialogue boxes look like standard OPEN LOOK dialogues, and so on. (DOS doesn't have a standard windowing interface, so Autodesk invented one that resembles Windows.) Figures 20.1 and 20.2 show the DDRMODES Drawing Aids dialogue box on AutoCAD DOS 386 and AutoCAD for Windows. Notice that the radio buttons under Isometric Snap/Grid look different. Also, Windows uses a proportionally spaced font, while DOS uses a fixed-width font.

While programmable dialogue boxes are an unmitigated boon for third-party developers, they're a mixed blessing for those who aren't already AutoLISP or ADS experts. Creating custom dialogue boxes requires a good deal of programming skill, and creating useful ones demands user interface

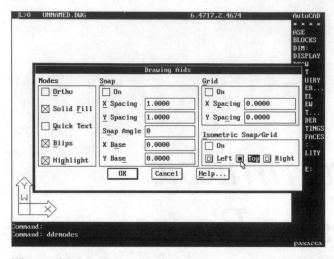

Figure 20.1   The DDRMODES PDB in AutoCAD DOS 386.

design talent. Many in-house customizers will be eager to take advantage of PDBs in order to make their LISP programs easier to use and more consistent with Release 12. Doing so will require ascending a whole new learning curve beyond the one presented by AutoLISP. Fortunately, there's a shortcut for displaying alert and file dialogue boxes—see the "PDB Techniques" section later in this chapter.

About This Chapter

This chapter introduces the Release 12 Programmable Dialogue Box facility and demonstrates it with a simple but useful example. The subject is a large and complex one, and there's much about it that we don't cover here, but we do show you how to get started. Chapter 9 of the *AutoCAD Customization Manual* documents the PDB facility, including Dialogue Control Language and controlling dialogues using AutoLISP and ADS.

A Programmable Dialogue Box Primer

Making your own AutoCAD dialogue boxes involves two activities: designing and specifying the dialogue box's visual layout, and controlling its behavior and consequences with AutoLISP (or ADS). You specify the visual layout in Release 12's new Dialogue Control Language (DCL), a C-like language that's somewhere between DIESEL and LISP in complexity. You control a PDB with the help of several new dialogue-handling functions that were added to AutoLISP in Release 12. Together, the .DCL file and .LSP program that you write will set up

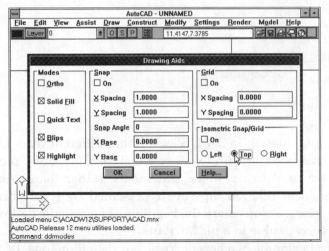

Figure 20.2 The DDRMODES PDB in AutoCAD for Windows.

the precise appearance of the dialogue box, present it on the screen, respond to user typing and picking, and carry out some presumably useful actions.

Dialogue Control Language

DCL is a language designed to specify the arrangement of components, or *tiles*, in a dialogue box. There are various kinds of tiles, including edit boxes, buttons, drop-down lists, and ordinary text. A .DCL file is an ASCII file that defines which tiles to use, what their characteristics are, and what their hierarchical relationship is. Shown below is a sample .DCL file, and Figure 20.3 shows the dialogue box that results from it.

```
// WELCOME.DCL - a sample .DCL file
welcome : dialog {
    label               = "My First Dialogue Box";
    initial_focus       = "response";
    : text {
        label           = "Welcome to PDB.";
        alignment       = centered;
    }
    : edit_box {
        key             = "response";
        label           = "Your Response:";
        allow_accept    = true;
    }
    : button {
        key             = "accept";
```

```
        label           = "OK";
        is_default      = true;
        fixed_width     = true;
        alignment       = centered;
    }
}
```

As you can see, punctuation in .DCL files is rather different from LISP's conventions. Comments begin with two forward slashes (//), not a semicolon. Semicolons are used to terminate statements, rather than to begin comments. Hierarchical relationships are represented by {curly braces} rather than parentheses. Colons mark the beginning of a new tile definition. The equal sign assigns a value to a tile attribute.

: dialog marks the beginning of a new dialogue box definition (one .DCL file can contain definitions for multiple dialogue boxes, but we'll stick with one dialogue per .DCL file). The dialogue's name is indicated by the word that comes before *: dialog*–in this case, *welcome*. The open curly brace after *: dialog* begins the first level of nesting, and is matched by the close curly brace at the very end of the file. As in LISP, you have to make sure all braces match properly. Nested inside of *: dialog {...}* are three tiles: a text tile, an edit box, and a button.

Tip

Note that Autodesk's documentation writers spell differently from their programmers. Most AutoCAD documentation uses "dialogue," while the new AutoLISP and ADS functions are spelled "dialog."

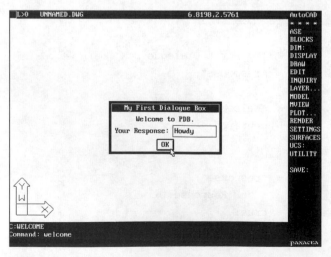

Figure 20.3   The sample .DCL file in action.

The two lines below *welcome : dialog* define attributes for the dialogue as a whole. The dialogue box's *label* attribute is displayed in the dialogue box title, as you can see in Figure 20.3. The *initial_focus* attribute tells AutoCAD where to put the cursor when the dialogue box opens. In this case, focus begins in the edit_box, whose key is *"response."*

The three tiles inside the dialogue have similar attributes, and the meaning of most of them should be apparent once you compare the above .DCL listing with the dialogue box in Figure 20.3. Note that strings are enclosed in quotation marks, and keywords such as *centered* and *true* are not. One important attribute that won't be obvious at this stage is *key*. The key attribute is the name by which that tile is known to AutoLISP programs that need to work with the tile. The *allow_accept = true* attribute says that if the user presses <Enter> while focus is in the edit_box tile, then AutoCAD should act as if the default button (the one that has *is_default = true*) were pressed. The combination of *allow_accept = true* and *is_default = true* lets users exit the dialogue without having to move the mouse and explicitly pick the OK button.

DCL supports many other types of tiles and attributes, and lets you arrange tiles in columns and rows. See the first part of Chapter 9 in the *AutoCAD Customization Manual* for complete listings of tiles and attributes.

Controlling PDBs with AutoLISP

Specifying a dialogue box layout is less then half the battle. By itself, a .DCL file can't do anything—it has to be loaded, initialized, displayed, and controlled by an AutoLISP or ADS program. Shown below is a bare-bones LISP program for controlling WELCOME.DCL. This program doesn't do anything very useful for the user—it simply displays the dialogue, waits for the OK button to be picked, and then prints the user's response on the command line.

```
; WELCOME.LSP - a sample program for showing WELCOME.DCL

(defun C:WELCOME ( / dcl_id resp)

   ;*Load .DCL file and select dialogue ——————————
   (setq dcl_id (load_dialog "WELCOME.DCL"))
   (if (not (new_dialog "welcome" dcl_id)) (exit))

   ;*Establish action expressions ——————————
   (action_tile "response" "(setq resp $value)" )
   (action_tile "accept" "(done_dialog 1)" )
```

```
;*Display dialogue on screen ─────────────────────
(start_dialog)

;*Unload .DCL file from memory ───────────────────
(unload_dialog dcl_id)

(princ "\nYou responded with: ") (princ resp)
(princ)
)
```

WELCOME.LSP defines a new AutoCAD-style command called WEL-COME. The program begins by loading the WELCOME.DCL file with the new (load_dialog) function. This step only loads the .DCL file; it doesn't actually do anything with the dialogue (or dialogues) defined in the file. It's similar to using (load) to load a LISP file containing a (defun); you still have to type the function name to make something happen. However, (load_dialog) does return an integer that you need to use in the next step.

The next line uses (new_dialog) to choose an individual dialogue definition from the .DCL file. As mentioned earlier, a .DCL file can define multiple dialogues, just as a single .LSP file can contain multiple (defun)s. The two step (load_dialog), then (new_dialog) sequence is required in order to accommodate this possibility. (new_dialog) returns t (for true) if it finds the specified dialogue in the .DCL file, and nil if it doesn't. Notice that the .DCL file is referred to by its integer handle, rather than by its name. If (new_dialog) can't find the dialogue definition, the (if) statement uses (exit) to abort the program.

So far, C:WELCOME has loaded the dialogue file and chosen the individual dialogue definition. Before actually displaying the dialogue on the screen, we must tell AutoLISP what to do when the user performs certain operations in the dialogue box. These operations generate what's called a *callback* to the LISP program: The dialogue box calls back the controlling program so that it can figure out how to respond. The program statements you write to handle callbacks are called *action expressions* (or, in ADS, *callback functions*). Action expressions are specified with the (action_tile) function, which associates a program action with a dialogue tile. In other words, an (action_tile) expression says "if the user does something in this tile, perform these steps."

WELCOME.DCL contains only two tiles that the user can do anything with: the Your Response: edit box, whose key is *"response,"* and the OK button, whose key is *"accept."* As a result, WELCOME.LSP contains two action expression lines—one for each tile. The action expression for the edit box, *"(setq resp $value),"* sets the LISP variable resp to the contents of the edit box (*$value* is a magic name that means the current value of the tile). The action expression for the edit box, *"(done_dialog 1),"* closes the dialogue box and specifies a return code of 1. Note that both action expressions are contained in quotation marks, like strings.

Now at last the dialogue box is ready to make its appearance. The (start_dialog) function displays the dialogue box on the screen, at which point the LISP program waits until the user picks OK or presses <Enter>. While the dialogue box is on the screen, the LISP program sits attentively in the background, waiting for callbacks. Each time the dialogue issues a callback, LISP jumps into action and carries out the action expression associated with the tile that generated the callback. Unless the action expression is (done_dialog), the dialogue box remains on the screen and LISP goes back to waiting.

When the user presses the button with a (done_dialog) action expression, (start_dialog) relinquishes control and returns the return code from (done_dialog)—in this case, 1. This program doesn't do anything with the return value, but most real programs will use it to determine how the user exited the dialogue (whether by picking OK or Cancel, for instance). Based on this information, the program decides what steps to take.

(unload_dialog) unloads the entire dialogue file from memory. Dialogues consume a fair amount of memory, and it's a good idea to unload them once their job is done. Note that (unload_dialog), like (new_dialog), uses the dialogue file's integer handle.

Finally, the (princ) statements in this simple program display a message on the command line in order to prove that the program really did something.

A PDB Tile and Function Minicatalogue

In this section, we present a minicatalogue of DCL tiles and attributes and AutoLISP functions for controlling PDBs. This listing presents only a subset of useful tiles and functions, but it will suffice for our tutorial and will get you started creating simple dialogues. Refer to Chapter 9 of the *AutoCAD Customization Manual* for more information about these and other tiles and functions.

DCL TILES

- `dialog{}`

The dialog{ } tile defines a new dialogue box layout. It is preceded by the dialogue box's name, and all tiles in the dialogue are nested inside the curly braces. Commonly used attributes are *label* and *initial_focus*. Example:

```
mydia : dialogue {
    label           = "Just a Test";
    initial_focus   = "my_box";
    ... tile definitions ...
}
```

- text{}

The text{ } tile defines a read-only text message. Commonly used attributes are *label* and *alignment*. Example:

```
: text {
    label       = "Eat at Joe's";
    alignment   = centered;
}
```

- edit_box{}

The edit_box{ } tile defines a text box in which the user can edit a string. Commonly used attributes are *key, label*, and *allow_accept*. Example:

```
: edit_box {
    key             = "my_box";
    label           = "Password, please:";
    allow_accept    = true;
}
```

- button{}

The button{ } tile defines a button the user can pick in order to carry out an action. Commonly used attributes are *key, label*, and *fixed_width*. Example:

```
: button {
    key             = "my_button";
    label           = "Push me";
    fixed_width     = true;
}
```

- ok_cancel

ok_cancel is not actually a tile but a standard *subassembly* of tiles defined in AutoCAD's BASE.DCL. Subassemblies, such as ok_cancel, are designed to make common DCL coding chores easier and to give dialogues a standard look and feel. Use ok_cancel at the end of your custom dialogue definition in order to place OK and Cancel buttons at the bottom of the dialogue (see Figure 20.8 later in the chapter for an example).

Predefined attributes for the OK button are:

```
key           = "accept"
label         = "OK"
is_default    = true
```

is_default = *true* means that this is the button AutoCAD "presses" when the user presses <Enter> while in a tile with *allow_accept* = *true*.

Predefined attributes for the Cancel button are:

```
key           = "cancel"
label         = "Cancel"
is_cancel     = true
```

is_cancel = *true* means that this is the button AutoCAD "presses" when the user presses <Esc> or <Ctrl>+C.

Tip

There are other useful subassemblies in BASE.DCL, including ok_only and errtile. Some of these are documented in Chapter 9 of the *AutoCAD Customization Manual*. Don't change anything in BASE.DCL; all of AutoCAD's stock dialogues rely on it, and changing the subassembly definitions can make a mess of the standard dialogues.

AUTOLISP PDB FUNCTIONS

- (load_dialog *dcl_file*)

(load_dialog) loads a .DCL file into memory and returns an integer handle that other dialogue-handling functions must use. Example:

```
(setq dcl_handle (load_dialog "MYDIAFIL"))
```

loads MYDIAFIL.DCL into memory and sets the variable dcl_handle to the dialogue file's integer handle.

- (new_dialog *dialogue_name dcl_file_handle*)

(new_dialog) selects an individual dialogue box definition from a .DCL file that has been loaded previously with (load_dialog). (new_dialog) returns t if it finds *dialogue_name* and nil if not. Example:

```
(new_dialog "mydiabox" dcl_handle)
```

selects mydiabox from the .DCL file whose handle is stored in the dcl_handle variable. Subsequent calls to dialogue functions, such as (action_tile) and (start_dialog), will refer to this dialogue.

- (action_tile *tile_key action_expression*)

(action_tile) associates an action with a tile callback. When the user selects or edits in the tile whose key is *tile_key*, AutoLISP evaluates the *action_expression*. Example:

```
((action_tile "my_edit" "setq str1 $value)")
```

associates an action with the edit box whose key is *my_edit*. This action causes AutoLISP to assign the current value of the edit box to the variable str1 whenever the user edits in this box. *$value* is a magic name that stands for a tile's current value. See Table 9.7 in the *AutoCAD Customization Manual* for a list of other magic names.

- (done_dialog *return_code*)

(done_dialog) is used in an action expression to close the dialogue box. *return_code* is a code that tells your LISP program how the user exited the dialogue. Typically, 1 means the user picked OK, 0 means the user picked Cancel, and any other codes are defined by the application. (start_dialog) returns this code after the dialogue closes, at which point the LISP program can decide what steps to take (whether to update variables, modify entities, etc.). Example:

```
(done_dialog 1)
```

closes the dialogue and tells (start_dialog) to return 1. You usually would assign this action expression to the OK key.

- (set_tile *tile_key tile_value*)

(set_tile) initializes a tile with a value. It's possible to "hard-code" an initial value in the .DCL file (with the value attribute), but (set_tile) lets you insert a value that's calculated at runtime. Example:

```
(set_tile "my_edit" (getvar "CLAYER"))
```

displays the current layer name in the tile whose key is *my_edit*.

- (start_dialog)

(start_dialog) pops up the dialogue that has been selected with (new_dialog). (start_dialog) then waits for the user to close the dialogue, after which it returns the return code specified by (done_dialog).

- (unload_dialog *dcl_file_handle*)

(unload_dialog) removes a .DCL file's dialogue definitions from memory. Example:

```
(unload_dialog dcl_handle)
```

unloads from memory the .DCL file whose handle is stored in the dcl_handle variable.

Tip

AutoLISP dialogue-handling functions are listed but not fully documented in the *AutoLISP Programmer's Reference Manual*. Refer to the "Function Catalogue" section of Chapter 9 in the *AutoCAD Customization Manual* for complete documentation of these functions.

PDB Techniques

In this section, we discuss the different ways of creating custom dialogue boxes, some techniques for testing and debugging, and user interface design issues.

Ready-Made AutoLISP Dialogues

LISP programmers who don't want to tackle full dialogue box customization have two ready-made and easy-to-use dialogues at their disposal: an alert box and the standard file dialogue box. The new AutoLISP functions (alert) and (getfiled) let you add a bit of dialogue box panache to your programs without your having to master DCL and callbacks. (alert) is similar to (princ), but it displays only strings and puts them in a dialogue box; see Figure 20.4.

(getfiled) is somewhat more involved, but still straightforward compared to creating your own dialogue from scratch. (getfiled) accepts four arguments: the dialogue box title, default filename, default file extension, and bit-coded flags that control various options. Figure 20.5 shows the result of the following call to (getfiled):

```
(getfiled "Select a Text File" "" "TXT" 2)
```

Chapter 4 of the *AutoLISP Programmer's Reference Manual* includes complete documentation for (alert) and (getfiled).

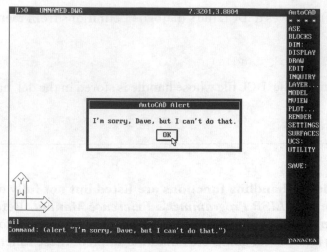

Figure 20.4   Using the (alert) function.

Building Your Own PDBs

Making dialogue boxes from scratch involves creating the DCL layout, writing the LISP program that controls it, and then testing and refining the two so that they work together effectively. This is a tricky process, since it involves at least two files (and two programming languages). In addition, you have to consider a larger number of user interaction and error possibilities than you do with command line programs. Ordinary LISP routines rigidly control the sequence of actions, so input validation and error trapping are comparatively straightforward. Dialogue boxes, on the other hand, let the user select tiles and make entries in any sequence—not just the one

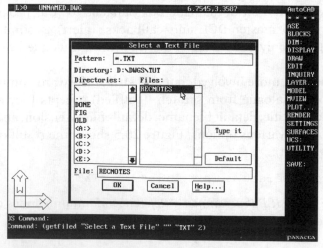

Figure 20.5   Using the (getfiled) function.

that you had in mind when you designed the dialogue! It takes time to adjust your thinking and programming approach to this new process, but with experience it becomes familiar.

Release 12 comes with over two dozen .DCL files in the \ACAD\SUPPORT and \ACAD\SAMPLE directories. Most of these .DCLs are quite involved, but you can look at some of the simpler ones (such as DDTYPE.DCL and DDOSNAP.DCL) for ideas. You might try modifying copies of some of the stock dialogues in order to get a feel for how DCL works. Whatever you do, don't modify BASE.DCL and ACAD.DCL, since everything else depends on these.

Testing and Debugging PDBs

Programming dialogue boxes, like ordinary LISP programming, benefits immensely from planning and a step-wise approach. You'll cut down on the time required to test and debug your dialogues if you adopt an organized approach. Sketch out your dialogue box's layout on a piece of paper (see Figure 20.6) and consider how users are likely to interact with it. Think about the callbacks that each tile will generate, and note the kinds of action expressions you'll use to respond to them. As with all LISP programs, write an outline before you start typing in the code.

Create the .DCL file with only a few representative tiles first, and use a simple loader program, such as the one shown earlier in the sample .LSP program for controlling WELCOME.DCL, to put the dialogue box on the screen. Then build up the full dialogue layout in stages so that you can correct mistakes as you go. Besides obvious layout mistakes, syntax errors will crop up as you modify your .DCL files. AutoCAD displays syntax error messages in a dialogue box, and tells you where to start looking (see Figure 20.7).

Once the dialogue layout has taken shape, start developing the accompanying LISP program. Work on one or two action expressions at a time, and test each one thoroughly. As you refine the LISP program, you'll probably find that you have to go back to the .DCL file and make modifications to it as well. At this stage, it's important to have a text editor that can open at least two windows at once, so that you can compare the .DCL and .LSP files. Once you have all of the pieces in place, you'll need to test the actual operation of the dialogue. Try different sequences, including erroneous ones that test error trapping.

As you begin to attain competence in dialogue box programming, you can take a more direct but still "safe" approach to dialogue box development. When developing a new dialogue, find the existing one that's most similar to it. Copy the .DCL and .LSP files from the existing dialogue, and then delete, modify, and add pieces as needed.

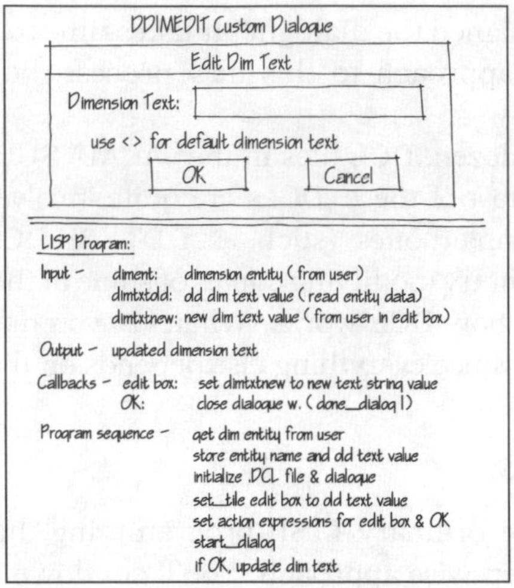

Figure 20.6 Planning a PDB.

User Interface Design

Just as knowing AutoCAD doesn't make someone a competent engineer or architect, knowing DCL and AutoLISP won't make you a competent dialogue box designer. User interface design is a combination of art and science, and it's quite easy to create dialogues that are awkward, confusing, or ugly. Make sure you have, or can develop, some talent at designing interfaces if you intend to create many of them.

Look at Autodesk's and third-party developers' dialogues for good and bad examples, and try to maintain consistency with the ones that your users are accustomed to. In fact, sometimes you can use a stock AutoCAD dialogue as the basis of your own custom one. This "borrowing" approach will prevent your dialogues from being too amateurish, save design time, and, if worse comes to worst, give you someone else to blame.

Chapter 9 in the *AutoCAD Customization Manual* includes a 14-page section called "Guidelines for Dialogue Box Design" that you can use to guide your efforts. This is one of the most useful (and straightforward) parts of Chapter 9, so take advantage of it.

PDB Tutorial

The tutorial below demonstrates developing a simple dialogue box interface to the DIM NEWTEXT command. It contains a minimum of error trapping in order to keep the example simple.

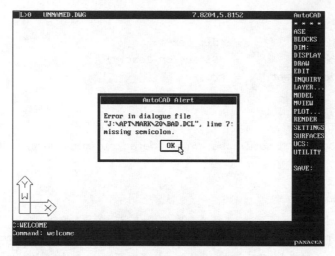

Figure 20.7   AutoCAD reporting a .DCL error.

Developing a PDB

1. Plan out the dialogue box.

Sketch the dialogue box design and outline the accompanying LISP program.

Our design is shown in Figure 20.6.

2. Change to \ACUSTOM\TEST and launch AutoCAD.

3. Create the .DCL file.

This dialogue is simple enough that we can create the .DCL file in one fell swoop. Of course, you'll want to experiment with different attributes (and tiles) on your first few dialogues, but we'll leave that to you.

Type in the text shown below.

Make sure you include all the colons, semicolons, and curly braces.

Save the file as DDIMEDIT.DCL.

```
// DDIMEDIT.DCL: PDB for editing Dimension text
// Version 1.0 14 June 93 by Mark Middlebrook


dim_edit : dialog {
    label               = "Edit Dimension Text";
    initial_focus       = "dim_text";
```

```
: edit_box {
    key            = "dim_text";
    label          = "Dimension Text:";
    allow_accept   = true;
}

: text {
    label  = " note: use <> for default dimension text ";
}

ok_cancel;
}
```

This .DCL file is similar to the sample presented in the sample .DCL file shown at the beginning of this chapter except that it uses the standard ok_cancel subassembly to define the OK and Cancel buttons.

4. Create an AutoLISP program that simply displays the dialogue.

In order to check the dialogue box layout, we just want to start with a loader program that puts the dialogue on the screen and lets us close it.

Begin a new file in your editor and type in the text shown below.

The only action expression we need right now is the one that responds to the OK button (whose key is *accept*).

Save the file as DDIMEDIT.LSP.

```
(defun C:DDIMEDIT ()

    (setq dcl_id (load_dialog "DDIMEDIT.DCL"))
    (if (not (new_dialog "dim_edit" dcl_id)) (exit))

    (action_tile "accept" "(done_dialog 1)" )

    (start_dialog)
    (unload_dialog dcl_id)
    (princ)
)
```

5. Test the dialogue box design.

Return to AutoCAD and load DDIMEDIT.LSP:

```
Command: (LOAD "DDIMEDIT")
```

```
C:DDIMEDIT
Command: DDIMEDIT
```

The dialogue box should appear on screen, as shown in Figure 20.8. Note that the edit box is blank. You can edit in it, but the text you type isn't saved anywhere or used for anything.

Test the dialogue.

Try opening and closing the dialogue several times. Use the OK and Cancel buttons, and also try <Enter> and <Esc>. Correct any problems in DDIMEDIT.DCL and DDIMEDIT.LSP before proceeding.

6. Add and test the code for extracting, displaying, and updating dimension text.

To make the dialogue perform some useful work, we must do three things:

- Prompt the user for a dimension entity and extract its text.

- Initialize the edit box with the current dimension text string and associate an action expression with this tile.

- Update the dimension text, but only if the user picks OK.

Open DDIMEDIT.LSP and add the code shown below in italics.

```
(defun C:DDIMEDIT ()
    (setq diment (car (entsel "\nSelect a dimension: "))
          dimtxtold (cdr (assoc 1 (entget diment)))
    )

    (setq dcl_id (load_dialog "ddimedit.dcl"))
    (if (not (new_dialog "dim_edit" dcl_id)) (exit))

    (set_tile "dim_text" dimtxtold)
    (action_tile "dim_text" "(setq dimtxtnew $value)" )
    (action_tile "accept" "(done_dialog 1)" )

    (if (equal (start_dialog) 1)
        (command "_.DIM1" "NEWTEXT" dimtxtnew diment "")
    )

    (unload_dialog dcl_id)
    (princ)
)
```

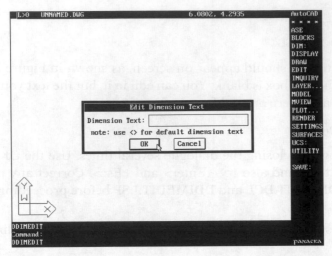

Figure 20.8   The dialogue defined in DDIMEDIT.DCL.

The first new section prompts the user for a dimension entity, stores its entity name in the variable diment, and stores the dimension text (DXF group code 1) in the variable dimtxtold. Note that, in order to keep the example simple, we haven't included any error trapping to check whether the user did in fact select a dimension entity. TEXTEDIT.LSP in the previous chapter shows how to do this.

The second set of additions loads the current dimension text value into the edit box and associates an action expression with this box. Whenever the user edits the text, AutoLISP will store the new value in the variable dimtxtnew.

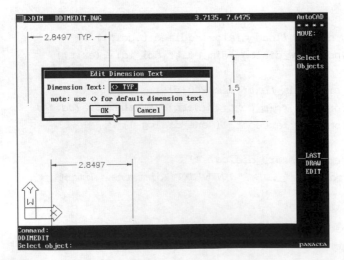

Figure 20.9   DDIMEDIT in action.

Finally, we wrap (start_dialog) in an if statement that says "if the user closed the dialogue by picking OK (or pressing <Enter>), then go ahead and change the dimension text."

Save DDIMEDIT.LSP, return to AutoCAD, reload the LISP program, and test.

Create several dimension entities and try editing them with DDIMEDIT. The completed PDB is shown in Figure 20.9.

7. Finish up DDIMEDIT.LSP by defining local variables and adding a header comment and load message.

As described in the previous chapter, you should make program variables local unless you need them to be global. Also, it's a good idea to identify the program.

Open DDIMEDIT.LSP and make the additions shown below in italics.

We've also replaced the (command "_.DIM1"...) line with a cleaner and more efficient line that uses (entmod) to modify the dimension entity directly.

Save, reload, and retest DDIMEDIT.

```
;DDIMEDIT.LSP: routine to edit Dimension text in a PDB
; Version 1.0 14 June 93  by Mark Middlebrook
; Requires DDIMEDIT.DCL

(defun C:DDIMEDIT ( / diment dimtxtold dcl_id dimtxtnew)
    (setq diment (car (entsel "\nSelect a dimension: "))
          dimtxtold (cdr (assoc 1 (entget diment)))
    )

    (setq dcl_id (load_dialog "ddimedit.dcl"))
    (if (not (new_dialog "dim_edit" dcl_id)) (exit))

    (set_tile "dim_text" dimtxtold)
    (action_tile "dim_text" "(setq dimtxtnew $value)" )
    (action_tile "accept" "(done_dialog 1)" )

    (if (equal (start_dialog) 1)
    (entmod (list (cons -1 diment) (cons 1 dimtxtnew)))

    )
```

```
          (unload_dialog dcl_id)
          (princ)
)


(princ "/nDDIMEDIT.LSP loaded. DDIMEDIT runs it.")
(princ)
```

Finishing Up

Once you've tested the dialogue box thoroughly, move DDIMEDIT.DCL and DDIMEDIT.LSP to your \ACUSTOM directory so that they're available in your normal AutoCAD editing sessions.

The *AutoCAD Power Tools* disk includes an enhanced version of DDIMEDIT that provides better error trapping and a link to the TEXTEDIT program from the previous chapter. If you prefer to use these versions, copy DDIMEDIT.DCL, DDIMEDIT.LSP, and TEXTEDIT.LSP from the disk to your \ACUSTOM directory.

PDBs and Workgroups

The primary workgroup issue with programmable dialogue boxes is consistency of interface. Your workgroup members (especially Windows or Macintosh users) will become more accustomed to using AutoCAD's and your third-party application's dialogues. Some users may begin to see in-house custom utilities that do everything at the command line as antiquated. Perception aside, there may be ease-of-learning and ease-of-use benefits to wrapping a dialogue box around some of your in-house programs. You'll need to decide whether it's worth the company's while to create dialogue box interfaces for custom programs. If so, this might be a good time to bring in a consultant with solid PDB experience.

On the other hand, command-line operation still is the most efficient approach for many tasks, especially for experienced users. Some power users resent having to navigate through dialogues and are slowed down by them. Take this concern into account when developing in-house programs or evaluating third-party applications.

As dialogue box programming becomes a more common skill, you'll see more dialogue-box-driven freeware and shareware. Comb the usual sources (CompuServe, *CADENCE*, *CADalyst*, etc.) for useful and well-designed dialogues, and incorporate them into your workgroup's AutoCAD system.

Tip

One good approach is to use CMDDIA to control whether your AutoLISP programs rely on dialogue boxes or the command line for input. CMDDIA controls AutoCAD's PLOT and ASE commands, but your applications can also use it. If the CMDDIA system variable is set to 1, pop up the dialogue box; but if CMDDIA=0, use command line prompts instead. An obvious disadvantage of this approach is that it requires more development time. However, if you already have an "old-fashioned" LISP program, it usually doesn't take long to incorporate the command-line code into a new dialogue box version.

Summary

Programmable dialogue boxes are a welcome enhancement to Release 12, but taking full advantage of them requires considerable programming and interface design skill. AutoLISP functions such as (alert) and (getfiled) let you add dialogues to your programs without having to learn AutoCAD's PDB facility. By becoming acquainted with DCL and a few PDB-handling AutoLISP functions, you can modify existing dialogues and perhaps write simple dialogues from scratch. With these skills, you'll be able to create a more sophisticated and user-friendly interface for your AutoCAD customization.

21

Panacea Device Independent Graphics Interface

The Panacea Device Independent Graphics Interface (PDIGI) is a direct interface to the AutoCAD display. It is provided by Panacea, the same company that produced the TurboDLD*Lite*™ driver included on the *AutoCAD Power Tools* disk. PDIGI—pronounced to rhyme with "Gee, did she?"—is a sophisticated C interface that allows experienced programmers to write programs that directly affect what shows up on the AutoCAD display screen.

Unlike earlier chapters, this one is not intended for use in simple, or even moderately complex, customization of AutoCAD. Instead, it describes powerful programming interfaces for use by experienced C programmers. If you want to use PDIGI to add power to your applications, you will first need to gain experience in writing C programs that work with AutoCAD, and in writing graphics programs that manipulate displays.

About This Chapter

In this chapter, we describe how to use PDIGI to directly access the AutoCAD graphics display through C and assembly-language programs. Then we list and describe the functions that make up the PDIGI interface. We also tell you how to make the PDIGI interface available on the machines of end users so that programs you write that use PDIGI will run.

Further information about PDIGI is not provided in the AutoCAD manuals; this is a third-party interface written and supported by Panacea. See below for information about how to get support.

555

NOTE

All the files described in this chapter, including the PDIGI library files and programming examples, are included on the *AutoCAD Power Tools* disk. See Chapter 22 for installation instructions.

A PDIGI Primer

Experienced AutoCAD programmers have a large and growing wish list for better and more powerful ways to customize AutoCAD. ADS is, of course, the answer to many requests. However, Autodesk has not yet provided an easy, powerful way to directly access the AutoCAD display.

PDIGI is the answer to this problem. It allows you to use C functions to directly access and update any part of the screen. With PDIGI, your applications can be a great deal more powerful.

Programming Knowledge Required

Just a quick note before we go any farther: It is assumed that in wanting to use PDIGI, you have some understanding of two topics:

1. C programming, which is a necessity for **ADS** programming.

2. Workings of pixel-oriented graphics work, including such topics as coordinate spaces, color look-up tables, and simple geometry.

You also should know enough about assembly language programming to type in and assemble the code, described below, that starts PDIGI. Alternatively, however, you simply can link in the PDIGISUB.OBJ file located on the *AutoCAD Power Tools* disk. More information and a PDIGI programming tutorial are provided later in the chapter.

What Is PDIGI?

PDIGI is a way to directly access your graphics display while using DOS versions of AutoCAD Release 11 or Release 12, using ADS routines from within AutoCAD.

PDIGI was created under Release 11 because there was no decent way to get access to the display, while under Release 12, the only Autodesk-supported method is a klunky, slow, and limited technique called the *ADS->ADI link*.

Since, by definition, PDIGI must have access to the display, it is best implemented in the display driver used for AutoCAD. All the products in

NOTE

For up-to-the-minute information on PDIGI, including information on the latest application support and enhancements to the PDIGI interface, you may want to check out Panacea's BBS and CompuServe's ACAD Forum. New versions of PDIGI for DOS AutoCAD are guaranteed to be fully backward compatible with earlier versions.

Panacea's TurboDLD product family, as of version 1.02, incorporate PDIGI, including the TurboDLD*Lite* software you acquired when you purchased this book. However, TurboDLD*Lite* is not freely distributable—your purchase of this book entitles you to a single user license of the software. Because of this, Panacea provides TurboDLD*Demo* on its BBS (603-432-5193) and in CompuServe's ACAD Forum.

TurboDLD*Demo* is a demonstration version of Panacea's full-featured TurboDLD*Deluxe* (TurboDLD*Lite* with several additional user interface features), allowing access to the full feature set of TurboDLD*Deluxe* for 20 minutes a day. After the 20 minutes expire, TurboDLD*Demo* reverts to being a plain AutoCAD (and 3D Studio) display driver (with no display list), but here's the important part: It still includes PDIGI in its most basic mode, and *is* freely distributable, with no obligation to the publisher of this book or Panacea.

Also, various TurboDLD products can be found with many of today's most popular graphics boards, and all of these custom versions of TurboDLD include PDIGI support as well. Ultimately, PDIGI support can be found, or can be legally made available, just about anywhere. And, because PDIGI is an open architecture interface, other display driver manufacturers can implement the interface as well.

A number of AutoCAD add-on applications are in the process of completing PDIGI compatible applications. The PDIGI logo (shown in Figure 21.1) is used by application vendors to certify that their applications are PDIGI compatible. If you're interested in licensing the logo for display on and in your software, contact Panacea Inc. at the address listed in back of this book. There is no fee involved in licensing PDIGI; just an obligation to maintain PDIGI compatibility in your software.

Figure 21.1   PDIGI Logo.

How PDIGI Works

PDIGI is implemented in a two-part mechanism. The first part, namely the dependency on the display driver, has been described above. The second part is a library for C and Assembly Language programs to link with in order to access PDIGI. Source code for the library can be found at the end of this chapter, so that you can use it with any protected mode ADS-compatible compiler you choose. The library was initially developed with MetaWare High C v1.7 and PharLap's 386ASM, but also can be used with Watcom C. The source code is provided for purposes of reference and for use with a library compiled with a different set of tools. The reason for this warning is that it is quite likely that the PDIGI interface documented in the following pages may appear on other platforms, such as Windows or UNIX, but would have library internals significantly different from those necessary for use with DOS.

The first step in accessing PDIGI is to confirm that it's, in fact, present. This is done by issuing the **PDIGIENTRY** or **PDIGIALTENTRY***XXXX:YYYYYYYY* commands at the AutoCAD command line. If the command is not recognized, then PDIGI is not available. However, if it is recognized, then a link can be established. For the **PDIGIENTRY** command, the driver will return an address, in *Selector:Offset* format, to an entry point in the display driver. For the PDIGIALTENTRY command, the *XXXX:YYYYYYYY* indicated above is a pointer to an address in the ADS application's memory where the driver should store the address of its PDIGI entry point. The reason for having both functions is to provide an option for a PDIGI application on how to interface to PDIGI. The PDIGIENTRY command requires the user to hit <Enter> during the link process, while the PDIGIALTENTRY does not. Full details can be found in the PDIGI.C library code listing at the end of this chapter.

No matter how the entry point is determined, it is then used for all information interchange, including executing graphics instructions. The information retrievable via this entry point ranges from display capabilities to current viewport settings. From a programming perspective, this entire initialization operation is performed by the *InitPDIGI()* function documented later in this chapter.

Since it is possible for AutoCAD or the user to have changed the environment between PDIGI screen accesses (i.e., when your PDIGI application relinquishes control back to AutoCAD), it's recommended that you query the current state of the display via the *InitPDIGI()* function every time your application gains control, to avoid unexpected results.

Conversely, it's recommended that your PDIGI application save all portions of the display that may be affected by PDIGI calls, perform its operations, and then restore the display to its former state. If modifying only a single viewport, you may suggest that the user use a REDRAW to restore the state of that viewport to what AutoCAD expects it to be.

An important note regarding all PDIGI graphics functions that require a drawing color is that the color must be in the right format for the display device. A look-up table reference is provided to ensure that you can translate an AutoCAD color into the appropriate device color. This is vital for accessing devices with more than 8 bits per pixel. Details on the color table, and how to access data buffers in the display driver's data selector can be found under the information for the *InitPDIGI()* function.

Before we list all the functions for PDIGI, it's important to understand the nomenclature and definitions used in the function explanations. A portion of the C include file for PDIGI is defined below, listing the definitions of various variable types. Another convention used by PDIGI is that all drawing coordinates are referenced with the origin (0,0) in the upper left corner of the display.

PDIGI Type Definitions

```
typedef         char               BYTE
typedef         unsigned char      UBYTE
typedef         short              WORD
typedef         unsigned short     UWORD
typedef         long               DWORD
typedef         unsigned long      UDWORD
typedef         void               VOID
typedef         UDWORD             COLOR
typedef         struct
    {
    UBYTE       red;
    UBYTE       green;
    UBYTE       blue;
    } LUTDATA;
```

PDIGI Reference

The following is a summary of all functions defined by PDIGI v1.0 and its associated library, listed in ascending alphabetic order. The intent is that you can read through the list of functions in order to get a feel for the language, then look up specific functions later when the need arises. Note that the function titles leave off the "PDIGI_" prefix for convenience, in order to make it easier to look up the functions. This approach also is used in the function descriptions to reference other PDIGI functions.

BitBLT (Bit BLock Transfer)—Copy a rectangle of screen data

```
VOID                PDIGI_BitBLT(UDWORD srcX, UDWORD srcY,
                    UDWORD width, UDWORD height, UDWORD dstX,
                    UDWORD dstY)
```

Description:

This function copies a rectangular portion of the display to another part of the display. No overlap checking is done, so if the destination rectangle overwrites portions of the source rectangle, the BitBLT will produce strange results. In TurboDLD, this function is used primarily to scroll the command text area at the bottom of the screen.

Parameters:

srcX, srcY
These specify the coordinate of the upper left corner of the source rectangle to be copied.

width
The width, in pixels, of the rectangle to be copied.

height
The height, in scan lines, of the rectangle to be copied.

dstX, dstY
The coordinate of the upper left corner of the destination rectangle.

Related Functions:

ReadRectArea, WriteRectArea

CalcRectSpace—Calculate byte size of screen rectangle

```
DWORD               PDIGI_CalcRectSpace(UDWORD x1, UDWORD y1,
                    UDWORD x2, UDWORD y2)
```

Description:

This function is used to calculate the amount of memory required when saving part of the screen via the *ReadRectArea()* function. The number of bytes required is the return value for this function, and should be used to allocate memory for the *ReadRectArea()* call.

For display modes less than 8 bits per pixel, PDIGI software should never assume it knows how much space a given screen rectangle will require to save; just knowing the size and bits per pixel will not always accurately determine size, based on the memory architecture of the current display device.

For display modes of at least 8 bits per pixel, the amount of memory required by a screen rectangle can be calculated by multiplying the width of the rectangle by its height by the number of bytes per pixel, although it is still recommended you use this function to avoid any potential incompatibilities.

Parameters:

x1, y1   The upper left coordinate of the rectangle whose size is to be calculated.

x2, y2   The lower right corner of the rectangle.

Related Functions:
ReadRectArea, WriteRectArea

ComplexPolygon—Draw a filled, complex polygon on the screen

```
VOID            PDIGI_ComplexPolygon(UWORD *vertexList,
                UDWORD vertexCnt, COLOR color)
```

Description:
This function draws a filled complex polygon on the screen. A complex polygon is basically defined as a polygon (or solid if using AutoCAD terminology) which is self-intersecting, such as an "hour-glass" or "bow-tie." However, this is the best function to call if you have no way of knowing if you have a complex or convex (simple) polygon. This function will automatically close the polygon (i.e., connect the first and last points in the vertex list). Polygons with up to 10 vertices are supported.

Parameters:

vertexList   This is a pointer to the list of points for the polygon, and is required to point to a data buffer in the display driver's data selector.

vertexCnt   The count of vertices in the polygon.

color   The desired color of the polygon, in device-specific color format.

Related Functions:
ConvexPolygon, DrawPattPolygon, DrawRect, DrawRectXOR

ConvexPolygon—Draw a filled, convex polygon on the screen

```
VOID                    PDIGI_ConvexPolygon(UWORD  *vertexList,
                        UDWORD vertexCnt, COLOR color)
```

Description:

This function draws a filled convex polygon on the screen. A convex (or simple) polygon is basically defined as a polygon (or solid if using AutoCAD terminology) which is not self-intersecting. All three-point polygons (triangles) are, by definition, convex, while some four-point polygons may be as well. This function will automatically close the polygon (i.e., connect the first and last points in the vertex list).

Parameters:

vertexList   This is a pointer to the list of points for the polygon, and is required to point to a data buffer in the display driver's data selector.

vertexCnt   The count of vertices in the polygon.

color   The desired color of the polygon, in device-specific color format.

Related Functions:

ComplexPolygon, DrawPattPolygon, DrawRect, DrawRectXOR

DrawChar—Draw a text character

```
VOID                    PDIGI_DrawChar(UDWORD x, UDWORD y, UDWORD
                        charVal, COLOR bgColor, COLOR fgColor)
```

Description:

This function will draw a text character on the display, using the default font for the current graphics mode, whose size can be determined at initialization time via the *InitPDIGI()* function.

Parameters:

x, y   The upper left corner of the cell location at which to draw the character, in pixel coordinates.

charVal   The character to draw. The range in value for the character is 0–255.

bgColor   The color to use for displaying the background portion of the text character.

fgColor   The color to use for displaying the foreground portion of the text character.

Related Functions:
DrawString, InitPDIGI

DrawHLine—Draw a horizontal line on the display

```
VOID                PDIGI_DrawHLine(UDWORD x, UDWORD y, UDWORD
                    length, COLOR color)

VOID                PDIGI_DrawHLineXOR(UDWORD  x,  UDWORD  y,
                    UDWORD length, COLOR color)
```

Description:
These functions draw a horizontal line on the screen. The reason to use them instead of the *DrawLine()* and *DrawLineXOR()* functions is that they execute faster and have one fewer parameter.

The *DrawHLineXOR()* function is identical to the *DrawHLine()* function, except that it uses an XOR raster operation to update the display. This is useful for highlighting an object or area, as once the highlight is no longer desired, all that needs to be done is a second identical XOR draw in order to remove the highlight.

Parameters:

x, y   The starting (left) coordinate of the horizontal line.

length   The length of the horizontal line, in pixels.

color   The color to draw the horizontal line in.

Related Functions:
DrawLine, DrawLineXOR, DrawPattLine, DrawPattLineXOR, DrawVLine, DrawVLineXOR

DrawLine—Draw a regular line on the display

```
VOID                PDIGI_DrawLine(UDWORD  x1,  UDWORD  y1,
                    UDWORD x2, UDWORD y2, COLOR color)

VOID                PDIGI_DrawLineXOR(UDWORD x1, UDWORD y1,
                    UDWORD x2, UDWORD y2, COLOR color)
```

Description:

These functions draw a regular line on the screen. *DrawLineXOR()* draws the line using an XOR raster operation.

Parameters:

x1, y1	The starting coordinate of the line.
x2, y2	The ending coordinate of the line.
color	The color in which to draw the line.

Related Functions:

DrawHLine, DrawHLineXOR, DrawPattLine, DrawPattLineXOR, DrawVLine, DrawVLineXOR

DrawPattLine—Draw a patterned line on the display

```
VOID            PDIGI_DrawPattLine(UDWORD x1, UDWORD y1,
                UDWORD x2, UDWORD y2, COLOR bgColor,
                COLOR fgColor)

VOID            PDIGI_DrawPattLineXOR(UDWORD x1, UDWORD
                y1, UDWORD x2, UDWORD y2, COLOR bgColor,
                COLOR fgColor)
```

Description:

These functions draw a patterned line on the screen. *DrawPattLineXOR()* draws the patterned line using an XOR raster operation. The pattern used is currently fixed, and is device-dependent as well.

Parameters:

x1, y1	The starting coordinate of the line.
x2, y2	The ending coordinate of the line.
bgColor	The color in which to draw the background portions of the patterned line. This is normally the screen's default background color, and can be determined as indicated in *InitPDIGI()*.
fgColor	The color in which to draw the foreground portions of the patterned line.

Related Functions:

DrawHLine, DrawHLineXOR, DrawLine, DrawLineXOR, DrawVLine, DrawVLineXOR

DrawPattPolygon—Draw a patterned filled polygon on the screen

```
VOID              PDIGI_DrawPattPolygon(UWORD *vertexList,
                  UDWORD vertexCnt, COLOR bgColor, COLOR
                  fgColor)
```

Description:

This function draws a filled patterned polygon on the screen. Both complex and convex polygons are drawn with this function. This function will automatically close the polygon (i.e., connect the first and last points in the vertex list). Polygons with up to 10 vertices are supported. The pattern used is currently fixed, and is device-dependent as well.

Parameters:

vertexList   This is a pointer to the list of points for the polygon, and is required to point to a data buffer in the display driver's data selector.

vertexCnt   The count of vertices in the polygon.

bgColor   The color in which to draw the background portions of the patterned polygon. This is normally the screen's default background color, and can be determined as indicated in *InitPDIGI()*.

fgColor   The color in which to draw the foreground portions of the patterned polygon.

Related Functions:

ComplexPolygon, ConvexPolygon, DrawRect, DrawRectXOR

DrawRect—Draw a filled rectangle on the display

```
VOID              PDIGI_DrawRect(UDWORD  x1,   UDWORD  y1,
                  UDWORD x2, UDWORD y2, COLOR color)
```

```
VOID              PDIGI_DrawRectXOR(UDWORD  x1,   UDWORD  y1,
                  UDWORD x2, UDWORD y2, COLOR color)
```

Description:

These functions draw a filled rectangle on the screen. *DrawRectXOR()* draws the line using an XOR raster operation.

Parameters:

x1, y1	The upper left coordinate of the rectangle.
x2, y2	The lower right coordinate of the rectangle.
color	The color in which to draw the rectangle.

Related Functions:
ComplexPolygon, ComplexPolygonXOR, ConvexPolygon, ConvexPolygon-XOR, DrawPattPolygon

DrawString—Draw a character string

```
VOID                PDIGI_DrawString(UDWORD x, UDWORD y, UBYTE
                    *string, COLOR bgColor, COLOR fgColor)
```

Description:
This function will draw a text character string on the display, using the default font for the current graphics mode, whose size can be determined at initialization time via the *InitPDIGI()* function.

Parameters:

x, y	The upper left corner of the cell location at which to start drawing the character string, in pixel coordinate space.
string	This is a pointer to a null-terminated string of characters (1 byte each), and is required to point to a data buffer in the display driver's data selector.
bgColor	The color to use for displaying the background portion of each text character.
fgColor	The color to use for displaying the foreground portion of each text character.

Related Functions:
DrawChar, InitPDIGI

DrawVLine—Draw a vertical line on the display

```
VOID                PDIGI_DrawVLine(UDWORD x, UDWORD y, UDWORD
                    length, COLOR color)

VOID                PDIGI_DrawVLineXOR(UDWORD  x,  UDWORD  y,
                    UDWORD length, COLOR color)
```

Description:

These functions draw a vertical line on the screen. The reason to use them instead of the *DrawLine()* and *DrawLineXOR()* functions is that they execute faster and have one fewer parameter.

Parameters:

x, y	The starting (top) coordinate of the vertical line.
length	The length (height) of the vertical line, in pixels.
color	The color to draw the vertical line in.

Related Functions:

DrawHLine, DrawHLineXOR, DrawLine, DrawLineXOR, DrawPattLine, DrawPattLineXOR

GetLUT—Get the color Look-Up Table (LUT)

```
VOID            PDIGI_GetLUT(LUTDATA *lutData, UDWORD count,
                UDWORD start)
```

Description:

This function interrogates the current display device to see how its hardware color palette is set up. The primary uses of this function are either to save the current palette for later restoration, or to determine what the closest match to a desired color might be for drawing or rendering. Note that some devices may not have a color palette, especially devices running in resolutions which have more or less than 8 bits per pixel. Palettes have no more than 256 entries.

Parameters:

lutData	This is a pointer to a data buffer in the display driver's data selector.
count	The number of color palette entries you want to get, ranging from 1 to 256.
start	The palette entry from which to start reading. May be a number from 0 to 255.

Related Functions:

GetLUTEntry, InitPDIGI, SetLUT, SetLUTEntry

GetLUTEntry—Get a color LUT entry

```
VOID              PDIGI_GetLUTEntry(UDWORD index, UBYTE *red,
                  UBYTE *green, UBYTE *blue)
```

Description:

This function returns the red, green, and blue subcomponent intensities of the digital color referenced by the index. Intensities range from 0 to 255 (8 bits). Note that some devices may not have a color palette, especially devices running in resolutions which have more or less than 8 bits per pixel. Palettes have no more than 256 entries or indices.

Parameters:

index
: The palette entry from which to retrieve the color palette information.

red,green,blue
: Pointers to byte data areas in the display driver's data segment.

Related Functions:

GetLUT, InitPDIGI, SetLUT, SetLUTEntry

InitPDIGI—Initialize the PDIGI interface

```
PDIGIDATA         *InitPDIGI()
```

Description:

This is the very first function a PDIGI application needs to call. Its purpose is to try to detect the PDIGI interface built into the display driver. It is recommended that a PDIGI application call this function.

Return Value:

The return value from this function reflects its success. If the return value is set to 0 (NULL), a PDIGI interface was NOT detected. If this return value is anything but 0, it points to the offset, in the display driver's code/data selector, of a 4KB buffer that the PDIGI application can use for transferring local data to and from the display driver. Note that it is assumed that the display driver's code and data selectors point to the same range of memory, except that when using the code selector for access, data can only be read and not written. The data selector must be used to write this buffer. Note that the PDIGI application may not assume that the contents of the 4KB buffer will remain constant as some functions, such as *ComplexPolygon()*, will modify the contents of this scratch buffer. At initialization, this buffer contains the following structure:

```
typedef struct

  {
  UWORD     PDIGI_VERS;        /* PDIGI Version */
  UWORD     PDIGI_DS;          /* Our DS */
  UDWORD    PDIGI_VPINF;       /* Pointer to the VP structures */
  UDWORD    PDIGI_CURVP;       /* Pointer to current VP */
  UDWORD    PDIGI_VPLEN;       /* Length of a VP block entry */
  UWORD     PDIGI_MAXVP;       /* The maximum number of VPs */
  UWORD     PDIGI_YBIAS;       /* The y-bias (for VP calcs) */
  UDWORD    PDIGI_SCRPT;       /* Pointer to active screen struc. */
  UWORD     PDIGI_CHRWD;       /* Character width */
  UWORD     PDIGI_CHRHT;       /* Character height */
  UWORD     PDIGI_SIDWD;       /* Side menu width (chars) */
  UWORD     PDIGI_CMDHT;       /* Command area, number of char lines */
  UWORD     PDIGI_TOPOF;       /* Flag for status line inactive */
  UWORD     PDIGI_XMAX;        /* Right edge of drawing area */
  UDWORD    PDIGI_CLRTB;       /* Pointer to colorTable */
  UDWORD    PDIGI_CLRLG;       /* Pointer to logical color table */
  UDWORD    PDIGI_CLRPH;       /* Physical color table (for <=8bpp) */
  UDWORD    PDIGI_CLRXR;       /* XOR Color (full width) */
  } PDIGIDATA;
```

Detailed Structure Information:

PDIGI_VERS

This 16-bit value contains the version number of this implementation of PDIGI, encoded with the major version number in the high byte, and the minor version number in the low byte. Version 1.00 (documented in this chapter) returns a version number of 0x0100.

PDIGI_DS

This 16-bit value contains the display driver's data selector, which is required for read *and* write access to the 4KB buffer local to the display driver. This buffer is used for functions like *GetLUT()* and *SetLUT()*.

PDIGI_VPINF

Display driver local pointer to the internal structures used to store information about the active viewports. The relevant part of the viewport structures used by PDIGI v1.00 is as follows:

```
typedef struct
  {
  UWORD       VP_NUM;          /* ID number AutoCAD knows this viewport
                                  by */
  UWORD       VP_XMIN;         /* Screen coordinates of this viewport,
                                  in */
  UWORD       VP_YMIN;         /* Y-bias adjusted coordinates. */
  UWORD       VP_XMAX;
  UWORD       VP_YMAX;
  UWORD       VP_RSVD0;        /* Reserved - do not use */
  UDWORD      VP_XWIDTH;       /* Dimensions of the viewport in pixels */
  UDWORD      VP_YHEIGHT;
  UDWORD      VP_MAXLXWID;     /* The maximum dimensions of the logical
                                  space */
  UDWORD      VP_MAXLYHGT;
  UDWORD      VP_LGXL;         /* Position of the viewport in logical
                                  space */
  UDWORD      VP_LGYL;
  UDWORD      VP_LGXH;
  UDWORD      VP_LGYH;
  UDWORD      VP_RSVD1[9];     /* Reserved - do not use */
  REAL64      VP_RXL;          /* AutoCAD's coordinates of the logical
                                  space */
  REAL64      VP_RYL;
  REAL64      VP_RXH;
  REAL64      VP_RYH;
  REAL64      VP_RWIDTH;       /* Width of logical space */
  REAL64      VP_RHEIGHT;      /* Height of the same */
  REAL64      VP_VRXL;         /* Coordinates of the viewport */
  REAL64      VP_VRYL;
  REAL64      VP_VRXH;
  REAL64      VP_VRYH;
  UDWORD      VP_ZOOMABLE;     /* Is this VP zoomable? 0 = no */
  UDWORD      VP_RSVD2[24];    /* Reserved - do not use */
  } VPBLOCK;
```

As you may notice, several different types of coordinates are specified in the above VPBLOCK structure. The first are *screen coordinates*, which use the *lower left corner* of the AutoCAD drawing area as an origin. To get upper-left-origin screen coordinates, as the PDIGI graphics functions expect, you must subtract the VP_YMIN and VP_YMAX values from the value of PDIGI_YBIAS—this procedure is known as a *Y-bias adjust*.

The next type of coordinate is referred to as the *logical space coordinate*, which is another way of referring to AutoCAD's internal integerized regen space. For faster display processing, whenever an AutoCAD regen occurs, AutoCAD determines what is visible and generates an integerized form of the drawing database. This integerized drawing information forms the core of the display list used by display list processing software. It uses coordinates which range from 0 to 0x7FFFFFFD for Release 12's 31-bit logical space, or from 0 to 0x7FFD for the less-memory consuming, and less-zoomable (i.e., causing more regens when zooming) 15-bit logical space in earlier versions of AutoCAD (Releases 10 and 11). The logical space coordinates provided in the VPBLOCK structure refer to the viewport's position in the current logical space. Logical space uses a *lower left origin*. This information is useful for PDIGI applications which also intercept ADI packets via the "Tee" Driver interface AutoCAD provides, and may be useful for future implementations of PDIGI.

The final type of coordinate system is AutoCAD's drawing coordinate system, specified in 64-bit floating point format. This information allows PDIGI applications to correlate a given viewport's contents in normal floating point coordinate space to its own needs. The viewport position in AutoCAD drawing coordinate space also can be used for transformations from data in the current drawing database to the display.

PDIGI_CURVP   This is a pointer to the current viewport structure in the display driver's local memory. The "current" viewport is the active viewport (i.e., the only viewport when one is up, or the one with cross-hairs in it in a multiple-viewport situation).

PDIGI_VPLEN   This field contains the length of an individual viewport structure, in bytes, and should be used to traverse the viewport structure list.

PDIGI_MAXVP   The total number of viewport structures allocated. This value is to be used when scanning the list of viewports.

PDIGI_YBIAS   The Y-bias, used for translating the viewport screen coordinates (found in the **VPBLOCK** structure) to physical screen coordinates.

PDIGI_SCRPT   Pointer to current screen information structure, stored local to the display driver, which is defined as follows:

```
typedef struct
  {
  UDWORD      SCR_XSIZE;          /* X width of the display (in pixels) */
  UDWORD      SCR_YSIZE;          /* Y height of the display (in scan lines)
                                     */
  UDWORD      SCR_BPP;            /* Number of bits per pixel */
  UDWORD      SCR_RSVD0[7];       /* Reserved - do not access */
  UDWORD      SCR_RGBORDER;       /* RGB order for 24 & 32 bpp modes */
  UDWORD      SCR_ALIGN8;         /* Flag to indicate need for alignment
                                     on 8 pixel boundaries. */
  UDWORD      SCR_RSVD1[2];       /* Reserved - do not access */
  } SCREEN;
```

Note that this structure is loaded into memory local to the ADS application by *InitPDIGI()*, for easier access.

The **SCR_RGBORDER** field has the following meaning when **SCR_BPP** is greater than or equal to 24 (listed in byte order, least significant first):

```
/*

  Types of RGB ordering is BPP >= 24.

*/

#define    RGB    0   /* 24 bpp data in red, green, blue byte order */

#define    BGR    1   /* 24 bpp data in blue, green, red order */

#define    BRG    2   /* 24 bpp data in blue, red, green byte order */

#define    RGBO   3   /* 32 bpp data in red, green, blue, alpha order */

#define    BGRO   4   /* 32 bpp data in blue, green, red, alpha order */

#define    ORGB   5   /* 32 bpp data in alpha, red, green, blue order */

#define    OBGR   6   /* 32 bpp data in alpha, blue, green, red order */

#define    OBRG   7   /* 32 bpp data in alpha, blue, red, green order */
```

The SCR_ALIGN8 field is non-zero if functions which are used to save and restore portions of the screen need to have their X positions and widths aligned to 8 pixel boundaries. This is required for some devices for hardware architectural purposes, when using the *CalcRectSpace()*, *ReadRectArea()*, and *WriteRectArea()* functions.

PDIGI_CHRWD	This field contains the width of the character cell in pixels.
PDIGI_CHRHT	This field contains the height of the character cell in scan lines.
PDIGI_SIDWD	Width of the AutoCAD side menu, in characters. If set to 0, there is no side menu. Multiply by **PDIGI_CHRWD** to get side menu width in pixels.
PDIGI_CMDHT	Command area height, in characters. If set to 0, there is no command area at the bottom of the screen. Multiply by **PDIGI_CHRHT** and add 1 to get the height in scan lines.
PDIGI_TOPOF	If non-zero, then there is no status area at the top of the display. If the status area is present, then its height is one character cell plus 1.
PDIGI_XMAX	This is the right edge of drawing area. If no side menu exists, then this will be the same as **SCR_XWIDTH** − 1. If a side menu is present, this will reflect its width plus whatever number of pixels is required for a border and other special areas.
PDIGI_CLRTB	This is a pointer, in the driver's local memory, to the physical color table. Each entry in this table is 32- bits wide, and is used to translate from internal 8 bpp psuedo-physical color to device-specific color. Its main use is for when the display device has more than 8 bpp. The range of values used for look-up is 0 to 255.
PDIGI_CLRLG	This is a pointer to logical color table, local to the driver's memory. This color table is used to translate an **AutoCAD** logical color, ranging from −18 to +255, into an 8 bpp psuedo-physical color.
PDIGI_CLRPH	This is a pointer, in driver local memory, to the current working palette, if the device is in 8 bpp mode or less. This palette is stored in exactly the same format as that returned by the *GetLUT()* functions.

PDIGI_CLRXR   This 32-bit field contains the device-specific color value used to XOR (highlight) data on the display. No translation through the table at PDIGI_CLRTB is required (or recommended).

Please note that additional data items may end up being defined for the PDIGIDATA structure for future versions of the PDIGI interface. Such additions would be placed after the end of the currently defined structure, so it's important not to assume anything about undefined data areas.

Related Functions:
All

ReadPixel—Read the color of a pixel on the display

```
COLOR          PDIGI_ReadPixel(UDWORD x, UDWORD y)
```

Description:
This function allows you to read the color of a pixel located on the display. The value returned is a device-specific color value. The purpose of this function is to allow an application to read a single pixel value for later modification or restoration. For doing this to a larger group of pixels, it's much more efficient to use *ReadRectArea()*.

Parameters:

x, y   The display coordinate from which to read the pixel color.

Related Functions:
ReadRectArea, WritePixel, WriteRectArea

ReadRectArea—Read a rectangle of data

```
VOID           PDIGI_ReadRectArea(UDWORD x1, UDWORD y1,
               UDWORD x2, UDWORD y2, UBYTE *dataPtr)
```

Description:
This function is used to read a rectangular area of display memory. The amount of data required for the read needs to be calculated via the *CalcRectSpace()* function (see the description of that function for more details). There is no consistency on how data of 4 bits per pixel or

smaller is stored. However, it can be assumed that 8-bit-per-pixel data, or larger, will be stored in a pure pixel format, based on the contents of the SCREEN structure, accessible via the *InitPDIGI()* function.

Parameters:

`x1, y1`	The upper left coordinate of the rectangle to read.
`x2, y2`	The lower right corner of the rectangle.
`dataPtr`	This is a pointer to a data area to which to save the read display data. Note that this refers to data in the GS selector (which is automatically set using the supplied PDIGI libraries, to be the same as the PDIGI application's DS selector).

Related Functions:
CalcRectSpace, WriteRectArea

RemoveCursor—Remove the raster cursor from the display

```
VOID                    PDIGI_RemoveCursor()
```

Description:
This function removes the raster cursor from the display. It should be called only if the raster cursor is already on the display. However, it is safe to call it if the current cursor state is unknown. The only pitfall in this latter case is that if a cursor happened to be displayed on the screen, and it was erased by some overlapping drawing process (such as a *DrawRect()*) without *RemoveCursor()* having been called first,) then a *RemoveCursor()* call after the unintentional cursor obliteration might result in an artifact being left on the display (showing the previous saved "underside" of the raster cursor prior to its obliteration).

Parameters:
None

Related Functions:
SetCursorData, ShowCursor

SetCursorData—Set the raster cursor shape

```
VOID                    PDIGI_SetCursorData(UDWORD hotX, UDWORD
                        hotY, UDWORD width, UDWORD height, UBYTE
                        *andPtr, UBYTE *xorPtr)
```

Description:

This function sets the raster cursor data and information for use by subsequent *ShowCursor()* and *RemoveCursor()* calls. The raster cursor is currently limited to a 16×16 size, and consists of two masks, an AND mask and an XOR mask, which are sequentially applied to a given display area to create a raster cursor, akin to the arrow cursor used in AutoCAD.

Parameters:

hotX, hotY   This coordinate specifies the *hot spot* of the raster cursor. The upper left corner of the raster cursor is the cursor "origin" (0,0). The "hot spot" is a coordinate relative to the raster cursor origin and specifies the point in the raster cursor, which is used for displaying the cursor, via the *ShowCursor()* function. For version 1.00 of PDIGI, the range of valid values for either subcoordinate is 0 to 15.

width, height   Both should be set to 16 for version 1.00 of PDIGI. Any other values may produce unexpected results.

andPtr   This points to a buffer in the driver's local memory, which contains the AND mask for the cursor. In version 1.00 of PDIGI, the mask is stored as 16 contiguous words (16 bits each), each one reflecting the AND mask for a single line of the cursor. Within each word, the most significant bit (bit 15) represents the first pixel to be ANDed at the left end of the cursor, with each subsequently decreasing bit representing another pixel going right. If the bit for a given pixel is 0, then the display pixel is zeroed, and if the bit is 1, the display pixel is left untouched.

xorPtr   This points to a buffer in the driver's local memory, which contains the XOR mask for the raster cursor. This buffer is laid out in exactly the same fashion as the AND mask buffer, except that a 0 bit indicates that the display pixel will be untouched, while a 1 bit indicates that the pixel will be XORed with the color specified in the *ShowCursor()* function.

Related Functions:

SetCursorData, ShowCursor

SetLUT—Set the color Look-Up Table (LUT)

```
VOID                    PDIGI_SetLUT(LUTDATA  *lutData,  UDWORD
                        count, UDWORD start)
```

Description:
This function sets the current display device's hardware color palette, and is the converse of *GetLUT()*. Note that some devices may not have a color palette, especially devices running in resolutions which have more or fewer than 8 bits per pixel. Palettes have no more than 256 entries.

Parameters:

height, lutData   This is a pointer to a data buffer in the display driver's data selector.

count   The number of color palette entries you want to get, ranging from 1 to 256.

start   The palette entry from which to start reading. May be a number from 0 to 255.

Related Functions:
GetLUT, GetLUTEntry, InitPDIGI, SetLUTEntry

SetLUTEntry—Set a color LUT entry

```
VOID                    PDIGI_SetLUTEntry(UDWORD index, UBYTE red,
                        UBYTE green, UBYTE blue)
```

Description:
This function sets the red, green, and blue subcomponent intensities of the digital color referenced by the index. Intensities range from 0 to 255 (8 bits). Note that some devices may not have a color palette, especially devices running in resolutions which have more or fewer than 8 bits per pixel. Palettes have no more than 256 entries/indices.

Parameters:

height index   The palette entry in which to set the color palette information.

red, green, blue   The values of the color subcomponents to set in the palette.

Related Functions:
GetLUT, GetLUTEntry, InitPDIGI, SetLUT

ShowCursor—Place Raster Cursor on the display

```
VOID              PDIGI_ShowCursor(UDWORD x, UDWORD y, COLOR
                  color)
```

Description:

This function displays the raster cursor, whose shape is defined by the *SetCursorData()* function. This function must not be called more than once for each associated *RemoveCursor()* call; i.e., each *ShowCursor()* must be paired with a subsequent *RemoveCursor()* without an intervening additional *ShowCursor()* call.

Parameters:

x, y
The coordinate on the display at which to place the raster cursor's hot spot as specified in the *SetCursorData()* function.

color
The color to XOR with when a bit in the XOR mask is set to 1. This most typically will be the XOR color value returned in the PDIGI structure by the *InitPDIGI()* function.

Related Functions:

InitPDIGI, RemoveCursor, SetCursorData

WriteMonoRectArea—Perform a color expansion from memory to display

```
VOID              PDIGI_WriteMonoRectArea(UDWORD x, UDWORD
                  y, UDWORD width, UDWORD height, UBYTE
                  *dataPtr, UDWORD bytePitch, COLOR colorIf0,
                  COLOR colorIf1)
```

Description:

This function is used to expand a monochrome mask located locally into a fully colored image on the display. Each 0 bit in the monochrome mask is expanded into one color, while each 1 bit is expanded into another color. This function is useful for displaying raster fonts and icons.

Parameters:

x, y
This is the upper left corner of the destination area on the display, at which to place the color expanded rectangle.

width, height	These are the dimensions, in pixels, of the rectangle to be color expanded.
dataPtr	This points to the monochrome source data in the selector pointed to by the GS selector register.
bytePitch	The length of one line of monochrome data, including any buffer bits at the end of a line, in bytes. Note that each new line of monochrome data *must* start on a byte boundary.
colorIf0	This is the color used when expanding a 0 bit in the monochrome mask.
colorIf1	This is the color used when expanding a 1 bit in the monochrome mask.

Related Functions:
   WriteRectArea

WritePixel—Draw a pixel on the display

```
VOID              PDIGI_WritePixel(UDWORD x, UDWORD y, COLOR
                  color)

VOID              PDIGI_WritePixelXOR(UDWORD x, UDWORD y,
                  COLOR color)
```

Description:
   This function draws a single pixel on the display. The XOR version of the function XORs the specified color with the one already on the display.

Parameters:

x, y	The position at which to draw the pixel.
color	The color in which to draw or XOR the pixel.

Related Functions:
   ReadPixel

WriteRectArea—Write a rectangle of data

```
VOID              PDIGI_WriteRectArea(UDWORD x1, UDWORD y1,
                  UDWORD x2, UDWORD y2, UBYTE *dataPtr)
```

Description:

This function is used to write a rectangular area of display memory. The main purpose of this function is to restore data to the display saved by the *ReadRectArea()* function. The amount of data required for the write needs to be calculated via the *CalcRectSpace()* function (see the description of that function for more details). There is no consistency in how data of 4 bits per pixel or smaller is stored, however, it can be assumed that 8-bit-per-pixel data, or larger, will be written in a pure pixel format, based on the contents of the SCREEN structure, (accessible via the *InitPDIGI()* function), allowing this function to be used to write raster data directly to the display.

Parameters:

`x1, y1`	The upper left coordinate of the rectangle to write.
`x2, y2`	The lower right corner of the rectangle.
`dataPtr`	This is a pointer to a data area from which to write the display data. Note that this refers to data in the GS selector, which is automatically set using the supplied PDIGI libraries to be the same as the PDIGI application's DS selector. See the library file listings in PDIGI.H, PDIGI.INC, PDIGI.C, and PDIGISUB.ASM, found in the next section.

Related Functions:

CalcRectSpace, ReadRectArea

PDIGI Core Library File Listings

This section contains listings of PDIGI's four library files: PDIGI.H, PDIGI.INC, PDIGI.C, and PDIGISUB.ASM. The next section, "PDIGI Techniques," describes how to use these files.

PDIGI.H, Include File for PDIGI 'C' Files

```
/* ---------------------------------------------------------------
PDIGI.H

  DESCRIPTION:
  This is the core library file for PDIGI v1.00.
  Copyright (c) 1993 by Panacea Inc.—All Rights Reserved.
  This file may be freely distributed, providing the above
  copyright notice remains wholly intact.
```

```
    Support for PDIGI can be found in the ACAD Forum on CompuServe.
    Revision History:

    When        Who    What

    ========    ===    ===============================================

    02/10/93    JBR    Original version created for PDIGI v1.00
    ------------------------------------------------------------------ */

    /* ----------------------------------------------------------------

       TYPEDEFS
       The following individual typedefs are used to clearly identify
       the type and size of a given variable.
       ------------------------------------------------------------- */

    typedef    char              BYTE;
    typedef    unsigned char     UBYTE;
    typedef    short             WORD;
    typedef    unsigned short    UWORD;
    typedef    long              DWORD;
    typedef    unsigned long     UDWORD;
    typedef    double            REAL64;
    typedef    void              VOID;
    typedef    UDWORD            COLOR;
    /* ----------------------------------------------------------------

       STRUCTURES
       The following are structures used for PDIGI access.
       ------------------------------------------------------------- */

typedef struct                 /* The PDIGI information structure */
    {
    UWORD      PDIGI_VERS;         /* PDIGI Version */
    UWORD      PDIGI_DS;           /* Our DS */
    UDWORD     PDIGI_VPINF;        /* Pointer to the VP structures */
    UDWORD     PDIGI_CURVP;        /* Pointer to current VP */
    UDWORD     PDIGI_VPLEN;        /* Length of a VP block entry */
    UWORD      PDIGI_MAXVP;        /* The maximum number of VPs */
    UWORD      PDIGI_YBIAS;        /* The Y-bias (for VP calcs) */
    UDWORD     PDIGI_SCRPT;        /* Pointer to active screen struc. */
    UWORD      PDIGI_CHRWD;        /* Character width */
    UWORD      PDIGI_CHRHT;        /* Character height */
    UWORD      PDIGI_SIDWD;        /* Side menu width (chars) */
    UWORD      PDIGI_CMDHT;        /* Command area, number of char lines */
    UWORD      PDIGI_TOPOF;        /* Flag for status line inactive */
    UWORD      PDIGI_XMAX;         /* Right edge of drawing area */
    UDWORD     PDIGI_CLRTB;        /* Pointer to colorTable */
```

```
        UDWORD      PDIGI_CLRLG;        /* Pointer to logical color table */
        UDWORD      PDIGI_CLRPH;        /* Physical color table (for <=8bpp) */
        UDWORD      PDIGI_CLRXR;        /* XOR Color (full width) */
    } PDIGIDATA;
typedef struct                          /* Defines a palette entry */
    {
    UBYTE       red;                    /* The red subcomponent */
    UBYTE       green;                  /* The green subcomponent */
    UBYTE       blue;                   /* The blue subcomponent */
      } LUTDATA;
typedef struct                          /* The structure for accessing viewport info */
      {
    UWORD       VP_NUM;                 /* ID number AutoCAD knows this viewport by */
    UWORD       VP_XMIN;                /* Screen coordinates of this viewport, in */
    UWORD       VP_YMIN;                /*  Y-bias adjusted coordinates. */
    UWORD       VP_XMAX;
    UWORD       VP_YMAX;
    UWORD       VP_RSVD0;               /* Reserved—do not use */
    UDWORD      VP_XWIDTH;              /* Dimensions of the viewport in pixels */
    UDWORD      VP_YHEIGHT;
    UDWORD      VP_MAXLXWID;            /* The maximum dimensions of the logical space */
    UDWORD      VP_MAXLYHGT;
    UDWORD      VP_LGXL;                /* Position of the viewport in logical space */
    UDWORD      VP_LGYL;
    UDWORD      VP_LGXH;
    UDWORD      VP_LGYH;
    UDWORD      VP_RSVD1[9];            /* Reserved—do not use */
    REAL64      VP_RXL;                 /* AutoCAD's coordinates of the logical space */
    REAL64      VP_RYL;
    REAL64      VP_RXH;
    REAL64      VP_RYH;
    REAL64      VP_RWIDTH;              /* Width of logical space */
    REAL64      VP_RHEIGHT;             /* Height of the same */
    REAL64      VP_VRXL;                /* Coordinates of the viewport */
    REAL64      VP_VRYL;
    REAL64      VP_VRXH;
    REAL64      VP_VRYH;
    UDWORD      VP_ZOOMABLE;            /* Is this VP zoomable? 0 = no */
    UDWORD      VP_RSVD2[24];           /* Reserved—do not use */
    } VPBLOCK;
typedef struct                          /* Information about the current display */
    {
    UDWORD      SCR_XSIZE;              /* X width of the display (in pixels) */
```

```
UDWORD       SCR_YSIZE;          /* Y height of the display (in scan lines) */
UDWORD       SCR_BPP;            /* Number of bits per pixel */
UDWORD       SCR_RSVD0[7];       /* Reserved—do not access */
UDWORD       SCR_RGBORDER;       /* RGB order for 24 & 32 bpp modes */
UDWORD       SCR_ALIGN8;         /* Flag to indicate need for alignment on
                                          8 pixel boundaries. */
UDWORD       SCR_RSVD1[2];       /* Reserved—do not access */


  } SCREEN;
/* -------------------------------------------------------------
   DEFINES
   ---------------------------------------------------------- */
/*
   Types of RGB ordering when SCR_BPP >= 24.
   The sequence of letters in the define is related to the byte order
   of the color subcomponents of the pixel. For example, for "RGB,"
   byte 0 of a pixel will be the red subcomponent, byte 1 will be the
   green subcomponent, and byte 2 will be the blue subcomponent.
*/
#define   RGB      0   /* 24 bpp data in red, green, blue byte order */
#define   BGR      1   /* 24 bpp data in blue, green, red byte order */
#define   BRG      2   /* 24 bpp data in blue, red, green byte order */
#define   RGBO     3   /* 32 bpp data in red, green, blue, alpha order */
#define   BGRO     4   /* 32 bpp data in blue, green, red, alpha order */
#define   ORGB     5   /* 32 bpp data in alpha, red, green, blue order */
#define   OBGR     6   /* 32 bpp data in alpha, blue, green, red order */
#define   OBRG     7   /* 32 bpp data in alpha, blue, red, green order */
/*
   Standard color definitions for AutoCAD displays
   Assumes user has made no color display changes
*/
#define   BLACK    0   /* Also background color */
#define   RED      1
#define   YELLOW   2
#define   GREEN    3
#define   CYAN     4
#define   BLUE     5
#define   MAGENTA  6
#define   WHITE    7
/*
   Definitions for object colors in AutoCAD—in logical color space
*/
```

```
/*                              -1    is reserved for internal XOR */
#define   SCRBACKCOLOR          -2   /* Graphics area background color */
#define   TXTBACKCOLOR          -3   /* Background color for text areas */
#define   TXTFORECOLOR          -4   /* Foreground color for text areas */
#define   TXTBRDRCOLOR          -5   /* Border color for text areas */
#define   ALRTBACKCOLOR         -6   /* Alert box background */
#define   ALRTFORECOLOR         -7   /* Alert box foreground */
#define   ALRTBRDRCOLOR         -8   /* Alert box border */
#define   MENUBACKCOLOR         -9   /* Menu bar background */
#define   MENUFORECOLOR         -10  /* Menu bar foreground */
#define   MENUBRDRCOLOR         -11  /* Menu bar border */
#define   POPUPBACKCOLOR        -12  /* Pop-up menu background */
#define   POPUPFORECOLOR        -13  /* Pop-up menu foreground */
#define   POPUPBRDRCOLOR        -14  /* Pop-up menu border color */
#define   DLOGBACKCOLOR         -15  /* Dialogue box background */
#define   DLOGFORECOLOR         -16  /* Dialogue box foreground */
#define   DLOGBRDRCOLOR         -17  /* Dialogue box border */
#define   DLOGLINECOLOR         -18  /* Dialogue box line drawing color */


/* ----------------------------------------------------------------
   External References
   --------------------------------------------------------------- */
/*
   The following is the entry point into our assembly language
   dispatcher, which then calls the display driver.
*/
extern    UDWORD                PDIGIEntryPoint(DWORD, ...);
/*
   This is the InitPDIGI() entry point.
*/
extern    UDWORD                InitPDIGI(VOID);
/*
   These two functions are used to read and write data from and to
   the 4KB data buffer located in the driver.
*/
extern    VOID                  CopyFromDriver(VOID *, VOID *, UDWORD);
extern    VOID                  CopyToDriver(VOID *, VOID *, UDWORD);
/*
   InitPDIGI() loads up the following two structures, and sets pdigiDataPtr.
*/
extern    PDIGIDATA  pdigiInfo;      /* Copy of the current PDIGIDATA struct */
extern    SCREEN     screenInfo;     /* A copy of the current SCREEN struct */
extern    UBYTE      *pdigiDataPtr;  /* The driver pointer to 4KB buffer */
```

```
/* ------------------------------------------------------------
   Macros
   ---------------------------------------------------------- */
/*
   The following are the Macros used to call PDIGI. Every PDIGI
   function, with the exception of InitPDIGI(), is actually a macro,
   which in turn calls our assembly language dispatcher, located
   in PDIGISUB.ASM. The PDIGI support stub in the display driver
   uses a dispatch number (the first parameter of the call to
   PDIGIEntryPoint) to determine what function to perform. Numbers
   not defined below are not to be called, as they are reserved.
*/
#define    PDIGI_GetPDIGIData() \
                ((UBYTE *)PDIGIEntryPoint(-1))     /* Special call for Init */
#define    PDIGI_WritePixel(x, y, color) \
                PDIGIEntryPoint(0, x, y, color)
#define    PDIGI_WritePixelXOR(x, y, color) \
                PDIGIEntryPoint(1, x, y, color)
#define    PDIGI_ReadPixel(x, y)   \
                PDIGIEntryPoint(2, x, y)
#define    PDIGI_DrawLine(x1, y1, x2, y2, color) \
                PDIGIEntryPoint(3, x1, y1, x2, y2, color)
#define    PDIGI_DrawLineXOR(x1, y1, x2, y2, color) \
                PDIGIEntryPoint(4, x1, y1, x2, y2, color)
#define    PDIGI_DrawHLine(x, y, length, color)   \
                PDIGIEntryPoint(7, x, y, length, color)
#define    PDIGI_DrawHLineXOR(x, y, length, color)   \
                PDIGIEntryPoint(8, x, y, length, color)
#define    PDIGI_DrawVLine(x, y, length, color)   \
                PDIGIEntryPoint(9, x, y, length, color)
#define    PDIGI_DrawVLineXOR(x, y, length, color)   \
                PDIGIEntryPoint(10, x, y, length, color)
#define    PDIGI_DrawRect(x1, y1, x2, y2, color) \
                PDIGIEntryPoint(11, x1, y1, x2, y2, color)
#define    PDIGI_DrawRectXOR(x1, y1, x2, y2, color) \
                PDIGIEntryPoint(12, x1, y1, x2, y2, color)
#define    PDIGI_WriteRectArea(x1, y1, x2, y2, dataPtr)  \
                PDIGIEntryPoint(15, x1, y1, x2, y2, dataPtr)
#define    PDIGI_ReadRectArea(x1, y1, x2, y2, dataPtr)  \
                PDIGIEntryPoint(16, x1, y1, x2, y2, dataPtr)
#define    PDIGI_WriteMonoRectArea(x, y, width, height, dataPtr, bytePitch,
color0, color1) \
```

```
                       PDIGIEntryPoint(17, x, y, width, height, dataPtr, bytePitch,
            color1, color0)
#define    PDIGI_ConvexPolygon(vertexList, vertexCnt, color) \
                       PDIGIEntryPoint(18, vertexList, vertexCnt, color)
#define    PDIGI_ComplexPolygon(vertexList, vertexCnt, color) \
                       PDIGIEntryPoint(20, vertexList, vertexCnt, color)
#define    PDIGI_DrawPattLine(x1, y1, x2, y2, bgColor, fgColor) \
                       PDIGIEntryPoint(23, x1, y1, x2, y2, bgColor, fgColor)
#define    PDIGI_DrawPattLineXOR(x1, y1, x2, y2, bgColor, fgColor) \
                       PDIGIEntryPoint(24, x1, y1, x2, y2, bgColor, fgColor)
#define    PDIGI_DrawPattPolygon(vertexList, vertexCnt, bgColor, fgColor) \
                       PDIGIEntryPoint(29, vertexList, vertexCnt, bgColor, fgColor)
#define    PDIGI_DrawChar(x, y, charVal, bgColor, fgColor) \
                       PDIGIEntryPoint(30, x, y, charVal, bgColor, fgColor)
#define    PDIGI_DrawString(x, y, string, bgColor, fgColor)   \
                       PDIGIEntryPoint(31, x, y, string, bgColor, fgColor)
#define    PDIGI_BitBLT(srcX, srcY, width, height, dstX, dstY)   \
                       PDIGIEntryPoint (35, srcX, srcY, width, height, dstX, dstY)
#define    PDIGI_CalcRectSpace(x1, y1, x2, y2) \
                       PDIGIEntryPoint (38, x1, y1, x2, y2)
#define    PDIGI_SetLUTEntry(index, red, green, blue)    \
                       PDIGIEntryPoint(40, index, red, green, blue)
#define    PDIGI_GetLUTEntry(index, red, green, blue)    \
                       PDIGIEntryPoint(41, index, red, green, blue)
#define    PDIGI_SetLUT(lutData, count, start) \
                       PDIGIEntryPoint(42, lutData, count, start)
#define    PDIGI_GetLUT(lutData, count, start) \
                       PDIGIEntryPoint(43, lutData, count, start)
#define    PDIGI_SetCursorData(hotX, hotY, width, height, andPtr, xorPtr) \
                       PDIGIEntryPoint(44, hotX, hotY, width, height, andPtr, xorPtr)
#define    PDIGI_ShowCursor(x, y, color) \
                       PDIGIEntryPoint(45, x, y, color)
#define    PDIGI_RemoveCursor() \
                       PDIGIEntryPoint(46)
/* ---------------------------------------------------------------
   End of PDIGI.H
   --------------------------------------------------------------- */
```

PDIGI.INC, Include File for PDIGI.ASM Files

```
; ---------------------------------------------------------------
; PDIGI.INC
;
```

```
; This file contains the structure and equate information for the
; PDIGISUB.ASM routine and any other assembly language routines which
; want to use PDIGI. Note that function calls from assembly language
; are not defined here in any way, as the form of parameter passing
; used for PDIGI is better suited for 'C.'
;
;
; Copyright (C) 1993  Panacea Inc.——All Rights Reserved.
;
; NOTICE:
;   This file may be freely distributed, as long as the above copyright
;    notice is kept wholly intact.
;
;Revision History:
;
;When       Who  What
;========   ===  ==================================================
;02/10/93   JBR  Created this file for PDIGI v1.0
;
;
; ----------------------------------------------------------------
;
; Structures
;
; ----------------------------------------------------------------
PDIGIDATA       struc           ; The PDIGI information structure
PDIGI_VERS      dw    ?         ; PDIGI Version number
PDIGI_DS        dw    ?         ; Display driver's data selector
PDIGI_VPINF     dd    ?         ; Pointer to the viewport structures
PDIGI_CURVP     dd    ?         ; Pointer to current viewport
PDIGI_VPLEN     dd    ?         ; Length of a VP block entry
PDIGI_MAXVP     dw    ?         ; The maximum number of VPs
PDIGI_YBIAS     dw    ?         ; The Y-bias (for VP calculations)
PDIGI_SCRPT     dd    ?         ; Pointer to active screen structure
PDIGI_CHRWD     dw    ?         ; Character cell width
PDIGI_CHRHT     dw    ?         ; Character cell height
PDIGI_SIDWD     dw    ?         ; Side menu width (in characters)
PDIGI_CMDHT     dw    ?         ; Command area height, in characters
PDIGI_TOPOF     dw    ?         ; Flag for status line inactive
PDIGI_XMAX      dw    ?         ; Right edge of drawing area
PDIGI_CLRTB     dd    ?         ; Pointer to physical color table
PDIGI_CLRLG     dd    ?         ; Pointer to logical color table
PDIGI_CLRPH     dd    ?         ; Current palette (for <=8bpp)
```

```
            PDIGI_CLRXR     dd      ?               ; XOR Color in device color
            PDIGIDATA       ends
            VPBLOCK         struc                   ; The struc. for accessing viewport info.
            VP_NUM          dw      ?               ; ID number AutoCAD knows this viewport by
            VP_XMIN         dw      ?               ; Screen coordinates of this viewport, in
            VP_YMIN         dw      ?               ; Y-bias adjusted coordinates.
            VP_XMAX         dw      ?
            VP_YMAX         dw      ?
            VP_RSVD0        dw      ?               ; Reserved—do not use
            VP_XWIDTH       dd      ?               ; Dimensions of the viewport in pixels
            VP_YHEIGHT      dd      ?
            VP_MAXLXWID     dd      ?               ; The maximum dimensions of the logical space
            VP_MAXLYHGT     dd      ?
            VP_LGXL         dd      ?               ; Position of the viewport in logical  space
            VP_LGYL         dd      ?
            VP_LGXH         dd      ?
            VP_LGYH         dd      ?
            VP_RSVD1        dd      9 dup (?)       ; Reserved - do not use
            VP_RXL          dq      ?               ; AutoCAD's coordinates of the logical  space
            VP_RYL          dq      ?
            VP_RXH          dq      ?
            VP_RYH          dq      ?
            VP_RWIDTH       dq      ?               ; Width of logical space in floating point
            VP_RHEIGHT      dq      ?               ; Height of the same
            VP_VRXL         dq      ?               ; Coordinates of the viewport (floating point)
            VP_VRYL         dq      ?
            VP_VRXH         dq      ?
            VP_VRYH         dq      ?
            VP_ZOOMABLE     dw      ?               ; Is this VP zoomable? 0 = no
            VP_RSVD2        dd      24 dup (?)      ; Reserved—do not use
            VPBLOCK         ends
            SCREEN          struc                   ; Information about the current display
            SCR_XSIZE       dd      ?               ; X width of the display (in pixels)
            SCR_YSIZE       dd      ?               ; Y height of the display (in scan lines)
            SCR_BPP         dd      ?               ; Number of bits per pixel
            SCR_RSVD0       dd      7 dup (?)       ; Reserved—do not access
            SCR_RGBORDER    dd      ?               ; RGB order for 24 and 32 bpp modes
            SCR_ALIGN8      dd      ?               ; Flag to indicate need for alignment on
                                                    ; 8 pixel boundaries.
            SCR_RSVD1       dd      2 dup (?)       ; Reserved—do not access
            SCREEN          ends
            ; --------------------------------------------------------------
            ;
```

```
; Equates
;
; ----------------------------------------------------------------
;
; Types of RGB ordering when SCR_BPP >= 24.
; The sequence of letters in the define is related to the byte order
; of the color subcomponents of the pixel. For example, for "RGB,"
; byte 0 of a pixel will be the red subcomponent, byte 1 will be the
; green subcomponent, and byte 2 will be the blue subcomponent.
;
RGB       equ     0   ; 24 bpp data in red, green, blue byte order
BGR       equ     1   ; 24 bpp data in blue, green, red byte order
BRG       equ     2   ; 24 bpp data in blue, red, green byte order
RGBO      equ     3   ; 32 bpp data in red, green, blue, alpha order
BGRO      equ     4   ; 32 bpp data in blue, green, red, alpha order
ORGB      equ     5   ; 32 bpp data in alpha, red, green, blue order
OBGR      equ     6   ; 32 bpp data in alpha, blue, green, red order
OBRG      equ     7   ; 32 bpp data in alpha, blue, red, green order
;
; Standard color definitions for AutoCAD displays
; Assumes user has made no color display changes
;
BLACK     equ     0   ; Also background color
RED       equ     1
YELLOW    equ     2
GREEN     equ     3
CYAN      equ     4
BLUE      equ     5
MAGENTA   equ     6
WHITE     equ     7
;
; Definitions for object colors in AutoCAD — in logical color space
;
;                      -1        is reserved for internal XOR
SCRBACKCOLOR     equ   -2    ; Graphics area background color
TXTBACKCOLOR     equ   -3    ; Background color for text areas
TXTFORECOLOR     equ   -4    ; Foreground color for text areas
TXTBRDRCOLOR     equ   -5    ; Border color for text areas
ALRTBACKCOLOR    equ   -6    ; Alert box background
ALRTFORECOLOR    equ   -7    ; Alert box foreground
ALRTBRDRCOLOR    equ   -8    ; Alert box border
MENUBACKCOLOR    equ   -9    ; Menu bar background
MENUFORECOLOR    equ   -10   ; Menu bar foreground
```

```
        MENUBRDRCOLOR      equ    -11    ;  Menu bar border
        POPUPBACKCOLOR     equ    -12    ;  Pop-up menu background
        POPUPFORECOLOR     equ    -13    ;  Pop-up menu foreground
        POPUPBRDRCOLOR     equ    -14    ;  Pop-up menu border color
        DLOGBACKCOLOR      equ    -15    ;  Dialogue box background
        DLOGFORECOLOR      equ    -16    ;  Dialogue box foreground
        DLOGBRDRCOLOR      equ    -17    ;  Dialogue box border
        DLOGLINECOLOR      equ    -18    ;  Dialogue box line drawing color
        ;
        ; The following are convenient definitions for aligning both data and
        ; code on boundaries designed to make 386/486 use much more efficient,
        ; relative to prefetch queue issues. See Appendix G of the i486 programmer's
        ; documentation for details.
        ;
        PROCALIGN          equ    16     ; Align all procs to 16-byte boundaries
        VARALIGN           equ    4      ; Align vars to dword boundaries
        JMPALIGN           equ    4      ; Align jmps/loops to dword boundaries
        ;
        ; Equates for DWord sized parms on the stack for near calls
        ;
        P_DWARG1           equ           dword ptr [EBP+8]
        P_DWARG2           equ           dword ptr [EBP+12]
        P_DWARG3           equ           dword ptr [EBP+16]
        P_DWARG4           equ           dword ptr [EBP+20]
        P_DWARG5           equ           dword ptr [EBP+24]
        P_DWARG6           equ           dword ptr [EBP+28]
        P_DWARG7           equ           dword ptr [EBP+32]
        P_DWARG8           equ           dword ptr [EBP+36]
        P_DWARG9           equ           dword ptr [EBP+40]
        P_DWARG10          equ           dword ptr [EBP+44]
        P_DWARG11          equ           dword ptr [EBP+48]
        P_DWARG12          equ           dword ptr [EBP+52]
        ;
        ; End of PDIGI.INC
        ;
```

PDIGI.C, Core 'C' File for Linking to PDIGI Applications

```
/* ------------------------------------------------------------
   PDIGI.C
```

```
    DESCRIPTION:
    This is the core library file for PDIGI v1.00.
    Copyright (c) 1993 by Panacea Inc.—All Rights Reserved.
    This file may be freely distributed, providing the above
    copyright notice remains wholly intact.
    Support for PDIGI can be found in the ACAD Forum on CompuServe.
Revision History:
When      Who   What
========  ===   =================================================
02/10/93  JBR   Original version created for PDIGI v1.00
04/30/93  JBR   Replaced PDIGIENTRY with PDIGIALTENTRY methodology
    ---------------------------------------------------------------- */
/* ----------------------------------------------------------------
    Necessary Include Files
    ---------------------------------------------------------------- */
#include   <stdio.h>
#include   <string.h>
#include   "adslib.h"        /* Necessary for ADS defs */
#include   "pdigi.h"         /* Necessary for PDIGI defs */
/* ----------------------------------------------------------------
    External Functions and data defined in PDIGISUB.ASM
    ---------------------------------------------------------------- */
extern  VOID     SetPDIGIAddr(UDWORD, UDWORD);  /* Sets the PDIGI buffer addr */
extern  VOID     CopyPDIGIData(VOID *);     /* Gets the PDIGIData */
extern  UDWORD   GetDS(VOID);               /* Gets our data selector */
/* ----------------------------------------------------------------
    Local Data
    ---------------------------------------------------------------- */
/* ----------------------------------------------------------------
    CODE
    ---------------------------------------------------------------- */
/* ----------------------------------------------------------------
    InitPDIGI()
    This is the InitPDIGI() function as described in the PDIGI
    documentation. If PDIGI is located, this function returns the
    offset of a 4KB transfer buffer in the display driver. In addition
    to the above, this function will also load the PDIGIDATA and SCREEN
    structures from the display driver into two local data areas,
    appropriately named "pdigiInfo," and "screenInfo," respectively.
    If PDIGI is not found, then this function returns 0 and the
    two structures defined above are uninitialized.
    ---------------------------------------------------------------- */
UDWORD InitPDIGI(VOID)
{
```

```
    BYTE       pdigiPtrStr[32];   /* Used to read the PDIGI entry point */
    BYTE       tmpString[32];     /* Used as scratch data area */
    UDWORD     pdigiSelector;     /* This is where we break down the entry */
    UDWORD     pdigiOffset;       /* point into */
    DWORD      i, j;              /* Local loop variables */
    UDWORD     pdigiEntry[2];     /* Place to stuff PDIGI addr */
    /*
```

The first step is to see if PDIGI is available. There are two ways
to do this.

The first is to issue the PDIGIENTRY command at the AutoCAD
command prompt. If the display driver understands the command,
then it will return the entry point in selector:offset format
via string input to the ADS application. Due to a bug in the
ads_cmd and ads_command functions, we unfortunately have no way
of telling if the command was understood.

Because of the aforementioned problem, we have to work a weird
workaround, namely asking the user to press <Enter>. The reason
this works is that we follow this by a call to ads_getstring.
If the PDIGIENTRY command is accepted, then the ads_getstring
call will return an ASCII string of the PDIGI entry point in
the driver, and the <Enter> the user hit will still be waiting
to be read. (Note that ads_getstring could be replaced by
a call to ads_grread, which would limit input to a single
character, but, according to the ADS manuals, is more error prone.)
If the PDIGIENTRY command is not recognized, then the
ads_getstring will just retrieve the user's <Enter>, which will
be tested to see if it's the proper length and if it has a
colon as the fifth character. The <Enter> will cause this
comparison to fail. The only time this mechanism could cause a
problem is if the user does one of the two following things
before pressing <Enter>:

1) The user enters more than 32 characters (the size of
    pdigiPtrStr).
2) The user enters exactly 13 characters with the 5th
    character being a ":" and all other characters being
    valid hexadecimal digits.

This is all documented in the excluded code sequence below.
    */

```
#ifdef OLD_ENTRY_STYLE
    if (ads_command(RTSTR, "PDIGIENTRY", RTNONE) != RTNORM)
        {                         /* Test in case bug ever fixed */
        ads_printf("PDIGI not found!\n");
```

```
      return(0);
      }
   ads_printf("\nPlease hit <Enter>...\n");
   if (ads_getstring(0, "", pdigiPtrStr) != RTNORM)
      {
      ads_printf("Could not obtain PDIGI Entry Point string!\n");
      return(0);
      }
   /*
      The format of the string we should get is XXXX:YYYYYYYY.
      The "XXXX" is the selector to use, while the "YYYYYYYY" is
      the offset. As indicated above, we need to check for the 5th
      character being a ':' to ensure validity of the returned data,
      and make sure that we have a 13-character long string.
   */
   if (pdigiPtrStr[4] != ':' && strlen(pdigiPtrStr) != 13)
      {
      ads_printf("PDIGI Not Found!\n");
      return(0);
      }
   ads_getstring(0, "", tmpString); /* Get the dummy <Enter> */
#ifdef DEBUG
   /*
      Used for debugging only...
   */
   ads_printf("\nThe PDIGI C Entry Point is at %s!\n", pdigiPtrStr);
#endif
   /*
      Now, convert from string to Hex values, doing the selector first.
   */
   pdigiSelector = 0;            /* Start with 0 in both variables */
   pdigiOffset = 0;
   for (i = 0; i < 4; i++)       /* Processing only 4 nibbles */
      {
      pdigiSelector <<= 4;       /* Shift contents up by one nibble */
      j = pdigiPtrStr[i] - '0';  /* Bring down to zero */
      if (j > 9)
         j -= 'A' - '0' - 10;    /* Convert A-F to proper value */
      if (j < 0 || j > 15)       /* Another error check... */
         {
         ads_printf("Invalid PDIGI Entry Point!\n");
         return(0);
         }
```

```
            pdigiSelector += j;     /* Add this digit to the result */
            }
        for (i = 5; i < 13; i++)    /* Processing 8 nibbles */
            {
            pdigiOffset <<= 4;      /* Shift contents up by one nibble */
         j = pdigiPtrStr[i] - '0';  /* Bring down to zero */
         if (j > 9)
            j -= 'A' - '0' - 10;    /* Convert A-F to proper value */
         if (j < 0 || j > 15)       /* Another error check... */
            {
            ads_printf("Invalid PDIGI Entry Point!\n");
            return(0);
            }
            pdigiOffset += j;       /* Add this digit to the result */
            }
    /*
       This function call tells PDIGISUB.ASM where to call the display
       driver in order to talk to PDIGI.
    */
    SetPDIGIAddr(pdigiSelector, pdigiOffset);    /* Tell comm. about address */
#else  /* Else do PDIGIALTENTRY—this is the default */
    /*
       The other way to link up with PDIGI is via the PDIGIALTENTRY
       command, which is sent to the driver with a local address
       concatenated to it. This address points to a two DWORD buffer
       (where the first DWORD is the offset and the second DWORD is
       the selector) of the PDIGI Entry Point in the driver.

       If the driver understands the PDIGIALTENTRY command, it places
       its entry point address at the location specified after the
       PDIGIALTENTRY command. We zero out the entry point address area
       first, however, so that we can determine if anything was
       actually placed there. The benefit of this approach is that it
       does not require the user to press any keys in order to
       establish the communications link.

       Both methods are documented, as there may be situations where
       one method is preferred over the other (i.e., dealing with real-
       mode ADS apps, perhaps?). Many thanks to Shannon Posniewski
       of Image Systems for coming up with this second method.
    */
    /*
       First, let's create the address string to send with the command
       to the driver. GetDS() gets the value of our local data selector
       so we can tell the driver where to stuff data.
```

```
     Note that the format required by the driver is ASCII-ized
     hexadecimal in uppercase in an XXXX:YYYYYYY format, just
     like what the other command documented above expects back
     from the driver.
  */
  sprintf(tmpString, "%0.4X:%0.8lX", GetDS(), pdigiEntry);
  strcpy(pdigiPtrStr, "PDIGIALTENTRY");  /* Set command in string */
  strcat(pdigiPtrStr, tmpString);   /* Append the address */
  pdigiEntry[0] = 0; /* Clear out our address recepticle */
  pdigiEntry[1] = 0;
  if (ads_command(RTSTR, pdigiPtrStr, RTNONE) != RTNORM)
     {             /* Send the complete command */
     ads_printf("PDIGI not found!\n");
     return(0);
     }
  if ((pdigiEntry[0] | pdigiEntry[1]) == 0) /* Check if either is != 0 */
     {             /* If not, abort */
     ads_printf("PDIGIALTENTRY not found!\n");
     return(0);
     }
#ifdef DEBUG
  /*
     Used for debugging only...
  */
  ads_printf("\nThe PDIGI C Entry Point is at %0.4X:%0.8lX!\n",
             pdigiEntry[1], pdigiEntry[0]);
#endif
  SetPDIGIAddr(pdigiEntry[1], pdigiEntry[0]);  /* Tell comm. about address */
#endif /* OLD_ENTRY_STYLE */
  /*
     Call the entry point and get the pointer to the 4KB data buffer.
  */
  pdigiDataPtr = PDIGI_GetPDIGIData();   /* Get the address of PDIGI data */
  /*
     Get the PDIGIDATA and SCREEN structure information from the driver.
     The reason for the separate function call to get the PDIGIDATA
     contents is that until we get that structure, we don't know what
     the driver's data selector is. Therefore, the CopyPDIGIData()
     function uses the code selector obtained above for reading the
     structure. Once the PDIGIDATA structure is moved over, we can
     use the CopyFromDriver() and CopyToDriver() functions, which
     rely on the PDIGI_DS field.
```

```
       */
    CopyPDIGIData(pdigiDataPtr);        /* Gets the PDIGIData */
    CopyFromDriver(&screenInfo,
            (UBYTE *)pdigiInfo.PDIGI_SCRPT, sizeof(SCREEN));
    return((UDWORD) pdigiDataPtr);    /* Everything went fine. */
}
/* -----------------------------------------------------------------
    End of PDIGI.C
    -----------------------------------------------------------------*/
```

PDIGISUB.ASM, Core ASM File for Linking to PDIGI Applications

```
;
; PDIGISUB.ASM
;
; This file contains the assembly language functions necessary to
; interface with PDIGI routines.
;
; Copyright (C) 1993  Panacea Inc.—All Rights Reserved.
;
; NOTICE:
;    This file may be freely distributed, as long as the above copyright
;    notice is kept wholly intact.
;
;Revision History:
;
;When       Who  What
;========   ===  =================================================
;02/10/93   JBR  Created this file for PDIGI v1.0
;04/30/93   JBR  Added the GetDS() function for use with PDIGIALTENTRY
;
;
;
; Include files
;
;
           includepdigi.inc       ; Necessary structure defs.
; -----------------------------------------------------------------
;
; Data Segment
```

```
;
; ------------------------------------------------------------------
DGROUP        group       pdigi_dseg
pdigi_dseg    segment     para use32 'DATA'
              assume      DS:pdigi_dseg
              public      pDigiDataPtr
pdigiDataPtr  dd          ?                        ; Pointer to 4KB buffer in
                                                   ; driver
pdigiOff      dd          ?                        ; FAR Pointer to PDIGI
                                                   ; Entry point
pdigiSel      dd          ?
callerOff     dd          ?                        ; Local save variables
saveGS        dw          ?
saveES        dw          ?
              public      pdigiInfo
pdigiInfo     db          size PDIGIDATA dup(?)  ; Allocate space for struc.
              public      screenInfo
screenInfo    db          size SCREEN dup(?)     ; Allocate space for struc.
pdigi_dseg ends
; ------------------------------------------------------------------
;
;  Code Segment
;
; ------------------------------------------------------------------
CGROUP        group       pdigi_cseg
pdigi_cseg    segment     para use32 'CODE'
              assume      CS:pdigi_cseg
; ------------------------------------------------------------------
;
; GetDS();
;
; Returns the current data selector.
;
; All registers except EAX are preserved (contains the selector).
;
; ------------------------------------------------------------------
              align       PROCALIGN                ; Best performance for 486
              public      GetDS
GetDS         proc
              mov         AX, DS
              movzx       EAX, AX
              ret
GetDS         endp
```

```
;   ------------------------------------------------------------------
;
;   SetPDIGIAddr(selector, offset);
;
;   Sets the selector and offset of the C Entry Point for calling PDIGI
;   functions.
;
;   All registers except EAX are preserved.
;
;   ------------------------------------------------------------------
            align       PROCALIGN               ; Best performance for 486
            public      SetPDIGIAddr
SetPDIGIAddr proc
            push        EBP
            mov         EBP, ESP
            mov         EAX, P_DWARG1
            mov         pdigiSel, EAX
            mov         EAX, P_DWARG2
            mov         pdigiOff, EAX           ; Store them.
            pop         EBP
            ret
SetPDIGIAddr endp
;   ------------------------------------------------------------------
;
;   PDIGIEntryPoint(functionNum, parms ...)
;
;   This is the entry point for PDIGI. Note that since the PDIGI function
;   requires all the right information on the stack, we need to remove our
;   caller return address before calling the PDIGI Entry point in the
;   driver.
;
;   EAX, ECX, and EDX are trashed. All other registers are preserved.
;   Note that EAX may have a valid return value.
;
;   ------------------------------------------------------------------
            align    PROCALIGN                  ; Best performance for 486
            public   PDIGIEntryPoint
PDIGIEntryPoint proc
            pop      [callerOff]                ; Save return address
            mov      saveGS, GS                 ; Save GS for a bit
            mov      saveES, ES                 ; Save ES for a bit
            mov      AX, DS
            mov      GS, AX                     ; Set GS for WriteMonoRect,
```

```
                                           ; WriteRect
               mov     ES, AX              ; Set ES for ReadRectArea
               push    CS                  ; Save CS for return
               push    offset PDIGIEP_Return ; Save return offset
               push    [pdigiSel]
               push    [pdigiOff]
FakeProc       proc    far
               ret                         ; Sneaky way to call PDIGI
                                           ; "far"
FakeProc       endp
PDIGIEP_Return:
               mov     GS, saveGS
               mov     ES, saveES          ; Restore them
               jmp     [callerOff]         ; Return to caller
PDIGIEntryPoint endp
; ----------------------------------------------------------------
;
; CopyPDIGIData(driverOffset)
;
; This function copies the core PDIGI structure from the driver to
; the local pdigiInfo structure, which can then be used by the PDIGI
; application.
;
; All registers are preserved.
;
; ----------------------------------------------------------------
               align   PROCALIGN           ; Best performance for 486
               public  CopyPDIGIData
CopyPDIGIData  proc
               push    EBP
               mov     EBP, ESP
               push    ES
               push    ESI
               push    EDX
               push    ECX
               push    EAX
               mov     EAX, pdigiSel
               mov     ES, AX              ; Set ES to driver's CS
               mov     ECX, size PDIGIDATA / 4 ; Get DWORD size of struc.
               mov     ESI, P_DWARG1       ; Get source data
               lea     EDX, pdigiInfo      ; Point to destination
CopyPDIGI_Loop:
               mov     EAX, ES:[ESI]       ; Faster than REP MOVSD on 486
```

```
                mov      [EDX], EAX                  ; Copy the whole structure
                add      ESI, 4
                add      EDX, 4
                loop     CopyPDIGI_Loop
                pop      EAX
                pop      ECX
                pop      EDX
                pop      ESI
                pop      ES
                pop      EBP
                ret
CopyPDIGIData endp
; -----------------------------------------------------------------
;
; CopyFromDriver(localOffset, driverOffset, numBytes)
;
; This function copies data from the driver's data selector to the
; PDIGI application's data area. "localOffset" specifies the address
; in the PDIGI application, "driverOffset" is the address of the source
; data in the driver, and "numBytes" is the number of bytes to copy.
;
; All registers are preserved.
;
; -----------------------------------------------------------------
                align    PROCALIGN                   ; Best performance for 486
                public   CopyFromDriver
CopyFromDriver proc
                push     EBP
                mov      EBP, ESP
                push     DS
                push     ES
                push     EDI
                push     ESI
                mov      AX, DS
                mov      ES, AX                       ; Set destination selector
                mov      DS, pdigiInfo.PDIGI_DS ; Get source selector
                mov      EDI, P_DWARG1                ; Destination
                mov      ESI, P_DWARG2                ; Source
                mov      ECX, P_DWARG3                ; Byte count
                rep      movsb                        ; Do the copy
                pop      ESI
                pop      EDI
                pop      ES
```

```
                        pop     DS
                        pop     EBP
                        ret
        CopyFromDriver endp
        ; ----------------------------------------------------------------
        ;
        ; CopyToDriver(driverOffset, localOffset, numBytes)
        ;
        ; This function copies data to the driver's data selector from the
        ; PDIGI application's data area. "localOffset" specifies the address
        ; in the PDIGI application, "driverOffset" is the address of the source
        ; data in the driver, and numBytes is the number of bytes to copy.
        ;
        ; All registers are preserved.
        ;
        ; ----------------------------------------------------------------
                        align   PROCALIGN
                        public  CopyToDriver
        CopyToDriver    proc
                        push    EBP
                        mov     EBP, ESP
                        push    ES
                        push    EDI
                        push    ESI
                        mov     ES, pdigiInfo.PDIGI_DS    ; Get source selector
                        mov     EDI, P_DWARG1             ; Destination
                        mov     ESI, P_DWARG2             ; Source
                        mov     ECX, P_DWARG3             ; Byte count
                        rep     movsb                     ; Do the copy
                        pop     ESI
                        pop     EDI
                        pop     ES
                        pop     EBP
                        ret
        CopyToDriver endp
        pdigi_cseg ends
          end
```

PDIGI Techniques

The section above describes the basic PDIGI functions and structures. This section contains some sample programs that demonstrate how to access PDIGI. It will teach you how to initialize PDIGI, access all its data structures in order to manage screen manipulation, and use most of its primitives.

Several sets of development tools are documented in this chapter as being well suited to developing ADS and PDIGI applications. First, the PharLap assembler is used to assemble PDIGISUB.ASM. Next, either WATCOM's C/386 or MetaWare's High C is used to compile both the PDIGI.C library and the PDIGI/ADS applications. Finally, WATCOM's linker (WLINK) can be used to link everything together, as can the one that comes with PharLap. The minimalistic approach is to use only WATCOM's C/386 package (we used v9.0 for testing) in lieu of the combination of PharLap and MetaWare's High C, since WATCOM's C/386 has everything you'll need except the assembler. The latter is not necessary if you have the disk accompanying this book, which includes the PDIGISUB.OBJ file you need to link with.

The First Step

The first thing you must do is set up your ADS application core. If you're planning to add PDIGI support to an existing ADS application, then you already have this core. However, if you are just starting to develop ADS applications, ADS Application Core, TSTPDIGI.C offers a core similar to that presented in Autodesk's ADS manual. All examples in this chapter are based on this core.

Note that the sample core code provided below defines a function called *TestPDIGI*, which is the function that we will be updating to exercise most aspects of PDIGI.

While the listing provides a framework for a PDIGI application, it doesn't actually do anything other than determine that PDIGI is installed and available.

ADS Application Core, TSTPDIGI.C

```
/* -------------------------------------------------------------
    TSTPDIGI.C

      DESCRIPTION:
      This file contains core ADS code to demonstrate use of PDIGI.
      Copyright (c) 1993 by Panacea Inc. — All Rights Reserved.
      This file may be freely distributed, providing the above
      copyright notice remains wholly intact.
      Support for PDIGI can be found in the ACAD Forum on CompuServe.
```

```
Revision History:
When      Who   What
========  ===   ==================================================
02/10/93  JBR   Original version created for PDIGI v1.00
 ------------------------------------------------------------------ */
/* ----------------------------------------------------------------
    Necessary Include Files
 ------------------------------------------------------------------ */
#include    <stdio.h>
#include    <string.h>
#include    "adslib.h"    /* Necessary for ADS defs */
#include    "pdigi.h"     /* Necessary for PDIGI defs */
/* ----------------------------------------------------------------
    Local Data
 ------------------------------------------------------------------ */
VPBLOCK     vpInfo;        /* The current VP information */
UDWORD      pdigiData;     /* Pointer to PDIGI Data Area */
/* ----------------------------------------------------------------
    CODE
 ------------------------------------------------------------------ */
/* ----------------------------------------------------------------
    TestPDIGI()
    This function is where we put our code that actually uses the
    PDIGI interface. Note that this function assumes it is the first
    ADS function defined in the ADS application (i.e., function code 0).
 ------------------------------------------------------------------ */
UDWORD          TestPDIGI()
{
  if ((pdigiData = InitPDIGI()) == 0) /* See if PDIGI is available */
    return (RSERR);
  ads_retvoid();              /* Absorb the "nil" return */
  return (RSRSLT);            /* Everything went fine. */
}
/* ----------------------------------------------------------------
    main()
    This is the entry point into the ADS application, and performs
    the necessary ADS function calls to register the application with
    AutoCAD. Most of this code was derived from Autodesk's ADS sample
    programs.
 ------------------------------------------------------------------ */
VOID   main(argc, argv)
DWORD  argc;
BYTE   *argv[];
```

```
{
  DWORD      stat;
  WORD       scode = RSRSLT;      /* This is the default result code */
  ads_init(argc, argv);          /* Initialize the ADS interface */
  for ( ;; )
    {                                  /* Note infinite loop condition */
    if ((stat = ads_link(scode)) < 0)    /* Try ACAD link, get req. */
      {
      printf("TEMPLATE: bad status from ads_link() = %d\n", stat);
      /*
        Can't use ads_printf to display this message,
        because the link failed
      */
      fflush(stdout);
      exit(1);
      }
    scode = RSRSLT;              /* Default return value */
    /*
      Check for all request cases here:
    */
    switch (stat)
      {
      case RQXLOAD:         /*
                            Register your ADS external functions.
                            Register your function handlers if you
                            want your ADS functions to be called
                            transparent to this dispatch loop.
                            Required for all applications.
                            In our case, we'll register "TestPDIGI."
                          */
        if (ads_defun("C:TestPDIGI", 0) != RTNORM)
          scode = RSERR;
        else
          ads_printf("Type 'TestPDIGI' to use this program.\n");
        break;
      case RQSUBR:          /*
                            This case is normally expanded to
                            select one of the application's
                            external functions.
                          */
        if (ads_getfuncode() != 0)
          {
          ads_fail("Received non-existent function code.");
```

```
            scode = RSERR;
            }
        else
            scode = TestPDIGI(); /* Call our PDIGI tester */
        case RQXUNLD:        /*
                              Do C program cleanup here.
                              Not required unless you need to
                              clean up your own allocated resources.
                              Note: You don't have to undefine ADS
                              functions. LISP does it for you.
                              */
            break;
        case RQSAVE:         /*
                              AutoCAD SAVE command notification.
                              You can use it for your own database
                              synchronization. Not required.
                              */
            break;
        case RQQUIT:         /*
                              AutoCAD QUIT command notification.
                              Not required.
                              */
            break;
        case RQEND:          /*
                              AutoCAD END command notification.
                              Not required.
                              */
            break;
        default:
            break;
        }
    }
}
/* ------------------------------------------------------------
   End of TSTPDIGI.C
   ----------------------------------------------------------- */
```

Building TSTPDIGI with MetaWare High C and PharLap

Using High C and PharLap, you build the above code into a loadable EXP file using the TSTPDIGI.MAK file found below in the MWMAKE File for PDIGI Test, TSTPDIGI.MAK, which is designed to be used by MetaWare's MWMAKE utility. To perform the MAKE operation, execute the following lines from the DOS command prompt:

```
SET  IPATH=C:\HIGHC\INC
MWMAKE  -F  TSTPDIGI.MAK
```

The above "SET" statement and the MAKE file assume that your HIGHC include files and libraries are located in C:\HIGHC\INC, and that you are executing the MAKE file from within your ADS subdirectory (located under the main AutoCAD directory). The contents of the MAKE file may need to change if you use other "make" utilities. We should point out, however, that while we were using v1.7 of the High C compiler, we found that the *malloc()* function was broken in the v1.7 libraries and had to resort to using the older v1.6 small model libraries in order to get memory allocation to work properly. Assumedly, this would not be a problem with v3.0 of High C.

Note that the MWMAKE file also makes mention of a SAMPLE.PRO file, which contains compiler directives for the High C compiler. This file is created by the MAKESAMP.BAT file provided by Autodesk in the ADS subdirectory mentioned earlier. SAMPLE.PRO is shown below in the Meta-Ware C PRAGMA File, SAMPLE.PRO.

MWMAKE File for PDIGI Test, TSTPDIGI.MAK

```
TSTPDIGI.EXP:  TSTPDIGI.OBJ PDIGI.OBJ PDIGISUB.OBJ
               386link TSTPDIGI.OBJ ADS.LIB PDIGI.OBJ PDIGISUB.OBJ
               lib d:\highc\small\hcc -sym -exe TSTPDIGI
PDIGI.OBJ:     PDIGI.C PDIGI.H
               hcd386p PDIGI.C -pr sample.pro -ob PDIGI.OBJ -noansi
TSTPDIGI.OBJ:  TSTPDIGI.C PDIGI.H
               hcd386p TSTPDIGI.C -pr sample.pro -ob TSTPDIGI.OBJ -noansi
PDIGISUB.OBJ:  PDIGISUB.ASM PDIGI.INC
               386asm PDIGISUB.ASM -o PDIGISUB.OBJ
```

MetaWare C PRAGMA File, SAMPLE.PRO

```
#define HIGHC 1
#define PROTOTYPES  1
pragma Memory_model(Small);
pragma On(Floating_point);
pragma On(Int_function_warnings);
pragma On(Parm_warnings);
pragma On(Struct_by_value_warnings);
pragma On(Prototype_conversion_warn);
pragma Off(PCC_msgs);
```

```
pragma Off(Prototype_override_warnings);
pragma On(Callee_pops_when_possible);
pragma Off(check_stack);
pragma On(Emit_line_table);
pragma On(Emit_line_records);
```

Building TSTPDIGI with WATCOM C/386 v9.0

Using the WATCOM tools is similar to using MetaWare and PharLap, except that WATCOM has added a few things to specifically support ADS programming. First, make sure to modify the WCADS.LIB as indicated in the WATCOM documentation. Next, to set the necessary environment variables, run the AUTOC386.BAT file created when you installed WATCOM's C/386. The MAKE file for TSTPDIGI appropriate for use with WMAKE (the WATCOM MAKE utility) is in the listing below. Note that it is assumed you have PDIGISUB.OBJ, found on the *AutoCAD Power Tools* disk, available to link with, instead of requiring PharLap's 386ASM to assemble the code. To execute WMAKE for TSTPDIGI, just type the following line at the DOS command prompt:

```
WMAKE  -F  TSTPDIGI.WC
```

WATCOM MAKE file, TSTPDIGI.WC

```
TSTPDIGI.EXP:  TSTPDIGI.OBJ PDIGI.OBJ PDIGISUB.OBJ
               wlink system ads file TSTPDIGI.OBJ,PDIGI.OBJ,PDIGISUB.OBJ
               name TSTPDIGI library c:wcads
PDIGI.OBJ:     PDIGI.C PDIGI.H
               wcc386p /fpi87 /3s PDIGI
TSTPDIGI.OBJ:  TSTPDIGI.C PDIGI.H
               wcc386p /fpi87 /3s TSTPDIGI
```

The PDIGI Environment

Once you have compiled TSTPDIGI and determined successful initialization of PDIGI, take a look at the various structures which help define the PDIGI environment, namely the PDIGIDATA, SCREEN, and current VPBLOCK structures. The code in the PDIGI Structure Display shown below, which should be inserted into the *TestPDIGI()* function shown earlier, switches to the text screen and then displays all the pertinent portions of the aforementioned structures.

PDIGI Structure Display

```
    BYTE      tmpString[32];    /* Used as scratch data area */
    DWORD     i, j, k;          /* Used by all examples */
/* ------------------------------------------------------------
   Example 1—Dumping the contents of the PDIGI structures:
   ------------------------------------------------------------ */
/*
   Since we'll be printing lots of stuff, let's switch to the text
   screen first. Note that you need to ensure that you are in
   the graphics mode in order to draw using PDIGI.
*/
ads_textscr();                              /* Go to text screen */
    /*
    Now, let's take a look at the data we have. The pdigiInfo
    structure is filled by the call to InitPDIGI, as is the
    screenInfo structure.
    */
ads_printf("\nPDIGIDATA Information\n");
ads_printf("Version:                %d.%d\n",
            (pdigiInfo.PDIGI_VERS >> 8), (pdigiInfo.PDIGI_VERS & 0xFF));
ads_printf("Data Selector:          %0.4X\n", pdigiInfo.PDIGI_DS);
ads_printf("VP Structures:          %0.8lX\n", pdigiInfo.PDIGI_VPINF);
ads_printf("Current VP:             %0.8lX\n", pdigiInfo.PDIGI_CURVP);
ads_printf("VP Size (bytes):        %ld\n", pdigiInfo.PDIGI_VPLEN);
ads_printf("# of VP structs:        %d\n", pdigiInfo.PDIGI_MAXVP);
ads_printf("Y-Bias:                 %d\n", pdigiInfo.PDIGI_YBIAS);
ads_printf("SCREEN structure:       %0.8lX\n", pdigiInfo.PDIGI_SCRPT);
ads_printf("Character Width:        %d\n", pdigiInfo.PDIGI_CHRWD);
ads_printf("Character Height:       %d\n", pdigiInfo.PDIGI_CHRHT);
ads_printf("Side Menu Width:        %d\n", pdigiInfo.PDIGI_SIDWD);
ads_printf("Command Area Hgt:       %d\n", pdigiInfo.PDIGI_CMDHT);
ads_printf("Status Line On?         %s\n", pdigiInfo.PDIGI_TOPOF ? "Yes":"No");
ads_printf("Max. Drawing X:         %d\n", pdigiInfo.PDIGI_XMAX);
ads_printf("Device Color Tbl:       %0.8lX\n", pdigiInfo.PDIGI_CLRTB);
ads_printf("Logical Color Tbl:      %0.8lX\n", pdigiInfo.PDIGI_CLRLG);
ads_printf("Color Palette Tbl:      %0.8lX\n", pdigiInfo.PDIGI_CLRPH);
ads_printf("Device XOR Color:       %0.8lX\n", pdigiInfo.PDIGI_CLRXR);
ads_printf("\nPlease hit <Enter>...\n");     /* Force pause */
if (ads_getstring(0, "", tmpString) != RTNORM)
    return (RSERR);        /* Abort the operation */
ads_printf("\nSCREEN Information\n");
ads_printf("X Size:                 %d\n", screenInfo.SCR_XSIZE);
```

```
    ads_printf("Y Size:              %d\n", screenInfo.SCR_YSIZE);
    ads_printf("Bits Per Pixel:       %d\n", screenInfo.SCR_BPP);
    /*
      We could search the whole viewport list to see which
      viewports are active, but for the sake of simplicity, we'll
      just display information for the current viewport, which
      we obtain via the following couple of lines:
    */
      CopyFromDriver(&vpInfo,
                    (UBYTE *)pdigiInfo.PDIGI_CURVP, pdigiInfo.PDIGI_VPLEN);
    ads_printf("\nVP Information\n");
    ads_printf("ACAD VP Number:      %d\n", vpInfo.VP_NUM);
    ads_printf("Screen Min. X, Y:    %d, %d\n", vpInfo.VP_XMIN, vpInfo.VP_YMIN);
    ads_printf("Screen Max. X, Y:    %d, %d\n", vpInfo.VP_XMAX, vpInfo.VP_YMAX);
    ads_printf("ACAD Min. X, Y:      %lf, %lf\n", vpInfo.VP_VRXL, vpInfo.VP_VRYL);
    ads_printf("ACAD Max. X, Y:      %lf, %lf\n", vpInfo.VP_VRXH, vpInfo.VP_VRYH);
    ads_printf("\nPlease hit <Enter>...\n"); /* Force a pause again */
    if (ads_getstring(0, "", tmpString) != RTNORM)
      return (RSERR);  /* Abort the operation */
    ads_graphscr();                          /* Go back to graphics mode */
```

As we dump out the current structure information, it's important to keep in mind that some of this data occasionally may change due to user interaction with AutoCAD, which is why use of the various additional states in ADS applications (RQXUNLD, RQEND, RQSAVE, and RQQUIT) may be a useful way to flag significant changes in the environment. In any event, at any time you hand back control to the user, you should reload the contents of at least the **PDIGIDATA** structure, via code similar to the following (taken from PDIGI.C):

```
    /*
      Get the current PDIGIDATA info.
    */
    PDIGI_GetPDIGIData();            /* Get driver to set PDIGI data */
    CopyPDIGIData(pdigiDataPtr);     /* Gets the PDIGIData */
```

It should be noted that any time you ask the user for input via one of the *ads_getxxxxx()* input functions, you are giving the user the opportunity to force a flip-screen (to or from the text screen in a single screen configuration) or to change the current viewport (in a multiple viewport setup). For the flip-screen, just calling *ads_graphscr()* after user input but prior to any **PDIGI** drawing operation, will be sufficient to ensure it will operate properly; executing a **PDIGI** graphics instruction while on the text screen may produce extremely undesirable results. For the current viewport change, you may need to recheck the current viewport information after user input via the sample code above.

The next example, given below in the sample PDGI Drawing Code, shows how to draw using the PDIGI interface, and also puts into practice our need to ensure that we are always on the graphics screen.

```
/* -------------------------------------------------------------
     Example 2—Draw in the current viewport
     ----------------------------------------------------------- */
/*
   The following are used by the drawing code in the TestPDIGI()
   function.
*/
UDWORD physColorTable[256]; /* Physical color table lookup */
union LOGICOLORS
   {
   UBYTE    overAll[274];
   struct
      {
      UBYTE    start[18];  /* Logical color table—negative values */
      UBYTE    table[256]; /* Logical color table—positive values */
      } split;
   } logiColor;
/*
   The following is a macro that converts a logical ACAD color into
   the proper display color for any display:
*/
#define  ConvColor(x) physColorTable[logiColor.split.table[(x)]]
   UDWORD xLo, yLo, xHi, yHi;  /* Used by Examples 2-4 */
   /*
      Although Example 1 gets a copy of the current viewport data,
      let's get it again for completeness.
   */
   CopyFromDriver(&vpInfo,
            (UBYTE *)pdigiInfo.PDIGI_CURVP, pdigiInfo.PDIGI_VPLEN);
   /*
      Now, since we are going to be drawing on the screen, we need to
      have knowledge of the color space layout of the current display
      device. So, first we get a copy of the physical color table.
      This is the table used to translate an 8-bit physical color to
      a display drawing color.
   */
   CopyFromDriver(physColorTable,
```

```
                 (UBYTE *)pdigiInfo.PDIGI_CLRTB, sizeof (UDWORD) * 256);
/*
   Then, we load the logical color table. Note that this table is
   a bit weird, as it has 256 nonnegative entries used for ACAD
   drawing colors, and 18 negative entries used for ACAD interface
   objects, such as dialogue boxes, pull-downs, side menus, etc.
   This means we need to copy 256+18 entries, from 18 positions
   prior to the start of the logical color table.
*/
CopyFromDriver(&logiColor,
           (UBYTE *)(pdigiInfo.PDIGI_CLRLG - 18), sizeof (UBYTE) * 274);
/*
   Let's take the viewport coordinates, and convert them to screen
   coordinates for easier manipulation. Note that Y coordinates
   have to be Y-Bias adjusted for conversion to screen coordinates.
   Such conversion causes the min/max relationship to change between
   the two Y coordinates.
*/
xLo = vpInfo.VP_XMIN;
xHi = vpInfo.VP_XMAX;
yLo = pdigiInfo.PDIGI_YBIAS - vpInfo.VP_YMAX;
yHi = pdigiInfo.PDIGI_YBIAS - vpInfo.VP_YMIN;
/*
   Next, let's clear the viewport. Each set of graphics operations
   will require the user to hit <Enter> in order to get to the next
   set of operations. Note that a logical color of 0 is the background
   color.
*/
ads_printf("\nHit <Enter> to clear viewport...\n");
if (ads_getstring(0, "", tmpString) != RTNORM)
   return (RSERR);  /* Abort the operation */

ads_graphscr();        /* Make sure we're in graphics mode */
PDIGI_DrawRect(xLo, yLo, xHi, yHi, ConvColor(0));
/*
   Now, let's fill the viewport completely with horizontal lines.
   The color value is forced to be between 0 and 255.
*/
ads_printf("\nHit <Enter> to fill viewport with H-Lines...\n");
if (ads_getstring(0, "", tmpString) != RTNORM)
   return (RSERR);  /* Abort the operation */
ads_graphscr();        /* Make sure we're in graphics mode */
```

```
for (i = yLo; i <= yHi; i++)
  PDIGI_DrawHLine(xLo, i, xHi - xLo + 1, ConvColor(i & 0xFF));
/*
  Now, let's clear the viewport completely with horizontal lines,
  drawing exactly the same sequence as above, but demonstrating
  the result of an XOR operation.
*/
ads_printf("\nHit <Enter> to clear viewport with H-Lines...\n");
if (ads_getstring(0, "", tmpString) != RTNORM)
  return (RSERR);  /* Abort the operation */
ads_graphscr();        /* Make sure we're in graphics mode */

for (i = yLo; i <= yHi; i++)
  PDIGI_DrawHLineXOR(xLo, i, xHi - xLo + 1, ConvColor(i & 0xFF));
/*
  Now do the same for Vertical lines
*/
ads_printf("\nHit <Enter> to fill viewport with V-Lines...\n");
if (ads_getstring(0, "", tmpString) != RTNORM)
  return (RSERR);  /* Abort the operation */

ads_graphscr();        /* Make sure we're in graphics mode */

for (i = xLo; i <= xHi; i++)
  PDIGI_DrawVLine(i, yLo, yHi - yLo + 1, ConvColor(i & 0xFF));
ads_printf("\nHit <Enter> to clear viewport with V-Lines...\n");
if (ads_getstring(0, "", tmpString) != RTNORM)
  return (RSERR);  /* Abort the operation */

ads_graphscr();        /* Make sure we're in graphics mode */

for (i = xLo; i <= xHi; i++)
  PDIGI_DrawVLineXOR(i, yLo, yHi - yLo + 1, ConvColor(i & 0xFF));
/*
  Now fill the viewport with a moire pattern sweep
*/
ads_printf("\nHit <Enter> to fill viewport with a line sweep...\n");
if (ads_getstring(0, "", tmpString) != RTNORM)
  return (RSERR);  /* Abort the operation */

ads_graphscr();        /* Make sure we're in graphics mode */
for (i = yLo; i <= yHi; i++)
  PDIGI_DrawLine(xLo, yLo, xHi, i, ConvColor(i & 0xFF));
```

```
    for (i = xLo; i < xHi; i++)
        PDIGI_DrawLine(xLo, yLo, i, yHi, ConvColor(i & 0xFF));
    /*
        Then XOR each pixel in the viewport, using a manual read/modify write.
    */
    ads_printf("\nHit <Enter> to XOR each pixel...\n");
    if (ads_getstring(0, "", tmpString) != RTNORM)
        return (RSERR);   /* Abort the operation */

    for (i = xLo; i <= xHi; i++)
        for (j = yLo; j <= yHi; j++)
            PDIGI_WritePixel(i, j, (PDIGI_ReadPixel(i, j) ^
            pdigiInfo.PDIGI_CLRXR));
    /*
        XOR each pixel again, using PDIGI's read/modify pixel write.
    */
    ads_printf("\nHit <Enter> to XOR each pixel again...\n");
    if (ads_getstring(0, "", tmpString) != RTNORM)
        return (RSERR);   /* Abort the operation */

    for (i = xLo; i <= xHi; i++)
        for (j = yLo; j <= yHi; j++)
            PDIGI_WritePixelXOR(i, j, pdigiInfo.PDIGI_CLRXR);
    /*
        Now do the same operation with a single filled rectangle.
    */
    ads_printf("\nHit <Enter> to XOR viewport...\n");
    if (ads_getstring(0, "", tmpString) != RTNORM)
        return (RSERR);   /* Abort the operation */

    ads_graphscr();          /* Make sure we're in graphics mode */
    PDIGI_DrawRectXOR(xLo, yLo, xHi, yHi, pdigiInfo.PDIGI_CLRXR);
    ads_printf("\nPlease hit <Enter> to continue...\n");
    if (ads_getstring(0, "", tmpString) != RTNORM)
        return (RSERR);   /* Abort the operation */
    ads_redraw(NULL, 0);   /* Restore viewport contents */
```

Sample PDIGI Drawing Code

Looking at the drawing example, you may immediately see a number of strange things happening. The first has to do with color. AutoCAD internally generally deals with "logical" colors, which range from –18 to 255 in value.

The negative values are used to refer to menu areas, dialogue boxes, and pretty much the whole color look and feel of the AutoCAD display.

The nonnegative logical colors are used for drawing colors. A display driver takes the AutoCAD logical colors and translates them into the device-specific physical colors, usually by way of a non-device-specific logical to physical translation mechanism. This latter is important, as display devices vary greatly in the number of colors supported and in the color format they use. Autodesk, by defining its color environment via a fixed but translatable scheme, permits AutoCAD to work with such diverse hardware.

Shown below is a list of some of the positive and all of the negative logical color values. This list also can be found in PDIGI.H and PDIGI.INC.

Normally, the object colors (logical colors −18 through −1) are not used for regular drawing by PDIGI applications; they are used instead to simulate the AutoCAD color scheme in custom user interface designs.

Logical Object Colors

```
/*
    Standard color definitions for AutoCAD displays
    Assumes user has made no color display changes
 */
#define    BLACK      0      /* Also background color */
#define    RED        1
#define    YELLOW     2
#define    GREEN      3
#define    CYAN       4
#define    BLUE       5
#define    MAGENTA    6
#define    WHITE      7
/*
    Definitions for object colors in AutoCAD—in logical color space
 */
/*                    -1      is reserved for internal XOR */
#define    SCRBACKCOLOR   -2   /* Graphics area background color */
#define    TXTBACKCOLOR   -3   /* Background color for text areas */
#define    TXTFORECOLOR   -4   /* Foreground color for text areas */
#define    TXTBRDRCOLOR   -5   /* Border color for text areas */
#define    ALRTBACKCOLOR  -6   /* Alert box background */
#define    ALRTFORECOLOR  -7   /* Alert box foreground */
#define    ALRTBRDRCOLOR  -8   /* Alert box border */
#define    MENUBACKCOLOR  -9   /* Menu bar background */
#define    MENUFORECOLOR  -10  /* Menu bar foreground */
#define    MENUBRDRCOLOR  -11  /* Menu bar border */
```

```
#define   POPUPBACKCOLOR   -12   /* Pop-up menu background */
#define   POPUPFORECOLOR   -13   /* Pop-up menu foreground */
#define   POPUPBRDRCOLOR   -14   /* Pop-up menu border color */
#define   DLOGBACKCOLOR    -15   /* Dialogue box background */
#define   DLOGFORECOLOR    -16   /* Dialogue box foreground */
#define   DLOGBRDRCOLOR    -17   /* Dialogue box border */
#define   DLOGLINECOLOR    -18   /* Dialogue box line drawing color */
```

There is, alas, yet another step in dealing with logical to device colors: via the physical color look-up table. This table is not really necessary when you're dealing with a display device that is in an 8-bit-per-pixel (BPP) mode or less; in such modes, the look-up table basically is an identity table (i.e., index X has a value of X), so it is safe to use with all pixel depths. However, the primary purpose of this device physical table is to translate a driver-internal physical color into a device physical color for 15, 16, 24, and 32 BPP modes. We recommend you use the *ConvColor()* macro shown in the above example at all times, as it executes faster and takes up less code than performing a comparison to the current device's BPP.

The two *CopyFromDriver()* calls in the sample PDIGI Image Save/Restore and Text Handling Code copy the two color translation tables from the driver into local memory, so they can be more easily accessed. The next strange thing we do in the example is calculate the actual screen coordinates of the viewport that was active when we first initialized the PDIGI interface (remember that users can change the active viewport when given control via ADS input functions, so the previously current viewport may no longer be the currently active viewport). Getting the minimum and maximum X coordinates is pretty simple—they just map the same way. The Y coordinates are different, however, as they assume an origin in the lower left corner (LLC) of the drawing area. In order to translate these coordinates into screen coordinates, we use the "Y-Bias" to perform the transformation. The Y-Bias is the Y position of the bottom of the drawing area, in screen coordinates. In order to perform the transformation, we subtract the LLC Y coordinate from the Y-Bias. Doing these viewport calculations ahead of time in the example saves us the effort of having to redo the translation every time we need the screen coordinates.

What follows next in the example is a series of actual (finally!) drawing examples using PDIGI. The only thing you may find to be of additional interest is that we show several different ways to XOR the whole viewport's contents, each method having different performance. Slowest is having the ADS application read the pixel, XOR it, and then write it back. While PDIGI overhead is insignificant compared to alternate methods available for some functions via AutoCAD, the amount of additional time it takes to manually perform a read/modify/write function such as the one described is still quite noticeable. A more direct approach is to use the *WritePixelXOR()* function, which performs the read/modify/write at the lowest level—this is visually faster than having the ADS application do it. Faster yet is using more advanced primitives, such as lines or even filled rectangles (the latter is shown in the example). Of course, this should not dissuade you from doing your own pixel-oriented manipulations, which can still be quite efficient if you process lots of pixels at once, as we'll see in the next example.

To finish the discussion of the first drawing example, note that we make a call to *ads_redraw()* to restore the contents of the current viewport (which, for our purposes, we assume to be the same as the one we started with). If you're modifying only portions of the screen occupied by viewports, then this will allow you to restore the contents of the screen, albeit slowly for complex images (since the whole drawing has to be redrawn), and even more slowly if no display list is present.

The next example shows several different things. First, it shows how to more quickly save and restore any part of the display. This is useful for performance reasons, as well as allowing you to modify areas outside the viewport drawing areas. Also, the example shows some rudimentary image-processing on several lines of data at a time, using a mechanism similar to the save/restore mechanism. Finally, the example shows two different ways to draw text on the display.

Sample PDIGI Image Save/Restore and Text Handling Code

```
UDWORD  saveSize;          /* Used by Example 3 */
UBYTE   *saveArea, *saveLine;/* "" */
UWORD   chrWidth, chrHeight; /* Used by Examples 3 and 4 */
/* -------------------------------------------------------------
   Example 3—Save/Restore display, image edit, show text
   ------------------------------------------------------------- */
ads_printf("\nHit <Enter> To Save Screen and XOR it...\n");
if (ads_getstring(0, "", tmpString) != RTNORM)
    return (RSERR);  /* Abort the operation */
ads_graphscr();     /* Make sure we're in graphics mode */
/*
   First, let's get the # of bytes required to save the whole
   display. Let's use the same variables from above, but reset to
   whole screen size.
*/
xLo = yLo = 0;
xHi = screenInfo.SCR_XSIZE - 1;  /* We want the max, not extents */
yHi = screenInfo.SCR_YSIZE - 1;
saveSize = PDIGI_CalcRectSpace(xLo, yLo, xHi, yHi);
ads_printf("Amount of space needed: %ld bytes\n", saveSize);
/*
```

```
      Now let's try to allocate space for the save and then perform
      the save to the allocated area. Note that we do not check
      the state of the SCR_ALIGN8 since all display devices have a
      physical display width that is a multiple of 8 anyway.
*/
if ((saveArea = (UBYTE *)malloc(saveSize)) != NULL)
  {
  PDIGI_ReadRectArea(xLo, yLo, xHi, yHi, saveArea);
  /*
     Now, we can really image edit only in 8-bit-per-pixel
     or deeper modes, as in 4bpp mode we cannot be sure of how
     the data is stored (i.e., it's not guaranteed to be in a
     packed-pixel format). However, we still can modify the 4bpp
     data just to prove that reading and writing image data
     really works.
     So, we need to get the number of bytes for one line of data,
     allocate a buffer to it, and start processing the display
     by performing an XOR on a byte-by-byte basis. Note that in
     some 32bpp modes this may set the alpha channel (the "O"),
     which may result in a really weird display.
  */
  saveSize = PDIGI_CalcRectSpace(xLo, yLo, xHi, yLo);
  if ((saveLine = (UBYTE *)malloc(saveSize)) != 0)
    {
    for (i = yLo; i <= yHi; i++)
      {
      PDIGI_ReadRectArea(xLo, i, xHi, i, saveLine);    /* Read */
      for (j = 0; j < saveSize; j++)
        if (screenInfo.SCR_BPP > 4)
          saveLine[j] ^= (pdigiInfo.PDIGI_CLRXR & 0xFF); /* Modify */
        else
          saveLine[j] ^= 0xFF;                           /* Modify */

      PDIGI_WriteRectArea(xLo, i, xHi, i, saveLine);   /* Write */
      }
    free(saveLine);  /* Good housekeeping */
    }
  else
    ads_printf("Malloc of line save area failed! Aborting example!\n");
  /*
     Now, let's display the current display and font information
     in the middle of the display. Putting a pretty border area
     up is an exercise left to the reader of this comment.
```

```
        */
        chrWidth = pdigiInfo.PDIGI_CHRWD;       /* Get the cell size for */
        chrHeight = pdigiInfo.PDIGI_CHRHT;      /* easier access */
        sprintf(tmpString, " Character Size: %d by %d ", chrWidth, chrHeight);
        i = ((xHi - xLo) - (strlen(tmpString) * chrWidth)) / 2;
        j = ((yHi - yLo) - (chrHeight * 2)) / 2;   /* Center it */
        /*
            Let's print the string out on a display, a character at a time.
        */
        k = 0;
        while (tmpString[k])
          {
          PDIGI_DrawChar(i + k * chrWidth, j, tmpString[k],
                    ConvColor(TXTBACKCOLOR), ConvColor(TXTFORECOLOR));
          k++;
          }
        /*
          Now let's print out the screen info via a full string.
        */
        sprintf(tmpString, " Screen Size: %d by %d by %d ",
            screenInfo.SCR_XSIZE, screenInfo.SCR_YSIZE, screenInfo.SCR_BPP);
        /*
          Copy the string to the driver's local memory. Copy trailing null.
        */
        CopyToDriver((UBYTE *)pdigiData, tmpString, strlen(tmpString)+1);
        /*
          Recenter horizontally and display.
        */
        i = ((xHi - xLo) - (strlen(tmpString) * chrWidth)) / 2;
        PDIGI_DrawString(i, j + chrHeight, pdigiData,
                    ConvColor(TXTBACKCOLOR), ConvColor(TXTFORECOLOR));
        ads_printf("\nHit <Enter> To Restore Screen (Do NOT Flip to Text!)..\n");
        ads_getstring(0, "", tmpString);
        /*
          Restore the contents of the display.
        */
        PDIGI_WriteRectArea(xLo, yLo, xHi, yHi, saveArea);
        free(saveArea);
        }
    else
        ads_printf("Malloc of screen save area failed! Aborting example!\n");
```

In the above example just about the first thing we do is determine the dimensions of the display, and then calculate the amount of memory required to save the whole display. That amount is then printed out. Next, we actually try to allocate the desired space, aborting if the memory is not available (which is possible with very high-resolution displays on systems with little memory).

If memory is available, we save the whole display, and then allocate enough space for a single scan line of display information. This single scan line buffer allows us to do some simple image processing on the display contents. In our case, we read the line, XOR the display data, and send it back. Note that this rather unscientific example makes a special case of 4-bit-per-pixel (16 color) modes, as we don't know their storage format. Such image processing as we are doing here should really be done only on 8-bit-per-pixel (256 color) or deeper color resolutions. Note that you could grab several scan lines at a time in such modes to perform smoothing or other real-image processing functions that depend on surrounding pixel information.

Once we have "image-processed" the whole display, we display two lines of centered text. The first indicates the font cell size we are using and is displayed a character at a time, while the second line shows the current display dimensions using a string function. Note that in the latter case, we have to copy the string to driver memory, making sure to include the trailing NULL string terminator before actually executing the string display function. After a response from the user, the whole display is restored from our saved memory area.

The final example, shown below in the sample PDIGI Point Selection/Polygon/Monochrome Code, is the most complex and perhaps the most interesting, as it is quite interactive. The purpose of this example is to show several things. First, it shows how to translate viewport pick coordinates into screen coordinates. Second, it shows how to use the monochrome to color memory expansion function, which allows you to take 1-bit-per-pixel source bitmap data and display it on the graphics device. Lastly, we show how to use the PDIGI polygon drawing engine.

Sample PDIGI Point Selection/Polygon/Monochrome Code

```
/* -------------------------------------------------------------
   Example 4—Point selection/Draw Polygon
   -------------------------------------------------------- */
struct resbuf  resBuf;                    /* Needed for GETVAR/SETVAR */
UWORD          snapVal, osnapVal, orthoVal; /* Save values */
ads_point      pickPoint;                  /* Pick point from ACAD */
UDWORD         pickX, pickY;               /* Screen pick position */
UWORD          vertList[6][2];             /* Polygon list */
UWORD          pointHand[16] =             /* Pointing hand icon data */
```

```
                         {
                         0x0000,   0x0008,   0x000C,   0x000C,
                         0x000C,   0xB00D,   0xB00D,   0xB60D,
                         0xFE0F,   0xFE37,   0xFC3F,   0xFC3F,
                         0xFC1F,   0xFC0F,   0xF80F,   0xF807
                         };
/*
    First, get the variables that affect point/position selection.
*/
ads_getvar("SNAPMODE", &resBuf);
snapVal = resBuf.resval.rint;
ads_getvar("OSMODE", &resBuf);
osnapVal = resBuf.resval.rint;
ads_getvar("ORTHOMODE", &resBuf);
orthoVal = resBuf.resval.rint;
/*
    Next, turn them all off... (we know that restype was set above).
*/
resBuf.resval.rint = 0;
ads_setvar("SNAPMODE", &resBuf);
ads_setvar("OSMODE", &resBuf);
ads_setvar("ORTHOMODE", &resBuf);
/*
    We're going back to using the viewport from the earlier example.
*/
xLo = vpInfo.VP_XMIN;
xHi = vpInfo.VP_XMAX;
yLo = pdigiInfo.PDIGI_YBIAS - vpInfo.VP_YMAX;
yHi = pdigiInfo.PDIGI_YBIAS - vpInfo.VP_YMIN;
/*
    Determine the size of the icon combined with the character.
    The icon is 16x16, and the character is added to the right side
    of it.
*/
j = 16 + pdigiInfo.PDIGI_CHRWD;
k = pdigiInfo.PDIGI_CHRHT > 16 ? pdigiInfo.PDIGI_CHRHT : 16;
ads_graphscr();     /* Make sure we're in graphics mode */
ads_printf("Enter 6 points to draw a polygon with...");
for (i = 0; i < 6; i++)
    {
    if (ads_getpoint(NULL, "\nSelect point: ", pickPoint) != RTNORM)
        break;       /* Abort if bad return code */
    /*
```

```
   Convert the input point into screen position. Assume only
   the single viewport. Note that Z coordinate is ignored.
*/
pickPoint[0] -= vpInfo.VP_VRXL;  /* Translate to VP origin */
pickPoint[1] -= vpInfo.VP_VRYL;
pickPoint[0] /= (vpInfo.VP_VRXH - vpInfo.VP_VRXL);  /* Get % into VP */
pickPoint[1] /= (vpInfo.VP_VRYH - vpInfo.VP_VRYL);
pickPoint[0] *= vpInfo.VP_XWIDTH; /* Calculate screen position */
pickPoint[1] *= vpInfo.VP_YHEIGHT;
pickX = (UDWORD)pickPoint[0] + vpInfo.VP_XMIN;  /* Get VP base */
pickY = pdigiInfo.PDIGI_YBIAS - ((UDWORD)pickPoint[1]+vpInfo.VP_YMIN);
if (pickX < xLo)   /* Make sure that our icon/char doesn't leak */
   pickX = xLo;        /*  over edges of viewport. */
else
   if ((pickX + j) > xHi)
      pickX = xHi - j;
if (pickY < yLo)
   pickY = yLo;
else
   if ((pickY + k) > yHi)
      pickY = yHi - k;
/*
   Write our icon and draw the character.
*/
PDIGI_WriteMonoRectArea(pickX, pickY, 16, 16, pointHand, 2,
               ConvColor(TXTBACKCOLOR), ConvColor(TXTFORECOLOR));
PDIGI_DrawChar(pickX + 16, pickY, i + '1',
               ConvColor(TXTBACKCOLOR), ConvColor(TXTFORECOLOR));
vertList[i][0] = pickX;  /* Save in vertex list for polygon */
vertList[i][1] = pickY;
   }
/*
   Copy vertex list to driver memory and draw it in yellow.
*/
CopyToDriver((UBYTE *)pdigiData, (UBYTE *)vertList, sizeof(vertList));
PDIGI_ComplexPolygon(pdigiData, i, ConvColor(YELLOW));
/*
   Since it's likely that our icons/chars were obscured by the
   polygon, let's redraw them all.
*/
for (i = 0; i < 6; i++)
   {
   PDIGI_WriteMonoRectArea(vertList[i][0], vertList[i][1], 16, 16,
```

```
              pointHand, 2, ConvColor(TXTBACKCOLOR), ConvColor(TXTFORECOLOR));
         PDIGI_DrawChar(vertList[i][0] + 16, vertList[i][1], i + '1',
                   ConvColor(TXTBACKCOLOR), ConvColor(TXTFORECOLOR));
     }
   ads_printf("\nHit <Enter> To Return to AutoCAD...\n");
   ads_getstring(0, "", tmpString);
   /*
     Restore the settings we changed...
   */
   resBuf.resval.rint = snapVal;
   ads_setvar("SNAPMODE", &resBuf);
   resBuf.resval.rint = osnapVal;
   ads_setvar("OSMODE", &resBuf);
   resBuf.resval.rint = orthoVal;
   ads_setvar("ORTHOMODE", &resBuf);
   ads_redraw(NULL, 0);        /* Restore viewport contents */
```

In order to prepare ourselves for accepting positional input from the user, we first turn off all AutoCAD options that might affect the actual pick position requested by the user. These three environment items are Snap, Object Snap, and Ortho modes. We save their states, turn them off, and at the end of our example, restore their settings.

To best illustrate our accurate conversion of the pick points to screen coordinates, we will put a little (16×16) monochrome icon at the pick position, followed by a number indicating which pick this is out of our six-pick sequence. Once all six picks are made, we'll draw a polygon using the six picks as the polygon vertices.

One correction we have to make to the pick points is to make sure our little icons and characters don't leak beyond the edges of the viewport we are supporting. To facilitate this, we calculate the maximum size the icon/character combo can take up, and adjust our screen positions (specified by the picks) accordingly.

The translation from pick position to screen position is perhaps one of the most vital things here, as it allows you to create your own special menus or sensitive areas in the drawing area of the display. The example here works well for a single viewport, but may pose some problems for multiple viewports. In the latter case, you'll need to check the current viewport number (obtainable from AutoCAD) or the current viewport structure pointer (obtainable from PDIGI) to determine if viewports have changed. If they have, you'll need to use new viewport structure data to track the pick point.

Back to the actual translation: What AutoCAD provides for a pick is the coordinate of the pick in floating point coordinates. Since we have access to the viewport structure, we know the floating point position of the viewport contents, as well as the physical screen position of the viewport, and can use this knowledge to do the translation. The translation process follows these steps:

1. Convert pick coordinates into coordinates relative to the viewport origin. This is done by subtracting the viewport origin coordinates from the pick coordinates.

2. Convert the viewport relative coordinates into a percentage of how far into the viewport the pick position is on each axis.

3. Multiply the percentage by the physical pixel dimensions of the viewport to get the relative pixel position of the pick position in the viewport.

4. Get the actual physical pixel location of the pick by adding the viewport origin and then Y-Bias adjusting the Y coordinate.

At the end, we have the screen position, which we then tweak to make sure we're not "leaking" outside the viewport. Once tweaked, the pixel position is saved in an array and used as the location at which to draw the icon (a hand with a pointing finger). Then, the current pick number is displayed to the right of the icon. This process is repeated until all six points have been handled.

Next, the point array is copied to driver memory and used to draw a complex yellow polygon. Since this polygon most probably will obscure all the little icon/character combos, we draw them all again one more time.

The pick controls are restored and we restore the display with a redraw, as in a previous example. Now all PDIGI examples are complete, almost all types of PDIGI functions have been exercised, and you're ready to try some things on your own.

In the event you run into problems with PDIGI, or have questions, the best place to ask them is in the API section of the ACAD Forum on CompuServe. PDIGI experts will be available on a daily basis to help you and learn from your experiences.

More on Cursors and Input

Before concluding this discussion of PDIGI, we would like to expand on the subject of cursors and positional input. Perhaps the most blatant omission in the series of examples presented in this chapter is information on using the raster cursor. This was intentional, alas, as currently there really isn't any simple way of tracking cursor motion without having AutoCAD's cursor physically tracking such actions.

While the pick example described above will suit the majority of PDIGI users, some of you may want greater access to the input stream. The only ways to do this require either your own digitizer input stream (separate from AutoCAD's) or direct access to the ADI (display or digitizer) via a Tee driver, the Release 12 ADS->ADI link, or a special back door into a driver. The Tee driver and ADS->ADI link were why PDIGI was written in the first place. However, the ADI back door does exist in PDIGI, but it's not guaranteed to work, especially if there is more than one active PDIGI application running at a time doing this sort of thing.

This ADI back door allows your ADS application to place small code stubs in the driver memory, and then modify the ADI packet table to call these stubs, which in turn should call functions in your ADS application, which should then pass back control to the original driver function after doing its bit. Since this method is extremely complex and possibly somewhat unstable, we will provide documentation and support for this back door only on a case-by-case basis. If you have a real need to use this mechanism (i.e., you find that PDIGI alone does not suffice), contact Jake Richter at Panacea Inc. via CompuServe (75130,2705), MCI Mail (351-5206), or FAX (603-434-2461) to discuss your needs. If this method is found to be fully stable and manageable, then it will be documented in a future release of PDIGI.

PDIGI and Workgroups

PDIGI is a powerful tool that works with ADS programming to make even more of AutoCAD customizable. Using it, you can write powerful applications that revamp AutoCAD to a previously unheard-of degree.

The development of such applications is no mean feat, however. Creating such a program may mean thousands of hours of work in creating specifications, development, and testing. The ongoing work to maintain the application as new requirements arise and new versions of AutoCAD are developed also is substantial.

You should do a fair amount of work in other areas of customization, including AutoLISP and ADS programming, before resorting to writing your own custom application. These smaller customization efforts not only provide quicker payback, they allow you to test out ideas for the custom application before you start writing it. If your needs to customize AutoCAD are really substantial, consider partnering with a medium-size or larger consulting firm, an existing third-party applications developer, or other companies with similar needs in order to make more development resources available and to reduce risk.

Summary

PDIGI is an advanced tool for experienced C and graphics programmers who want to directly access the AutoCAD display from within their ADS programs. It is available through several means, so programs developed under PDIGI can be used with any of a variety of display-list products that support it.

When ADS isn't enough for the graphics programming you need to do, PDIGI is available to help you make your applications more powerful. It may become a standard that is widely seen in third-party AutoCAD applications of the future.

PART IV

AutoCAD
Power Tools

22

Using the Software on Disk

One of the most valuable parts of *AutoCAD Power Tools* is the software provided on the accompanying disk. The major software includes a display driver, quick drawing viewer, and drawing management utilities. Also included are several AutoLISP programs that you can use as is or modify to suit your needs. All programs on the disk have been prelicensed for your immediate use.

About the Programs

The program disk includes the following software:

- The TurboDLD*Lite*™ display list processing driver

- The SirlinVIEW/Lite™ fast .DWG file viewer for DOS and Windows

- The DWGDB program for storing information about, locating, and loading .DWG files

- The SHOWREFS and DWGLIST utilities for reporting on drawing contents

- Miscellaneous AutoLISP programs

Refer to the remainder of this chapter for brief summaries of each program. Subsequent chapters document the major software programs in detail. Also see the README.TXT file contained on the disk.

629

Windows Tip

All of the software except for the TurboDLD*Lite* display list driver works equally well for AutoCAD DOS 386 and AutoCAD for Windows users. TurboDLD*Lite* is designed for AutoCAD DOS 386 only; Release 12 for Windows includes its own display list processing driver. Some of the other utilities, such as SHOWREFS and DWGLIST, need to be run from a DOS window.

Installation

The *AutoCAD Power Tools* disk contains a large number of files that have been compressed to save space. You will need to use the automatic installation program located on the disk to extract the files and copy them to your hard disk. This installation program is designed to be both easy to use and flexible. It gives you the choice of installing everything or only those utilities that you choose. It also can make changes to your system files (e.g., AUTOEXEC.BAT) when necessary, but it always will ask your permission before doing so.

To run the installation program, insert the disk into your floppy drive and type:

    A:INSTALL

(or B:\INSTALL if the *AutoCAD Power Tools* disk is in your B: drive). The installation program will prompt you to select the utilities you want installed, and then will ask where to copy them. Select the hard-disk drive and subdirectory names to install to. A complete default installation will create the following directories:

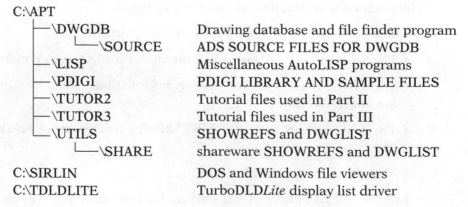

```
C:\APT
   ├──\DWGDB              Drawing database and file finder program
   │      └──\SOURCE      ADS SOURCE FILES FOR DWGDB
   ├──\LISP               Miscellaneous AutoLISP programs
   ├──\PDIGI              PDIGI LIBRARY AND SAMPLE FILES
   ├──\TUTOR2             Tutorial files used in Part II
   ├──\TUTOR3             Tutorial files used in Part III
   └──\UTILS              SHOWREFS and DWGLIST
          └──\SHARE       shareware SHOWREFS and DWGLIST
C:\SIRLIN                 DOS and Windows file viewers
C:\TDLDLITE               TurboDLDLite display list driver
```

If you choose to install TurboDLD*Lite,* the installation program will ask you which AutoCAD version you are using. If you install TurboDLD*Lite* for

Release 12, the installation program will ask for the name of your Release 12 driver subdirectory (usually \ACAD\DRV). This subdirectory is where the Release 12 TurboDLD*Lite* driver and configuration files will be copied. These files will not overwrite any of your standard AutoCAD files.

AutoCAD Releases 11 and 10 didn't use a driver subdirectory; if you install TurboDLD*Lite* for use with one of these older AutoCAD Releases, the installation program will ask you for a separate subdirectory, like C:\TDLDLITE.

After you've specified the utilities and directories, the installation program will copy files to the appropriate locations.

Depending on the utilities you choose to install, the installation program may ask you whether you want it to make changes to your AUTOEXEC.BAT or AutoCAD batch file. You can let the installation continue without the changes. Of course if you choose not to let the program change the original files, you'll need to incorporate the changes after installation is completed.

Once you've completed the installation procedure, please glance at README.TXT on the disk or in the \APT subdirectory of your hard disk for any last-minute changes. You can view or print this file with any ASCII text editor, such as DOS's EDIT or the Windows Notepad.

Before you use TurboDLD*Lite*, Sirlin VIEW/Lite (for DOS or Windows), or DWGDB, see Chapters 23, 24, or 25, respectively, for additional configuration information that pertains to each utility.

If you later decide to install other utilities from the *AutoCAD Power Tools* disk, simply rerun the installation program and select the additional utilities.

Copyright

All software provided on the disk accompanying this book is protected by U.S. and international copyright laws, and as such, may be used only on a single machine at a time, much in the same way that only one person can read this book at the same time. Respecting software copyrights allows software developers to afford to keep on developing great software.

A Summary of the Programs

In this section, we summarize the programs and tell you where to learn more about them.

Panacea's TurboDLDLite

TurboDLD*Lite* is Panacea's software-only AutoCAD accelerator. It's a special kind of display driver called a display list processor, and it works with AutoCAD to speed up zooms, pans, and redraws. Chapter 23, *Panacea's*

*TurboDLD*Lite, describes the driver in detail, so refer to that chapter for information about how to configure and use TurboDLD*Lite*.

SirlinVIEW/Lite Drawing File Viewers

The SirlinVIEW/Lite drawing file viewers for DOS and Windows let you view AutoCAD drawings more quickly and efficiently than AutoCAD does. These viewers use special techniques to display drawings quickly, which makes them ideal for looking at a single drawing or browsing through a group of drawings. Chapter 24, *SirlinVIEW/Lite Drawing File Viewers*, documents these programs.

DWGDB File Finder

The DWGDB file finder lets you store information about your drawing files in a simple ASCII text database, and then helps you locate and load drawings. With it, you can search for drawings by name, description, date, author, or keywords. You also can get a list of the last 10 drawings you worked on. Once you've located a drawing you want to work with, you can open, insert, xref, or view it. See Chapter 25, *DWGDB File Finder*, for more information.

SHOWREFS and DWGLIST

SHOWREFS and DWGLIST are Mike Dickason's popular DOS command-line utilities for managing drawing files. Together they let you report on the Xrefs, Blocks, layers, text fonts, and menus used by one or more drawings. Chapter 26, *SHOWREFS and DWGLIST*, gives a complete rundown of these two valuable utilities.

Miscellaneous AutoLISP Programs

We've included several miscellaneous AutoLISP programs in addition to the major software programs described above. The LISP programs will be useful as is for many people, but they also can serve as examples and idea-generators for users who customize. See Chapter 19, *AutoLISP*, for more information on how to modify or create your own LISP programs.

During installation, the miscellaneous AutoLISP programs are installed in the \APT\LISP subdirectory. You can leave them there and add \APT\LISP to your ACAD= support file search path, or you can copy them to another directory that's already included in the ACAD= path. See Chapter 14, *Getting Ready to Customize*, for more information about AutoCAD support file locations.

Each LISP program contains brief documentation and copyright information as a comment at the top of the .LSP file, so view or print out the files in order to find out more.

EDITXREF.LSP

EDITXREF streamlines the process of editing an externally referenced drawing and then returning to the parent drawing. As you work with Xrefs, you'll often discover that you want to make changes to them. Doing so involves loading the externally referenced file, making the editing changes, and then reloading the original parent file. EDITXREF lets you open an Xref (or Block) by picking it, rather than typing its name, and also provides a quick way to return to the parent drawing.

UPDBLKS.LSP

UPDBLKS automates the job of updating Block Definitions. Even with the advent of Xrefs, you sometimes need to update Blocks, and if you have more than one to update, the process can be a long and tedious one involving lots of typing. UPDBLKS automatically updates all Blocks in the current drawing that have matching .DWG filenames in the current directory.

TEXTEDIT.LSP

TEXTEDIT is a simple program for making the editing of text-type entities more sensible in AutoCAD. This program ties the DDEDIT, DDATTE, and DIM Newtext commands into a single command, so that you don't have to think about whether the strings you want to edit happen to be Text entities, Block Attributes, or Associative Dimensions. TEXTEDIT also provides a dialogue box for DIM Newtext, so that it works similarly to DDEDIT and DDATTE (see Figure 22.1).

FLATTEN.LSP

FLATTEN sets the Z coordinates of all Lines, Polylines, Circles, Arcs, Text, Block Inserts, and Points in the current drawing to 0. This procedure is useful when drawing entities that contain differences in Z elevation that prevent you from object-snapping to intersections. Such differences in Z elevation sometimes occur in drawings translated from other CAD systems, or when an inexperienced AutoCAD user sets the ELEV system variable or creates a different UCS without realizing it.

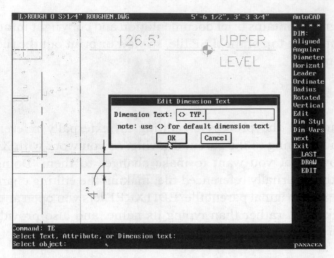

Figure 22.1   TEXTEDIT's dialogue for dimension text.

ROUGHEN.LSP

ROUGHEN turns a straight Line or Polyline into an irregular, wiggly line. It's a quick way to create an irregular surface or other line that looks "hand-sketched" (see Figure 22.2).

ARCDOT.LSP

ARCDOT draws an arc leader with a heavy "dot" at the end of it (see Figure 22.3). Architectural drafters often use an arc and dot to point from dimension text to a dimension line when the text falls outside the extension lines.

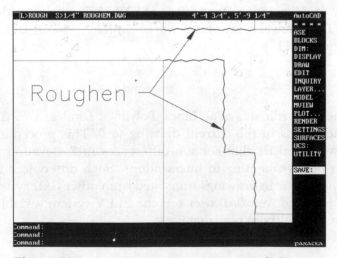

Figure 22.2   Use ROUGHEN to create wiggly lines.

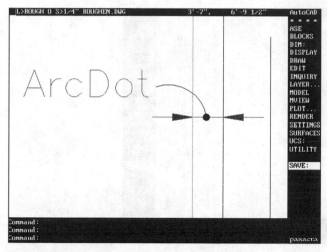

Figure 22.3   ARCDOT is useful for pointing to dimensions.

This routine makes it easy to add such a symbol. The arc and dot are drawn as a single Polyline for ease of picking.

LEADELPS.LSP

LEADELPS draws a straight line leader with a small ellipses at the end of it (see Figure 22.4). The ellipses is used by some drafters to "lasso" an entity or dimension line that they're calling out. For ease of picking, LEADELPS creates a single Polyline out of the ellipses and all the segments of the leader.

The Programs on Disk and Workgroups

If you've read most of the book up to this point, and especially the "Workgroups" sections at the end of most of the chapters, congratulations! You've taken advantage of a rare opportunity to step back from the details and take a look at the way AutoCAD is really used in your discipline and workplace.

While there are workgroup sections in several of the remaining chapters, different readers will skip among them, depending on whether the specific software package that's being described interests them. We would like to extend an invitation to all readers, and especially those who have been reading the workgroup sections, to contact us on CompuServe and share your ideas about how this book and the software on disk can be made better in future versions. Each of the authors is interested in various aspects of making use of AutoCAD faster, more productive, and easier. You can find us in the ACAD forum, or send mail directly to any of us; see Appendix B, *AutoCAD Resources*, for details. We look forward to your comments.

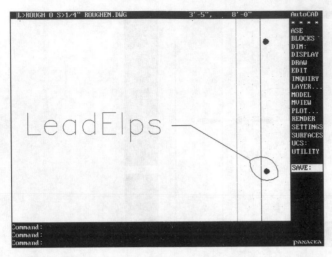

Figure 22.4 LEADELPS draws a leader with a "lasso."

The programs included on the *AutoCAD Power Tools* disk are a great resource for a workgroup. Between the speed increase of TurboDLD*Lite*, the convenience of the file viewer and file finder, the SHOWREFS and DWGLIST routines for improved drawing management, and the several AutoLISP utilities, there are a number of opportunities for improving the power and usefulness of AutoCAD.

As with the many routines included with AutoCAD itself, you will get the most from the *AutoCAD Power Tools* programs if you manage the process of learning and absorbing them. Try the routines and see which ones make the most sense for your workgroup. Modify those that come with source code if that makes them more useful.

Once you have the copies, get the members of your workgroup to install them (or the modified versions you've created). Hold a short training session to demonstrate how to get the most out of each program. Answer questions and get suggestions for further improvements in the programs that you or someone else can make later.

Once you've done all this, watch how these programs, and indeed the many parts that make up your group's overall AutoCAD experience, are used. Plan changes you would like to make in software and procedures to get the most out of the AutoCAD environment. Then look for opportunities to implement these changes. (AutoCAD upgrade time, harried as it may be, is a good time to introduce your own new ways of doing things.) Over time, you can do a great deal to make the experience of using AutoCAD more productive and even more fun for everyone involved.

C H A P T E R

23

*Panacea's TurboDLD*Lite™

This chapter documents the installation and use of Panacea's TurboDLD*Lite* software-only AutoCAD accelerator. The first major section is a Quick Start that should be enough information to get you going; the remainder of the chapter has more detailed information about using TurboDLD*Lite*.

Please note that TurboDLD*Lite* works with AutoCAD DOS Releases 386/10, 11, and 12, but does not work with AutoCAD Release 12 for Windows, which already has a built-in display-list driver. AutoCAD Release 12 for Windows *with* its built-in display-list driver achieves roughly the same performance as AutoCAD Release 12 for DOS *without* a display-list driver. Adding TurboDLD*Lite* to your AutoCAD Release 12 for DOS setup gets you the fastest possible level of performance with less memory usage than the Windows version.

 NOTE

As with all software provided on the disk accompanying this book, TurboDLD*Lite* is protected by U.S. and international copyright laws, and as such, may be used only on a single machine at a time, much in the same way that only one person at the same time can read this book. Respecting software copyrights enables software developers to afford to keep on developing great software.

637

TurboDLD*Lite* Quick Start

The following few pages sum up the basics of installing and using TurboDLD*Lite*. Please read the rest of the chapter for details.

What Does TurboDLD**Lite** Do?

TurboDLD*Lite*'s main function is to speed up AutoCAD pans, zooms and redraws. The driver accomplishes this by creating and maintaining a display list—a fast-displaying object list of the current drawing—dramatically increasing performance on pans, zooms, and redraws.

What's the Catch?

The only resource used by TurboDLD*Lite* is memory. The driver actively uses about 300KB of RAM from extended memory for its operation. This memory is drawn from AutoCAD's memory pool and therefore does not affect normal DOS operation. The driver is loaded by AutoCAD at AutoCAD load time and is unloaded when AutoCAD is exited.

Additionally, the display list size can vary from one tenth to three times the size of the current drawing file, particularly when using AutoCAD Release 12's 31-bit regen space. Memory for the display list is also drawn from AutoCAD's memory pool. If insufficient RAM is available and virtual memory is in use, the display list may be stored partly or entirely on disk. It is accessed much more slowly from disk than from RAM.

You may wish to purchase and install additional RAM before installing TurboDLD*Lite*, since it shares memory with AutoCAD. If AutoCAD is using a lot of memory, TurboDLD*Lite* may not have enough. If there is significant hard disk activity while you are using TurboDLD*Lite*, it may be an indication that you should add more memory to your system. (See Chapter 3, *Performance,* for more details.)

Starting the Installation: Release 12/386

First install the TurboDLD*Lite* files as described at the beginning of Chapter 22, *Using the Software on Disk*.

If you choose to install TurboDLD*Lite* into a subdirectory other than ACAD\DRV, be sure to modify the ACADDRV environment variable to include that subdirectory. Otherwise, the TurboDLD*Lite* selection will not appear in the list of available drivers. You will find this environment variable in the ACADR12.BAT file created during your original AutoCAD Release 12 installation.

Once the files are installed, begin AutoCAD with the −R reconfigure switch. For instance, if your AutoCAD batch file is named ADADR12, type the following:

```
ACAD R12-R
```

Choose option 3, Configure Video Display from the AutoCAD configuration menu. Type Y at the "Do you want to select a different one?" message to display the available video options for AutoCAD. Select "TurboDLD*Lite* by Panacea Inc." from the list of display options. Continue installation at the Driver Configuration section below.

Starting the Installation: Release 10/386 and Release 11/386

First install the TurboDLD*Lite* files as described at the beginning of Chapter 22, *Using the Software on Disk*. Run FASTACAD.BAT and then start AutoCAD. Reconfigure AutoCAD to use TurboDLD*Lite* by selecting option 5, Configure AutoCAD, from the AutoCAD main menu. From the next menu, select option 3, Configure Video Display. Choose Item 1, P386 ADI 4.0/4.1 (Release 11) or ADI P386 (Release 10), as your display device. (For more information, see your AutoCAD *Installation and Performance Guide*.)

After you select the proper display device, the TurboDLD*Lite* Driver Configuration menu will appear.

Completing the Installation: Driver Configuration

The following information applies to installing TurboDLD*Lite* for AutoCAD386 Releases 10, 11, and 12:

Setup of TurboDLD*Lite* requires configuration of its various operating parameters. These parameters have been logically grouped into menus based on their interaction with AutoCAD. A quick trip through each menu will complete the configuration process. Context-sensitive help can be obtained by typing "?" at any menu option.

The first menu, *Select Graphics Board/Resolution*, configures TurboDLD*Lite* for the graphics board, and display and rendering resolutions to be used.

Select Graphics Board. Selects graphics platform to be used.

Select Display Resolution. Selects AutoCAD, 3D Studio, and AutoShade main display screen resolutions.

Select Rendering Resolution. Selects AutoCAD Release 12, 3D Studio, and AutoShade rendering resolutions.

NOTE

You will have either a Display *or* a Rendering configuration option available during configuration. The correct menu choice will automatically appear, depending on whether you are configuring AutoCAD's display screen or its rendering capabilities. Configuring AVE Render is described under the section on reconfiguring TurboDLD*Lite* below.

Basic Configuration options set AutoCAD screen characteristics, number of text lines in the command-line area, font size, and dual screen mode.

AutoCAD Text Lines. Selects number of lines in AutoCAD command prompt area.

Font Size. Selects AutoCAD display screen font or font file to be used.

Dual Screen Mode. Enables or disables dual screen operation of AutoCAD. The Expert Configuration menu controls the operation of TurboDLD*Lite* itself. This menu allows for customization of the driver for speed or to adjust for memory constraints.

Display List. Enables or disables the display list feature of TurboDLD*Lite*.

Drawing Cache. Enables or disables TurboDLD*Lite*'s internal drawing cache.

AutoCAD Logical Drawing Space. Sets AutoCAD's logical space to 15 or 31-Bits (Release 12 only).

Internal Command Echo. Enables or disables the echo of TurboDLD*Lite* internal commands at the AutoCAD command line when executed.

Regen Mode. Selects TurboDLD*Lite*'s regen method.

After all options have been set, use the arrow keys to scroll down to the Save and Exit option, and then press the ENTER key to continue. Next, configure the AutoCAD screen display characteristics and then type Y to accept the changes. Exit to the AutoCAD drawing editor to begin using TurboDLD*Lite*.

The last step in setting up TurboDLD*Lite* is to configure the colors for AutoCAD. From the AutoCAD Command Line, type DLDCOLOR to start *CustomColors*™, TurboDLD*Lite*'s color configuration utility. Make any desired color changes, Save the new color palette, then Exit to return to the drawing editor.

If you encounter a problem or abnormality, please try to duplicate and document the steps required to reproduce it. As you document the problem, list your current system configuration, including video board, resolution, number of colors configured, etc. Also, if possible, try to duplicate the problem with an AutoCAD sample file so that we can easily try to re-create the problem on our equipment. Follow the steps at the end of this chapter to obtain technical support.

End of Quick Start

This is the end of the Quick Start section. Please see the sections below for more detailed information about TurboDLD*Lite*, problem-solving, getting support, etc.

What Does TurboDLD*Lite* Do?

AutoCAD supports graphics boards via a mechanism called ADI (Autodesk Device Interface). TurboDLD*Lite* is technically an ADI driver—a software program that takes requests from AutoCAD to display items on your graphics screen and does so, caching in the process the information for quicker access. In particular, there exists a class of ADI drivers known as display list processors—TurboDLD*Lite* is such a product. The term "display list" refers to the special type of caching the driver performs.

As the display list is created from the drawing information AutoCAD sends, the drawing information is usually specially encoded so that portions of it can be located very quickly for zoom and pan operations within AutoCAD. TurboDLD*Lite* uses a patented display list technology (Patent #5,101,444, in case you want to see how it works) to encode and retrieve its display data.

Using the display list, AutoCAD zooms, pans, and redraws can be significantly accelerated by as much as 25 times in some situations, but more like 8 to 10 times for casual usage. Also, the display list can be used to provide advanced features like a spyglass or magnifying glass, which allows you to enlarge a small section of your drawing dynamically; a bird's-eye view that lets you see your whole drawing for quick access to any part of the drawing; and real time panning and/or zooming for greater interactivity. (Look in the back of this book for more information on Panacea products that offer this advanced functionality.) Panacea's TurboDLD*Lite* has only one purpose: to speed up AutoCAD functions, including REDRAWs, PANs, and ZOOMs.

The driver is memory-resident and inserts itself between AutoCAD and the graphics board. It has no other effect on AutoCAD's operation besides speeding up the program; it runs with AutoShade 2 with RenderMan and 3D Studio to provide enhanced rendering support, but does not affect the speed of these programs, since they do not support display lists.

Installing TurboDLD*Lite* does not change any of the AutoCAD program files or alter any of the drawing files stored on disk. TurboDLD*Lite* was designed to be an easy-to-use product that makes using AutoCAD faster and more productive, not one that makes AutoCAD more complicated and difficult to use.

How does TurboDLD*Lite* make AutoCAD run faster? There are three things the driver does to speed operation. AutoCAD stores drawings in a hierarchical structure, with simple and complex elements intermixed. Every time the screen is updated, AutoCAD must decode this structure. TurboDLD*Lite* works differently. While you are working, it translates the normal hierarchical structure into a display list, a series of vectors or polygon fills. (The ability to support display lists was specifically added to AutoCAD with Release 10 via the ADI 4.0 interface.) When you pan or zoom, TurboDLD*Lite* uses the display list, then writes the resulting vectors to the video board hardware. Since the hierarchical structure does not have to be decoded, drawing proceeds very quickly.

In addition to the display list, TurboDLD*Lite* also maintains a drawing cache, which is a compressed list that contains the current contents of a viewport. This prescaled portion of the display list allows for even faster pans, zooms, and redraws.

By how much does TurboDLD*Lite* increase the speed of AutoCAD? Pans and zooms, aided by only the display list, run from 2 to 12 times faster than a nondisplay list driver. The drawing cache further speeds up things to the point that redraws can be up to 25 times faster with TurboDLD*Lite*, compared to the graphics drivers shipped with AutoCAD.

System Requirements

TurboDLD*Lite* requires the following:

- A '386-, '486-, or Pentium-based PC, which supports AutoCAD DOS 386 Release 12, 11, or 10, AutoShade 2 with RenderMan, or 3D Studio V1.x/2.x.

- A compatible graphics board. TurboDLD*Lite* will work with most graphics boards—including VGA, SuperVGA, 8514/A, TIGA, XGA, S3, Weitek P9000, and Compaq QVision.

- Additional extended memory is recommended for optimal performance.

Features

The following is a convenient list of features of TurboDLD*Lite:*

- Accelerates redraws, pans, and zooms.

- Easy to use—no new commands or special menus to learn.

- Protected-mode ADI 4.2 driver—completely compatible with AutoCAD DOS 386 Release 12, 11, or 10, 3D Studio, and AutoShade 2 with Render-Man.

- No memory conflicts. Works with AutoCAD's built-in Virtual Memory Manager.

- Includes *CustomColors*, which lets you interactively customize your logical and physical colors from within AutoCAD.

- Completely compatible with all AutoCAD ADI 4.2 compatible third-party software.

- Will support higher resolutions on many popular graphics boards.

- Supports all AutoCAD Release 12 features, including rendering to viewports and 31-Bit regen space.

Copyright Information

Please read and observe the following copyright information:

Copyright (c) 1989-1993 by Panacea, Inc. All rights reserved.
Portions of TurboDLD*Lite* are patented under U.S. Patent No. 5,101,444.

Detailed Installation/Configuring Information

Before starting, please make a backup copy of the distribution disk, using the DOS DISKCOPY command, and put it in a safe place.

The TurboDLD*Lite* installation procedure below is exact and describes what to do at each step. Installation is slightly different for older releases of AutoCAD than it is with AutoCAD Release 12. Be sure to follow any directions that may be specific to your particular AutoCAD release. For brief installation instructions, see the Quick Start section above.

Installation

First install the TurboDLD*Lite* files as described at the beginning of Chapter 22, *Using the Software on Disk.*

NOTE

For TIGA installations only, you must copy the file DLDEXT.RLM from your
TurboDLD*Lite* subdirectory to your TIGA software subdirectory.

For AutoCAD 12 installations, if you choose to install TurboDLD*Lite* into a
subdirectory other than \ACAD\DRV, be sure to change the ACADDRV
environment variable to include that directory. If ACADDRV is not set
properly, you will have problems following instructions later in this chapter.
See Chapter 4 of the *AutoCAD Interface, Installation, and Performance Guide*
for more details about ADADDRV.

After all of the program files have been successfully transferred, it is necessary to reconfigure AutoCAD to use TurboDLD*Lite*. Follow the steps below for
either Release 12 or Release 11/10 of AutoCAD, and then proceed to the "Driver
Configuration" section of this chapter to finish the installation.

For Use with AutoCAD Release 12

Once the files are installed, begin AutoCAD with the –R reconfigure switch.
For instance, if your AutoCAD batch file is named ACADR12, type the
following:

```
ACADR12 -R
```

Choose option 3, Configure Video Display, from the AutoCAD configuration menu. Type Y at the "Do you want to select a different one?" message to
display the available video options for AutoCAD. Select "TurboDLD*Lite* by
Panacea Inc." from the list of display options. Continue installation at the
"Driver Configuration" section below.

 NOTE

If TurboDLD*Lite* does not appear in the list of available video drivers, be sure
that the AutoCAD environment variables, ACADDRV in particular, have
been properly set before typing ACADR12 –R.

For Use with AutoCAD Releases 11 and 10

Run the FASTACAD.BAT file that was copied to the TurboDLD*Lite* subdirectory by typing:

```
C:\TDLDLITE\FASTACAD
```

The above example assumes that TurboDLD*Lite* was installed on drive C: in a subdirectory named TDLDLITE.

FASTACAD sets up the necessary environment variables for AutoCAD. For more information on FASTACAD.BAT, refer to "Configuring the AutoCAD Release 10 or 11 Operating Environment" found on page 650.

Start AutoCAD and reconfigure the program to use TurboDLD*Lite* by selecting option 5, Configure AutoCAD, from the AutoCAD main menu. From the next menu, select option 3, Configure Video Display. Choose Item 1, P386 ADI 4.0/4.1 (Release 11) or ADI P386 (Release 10) as your display device (for more information, see the AutoCAD *Installation and Performance Guide*).

Driver Configuration

Once you have selected the proper display device, the TurboDLD Driver Configuration Menu will appear. Simply follow the instructions on-screen to configure the driver.

Help during TurboDLD*Lite* setup is only a keystroke away. At any time, you may press the question mark ("?") key, then <Enter>, to get help information pertaining to the current prompt. Please note that the DLDSETUP.HLP file must be present in order for help to appear. If you get an error message, be sure that the file DLDSETUP.HLP is in the ACAD\DRV subdirectory (Release 12), or in the TURBODLD subdirectory. (Release 10 and 11).

The first screen to appear is an information screen explaining what the TurboDLD*Lite* setup program does. Press any key to continue once you have read the overview.

If at any point during the configuration process you want to change an item on a previous screen, just press the ESC key to back up. Selecting NO SAVE, EXIT at the main configuration menu will return you to the AutoCAD configuration menu, without making any changes.

Setup of TurboDLD*Lite* requires configuration of the various operating parameters of the driver. These parameters have been logically grouped into four menus based on their interaction with AutoCAD. A quick trip through each menu will complete the configuration process.

At a minimum, a graphics board and screen resolution must be chosen from the Select Graphics Board/Resolution menu. If no display options are configured, the driver will be automatically configured for Generic VGA, 640 x 480 resolution at 16 colors.

Select Graphics Board/Resolution Menu

The Select Graphics Board/Resolution menu configures TurboDLD*Lite* for video parameters. From this menu, graphics board type and display and rendering resolutions for TurboDLD*Lite* will be determined.

Select Graphics Board allows you to manually select your computer's graphics board. A list of video cards is given based on the findings of TurboDLD*Lite*'s built-in graphics platform detection utility. Use the up and down arrow keys and the PgUp and PgDn keys to scroll through the list and highlight your graphics board. Please note that graphics boards are listed alphabetically, therefore you may need to scroll through the list in order to find your particular board or graphics platform.

If your graphics board is not listed, you may choose the generic board option for your video chip type if available.

Press <Enter> to accept your choice and return to the Select Graphics Board/Resolution menu.

Select Display Resolution configures the resolution of the AutoCAD drawing screen. Display screen options are made available based on the findings of TurboDLD*Lite*'s graphics platform detection utility. Use the up and down arrow keys and the PgUp and PgDn keys to scroll through and highlight the resolution and color option you wish to use.

Press the <Enter> key to accept your resolution choice and return to the Select Graphics Board/Resolution menu.

When configuring TurboDLD*Lite*'s display options, the Rendering Board/Resolution options described below will automatically appear *only* when configuring AVE Render, 3D Studio, or AutoShade 2 with RenderMan. Otherwise, the Display Board/Resolution options will be the only menu choices available.

Similar to the Select Display Resolution menu, *Select Rendering Resolution* configures the resolution of the AutoCAD rendering screen. Rendering screen options are also based on the findings of TurboDLD*Lite*'s detection utility. Use the up and down arrow keys and the PgUp and PgDn keys to scroll through and highlight the resolution and color option you wish to use.

Press <Enter> to accept your choice and return to the Select Graphics Board/Resolution menu.

TurboDLD*Lite* includes a graphics platform detection utility that queries the graphics card for type, Hi-Color support, and installed memory. Based on the graphics platform detector's information, TurboDLD*Lite* will list a set of display and rendering resolutions. Due to the variety of graphics boards and their specific implementations of platform chip sets, the detector is not always 100 percent accurate. Therefore, when selecting a display or rendering resolution, be sure to use only resolutions that your graphics board will support. If you are unsure which resolutions are supported by your graphics board, refer to your owner's manual.

Highlight *Return to Previous Menu* and press the <Enter> key to return to the Main Configuration menu.

Basic Configuration Menu

The Basic Configuration menu configures TurboDLD*Lite*'s AutoCAD screen characteristics: text lines, font size, and dual-screen mode.

The first Basic option is the number of *text lines* you wish to use for the AutoCAD command line. The default is 3 lines, but values from 1 to 10 can be specified. A number larger than 3 might be useful if you are using this driver in a high-resolution mode with small fonts, since more text lines can reduce the need to flip between the text and graphics screens.

If you do not want any lines of text at the bottom of the display, use AutoCAD to disable the command area (see the AutoCAD *Interface, Installation, and Performance Guide* for more information). Press Return to continue with font selection.

Choose the *Font Size* you would like to use for your AutoCAD menus, pulldowns, and dialogue boxes: 8x8, 8x14, 8x16, 12x20, and 12x24. For resolutions over 800x600 we recommend the 12x20 or 12x24 font size. The default is the 8x14 size. XGA and 8514/A platforms provide only 7x15, 8x14, and 12x20 font size options. TIGA-based graphics boards will allow you to use only two different font sizes—8x16 and 12x24.

The *Dual Screen Mode* command is used to tell the driver whether you want to operate with one screen for combined text and graphics, or with two: one screen for graphics and a second for text. Choose *Disable* to run AutoCAD in single-screen mode. Select *Enable* to run in dual-screen mode—don't select Enable mode if you don't have a Monochrome board (VGA board for TIGAs, XGAs, or 8514/As) in your system.

Highlight *Return to Previous Menu* and press the <Enter> key to return to the Main Configuration menu.

Expert Configuration Menu

The Expert Configuration menu sets the basic internal functions of TurboDLD*Lite*. Options in this menu allow for customization of the driver for speed or to adjust for memory constraints.

Display List, the core of TurboDLD*Lite*, enables or disables the display list feature of the driver. This option should always be set to enable, as disabling the display list will cause TurboDLD*Lite* to run as an ordinary nondisplay list driver (i.e., slowly).

The Drawing Cache option enables or disables TurboDLD*Lite*'s internal drawing cache, a compressed display list of the current viewport, which speeds up pans, zooms, and redraws. As in the display list option, Drawing Cache should normally be enabled. In low memory situations, it may be desirable to disable the Drawing Cache, which will free up memory for AutoCAD but may or may not have a visible effect on your zoom and pan performance. For example, on VGAs, the performance benefit of the Drawing Cache is as little as five percent. With a TIGA-based graphics board, however, the performance benefit of the Drawing Cache is as high as 400 percent.

The Use AutoCAD 31-Bit Space option configures TurboDLD*Lite* for use with AutoCAD R12's 31-Bit logical drawing space. When this option is set to Yes, the driver will use AutoCAD's extended 31-Bit drawing space. Selecting No will use a 15-Bit drawing space, similar to that of AutoCAD Release 10 or 11.

The 31-Bit logical space allows you to extend your regenless zooming ability by a factor of several million, at the cost of more memory. Additional memory is used by AutoCAD for the drawing space, and by TurboDLD*Lite* for the display list. 31-Bit zooming and panning is about 10 to 20 percent slower than for 15-Bit logical space. The Use AutoCAD 31-Bit Space setting is ignored for AutoCAD Release 10 and 11 installations.

The echo of TurboDLD*Lite* internal commands can be enabled or disabled with the Internal Command Echo option. If you would like to see TurboDLD*Lite*'s internal commands displayed at the AutoCAD command line as they are executed, enable this option.

As a convenience feature, a Regen Mode option has been added to TurboDLD*Lite*. A Fast Regen will store the AutoCAD drawing until the display list has been created, and then display it all at once. The Incremental mode displays the drawing in "chunks" as the display list is created. The Fast mode causes Regens to process approximately 5 to 10 percent faster than the incremental. Neither mode changes memory requirements.

After all Expert options have been set, highlight Return To Previous Menu and press the <Enter> key to return to the Main Configuration menu.

Saving Configuration Information

Once all of the TurboDLD*Lite* parameters have been configured, select SAVE, EXIT to save the configuration information and create DLDSETUP.DAT in either the ACAD\DRV subdirectory (Release 12) or the TURBODLD (Release 10 or 11) subdirectory. DLDSETUP.DAT is Turbo-DLD*Lite*'s configuration file.

After answering AutoCAD's standard driver configuration questions, you will return to the AutoCAD configuration menu. To begin your accelerated AutoCAD do one of the following: For AutoCAD Release 12, select option 0, Exit to Drawing Editor; for AutoCAD Release 10 or 11, select option 0, Exit to Main Menu, and then option 1 or 2, Open New or Existing Drawing.

Verifying Your TurboDLDLite Installation

To verify that TurboDLD*Lite* is running and installed correctly, follow one of these two simple tests:

- If you have the AutoCAD side menu enabled, look for the Panacea logo in the lower right-hand corner.

- If you are running AutoCAD without a side menu, type DLDVER at the AutoCAD command prompt. If TurboDLD*Lite* is loaded and running, this command should return your current version, serial number, and registered user's name.

Reconfiguring TurboDLD*Lite*

To reconfigure TurboDLD*Lite*, follow the instructions below for your version of AutoCAD, Release 12 or Release 11/10, or AutoShade 2 with RenderMan, 3D Studio, or AVE Render.

AutoCAD Release 12

If you need to make changes to your Release 12 TurboDLD*Lite* configuration, type CONFIG at the AutoCAD command prompt or use the –R reconfigure switch when starting the program. Select option 3, Configure Video Display. Answer No to the "Select a new video driver ..." prompt to start the TurboDLD*Lite* configuration program. Make the desired changes to the driver and then Save and Exit to continue to the AutoCAD drawing editor.

AutoCAD Release 10 or 11

To change a Release 10 or 11 configuration, select option 5, Configure AutoCAD, from the AutoCAD main menu. Then from the configuration menu, select option 3, Configure Video Display. Answer No to the "Select a new video driver ..." prompt to start the TurboDLD*Lite* configuration program. Change the desired driver options. Save and Exit to return to the AutoCAD configuration menu. Open or begin a new drawing.

To completely reconfigure TurboDLD*Lite* using Panacea's defaults, delete DLDSETUP.DAT from either the \ACAD\DRV subdirectory (Release 12) or the TURBODLD subdirectory (Release 10 or 11) and then follow the Driver Configuration instructions at the beginning of this chapter.

Configuring the AutoCAD Release 10 or 11 Operating Environment

During the TurboDLD*Lite* installation process, a FASTACAD.BAT file is created and placed in the TDLDLITE subdirectory. FASTACAD.BAT contains four lines that set four separate environment variables: DLDCFG—used by TurboDLD*Lite* to find all of its configuration files; and DSPADI, RCPADI, RDPADI—used by AutoCAD, 3D Studio, and AutoShade 2 w/ RenderMan, respectively, to find the driver file. FASTACAD.BAT must be run prior to starting AutoCAD R10 or R11 and needs to be run only once per system boot. For automatic loading of the environment variables, FASTACAD.BAT may be added to the AUTOEXEC.BAT file or an AutoCAD startup batch file.

To add FASTACAD.BAT to your AUTOEXEC.BAT file, insert the line

```
CALL D:\TDLDLITE\FASTACAD
```

anywhere in the file. The above example assumes that FASTACAD.BAT resides in a subdirectory on drive D: called \TDLDLITE.

If you don't wish to put FASTACAD in your AUTOEXEC.BAT file, you may put it in a batch file that also starts AutoCAD, or simply remember to run the file before starting AutoCAD. (You should also stop using any ADI driver that may have come with your graphics board, since TurboDLD*Lite* is a superset of that type of driver.)

If you get the message

```
Out of Environment Space
```

when you run FASTACAD.BAT, you will need to enlarge your system's environment. This is accomplished by adding the line

```
SHELL=C:\COMMAND.COM /P /E:768
```

to your CONFIG.SYS file. The /E:768 specifies an environment size of 768 bytes. Change this number as needed. If you modify your CONFIG.SYS file, you will need to reboot in order for the changes to take effect.

Configuring for AutoShade 2 with RenderMan

To configure AutoShade 2 with RenderMan to use TurboDLD*Lite*, first run the FASTACAD.BAT file from your TurboDLD*Lite* subdirectory to set the AutoShade environment variables. Next, start AutoShade with SHADE /R, which will allow you to reconfigure AutoShade. For the display device, select P386 Autodesk Device Interface display driver; for the rendering display, select the P386 Autodesk Device Interface rendering driver. If you are running the display and rendering screen on the same monitor (i.e., single monitor), make sure to tell AutoShade this. A single-monitor approach will require a redraw of the display screen after a rendering screen.

Next, follow the same installation steps that were used to select the graphics board and display and rendering resolutions for AutoCAD (see above).

Configuring for 3D Studio

Configuring TurboDLD*Lite* for 3D Studio requires three steps: First, you need to set the environment variables for 3D Studio by running the PANA3DS.BAT file that was copied into your TurboDLD*Lite* subdirectory. Next, edit the 3DS.SET file located in your 3DS directory. The following three lines may be changed to use the RCPADI rendering driver. Locate the lines that begin with:

```
RENDER-DISPLAY
MAIN-DISPLAY
MATERIAL-DISPLAY
```

and change them to read:

```
RENDER-DISPLAY=RCPADI
MAIN-DISPLAY=RCPADI
MATERIAL-DISPLAY=RCPADI
```

Make sure to remove the ";" or any spaces that may be present at the beginning of the line.

Note that it is necessary for the RENDER-DISPLAY line to be set only to RCPADI in order to render at high resolution. If you do not need a high-resolution main display screen or if you will not be using the materials editor, you may keep MAIN-DISPLAY and MATERIAL-DISPLAY set to their defaults.

The MATERIAL-DISPLAY should be configured for RCPADI only when *both* the Display *and* Rendering Resolutions of TurboDLD*Lite* are configured for 256-color resolutions. An unpredictable Materials Editor screen will appear if anything other than 256 colors is selected. If you are unsure about the function of the Materials Editor screen, use the Materials Editor as VGA, and you should not have any problems at all. Please also note that the use of the Materials Editor will not give you any more colors to choose from.

Save the above changes, start 3D Studio, and begin the last part of the configuration procedure.

From your 3D Studio directory, delete the file 3DADI.CFG by typing:

```
DEL 3DADI.CFG
```

This will cause 3D Studio to start in its reconfiguration mode. Start 3D Studio by typing:

```
3DS
```

During the 3D Studio reconfiguration startup, you are prompted with a series of questions. After the first 3D Studio question appears and is answered, the TurboDLD*Lite* Configuration program will appear. Select a graphics board and display and rendering resolutions as you would for AutoCAD use. (See above for complete details.)

Because RCPADI device drivers, by definition, are combined display and rendering devices, during 3D Studio reconfiguration you will be brought to the TurboDLD*Lite* Configuration Menu more than one time, once each for Display and Rendering. It is not necessary to select display and/or rendering resolutions a second time. Simply press the <Enter> key to remove the help screen and then highlight Save and Exit to continue to the next question. Also, if FASTACAD.BAT is used instead of PANA3DS.BAT to define the AutoCAD operating environment, the TurboDLD*Lite* Configuration Menu also will appear for RDPADI and DSPADI devices if they are present.

DIFFERENCES FOR 3D STUDIO 1.X

For 3D Studio 1.x, there is no RENDER-DISPLAY line. The corresponding line is DEFAULT-DISPLAY, and should be changed to read DEFAULT-DISPLAY="RCPADI", The quotes around RCPADI must be used for this version of 3D Studio.

SOME 3D STUDIO LIMITATIONS

TurboDLD*Lite* provides only still rendering support for 3D Studio. TurboDLD*Lite* will not play back rendered FLI or FLC files. This is a limitation of 3D Studio.

Under 3D Studio v1.x, the Mapping Icon color and shaper arrows, usually yellow and green, will appear black when using any external ADI driver. TurboDLD*Lite* does resolve this issue under 3D Studio v2.x, however.

Configuring AVE Render

AutoCAD Release 12's AVE Render uses TurboDLD*Lite*'s rendering capabilities to render objects and drawings. If AVE Render has never been configured, when you select the AutoCAD render command you will be forced to run through the configuration process. You will be prompted as follows:

1. Select a Rendering Display device. Since TurboDLD*Lite* is a combined display/rendering device, choose item 1, P386 ADI Combined Display/ Rendering Driver from the available choices.

2. Configure the Rendering Graphics Board and Resolution. Here the TurboDLD*Lite* configuration program will appear on the screen. Press the Return key to continue past the help screen and display the Rendering Configuration menu. Choose Select Graphics Board/Resolution to display graphics board and resolution menu selections. First, choose Select Render Graphics Board to select the graphics board to be used for renderings. Next, choose Select Render Resolution to select the desired rendering resolution from the list of available choices. Select Return to Previous Menu and then Save and Exit.

3. Select Render Mode. The next step is to select the rendering mode for TurboDLD*Lite*. Select either Render to Viewport or Render to Screen depending on how you wish to view your renderings. Note that in order to render to a viewport, you must be using a Display resolution of at least 256 colors. Otherwise, AVE Render will not allow a render to viewport selection.

4. Select a Render Hard Copy Device. If you are using a render hard copy device, select your device type from the list of choices. If you are not using a hard copy device, accept the default of NULL.

After configuring AVE Render, return to the AutoCAD drawing editor to render the current drawing.

If you have previously configured AVE Render, type RCONFIG at the AutoCAD command prompt to manually display the Render Configuration Menu. Follow these steps to reconfigure AVE Render.

1. Select option 2, Configure Rendering Device to choose a new rendering driver. Answer Yes to the "Select Different Rendering Device" question.

2. Select option 1, P386 Combined Display/Rendering Driver.

3. Configure the Rendering Graphics Board and Resolution. Here the TurboDLD*Lite* configuration program will appear on the screen. Press the Return key to continue past the help screen and display the Rendering Configuration menu. Choose Select Graphics Board/Resolution to display graphics board and resolution menu selections. First, choose Select Render Graphics Board to select the graphics board to be used for renderings. Next, choose Select Render Resolution to select the desired rendering resolution from the list of available choices. Select Return to Previous Menu and then Save and Exit.

4. Select Render Mode. The next step is to select the rendering mode for TurboDLD*Lite*. Select either Render to Viewport or Render to Screen, depending on how you wish to view your renderings. Note that in order to render to a viewport, you must be using a Display resolution of at least 256 colors. Otherwise, AVE Render will not allow a render to viewport selection.

5. Select Exit to the Drawing Editor from the Render Configuration menu and then type Y to keep the changes you've just made. Press the <F1> key to change back to the graphics screen if necessary.

Changing Colors with DLDCOLOR

Included with TurboDLD*Lite* is Panacea's revolutionary *CustomColors* color configuration utility. What's so unique about *CustomColors* is that it gives you the ability to modify all your changeable AutoCAD colors, including menu colors, text colors, dialogue box colors, and even drawing colors, while running AutoCAD.

CustomColors simulates an AutoCAD screen, complete with all possible objects. At the AutoCAD drawing editor command line, type DLDCOLOR to edit the color configuration. Once you enter the utility, you are provided with the following configuration menu at the bottom of the screen:

- (O)bject
- (D)rawing
- (P)hysical
- (A)DI reset
- (V)GA reset
- (L)oad
- (S)ave
- (E)xit

The menu items perform the following functions.

Object

Selecting this option will allow you to change the color of any AutoCAD screen object, such as the graphics area background color, the menu area text color, or the border line color.

Select the object whose color you want to change by moving the highlight box around with the left and right cursor control keys and pressing <Enter> when you have highlighted the desired object. Note that a one-line description of the object type is displayed at the top of the screen as you move the box around.

Once you have selected the object, another highlight box will appear around the color boxes nearest the bottom of the screen. These are the physical colors that the video board supports. Use the left and right cursor keys to select the color to be used for the object you have selected and press <Enter>. The screen will quickly redraw with the new color selection for the object you have chosen, and you will be back at the start of object selection in case you want to change the color of another object.

Note that at any time during color configuration, you can press the <Esc> key once or twice and return to AutoCAD. Also, pressing the question mark (?) key will provide you with context-sensitive help.

Drawing

This option allows you to modify all AutoCAD drawing colors in a fashion similar to the way you change object colors. When this option is selected, a highlight square appears in the drawing color area of the simulated AutoCAD display. The square can be manipulated using the four cursor keys. You may notice that the drawing color portion of the display is laid out just like the CHROMA drawing supplied with AutoCAD. When you press <Enter>, the highlight moves down to the 16 physical colors, just as it does during the object color selection. Using the arrow keys, pick the physical color you want to represent the selected drawing color. Press <Enter> to have your selection take effect. Note that if you are running your board in a 256 or greater color mode, Physical and drawing colors are identical and the Drawing color option disappears.

Physical

Choosing the Physical option from the menu allows you to alter the red, green, and blue components of the physical colors. A highlight box will appear in the row of 16 physical colors at the bottom of the screen. Note that if you are running your board in a 256 or greater color mode, Physical and Drawing colors are identical and the Drawing color option disappears.

Use the arrow keys to select the color you wish to edit and press ENTER. Three "sliders" will appear near the bottom of the display, with the horizontal position of the slider for each of the color components (red, green, or blue—RGB) indicating the relative intensity of the component. You can use the left and right arrow keys to move the slider for the selected component, or type in a number from 0 to 255.

Many graphics boards do not support 255 different intensities for each color component. Therefore, when you enter an intensity, *Custom Colors* will round it to the nearest intensity which your graphics board supports. For example, VGAs support 64 intensities per RGB color component. This means intensities increase in multiples of 4 (256/64), therefore an intensity of 0 is the same as an intensity of 3.

The up and down arrows allow you to select which component you want to alter. As you manipulate the sliders, all objects on the display that are of the same color as the selected physical color will change in hue. This way you can visually determine the most appropriate setting for your display. Pressing <Enter> will set the RGB values you have selected for the physical color you were modifying.

Please note that when your graphics board is running at more than 8-bits-per-pixel (256 colors), setting physical colors via DLDCOLOR generally will not have a visible effect until a SAVE and EXIT occurs.

ADI Reset

This choice constructs a default ADI color palette, as defined in the *Autodesk Device Interface Driver Development Kit*, and in Panacea's 8514/A and XGA nondisplay list drivers shipped with AutoCAD Release 12.

VGA Reset

This choice constructs a default VGA color palette in the first 16 color entries. The remaining palette colors remain identical to those used for ADI devices.

Load

This choice reloads the color information from the file DLDCOLOR.DAT. It will be loaded from the directory pointed to by DLDCFG (AutoCAD Release 10 or 11), or from the AutoCAD Release 12\ACAD\DRV directory. If DLDCOLOR.DAT cannot be found, an error message will be displayed.

This command is useful because it allows you to go back to your previously edited color configuration in case you have made some mistakes in configuring colors that you want to undo.

Save

Saves the current color palette to DLDCOLOR.DAT. It will be saved to the directory pointed to by the DLDCFG environment variable in FASTACAD, or to the Release 12 \ACAD\DRV (R12) directory if FASTACAD is not used.

NOTE

Don't Accidentally Wipe Out Your Changes! Selecting ADI reset, VGA reset, or Load will irrevocably wipe out any current color changes you may have made, unless you have just saved your new settings. Use them only when you really need to, such as when you have made so many color changes that you can't seem to get back to a reasonable place and just want to start over.

Exit

Exits *CustomColors*. If you have made palette changes but not saved them, you will be asked if you want to save your changes before exiting.

Using TurboDLD*Lite* Special Commands

TurboDLD*Lite* offers AutoCAD users many features and productivity options. This chapter alphabetically lists the basic commands found in TurboDLD*Lite* and provides the correct syntax for their usage. For a brief summary of TurboDLD*Lite* commands, type DLDHELP at the command prompt. Note that in order to use these commands, you must enter them at the AutoCAD command line.

DLDCOLOR

Invokes *CustomColors*, Panacea's color configuration program. See the previous section for more information on configuring TurboDLD*Lite* colors.

DLDCOMPACT

Forces a manual garbage collection of display list memory, thereby returning unused display list memory back to the AutoCAD memory pool.

DLDDCACHE

This command toggles the TurboDLD*Lite* drawing cache on and off. The drawing cache is a compressed form of the current viewport, and it speeds, pans, zooms, and redraws.

DLDDLIST

This command toggles the display list function of TurboDLD*Lite* on and off. Please note that if the display list is turned off, you will be running AutoCAD as though you were using a standard nondisplay list driver—pans, zooms, and redraws will be *much* slower with DLDDLIST disabled.

DLDECHO

Toggles internal TurboDLD*Lite* command echoing at the AutoCAD command line. When TurboDLD*Lite* commands are executed via the digitizer or pop-up menus, they generate internal commands which will be displayed at the AutoCAD command line if DLDECHO is enabled. Disable DLDECHO to simplify the command line.

DLDHELP

Provides a list of TurboDLD*Lite* commands with one-line descriptions of each within AutoCAD. It's recommended that you flip to the text screen by pressing the <F1> key to view the output.

DLDSTAT

Displays the current TurboDLD*Lite* status. A listing of the current TurboDLD*Lite* parameters will be displayed at the AutoCAD command line. A flip to the text screen is recommended for this command.

DLDUSAGE

Use DLDUSAGE if you want a to-the-byte breakdown of how memory is being used specifically for display list processing. DLDUSAGE returns information regarding the memory each viewport is occupying. (Since AutoCAD supports multiple viewports, it is possible to have multiple display lists.)

DLDVER

Displays the TurboDLD*Lite* version, serial number, and registered user's name at the AutoCAD command line.

DLDVISREGEN

Toggles between the Fast and Visible Regen modes of TurboDLD*Lite*. A Fast Regen will create the display list and then display the drawing all at once. A

Visible Regen will display the drawing in "chunks" as the display list is created. This command is a dynamic form of the Regen Mode parameter in the Expert Configuration Menu. Since TurboDLD*Lite*'s Fast Regen mode is faster than AutoCAD's, we highly recommend its use.

Note that all the commands above, when issued within AutoCAD, will override the selections made during TurboDLD*Lite* configuration for the current drawing session only. Exiting AutoCAD and subsequently restarting will cause all feature settings to revert back to those selected in the TurboDLD*Lite* configuration menu. If you wish to make the current changes permanent, reconfigure TurboDLD*Lite* by following the reconfiguration instructions given earlier in this chapter.

Memory Usage and Lists

TurboDLD*Lite* shares extended memory with AutoCAD via the PharLap Virtual Memory Manager. This means that TurboDLD*Lite* will automatically page to disk if it consumes all the RAM that AutoCAD has left for its use. See the AutoCAD *Installation and Performance Guide* for more information on virtual memory management.

DLDCOMPACT Redux

Note that if you start seeing excessive hard disk accesses during pans, redraws, and zooms while using AutoCAD with TurboDLD*Lite*, try using the DLDCOMPACT command. You can add this command to a pull-down menu or the cursor menu using the how-to information in Chapter 17. If the DLDCOMPACT command doesn't affect the amount of disk access, it's probably time to add more memory to your system. Contact your AutoCAD dealer for assistance in upgrading your memory.

How Much Memory?

For production use, we recommend that at least 4 megabytes of memory are available for TurboDLD*Lite*, above and beyond what's recommended for AutoCAD. For example, it's recommended that AutoCAD Release 12 have at least 8MB of RAM to itself, which means that your system should have a minimum of 12MB for proper use with TurboDLD*Lite*.

To determine how much memory AutoCAD is using, use the status command while in AutoCAD (refer to the AutoCAD *Installation and Performance Guide* for more information). The display list for a simple drawing like the shuttle *Columbia* might require only 20 KB for the display list. Complex drawings may require several megabytes. We have seen display lists for a drawing range from one-tenth the size of the drawing file to three times the size; in general, the display list averages about the same as the DWG file size. Also, complex objects such as circles and text "expand" when translated into display list format, so a drawing with a lot of complex objects and text will have a larger display list than a simpler drawing.

The amount of display list memory a circle consumes can be controlled by the AutoCAD VIEWRES command. Text takes up a disproportionate amount of space in the display list. To keep the list small, put text on its own layer of the drawing and turn this layer off when you don't need to see the text. This will keep memory consumption down, and speed up pans, redraws, and zooms.

The *AutoCAD Interface, Installation, and Performance Guide* has an excellent section on performance, concentrating on memory usage. Chapter 3 of this book also discusses memory and other performance issues.

Tips and Tricks

Because TurboDLD*Lite* supports such a wide range of graphics board platforms, it is necessary to be aware of certain idiosyncrasies. This chapter outlines known configuration and usage problems of TurboDLD*Lite* and of various graphics platforms. Also included are tips to help gain performance from AutoCAD itself. These tips and tricks are a compilation of the most commonly asked technical support questions. Therefore, if you are having problems, please review this chapter; you may be able to quickly answer your own question.

Memory Management

System lock-ups, random reboots, or missing displays indicate that you may have a memory conflict on your system. Different video platforms access different specific portions of upper memory blocks. If these memory addresses are in use by TSRs or other programs or memory managers, the above symptoms will occur. To avoid these problems, it is necessary to use an expanded memory manager to allocate the specific address range to the graphics board. The address to exclude usually falls within the range of A000 to C7FF. XGAs, and some TIGA boards go beyond C7FF up to DFFF.

Some common expanded memory managers are QEMM, 386Max, and EMM386, which comes with DOS 5.0 and 6.0. QEMM and EMM386 use similar commands to perform the exclusion.

```
X=B000-B7FF
```

is added to the QEMM386.SYS or EMM386.EXE command line in the

CONFIG.SYS file. 386Max uses a video memory parameter that looks like this:

```
VIDMEM=B000-B7FF
```

Note that it may be necessary to run an optimization utility with some memory managers in order for the exclusion to take effect. Refer to your memory manager's documentation for specific details.

If the range of A000-C7FF seems like a large area to exclude, you may decrease the range by changing the ending address to determine the exact range that you need to exclude. Typically B000-B7FF, as shown in the examples above, will be sufficient. You may try other ranges, by altering the beginning and/or ending address, to isolate the exact region the graphics board requires. Remember to reboot after changing the CONFIG.SYS file. Some common graphics board requirements are described below.

Due to the manner in which they remap video BIOS memory regions in RAM, memory optimization utilities such as QEMM's Stealth feature should be avoided. If these utilities must be used, video BIOS regions should be made known to them if possible. For example, QEMM's XST= parameter may allow Stealth to be used without a lot of problems. Again, consult your memory manager's manual for specific details.

XGA

XGA-based graphics boards must have at least the range of B000-DFFF available. Your XGA manual and/or systems diagnostics should be able to tell you specifically which 8KB area needs to be set aside for your XGA board.

SVGA AND S3

SVGA and S3 boards usually use the area of B000-B7FF.

34020-BASED TIGA BOARDS

TIGA boards based on the 34020 graphics chip request the range of A000-DFFF. However, C000-C7FF usually is sufficient. Again, check your TIGA board's manual for details.

Upgrading from Older Panacea DLD Drivers

Be sure to remove any reference to previous DLD driver commands (FASTACAD calls or SET parameters) or subdirectories that may be in your AUTOEXEC.BAT file or in AutoCAD startup batch files. Such references could cause AutoCAD and TurboDLD*Lite* to look in the wrong place for setup information.

If you have been using a previous Panacea DLD driver and wish to use the color palette you customized for it with TurboDLD*Lite*, you may copy the DLDCOLOR.DAT file from your older DLD's subdirectory to the subdirectory you specified during the TurboDLD*Lite* installation process.

Maneuvering Through AutoCAD: Zooming

When zooming into an image, be aware of your AutoCAD Snap setting. If you are zoomed extremely far into a drawing and you are having trouble moving your digitizer cursor, you may be snapping to a point which is not part of the zoomed viewport. If the cursor moves only to a single point or is not on-screen at all, try toggling Snap off.

Switching Color Modes

When switching color modes (e.g., from 16 to 256 or vice versa), the DLDCOLOR command should be run in order to reconfigure your color palette for the number of colors selected. A black cursor and disappearing cross hairs are both symptoms of a color palette problem.

Using AutoCAD Commands

Since TurboDLD*Lite* is totally transparent with respect to using normal AutoCAD commands to redraw, pan, and zoom, you must still suffer some of AutoCAD's quirks, one of which is that ZOOM All and ZOOM Extents both force a regen, because AutoCAD does not keep track of various boundaries necessary to avoid the regen. And regen are rather time-consuming and don't use any display list processing to speed themselves up. One way around this problem is to use another of AutoCAD's built-in features; namely, the VIEW command.

When you first load your image and see the whole drawing on the screen at once, just type VIEW Save ALL, which will save the display position you see under a view named "All." Then after you've done some detailed editing and want to return to the big picture, type VIEW Restore ALL, instead of ZOOM All or ZOOM Extents, and the full drawing will be restored to the display at display list speeds, without a regen.

Another nuance of AutoCAD's is that if you zoom in or pan over too far, you may inadvertently cause a regen. AutoCAD again provides a very simple solution: the REGENAUTO command. Just type REGENAUTO OFf at the AutoCAD command prompt, and automatic regen will be disabled. The REGENAUTO setting is also saved as part of your drawing file, so you need to execute it only once per drawing. You may even want to set REGENAUTO off in your ACAD.DWG prototype so that all your drawings are created with REGENAUTO set off.

Third-Party Software

If you are having trouble with TurboDLD*Lite* and a third-party AutoCAD application, be sure that the third-party application supports ADI 4.2. In order to use the ADI 4.2 specification, third-party applications require new T-drivers and therefore must be revised. If an application does not specifically say that it is ADI 4.2-compatible, it probably is not. Check with the manufacturer to be sure.

If your third-party application is ADI 4.2-compatible and you are having trouble using TurboDLD*Lite*, try running AutoCAD without the third-party application to try to isolate the problem. Also, try the third-party application with the SVADI driver shipped with AutoCAD; this also will help to isolate the source of the problem.

Also note that any third-party TSR that needs to access the display may not work properly when using AutoCAD with any advanced ADI display driver, especially if the TSR switches graphics modes. Most TSRs will not support the same graphics platforms as TurboDLD*Lite* and, therefore, will not be able to accommodate mode switching back and forth.

Troubleshooting TIGA Installations

TIGA board software version 2.0 or later *must* be loaded prior to installing and using TurboDLD*Lite*. Usually with TIGA boards, the problem is with the TIGA software initialization and not with TurboDLD*Lite*.

If you are having trouble configuring your TIGA graphics board, check the following:

1. Make sure that the TIGA software is the correct version and is loaded properly by changing into the TIGA software subdirectory and typing TIGACD. This command will return the version and status of the software.

2. Make sure that the TIGA environment variables are pointing to the correct TIGA subdirectory and that a system compatible interrupt is being specified. For example, you may have a statement like the following in your AUTOEXEC.BAT file:

   ```
   SET TIGA = -mC:\TIGA  -lC:\TIGA  -i0x60
   ```

   Using the example above, the -m and -l parameters point to a TIGA 2.0 software subdirectory named TIGA. The -i parameter indicates that the hexadecimal value of 0×60 is being used as the TIGA's interrupt. Another common interrupt is $0\times7F$.

If you have upgraded your TIGA software, and are using your AUTOEXEC.BAT file to initialize the TIGA board, be sure that the path (see above example) is pointing to the new software and not the previous version. Try remarking out the TIGA initialization line(s) from the AUTOEXEC.BAT and entering them manually at the DOS prompt, so you can easily test new values.

3. Make sure that the DLDEXT.RLM file from the TurboDLD*Lite* subdirectory has been copied into the TIGA subdirectory.

4. Try running your TIGA demo program if you have one. If you get errors similar to "Can't initialize TIGA ...," verify the installation per the steps above.

Support Information

Support for Panacea's TurboDLD*Lite* is available in the ACAD Forum on CompuServe. Type GO ACAD at the CompuServe prompt to reach this forum, and post your message in Section 5 (Hardware/Drivers/ADI). See Appendix B for more information about CompuServe.

Note that many of the problems that may occur in setting up and using TurboDLD*Lite* are not really problems with the driver; instead, the problems occur in installing and getting access to additional memory for the driver.

Memory management programs, such as QEMM, 386Max, and EMM386, can cause memory conflicts on certain graphics platforms. In order to avoid these conflicts, it may be necessary to exclude certain memory regions from being used by the memory manager.

Also, if you are using a memory manager, avoid using any switches or utilities of the manager that may remap upper memory blocks in order to load as many programs and TSR's as "high" as possible (e.g., QEMM's "Stealth" mode). These features can make it difficult or impossible for TurboDLD*Lite* utility programs to locate certain video BIOS information. If you have memory problems, carefully check both the system documentation and the memory manager documentation before contacting technical support. System memory problems probably won't be solvable by us.

We aren't able to fix incorrectly set jumpers and configuration options from CompuServe. Please be sure that all hardware is installed and operating correctly before assuming that the driver is at fault. Carefully check your hardware documentation for the correct switch and jumper settings.

It also may be necessary for you to post additional information if your problem cannot be easily resolved by just providing the symptoms. In the event more information is needed, please supply the following:

- A list of what appears on the screen when you type "SET" at a DOS prompt.

- Printouts of your DLDSETUP.DAT and FASTACAD.BAT files.

- Printouts of your CONFIG.SYS, AUTOEXEC.BAT, and any AutoCAD startup files.

In any event, you should always provide a complete description of what the problem is, how many times it has occurred, and under what circumstances it has occurred. We can help you most efficiently if you can re-create the problem with some consistency.

24

Sirlin VIEW/Lite™
File Viewer

The *AutoCAD Power Tools* disk includes two different implementations of the SirlinVIEW/Lite drawing viewers, both developed by Sirlin Computer Corporation, which allow you or your clients to view .DWG files without AutoCAD. The first is a stand alone DOS-based viewer (Figure 24.1), while the second is a Windows-based version of the same software (Figure 24.2). The documentation provided for the viewers in this chapter will focus primarily on the DOS version, as it is virtually identical to the Windows version. Differences will be pointed out where appropriate.

Installation

By default, the installation program described in Chapter 22, copies the DOS and Windows viewer files to the C:\APT\SIRLIN directory. In order for the viewers to run properly in DOS or Windows, you must do two things:

• Add the SirlinVIEW/Lite directory to the DOS path.
• Set the SIRLIN=DOS environment variable to point to the Sirlin VIEW/Lite directory.

The installation program described in Chapter 22 normally performs these steps for you, but if not, you will need to edit your AUTOEXEC.BAT file and make changes similar to these:

```
SET PATH=C: \;C:\DOS;C:\WINDOWS; C:\SIRLIN
SET SIRLIN=C:\SIRLIN
```

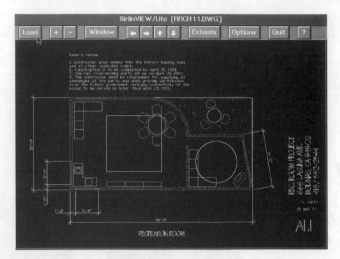

Figure 24.1   SirlinVIEW/Lite for DOS.

Be sure to reboot after editing AUTOEXEC.BAT. Once these changes have been made, you can start the DOS viewer by typing SVDWG. See page 670 for a list of optional command line parameters.

To create a program icon for the Windows version, use the New option on the Program Manager's File menu. Select Program Item, and then use the Browse… button to locate \SIRLIN\WINLITE.EXE. Refer to your Microsoft Windows manual if you need more information about setting up a Windows program.

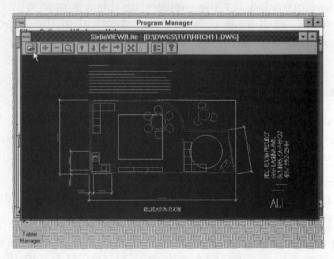

Figure 24.2   SirlinVIEW/Lite for Windows.

Overview

The drawing viewer is a piece of software that allows you to view an AutoCAD .DWG file outside of AutoCAD, providing a low-cost way to allow others to take a look at drawings you and others have created. The viewer allows the selected drawing to be zoomed, panned, and viewed in both paper and model space using either the keyboard or the mouse. If you need more capabilities or are interested in adding viewing support to your own applications, you can find an overview of Sirlin's other tools at the end of this chapter.

Tip

Try it! Just change to the SIRLIN subdirectory, type SVDWG, and select a drawing from the Load File dialogue box. SirlinVIEW/Lite has a unique button bar interface that can be accessed by the mouse or by pressing the keys indicated on the button bar. While this chapter documents each of the options, you can learn most of what you need to know in just a few minutes of experimenting. Note that the question mark button brings up on-line help.

Why DOS Users Need SirlinVIEW/Lite

If you're a DOS AutoCAD user, you need SirlinVIEW/Lite so that you can quickly view other drawings. With SirlinVIEW/Lite you can shell out to DOS from AutoCAD, look at a number of drawings, then return to AutoCAD. When you don't have AutoCAD loaded and just need to check something in a drawing, SirlinVIEW/Lite is much quicker and easier to use than AutoCAD.

One of the biggest benefits is that people who don't own or know how to use AutoCAD can look at AutoCAD drawings with SirlinVIEW/Lite. Now you can make your AutoCAD drawings viewable by anyone in your workgroup or company. Just make sure to get as many legal copies as you need; see the licensing information below for more information.

Why Windows Users Need SirlinVIEW/Lite

If you're a Windows AutoCAD user, you also need SirlinVIEW/Lite so that you can quickly view other drawings. Yes, the Windows version of AutoCAD Release 12 does this for you too, but each drawing you open takes up many megabytes of memory. SirlinVIEW/Lite is much faster and easier on your system's memory usage.

As with the DOS version, when you don't have AutoCAD loaded and just need to check something in a drawing, SirlinVIEW/Lite is much quicker and easier to use than AutoCAD. Again, as with the DOS version, those who don't use AutoCAD can look at AutoCAD drawings with SirlinVIEW/Lite. You can mix and match the DOS and Windows versions among the users in your company who need to view AutoCAD drawings. See below for licensing information.

Using the Drawing Viewers

The DOS version of SirlinVIEW/Lite, SVDWG.EXE, can accept a filename on the command line, along with optional command-line arguments that allow the viewer to run more optimally with your existing hardware configuration. In most cases though, you can start the program without any arguments: SVDWG will present a Load File dialogue from which you can select a .DWG file (see Figure 24.3). After you've viewed one .DWG file, use the Load button on the button bar to select others.

To select a drawing to view with the Windows version of SirlinVIEW/Lite, you just pick on the Open File icon.

The command-line syntax for the DOS version of SirlinVIEW/Lite (the file called SVDWG.EXE) looks like this:

```
SVDWG [options] [file.DWG]
```

The following are the available options, of which more than one may be used on the command line at once, providing they are separated by spaces:

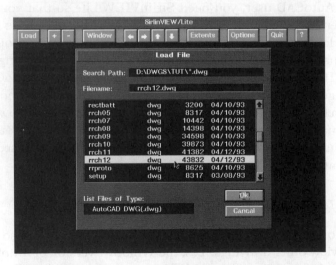

Figure 24.3 The Load File dialogue.

–NOEMS	Disable use of Expanded memory. Use this option if you are having problems with utilizing expanded memory on your system.
–NOXMS	Disable use of Extended memory. Use this option if you are experiencing memory conflicts with RAM disks, or if you are running under Windows with the DOS version of the viewer.
–PAPER	Force paper space view of the drawing. This is the opposite of –MODEL below.
–MODEL	Force model space view of the drawing. This is the opposite of –PAPER above.
–D?	Select video display mode. You will be prompted for input with a hardware configuration menu, which will allow you to specify if you want to change the current display device and mode or the input device. If you opt to do so, a list of supported devices is shown with the possible modes of operation highlighted, and modes that the software thinks are not available are not highlighted. Note the number after the –D or –I for future use of the viewer.
–I?	Select input device. Operates the same as the –D? option.

Note that these options must be typed in uppercase, and that –PAPER and –MODEL are mutually exclusive and should not be used at the same time.

Auxiliary Files

The SirlinVIEW/Lite program needs several auxiliary system files to run properly. Normally, these files reside in the same directory as the program itself. These system files will be found if (a) the program directory is listed in the PATH= environment variable, or (b) the SIRLIN= environment variable is defined to point to the program directory.

AutoCAD drawing files sometimes reference external files for shapes (text fonts) and external drawing files (Xrefs). The program will search for these files, first in the same directory as the drawing being viewed, and then in the path defined by the ACAD= environment variable.

Keyboard and Mouse Commands

SirlinVIEW/Lite can be controlled using the keyboard or the mouse. The following options can be chosen from either the keyboard or the button bar across the top of the screen. Where the key and button are different, both are listed. (The key is the first letter of the word on the button.)

Key (Button)	Function
L (Load)	Load a new drawing.
+, –	Press the + or – control button or keys to zoom in or out.
W (Zoom Window)	To zoom to a selected area of the drawing using the directional keys to move and size the window, or use the mouse to select the area to zoom.
Arrow keys	Use the arrow control buttons or directional keys to pan around the drawing.
E (Extents)	Zoom to the drawing's extents.
O (Options)	Select viewing options.
Q (Quit)	Exit the program.
?	Display help.
<Esc>	Press the ESC key at any point to interrupt drawing.

Additional Features for Windows

There are a few additional features for the Windows version, described here.

Open File	Use this button to select a file to load. (In the DOS version, Load is the equivalent button.)
Paper/Model Space	This button toggles between Paper Space and Model Space; in the DOS version, this is done by a command-line switch.
Close	Use Close on the system menu to quit, instead of the Quit button found on the DOS version's menu bar.

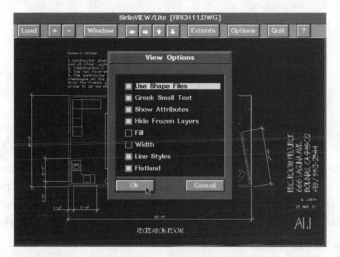

Figure 24.4 The View Options dialogue.

Viewing Options

The following options are available in the View Options dialogue box, which you can bring up by picking the Options button or pressing the O key (see Figure 24.4). When the check box is marked (filled in), the option is ON; when it is empty, the option is OFF.

Most of these options are designed to increase redraw speed at some cost in the amount of detail shown. Start by selecting the option settings that show the most detail, then change them if needed to improve performance.

Use Shape Files	ON to use shape files (more accuracy), OFF to ignore them (more speed).
Greek Small Text	ON to display small text as a line (more speed), OFF to draw all text (more accuracy).
Show Attributes	ON to display visible attributes (more accuracy), OFF to hide them (more speed).
Hide Frozen Layers	ON to hide frozen layers (more speed), OFF to show them (more detail).
Fill	ON to draw area fills such as wide polylines (more accuracy), OFF to draw the outline only (more speed).
Width	ON to draw wide polylines as wide (more accuracy), OFF to draw them single width (more speed).

| Line Styles | ON to draw line styles correctly (more accuracy), OFF to draw all lines solid (more speed). |
| Flatland | ON to ignore 3D information (more speed), OFF to show it correctly (more accuracy). |

Registering the Drawing Viewer

Please take the time to register your drawing viewer with Sirlin. This will entitle you to technical support, notification of product updates, special offers, and new product announcements. When you register, you will receive discount coupons for the purchase of other Sirlin products. Contact Sirlin at:

Sirlin Computer Corporation
25 Orchard View Drive, Suite 14
Londonderry, NH 03053 USA
Phone: (603) 437-0727
Fax: (603) 437-0737
BBS: (603) 437-0765
CompuServe: 70743,3136
Internet: 70743.3136@compuserve.com

Shareware Information

SirlinVIEW/Lite normally is provided as shareware; users are expected to try it, then register and pay a fee if they like it. The copies of SirlinVIEW/Lite you receive with *AutoCAD Power Tools*—one for DOS, one for Windows—are free of further shareware fees. Use the version you need, or use each in turn as you move from DOS to Windows, and don't worry about paying any fees. You still should register at the address above, however, to receive the other benefits of being a registered user.

If you share SirlinVIEW/Lite with other users, however, normal shareware rules apply. If that user is satisfied with the program and continues to use it, he or she should register it. If you feel that SirlinVIEW/Lite is of general value to many members of your workgroup or company, please contact the company about a site license; terms are reasonable, and upgrades and support are much easier with a site license.

The information below should be read by all users of SirlinVIEW/Lite, either those trying the product or those who continue to use it.

DEFINITION OF SHAREWARE

Shareware distribution gives users a chance to try software before buying it. If you try a shareware program and continue using it, you are expected to register. Individual programs differ on details—some request registration while others require it, and some specify a maximum trial period. With registration, you get anything from the simple right to continue using the software to an updated program with a printed manual. Copyright laws apply to both shareware and commercial software, and the copyright holder retains all rights, with a few specific exceptions as stated below.

Shareware authors are accomplished programmers, just like commercial authors, and the programs are of comparable quality. (In both cases, there are good programs and bad ones!) The main difference is in the method of distribution. The author specifically grants the right to copy and distribute the software, either to all and sundry or to a specific group. For example, some authors require written permission before a commercial disk vendor may copy their shareware.

Shareware is a distribution method, not a type of software. You should find software that suits your needs and pocketbook, whether it's commercial or shareware. The shareware system makes fitting your needs easier, because you can try before you buy. And because the overhead is low, prices are also low. Shareware has the ultimate money-back guarantee: If you don't use the product, you don't pay for it.

DISCLAIMER AND AGREEMENT

Users of SirlinVIEW/Lite must accept this disclaimer of warranty: "SirlinVIEW/Lite is supplied as is. The author disclaims all warranties, expressed or implied, including, without limitation, the warranties of merchantability and of fitness for any purpose. The author assumes no liability for damages, direct or consequential, which may result from the use of SirlinVIEW/Lite."

SirlinVIEW/Lite is a "shareware program" and is provided at no charge to the user for evaluation. Feel free to share it with your friends, but please do not give it away altered or as part of another system. The essence of "user-supported" software is to provide personal computer users with quality software without high prices, and yet to provide incentive for programmers to continue to develop new products. If you find this program useful and find that you are using and continue to use SirlinVIEW/Lite after a reasonable trial period, you must make a registration payment of $25 (U.S.$) to Sirlin Computer Corporation. The $25 registration fee will license one copy for use on any one computer at any one time. (As described above, this requirement does not apply to single computer use by owners of this book. *AutoCAD Power Tools* includes a license to use SirlinVIEW/Lite on one computer.)

You must treat this software just like a book. An example is that this software may be used by any number of people and may be freely moved from one computer location to another, as long as there is no possibility of its being used at one location while being used at another. Just as a book cannot be read by two different persons at the same time.

Commercial users of SirlinVIEW/Lite must register and pay for their copies of SirlinVIEW/Lite within 30 days of first use or their license will be withdrawn. Site license arrangements may be made by contacting Sirlin Computer Corporation.

Anyone distributing SirlinVIEW/Lite for any kind of remuneration must first contact Sirlin Computer Corporation at the address above for authorization. This authorization automatically will be granted to distributors recognized by the Association of Shareware Professionals (ASP) as adhering to its guidelines for shareware distributors, and such distributors may begin offering SirlinVIEW/Lite immediately (however, Sirlin Computer Corporation still must be advised so that the distributor can be kept up to date with the latest version of SirlinVIEW/Lite). You are encouraged to pass a copy of SirlinVIEW/Lite along to your friends for evaluation. Before you do, please delete the registration file SVLITE.REG, and encourage them to register their copies if they find that they can use them. All registered users will receive a copy of the latest version of the SirlinVIEW/Lite software.

Other Sirlin Products

Would you like to be able to select layers? View other file formats, including .DXF, .PCX, .TIF, and more? Print and plot? Attach notes and redline (markup) your drawings for annotation?

Sirlin Computer Corporation produces a number of products for the access, display, and management of graphics files. Products are available for DOS, Microsoft Windows, SUN UNIX/Solaris, and other UNIX platforms:

- SirlinVIEW/POP

- SirlinVIEW/SE

- SirlinVIEW/PLUS

- CAD++ ENGINE Developer's Toolkit

- Other CAD utilities

SirlinVIEW/POP

SirlinVIEW/POP makes viewing an extension of off-the-shelf software. It's a simple viewer which enables users to view CAD drawings and raster images at any time with a press of a button, even while working in other programs. With complete viewing flexibility, you can pan, zoom, and select layers. SirlinVIEW/POP lets you seamlessly integrate viewing features into existing applications with no special programming required, and it supports viewing

of AutoCAD's .DWG file format, industry standard .DXF files, HPGL formatted plot files, and Raster Image files.

SirlinVIEW/SE (Standard Edition)

SirlinVIEW/SE is a fast, accurate, full-featured, intelligent drawing viewer.
It's a full-featured viewing application that lets you quickly review and use
CAD drawings without an expensive CAD workstation. Loading a drawing is
as simple as selecting from a list, or, even easier, by selecting a HyperLink
region of one drawing to load another related drawing. You can add notes
(both graphical "redlines" and pop-up note cards) and print to over 300 dot
matrix and laser printers, and plot to HPGL plotters. SirlinVIEW/SE supports AutoCAD's .DWG file format, industry standard .DXF files, HPGL
formatted plot files and Raster Image files.

SirlinVIEW/PLUS

SirlinVIEW/PLUS is a low-cost visual information management system. Use
it to build low-cost GIS, FM, AEC, and manufacturing systems by combining
CAD drawings with existing database files. Look up data records by clicking
on locations, shown in a pop-up window. Highlight objects in the drawing
that match a selection criteria. Multiple queries may be visible at a time, and
queries can be saved and selected like layers in the drawing. SirlinVIEW/
PLUS has full viewing support, Posted Notes, HyperLinks, print/plot, graphical redlining, and customization capabilities. SirlinVIEW/PLUS supports
AutoCAD's .DWG file format, industry standard .DXF files, HPGL formatted
plot files and Raster Image files. Runs outside of AutoCAD.

Sirlin CAD++ Engine

The Sirlin CAD++ Engine is a powerful, modular programmer's toolkit. It
supports the access, manipulation, and display of popular CAD drawing
files, including the industry standard .DXF and AutoCAD's .DWG. Use it to
import and export .DWG and .DXF data and convert CAD data to Raster
Image format. Both sequential and random access are supported for reading
and writing files, and you can search and replace entities in drawing files.

The Sirlin CAD++ Engine supports most computer environments and
compilers, including languages from Microsoft, Borland, Zortech, Watcom,
and Metaware. DOS graphics support includes MSC, BGI, and Metagraphics
libraries. Sun C and ANSI C compilers are supported on Sun using X
Windows. The Windows version is a set of Dynamic Link Libraries callable
from any of the many languages that support DLLs.

Sirlin DWG-DXF Conversion Utilities

The Sirlin DWG-DXF Conversion Utilities convert drawings between .DWG and .DXF formats. The Utilities include two programs: DWG2DXF converts AutoCAD's .DWG files into industry standard .DXF format; DXF2DWG converts .DXF files into AutoCAD .DWG format. Both operate from the command line or batch mode, outside of AutoCAD.

25

DWGDB File Finder

AutoCAD .DWG files, like other types of data files, have a way of accumulating on your hard disk until finding the drawings in which you're interested becomes a big hassle. The DWGDB file finder is a simple but handy utility that helps you keep track of and load your drawings easily. DWGDB allows you to save a drawing description, dates, keywords, and author for each .DWG file, and then lets you search for drawings based on this information. DWGDB also stores a list of the last ten drawings you opened, so that you can access them again quickly.

About the Program

AutoCAD Release 12's OPEN file dialogue box is a big advance over the primitive Main Menu in previous versions, but it still forces you to locate files based on the cryptic eight-character names imposed by DOS. Release 12 for Windows includes a rudimentary Find File dialogue that allows you to search for drawings by location, name, or DOS date, but you can't attach descriptions or keywords.

DWGDB was inspired by the easy-to-use document management tools available in other types of application software, such as word processing programs. These programs let you log information about each document and then use this information later to locate the document (see Figure 25.1).

DWGDB comes in two versions: one for AutoCAD DOS 386 and another for AutoCAD for Windows. The versions work identically and share the same

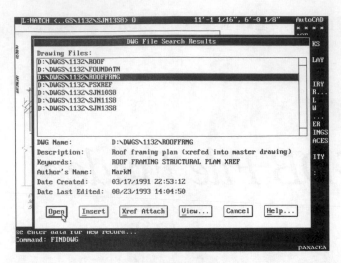

Figure 25.1   The DWGDB file finder.

dialogue boxes, so the descriptions we give for the DOS version apply equally well if you're running DWGDB with Release 12 for Windows.

Installation and Loading

DWGDB consists of the following files:

DWGDB.EXP	The DOS 386 ADS program
DWGDB.EXE	The Windows ADS program
DWGDB.DCL	The dialogue boxes

The installation program copies these files to the \APT\DWGDB subdirectory. You can move these files to a different subdirectory, but be sure to keep them all together. The installation program also installs the ADS source files in \APT\DWGDB\SOURCE. Accomplished ADS programmers can use these files to modify and recompile DWGDB. If you won't be modifying DWGDB, you can delete this subdirectory.

In order to use DWGDB, you need to do two things:

1. set the DWGDB environment variable from DOS, and
2. load the ADS program in AutoCAD.

The DWGDB environment variable tells the program where to store its database (DWGDB.DAT) and where to look for its support files. Loading the ADS program allows DWGDB to intercept drawing saves and also creates two new commands: FINDDWG and LAST10.

We describe two ways of carrying out these two steps. The first approach is a "manual" one that you can use to experiment with DWGDB without altering your AutoCAD support and DOS system files. The second approach is the "automatic" method; it ensures that DWGDB is always loaded, and requires that you edit your ACAD.ADS file and a DOS batch file.

LOADING DWGDB MANUALLY

To set the DWGDB environment variable manually, type the following at the DOS prompt:

```
SET DWGDB=C:\APT\DWGDB
```

If you're using DWGDB with AutoCAD for Windows, perform this step before starting Windows. This example assumes that you installed the program files on the C: drive and left the DWGDB files in their default subdirectory; modify the disk and subdirectory name accordingly if your system is different.

Once you've set the DWGDB environment variable and launched AutoCAD, load the DWGDB ADS program with the (xload) function:

```
Command: (XLOAD "DWGDB")
```

If you prefer, you can use the Release 12 APPLOAD command instead of (xload); see Chapter 9, *Adding Dimensions and Text*, for more information about APPLOAD.

If you performed these steps correctly, you'll see a sign-on and copyright message for DWGDB. If not, return to DOS and check your typing and subdirectory name carefully.

LOADING DWGDB AUTOMATICALLY

If you decide to use DWGDB regularly, you should add the SET statement shown above to your AutoCAD batch file or AUTOEXEC.BAT file, so that the DWGDB environment variable always is set automatically. For instance, if you want to put the statement in your ACADR12.BAT file, place it with the other SET statements:

```
SET ACAD=C:\ACAD\SUPPORT;C:\ACAD\FONTS;C:\ACAD\ADS
SET ACADCFG=C:\ACAD
SET ACADDRV=C:\ACAD\DRV
SET DWGDB=C:\APT\DWGDB
C:\ACAD\ACAD %1 %2
```

If you're using DWGDB with AutoCAD for Windows, you won't be using a batch file to start AutoCAD, so add the SET statement to your AUTOEXEC.BAT file.

In order to load the ADS program automatically each time you launch AutoCAD, you need to add the location and name of the DWGDB.EXP file (or DWGDB.EXE for Windows) to the ACAD.ADS file. ACAD.ADS is an

ASCII file in your \ACAD subdirectory; it stores the names of ADS programs you want AutoCAD to load each time it launches. (See Chapter 14, *Getting Ready to Customize*, for more information.)

The stock ACAD.ADS file that comes with AutoCAD contains only one ADS program name: ACADAPP. To add DWGDB, open ACAD.ADS in a text editor and, on the line after ACADAPP, add the complete DWGDB file specification for the DWGDB.EXP file. (You don't need to add the .EXP or .EXE, though.) Because of the way that AutoCAD deals with slashes, you must convert the backslashes to forward slashes. Here's an example:

```
ACADAPP
C:/APT/DWGDB/DWGDB
```

After you've made these two changes, launch AutoCAD. DWGDB now should load automatically.

Tip

If you don't set the DWGDB= environment variable, DWGDB uses the first subdirectory on the ACAD= support path.

How the Program Works

DWGDB comprises three parts:

1. a procedure and dialogue box for saving information to the DWGDB.DAT database each time you save a drawing,

2. a dialogue box for specifying search parameters, and

3. a dialogue box that shows the results of the search and lets you open, insert, attach, or view drawings.

Each time you save a drawing in AutoCAD, DWGDB checks whether the current drawing has been logged in the database. If not, DWGDB presents you with a dialogue in which you can enter a description, a set of keywords, and the author's name. If the drawing was logged previously, DWGDB simply updates the "last edited" time.

After you've logged at least one drawing into the database, you can use the FINDDWG and LAST10 commands to look for and load .DWG files. With FINDDWG, you enter a search specification that tells the program what information to look for. Once you pick OK, DWGDB displays a list of files that matches the specification. With LAST10, DWGDB goes directly to the search results dialogue; you don't have to specify anything. With either

FINDDWG or LAST10, you can scroll through the drawing names and see the database information for each file. Assuming you find the file you're looking for, you can open it, insert it as a Block, attach it as an Xref, or view it with the SirlinVIEW/Lite drawing viewer that's included with this book (see Chapter 24, *SirlinVIEW/Lite File Viewer*).

DWGDB's database is stored in an ordinary ASCII file called DWGDB.DAT (located in the DWGDB= directory). You can view, edit, and print this file with standard DOS utilities like EDIT.

Using the DWGDB File Finder

This section describes in more detail how to use DWGDB. It also documents the DWGDB.DAT file, in case you want to edit it or import it into other programs.

Saving

As described above, DWGDB sits in the background waiting for drawing saves. After one occurs, it checks the saved name and compares it to the list of drawings logged in DWGDB.DAT. If the saved name isn't in the database, DWGDB displays the Add Info to Database dialogue box, as shown in Figure 25.2.

This dialogue displays the drawing name, date created (based on the TDCREATE system variable), and last edited date (based on the DOS system clock). The dialogue also provides edit boxes in which you can enter a description of the drawing, a list of keywords, and the author's name. As a convenience, DWGDB automatically enters your AutoCAD login name in the Author's Name field, although you can change this value.

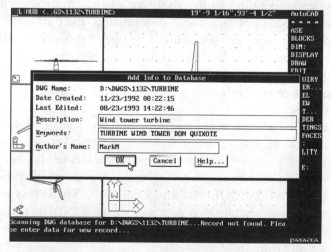

Figure 25.2   Adding a file entry to the DWGDB database.

Assuming that you want to log the current drawing into the database, type in any description and list of keywords (separated by spaces), verify the author's name, and then press OK. If you prefer not to log the current drawing, pick Cancel instead.

Tip

If you later want to change any of this information, you'll need to edit DWGDB.DAT with an ASCII text editor, such as DOS's EDIT or the Windows Notepad.

Once you have a few drawings logged into the database, you can start taking advantage of DWGDB by using the FINDDWG and LAST10 commands.

FINDDWG

The FINDDWG command lets you conduct searches using the information stored in DWGDB.DAT. After FINDDWG locates a group of drawings that match your search specification, you can view the database information for each drawing and select a drawing for loading or viewing.

THE SEARCH SPECIFICATION

When you start the FINDDWG command, it displays the DWG File Search Specification dialogue box, as shown in Figure 25.3. This dialogue contains six specification areas corresponding to the six fields in the database: drawing name, description, keywords, author's name, date created, and date last edited.

To create a search specification, type values into one or more of the six edit boxes. If you specify a created or last edited date, you also need to pick the radio button that indicates how FINDDWG should treat the date. Once you've entered at least one search value, pick the Start Search... button in order to see the results.

As you're constructing search specifications, it helps to understand the rules FINDDWG uses when it looks for matches. FINDDWG is case insensitive, so you don't need to worry about upper- or lowercase. It also finds partial matches, which means that a drawing name search specification of "BOO" will match C:\DWGS\BOOLEAN and C:\SUB\DASBOOT as well as C:\BOO. Finally, when you specify two or more fields, FINDDWG uses an implied "and": All the fields in which you've specified a search value must match in order for a drawing to be selected.

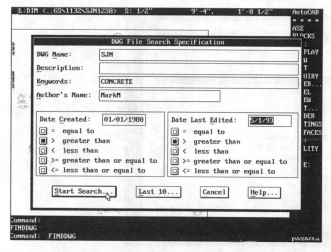

Figure 25.3   Entering the search specification.

For example, the search specification shown in Figure 25.3 selects all drawings that contain the string "SJN" in their name, have "CONCRETE" as a keyword, have "MarkM" as the author, and were last edited after May 1, 1993.

The DWG File Search Specification dialogue also includes a Last 10... button, which works the same as the LAST10 command. See the next section for a description of LAST10.

THE SEARCH RESULTS

After you pick the Start Search... button in the DWG File Search Specification dialogue, FINDDWG displays any matches in the DWG File Search Results dialogue box (see Figure 25.4). The names of the matching files are displayed in a list box, and you can see the database information for any file by selecting its name in the list.

If you want to use one of the matching files, select its name and then pick the Open, Insert, or Xref Attach button in order to run the appropriate command with the selected drawing. If instead you just want to view the drawing, select the View... button. FINDDWG will temporarily shell out to DOS and launch SirlinVIEW/Lite with the currently selected drawing.

Tip

In order for the View... option to work, SirlinVIEW/Lite's program subdirectory must be included on the DOS path, and the SIRLIN= environment variable must be set properly. See Chapter 24 for more information.

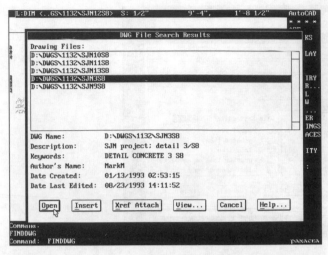

Figure 25.4   Viewing the results of a database search.

LAST10

The LAST10 command works much like FINDDWG, except that you don't have to specify any search parameters. Simply type LAST10 (or pick the Last 10... button on the DWG File Search Specification dialogue box), and DWGDB will automatically select the last ten drawings you've saved. The drawing names are displayed in the DWG File Search Results dialogue box, as described in the previous section and shown in Figure 25.5.

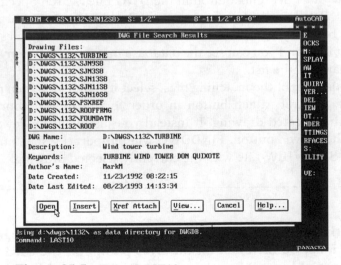

Figure 25.5   Using LAST10.

Tip

If you use the FINDDWG and LAST10 commands often, add them to the File menu or to your custom pull-down menu page. See Chapter 17 for details.

About the DWGDB.DAT File

As described above, the DWGDB.DAT file contains DWGDB's database in ASCII format. Each record contains six fields, as shown in Table 25.1. The records are separated by a row of dashes preceded by a semicolon.

Table 25.1   DWGDB.DAT's Field Structure

Field Name	Maximum Length
FILE:	61
AUTHOR:	31
DATE CREATED:	20
LAST EDITED:	20
DESCRIPTION:	61
KEYWORDS:	61

You can edit field values and delete or add records with an ASCII editor as long as you preserve these formatting conventions. We recommend that you make a backup copy of DWGDB.DAT before editing it, (at least for the first couple of times). Below is an example of a DWGDB.DAT file containing three drawing records.

```
;-------------
FILE: D:\DWGS\1132\ROOFFRMG
AUTHOR: MarkM
DATE CREATED: 03/17/1991 22:53:12
LAST EDITED: 08/23/1993 14:04:50
DESCRIPTION: Roof framing plan (xrefed into master drawing)
KEYWORDS: ROOF FRAMING STRUCTURAL PLAN XREF
```

```
;-------------
FILE: D:\DWGS\1132\SJN9S8
AUTHOR: MarkM
DATE CREATED: 01/13/1993 02:53:15
LAST EDITED: 08/23/1993 14:12:39
DESCRIPTION: SJN project; detail 9/S8
KEYWORDS: DETAIL CONCRETE 9 S8


;-------------
FILE: D:\DWGS\1132\TURBINE
AUTHOR: MarkM
DATE CREATED: 11/23/1992 08:22:15
LAST EDITED: 08/23/1993 14:22:46
DESCRIPTION: Wind tower turbine
KEYWORDS: TURBINE WIND TOWER DON QUIXOTE
```

DWGDB and Workgroups

DWGDB is designed as a straightforward and simple "personal logbook" for keeping track of and loading drawings. Although DWGDB was not designed to be network-aware, other members of your workgroup might find it to be a valuable tool for managing their drawings. Experiment with FINDDWG and LAST10, and if you find them useful, consider purchasing copies for other workgroup members.

Tip

If your workgroup is connected with a network, make sure that the DWGDB= environment variable points to a local or personal subdirectory for each user. If two users try to share the same DWGDB= subdirectory, they'll either overwrite one another's DWGDB.DAT file or encounter file sharing violations.

26

SHOWREFS and DWGLIST

Managing the Xrefs, Blocks, layers, and text fonts in a group of drawings is a big and important job. Unfortunately, AutoCAD doesn't include much in the way of tools for doing this, especially when more than one drawing file is involved. Two utility programs included on the AutoCAD disk, SHOWREFS and DWGLIST, address this shortcoming. They let you generate reports that show the Xrefs, text fonts, menus, Blocks, and layers on which one or more drawings (in one or more subdirectories) depend.

About the Programs

AutoCAD provides a great deal of flexibility in how you can use Xrefs, Blocks, layers, and text fonts, but with that flexibility come potential file and CAD standards management problems. For instance, if you forget to include an externally referenced drawing or custom .SHX file when you send drawing files to a service bureau or consultant, the recipient won't be able to view or plot your drawings accurately. This problem will fray everyone's nerves, and may cost valuable days and dollars. Or suppose your company is required to make an electronic submittal of a large number of .DWG files that are supposed to adhere to specific layer and Block naming standards—how will you efficiently check that only the proper names were used?

SHOWREFS and DWGLIST are invaluable tools for carrying out these sorts of drawing file management tasks. Both programs are DOS command-line utilities that inspect .DWG files and report on their contents. SHOWREFS

689

reports on all the external files on which one or more drawings depend: Xrefs (.DWG), fonts and shapes (.SHX and .PFB), and menus (.MNU/.MNX). DWGLIST reports on the layers and Block Definitions contained in one or more drawings.

SHOWREFS and DWGLIST were developed by Mike Dickason, a CAD consultant and civil engineer who has authored several general-purpose and discipline-specific AutoCAD utility programs. See the advertisements in the back of this book for information about other products and services from Mike's company, MD Computer Consulting.

SHOWREFS and DWGLIST have been distributed as shareware through the ACAD forum on CompuServe and through other sources, but each copy of *AutoCAD Power Tools* includes a license to use one copy of each program on one computer—no shareware registration fee is required for owners of this book. (See the "Shareware Information" section of Chapter 24 if you're not familiar with the shareware method of software distribution.) Of course, if your office requires additional copies, you will need to arrange to purchase them. Contact Mike Dickason at the address shown in the program banner or at the end of this book for information about additional individual or site licenses.

Installation

SHOWREFS and DWGLIST consist of just two files, SHOWREFS.EXE and DWGLIST.EXE. The installation program copies these files to the \APT\UTILS subdirectory by default. You might want to move the files to a subdirectory in your DOS path, so that you can run the programs easily from any directory.

Note that the files SHOWREFS.EXE and DWGLIST.EXE in the \APT\UTILS subdirectory are your licensed versions, and therefore are not to be distributed to others. The installation program also creates SHOWREFS.ZIP and DWGLIST.ZIP in the \APT\UTILS\SHARE subdirectory. These .ZIP files contain shareware versions of the programs, so feel free to distribute them to others.

How the Programs Work

As described in Chapter 10, *Xrefs, Blocks, and Attributes*, AutoCAD maintains in each drawing file a series of tables of "named objects": Layers, Block Definitions, text styles, and so on. These data, like the rest of the .DWG file, are encoded in a binary format, so you can't directly read them from DOS. SHOWREFS and DWGLIST understand the binary format of this part of the .DWG file format, and thus the programs are able to decode the names of Blocks (including Xrefs, which are listed in the Block table), layers, and text fonts. Both programs can extract this information from one or many drawing files, and can display it on the screen or save it in an ASCII text file.

Because SHOWREFS and DWGLIST are only *reading* your drawing files (and not writing to them), there's no danger that any .DWG files could become corrupted.

SHOWREFS

SHOWREFS shows all the external files that one or more .DWG files reference. The external files on which an AutoCAD drawing can depend are:

- Xrefs (.DWG)

- Text fonts and shapes (.SHX and .PFB)

- Menus (.MNU or .MNX)

SHOWREFS reads the header portion of each drawing you specify and determines which Xrefs, fonts and shapes, and menus are referenced. It then displays the information in a format that you can control with command-line switches. The syntax for SHOWREFS is:

```
SHOWREFS filespec[;filespec][/A][/F][/G][/I][/M][/P][/S]
```

All parameters in [square brackets] are optional.

Tip

By default, SHOWREFS sends its report to the screen. If you want to save the results to a file or send them directly to the printer, use the DOS redirection symbol (>). For example,

```
SHOWREFS *.DWG /G > REFLIST.TXT
or
SHOWREFS MYPLAN  > PRN
```

If you type SHOWREFS without any parameters and press <Enter>, the program will display a series of three text screens. These screens remind you of the meaning of the program switches and give other information about the program. SHOWREF's program parameters are defined as follows:

filespec[;filespec]   Defines the drawing files that SHOWREFS will scan. You can specify a single drawing, a group of drawings separated by semicolons, a group of drawings that match DOS wildcards (? and *), or any combination of these three. You don't need to supply an extension; SHOWREFS assumes an extension of .DWG. You can, however, supply an extension of .DWG or .BAK if you like.

/A (ACAD)   Searches the path pointed to by the DOS environment variable ACAD= for .MNU and .MNX files that match the menu names referenced by the drawings being scanned. This switch allows you to find out in advance whether AutoCAD will be able to find all the menus referenced by a group of drawings. If the variable ACAD= is not set, SHOWREFS will exit with an error message.

/F (parent File only)   Suppresses the display of nested Xrefs. By default, when SHOWREFS locates an Xref, it checks to see whether that Xref refers to any other Xref, and so on down the line. /F tells SHOWREFS not to look any deeper than one level.

/G (Graphical)   Displays the structure of nested Xrefs using a "graphical" tree, rather than just indenting each Xref name.

Tip

The "graphical" lines are extended ASCII characters. If your printer displays funny characters when you send SHOWREFS /G output to it, then you need to configure the printer to use a different character set, such as PC-8.

/I (Individual)   Outputs results for each file processed. By default, SHOWREFS displays a summary of the fonts, shapes, and menus referenced by all drawings that match the filespecs. /I tells the program to list this information individually for each drawing file.

/M (Menu)   Creates "dummy" menus in the filespec directories to match the menu names referenced by each drawing in the given filespec. If you use the /a option with /m, SHOWREFS will create dummy menus only if it doesn't locate a matching menu name somewhere in the ACAD= support path.

This option is provided primarily for users of versions prior to Release 12. In Release 11, a missing menu would cause a script to stall, which created big problems for users who processed batches of drawings with scripts (e.g., to plot). The dummy menus created by SHOWREFS prevented this problem from occurring. Release 12 is smart enough to ignore missing menus when a script is running, so Release 12 users won't need this switch.

/P (Pause)   Pauses after each screen full of text.

/S (Subdirectories) Includes all subdirectories of each filespec. By default, SHOWREFS scans only the filespec in the directories you specify. This switch causes the program to also look in subdirectories of the directories you specify.

/U (Unsorted) Suppresses alphabetical sorting of names. By default, SHOWREFS sorts Xref, text font and shape, and menu names alphabetically. This switch causes the program to display the names in the order it finds them instead.

Examples

Here are several examples showing how you might use SHOWREFS. Sample output from the program is shown below.

SHOWREFS PLAN01 Scans PLAN01.DWG in the current directory and displays SHOWREF's normal report on the screen.

SHOWREFS * > COMPLETE.REF Scans all .DWGs in the current directory and saves SHOWREF's normal report to a text file called COMPLETE.REF.

SHOWREFS D:\DWGS\TYP* /S > PRN Scans all drawings beginning with TYP and located in D:\DWG or any of its subdirectories and sends SHOWREF's normal report to the printer.

SHOWREFS PLAN01;PLAN02 /I /P Scans PLAN01.DWG and PLAN02.DWG in the current directory and displays a report broken down by drawing to the screen (pausing at each screenful).

Sample SHOWREFS Output

```
SHOWREFS 1.2 Copyright (c) 1992-93 MD COMPUTER CONSULTING  All rights reserved.
Lists externally referenced files for the given ACAD drawing(s).


The following filespecs were used by SHOWREFS:
S2-5?.DWG


The following menus are referenced in the above filespec(s):
ACAD
DESIGNER


The following fonts are referenced in the above filespec(s):
ARCHQUIK.SHX
```

```
ROMANC
ROMANS

The following bigfonts are referenced in the above filespec(s):
SPECIAL

The following XREF's were encountered in the above filespec(s):
J:S2-5A.DWG
   References:
   TBLK.DWG
   HR-1.DWG
     References:
     ALLGRID.DWG
       References:
       PSBORDRS.DWG
   NOTE2-5A.DWG

J:S2-5B.DWG
   References:
   TBLK.DWG
   HR-1.DWG

J:S2-5C.DWG
   References:
   TBLK.DWG
   HR-1.DWG
   321DS74.DWG

J:S2-5D.DWG
   References:
   TBLK.DWG
   HR-1.DWG
```

DWGLIST

DWGLIST reports on the names of layers and Blocks defined in one or more
.DWG files. DWGLIST works similarly to SHOWREFS—it reads the header
portion of each drawing you specify—but DWGLIST's output is sent by
default to individual files that match each .DWG file and have an .LIS
extension. You can control the format of the output and where it's sent with
several command-line switches.

The syntax for DWGLIST is:

```
DWGLIST filespec[;filespec] [/L] [/B] [/FB=blockname]
[/FL=layername] [/A] [/O] [/O-] [/S] [/U] [/V]
```

All parameters in [square brackets] are optional, but you must specify at least one of the switches /L, /B, /FL, or /FB.

As with SHOWREFS, if you type DWGLIST without any parameters and press <Enter>, the program will display a series of informational text screens. DWGLIST's program parameters are defined as follows:

filespec[;filespec] Defines the drawing files that DWGLIST will scan. You can specify a single drawing, a group of drawings separated by semicolons, a group of drawings that match DOS wildcards (? and *), or any combination of these three. You don't need to supply an extension; DWGLIST assumes an extension of .DWG. You can, however, supply an extension of .DWG or .BAK if you like.

/L (Layer list) Lists layers in the specified files.

/B (Block list) Lists Block Definitions in the specified files.

/FL=*layername* (Find Layer) Finds each drawing in the filespec that contains the layer called *layername*. You can use wildcards to specify the layer name.

/FB=*blockname* (Find Block) Finds each drawing in the filespec that contains the Block Definition called *blockname*. You can use wildcards to specify the Block name.

Tip

As mentioned above, you must specify at least one of the switches /L, /B, /FL, or /FB. Using /FL or /FB suppresses the /L or /B switch.

/A (Append output) Appends output to the file(s) if they already exist. By default, DWGLIST overwrites any existing output files (see /O below).

/O=*filename* (Output to specified file) Sends all output to the specified filename. By default, DWGLIST creates a file called *dwgname*.LIS for each drawing file it processes and writes the output to these files. The /O switch tells DWGLIST to send all output to a single file instead.

/O- (disable Output to file)   Sends output to the screen, rather than to individual *dwgname*.LIS files.

/S (Subdirectories)   Includes all subdirectories of each filespec. By default, DWGLIST scans only the filespec in the directories you specify. This switch causes the program to also look in subdirectories of the directories you specify.

/U (Unsorted)   Suppresses alphabetical sorting of names. By default, DWGLIST sorts layer and Block names alphabetically. This switch causes the program to display the names in the order it finds them instead.

/V (Verbose output)   Creates "verbose" output. By default, DWGLIST displays only the drawing filename, the labels "*LAYERS" and "*BLOCKS", and the names of the individual Layers and Blocks. The /V switch causes the program to add a count of Layers and Blocks, an indication of the AutoCAD .DWG file version, and separator lines (see below).

Examples

Here are several examples showing how you might use DWGLIST. Sample output from the program is shown below.

DWGLIST PLAN01 /L   Scans PLAN01.DWG in the current directory and creates a file called PLAN01.LIS containing the layers found in PLAN01.DWG.

DWGLIST PLAN* /B   Scans all drawings in the current directory whose names begin with PLAN and creates a file called *dwgname*.LIS for each of them. Each *dwgname*.LIS file contains a list of the Block Definitions found in that drawing.

DWGLIST * /L /B /O=COMPLETE.LIS   Scans all .DWGs in the current directory and creates a single file called COMPLETE.LIS that contains a listing of the Layers and Block Definitions for each drawing.

DWGLIST D:\DWGS\TYP* /FB=IMLOST /S   Scans all drawings beginning with TYP and located in D:\DWG or any of its subdirectories. DWGLIST looks for a Block called IMLOST in each of the drawings and reports the names of any drawings that contain it.

DWGLIST PLAN01;PLAN02 /FL=DIM* /O-   Scans PLAN01.DWG and PLAN02.DWG in the current directory and displays on the screen a list of layers in each drawing that begin with DIM.

Sample DWGLIST Output

```
--------------------------------------------------------
**D:S2-5A.DWG
AutoCAD Version 11/12
There are 4 blocks.
*BLOCKS
HR-1
NOTE2-5A
TBLK
TBLKATT
--------------------------------------------------------
There are 31 layers.
*LAYERS
0
ALLGRID|DIM
ALLGRID|ML
ALLGRID|NOPLOT
ALLGRID|OBJ06
ALLGRID|S1
ALLGRID|S3
DEFPOINTS
HR-1|ARCH
HR-1|BRACE
HR-1|DIM
HR-1|OBJ06
HR-1|S1
IIR-1|S10
HR-1|S2
HR-1|S3
HR-1|S4
HR-1|S5
HR-1|S7
HR-1|S8
NOTE2-5A|DIM
NOTE2-5A|OBJ06
NOTE2-5A|S3
PSBORDRS|NOPLOT
S2
S3
TBLK|3
TBLK|HATCH
```

```
TBLK|NP
TBLK|TXTS
VIEW
```

SHOWREFS, DWGLIST, and Workgroups

SHOWREFS and DWGLIST are excellent tools for managing workgroup drawing files. You can use these programs to check drawings as a project progresses, and to verify accuracy and completeness of electronic submittals or archives.

Use SHOWREFS when you need to ensure that a set of drawings is complete. Run SHOWREFS on the set of drawings, redirect output to a file, and print the listing. Then use the printed listing as a checklist for assembling an archive, electronic submittal, or package of drawings to be plotted by a service bureau. SHOWREFS also is useful for showing the Xref structure of a group of drawings—it gives you an "at-a-glance" view of how your drawings are related to one another.

Use DWGLIST to inspect a group of drawings for adherence to layer and Block name standards. DWGLIST also is helpful when you can't find a Block that you know is defined somewhere in a group of drawings.

Both SHOWREFS and DWGLIST can serve as tools for documenting drawings. Print the output from each program and include the printout with project archives. When you return to a set of drawings you haven't worked on for awhile, this documentation will make it much easier to reacquaint yourself with them.

Remember that your copy of *AutoCAD Power Tools* includes a license to use one copy each of SHOWREFS and DWGLIST. If others in your workgroup would benefit from using these programs, contact Mike Dickason about a site license.

A

Making the Upgrade Decision

Although most readers of this book are likely to have upgraded to Release 12, some still may be working with Release 11 (or earlier versions). The reasons for not upgrading are many: upgrade costs, skepticism about the value of the new release, concerns about bugs, or plain old inertia. In this chapter, we suggest some strategies for making the upgrade decision.

Deciding whether and when to upgrade your software package has become a big problem for all computer users; but if the upgrade decision is a headache for users of other software, it's a migraine for AutoCAD users. AutoCAD is 10 times as expensive as a typical productivity package, requires that you own and maintain a system about twice as powerful as the average user's, and is at the center of a whole industry of third-party add-ons. So upgrade-related decisions are bound to be complicated for many AutoCAD users.

This chapter discusses in detail the pros and cons of upgrading. It focuses on whether you should upgrade to AutoCAD Release 12, but the principles in it are applicable to other software and to future AutoCAD releases. Read through it to help yourself make the right upgrade decision.

If you have already upgraded, you're still not off the hook. You may well be asked to make formal or informal upgrade recommendations to others—consulting clients, peers, or people you supervise in a workgroup. Again, reading through this chapter will help you make the right recommendation.

Whether to upgrade is a key question, but when to upgrade is just as important. If you understand the issues involved in deciding whether to upgrade, you can more easily decide the right time to get on with it. You also can justify this decision to others in concrete, bottom-line terms. So here's a close look at the many factors that add up to the right upgrade decisions for you and people who listen to you.

Benefits of Upgrading to Release 12

Each previous release of AutoCAD has had a file format that was incompatible with other releases. So the upgrade decision was easy: You had no choice but to upgrade as soon as your key colleagues, customers, and coworkers did. But since Release 11 and Release 12 files are compatible, your decision as to which one to use doesn't depend on what others are using. Instead, you need to look at all the costs and benefits of upgrading. This section will help you identify the key benefits.

Table A.1 contains a short checklist to help you identify the most important new features in Release 12 for your own work. Take a moment to rate the importance of the features already in the checklist, and add in others that are important to you. If you are looking at an upgrade from Release 10, you also need to add to your list key features that were introduced in Release 11. (Refer to Parts I and II of this book if you're not familiar with the new features listed in Table A.1.)

If it's hard for you to identify which features might be most important to you, browse through Parts I and II of this book to get a feel for how we've used them. Also, check with coworkers, consultants, CompuServe, and other sources to see what they say. Those who use AutoCAD in ways similar to yours are probably in the best position to help identify the key features that will make the most difference in the way you work.

Using the table to identify the most beneficial features of Release 12 has probably convinced you that it's worth upgrading. But the changeover is not without problems. These are discussed in the section below.

Problems with Upgrading to Release 12

Nearly all AutoCAD users will find it worthwhile to invest the time and money to move up to Release 12. But there are several concerns you will encounter in upgrading, which may affect your decision on whether to upgrade or at least influence the timing of when you make the move. These include:

- **Time to perform the upgrade.** You should set aside a half to a full day to do the upgrade. You may wish to do it on a weekend morning when things are quiet, or on a weekday when colleagues and technical support people can be reached easily. Consider involving your dealer or a

Table A.1   Rating New Features in Release 12

Feature	Must have	Important	Nice
Better file handling (no Main Menu)			
Cursor pop-up menu			
Hatching improvements			
Selection enhancements			
Grips			
Noun/verb editing			
Plotting improvements			
Rendering built in			
Faster entity selection and osnaps			
Layer locking			
Fewer regenerations			
More and better dialogue boxes			
Customization improvements			

consultant in order to reduce time spent and risk of being left without a functioning system for some period of time. In any case, don't put yourself in a position where the upgrade has to go well and quickly or you're left unable to work.

- **Hardware upgrade costs.** To run Release 12 effectively, you'll need at least a 386DX processor, 8 MB of memory, and VGA graphics. You may need to upgrade your hardware to meet these minima, and if you're going to bother, you might as well get a 486DX processor and super VGA graphics (see Chapter 3, *Performance*, for more detailed hardware recommendations). To maintain performance on large drawings, you may need to upgrade to about double the amount of memory you're currently using (Release 12's 32-bit display lists are twice as large as 16-bit ones; programmable dialogue boxes take up memory, too).

- **Software upgrade costs.** The AutoCAD upgrade itself is not free; you're likely to pay about $500 for an upgrade from Release 11 to Release 12. You probably will need to upgrade video and other drivers to the latest versions to ensure compatibility with and optimal performance under AutoCAD. You'll want to upgrade to DOS 6 and, if you use Windows, Windows 3.1 in order to get the best memory management features and general compatibility with AutoCAD.

- **Third-party application upgrades.** You need to be sure that all the third-party applications you use work "as-is" with Release 12, or are available in Release 12 versions, or that you can live without them until they are upgraded. Then you have to go to the trouble and expense of getting the upgraded versions. Likewise with third-party drivers and utilities.

- **Customization upgrades.** You will have to move any custom tools or modifications of your previous AutoCAD environment up to the new version. The new features available for AutoCAD programming may help you create a better program, but in the short run, making such changes is just another time hit.

- **Initial lowered productivity.** You can do the same things in Release 12 that you used to do in Release 11 and they will work the same way, so there isn't a direct productivity hit for doing the same tasks using the new release. But to the extent that you take the time to experiment, you will get less done in Release 12 than you would have in Release 11 for a little while. The tutorials in this book are designed to minimize the learning curve, but only practice will get you to the point where you're really doing better with the new version. Count on a couple of weeks of occasional experimentation before you really get on top of the new release.

- **Slower performance.** Some AutoCAD operations, such as loading drawings, are slightly slower under Release 12 than Release 11. Depending on your working style and drawing size, the performance improvements in Release 12 (e.g., reduced regens and faster object selection) might or might not outweigh the slower operations.

- **Costs of benefits.** Very little is free. The greater ease of setup in Release 12 won't benefit you until you reorganize your setup procedures; customization improvements won't help until you upgrade your third-party application or modify your in-house customization. In a larger group, you may find yourself losing good drafters and lead people to the care and feeding of AutoCAD.

- **Bugs and incompatibilities.** Just as there probably is some feature in Release 12 that you would kill for, there may be a bug or incompatibility that will make you wish you were dead. The list of bugs, workarounds, patches, and bug-fix releases changes from month to month, so you need to be vigilant to stay informed. Check the tips in this book, Mike Dickason's bug report files in the ACAD forum on CompuServe, and *CADalyst* magazine's Bug Watch column. Also, you can ask colleagues, users' groups members, and your dealer for current information.

If you are concerned about the impact of these factors (and you should be), take a moment to plug some estimates into Table A.2, "Factors to Consider in Upgrading to Release 12." A high degree of accuracy is less important than identifying key problem areas and getting an overall feel for whether the costs and time investment of upgrading are a major, moderate, or minor concern to you.

Use the table to assist in making the upgrade decision and in identifying important factors to consider as you perform the upgrade.

Table A.2   Factors to Consider in Upgrading to Release 12

Factor	Time cost	Dollar cost
Time to perform the upgrade		
Hardware upgrade costs		
Software upgrade costs		
Third-party application upgrades		
Customization upgrades		
Initial lowered productivity		
Slower performance		
Bugs and incompatibilities		
Learning new features		

Should You Upgrade?

If you've plugged some numbers into Table A.2 above, the results are probably sobering. This is especially true because it's much easier to put a dollar value on costs than on benefits. But even one or two of the major improvements, such as plot preview and hatching preview, may be enough to make the upgrade pay for itself over time. If upgrading is in the cards for you, the sooner you make the move, the sooner you'll start to enjoy the benefits.

But now that you know the costs and time requirements of upgrading, you can better plan and budget for the upgrade process. Having identified the benefits, you'll be more motivated to get the upgrade started and done when it makes the most sense. For instance, the next project you're taking on may benefit greatly from one of the new Release 12 features; this argues for upgrading sooner. Or, you might be scheduled tightly for the next several weeks; having looked at the time required, you may upgrade later. Timing the upgrade correctly allows you to get the benefits of Release 12 as painlessly as possible.

Another factor to consider is the 90-day overlap that the Release 12 upgrade license agreement allows between the day you install Release 12 and the day you should erase Release 11. If you have the hard disk space to allow it, you can run both releases at once for a period of time. The ability to move back and forth between releases is made especially valuable by the fact that their files are compatible. But don't be lulled by this grace period; the work of upgrading to Release 12 has to get done eventually, and you'll make much better use of the 90-day overlap period if you're trying to get over to Release 12 quickly and use Release 11 only in a pinch until the day you have to erase it.

If you decide not to upgrade now, you might feel that this book will be gathering dust on your bookshelf until then, but it actually still has a lot of benefits. The tutorials on new AutoCAD features and 3D features include a lot of information that can be adapted for use with Release 11. Most of the content of the customization chapters relates almost as well to Release 11 as to Release 12. And most of the packages on disk work with both releases. The TurboDLD*Lite*™ package in particular will accelerate AutoCAD performance under either release.

Performing the Upgrade

This section lists a few key things that you should do in conjunction with the upgrade process to make it easier and more likely to succeed.

1.   Get driver and third-party updates or problem reports before starting.

Failure to do this can cause you to make frenzied requests of one or more vendors to send you disks via overnight delivery, patches on CompuServe, instructions by fax, etc. Even after the needed information arrives, you may not have a working system. Get the software and information you need before you start the upgrade.

2. **Install and test incrementally.**

   Start by installing AutoCAD alone without any third-party applications or drivers (unless you can't use video without one). Then add in drivers for your hardware, one at a time, and test that each piece works. Finally, add and test third-party applications and your in-house customization. Following these steps will prevent a great number of problems and make the ones that do occur far easier to fix.

3. **Schedule training immediately.**

   Users will develop strategies to avoid, disable, or otherwise ignore the new features of Release 12 if they aren't shown how to use them. Make sure that users, especially those in workgroups, get immediate training to help them take advantage of Release 12.

Upgrading and Workgroups

If you're responsible for the upgrading decision of others, such as other members of your workgroup, clients, or even friends with whom you share AutoCAD tips, you may need to plan a strategy for upgrading a number of people as painlessly as possible.

We suggest that one person in a workgroup be made responsible for investigating the costs and benefits of upgrading, advising others on the best time to upgrade, and assisting with the upgrade itself. This approach amortizes the costs of investigation and analysis over a number of people, and ensures that only one person has to undergo the full learning curve required to perform the upgrade in different circumstances.

The designated person should perform the costs and benefits analysis indicated above, and then do the upgrade for himself or herself as soon as reasonably possible. This person can then use the experience gained to give solid advice to others about upgrading, and lend a hand in doing the upgrade.

Once one person has gone through the upgrade and worked with Release 12 for a little while, an upgrade strategy for the rest of the group can be decided on. One strategy is to have most or all of a group upgrade at once; set aside a few days as "Upgrade Week" and devote that period to doing the upgrade and practicing with the new features. Another strategy is to upgrade one or two users every few days, in order to keep disruption to a minimum. There are three things that you should avoid:

- Assuming the upgrade will not cause any loss of time.

  Include time for the upgrade in your schedules, or you may miss deadlines.

- Upgrading most but not all of a workgroup.

  It's frustrating for support people and users to have a mixed group of users who are on different releases. The fewer the users of an older release that remains, the harder it will be for them to get support. Once you've gotten a good start on the job, finish it.

- Making one or more key people unavailable for a long time.

  Once the upgrade process has begun, it can become a big priority for all concerned. The one or two people most responsible for it can get very bogged down. Don't let yourself or someone else get stuck in the middle of a seemingly endless upgrade. Stage the effort and get the help you need to make sure that it proceeds quickly.

B

AutoCAD Resources

The AutoCAD community is huge, energetic, and widespread. It is very much worth your effort to reach out to other AutoCAD users. The chances that you can get that piece of AutoLISP code you need or an answer to an AutoCAD-related question (even one specific to your discipline) are surprisingly high. But first, you have to know where to look.

The premiere resource for AutoCAD users is the ACAD forum on CompuServe. Once you're on CompuServe and have learned your way around, you can find all the resources available elsewhere just by asking. CompuServe is the first resource described below.

Local AutoCAD users' groups and the Autodesk-sponsored North American AutoCAD User Group (NAAUG) also are valuable resources. Local users' groups give you the opportunity to meet and share expertise with other users. NAAUG helps you stay connected with other users through newsletters, annual conferences, and utility disks.

Read the section on CompuServe if you're not already on-line, and scan the rest. Just knowing what's available can be helpful in a pinch.

CompuServe's ACAD Forum

The ACAD forum on CompuServe is home to a thriving community of AutoCAD users, consultants, dealers, and Autodesk employees. The forum consists of a "message base" and "file libraries." The message base contains electronic conversations in the form of ASCII text messages linked together into "threads." The file libraries contain thousands of useful shareware and freeware AutoCAD-related files, including AutoLISP and ADS programs, drivers, and utilities.

The large amount of message traffic (currently over 200 messages per day) makes the ACAD forum an overwhelming resource at first. Fortunately, there are many CompuServe-specific communications programs that help make the process of reading and responding to forum messages more manageable. See below for a listing of some of these programs.

To access CompuServe, you need four things: a modem, a communications program, a phone line, and a CompuServe membership kit. Most ordinary modems and communications software will work fine, though setting the two up to work together can be tricky if you haven't done it before. Refer to the documentation or a book on communications, or ask an experienced friend for help.

To sign up with CompuServe, get one of the Introductory Membership booklets that are included with many pieces of software. Alternatively, you can purchase a CompuServe kit from many software stores or call CompuServe customer service at 800/848-8990. In most cases, you'll receive a usage credit (usually about $25) to get you started.

Once you're connected to CompuServe, use the command GO ACAD to enter and join the ACAD forum. You also might be interested in two other Autodesk forums on CompuServe: ASOFT and ARETAIL. ASOFT covers 3DStudio, Animator, and other Autodesk multimedia products, while ARETAIL is for users of Autodesk Retail Products software, including Generic CADD and AutoSketch.

Message Sections in the ACAD Forum

Here's a list of the message sections available in the ACAD forum:

1. AutoCAD
2. AutoCAD API
3. AME/AutoSurf/MCAD
4. Shade/Flix/RMan
5. Hrdware/Drvrs/ADI
6. OpSystms/Networks
7. NAAUG/UsrGps/AdeskU
8. Applications
9. What's New/Want Ads
10. Shipping/Receiving
11. AutoCAD for Windows
12. GIS/Civil/AEC
13. Take 5

Most of the section names are self-explanatory. Section 1, AutoCAD, is for general AutoCAD discussions that don't fit into any of the other categories. Section 2, AutoCAD API (Application Programming Interfaces) is for programming and customization messages. On most forums, including ACAD, a camaraderie develops among the forum regulars and people soon start discussing things that have nothing to do with the subject of the forum. Section 13, Take 5, is the place for these conversations. Popular topics in Section 13 include beer, grammar, automobiles, politics, and baby announcements.

You should post questions or comments in an appropriate section, and then check back within the next couple of days for replies.

Tip

If you have a large hard disk, you can use the ACAD forum's message traffic as an on-line help database. Use a script or other automated communications program function to download the message periodically (at least twice a week if you want to catch everything—that's about how long it takes during busy times for old messages to "scroll" off and be replaced by new ones). Store the messages on your hard disk, and then use a file search program to look for keywords that interest you. You'll not only find out whether there's an answer to your question, you'll identify people who can help you with more detail.

Data Libraries in the ACAD Forum

Here's a list of available data libraries in the ACAD forum:

1. AutoCAD
2. AutoCAD API
3. AME/AutoSurf/MCAD
4. Shade/Flix/RMan
5. Hrdware/Drvrs/ADI
6. OpSystms/Networks
7. NAAUG/UsrGps/AdeskU
8. Applications
9. What's New!
10. Utilities
11. AutoCAD for Windows
12. GIS/Civil/AEC
13. Adesk Files/General

As you can see, the data libraries pretty much follow the message sections. New files always appear first in Data Library 9, What's New!, and then reside there for about a month before being moved to their final resting place.

You can browse the libraries on-line and search for filenames and key-words, but this can be slow work in libraries that contain a large number of files. Each library includes an ASCII file listing the library's contents. These files are compressed in ZIP files called CAD-*XX*.ZIP, where *XX* is the library number (01 through 13). Once you download and unzip a CAD-*XX* file, you can browse, search, or print it out.

Many of the data library files are compressed with PKZIP or another compression utility. You'll need PKUNZIP or an equivalent program to extract them. The current version of the PK utilities is available in Library 10, Utilities.

CompuServe Costs

Regular use of CompuServe can become expensive if you're not careful. A basic monthly charge covers a few services such as CompuServe Mail (the place where you can exchange private messages with other CompuServe members). CompuServe charges by the minute for access to most forums (including the ACAD forum). Two plans are available: the Standard Plan and the Alternative Plan.

At this writing, the Standard Plan has the following costs: $8.95/month for Basic Services, plus $8.00/hour for your on-line time at 1200 or 2400 baud. It's $16.00/hour if you connect at 9600 baud, which is worth it if you're downloading files or automatically downloading messages.

The Alternative Plan has the following costs: $2.50/month for Basic Services, plus $12.80/hour at 1200 or 2400 baud, or $22.80/hour at 9600 baud.

At 2400 baud, the Alternative Plan is cheaper only if you're on-line for less than 90 minutes a month. For anyone who uses CompuServe forums much, the Basic Plan is more economical. See the CompuServe booklet for current pricing, lists of services, and other details.

Tip

You can use CompuServe Mail to exchange private messages with people who use other on-line services, including America Online and the Internet. For instance, to send a message via the Internet, address it to >INTERNET:*someone@somewhere.domain*, where *someone@somewhere.domain* is the person's Internet address. Conversely, someone on the Internet can send you a message via CompuServe Mail by addressing it to *XXXXX.YYYY*@compuserve.com, where *XXXXX.YYYY* is your CompuServe user ID (with the comma replaced by a period).

Specialized Communications Programs

Although most any communications program will work with CompuServe, it's far preferable to use one of the packages designed specifically for working with CompuServe forums and Mail. Most of these programs are either shareware or freeware, and they automate various aspects of using CompuServe. By doing so, they insulate you from CompuServe's primitive interface and help you save money by minimizing connect time.

Program	How to Get It
ATO (freeware)	GO IBMCOM (also available from Autodesk)
NavCIS (freeware)	GO DNAVCIS for DOS version GO WNAVCIS for Windows version GO NAVCIS for questions and support or 303/494-0298
OzCIS (freeware)	GO IBMCOM, section 14
TAPCIS ($79 shareware)	GO TAPCIS or 800/872-4768
WinCIS ($25 shareware)	GO WUGNET, section 12
CIM ($25)	GO CISSOFT (DOS, Windows, and Mac versions— from CompuServe)

CompuServe's three versions of CIM (DOSCIM, WinCIM, and MacCIM) are mouse-driven and easy to use, but they don't automate the most time-intensive part of using CompuServe: reading messages in forums. As a result, CIM is good for occasional users of forums, who want to browse the message base on-line; but the other packages listed above are better for regular forum users.

OzCIS, TAPCIS, and ATO are all popular CompuServe access programs for DOS users. OzCIS has the most modern interface, but it also requires more hardware resources than do the other two programs. WinCIS (not to be confused with CompuServe's WinCIM), has gained popularity with Windows users, but Windows versions of TAPCIS and OzCIS are in the works.

Some Other Resources

Some of the other resources available to AutoCAD users are listed below. There are many more, which you can find out about from CompuServe or from another one of the resources listed here.

Users' Groups

There are local users' groups in many cities. We cannot recommend these highly enough. They're even a great resource if you ever find yourself job-hunting. If you don't know whether there's a users' group in your area, ask other users or your dealer, or call Autodesk at 800/964-6432.

The North American AutoCAD User Group (NAAUG) is administered by Autodesk, but its officers are real AutoCAD users. It has a quarterly newsletter, an annual conference, AutoLISP utility disks, and input to the AutoCAD wish list. Dues are $25 per year, which includes the utility disk, newsletter, and a T-shirt. To join, write:

NAAUG Membership
P.O. Box 3394
San Rafael, CA 94912

Or call Autodesk's main number (415/332-2344) and ask for Kelly Daniels.

CADalyst and CADENCE Magazines

There are two monthly AutoCAD-specific magazines: *CADalyst* and *CADENCE*. You can reach *CADalyst* at 503/343-1200, or 73417,167 or 70302,2531 on CompuServe. *CADENCE* is at 800/486-4995, or 76703,4326 on CompuServe. *CADENCE* also maintains its own forum on CompuServe: GO CADENCE.

Both magazines offer a mix of product reviews, tutorials, AutoLISP programs, news, and editorial commentary. Both are available on well-stocked newsstands, so pick up a copy of each and see which you prefer. If you're serious about AutoCAD, it's worth subscribing to and reading both magazines.

Autodesk Global Village

The Autodesk Global Village is a CD-ROM and a network of local computer bulletin board services (BBSs) that make the contents of the CD-ROM available for downloading. The CD-ROM is produced by Autodesk, and it includes AutoLISP programs, sample drawings, and other information and data related to Autodesk's products.

You can access the Autodesk Global Village on Autodesk's own BBS in Sausalito, CA (415/289-2270), and on local BBSs in many parts of the world. Check local computer magazines and giveaways for BBS listings; often there will be a local BBS that caters to AutoCAD users and that is part of the Autodesk Global Village.

The AutoCAD Resource Guide

Autodesk publishes *The AutoCAD Resource Guide*, a listing of AutoCAD applications, developers, peripherals, books, and training centers. *The AutoCAD Resource Guide* comes with every copy of Release 12, and beginning in the fall of 1993, an expanded version will be available from Autodesk on CD-ROM.

Programs Mentioned in This Book

Here's a listing of the shareware, freeware, and commercial software that we've mentioned in this book.

Shareware and Freeware

The following listings give the program name followed by CompuServe ACAD forum data library information: filename, library number, download size, and shareware registration fee.

CHAPTERS 9 AND 14

- AutoED v.1.0: AUTOED.ZIP, Library 2, 88 KB, $35
  Walt Craig 76517,2466
  P.O. Box 3069
  St. George, UT 84771

- WCEdit v.2.04: WCEDIT.ZIP, Library 2, 433 KB, free
  ELSA, Inc.
  400 Oyster Point Blvd., Suite 109
  South San Francisco, CA 94080

CHAPTER 16

- SCRIPT v.2.5: SCR25.ZIP, Library 10, 45 KB, $35
  David A. Roman 70671,1546
  7625 King Richard Ct.
  Charlotte, NC 28227

CHAPTERS 16 AND 17

- SlideManager v.5.20: SLIDEM.EXE, Library 10, 163 KB, $25

- HyperSlide v.1.01: HYPSLD.EXE, Library 10, 280 KB, $50

- PlotManager v.2.31: PLOTM.EXE, Library 10, 200 KB, $50

John Intorcio 73417,155
5 Gladstone Street
Wakefield, MA 01880

Commercial Software

See the ads in the back pages of this book for information on how to contact the individuals and companies whose software is included in this book. Other commercial software mentioned in the book are listed below.

CHAPTER 10

- AutoTOOL dB
  Robert McNeel & Associates
  3670 Woodland Park Avenue North
  Seattle, WA 98103
  206/545-7000   Fax 206/545-7321

- PDB-ACAD
  CADology Limited
  Meach House, 71 Nonsuch Walk
  Cheam, Surrey SM2 7LF Great Britain
  +44 81 786 7774   Fax +44 81 786 7775

CHAPTER 13

- Allegro Basic
  Robert McNeel & Associates
  3670 Woodland Park Avenue North
  Seattle, WA 98103
  206/545-7000   Fax 206/545-7321

- Cadpanion
  LANDCADD
  7388 S. Revere Parkway, Building 900
  Englewood, CO 80112
  303/799-3600 or 800/876-5263   Fax 303/799-3696

- Productivity Tools
  Softdesk, Inc.
  7 Liberty Hill Road
  Henniker, NH 03242
  603/428-3199   Fax 603/428-7901

Contacting the Authors of This Book

As mentioned in Chapter 22, we'd enjoy hearing from you. Send your messages via CompuServe Mail or on the ACAD forum:

- Mark Middlebrook   73030,1604

- Jake Richter   75130,2705

- Bud Smith   71774,3321

Index

DÆDALUS CONSULTING

Computer Consulting for Structural Engineers and Other Smart Folks

Daedalus Consulting offers a wide range of AutoCAD consulting services and specializes in the needs of structural engineering firms. The company's principal is Mark Middlebrook, who founded Daedalus Consulting in 1988 after earning a Master's degree in structural engineering from U.C. Berkeley and working as a structural designer in the San Francisco Bay Area. He has consulted for many engineering firms, computer dealers, and software developers in California and throughout the U.S.

Mark's areas of expertise include using AutoCAD and related third party software for structural drafting, design, and analysis, as well as linking databases with CAD. Besides being principal of Daedalus Consulting, Mark is Contributing Editor of *CADalyst* magazine, Assistant Sysop on Autodesk's CompuServe forums, past Chairman of the Structural Engineers Association of Northern California's Electronic Computation Committee, and Co-chairman of the San Francisco AutoCAD Users Group.

Services:

- Training and support for AutoCAD and structural third party applications
- AutoCAD customization: AutoLISP, custom menus, etc.
- Computer management and standards consulting
- Help with specific projects or implementations
- Hardware and software recommendations and tuning
- Technical writing for magazines and software firms
- Beta testing and software design assistance

For more information, please contact:

Mark Middlebrook
Daedalus Consulting
435 Clifton Street
Oakland, CA 94618
510/547-0602

CompuServe 73030,1604

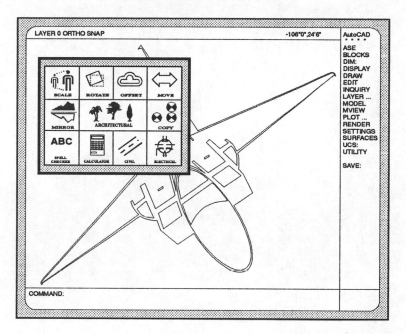

MD COMPUTER CONSULTING
2481 Belmont Drive
Anchorage, AK 99517

Discover these DOS based AutoCAD utility programs available through MD Computer Consulting or on the ACAD forum of Compuserve:

ATTEXT

An attribute extract program that mimics the AutoCAD command of the same name. Use the same template files you use within AutoCAD to extract attribute values from your drawings without having to load AutoCAD.

DWGLIST

List the block and layer names contained within the specified drawings. Can be used to search for drawings containing specific blocks or layer names. Great QA/QC tool for confirming that the layers meet your naming conventions.

DWGPATHS

Modify the drawing file to change or remove embedded paths for fonts, menus, and XREF's. This is an invaluable utility if you regularly receive drawing files from outside consultants and then have to spend your valuable time answering AutoCAD's prompts for the location of the font files.

SHOWREFS

List the directory tree of all the XREF'ed drawings used by a particular drawing file, including any nested XREF's. Quickly ensures that you have included all the necessary AutoCAD files on a disk before you send it to a client and discover you forgot a file.

MD Computer Consulting also sells PROPAK, an add—on package that works in conjunction with the R12 Softdesk Civil/Survey product line. Generate coordinate schedules, manipulate points, text, blocks, layers, plus much, much more. A great productivity enhancer that will quickly pay for itself.

For more information on any of these programs, please send your inquiries to MD Computer Consulting at the above address, or via Compuserve to Mike Dickason [72711,3404].

AUTOCAD® POWER TOOLS®
SOFTWARE LICENSING AGREEMENT